A CRITICAL AND EXEGETICAL COMMENTARY ON THE REVELATION OF ST JOHN

A CRITICAL AND EXEGETICAL COMMENTARY ON THE REVELATION OF ST JOHN

R. H. Charles

General Books

www.General-Books.net

Publication Data:

Title: A Critical and Exegetical Commentary on the Revelation of St John
Author: R. H. Charles
Reprinted: 2010, General Books, Memphis, Tennessee, USA
Publisher: Charles Scribner's Sons
Publication date: 1920

1

A CRITICAL AND EXEGETICAL COMMENTARY ON THE REVELATION OF ST JOHN

Th Right TVimMtoto andtf 099

99 M the Millennial Kingdom 236-385 386-446 447-451 45 453-455 45M57 Index L to the Greek words used in the Apocalypse 459-473 II. to Hebraisms used in the Apocalypse. 473 III. Passages in our Author based on the O. T., Pseudepigraphaaadthen. T. 474

M IV. to the Introduction, Commentary and Notes. 474-499

ADDENDA ET CORRIGENDA.

VOLUME IL

Page 10, line z. See Abbott, Notes onn. T. Criticism, p. 104, for passages in Origen and Clement of Alex, in which vopmm are applied to men, and in Ignatius (Smyrn. 13) to widows. But nothing that he says can explain the application of A fi r ywoucwr ofe tyuavrftpw to women.

Page 27, line 9. r "Only the faithful. fifth seal" read "The faithful suffer physical martyrdom, but their prayers become an instrument of wrath in the hands of God." See vol ii 403, note 2.

Page 49 line 7 ab fmo. Transpose the subject-matter of the fifth and sixth beatitudes. See vol ii. 445, note z.

Page 72, line 3 ab fmo. Debt "Again we should expect. iil 21." Our author only uses the participle of but his sources (xvii. 9, 15, xviii. 7) use the pres. ind. In the LXX the pres. and imperf. forms of Koftfr have disappeared, their place being taken by ico fuu, feoftpup. See Thackeray, Gram. 271 sq.

Pag 75, line 8. After "first" add "either in Dan. iv. 34 (LXX), ftfe r. fa icol insymOfi r. vptw mu fturixc r. Soo-ixcwv, or (rather in the pre-Maccabean section of z Enoch see my second edition, p. lii sq.). M

Page 90, lines 25-27. Delete "icdcAffuu. UL 21; and. 19 See note abore on p. 72, L 3.

Page 168. On the twelve precious stones see British Museum Guide to. Minerals mentioned in the Bible, 1911.

Page 203, line 4 ab im. The line " ml Xrfyci. should not be bracketed, but read immediately before xxi. See vol ii. 379, 444, where it is restored to its right place.

fiii ADDENDA ET CORRIGENDA

Page 219, line 3 abimo. After world n add of the living," Christ judges the living: God Himself judges the dead according to our author's view.

Page 234 line 18. Add " Where no reading of Tyc is quoted, Tyc agrees with vg."

Page 234, line 20. Add "From 20 to 21 (nova fiudo omnia) Pr in his comm. has copied verbatim the work of Augustine (de Civ. Dei, xx. 7-17), retaining Augustine's Italian text In the App. Crit. these verses are quoted without any mark of distinction

Page 240, ver. i x, line a. After 2020: add xownpr 181: yy ix, xi. For post Stiarccp. pon read tr after 0varctp. Similarly elsewhere.

Page 256, ver. 7, line 30. Delete (+ KCU ouscur ovot ci Or 1), and Or 1 in next line. Or conflates A 025 and 046 here. See vol. L p. clxxvl

Page 279, ver. 2, lines 5, 8, 9. Delete et M. Similarly elsewhere.

Page 288, ver. 12, line ix. Delete (M Or conflates 046 al and AM 025: and reads KOI TO rpirw avnpr fwy mn r jxpa (so 046 al) KCU 17 ijfjapa M ony TO TWTOV (Trroftov A) mmpr (s AM 025).

THE REVELATION

OF ST. JOHN.

CHAPTER XIV.

INTRODUCTION. i. Character and Object of this Chapter.

The entire chapter is proleptic in character. That is, the orderly development of future events as set forth in the successive visions is here, as in two sections heretofore, abandoned, and all the coming judgments from xvi. 17 to xx. 7-10, are summarized in xiv. 6-11, 14, 18-20. To this summary is prefixed a short description of the blessed (who are identical with the 144,000 in vii. 4-8) in the Millennial Kingdom established on the earth with Mount Zion as its centre, xiv. 1-5. Thus we have in this chapter a general introduction to xvi. ly-xx. i-io. It is therefore of the nature of an intermezzo.

The object of xiv. is to encourage the faithful to endurance in the face of impending universal martyrdom. Hence in xiv. 1-5 the veil is lifted for a moment from the future and to the Seer is disclosed a vision of the martyrs enjoying the blessedness of the Millennial Kingdom on Mount Zion in attendance on their Lord. We have here a later stage of their blessedness than that depicted in vii. 9-17, where the martyrs are represented as having arrived or arriving in heaven straight from the scene of martyrdom. See Chapter vii., Introduction, 10.

But the faithful are further encouraged to endurance and loyalty by the proclamation of the doom of the proud anti-christian power, xiv. 8-n, and of all the heathen powers whether confederate with it or not, xiv. 14, 18-20.

This chapter 1 thus contains three visions, which are all proleptic.

1 xiv. 12-13 belong to xiii., and are read immediately after adii. 18 in thit edition. They are from the hand of our author. VOL. II. I 1. xiv. 1-5. Vision of the glorified martyrs with the Lamb on Mount Zion during the Millennial reign. Cf. xx. 4. The greater part of xiv. 4-5 is interpolated.

2. xiv. 6-11. Vision of the judgment on the antichristian Roman Empire and its adherents and their everlasting torment. Cf. xvi. xy-xviii.

3. xiv. 14, 18-20. Vision of the judgment executed by the Son of Man on the heathen nations. Cf. xix. 11-21 and xx. 7-io(?). The paragraph xiv. 15-17 is an interpolation. See pp. 19-21.

2. This chapter, with the exception of certain interpolations (cf. xiv. 4-5, 15-17), is from the hand of our author; for (i) the order of the words is Hebraic: (2) the diction and style are decidedly his.

The first question needs no discussion: the fact is so obvious. Hence we shall limit our consideration to (2).

(2) The diction is that of our author except in xiv. 15-17, which in the first place is a doublet of xiv. 14, 18-20 and in the next exhibits three constructions, which are against the usage of our author (see notes on TW Kaihiiwy! rrjs ve Aiys in xiv. 15, 6 ica icvos ri rrys ie caqs and 3axcv. ri rrjv yr)v in xiv. 16) Of xiv. 3 C 5 only 01 yopooyxcvoi dwro rwv dvtfpeotrwv a-rrap rj T 0c dAoMfc cwriv seems to be original. The interpolations in those verses are, however, in the style of our author, except, perhaps, oirov? vrrayci in xiv. 4, but the thought conveyed is wholly against the context.

I will now enumerate some of the phrases characteristic of our author, though not, except in a few cases, peculiar to him.

1. Kdl etw ica! I8ou. See iv. i, note, ytypa vov M rwv jlCTriirw afav. See vii. 3, note. 2. on K TOU oupakou, x. 4, 8, xi. 12, xiv. 13. 6s + KV dsdrw maXac; cf. i. 15, xix. 6.)W K Kioapuw. Cf. xviii. 22. 2-3. In Kadapitrfirw. KOI Soucrik we have the familiar Hebrew idiom reproduced already in i. 5-6, ii. 2, 9, etc. (see note in loc.). OUTIK 6s usf)? Katv K; cf. v. 9. trimo? TOU OP KOU; cf. iv. 5, 6, etc. 4. The use of atrapxn = " sacrifice," though not found elsewhere in our author, is in keeping with his frequent use of Greek words in the same sense as in the LXX. 5. The asyndetic addition of the clause O UDWH clow (cf. xvi. 6). 6. irtrrfpciw Iv facooupai fiati. Already in viii. 13. With cftayycxuroi im rods Katoikourras (A., KC OUS, CPQ); cf. x. 7. The enumeration my KOS nal 4u V KT. (see note on v. 9) and the grammatical irregularity Xeyov in 7 instead of Afyovra are both characteristic of his style. 7. Xlyw 4wrp ficydx. Cf. xiv. 9. tv is used also before uv icy. after crpv-o-ccv (v. 2), but after Kpofctv only in passages from another hand (xiv. 15, xviii. 2). On the other hand it is absent after X yciv in this phrase (v. 12, viii. 13), after Kpdfav (vi. 10, vii. 2, 10, x. 3), after fwv w (xiv. 18). Hence our author varies in his use of this phrase in connection with A. cyeu. See note on x. 2. o0TJ0T)Tc TOK 6cov. So xv. 4, xix. 5 (cf. xi 18, foftovficvovs TO oyoui crov). 8o T OUTW S4 ak. Cf. xvi. 9, xix. 7 also in the incorporated source, xi. 13. fj 0ci 4 upa-njs xpurcus. Cf. similar phrases: vi. 17, fi Bcv f rj pa. TJS pyi s avrw; xi. 18, jyalcv. 6 icaipos TWV vctcMop Kpiotyai; xviii. 10, A0ev ij jcpuri? crov: also in interpolated section, xiv. 15. irpocricuk crate, c. dak of God: cf. iv. 10, vil n, note, xi. 16, xix. 10, xxii. 9, whereas it takes the ace. of TO Qrjpiov in 9 in both respects exhibiting our author's usage, inryds drfiw: cf. vhi. 10, xvi. 4.

8. ofrou TOU Oupou TYJS iroppcias. So xviii. 3. See note ivi v. 9. irpocncuici T 6t)piok. See note on 7. Xapj3Kci xpayiui. Cf. xiv. 11, xix. 20, xx. 4. But we should probably read TO dpayfia. See note A? r. m TOU ficrwirou. We should most probably read iiri TO xerwirov, since the context clearly comes from our author's hand. See note on vii. 3. reads the dative. M, iv Xcipa. Cf. xx. i, 4. See note on xiii. 16. 1O. ical afiros iricrau For the use of KOL see note on xiv. 10. parraiaao actat Iv irupl Kat Oeiu. Pao-avi o) is found four times elsewhere in our author, while ftaa-avurfjlo (see next verse), which occurs four times, is not attested elsewhere in the N. T. With irvpl KOI 0ctp cf. xx. 10, xxi. 8, xix. 20. 11. 6 KattKOs. apapaivci. Cf. viii. 4, ix. 2, xix. 3. oux xooaik avdirauo'ik KT. Already in iv. 8. ol vpooitu-Kourres T Oijptok. Characteristic of our author both as to grammar and diction. 12. woe thropoyi) KT. Cf. xiil 10. Tw dywak. ot rnpouttcs rs Jrrokas. For the phrase cf. xii. 17. The irregularity is characteristic of our author. 13. X yei TO irveujicu Cf. ii. 7, etc., xxii. 17. 14. KCU etsok ical ISou. See iv. i, note, jirl T JK v tf i v Kao rak. Characteristic of our author: see note on iv. 2, and contrast the non-Johannine constructions of this phrase in 15, 16. 8 ioiov ulok dfoprfirou. This unique constniction is found only in our author. It has already occurred in i. 13, and, as we have seen in the Additional Note on i. 13, vol. L p. 36, might be regarded as a further development of other linguistic constructions, to which attention is called in that note.

Interpolation 15-17. In this short section there are four constructions which are foreign to our author's use. These are given in the note on 15-17, p. 21. Other grounds for regarding 15-17 as interpolated are given in the note on 14-20, p. z 8 sq.

18-20. These verses are in keeping with the diction and style of our author. They contain, it is true, several words not found elsewhere in our author covctv, rpvyav, iorpv?, fynrcao?, Aa civ, ora vai?, xaauof, but these help to delineate his subject

THE REVELATION OF ST. JOHN XIV.-3.

18. 4 t)0 K twjj pcydxg. Though oweiv is not found elsewhere in our author the construction is always that which he uses with Kpafciv, and in two cases out of four with Aeyeiv. IT OP oou T Spfawok. The vernacular use of the pronoun here is elsewhere in our author not infrequent. 19. cflaxey. cis TTJK yrjK. See note in loc. XIJHOF TOO Oufou TOO Ocou. Cf. xix. 15. iirar di) 6 Xqitos. Cf. xix. 15. xpi TWK x f""- "XPi occurs six times in our author as a preposition and five times as a conjunction, but not once in the other Johannine writings in the N. T.

3. Interpolated passages, 3 C-4 C (hro rip yijs. iyopao-fliy-crav), 4 C, icat TW dpvtw, and probably 5, icat cv T f crrdxati avrwv oux vp 0i7 cvoos. See the grounds for this conclusion in lot. 15-17. That these verses are an intrusion is manifest on many grounds. See the general grounds in the note on 14-20, p. 18 sq., and the grammatical grounds in the note on 15-17, p. 21.

XIV. 1-6. A proleptic vision of the 144,000 with the Lamb on Mount Zion . of the risen martyrs with Christ during the Millennial reign. That these are the same as the 144,000 in vii. 4-8, i. e. the spiritual Israel, the entire Christian community, alike Jewish and Gentile, which were sealed to protect them from the demonic woes, that are to follow speedily, we hope to prove in the course of our criticism of verses 1-5 (see also vol. i. p. 199 sqq.). In vii. 9-17 this same body of the faithful is represented as arriving in heaven during the great final tabulation, or as already assembled there at its close. Here they aie represented as having at a later stage come down to earth for the Millennial reign (cf. xx. 4). The vision is therefore proleptic. There is a progressive note in each vision.

1. ita! ctook KCU ISou. See note in iv. i.

TO dp iok. The Lamb is here set over against the Beast in xiii., and the followers of the Lamb with His name and that of His Father over against the followers of the Beast with his mark on their forehead.

From O. T. times Mount Zion was associated in the minds of the faithful with divine deliverance. Thus Joel ii. 32 (iii. 5) writes: " And it shall come to pass, that whosoever shall call on the name of the Lord shall be delivered; for in Mount Zion and Jerusalem shall be those that escape, as the Lord hath said." In the 8th cent B. C. there existed for a time the belief that Jerusalem could not be destroyed. In later times it was held that a special blessing attached to residence in Palestine. It alone was to escape the woes that would befall the rest of the earth: cf. 2 Bar. xxix. 2 (where see my note), xl 2, Ixxi. i; 4 Ezra xiii. 48, 49, vi 25. This idea was revived in Talmudic literature.

This appearance of the Messiah with a mighty multitude on

XIV. L 144,000 HERE SAME AS 144,000 IN VII. 4-8 5

Mount Zion was a Jewish expectation, as we see in 4 Ezra xiil 35, 39, 40, "But he shall stand upon the summit of Mount Zion. And whereas thou didst see that he summoned and gathered to himself another multitude which was peaceable, these are the ten tribes." In 4 Ezra il 42 (Christian or Christian recast of Jewish material) we have a close parallel to our text: " I Esdras saw upon Mount Zion a great multitude which I could not (dst. c, no man could) number, and they all praised the Lord with songs. 43. And in the midst of them there was a young man of high stature, taller than all the rest, and upon every one of their heads he set crowns. 44. So I asked the angel and said: Who are these, my Lord? 45. He answered and said unto me: These be they that have put off the mortal clothing and put on the immortal, and have confessed the name of God."

This last work was probably written about 200-250 A. D., and therefore forms an early testimony to the right interpretation of the 144,000 on Mount Zion in our text; for it appears to identify the multitude described in vii. 9-17 and that in our text. In accordance with vii. 9-17 the writer of 4 Ezra ii. 42-47 represents them as having confessed and stood out stoutly for the name of God, and so as now clad in the garments of immortality, and in accordance with xiv. 1-5 of our text they stand on Mount Zion with the Messiah.

IKCTOV Tcao-cpdkOKra icrx. The answer to the question as to the identity of the 144,000 that accompany the Lamb has in pan been given in the introduction to Chap. vii. where we have found them to be the same as the 144,000 in vii. 4-8 and the great multitude in vii. 9-17. But, though the constituents of the multitude are the same, the circumstances are different. In the vision before us the scene is upon earth (cf. ver. 2). The blessed faithful follow the Lamb on Mount Zion. And yet they have already passed through the gates of death, and have been presented as an offering (atrapxn) to God (xiv. 4). Hence we have here a momentary vision of the saints, who have returned to earth to share in the Millennial reign. (Cf. xx. 4-6.)

But the above identification of the 144,000 in vii. 4-8 and xiv. 1-5 is apparently rejected by every modem scholar, save Alford, who has clung fast to it, although unable to surmount the chief difficulty that stands in its way. A minor difficulty, i. e. the absence of the defining article to identify these 144,000 with those spoken of in vii. 4, he treats as negligible on the ground that the reader was meant to identify the two hosts, seeing that they consist of the same number and are both marked on the forehead as God's own possession.

Alford may be right in ignoring the absence of the article (cf. xv. 2, where the expected article is missing, fc Ooaarrav instead of rrjv Ooaarcrav, and xiv. 9, where TO is wanting before Xapayxa), but the present writer is of opinion that the real explanation is that it was excised by the interpolator of the introductory sentences in xiv. 4-5, who sought by his manipulation of the text to destroy the identity of the 144,000 in vii. 4-8 and the 144,000 in the present passage, and to transform them into a body of monkish celibates. Having thus explained the absence of the article, there is another and greater difficulty, which stands in the way of this identification, and this is that the 144,000 are described as "first-fruits" to God and to the Lamb. If these 144,000, as the present writer holds, are identical with the entire body of Christians living in the last days, who have been sealed with a view to their protection against the demonic woes, how is it that they are designated as " first fruits "? It is the interpretation set on this word ir p Tq by all scholars in the past that has misled them into differentiating the 144,000 in vii. 4-8 and in xiv. 1-5. This word has hitherto been taken universally to mean "first fruits" in this passage. That in the Pauline Epistles and in St. James it bears this meaning is indubitable. But this is by no means the case in the LXX, although Grimm's Lexicon and Thayer's enlarged edition of Grimm state that avapxti i generally the equivalent of rpBW. So far is this from being the case that it is generally not the equivalent of this word. Thus whereas airapxy occurs about 66 times in the LXX, it is a rendering of rwN") only 19 times. In the remaining 47 times, it is once a rendering for the Hebrew word for "tithe," 4 times of n (= "fat,"in which case it means "the best of"), and 40 times a rendering of ntttin (= " offering" or " oblation "), and once of ribun (= " offering "). Thus we see that in the LXX oftener than twice out of three times it means "an offering." In Sirach it occurs four times, but only once with the meaning of "first fruits," while in the other three passages it signifies either an "offering "or "gift" Hesychius also notes that one of its Greek meanings is irpocr opo. It is clear, then, that in the Greek Bible of Judaism airapxq meant "offering," "sacrifice," or "gift" nearly 3 times out of 4. 1 Now 1 The above note was written before the publication of Moulton and Milli-gan's Vocabulary of the Greek Testament. Though these editors have not corrected the misstatements in Grimm's and Thayer's lexicons, to which they give their imprimatur in their preface, they have shown from the Magnesian inscriptions (ed. Kern. 1900), that ai-apx is very commonly used as as a " gift" to a deity, and that this use occurred as early as the 6th cent. B. C. in Athens (Syll. Inscr. Grate, Dittenberger, 1888-1901). They conclude that in the N. T. " we are perhaps at liberty to render sacrifice or gift where it improves the sense, though they do not specify any individual passage save Rom. viii. 23. The Magnesia above referred to was in the neighbourhood of Ephesus. Hence the local and Kowij use of drapx confirms the conclusions arris ed at above.

XIV. 1-3. VISION OF 144,000 ON MT. ZION f it is just this meaning that our text requires. The faithful, whether as martyrs or confessors, are sacrifices to God As such they are offered on the heavenly altar, vi. 9. A further sacrificial reference is discoverable in the epithet in xiv. 5, where they are said to be fyuiioi, that is, " unblemished, 1 sacrificially perfect.

SXOUCNU TO SKOJJLO- afrrog ical TO ovopa TOO irarpos aoroc rrx. With this clause we might compare iii. 12, where a threefold inscription on the foreheads of the faithful is mentioned. But, if we compare xxii. 4, where the name is simply said to be that of God, and 4 of the present chapter, where KOI rw fyvfa appears to be an interpolation, it is possible that dvrov al TO hop. is also an interpolation. The seal consists in the name of God inscribed on the brow. This inscription declares that the person so inscribed is God's own possession: it is at the same time evidence that his character is such as befits a servant of God.

2. wri v IK TOO oupakou KT. The singers are the angel choirs in heaven and not the 144,000 in Mt. Zion, but the new song is intelligible to the 144,000 and to them alone owing to their fellowship with Christ.

Most of the phrases of this verse occur elsewhere in our author, see p. 2.

Kioapwuf Ki6api 6ttw. 3. ital OOUOIK. These words should be rendered: "harpers harping. and singing." It is another instance of the literal reproduction in Greek of a familiar Hebrew idiom, which we have found already in i. 5-6, ii. 2, 9, 20, vii. 14, xv. 3. Thus the style is very characteristic of our author. Here the new song is at first sung not by the redeemed (as in xv. 3; 4 Ezra ii. 42), but by angelic choirs before the throne.

3. KU OOUOIK = KCU otsovrcuv. See preceding note. 6s wv K. air! v. See note on v. 9.

ivwiriqv TOU 6p6fou. See Introd. to Chap. xiv. 2.

ouoyis ftuvoto KT. Only those who are redeemed from the earth can learn the song; for the soul apprehends only that for which it has an affinity. Their spiritual experience won through travail and tears is the mother of understanding. The song is the expression of the inner life, and so in the measure of their spiritual growth is likewise the measure of their spiritual apprehension.

ot 4jyopao Uioi Airo rfjs yip. The diction and thought here have already occurred in v. 9, 10. That passage is of supreme importance in dealing with the text immediately before us. Now the leading thought in v. 9, 10 is that the faithful are bought by Christ for God, and consecrated to His service as kings and priests. Here also, whether we retain or omit the disturbing clauses airb rrp y s ovroi ciow ot.-rjyopa(r6i)rclv y the idea is of a like nature. The 144,000 have been bought to be an offering or sacrifice (Snrapxq, xiv. 4: see note on i) unto God: cf. vi. 9.

This verse, with the exception of the words TTO rv foopwrw farapxr) T g 0 or yopcur iorav faro rwv dvfyeo7rav airapxy Tg Otto, seems to be a later addition due to the incorporation of a marginal explanatory gloss. In support of the aorist we might adduce our author's usage elsewhere: see v. 9, ydpacra? TW 0 w. IK iraanrp fv rp KT. If, on the other hand, we adopt the former view, then in ot rjyopao-ficvot. KOL. ov cvptorj we have, if the latter clause is original, another instance of our author's reproduction in Greek of a Hebrew idiom: see ii. 2, 9, 20, vii. 14, xiv. 2-3. This combination of the perfect and aorist is found often in our author: cf. ii. 3, 5, in. 2, 3, 17, xvi. 6. That ai ru apvta) is an addition appears to be clear from the fact that the 144,000 have been bought by the Son for the Father; and not by the Son for the Father and for Himself: cf. v. 9. The Church is the bride of the Lamb: cf. xix. 7, 8; Eph. v. 27, not an offering presented to Him. If the above clauses are interpolated, the original of 3 c-4 may have run as follows: ot rjyopaa-JL vot euro rsnr dvfyoriraiy dirao rip 0cw. We shall now deal with the clauses, which for the time being we have assumed to be interpolations.

But let us waive for the moment the question of the authenticity of these clauses and study them in themselves and with regard to their immediate context. Now, fir t of all, it is admitted, so far as I am aware, on all hands that the 144,000, whether identical with the 144,000 in vii. 4-8, or representing the llite of the saints composed of Christian ascetics (Bousset, Moffatt), must embrace both men and women. That vapowot can be used of men is of course acknowledged. So far all is clear. But when we start from these premises and try to explain ovroi ciow ot fjicra ywauecw OVK Ip. okw6r)rav we are plunged into hopeless difficulties. For, if we take these words literally, it is obvious that they cannot be used of women. Nor indeed can they be applied to women in any intelligible sense, whatever the metaphorical meaning may be that we attach to the words. Had the writer wished, he could easily have found a phrase applicable literally and metaphorically alike to men and women, such as ot rg iropvcty, ofa Ipo w0rirav. iropvcia is used metaphorically in xiv. 8, xvil 2, 4, xviii. 3,

xix. 2, and ironwco in xvii. 2, xviii. 3, 9 in the sense of idolatrous worship. Such a clause could be used both of men and women, in a literal or metaphorical sense, and the same idea could have been expressed in other ways. Hence we conclude either that men alone are referred to in the text, or that this passage is interpolated. Since we cannot accept the former alternative, we are forced to adopt the latter, and the task devolves upon us to settle, so far as we may, the ground of the interpolation, its extent and meaning.

Now the chief ground for this interpolation is most naturally to be discovered in the misunderstanding of the word x pxn "first fruits." The monkish interpolator, convinced that the highest type of the Christian life was the celibate, naturally identified the 144,000, who form the "first fruits" (or best portion of the Christian Church), with the celibates. The superiority of the celibate life, though un-Jewish and un-Christian, was early adopted from the Gnostics and other Christian heretics. Thus Saturnmus and Basilides declared that "marriage and generation are from Satan" (Iren. Adv. Haer. i. 24), while Tatian (Ens. H. E. iv. xxix. 3) pronounced marriage to be " corruption and fornication." Marcion (Hipp. Phil. vii. 17-19) established churches of celibates, while the Encratites claimed a self-restraint in advance of that of the Christians. Similarly the religions of Isis and Mithra had their celibates throughout the Roman Empire, as Buddhism in the far East, certain orders of the Aztec priesthood in Mexico, the Vestal Virgins in Rome, and the "Virgins of the Sun" in Peru. The pressure of such ideas from without early made itself felt, not in the N. T. but in early Chiistianity, as we see from Polycarp, Ad Phil. ii. iv. v.; Hennas, Vis. ii. 2, 3, Sim. ix. n (see Hastings, Encyc. of Ethics wd Religion iii. 271-273, from which the above facts are drawn). The interpolation was probably made by John's editor.

It is, of course, possible that the interpolated passage appeared first as a marginal gloss on the passage, and that it was subsequently incorporated into the text with a necessary change or two.

As regards the extent it appears to begin with bro rjjs yrp and end with yopoo- o-av. The repetition of the dyopa a with two different adverbial phrases is remarkable. That Awd TW avopwvw is to be preferred to awo 7 yip seems clear from v. 9, where we have iydMura?. lie Trcun vajp;

The meaning of the interpolation we have already gathered from the foregoing criticism of the passage. The glosser or interpolator, as the case may be, tcok the passage to refer to celibates, and, as the peculiar clause tos tcra ywawcwv od fyioavk-Orprav) proves, made it refer to male celibates. They were the "first fruits" of the entire Christian Church (for such, of course, he conceived the meaning of farapxn)

This word as used by the interpolator carries with it the degradation of marriage an idea inadmissible in the N. T. The use ot the aorist here shows that their life on earth regarded as a diciphne belongs to the past.

4. iropo Koi. The word irapOeios was applied to men also: cf. Life of Asftiath, 3. coriv Sc ovros 6 Ion; av p fcocrcjffi??. cat irapqcvas. 6. Store ical avros 7ra06os. In Suidas it is applied to Abel: A? ex ovro?-rrapqcvo? KOLL SIKCUOS wnjpx Cf. also Epiph. i. 385 C. iraj0 V vo is used of males in Just. Frag. 1577 A.

oflroi ot AKoxouoouires irrx. These words can hardly fail to be an echo of our Lord's: cf. Mk. ii. 14, x. 21; Luke ix. 59; John i. 43, xxi. 19. For another echo cf. i Pet. ii. 21, Iva. erra-icoaovOi? o-i? rc rot? t pco-iv avrov. In vii. 17 it is said that the Lamb will be the shepherd of the blessed described in vii. 14-15. This means according to oriental conceptions that the blessed follow Him. Thus to follow Christ is characteristic of the faithful, whether on earth, on which they were called to follow Him even unto death (Matt. x. 38, xvi. 24, 25), or in the Millennial kingdom, or in heaven. But it would be possible to take dicoaovloiwcf as referring to the past, and the subsequent words as implying that in such following of the Lamb they underwent martyrdom. Cf. vii. 14, xii. n. But the context does not favour this interpretation. chrou K factyei. OTTOV elsewhere in the Apocalypse means "where," but with verbs of motion it was used as the equivalent of ovoi. Cf. John vni. 21, 22, xiii. 33, 36. The av in this connection is impossible in classical Greek. In viii. i we have orav fyoi(cv, and in Mk. vi. 56 Lv occurs after oirov with the past imperfect indicative. The construction seems to imply an action of indefinite frequency: cf. Robertson, Gram. 958.

ir6 rsw dityfisirw. This phrase summarizes the full enumeration given in v. 9. dirapx = " sacrifice " or " offering." See note on i. KU TW Ap uo. An addition. See note on 4.

5. KCH t TW orojicm aura? oux cdpt) i rcgSos This clause recalls most nearly Zeph. iii. 13, u ov firj vp Ofj lv TW orourn avrv yxSxrou Soxwi, and Isa. liii. 9. In i Pet. ii. 22 we have the latter reproduced: ovsc fvpeorj 80X09 rf ordian avrov. Cf. John i. 47. It must, however, be confessed that this clause follows weakly after ot yopoo-yu-evot. rrap q ro eo.

2 u Mi cicrik. This sentence introduced asyndetically is in the style of our author: cf. xvi. 6. 5iwxos = D Dn describes best the character of the airo; in the LXX it has three times out of four a sacrificial reference, and affirms the (lawlessness of the victim. It is that which is unblemished, sacrificially perfect. Tn i Pet. i. 19 Christ Himself is described as dxvov ducofiov, and in Heb. ix. 14 as offering Himself as an unblemished sacrifice unto God (lavrov irpcxn cykcv fyuonov TW cji). In the present context the 144,000 who had been offered in sacrifice to God (irapxrj rf 0c3) are likewise described as aAwxot. In the five other passages, where it occurs in the Pauline Epistles and Jude, the clause has an ethical meaning and connotes "blameless-ness."

Note on xiv. i-S This section has been an occasion of great difficulty to scholars. I have sought to show that much of this difficulty arose from misconception of the word farapxq. But, as we have seen, there are other difficulties, which cannot be got rid of save by the excision of certain clauses. Volter (iv. 38 sq., 139 sq.) excises xiv. 4-5 and a phrase in xiv. i, and then identifies the 144,000 here with the 144,000 in vii. 4-8. Weyland excises xiv. i, 4-5, Erbes xiv. 4 ab, and a phrase in 4. Spitta is the most drastic of all He changes TO ovoia. irarpos avrov into TO ovoxa rov 0cov uvros: excises 2 C 3 and reduces 4-5 to the following form: ovroi rjyopao-fojo-av diro Twavoptb-wov oitrapxn rg Oe. (See pp. 144 sq., 147 sq., 536.) Wellhausen recognizes the fact that the text shows undoubted signs of interpolation. Bousset admits the possibility of a source underlying xiv. 1-5, but he thinks it impossible to recover it. He therefore takes the text as it stands and interprets the 144,000 to be a body of Chiistian ascetics and, therefore, different from the 144,000 in vii. 4-8. He thinks, however, that there are signs in the Apocalypse that these two bodies were originally identical.

In the above study of xiv. 1-5 I have attempted to show that xiv. 1-3 comes from the hand of our author (see also Introd. p. 2) save probably one phrase (TO ovoxa avrov KO) in xiv. i. As regards xiv. 4-5 the case is different. Here the diction is not much of a guide to us, but the ideas and the irregularity of the order of the sentences are. Thus of the various descriptions of the 144,000 in 4-5 it is clear from the earlier chapters that the essential one is, without doubt, that which describes them as a sacrifice to God.

At the close of 5 this idea recurs in the words, aftwiot eio-iv, but a purely ethical description intervenes KOI cv TO orourn. revsos. This appears irregular, but greater difficulties have already emerged in connection with 4, where the un-Jewish and un Christian idea is presented, that the very elite of the blessed consists of ascetics, and that, too, male ascetics. On these and other grounds we have excised certain clauses and concluded that, before the monkish glosser went to work, our author's text read as follows in xiv. 3-5, oi yopooyxo'oi faro T K dv0poiray airupxrj TO) 0cjr auoAOt cto'tv. But ai Tp ord art. rcvos may be original. To the interpolator of the above clauses we may owe also the removal of the article before the 144,000, which identified this 144,000 with the 144,000 in vii. 4-8.

6-11. Vision of the judgment to be executed on the Roman Empire and its wor-shippers, in which three angels make proclamation. The first proclaimed to all men an eternal Gospel, the burden of which was that all men should worship the one God who had created heaven and earth, for that the hour of judgment had come (6-7). The second announced, as though already accomplished, the fall of Rome, which had made all the nations to drink of the wine of her fornication (8). The third proclaimed that those who submitted to the mandates of Rome would share in the everlasting torment that awaited her (9-11).

6. oxXok ayycxw. The presence of the a Xov occasions some difficulty. It is supported by the best textual authorities. If it is original, we might, perhaps, with Diisterdieck explain the word as used in contradistinction to the angels that had appeared in earlier scenes. He compares x. i where oxXov ayycaov has already been mentioned, who, as in the present instance, proclaims the impending end of the world. Erbes and J. Weiss suppose we have here a reference to viii. 13, where the phraseology is certainly similar: fro? dcrov TTCTOX OV iv lecrovjoaviyxan Xeyovros tfmwjj flcyaap. Bousset suggests that in oaAov ayycaov we have a dittography, and J. Weiss that it is a corruption of A. OV aterov. Cf. viii. 13. It seems best to explain oaA. ayy. as- "another, an angel" See note on 15 below. The difficulty recurs in 8, 9.

irmtyicvov ir imooupom um. Cf. viii. 13, xix. 17. In the O. T. the angels are not represented with wings save in its latest books: cf. Dan. ix. 21.

cdayytxtof atrfiw. This phrase is found here only in the Johannine writings, whereas the cognate verb occurs here and in x. 7. cwayyexiok here is not to be translated as if it were TO cvay-ycaiov. Its character is defined by its present context and x. 7. It is a proclamation of the impending end of the world and of the final judgment, which, while it is a message of good tidings to the faithful, constitutes for all nations a last summons to repentance.

In x. 7 it was made known to His servants the prophets, here it is proclaimed te all the world. This gospel is termed altwuw because possibly our author wishes to emphasize its unchangeable validity for all eternity.

rods Kdtotkouftaf M Ttjs ytjs (A and some cursives). KCPQ read T. jca0wlciov? M r. yifc. The textual evidence is here indecisive. Difficulties beset both readings. The second reading is against the normal usage of our author. We should expect rl r. yijv=after the Koftievovs. But krl r. yrp is the universal construction in our author after jrarouccu. Hence if we could discover any good ground for the change of jcaroucovrra? into ica0?7ucvovs, we shall have little hesitation in recognizing A as right. Now, though the scribes of KCPQ were occasionally doubtful as to our author's constructions after 6 a0i;uvos, rov they could have had no doubt as to the meaning of the phrase ol Karotfcovvrc? rl rip yrp (always so except in xiii. 12, xvii. i, 2, where these constructions are found in sources) elsewhere in our author, i. e. iii. 10, vi. 10, viii. 13, etc. And since this meaning was always bad in all other passages, and since it could not bear such a meaning here, some early scribe may have been led to substitute Ka icvovs for Karoucavvras and thus give the phrase the neutral colour it required here. But, if this hypothesis of the origin of ca0i?Acvovs is right, its presence here can only call for condemnation. It is against our author's usage wholly in this construction: indeed, according to his usage it could only mean " those who sat on the earth." l If, then, we accept the reading of A, we must in this one passage attach a purely neutral or geographical sense to the phrase, such as it bears not infrequently in i Enoch (see xxxviii. 5, note). See note on xi. 10.

iray fro? ical u V KT. See note pn v. 9.

Xfywk. The grammatical irregularity is characteristic of our author. See iv. i, xi. i.

7. X y K Iv 4wrfj jieydxfl. See Introduction to this Chapter, 2: also note on x. 2.

foptJ0t T TOP Oedk KT. This gospel is based on a purely theitic foundation. But, when the last hour has come, a man's chief concern is not dogmatic fullness or correctness of creed, but only self-humiliation before and self-surrender to the Lord of all. With this announcement we might compare the gospel as preached by our Lord in Mark i. 15, Acravoctrc tcai iriorcvcrc tv

But a really excellent parallel is to be found in St. Paul's speech at Lystra, Acts xiv. 15: cvayyexi(dicvoi vufc faro TOUTCOV TUP larcuw evtotx uv Ctrl Bcbv (ura of ciroii orcv rov oupavoy Kai rrjv yyv Kai TJJV 0d acrrav icrx On the creation idea, cf. x. 6 of our text.

The clause o3. r. 0eov is found in Eccles. xii. 13, and Sore avrw 3d av in Josh vii. 19; i Sam. vi. 5; Isa. xlii. 12; Jer. xiii. 16, but they both belong to our author's phraseology: see Introd. to Chap, xiv., p. 3.

fjxOcp pa Tt) Kpurews dhrou. The diction and form of this sentence are characteristic of our author, but are of still more frequent occurrence in the Fourth Gospel. Cf. ii. 4, iv. 21, 23, 1! Karoncovvtct M r. yijt is a rendering of pun hy O3e and this is the normal rendering of it in the LXX. In a few cases in the LXX of Jeremiah only do we find ol icaftftieioc M r.-yijr or T. 7: cf. xxxii. (xx v.) 29, 30. With definite localities it occurs more frequently: cf. Dan. ix. 7, where we have Kabrj vm fr lepourax M

(LXX Karoucownv tv lepo., Theod. (A)). See note on this phrase in xiii., Introd. S 4 v. 25, 28, vii. 30, viil 20, xii. 23, xiii. i, xvi. 2, 4, 21, 25, 32, xvii. i.

irou am. This is the usage of our author: contrast 9 where this verb takes the ace. of TO also the usage of our author. See note on vii. 1 1.

vpookUp fratC r iroi aarn TF odpapo? KT. Since God has created the world, man's allegiance is due to God. The fact of God as creator has already been brought forward in iv. ir, x. 6, but in both these passages KTI V and not irocczv has been used. References to the creative activity of God are rare in the N. T. but frequent in the O. T. See note on iv. n.

irrjyds dsdrw. The absence of the article is noteworthy, contrast xvi. 4, viii. 10. The phrase is a familiar O. T. one: cf. i Kings xviil 5; 2 Kings iii. 19 (OD WVD), 25; Ex. xv. 27; Num. xxxiii. 9.

8. The second angel proclaims the fall of Rome.

axXos Scutepos ayycxo?. So the best MSS. But we should rather expect simply ayycao? Scvrcpo? or a Ao ayy. 8evr.; for when our author uses another adjective in addition to oaAos it is added after the noun: cf. vi. 4, x. i, xiv. 9, xv. i: i. e. "another angel, a second one."

faccrer, fhrecrek Ba0uxfifr. These words are already found in Isa. XXI. 9. 733 nbd3 r6B3, LXX, irarrukw wewcoicei Kafivxtov. Cf. Jer. li. 8. But the two clauses circo-cv. ra Wvj seem to be derived by our author immediately from xviii. 2-3 (a source). To Eapvxw our author always attaches the epithet 17 ficyaai?, an epithet which goes back to Dan. iv. 27 (ran t23); cf. xvi. 19, xvii. 5, xviii. 2, 10, 21. That Babylon was already a synonym for Rome in the first century A. D. is clear from 2 Bar. xi. i; Sibyl Or. v. 143, 159; i Pet. v. 13 (?). Cf. also xvi. 19, xvii. 5, xviii. 2, 10, 21.

TJ K TOO ofrou TOO OUJAOU rfjs iroppctos adrfjs TTCITOTIKCK inform ra I6mfj. This very extraordinary form of speech, which recurs in xvni. 3, can hardly be original. The text as it stands combines two wholly disparate ideas. The first is IK TOV olvov rip Tropvetas aur75 a phrase which occurs in xvii. 2 i. e. " the wine of her fornication," which Babylon has made all the nations to drink. This wine symbolizes the intoxicating power, the corrupting influence of Rome. The second is c rod olvov TOV Ovpjov (TOV Ocov) a phrase which occurs in xiv. 10 i. e. "the wine of the wrath of God," which He will give Babylon to drink. This latter phrase recurs in a fuller form in xvi. 19, xix. 15, TOV olvov TOV 0vuv rrp opyris avrov. But in the O. T. it is God Himself that presents through His prophet this wine of wrath to the nations: cf. Jer. xxv. 15, which seems to have been in the mind of our author, Aajffc TO ironqpuv TOV olvov TOV axparov TOVTOV IK etxk fjtov

XIV. 8-9. DOOM OF WORSHIPPERS OF BEAST

Kal TTonets Trdvra ra Iflny. In xxviii. (li.) 7 Babylon is said to be a cup in the hand of the Lord whereof the nations have drunk and become mad: irorrjpiov pwrwv Bu3uaov lv x L P l wpiov tcxncw nturav TT)V y v. ATTO rov ozvov avrj? fcrfoorav i. Qvi. Sia rovro

As we study the above facts two ways of dealing with the text appear to be open to us. i. Excise rov dviov as an interpolation due to the occurrence of the phrase rov oivov rov Ovpav in 10. The extraordinary divergence of the MSS in xviii. 3, where the phrase recurs, points either to an interpolated or a very difficult text. 2. Since our author appears to have had Jer. xxv. 15 sq. in his mind, and since the text there has r n nonn (= "the wine which is wrath," i. e. wine of wrath), it is possible that he took non in the sense of " poison," which it sometimes bears (cf. Deut. xxxii. 24, 33; Ps. lviii. 5, cxl. 4). The fact that it maddens the nations (Jer. xxv. 16, li. 7; Hab. ii. 15) might be taken to favour this meaning. If this be right, then our text would mean " the wine of the poison of her fornication." But it seems best to regard TOV 0vuv as an interpolation. The nations, having drunk of the wine of the fornication of Babylon, have really therein drunk the wine of the wrath of God.

0. The third angel proclaims a doom of everlasting torment for adherents of the Imperial cult This forms a counter proclamation to that in xiii. 15, 17.

lv +wi) pcyrfxT). See note on x. 2.

irpoakUKci TO Orjpioy. See note on 7.

t Xoppdpci xpayP a t- Cf. xii. n, xix. 20, xx. 4. On XapayAa, see xiii. 16, note. The absence of the article before O L-ypol is suspicious. The context leads us to expect it. First it immediately follows the definite mention of the Beast (TO fcjptov), whose mark it is. Next this mark has already been twice mentioned in xiii. in the first instance in xiii. 16, without the article because mentioned for the first time, and again in xiii. 17 with the article. Finally the angel would not speak in this indefinite way of this brand of hell Contrast xx. 4. All mankind knew "the mark." We must suppose the angel knew so also. Hence we should read TO xapayui or excise Kal Aa avci. Xctpa avrov as an interpolation.

t irl TOO jtcttsirou f This construction of ciri with ftcronrov is against our author's usage We should expect cvt TO teironrov. See notes on vii. 3, xiii. 16. When we combine these two irregularities just dealt with, we are forced, it seems, to infer either that the text is corrupt or that we have in cu Xa ovci. xcp arov a marginal gloss. The closing words of 1 1 support the former con- elusion. Hence we should probably read cu M TO ftrrcuirov airrov 17 rl T V X" 1 ovrov.

1O. xai afoot vcrrai, " he too (the man who has received the mark) shall drink." To Rome herself finally this cup is given in xvi. 17. The al introduces the apodosis as in x. 17 (iii. 20 tcq) in-roo olpou TOU Oupog Toc Ocou TOU KCKCpao- Kou dkpdrou Iv T TTJS 6py? 1- Parallel expressions to vorjpiov TTJJ opyip found in Isa. li. 17, 22; Jer. xxv. 15, and in xviii. 6 in our text. The subject has in part been discussed under ver. 8 above. The only real difficulty lies in the words TOU ojVov TOV 0vuv. rov K K pa(Tfji vov ojcpdrov. The source of the expression appears to be Ps. lxxv. 9, ovi vonqpiov Iv x L P L vptov, oivov ojcpdrov irx pcs iccpacrfiaroc. Here the Mass, has DD N7D ion P 1 for the last four words. We should also compare Jer. xxxii. i (xxv. 15) TO irorqpioy TOV ozKov TOV fapdrov n TH noHH P n D13. We have still another parallel in Pss. Sol. viii 15, Sta TOVTO Mpacrw aurot9 0eds Trvcvia Trxan rccuc iirorurfv avroir? irvrrjptov otvov Kpatov cis flc0? v. From the last passage it follows that there can be no inconsistency between ciccpao-ev and cfcparov. The verb refers to the mingling of this wine with elements (as the literal wine with spices) that will not weaken it but render it noxious or poisonous, whereas the adjective (cparov) states that it is unmixed with water. For this use of aicparos cf. 3 Macc. v. 2; Galen (in Wetstein): otvov faparov clvat Xeyoxev, py fufuKrai TO vovop. o iyov fjltfjlucrai.

In Ps. lxxv. 9 the same explanation of the LXX would hold good, though in that case we have to read "ion p In Jer. xxxii. i (xxv. 15) okparov therefore implies ignn p and not the Massoretic reading given above. On the other hand, it must be stated that modern scholars, though they accept "ionn as the reading in Jer. xxv. 15, do not attribute to it the same meaning either here or in Ps. lxxv. 9 as the LXX.

From the above authorities we conclude that the passage is to be explained " the wine of the wrath of God which is mingled sheer in the cup," etc. But for the close parallels given above we might accept the proposal of Ewald, Alford and others that from the almost universal custom of mixing wine with water the common term for preparing wine came to be Kcpavivu. Thus E us tat hi us says on Od. v. 93 that in fclxunrc 3c vcvcrap Ipvqpov the verb Kcpaoxrc = ve ei. A further suggestion may be offered. Our author, we know, was better acquainted with Hebrew than with Greek. It is possible, therefore, that judging from the LXX he took 8. Kparos to be a right rendering of idn just as the author of Pss. Sol. xvi. n took 6 tyo lrvx a (which really means " faintheartedness ") to be a right rendering of nn t p (= " impatience "), a misrendering that is also found in the LXX. If th s be so, then we might assign to paro? the meaning of TOPI, and render " the wine of the wrath of God which is mingled foaming in the cup." The "foaming" or "fermentation" is still going on; for God has just mingled this cup of judgment for the nations.

pa7ayih) rttat iv mipl ical 0ci. The imagery goes back to the torments to be inflicted on Edom: Isa. xxxiv. 8-10. The punishment of brimstone and fire appears first in connection with Sodom and Gomorrah (Gen. xix. 24). As Anderson Scott writes in loc., " it is instructive to trace the development of the symbolism springing from the circumstances of an event in history, providing the traditional features, first of any great judgment, then of the day of the Lord, and, finally, of the judgment of Christ." Our author uses this symbolism again in xix. 20, xx. 10, xxi. 8.

iitftinoi TWK ayycxw. The idea has occurred already in T Enoch xlviii. 9 in another form:

"And I will give them over into the hands of Mine elect: As straw in fire, so shall they burn before the face of the holy: As lead in water, so shall they sink before the face of the righteous, And no trace of them shall any more be found."

In i Enoch xxvii. 2, 3, xc. 26, 27, 4 Ezra vii. 36, as in the passage before us, the sufferings of the wicked form an ever-present spectacle to the righteous; but not so in the Parables of i Enoch. There Gehenna and its victims form only a temporary spectacle. Then they vanish from the presence of the righteous for ever, as in the later sections of the Apocalypse. See i Enoch xlviii. 9, note, lxil 12, 13. This is not due to any moralisation of the idea but to the conception of a new heaven and a new earth, which exclude the possibility of the Gehenna conception. In Luke xii. 9 the wicked are to be disowned by Christ in the presence of His angels. This idea of Gehenna as an ever-present spectacle over against Paradise arose through a mistaken etymology of the phrase Q iy pfern in Isa. lxvi. 24 and Dan. xii. 2. In the ist cent B. C. or as early as the close of the 2nd cent B. C. Jewish scholars regarded p VT as derived from nto. Thus the LXX of Isa. lxvi. 24 renders this word TOVTCU cic opoo-tv.

xal twsmok TOO Apriou. Many critics remove this phrase as a gloss owing to the position after TWV yyav. If it is original it is best to render the phrase: "even before the Lamb." fiousset suggests that the phrase " before the angrls " is a late Jewish periphrasis for " before God." Cf. Luke xv. 10, xii. 8, 9; VOL. II. 2 and Bousset's Rd. des Judcntums, 308, but in the present context this is unlikely.

11. KOI 6 Kairps TOO Pacnmcrpou afirv. akaffaifci. Cf. xviii. 9, xix, 3, xx. 10; Isa. xxxiv. 10, forcu 7; yrj av-rfjs s Trcra Kuop. vr) VVKTOS Kal xcpas, KOL ov r? e(r0i7r rat cfe TOV alcova xpovov, KOL Juaj3i? crcrai 6 Jca7ryo? aflrj s 5ia. The word faravior s is used here as denoting the condition of those in torment, and similarly in xviii. 7, 10, 15, whereas in the gloss (?) in ix. 5 it has an active meaning. In Luke xvi. 23, 28 (Wisd. iii. i; 4 Macc. xiii. 15) ftdo-avos is used to denote passive suffering.

X X wnv AKdirauot? KT. Cf. iv. 8, where the same Greek clause occurs, but there it means the deliberate and willing surrender on the part of the Cherubim of their entire time to the praise of God, whereas here it denotes the involuntary endurance of ceaseless torment on the part of those who worship the Beast: cf. i Enoch lxiil 6.

"And now we long for a little rest but find it not: We follow hard upon and obtain it not"

ct TIS Xappdm = ol Aax? a ovt 9.

XIV. 12-18. These verses do not belong here but have in this edition been restored to their original position after xiii. 15. Just as at the close of xiii. 10 our author enforced the need of patience and faithfulness under the persecutions described in xiii. lo 1, so after he has foretold universal persecution and martyrdom for the saints in xiii. 15, and in xiv. 12 has enforced the need of patience on the part of the saints, a voice from heaven is heard declaring the blessedness of those who die in the Lord. For a full treatment of these verses see the section that follows immediately after xiii. 15, vol. i. pp. 368-373.

14, 18-2O. A proleptic vision of the preliminary Messianic judgment executed by the Son of Man on the heathen nations, which is described in detail in xix. 11-16, and further apparently in xx. 7-10, and under another form in xvii. 14. Although nearly all scholars have taken 14-20 to be the work of one hand, it is clear, as Wellhausen has already recognized, that in 14-20 there are doublets. Wellhausen takes these to be 14-16 and 17-20, but a study of the text and context shows that this analysis of the passage cannot be sustained. No more can that of Bousset, who regards xiv. 14-20 as originally from a foreign source, like xi. 1-13, and considers xiv. 17-18 as the addition of a reviser. For (i) since in xiv. 15-17 there are constructions (see notes on 15-17, p. 21) which are against our author's use, we conclude that these verses are an intrusion here, and that xiv. 14, 18-20 represent the original text. (2) Again the phrase axXos ayycaos (15) is noteworthy. It shows that the interpolator failed to recognize the " One like a Son of Man "in 14 as Christ, and took Him to be simply an angel, and hence assigned a mightier role to this second and unnamed angel. But to place beside the Son of Man a second figure, and that merely an angelic one as the judge of the earth, is hardly intelligible from any point of view.

(3) When 15-17 are removed, the text describes the Son of Man reaping the vintage of the earth just as in xix. 11-i 6, where He treads the winepress of the wrath of God. This fact is also against Wellhausen's analysis which would connect the Son of Man

with the harvesting of the earth and an angel with the gathering in of the vintage of the earth. (4) Again, neither 0cpt u (Matt. xxv. 24, etc.) nor any of its derivatives (Matt. ix. 37 sq., xiii. 30, xxv. 24; Mark iv. 29; John iv. 35 sqq.) is used elsewhere in the Apocalypse in regard to divine judgment, whereas in xix. vintage terms are applied metaphorically as in xiv. 18-20 to this judgment. (5) Again, instead of TO opetravov crov in 15 we should expect crow TO Spciravov TO o u, as rightly in 18, seeing that the Spcvavov is already described as 6 r in 14. (6) Finally, when the intrusive doublet (15-17) is removed, we understand why it is that the angel from the altar conveys the command to the Son of Man to gather in the vintage of the earth. The angel of the altar has had to do with the souls of those who had been martyred, and whose souls had cried in vi. 9 from beneath the altar to God for judgment on the inhabitants of the earth. This act of Messianic judgment is thus connected with the prayers of the martyrs: cf. Luke xviii. 7, 8.

14. There can be no question as to the identity of the divine figure seated on the cloud. He is described as "One like a Son of Man." The phrase oiotov viov avopunrav is a solecism so far as regards form, and is found only in our author here and in i. 13. The O. T. source of this expression is undoubtedly Dan. vii. 13, "I saw in the night visions, and behold, there came with the clouds of heaven one like unto a son of man (LXX, J vios avowirov)." But the expression, though identical in both works, so far as language goes, is dissimilar in meaning. According to the interpretation of the angel in Dan. vii. 18, 22, 27, the phrase denotes the saints of the Most High. But this is not all. In apocalyptic visions, where men or bodies of men are symbolized by beasts (as in Daniel, i Enoch, Testaments of the XII Patriarchs, etc.), angels and supernatural beings are symbolized by men. If, therefore, the expression " Son of Man " is to be taken strictly in Daniel, it undoubtedly suggests a supernatural being or body of such beings supernatural beings but not angels; for the form of the phrase excludes this possibility. In the apocalyptic vision an angel is simply designated " a man." Hence the words "like a man "- "like an angel," i. e. a being who is of a supernatural character but not an angel Thus in Daniel we are to infer that the faithful remnant in Israel are to be transformed into supernatural beings as in i Enoch xc. 38 (161 B. C.). That this is the meaning of the text is proved by the adjoining clause, "there came with the clouds of heaven." This clause implies beyond question supernatural authority.

Thus in Daniel the phrase is a collective designation of the righteous Israelites after they have undergone a heavenly transformation.

But a further development was necessary before we arrive at the conception conveyed by this phrase in pur author, and this development was reached first, so far as existing literature goes, in i Enoch xxxvii.-lxxi., the author of which interpreted "one like a son of man " of an individual, i. e. the Messiah, and by so doing rose to the conception of a supernatural Messiah. Thus the way was prepared for the N. T. designation "the Son of Man " (6 vtfo rov dvlpuirov) which in the Gospels has thrown off its distinctive apocalyptic form " like unto a Son of Man " (d s viot foopwrov), a form, however, which has been retained in the Apocalypse. On this use of fc in apocalyptic see additional note on L 10, vol. i. p. 35 sq. For a like transition inside our author, cf. xv. 2, where we have first 0a arrav vaxbnqv and then TTyv Bdxcurarav rrjv vaxtwfv.

In 4 Ezra xiii. 3 (before 70 A. D.?) we find the very same expression. The Latin here is wanting, but the Syriac = J? 6Aotuia vtov dv0xu7rov, where, however, the Syriac is only a paraphrastic rendering of OKHOV as in the Peshitto of Ezek. i. 5, 22, 26, x. i; and of Rev. L 13, xiv. 14. See Gwynn, Apocalypse of St. John i. 13, note. Thus the Syriac of the Peshitto in Rev. i. 13, xiv. 14, and 4 Ezra xiii. 3 is exactly the same, and both presuppose oiotov vtov (i. e. vtp) avqpuirav. Hence 4 Ezra xiii. 3 should be rendered as follows:

"And I beheld and lo I the wind caused to come up out of the heart of the seas one like a son of man. And I beheld and lo! this son of man flew with the clouds of heaven." The Ethiopic version supports this rendering.

fytotok uu?. See the last note but one.

M T V KC AIJK KooVjfmKor. Cf. Dan. vii. 13. See note on i. 7.

rrto w xpwrf"- We have here the golden wreath but not the Sto Lurro, which he wears in xix. 12. Even in the Apocalypse the orc aios has many associations. Probably it carries with it here the idea of victory as in ii. 10, iii. n, vi. 2.

15-17. We have seen already in note on p. 18 that these verses are a doublet of 14, 18-20. We have found that 14, 18-20 come from the hand of our author and form a uniform picture, the unity of which is broken up by the interpolated verses 15-17. This doublet was probably suggested by the poetic parallelism in Joel iii. 13.

11 Put ye in the sickle, for the harvest is ripe: Come, tread ye, for the winepress is full."

In 15-17 the judgment is represented as a harvesting of the earth. This figure is used both in the O. T. and in the Gospels in relation to the last judgment: cf. Matt. xiii. 30, 39, but not in the Apocalypse, save in the present interpolated passage, where the figure is worked out fully and vividly. The interpolator of 15-17 has, of course, imitated the phrasing and diction of the Apocalypse, but he betrays his ignorance in four constructions, i. e. in 15, po av iv wijj pcyoa.0, whereas our author would have written pa av f vy Acyaxg (see Introd. to this Chap. 2); TW Kafrrjfjlwy iirl-rip vc c ip (whereas our author would have written brl rfi V ty see vol. i. p. II2 sq.): in 16, 6 a0i?AcioS crrl TJ?? vc cxis (whereas our author would have used M rrjv v f r)v); and ? oacv. hn-rijv yfjv (whereas our author would have written ? oacv. cis rrjv yfjv).

15. clxXos olyycxos. The attempt to explain the AAo? here as looking back to 6 or 9 can hardly be justified, since 6-11 and 14-20 are quite distinct visions. Even the use of KOI clsov KOI IBov in xiv. 14 (see note on iv. i) is sufficient to prove that this is so.

It is most important to distinguish the different meanings of XAos in xiv. 8, 9, 15, 17, 18. In xiv. 8, 9 there is no difficulty. AAo? is used idiomatically as in classical Greek, and the phrase = " another, the second angel," etc. But in xiv. 15, 17, 18 there is this use and another. In 15, 17 we have the ordinary use, where the phrase = " another angel." For the interpolator of xiv. 15-17 regarded the Son of Man in xiv. 14 merely as an angel, since in xiv. 17 he makes an angel hold joint authority with Him in the Messianic Judgment and discharge in xiv. 19-20 the duty assigned to the Messiah in xix. 11-16. Hence in xiv. 15 5AXos ayycao?=" another angel." But in xiv. 18 the phrase is to be rendered differently. There, on the excision of xiv. 15-17 as an interpolation, the oaAos in ixX. ayy. refers back indeed to the Son of Man in xiv.

14, but at the same time it distinguishes this angel from the Son of Man, as a different kind of being; for nowhere throughout our author is the Son of Man conceived of as an angel. Hence oxX. yy. = " another, an angel." Cf. the use of crcpos in Luke xxiii. 32.

K TOU KOOU. I. e. the heavenly temple. See note in vol. L p. 111 sq.

iv tori) jteydxg. Our author does not insert the ev: cf. vi. 10, vii. 2, 10, x. 3, xix. 17, where we have Kpaw tfrwr-fj ieyoafl. It is true that in xviii. 2 we have Kpafeiv cv urxvpp tuvy. But this latter passage is from another source.

T Kdhiiifop ivi Ttjs Kc cxr s. Here and in the next verse the construction is against the usage of our author, though it is the more usual in classical Greek. See note on iv. 2.

In the three lines beginning with iripfrov TO Spciraidv o-ov we have apparently a paraphrase of Joel iv. 13, 3 3 ao rtr TVp, the first line being an expanded translation of the first two words in Joel, and the second and third lines being probably duplicate paraphrastic renderings of the last three words, though, like the LXX and the Targum, they presuppose a text differing from the Massoretic. Thus line two, on r) Qev fj opa 0 ptrat, presupposes by 5 A,0cv some Hebrew verb = " has come " as also does the LXX by vapcorrikcv (cf. Mark iv. 29, ATI-GOT AAei TO opeiravov, OTI irapconykCv 6 Ocptcrfws) and the Targum by KDO. In line three, OTI f e pav f o 0cptrfio? rfc yijs, Ifypavoy presupposes E?2 Is this a corruption of 7KO? (rjpaiv is unexampled in the sense of "to ripen," so far as I am aware, but might be explained as a rendering of a corrupt text. Iqpaivu means " to dry up," as in xvl 1 2, or " to wither " when used of plants (cf. Matt. xiii. 6, etc.) or of crops (cf. Joel i. 17, cfypavtfij O-ZTOS), but not "to ripen." It will be observed that the writer of 15-17 uses some form of the Hebrew text and not the LXX.

TO Speirarov croo. We should observe two things here. First, we should expect the addition of TO 6 v here, since the epithet is already attached to Spcvavo in 14. In 18, which we hold to be the original sequel to 14, we find, as we should expect, ireplrov crow TO Spevavov TO o v. Next, in 15 we note the position of the crov after its noun, in which case the emphasis is laid on the pronoun, whereas in 18 the o-ov stands before its noun, in which case the emphasis is laid on TO Bpcvavovro 6 v a fact which points to the thoroughness with which the vintage is carried out in 19-20.

Spa Ocpunu. For the construction cf. v. 5, ix. 10, xi. 6, xvi. 9.

16. This verse is modelled on 19, the judgment being referred to under the figure of a harvest instead of a vintage. But, as I have already pointed out on 15, the construction 6 jca Acio? r rfc vff r)s is against the usage of our author. ifia tv. cvi TTJV yrjy is unexampled in our author. In such a construction cfc not cw is always used by him. See note on 19.

17. TOU POOU IK r oflpovw. See note in vol. i. p. HI sq.

18. We here resume the original vision into which 15-17 were interpolated. In this verse oaAoc fyycaos is to be rendered

"another, an angel" See note on 15 above. The phrase 6 IXP V c(ovriav cvi TOV irupos appears to be interpolated. At all events it makes no contribution to the context If it had any right to a place in our text it might have been in viii. 3, but even there it would have been meaningless. Lists of angels who were set over the natural elements will be found in i Enoch Ix. 11-21; Jub. ii. 2. See Bousset, Religion des Judentums l 317; Eneyc. Bib. ii. 1258 sqq.; Jeivish Encyc. i. 589 sqq.

ftyycxo?. K TOU Ouaiaortjpiou. When the disturbing interpolation, 15-17, is removed, the role of the angel, who came forth from the altar, is at once intelligible. The number of the martyrs is at last complete, and now their prayer (vi. 10) from beneath the altar can be fulfilled, and so the angel, who has to do with the souls of the martyrs beneath the altar, is entrusted by God with the task of carrying to the Son of Man the command to undertake the judgment of the earth to thrust in the sickle and reap the vintage and tread the winepress of the wrath of God (cf. xix. 15). This judgment is the Messianic judgment that precedes the Millennial reign of the Messiah. In xvi. 7 the altar itself proclaims the truth and righteousness of God's judgments. In ix. 13 a voice from the altar commands the letting loose of the first demonic woe against those who had not the seal of God in their foreheads. On this the one heavenly altar see note in vol. i. p. 224 sq. Only one angel is mentioned here in connection with the righteous martyrs beneath the altar. But in contemporary and earlier apocalyptic many angels were said to keep guard over the souls of the departed righteous: cf. i Enoch c. 5; 4 Ezra vii. 85, 95.

6 SXWH ouaiar icrx. See note at the beginning of this verse.

riit)(rcp 4w jicy Xj). uictv is found only here in our author. For the entire phrase cf. Mark i. 26; Acts xvi. 28.

T BpcirakOK rft 6 u, i. e. the sharp sickle mentioned in 14.

Wfi ok crou T Spcirako?. Here (cf. 15) we have a tristich, of which the first and third lines are largely a reproduction of Joel iv. 13. The first line consists simply of the words in Joel, with the addition of the epithet "sharp," which the context requires (cf. 14 ad fin., while the third line is in part a translation and in part a transformation of the clause in Joel, Q 3 T p; for fjkpacrav is a good rendering of? fi?2, whereas ol ora vxat avr s is simply substituted instead of 06pirjus=TVp. And yet this tristich gives the impression of the master hand, and drives home in each line with ever-increasing force the thought of the Seer, who does not quote but simply transforms an O. T. couplet to serve his present purpose. What a contrast it presents to the feebleness of the tristich in 15! It should perhaps be mentioned here that some scholars have taken 15-16 to refer to the ingather- ing of the saints, and 17-20 to the judgment that befalls the wicked, and thought that there is a delicate propriety in the fact that the former is assigned to the Son of Man, and the latter to a nameless angel. But there is no support for this view in-our author; for in xix. 11-16 it is this very treading of the winepress of the wrath of God that is especially the role of the Son of God. Moreover, in the rest of the N. T. the words Otp w and 0 uouh are used of reaping harvests good or bad, alike as regards man (cf. Matt. xxv. 24, 26; Gal. vi. 7, 8; i Cor. ix. n) and the angels, who are termed the 0cptrnfc (see Matt. xiii. 30, 39: cf. Mark iv. 29). As a man sows good or evil, he reaps accordingly. Similarly in the judgment, the angels gather alike the tares and the wheat in the last great harvesting (Matt. xiii. 30, 39). The word O-ZTOS, " wheat, 11 as a symbol of the righteous is not found in our author. Finally to resume once more in xiv. 6-20 we have a proleptic summary from the divine standpoint of the Messianic judgments which are represented on a larger canvas in xvi. i8-xviii. and xix. 11-21, xx. 7-10. Thus there is no ground for the attempt to differentiate and justify the occurrence side by side of what are really doublets. 15-17 are, from whatever standpoint we regard them, a disturbing element in the text.

19. Spaxck. cis tv YVJK. Our author uses either rt-rip yjs, v. 3, 10, 13, vii. i, x. 2, 5, 8, xvi. 18, xviii. 24, or cfc tip yfjv, v. 6, vl 13, viii. 5, 7, ix. i, 3, xii. 4, 9, 13, xiii. 13, xvi. i, 2. ? oacv. brirrjv yrjv is found only in the interpolated passage, xiv. 15-17.?foacv is here another rendering of r6t? in Joel iv 13.

6 Syycxos. An interpolation due to the hand that inserted 15-18. The Son of Man is never described as an angel. See note on 15.

TV XIJKOV. TOV AC OK. This irregularity is probably to be explained by the fact that Aipo? in classical Greek is sometimes masculine (Winer, lix. 4, p. 661; cf. Kautzsch's Gesenius' Hcb. Gram, for similar anomalies in Heb.: no k, 135 0, 1440, 145 , , u). Analogous solecisms are characteristic of our author: cf. xxi. 14, TO rectos. l cuv.

Xi)pfr TOO Oupou TOO Ocou. Here and in xix. 15 only in the N. T. The phrase rov Iviov TOV 0eov is rather frequent: cf. xv. i, 7, xvi. i, 19, xix. 15.

90. Though the Messianic judgment as executed by the Son of Man is here described in awful terms, it is not the final judgment, which is regarded by our author as the prerogative of the Father: cf. xx. 11 sqq. The diction appears to be influenced by Isa. Ixiii. 3, where Yahweh declares, "I have trodden the winepress alone," and in i Enoch c. 3, "And the horses shall walk up to the bieast in the blood of sinners, And the chariot shall be submerged to its height." This phraseology reappears in Talmudic writings in connection with the carnage at Bether in the time of Hadrian: see my note in i Enoch c. 3: also 4 Ezra xv. 35, erit sanguis a gladio usque ad ventrem equi; 36, et femur hominis et poplites cameli.

Quocy T j-nrfxcus. There can be no question as to the identity of " the city." It is not Rome (for its destruction has already been announced in the hearing of the Seer in 9), but Jerusalem. It is, moreover, most probably not the earthly Jerusalem but the heavenly Jerusalem which is to descend from heaven to be the centre of the Kingdom of Christ for the 1000 years. For in the notes on xx. 1-6 we shall see that the heavenly Jerusalem described in xxi. Q-xxii. 2 is in reality the city that is to come down from heaven to take the place of the old Jerusalem and become the capital of Christ's kingdom for the 1000 years. Ifxiv. 14, 18-20 is a proleptic summary of xix. 11-21 only, then the city referred to might be the historic Jerusalem, or rather its ruined site: but if this is a summary of xix. 11-21 and also xx. 7-10, then the city can be none other than the city that came down from heaven the seat of the Messianic Kingdom.

Jewish tradition had long associated the neighbourhood of Jerusalem with the scene of the judgment of the Gentiles. According to Joel iii. 2, 12, God was to assemble and judge the Gentiles in " the valley of Jehoshaphat," a phrase which Theodotion renders by rqv i pav-rijs Kptvccas. According to the Midrash Mishle, 68 d, God was to judge the whole world in this valley. It is referred to in i Enoch hii. i (where see my note). Zechariah speaks also of the judgment of the Gentiles, who laid Jerusalem desolate, being executed on the Mount of Olives (xiv. 2 sqq., 12 sq.). In our author it is all the heathen nations that are to be similarly judged.

fjx0ey atpa KT. See preceding notes.

diro otasiw KT.- "to a distance of 1600 furlongs." This peculiar use of diro is found also in John xi. 18, xxi. 8 (diro m? x"" Staicoo-tw). Abbott (Gram. p. 22 7) describes it as " a natural transposition arising from the desire to give prominence to the notion distant, as in our distant two hundred cubits, and then illogically allowing the preposition that signifies distance to govern cubits. 1 " Similar transpositions occur in the case of wpo, as in John xii. i, irpo I LCM? rov ircco a; LXX of Amos L i, iv. 7, Hippocrates, wpo rptuv ijptpw ri rcacvrip (this last is quoted from Moulton, Gram. 101, note): and also in the case of xrra: cf. Test. Reub. i. 2; Test. Zeb. i. i; Plut. Coriol n. These idioms are not Latinisms but of Greek origin.

As regards the number itself various explanations have been offered, but none is absolutely convincing. Some have found in 1600 the idea of completeness, and therefore inferred that the deluge of blood swept over the whole earth (as Victprinus per omnes mundi quattuor partes), the holy city alone being exempt. Others have conceived that Palestine only was designed by the number, since according to Jerome (Ep. 129, Ad Dard.) the length of Palestine from Dan to Beersheba was 160 miles. But 160 miles = only 1280 stades. A nearer approach to the number in our text is to be found in the Itinerarium of Antoninus, according to which Palestine was said to be 1664 stades from Tyre to El-Arish.

Of the two above interpretations I am inclined to adopt the former. The more we study xiv. 14, 18-20 the more clear it becomes that it deals with the same subject as xix. 11-21, for xiv. 18-19 clearly state that the judgment is of the whole earth. Hence it is not merely the heathen nations that had submitted to the antichristian empire of Rome that are destroyed in xix. 11-21, but likewise all the remaining heathen nations that rebel against the kingdom of Christ (xx. 7-10) after the lapse of the TOGO years. Hence the slaughter is commensurate with the inhabited world.

axpt TUP xa tca? TUP Tirirw. These words apparently refer to the heavenly horsemen who are mentioned definitely (xix. 14) in another vision dealing with the same events, .?. xix. 11-21.

CHAPTER XV. i. Character and object of this Chapter.

The chronological order of events in the Seer's visions of the future is here resumed. In other words, this chapter, so far as chronological order goes, follows immediately on xni.; for, as we have seen (see p. i: cf. 32), xiv. broke away from this order and was wholly proleptic, passing over as it did the first six Bowls and summarizing the divine judgments from the seventh Bowl (xvi. 17) to xx. 7-10. In order, therefore, to recognize the connection between xiii. and the present chapter, we have only to remember that in xiii. 15 the second Beast caused all that refused to worship the first Beast to be put to death. Thus all the faithful were put to death and the roll of the martyrs was complete with the close of xiii.; and when we come to xv. we find that xv. 2-4 looks upon the destruction of the entire body of the faithful as already an event of the past (see note on xv. 2-4), and represents the entire martyr host as standing on the sea of glass before God and singing a song of praise to the Lord God of Hosts, xv. i is an interpolation (see 7). In xv. 5-xvi. i the Seer has a vision of the appointment of seven angels with seven

Bowls to execute the last series of cosmic woes upon the earth. It is to be observed that in these three series the Seals, the Trumpets, and the Bowls there is a distinct development and not a mere recapitulation as has hitherto either wholly or in part been assumed by students of the Apocalypse. This will be clear as we advance.

For to the first four Seals and the sixth all men saints and sinners, Christians and heathen alike are subject. Only the faithful are the victims of the fifth Seal. The sixth Seal describes in hyperbolic language the signs which precede the end, which, however, is not so near as the unbelievers apprehend. But there are worse things to come, the fifth, sixth and seventh, or rather the first, second, and third, Trumpets, 1 that is, the three demonic Woes, viii.-ix., xi. i4 b, 15, xii.-xiii. In vii. the faithful are sealed in order to secure them from these Woes. Hence these Woes did not affect the faithful, but only those that were without the seal of God. When we come to the Bowls we have arrived at a fresh stage of development. Since the martyrdom of the faithful is complete in xiii. and all the martyrs are represented as already in heaven in xv. 2-4, it is clear that only the heathen nations, that form the Roman Empire or hold aloof from it, survive.

On this heathen world, limited in the fifth Bvwl to the empire of the Beast, are poured down the plagues of the seven Bowls. Whilst the Seals and the Trumpets or Woes could be regarded as having a disciplining effect on the faithful, however they might affect the unbelievers, the Bowls cannot be regarded in any other light than that of punishments, though such expressions as those in xvi. 9, n, which refer to the refusal of men to repent notwithstanding these plagues, point to the fact that repentance was still possible for them. That the plagues, which are universal and not local (except the fifth), do not annihilate the heathen nations is clear from the fact that the eternal gospel (xiv. 6) is to be preached to the surviving nations after the close of the seven Bowls and the Messianic judgment (xix. 11-21).

2. Relation of xv. to xiv. and xvi.-xx. In xiv. our author has given three proleptic visions the first portraying the blessedness awaiting the martyrs in the Millennial kingdom, while the second and third describe the judgments about to befall Rome and the heathen nations. Thus xiv. summarized the outstanding events from the close of the universal martyrdom of the faithful to the final judgment. From this prelude the Seer now returns to describe in detail the events thus briefly foreshadowed, and first of all the blessedness into which the martyred faithful enter immediately on death, xv. 2-4, and the subsequent 1 We have seen that the first four Trumpets are an interpolation in the text (see p. 219 sqq).

Millennial reign on earth, xx. 4-6 (cf. xiv. 1-5). Next we have the vision of the seven last Plagues, which are to descend on the heathen world, from which all the faithful had already been removed, xv. 5-xviil (cf. xiv. 6-n). The doom of antichristian Rome, which does not come to pass till the seventh Plague, is portrayed with great fullness in xvii.-xvni. On the destruction of Rome there follow thanksgivings in heaven, xix. 1-8. The next act of judgment is that executed by the Son of Man on the heathen nations, xix. 11-21 (cf. xiv. 14, 18-20).

3. This chapter consists of two visions. The first, xv. 2-4, deals with the triumphal song sung by the martyrs as they stand round the sea of glass in heaven. It is a song of unmixed praise and thanksgiving; for the last martyrdom on earth is over and the ranks of the martyrs in heaven are now complete. l he second vision relates to the

Seven Angels who come forth from the heavenly Temple and are thereupon furnished with the seven Bowls which are full of the wrath of God.

4. The diction of xv. 2-8 iv, except in the case of one phrase in 6 9 that of our author. This will be apparent as we proceed.

1. This verse could be assigned to him in point of diction but not the phrase dyyous fnra? x onra irxijys irrc, because of the context. As I shall show in 7 ad fin., our author could not use this expression here or in 6. Otherwise the language recalls that of our author, but yet in certain respects with a difference. KOU cfto? is, of course, attested throughout the book, cnjjicto. This word has already been used in a like (and yet not altogether like) connection in xii. i, 3. A perfect parallel to its present usage would have led us to expect it in vni. 13. pcya xal Oaufuurnsy: cf. xv. 3. dyyaous tirrd. This is the right order for the numeral in our author. TOS rx Ta seems borrowed from xxi. 9. 3n lv aurais ircxcogi) KT.: cf. 8 But the subject-matter is open to objection (see note in loc.).

9. KKwras IK. A pregnant construction. Though VLKO. V is a favourite verb with our author the construction here is unique in Greek. TOO Oijpiou KOI. TTJS CIK KOS aurou KCU. TOO apiopou T. iwfywrros. Cf. xiil 17, xiv. II. laruras iirl T. Odxcuraa. Our author in x. 5, 8 writes M with the gen. in this phrase. But his usage is not fixed. See note on xv. 2. Kiodpas TOU Ocog a Hebraism.

3. KCU (jtSoucrtk. Here, as in xiv. 3, KU ovrii is to be taken as KOL vra. In fact this is the reading of Prim. Vg. and S 1. See note on xiv. 3. xjpic 6 Ocos 6 mrrokpcitup. A familiar title of God in our author: cf. i. 8, iv. 8, xi. 17, xvi. 7, xix. 6, xxi. 22. SUCOKU KU d T)0iku recurs in converse order in xvi. 7, xix. a.

4. nos. Used only in xvi. 5, as here of God, but not in the rest of the N. T. irdtra ra 20it). irpoo-Kum aouai. Cf. xiv. 7, where all the nations are bidden u-pooncwijcratc rp Troiijo-airi. tyav pu9i ra. v. Cf. iii. 18. 5. nal ftcra raura ctw. A clause used in our author introducing a new vision: cf. iv. i n. Hence i cannot be right, since it has already introduced the vision. Voiyi oupovw. Cf. xi. 19.

6. Torres ra? lirra irxt yfe. This phrase descriptive of the seven angels, as also in xv. i, is against the usage of our author as well as against the context. See below, 7. yscsupfoi Xiook. KU irepicluxtfifw. (rfyas xp ua 5. Cf. i. 13, xix. 14. 7. ycpouaa?. Cf. iv. 6, 8, etc. TOO IPTOS els aluvas TUK alwkwy. Cf. iv. 9., x. 6. 8. XP 1 Cf. xvii. 17, xx. 3, for the same clause.

5. Strongly Hebraic character ofxv.

This chapter is Hebraic in character, i. The writer translates in xv. 4 the Hebrew of Jer. x 7, where the LXX is lacking: 6 poaixeus. TIS 06 pi) o0i)(vj; Here Theodotion and Aquila render TIS ov py QofiriqTJcrttai ere fcurtxcv TWV iqvv; It is true that the words irdrra ra c6mr). tottdv aou in 4 agree verbatim with the LXX of Ps lxxxvi. 9, save that it omits om fcroivas after ny. But there is nothing distinctive in the LXX rendering.

2. As regards the order this is also Hebraic. The verb nearly always begins the clause or follows immediately on the subject as in 4, 7, 8. In 4 the position of ifav p!6vjtav serves to gives emphasis.

3. There are some Hebraisms. Thus in 2-3 we have TOS KikWKras = r. vcvtft-tffcora?. after the model of the Hebrew participle: lorahras a! oucriy = cororas.

ccuasovras (see in loc.): and Kiodpos TOU Ococ = Dn Mn nroD. Possibly vucuhrac IK may be due to a Hebraism.

4. In 5, 6 there are two phrases which apparently cannot be satisfactorily explained except on the hypothesis that 6 vofo T S O-KTJVTS TOV fwprvpiov in 5 is a translation from a Hebrew text, and that a corrupt one, and that the second phrase in 6 is due to the translator taking VV to mean Aflov, whereas in this context it could only=3vrcrivoi. See text in facts.

6. xv. 2-8 appears to be a translation by our author from a Hebrew source.

Since xv. 2-8 is from the hand of our author (4), and since, according to 5, xv. 2-8 is not only strongly Hebraistic but appears to imply a Hebrew source; and, finally, since in xv. 5, 6 the text can be best explained on the hypothesis of a corrupt

Hebrew source, this section appears to be a translation by our author from a Hebrew source.

7. xv. I appears to be an interpolation the chapter having originally begun with xv. 2: further, for ot erra ayycaot ot fyoircs ras euro. Trxiyyas in 6 we should read simply ayyexot eirra. (Cf. xv. 7, xvi. i.) The question has naturally been asked, how can the Seer have seen the angels in xv. i, before they came forth from the Temple, which was not opened till xv. 5? This fact has caused much difficulty, and, as we should expect, a variety of explanations has been offered. Volter in his last works assigns xv. 5-6 to the Apocalypse of Cerinthus and xv. 1-4, 7 to an editor in Trajan's time. Weyland ascribes xv. i, 6- 8 to an editor and the remaining verses to two different sources. Spitta traces xv. i and fragments of 2, 3, 5 and 7 to an editor: Erbes, xv. i, 5-8 to an editor of the year 80 A. D., and J. Weiss, xv. 1-4, 6-7 to an editor of the year 95 A. D.

None of these solutions of the difficulty has gained acceptance, and so Bousset thinks there is no need to excise any part of the text, and that xv. i is simply to be regarded as a superscription. But this explanation is, if anything, less satisfactory than the preceding. For (i) a superscription should not be introduced by the words al cftw, but rather be something of the nature of 17 opoo-ts TWV cirra dyyexwi icrx. (2) If it were a superscription it ought to have been inserted immediately after 4 and not before 2, seeing that 2-4 constitute an independent and absolutely different vision. (3) That a new and important vision is introduced by xv. 5 is shown by the use of the clause fjl ra TOvra e78ov. See iv. i. (4) Again, as I have shown below, the Seven Angels are wrongly described in this verse as "seven angels having seven plagues the last." Their right description would be " seven angels having seven bowls." (5) The clause Sri cv avrats crcxco-tfi? 6 Ovfjws rov 0cov is unjustifiable. The wrath of God cannot be conceived as coming to an end till sin is at an end or adequately punished. And this does not take place tili the final judgment. (6) The scene of the Seer's vision is wrongly represented as having been experienced on the earth etsov Xo oypelov rp ovpavui (cf. xii. i, 3) whereas it was undoubtedly in heaven: cf. xv. 5 sqq. Accordingly there appears to be no other way of solving the difficulty than to suppose either that xv. i is due to a marginal gloss subsequently incorporated in the text, or that it was an early interpolation by a scribe. Hence the chapter really begins with the vision of the triumphant martyrs in heaven, xv. 2-4, while xv. 5 introduces the vision of seven angels coming forth from the Temple in heaven. In xv. 6 instead of ot rra ayyexot ot cgoires ras rra we should simply read ayycxot fora. The change was made when xv. i was incorporated in the text. The interpolator, moreover, made a very inept addition. He did not know his text For, as is clear from xv. 7, the Seven Angels did not receive "the bowls full of the wrath of God " till after they had left the Temple, whereas in 6 they are represented as having the plagues before doing so. Again, these Seven Angels, when they are mentioned subsequently, as they are four times, are never described as "the seven angels having the seven plagues," but simply as "the seven angels," xv. 7, xvi. i, or "the seven angels which had the seven bowls," in xvii. i, xxi. 9. Each bowl contains a plague, and so the seven plagues, xv. 8, result respectively from the pouring forth in succession of the seven Bowls.

1. This verse cannot be original, as we have already seen in the Introd. to this Chapter, 7. It is true that the style resembles that of our author, but there are strong grounds against its being from his hand. The first is that the Seer cannot have seen the angels in i, seeing that the Temple is closed till 5, and the angels do not emerge from it till then. But there are other and more radical grounds for the rejection of this verse, (i) First, as we are aware (see note on iv. i) the clause icai tcra ravra ctSoi (xv. 5) always introduces a new and important section in the Apocalypse; but, if it had already been introduced in xv. i, then this clause would be out of place. Moreover, in xv. i the clause nal ttbov is used by our Seer to introduce the less important sections. The interpolator of xv. i does not seem to have been aware of this usage. If we excise xv. i and remember that xiv. is wholly proleptic in character, ivfeiring as it does to events subsequent to xvi. 17 (see p. 2), then the blessedness of the martyred faithful is set forth in contrast to their terrible plight in xiii. (2) The expression dyycxov? 7rra fyovras Trxiyyas kirra. is not that used by our author elsewhere, save in 6 where it appears also to be an interpolation, though it may have been suggested by the last clause in xv. 8. For the last three words we should have fyovras xaas eirrd: cf. xv. 7, xvii. i, xxi. 9. See also 8. The phraseology throughout xvi. also supports this objection. (3) The words ras rxira9 (probably derived from xxi. 9) are generally explained as the last plagues in contrast to the plagues mentioned in ix. 20; but that this is not the meaning of the writer of this verse is clear from the clause which follows, with which we shall now deal. (4) The clause just "referred to ort avrats frcaccrft; 6 0vios TOV Ofov cannot be given any satisfactory explanation. It manifestly states that the wrath of God will be consummated in these seven Bowls, whereas the last and most terrible of the divine judgments do not take place till after their close. The right expression is found in XV. 8, axw rca. cr6arii al cirra Aiytu, which is probably the source of the interpolator's phrase. These seven Plagues can be described as wholly consummated in xvi.-xviii., but not so the wrath of God.

On the above grounds we cannot but regard xv. x as an interpolation. When this interpolation was once effected, jyycxot hrrd in 6 was changed into o! rra fyycaot 01 IX OVT T "? "" Traiyas in order to adapt the context to the text thus interpolated. The incongruity of the addition ol fy 0 "? T- rra iraiyas is very glaring, seeing that the seven angels do not receive the plague-bearing Bowls till the next verse.

itai ctsof. See notes on iv. i.

xal etftok. iv T oupakw. This clause seems to have been suggested by xii. i.

ftaXo cnjjjleiok IK TW ofiparo. Cf. xii. i, 3, where this phrase implies that the Seer is on earth. But clearly in the vision of the Seven Angels he is in heaven: see xv. 5, xvi. i. This fact the interpolator failed to recognize.

plya KOI Oaujuumfo. Suggested (?) by the phrase tcyoan KU Oavfjmtrrd in 3. yyl ou irr. TOO Ocou. This passage has already been dealt with above. See also note on 7.

8-4. With this vision the march in the development of future events is resumed. The line of advance was abandoned for the time being in xiv., which, as we have seen, is wholly pro-leptic, and summarized all the coming judgments from the seventh Bowl to the immediate advent of the final judgment. Hence xv 2-4 is to be taken in close connection with xui. In xiii. 15 the second Beast is represented as exterminating the entire body of the faithful, and xv. 2-4 looks upon that extermination as already an event of the past. The roll of the martyrs is at last complete, and no longer are any of the faithful to be found on the earth, but only the heathen nations, which are either devoted followers of the Antichrist or occupy a neutral position, xv. 2-4 thus forms a companion picture to vii. 9-16. In both these the roll of the martyrs has just been completed or is on the eve of completion in heaven. The final judgment is still in the distance; for the conversion of the nations (cf. the announcement of the glad tidings in xiv. 6) is foretold (xv. 4) as an event of the future. In xiv. 1-5 and xx. 4, which depict a later stage, the martyrs have descended with Christ to the earth to share with Him the Millennial reign.

2. 6s (see Additional Note, i. p. 35 sq.) Orfxaaaa? da iit)K (= D?3 rvotot). This sea has already been referred to in iv. 6. The absence of the article is what we expect in this Hebraistic expression, which- " the likeness of a sea of glass."

vupi. This description is not attached to the heavenly sea when it is mentioned in iv. 6. But the difference of context is a sufficient explanation. In iv. 6 the vision is one of peace, whereas here it is one of judgment This phrase, therefore, may refer either to the sea as glowing with the wrath of God, or as reflecting the lightnings that proceeded from the throne of God, though there is here, it is true, no mention of these lightnings. In 2 Enoch xxix. 1-2 there is a passage that may be quoted, though it does not throw any real light on the text "From the gleam of My eye the lightning received its wonderful nature, which is both fire in water, and water in fire."

TOUS KikKras IK TOU Oqpiou. This is a very difficult phrase. There is no difficulty with the participle. Here VLKWVTOS = vcvuctjicoras. The great tribulation is over, and the martyre have triumphed over the Beast by proving faithful unto death. As our author thinks in Hebrew, his use of the Greek participle reflects that of the Hebrew participle, which, as we are aware, can = vikowae, vciuctyfcoras or VIKTCTOXCVOUS according to the context Here vikwiras is to be taken as a perfect participle. The roll of the martyrs is at last complete, but it has only just been completed. The Antichristian powers have not yet been judged, nor has the Millennial Kingdom been as yet established. When this kingdom is established the martyrs shall descend and reign (v. 10) with Christ for 1000 years (xiv. 1-5, xx. 4), and all the nations of the earth, which had not been leagued with Rome, shall come and worship before God (xv. 4, xxi. 24-26).

pikiras K. The use of CK after vucwiras is very difficult Winer (p. 460; quotes this passage in connection with a number of other passages where c is found, but not one of them has the same source as CK here. He compares the Latin expression " victoriam ferre ex aliquo," Livy, viii. 8, etc. But it would be difficult to justify the occurrence of a Latmism in our text. There is just the possibility that our author was here reproducing the Hebrew idiom nwrp onajn (cf. 2 Sam. i. 23; Ps. Ixv. 3) = "those who had been stronger than the beast. 1 But no adequate explanation has as yet been offered.

As Swete (in loc.) has pointed out, the martyrs show themselves as conquerors up to the moment of death: cf. Ep. Smym. 1 9, 8ia TJ S VTTOfioi s xaraycuvkrafievos TOV OKOV apxpvra at ovra? rov rip atfroapcrtas rrc aiov airoaafrov. Passio S. Perpetuae 1 8, "illuxit dies victoriae illorum, et processerunt de carcere in amphitheatrum quasi in caelum, hilares et vultu decori." But our Seer follows them into the life beyond and sees the exultant host celebrating not their own victory but the praises of God.

CK TOU Orjptou ical C K TTJS ciklros rrx. Cf. xiiu I, 14, 17, xiv. 9, ii, xix. 20, xx. 4. VOL. ii. 3 1-A iv Odxouaak. This phrase could mean "standing on" (cf. x. 5, 8, xii. 1 8, xiv. i) or "standing by" (cf. iii. 20). This scene of the victors standing on the heavenly sea with harps in their hands and praising God recalls Israel's song of triumph over Egypt on the shore of the Red Sea. The phraseology is unusual. In x. 5, 8 Zon?u is used with cvi TT? Oaxdo–criyc. Further, our author prefers generally the phrase eirt TTJS tfaadurftTs to iwl r v 0a currav: cf. vii. i b, x. 2, 5, 8. But the fact that tor u 7ri is in the case of all other nouns followed by the accusative (iii. 20, vii. i, viii. 3, XL n, xii. 18, xiv. i) may have led to the use of the accusative (instead of the gen.) of Oaxaura-a in the present instance after rnuras cvi.

itioclpas TOU Ocou = " harps belonging to the service of God." The omission of the article before t0opas is a Hebraism. On this idea cf. v. 8, xiv. 2. With this phrase we might compare i Thess. iv. 16, ev ouaTnyyi 0eoi), and i Chron. xvi. 42; 2 Chron. vii. 6, Dn tn "W 3 = " instruments to accompany the songs of God."

3. Kal fsouaii. These words are to be taken as = Kal psoira? and the passage to be rendered: " I saw. standing on the sea. and singing." This Hebraism has occurred several times already: see note on xiv. 2-3.

TV wv Muuolus TOU oouxou TOU Oeou Kal T P pv TOU PKIOU. Now that the martyr host is completed, and are already standing before God, they sing a song of praise to God, but not one of triumph over their enemies a fact which differentiates this song from that in Ex. xv. The first words, " the song of Moses the servant of God," recall Ex. xiv. 31, xv. i, where Moses and the children of Israel sang a song of thanksgiving to God, but still more a paean of triumph over the Egyptians and of joy at their destruction (Ex. xv. 2-19).

As that song was sung on earth, on the shore of the Red Sea by Israel after the flesh, so this song is sung in heaven by the Sea of Glass before God by the spiritual Israel.

The expression TTJV WTJV Moowew. cat r. taqv rov pviov creates insuperable difficulties. To excise (as most editors have done) KCU T. p8 v TOV apvtbv as an interpolation would only aggravate the difficulty in the present context. For, since it was through the Lamb that the Christian martyrs triumphed, if the song that followed was associated with any name, that name must have been that of the Lamb. Hence the difficulty does not originate in connection with this phrase, but rather with r. p8V MQWO-D?. How then are we to explain the collocation of the two phrases? Bousset is of opinion that the repetition of the phrase suggests that the victors sang first the old Song of Moses (Ex. xv. 2-19) and then a new song that of the Lamb, which is then given. This apparently is the view of Swete.

"St. John does not write r. 8rjv Mowo-cwc icat rov apwbv, for the notes are distinct though they form a harmony." This view can hardly be regarded as satisfactory. That the old dispensation is superseded is the essential belief of our author, and it can no less have been his conviction that in heaven the faithful members of the old dispensation would accept the teaching of the new. Moreover, if our author deliberately omits all reference to the Law throughout the Apocalypse, it would be surprising if he referred here to its author Moses, and placed him before the Lamb. This being so, we can hardly suppose that our author implies that the song of Mo es, given in Ex. xv. 2-19, was actually sung by a body of Christian martyrs before the throne. We, therefore, expect that, if the text is original, the song given in our text, which makes no definite mention of either Moses or of the Lamb, was sung alike by the martyred faithful of Judaism and Christianity, and that too led by the Lamb, as the song in Ex. xv. was led by Moses. But the form of the text is against this conclusion, and implies that the song or songs are led by Moses and the Lamb.

Thus there seems to be no way out of the difficulty save by assuming that the words r. tffiv Mowo-cu? rov Bovxov rov 0cov originated in a marginal gloss, which was subsequently incorporated in the text. Moreover, the nature of the song supports this assumption, since it is not a song of triumph, but simply a paean of thanksgiving, which the martyrs sing, when in the first perfect unclouded vision of God they wholly forget themselves and burst forth into praise of the Lord God of Hosts, who alone is holy, whose works are great and marvellous, whose ways are righteousness and truth, and to whom all the nations shall do homage, because of the coming manifestation of God's righteous judgments.

Not until this stage does the Seer behold the complete spiritual transformation of the faithful in heaven. At the same time by its mention of divine judgments to come, it prepares the way for the advent of the Seven Angels with their plagues. This song, therefore, though sung by the victorious Christian host of martyrs, could not be more fittingly conceived. Its sole theme is God; for, in the perfect vision of God, self is wholly forgotten, and so far as there is a reference to the earth from which they have been delivered, it is one of hopefulness: "the nations shall come and worship before Thee."

The gloss r. cpsqv Monwws icrx. in this context is probably due to the fact that the triumph of the actual Israel over the Egyptians at the Red Sea was certainly regarded by the Christians of the first century as prefiguring the triumphs of the spiritual Israel, as we see from the Pauline Epistles.

This song of Moses in Ex. xv. had already been incorporated in the Temple Services. Thus it was sung at the evening sacrifice on the Sabbath (Edersheim, The Temple p. 188), and in the benediction that followed the Shema there is a reference to it: "A new song did they that were delivered sing to Thy name by the seashore" (Encyc. Bib. iv. 4954). According to Philo (De Vita Contempl XL) this song was sung by the Therapeutae, the men forming one chorus and the women the other, while in the DC Agriculture xvii., he writes: "the chorus of men will have Moses for their leader and that of the women will be under the guidance of Miriam. Accordingly all the men sing the song on the seashore. Moses being the leader of their song; and the women sing Miriam being their leader."

The Martyrs' Song is formed almost wholly of O. T. expressions.

pcydxa KCU Oaujiaard T pya aou. The first epithet as describing the works of God is found in Ps. xcii. 5, cxi. 2, and the second in Ps. xcviii. i, cxxxix. 14; i Chron. xvi. 9.

Kispic, Oeos o irouroicpdtwp. See Amos iv. 13, but the phrase occurs several times elsewhere in our text (see note on i. 8).

Biicaiai ical d T Oikal at 6oi roo. Cf. xvi. 7, xix. 2; Ps. cxlv. 17, Sucatos fcvpio? iv Trao-ats rats 68019 avrov: Deut. xxxii. 4, axfjoiva. ra cpya avrov.

6 paaixcus TWK ttvw. 4. TIS ou pj +o0T)6jj. These clauses are a rendering of Jer. x. 7, which, though present in Aquila and Theodotion, are wanting in the LXX. The title " king of the nations " is here peculiarly appropriate, since it is God's dealings with the nations alike in the way of condemnation and of mercy that is the theme of this song and of the chapters that follow.

xal 8o (aci rd okopd aou. Cf. Ps. lxxxvi. 9, 8o ao-oixriv TO ovoxaoxru; see also 12; Mai. i. n, TO ovomd crov 8e8o aorai cv rois c vccrtv. PSKOS Sorios. Cf. I Sam. li. 2, ori OVK Icrriv ayu9 w? Kvpios. With the expression xovos 00-109 cf. Rom. xvi. 27, fjLQVIp 0-0)0).

STI irdrra T ffonr) rjfouaik. ikism K otu. From Ps. lxxxvi. 9.

T Sucauspata KT. Cf. Ps. xcviii. 2. fcatc!uara here means the judicial sentences of God in relation to the nations either in the way of mercy or condemnation. On Rome and all the adherents of the Empire will be manifested the judgments of God; whereas during the Millennial period the rest of the nations will experience His mercy. Cf. xiv. 6-7, which refer to the Millennial period. On the other hand, some scholars take aiofiara in the sense of "righteous deeds" a meaning which it undoubtedly possesses in the gloss in xix. 9 But xvi. i, 4aaa? ro? Qvpov TOV 0cov, xvi. 7, SIKCLUU at icuo-cif orov, and other analogous expressions are in favour of the interpretation given above.

irdmra T 0w TJ OUOIK rrx. These words point forward to the conversion of the nations during the Millennial reign: cf. xxi. 24 sq,, xxii. 2. In xiv. 7 the nations are exhorted to repent and worship God. Of course it is only the nations that survive the judgments in xvl-xix. that are so converted.

5n. i+ai fxs0i)rai. This clause gives the ground for the clause that immediately precedes: " for Thy righteous judgments shall have been made manifest."

XV. 5-XVI. L The commission of the Seven Angels with the Bowls.

5. ita! JJLCT Tdura ctw. As has been shown on iv. i, this phrase is never used except at the beginning of an important section. Thus the insertion of xv. i, which already deals with this subject, is wholly against the usage of our author. See also above on i.

Koiyvi 6 HOOS. Iv T ofipewfi. So in xi. 19.

6 KO9 t TTJf rk1)K1)S TOO fjLOptUploU f.

This designation of the heavenly Temple is certainly strange " the temple of the tabernacle of the testimony." It appears either to be an interpolation or the rendering of a corrupt Hebrew source. If we translate the phrase into Hebrew it is clear that vac? must be rendered by tan, cvciyn generally by bnk (occasionally by 3Bto), and frnprvptov by "Ijrfo (or possibly by rrny). But it must certainly be confessed that Ijmd fci fan is an absolutely unexampled designation, and difficult to justify.

The phrase in the text cannot be a rendering of biik pfipD (cf. Ex. xl. 2, 6, 29, since voos is never used to translate

Ziillig thinks that this expression is used in order to recall the fact that, when the Tabernacle with all its holy vessels was brought up to Jerusalem by the order of Solomon, the Ark was removed from it and set up in the most holy place in the Temple (2 Chron. v. 5; i Kings viii. 4), and that from that time forward the temple could also bear the name of the Tabernacle, and that in fact it is called mishhkan (pp) in Ps. lxxxiv. 2, cxxxii. 5, and ohel (HK) in Ezek. xll i. Hence he would, as Bousset, render the entire phrase as " the temple, that is, the tabernacle of the testimony." The genitive would in this case be one of apposition. But against the identification of the va6s and owny in our text there is the very great objection, that in Apocalyptic, from the vision in Isa. vi. to the latest times, it is the Temple whether in heaven or on earth, and not the Taberna-le that is referred to as the scene of apocalyptic vision. See note on viii. 3. Hence, since throughout the rest of the Apocalypse this usage is followed, the natural inference is that it is followed here. If this be so, then it is to be concluded that rijs o-Krjvijs rov fuiprupiov is an addition. If we might here assume a Hebrew original, we could dispose of the difficulty. Thus vaos rfaffkr stovJMprvpiovlvtQo pai(i)=xftw3 1JDD Slk WH, which might easily be a corruption of DBBOP DWK iovi = 6 vacs rov 0 ov iv rip ovpavw the very phrase that is found in xi. 19, with the same verb in both cases, i. e. fyoiyr).

6. oi irr yy. ol x- T- irra irxtiyds. As we have already seen on i, we should excise oi fa T "" irxiyyos as an addition from the hand that added i and read simply ayyeaoi cirra.

ScsuJL KOi txiooyf. ircpic ftxrjilioi. (t See note on the diction in i. 13.

ipesufupoi fxiookf icaOapi Xaprprfk. AC, a few Cursives, and the MSS of the Vulg. read AiOov for Aivov, which is found in the lesser authorities. That AiOov would more readily be changed into ivov and not vice versa is evident in itself. Besides, though thu best Codd. of the Vulg. have lafide the official text has linteo. WH adduce Ezek. xxviii. 13, vdvra L6av xpriavbv cyscdco-at in support of i9ov. Further, Xtvov (= flax) is not used as the equivalent of Aivow (= a garment made of flax) except in a few passages throughout Greek literature: cf. Homer, . ix. 661, Od. xiii. 73, 118; Aesch. Suppl 120, 132, Etym. Magn. The evidence, therefore, is strongly in favour of i6ov. But, notwithstanding the advocacy of WH, AiOov cannot be right. We must, therefore, assume either that, despite the very great improbability, A. iOov is a primitive corruption of the all but unexampled word ivov (= "linen garment" a most unusual meaning), or that we have here a mistranslation from the Hebrew. erscsvACpot ioov = W D Z. But as we know, means either fivo-o-ivo?, Gen. xli. 42; Ex. xxviii. 35 (39), or X os (cf. Esth. i. 6) or uxpiapos (Cant. v. 15). In fact, in later Hebrew it generally means "alabaster" or "marble." In the Epistle of Jeremy 71 the same mistranslation, as Ball has shown, occurs: "Ye shall know them to be no gods by the purple and the marble (rq? uapiapov) which rotteth upon them." Here uapiapo? w, which should have been rendered by rov fiwrcrivov= n fine linen." "Marble doesn't rot," as Ball remarks. Now returning to our text, if we may assume a Hebrew original, then instead of frscsvicpoi Xloov Kaoapov afjlirp6v we should read ipscbufupoi 0iwikOK naoap K Xojlirp6K, To confirm this conclusion we have only to turn to xix. 8, where we find ircpifia r Tcu fivo-crivov Xafjarpov Kaqapov, Or to xix. 14, where we have the clause that should be in our text,

XCVKOV Ka.6a. p6v. Hence we render "clothed in fine linen pure bright. 91 On the significance of this expression see note on lii. 5.

irepielfcmTjj Koi KT. Cf. i. 13.

7. IK K TWK rcaorfpw ljw, . one of the Cherubim. See note on iv. 6. The Cherubim in the Apocalyptic of the ist cent. A. D. have come to be the chief order of angels. It is fitting therefore that one of them should act as an intermediary between God and the Seven Angels of the Bowls. Even in Ezek. x. 7 it is one of the Cherubim that hands over to one of the seven angels of judgment coals of fire to be sprinkled on the earth.

firra +i Xa xp U(r te On the position of cirrd before its noun see note on viii. 2.

4idxas. ycpouaas TOO 6u iou TOO 0eou. It is highly probable that the Greek word 10X77 was adopted into both Hebrew and Aramaic as early as the beginning of the Christian era: see Levi's two Lexicons in loc. It is noteworthy that it is used in connection with the same idea as in our text in the Targum on Isa. li. 17, where the Hebrew tfldPl ra (= "the cup of His wrath") is explained by KBI l KD3 D and in 22 nn DVD by nom KD3 D. Again in the Targum of Jon. on Gen. xl. 12 we have KTJni b"D = " the bowl of wrath " (i. e. of the divine wrath). The word thus appears to have had the same idea associated with it as in our text With the present passage cf. xiv. 8, 10.

TOU IKTOS cis TOUS aiwa. See note on iv. 9.

8. cycpuror) 6 Kaos Kairrou K rfjs 6 i)S TOU Ocou. yeu a belongs to the vocabulary of our author but is not used in this connection in the LXX. The first four words recall the statement in Isa. vi. 4, where in connection with the great vision of Isaiah it is said that "the house (i. e. the Temple) was filled with smoke" (6 oticos 7rxijo-0T7 Katrvav LXX). The combined ideas of the Temple being filled with smoke and with the glory of the Lord are found in Ezek. x. 4, "The house (i. e. the Temple) was filled with the cloud, and the court was full of the brightness of the Lord's glory ": Ex. xl. 35, "Moses was not able to enter into the tent of meeting because the cloud abode thereon, and the glory of the Lord filled the tabernacle." See also i Kings viii. 10. The glory of God is spoken of as filling the temple in Ezek. xliv. 4; 2 Chron. vii. 2-3. During such manifestations of God's presence no one could enter the earthly temple. In all the O. T. passages above cited the presence of God is a mark of His gracious purposes. Hence the inability of humanity to approach God in these passages was due to the infinite transcendence of God and His unapproachableness by merely finite creatures. But that cannot be the meaning of the clause in our text in TTJS Wl jl ws. This attribute of God is here set parallel with His glory. It is to be manifested in the plagues that follow.

oscls ftupato clacxOcik KT. As we have seen in the first note on this verse, none could enter the earthly Temple in the O. T. during special manifestations of God's presence therein. But, since this cannot hold of the heavenly Temple, inasmuch as in heaven the heavenly hosts are constantly represented as standing in God's immediate presence, it seems necessary to attach a figurative meaning to the clause o 6cl? cwro cio-cx civ rra., and to interpret these words as meaning that, until the plagues were accomplished, none could avert by prayer the doom about to befall the earth through these plagues. At the close of these judgments God's gracious purposes with regard to the nations would take effect: see xiv. 6, xxi. 24, 26.

CHAPTER XVI. i. The object of this Chapter.

The object of this chapter is to set forth the last series of plagues that are to befall the earth. These plagues are symbolized under the seven Bowls which are poured forth by Seven Angels.

In these seven Bowls we have no mere repetition of the divine visitations in the Seals and Woes. Not only are they different in themselves from the Seals and Woes, but they differ further in respect of time and the people affected by them. Although these facts have been brought forward in the Introduction to XY., it is necessary here to emphasize them anew, since the prevailing view is that in the Bowls we have not advanced chronologically, but that in the Seals, Trumpets (Woes), and Bowls the same great principles of God's government are displayed under different aspects. Even scholars, like Bousset, who are opposed to the Recapitulati n Theory, are disposed to acknowledge in some degree its validity in regard to the Seals, Trumpets, and Bowls. Though the reader should consult the Introduction to xv., I will here repeat the two chief differentiae between the Bowls and the Seals and Woes. These are that the people affected in each series is different and that their order is alike logical and chronological. Under the Seals (save the fifth to which only the Christians were subject) Christian and heathen alike suffer. Then after the sealing of the faithful takes place, all those who had not been so sealed are exposed to the thive demonic Woes. In the course of the thiid Woe the last of the faithful are martyred, and at its close the world is inhabited only by the heathen nations. Then follows the last series of cosmic and other plagues, which are all embracing in their incidence with the exception of the fifth Bowl, which is confined to the kingdom of the Beast, just as the fifth Seal affected only the faithful.

2. State of the Text.

The text of this chapter has suffered much through faulty transcription and deliberate alteration, xvi. i has tcyaai? fwrj; an abnormal order of words in our author. Both the context and the diction of xvi. 2 C, and certain clauses in 13-14 are against their authenticity, as is shown in the notes on these passages. The apparently meaningless interchange of efe and ctTt after CKXCU is strange, xvi. 10 has sustained the loss of several clauses, xvi. 5 b-7, which belongs to xix., has been restored in this edition to its original position after xix. 4; xvi. 15, which belongs to iii., has been restored after iii. 3.

3. Diction and Idiom.

When the interpolated clauses in xvi. 2, 13-14 are removed, the entire phraseology and constructions are those of our author, with the exception of xvi. i. There are, as was to be expected, phrases not found elsewhere in our author, but these are not against any established usage on his part (a) Diction.

1. jjKoura. MPTJ: cf. iii. 20, xiv. 13, xxi. 3. Elsewhere in our author wnyv after KOVCIV. TOLS irrd dyyots: cf. XV. 6, 8, xvii. I, xxi. 9. flitd-yc-re K. IICXTC: cf. x. 8, virayc Aa3c. XTC. cis: cf. 2, 3, 4, but c x. ri in 8, 10, 12, 17. TOU Oufiog rog Ocou: cf. xiv. 10, 19, xv. 7.

2. irijx6ck. xal lx cc ": c f- v 7 5 0 " " czXi cv: xvii. i, xxi. 9 (a Hebraism). Cf. John v. 15, ix. 7, u, xii. 36. tytvcro 2Xicos. iiri. Here only in our author. On the interpolation rov? c ovras. avrov, see note in loc.

6 b-7. See Introd. to xvi. 5 b-7 on p. 120 sqq.

9. Kagfia: cf. vii. 16. Ipxao fuioak TO opopa: cf. xiil 6. Sourai aori 84 ak: cf. iv. 9, xi. 13, xiv. 7, xix. 7.

10. TK Oprfpop TOU Orjpiou: cf. xiii. 2. ioncotOilim): cf. ix. 2, where the word refers to the same phenomenon. TOU irovou: cf. ii, xxi. 4. Only once elsewhere in N. T., i. e. Col. iv. 13.

11. TOP 6cof TOO oupakou: cf. xi. 13 (a source). 06 IK T. cpywk atv: cf. 11. 21, 22, ix. 20, 21.

Id. Toipaoofj. A frequent word in our author, ou: cf. vn. 2. 13. TOU Spuorros. TOU Oqpiou: cf. xiii. 4. TOU : cf. xix. 20, xx. 10. irveupara rpia: such is our author's order: see note on viii. 2.

14. rfjs ououjarjs 5Xrjs: cf. iil 10, xii. 9. owayayety afrrouf cts T. msXeuxw: cf. xx. 8, where the same words recur: see also xix. 19. rfjs Wpas T. pcyrfxr)?: cf. vi. 17. TOU Ocou TOU irarro-icpdtopos: cf. i. 8, iv. 8., xi. 17, xv. 3, etc.

15. This verse should be read after iii. 3. Every phrase of it has its parallel in iii. See notes in loc.

16. TOF KoxotfpckOK: cf. i. 9, xi. 8, xii. 9, xix. n. Emporium: cf. ix. 11.

17. w. IK TOU POOU dird TOU 0p6Vou: cf. xx. 2, 10 for this combination of prepositions. Elsewhere we have fayy cwro T. Opovov in xix. 5 and . cv r. Op. in xxi. 3 and c r. Op. with other nouns iv. 5, xxii. i. ytyovtv: c xxi- 6.

18. dorpairal ical cwal ical pporrai: cf. viii. 5, xi. 19. o-curjtos. plyas. Cf. vi. 12, viii. 5, xi. 19, xvi. 18.

19. TO irotTjpiov TOU ofrou TOU Oujou TTJS opytjs: cf. xiv. 8, 10, xix. 15.

20.! uy K, xal. ofy c6pc f Or)aak: cf. xx. 1 1.

21. x Xd(a pcyaxij: cf. xi. 19. lpxaa u. T o ak: see above on 9. (b) Idiom.

1. pcyaxT) fwkTJs: the order of the words in this phrase is unique in our author. It is certainly abnormal and is corrected in fctp into uvi? ueyoais. But there are a few instances where the adjective precedes its noun in our author: cf. i. 10, iii. 12 (in both passages, however, between art. and noun), and daiyo? in three cases.

2. IY KCTO. iri: unique in our author.

3. atfjia ws Kcxpou, i. e. alxa us atxa vcicpov: see Additional Note in vol. i. p. 35.

8. 80 61) au-ru cum inf.: cf. vi. 4, vii. 2, etc.

9. CXOKTOS ri v ouo-iap liri: cf. note on ii. 26 on this idiomatic use of art. with c owriav. 06 fictcvrjcray. SOUPCU: cf. xi. 18, fafav. 6 jcatpo?. Sawai, xvi. 19, Cfj. vrjrOrj. Sovvat.

1. jiey ATJS 4wkTJs. In every other instance of this phrase, in the Apocalypse, i. 10, v. 2, 12, vi. 10, vii. 2, 10, viii. 13, x. 3, xi. 12, 15, xii. 10, xiv. 7, 9, 15, 18, xvi. 17, xix. i, 7, xxi. 3, the noun cony precedes the adjective. This "great voice," as that in 17, seems to be that of God Himself and not of an angel. According to xv. 8 none could enter the Temple till the plagues were accomplished. But it is possible that it is the voice of the angel of the altar, as in xiv. 18.

IKXTC TS IITT idxas icrx. Cf. Dan. ix. n, Jer. x. 25, xlii. 1 8, xliv. 6, on this Semitic use of the verb irid or W. C XCCD occurs repeatedly in this chapter and not elsewhere in the Apocalypse,

KXTC (see Winer, 13, 23. Blass, p. 41, would read. cis T. yvji. So also in 2. Cf. tfcxccv k T- Baxaaraav in 3, and the same verb with ts TOUS iroraiovs in 4. On the other hand, we have the same verb with ri r. irorapjov in 12, and with Ari T. ijAiov (8), liri T. 0pdvoi (10), and rl T. Aepo (17).

ra lirra +u Xos TOO Oupou. On the first four Trumpets, which can hardly on any hypothesis be regarded as the work of our author, see Introd. to viii., vol. i. p. 219 sq.

2. This plague recalls the sixth Egyptian plague: Ex. ix. 10-11; Deut. xxviii. 35.

tyrro cfxicos. Tronrjp(K. The first two words we have in Ex. ix. 10, PHP rn, and the two latter in Deut. xxviii. 35 and Job ii. 7, IP JW2U In the last two passages the LXX renders . m rods d pwirous. In Ex. ix. 10 we have iv rots avoputrois (i. e. D"1N3). Thus our author is independent of the LXX. For the construction, Luke i. 65, iii. 2 are generally quoted, eiri TOVS avtfpuwrovs, " upon men," f. e. on all mankind: cf. xvi. 8, 21.

T. fyotras T xdpaypa TOU Or)piou KU rods irpoo-KUKourras T eu Ki aurou. Cf. xhi. 17, xiv. 9, n, xk. 20.

This clause has been assigned by Spitta (p. 163) to the final editor of the Book, though he does not specify the grounds. There are, however, good reasons for regarding them as a gloss. i. The fourth Plague is universal in its incidence as regards the sun, and also the second so far as those on the sea are concerned. That the third is so likewise as regards all fresh waters is clear. Such also is the sixth and the seventh as regards the Euphrates and the air. Hence it is natural to expect that the first Plague is of the same character as in the second, third, and fourth, i. e. universal in its incidence. 2. The construction TOVS irpoo-Kwovvra? rg CIKOII avrov is against our author's usage. See note on vii. 1 1.

If the above conclusion is not valid, then we must assume that only the adherents of the Roman Empire, and not the rest of the heathen, are affected by the first Plague. In this respect the first and fifth Plagues would have the same incidence. But not only are the followers of the Beast subject to certain physical evils, but they alone are susceptible to the deceitful signs wrought by the false prophet (x:. 20). With this susceptibility to evil influence we should contrast the security against demonic influences enjoyed by those who were sealed by God in vii. 4-8, ix. 4. But all the faithful have already been removed from the earth (see Introd. to xv. p. 26).

8. This Plague recalls the first Egyptian plague, Ex. vii. 17-21, though in the latter the Nile alone is smitten.

atpa. Cf. Ex. vii. 19, 01 JTH.

iracra tu i l fjs. (Cf. rrnn C D, Gen. i. 21, or rw PW, i. 30.) ra fr TJJ Oaxdunrj). In viii. 9 only a third of the things in the sea perished. Here the destruction is complete.

4. elf r. irorapous ical r. tnjyaf TK dsdrwk. See note on viii. 10.

IY KCTO atpa, i. e. the fresh waters became blood.

5. KOI tjicoixra TOO Ayyaou TK torw Xlyoiros. An interpolation to introduce xvi. 5 b 7, which originally followed after xix. 4, and to which context it is restored in this edition. Cf. i Enoch Ixvi. 2. "Those angels were over the powers of the waters." In vii. i of our text the angels who had control of the winds are referred to, and in xiv. 18 the angel over fire, though the latter appears to be a gloss. On the various classes of angels see the Index to Charles' The Apoer. and Pseudep. vol. ii.; Bousset, Rcl. des Judenthums, 317, also Jewish Encyc art. "Angelology."

5-7. This passage has been restored after xix. 4, where the grounds are fully stated for this restoration.

8. The fourth Bowl takes effect on the sun, and causes a plague of excessive heat.

lx ck m rdr tfxiok. On the use of iirl here instead of cfc as in the preceding verses, see note on i. The construction Koqrj aurw is a frequent one in our author: see Introd. to Chap. vii., vol. i. p. 191.

9. iicaufiatiff0i orak. tcagfta. (See Blass, Gr. p. 91 sq.) Contrast vii. 16, o 5c M?-01077 Irt (emended) avrov? 6 jfaiosoic vav fcavia.

pxcur py)rak r6 orojia TOU Ocou. Cf. xiii. 6; Isa. lii. 5; Rom. ii. 24; i Tim. vi. i; Jas. ii. 7.

IXOKTOS T tgoucriak. See note on ii. 26 on the significance of the article with cfowiav. Bousset brackets here with the inferior MSS the article. This is strange, since he is aware that when cfovo-ia is accompanied by the art. it connot s full authority or power, and this is certainly the meaning in the present passage.

ou ficTCKOTjiray. Cf. ix. 20, 21, xvi. ii. In xi. 13 the Jews repent owing to the earthquake.

OUKCU afrr 6 ak. Cf. xi. 13, xiv. 7, xix. 7.

10-11. The fifth Bowl. If we compare this Bowl with the first Woe it is clear that they are developments of the same tradition, though they refer to different periods, the Christians being still upon the earth during the Woes, but not during the Bowls. Thus both affect only the adherents of the beast (xvi. 10: cf. ix. 4). In xvi. 10 the kingdom of the beast is darkened; in ix. 2 the sun is darkened by the smoke issuing from the pit, and from this smoke issued the demonic locusts. In xvi. 10-11 men gnawed their tongues through pain and blasphemed the God of heaven; in ix. 5-6 men were tormented by the locusts and sought death but could not find it.

Similarly we shall find that the sixth Bowl agrees closely with the second Woe (see note on xvi. 12-16), and the seventh Bowl with the third Woe (see note on xvi. 17-21). These facts will help us in the elucidation of the difficulties affecting the fifth Bowl.

But there is another point worthy of consideration. If we compare the seven Bowls with the Seven Seals, we find that, whereas only the faithful were the victims of the fifth Seal, only the followers of the beast are affected by the fifth Bowl.

10. The visitation on the kingdom of the Antichrist.

TOP Ooovop TOO dr)piou, i. e. Rome. Cf. xiii. 2, owcv avro (i. e. T5 Biffpiw) 6 3pajcay. TOV Qpovov avrov. The first four Bowls had affected the world at large; the fifth assails only the kingdom of the Beast.

v) patrixcia aurou TKOTW KT). Owing to this clause the fifth Plague has been taken to be one of darkness recalling the Egyptian one, Ex. x. 21 sqq. But this interpretation cannot be upheld. A plague of darkness would be wholly insufficient to explain the agony experienced by the adherents of the Beast after the pouring out of the fifth Bowl. Hence something else than the darkness that ensued on the pouring out of the fifth Bowl must be presupposed as the cause of this agony. Now, if me turn to the first Woe of which the filth Bowl is in some sense an abbreviation, we can explain both these statements. There we find that the sun was darkened by the smoke that issued from the pit (ix. 2). There is every reason for supposing that we have here the true explanation of the darkening of the kingdom of the Beast Further, the cause of the torments endured by the adherents of the Beast (xvi. 10, euuurahro ras yxwoxra? auruv eic TOV irdvov) is to be traced to the demonic locusts which issued from the smoke that ascended from the pit. Men were so tortured by the scorpion-like stings of these locusts (ix. 10) that they longed for death to end their agony (ix. 5-6). Hence we infer that after lotcorayicn; several clauses have been lost, in which the causes of the darkness and the sufferings of mankind were given. The hypothesis that certain clauses of the nature suggested originally stood after fokOTujlwr) is established by a clause in n, i. e. jcal IK rw I KW avtv. These sores could not have been caused by the darkness. Spitta and, so far as I am aware, Spitta alone (p. 171) has recognized this fact that the fifth Bowl originally treated of demonic locusts as the first Woe does. But he rejects (171, 576) TOV Bporov TOV Qrjpiov KCU tyfvtro vj patrtxtta avrov eworoyteviy as an addition from the hand of the final editor on the ground that the throne of the beast is not to be identified with Rome but with the abyss as in ix. n, and that accordingly the place on which the fifth Bowl is to be poured should be named, where the plague in question is to be developed, analogously with the rest of the plagues (xvi. 2, 3, 4, 8, 12, 17). He also excises the clause KOI K row excwv aurwv to the weakening of his own hypothesis. But I have already shown above that rj J3ao-i fia avrov ncoriAcm? can be fully justified. Nor can any valid objection be taken to rov Opovov rov Oyplov, seeing that already in xiii. 2 the Dragon had given his throne to the Beast. Thus it is only necessary here to suppose a lacuna in the text.

iorukTo inx. In the LXX only in Job xxx. 5.

11. Their sufferings drove the followers of the beast to fresh blasphemy instead of to repentance.

TK Ock TOU OpapOU. See XI. 13.

Kal IK TUP KWP aurwk. This phrase proves that the sufferings of the subjects of the Beast are not intelligible from the text as it stands after the loss of the clauses referred to in the note on 10. Some scholars explain it as referring to the phrase c cos KOKOV in a.

ou p TCKr)rai K TW? pya K. So already in ii. 21, ix. 20.

12-16. The sixth Bowl at all events xvi. 12 is related to the second Woe, ix. 13-21. In the latter passage we have an account of the demonic horsemen from the Euphrates, whose objective is the heathen unbelieving world. In the present context the river Euphrates is dried up in order that the way may be prepared for the kings coming from the East under Nero rcdivivus, and their objective is Rome, the throne of the Beast. This forecast reappears in xvii. 12-13, 7 x The powers of the Beast are therefore at variance. On the other hand, the gathering together of the kings of the earth to Armageddon is a distant echo of the onslaught of the forces of Gog in Ezekiel on Jerusalem. This expectation has undergone many developments in the interval, and reappears in a duplicated form under the actual designation of Gog and Magog in xx. 7-10, where it represents the last uprising of the powers of evil before their final destruction by fire from heaven. But the present context (xvi. 13-16) reproduces an earlier form of this expectation, and this form of it is referred to twice elsewhere in the book in xiv. 14, 18-20, and xix. 11-21. In these three passages, which refer to a universal insurrection of the heathen nations at the instigation of the demons and the Beast and the False Prophet, before the Messianic Kingdom the forces of evil are destroyed by the Messiah, and the Beast and the False Prophet cast into the lake of fire, whereas in the final insurrection of the heathen nations due to the direct instigation of Satan at the close of the Messianic Kingdom they are annihilated

XVI. 12-14. PARTIIIANS AND KINGS OF THE EARTH 47 by fire from heaven, and Satan himself cast into the lake of fire, where already were the Beast and the False Prophet.

Further, it is to be observed that the uprising of the kings of the East against Rome is only the preparatory step to their conflict with the Lamb, as we see in xvii. 12-17. Hence their combination here (xvi. 12) with the kings of the whole earth (xvii. 14) to resist the Lamb.

12. The march of the kings of the East against Rome, which is desciibed more fully in xvii. 12-13, J 7 6-

TP irotO t. Eu4pdtT K. Cf. ix. 14.

tzi pvqi T u8wp afirofl. For the idea cf. Ex. xiv. 21; Josh. iii. 13-17; Isa. xi. 15 sq., xliv. 27, li. 10; Jer. xxviii. (li.) 36; Zech. x. ii; 4 Ezra xni. 43 47- froijjLCuhHj. Cf. Isa. xl. 3, ITCHACLO-CITC rrjv 68ov. For the use of this verb in the second Woe, cf. ix. 15. It is a favourite with our author: cf. viii. 6, ix. 7, xu. 6, xix. 7, xxi. 2.

13,14, 16. The gathering together of all the kings of the earth to war against God and Christ Cf. Ps. ii. 2. See note above on 12-16.

13. Three unclean spirits from the Dragon (i. e. Satan: cf. xii. 3, 9)1 the Beast, and the False Prophet (i. e. the second Beast) go forth to call together the kings of the earth. Cf. i Kings xxii. 22. Contrast the three angels in xiv. 6 sqq.

TOU tlrcuoirpo Tou. Here for the first time the second Beast (xiii. 11 sqq) is so designated.

irpcupatci. dkdoapra. Cf. Matt. x. i; Mark i. 23, etc.

s pdrpaxou First we observe that the construction is unique in the Apocalypse. According to the universal usage outside the present passage we should here have os Sarpaxov?, as indeed and many cursives actually do read. But the best authorities support the abnormal text. However, as we shall see on the next verse, the context requires the excision of us pdrpaxot. o xeia as a marginal gloss subsequently incorporated in the text. As regards the use of the phrase, it may be observed that frogs were regarded in the Zend religion (see S. B. E. iv. 171, note) as the source of plagues and death. In Hennas, Vis. iv. i. 6, locusts of a fiery colour are seen by the Seer coming forth from the mouth of a great monster: Moi 3 iri frrjpiov xeyiorov. icai CK rov o-roxaros avrov ixpises vvptvai ctTopcvovro. This conception combines the ideas underlying ix. 3 and xvi. 13. Frogs were regarded as the agents of Ahriman: cf. TV , de hide, 46 (Moffatt).

14. cloiv Yp irvcujaara Saifioyiw iroioutra or)jj, cla. There are difficulties attaching to this clause, i. It has been taken parenthetically by Bousset and Holtzmann as an explanatory remark of our author: " there are, to wit, demonic spirits, sign workers " (as their masteis, xin. 13,14). The phrase nvcviara SaiAovtw should be rendered " spirits, that is, demons," i. e. " demonic spirits," as in Luke iv. 33, irvcvfui Satjwov txa0 prov "a spirit, that is, an unclean demon." The genitive is one of apposition or definition: cf. ii. 10,6 ow avos r s i. Demons have no spirits, but are themselves spirits. According to i Enoch xv. 8, 9, IT, xvi. i, xix., xcix. 7, the demons were the spirits which went forth from the antediluvian giants on their destruction, these giants being the children of the fallen angels and the daughters of men (cf. Gen. vi. i). These demons were not to incur punishment till the final judgment: cf. Matt viii. 29; i Enoch xvi. i; Jubilees x. 5-11. They were subject to Satan as in our text: cf. Matt, xi i. 24-28. 2. Or it may be rendered: " they are, to wit, demonic spirits, sign workers." But however we take this olause it is of the nature of a gloss.

t Kiropeoctoi t. This the best attested text is wholly unsatisfactory. K and several cursives read liaropcvetroai. Though this is less unsatisfactory it is against our author's u age as well as against Greek idiom. The context undoubtedly requires ewopcuoicvo, since without this participle the construction and meaning are both defective. For the preceding words ct3ov etc rov ordmaro? rov Spaicovros. n-pcisiara rpta are incomplete in both respects without the participle cwopcvdAcva. The phrase evc r. ordtaro?. Kiropcvtr0ai is of frequent occurrence in our text: cf. i. 16, ix. 17, 18, xi. 5, xix. 15, 21. Thus we should read ctsov c c r. ordiaros r. Spafcovro?. irvcviara rput. cfciropcvdAcva (cf. i. 16 for the same separation of c r. otoAaro? and the verb), and translate: " and 1 saw from the mouth of the dragon. three unclean spirits going forth. 1 The present text ciSov c c r. ordAaros. irevxara rpta without a participle, which at once explains the CK and completes the sentence, is, so far as I am aware, unexampled, and yet it has been thoughtlessly accepted by every grammarian and student of the Apocalypse, perhaps in many cases from the idea that any construction is possible in this Book.

Hence, since for ifciropcvmu we must read cwopeuoxera and connect it with ciSov c icrx., we conclude that curip yap. arrjfuiia is a marginal gloss, and likewise o? pdrpa ot if this is the earliest form of this phrase. Thus us arpa oi. o-rj la was originally a marginal gloss which on its incorporation into the text brought about the change of faropcvdfwa into cwopcvcrat.

rijs ouou Uni s 8Xi) Cf. iii. 10, xii. 9, for the same phrase and the same thought connection.

owayaytik afaofo KT Cf. xx. 8.

TTJt Vjfupas rfjs fieydxtjs TOU Ocou. This is the great day of Yahweh's reckoning with the ungodly nations. Cf. 2 Pet iii. 12,

XVI. 14-16. XVI. 15 TO BE RESTORED BEFORE III. 3 b 49

MLaln rjrov Ocov Tjptpa. See Charles 1 Eschatology (see Index), also the authorities quoted in the note of vi. 17 of our text.

Too 0too tog wiroicfirftopo. A divine title frequently found in our author: cf. L 8, iv. 8 (note), XL 17, xv. 3, xvl 7, xix. 6, 15, xxi. 22.

16. With Konnecke (Emendationcn zu Stellen NT. 35-37, whose work I have not seen; the reference I owe to Moffatt) this verse is to be taken as an intrusion here. Originally either it stood between iil 3 and 3 b, where it would complete the isov series of ii. 22, iii. 9, 20, or it should with Beza be transposed before iii. 18. I therefore bracket it with most modern critics in its present context.

What Konnecke's arguments are I do not know, but the cogency of his suggestion manifests itself on a comparison of 15 with iii. 2-4. To see how fitly it comes in after iii. 3 we have only to compare I8ov Ipxotai with the series of verbs so introduced in ii. 22, iii. 9, 20: w K limp m mxapios 6 yprjyopv Kal TTjpv TO. Jiparul avrov (xvi. I5 b) with yivov yp-rjyopuv in ill. 2 and cav ovv farj ypiryopijcrfls, yfa w? icxeimys in iii. 3 b (observe also the use of rrjpf. lv though without an expressed object in iii. 3 and OVK cxoawav TO, Ifidna avrwv in ill. 4): tva ULT) yvmvos ircpiirarjj (xvi. 15) with irepiira. Trirovriv ACT cuiot) ev A. CVKOIS in iii. 4, and the remaining words Kal jsAcrnixriv TTJV durx fuxrvi avrov with tva. p, vf tfravepvfrfj rj aio- vvi; rfjs yvivortros crov, iii. 18. tfacvns and yprjyoptlv occur only in xvi. 15 and ni. 2-3 in our author.

This verse implies that the sixth Bowl will take the world by surprise. But it is hard to see how the elaborate preparations of the kings of the East followed by those of all the kings of the world could do so. Finally, the utter inappropriateness of 15 in its present context is further evident from the fact that all the faithful have already been removed from the earth.

This verse forms one of the seven beatitudes in the Apocalypse: i. 3 (iii. 3) (xiv. 13), xix. 9, xx. 6, xxii. 14, 7. When xvi. 15 is restored to its original context, we find a special appositeness in their order: first beatitude (i. 3) deals with those who read the prophecy; the second (iii. 3, i. e. xvi. 15) with those who watch and keep their garments clean: the third, xiv. 12-13 (to De rea d after xiii. 15), with those who die in the Lord in the last persecution: the fourth, xix. 9, with those who are invited to the marriage supper of the Lamb: the fifth, xx. 6, with those who share in the first resurrection: the sixth, xxii. 14, with those who had washed their garments and had permission to eat of the tree of life during the Millennial Kingdom: the seventh, xxii. 7, with those who keep the words of this Book.

16. This verse should follow immediately on 14, and 15 be transferred to its original context between iii. 3 and iii. 3 b. VOL. ii. 4

Neuter nouns in the plural are followed either by the singular (viii. 3, xiii. 14, xiv. 13, xvi. 14, etc.) or plural verb in the Apocalypse, but mostly by the latter.

rbv KaxorfflCPOK. Cf. i. 9, xl 8, xii. 9.

Eppatcrrl Seeix. ii.

Ap Mayesrfp. No convincing interpretation has as yet been given of this phrase, which should probably be translated "the mountains of Megiddo." The city Megiddo was notable as the scene where Barak and Deborah overthrew the forces of Sisera by "the waters of Megiddo" (Judg. v. 19-21), and Pharaoh Necho defeated and slew Josiah, ., in " the plain of Megiddo " (2 Kings xxiii. 29, 30; 2 Chron. xxxv. 22; Herod. ii. 159). But the phrase " mountains of Megiddo " is not found elsewhere. Owing to this fact it has been proposed by Htlgen-feld to take Ap Mayeswv as- TWO ifc where, iy=Ty = "ciiy of Megiddo." Volter regards Ap as = JHK, " land." But both those conjectures have failed to meet with acceptance. It is best at present to regard the first element in the phrase as = "mountains"; for the final conflict in Ezek. xxxviii. 8, 21, xxxix. 2, 4, 17 a passage which influenced our author in xx. 8-1 1 was to take place on "the mountains of Israel." In Dan. xi. 45 the writer expected that Antiochus would meet his end "between the sea and the glorious holy mountain." Since Megiddo is not associated with any eschatological expectation, it is possible some corruption underlies this word. Hence the phrase in Daniel, "glorious holy mountain" (= ML Zion), as well as the expression in Ezekiel, " mountains of Israel," may give some support to the conjecture cited by Cheyne (Encyc. Bib. i. 311) that Ap Maycov = rup in, his "fruitful mountain." This would associate the battle scene with Jerusalem as in Joel iii. 2; Zech. xiv. 2 sqq.; i Enoch lvi. 7, xc. 13-19. As Rome was to be laid desolate by the kings of the East, xvi. 12, xvii. 16-17, so (after the destruction of the kings of the East see xix. 13 n.) the kings of the whole earth were to be destroyed in the neighbourhood of Zion. Now, since xvi. 1 4, 1 6 and xx. 8-10 are both ultimately derived from Ezek. xxxviii.-xxxxix., and since in xx. 8-10 the scene of the last great struggle at the close of the Millennial Kingdom is placed in the neighbourhood of the Heavenly Jerusalem (which has taken the place of the Old), it is possible that Ap Maycsdw may be a corruption either for tajp in = " his fruitful mountain," as above suggested, or for mjpn-iy, "the desirable city " (i. e. Jerusalem: cf. mon pk, " the desirable land," . Palestine, Jer. iii. 19; Zech. vii. 14). The latter suggestion derives some countenance from xx. 9, rrjv vo iv v, which is there surrounded by the hostile armies of Gog and Magog. But everything connected with the text and meaning of the phrase is uncertain. Hence Gunkel, followed by Cheyne and Bousset, conjectures in his Schopfung und Chaos, 263-266, that we have in this mysterious phrase a survival of some ancient myth no longer intelligible to our author which associated the final conflict of the gods with some ancient mountain. Rommel's suggestion that the phrase goes back to TjdD " n (Isa. xiv. 13) = " the mountain in the north where the gods meet," springs from the same view of the passage. Hence Bousset concludes that the context here goes back to an ancient myth which described the assault on the holy mountain of the gods by an army of demons mustered by certain evil spirits. To this myth our author in Bousset's opinion gave an historical character by connecting it with the Parthians. See Nestle's art. in Hastings' D. B. li. 304 sq.

17-21. The seventh Bowl. Just as the fifth and sixth Bowls showed undeniable affinities with the first and second Woes, so the seventh Bowl appears to be slightly related to the third Woe, xi. 14-19. In xvi. 17 a voice from heaven declares that the punishment of the heathen and of the great city of Rome is now completed in the pouring out of the seventh Bowl with the results about to be recounted. In xi. i8 h it is said that the time has come for "destroying those who destroy the earth ": cf. xix. 2. This connection is indeed slight in itself, but there are others, for the "earthquake and great hail" in xi. 19 are described at some length in xvi. 18-21.

4 lx cc " P- On this visitation on the air cf. ix. 2. The construction with cvt here is extraordinary: see note on i.

K TOO Kooo dir TOO 6pkou. A divine voice was heard coming from the Temple in xvi. i. Here the place whence it comes is more nearly defined. Throughout the Apocalypse the throne is connected with the Temple, though at times it is impossible to visualize the vision. But, as we have seen in the note on iv. 2, the combination of the Temple and throne scenery goes far back into Judaism.

+UK? I. ir TOU Opfrou. So also in xix. 5. It is noteworthy that in exactly a similar connection our author uses CK rov Bpovov in xxi. 3.

ylyopci. Cf. xxi. 6. The great voice from the throne, which had commanded these plagues, xvi. i, now proclaims that they are at an end.

18. Aorpairal KOI +wai nai Pporrcu. See notes on iv. 5, viii. 5.

acurpte. filyas. Cf. viii. 5, xi. 19.

olbs OUK. fyfrcro f 08 ftropwiroi iyfauto im rip yip. The phraseology is borrowed from Dan. xii. i. Cf. Theod. OCA ov yeyovcv ty ijs ytytvijtat IBvo ivrfj yg (evi Tijs yi s, AQ), and the LXX out ov cyevqlq ty ov cyevr o-ai. Here the cvl ri s yifc is found both in our text and Theod. a fact which may point to the presence of pk3 in the text of Daniel in the ist cent A. D. Our text is clearly an independent rendering of Dan. xii. i. Cf. Ass. Mos. viii. i, " ira quae talis non fuit in illis."

19. ical lylkcro. cis rpia fupt KCU oi iroxcis rwv iqvw lircarok. I have bracketed the first clause; for cfc rpia ACDI? is against the usage of our author, who would have written efe fl prj rpui: cf. xvi. 13, xxi. 13 (four times). Moreover, there is no hint in xvii.-xviii. that Rome had suffered from a violent earthquake. Rome is dealt with in the words which follow KOI Ba? vauv rra. These words prepare the reader for xvii.-xviii.

tylycto. els. Cf. Acts v. 36. In viii. 1 1 of our author the text is corrupt.

4j ir6Xis pcyt). Here as in xiv. 8 (see note) it is Rome, not Jerusalem, that is designated as "Babylon the Great." Jerusalem had already been in part overthrown by an earthquake in xi. 13: 7000 of its inhabitants had been thereby destroyed and the rest had repented. Here, according to the interpolator, it is Rome that is visited by an earthquake, and that an earthquake such as had never yet been experienced on earth, and yet in xvii. 3-4 Rome appears not to have suffered in this earthquake in the least degree. Its final overthrow and destruction are yet to come in xvii.-xviii. This judgment and that of the great hail do not lead men to repent: rather they blaspheme the more: cf. ver. 21. To identify Babylon here with Jerusalem, as is done by J. Weiss, Moffatt, and some other scholars, is against the whole context and the right conception of ftourai. The passive use of An? o-0i? vai is found in Ezek. iii. 20 (ov fty mviprtfukrii ai Sikaicxrvvai avrov), xviii. 22, 24. It is found also in Acts x. 31 and elsewhere. As regards the construction we should compare xi. 18, yxSw 6 atpos. 8ovvat, xvi. 9, oi nercvotjo-av Sovvai. In Ps. cix. 16 and ciii. 18 we find the infinitive in Hebrew after IDT.

T wnfjpiok TOO OIKOU TOU Oujxog Ttjs fyyt)? ofirou. See notes on xiv. 8, 10. The expression TOV 0uios T S pyfj recurs in xix. 15. In Isa, vii. 4; Jer. iv. 26, xxv. 16 (xlix. 37), xxxii. 23 (xxv. 37); Lam. i. 12, ii. 3, iv. n; Ezek. xxiii. 25; Hos. xi.

9; Nah. i. 6, we find the combination pyrj Ov ov (= K pin). The order 0v os 6pyfp is infrequent in the LXX but it is found: cf. Isa. ix. 1 8.

80. iroora njaos fyuycf. Cf. VI. 14, vav opo? ai 70 05.

ox cdploijo-ar. Cf. v. 4, xii. 8, xiv. 5, xviii. 21, xx. 11 17 yi;. cal rovo? ofy cupe) a familiar Hebrew expression (WVtdD 6): cf. Ps. xxxvi. (xxxvii.) 36.

ftpi) oflx cap Ov)ray. This disappearance of the mountains is one of the signs of the end of the world: cf. vl 14; also Ass. Mos. x. 4, "And the high mountains shall be made low, and the hills shall be shaken and fall," also i Enoch i. 6. In later Christian Apocalyptic this idea is found not unfrequently: cf. Sibyl. Or. viii. 234, 236, vt oo-ci 3c opayyas, 6Xct 8" vi fowajv, vtyos 8 owccrt AOITTOV (so Rase) cv Avbpwirouri Itra 8 opi; ircstot? rrai KOL iraara 0aaarcra OVKCTI ira. ovp Ifei.

A Latin translation of viii. 217-250 is given in Augustine, De Civitate Dei xviii. 23:

"Dejiciet colles, valles extollet ab imo. Non erit in rebus hominum sublime vel altum. Tarn aequantur campis montes et coerula ponti Omnia cessabunt."

Lactantius, Div. Instit. vii. 16, n, "Montes quoque altissimi decident et planis aequabuntur, mare innavigabile constitue-tur."

The idea underlying these passages is to be carefully distinguished from that which appears in the Zend religion to the effect that the mountains, being the work of the evil spirit Ahriman, would disappear with him, and the new earth would be " an iceless, slopeless plain; even the mountain whose summit is the support of the Kinvat bridge they keep down, and it will not exist," Bund. xxx. 33 (S. B. E. v. 129 sq.). The object of the earth being made a smooth plain was, as Boklen states (Eschat-ologte, p. 133), to make intercourse easy for the renewed humanity. In this connection, cf. Sib. Or. iii. 776 sqq.

Yet another idea underlies the use of analogous phrases in Isa. xl. 4; i Bar. v. 5-9; Pss. Sol. xi. 5.

SI. x la pcydxi). So also in xi. 19. Probably the Tia 123 of Ex. ix. 24 the seventh of the Egyptian plagues.

69 Toxamaio. A talent (rdxavrov = 133) weighed something between 108 and 130 Ibs. The word Toaavruuo? is found in Polybius and Josephus, as Swete points out.

4 3Xar AT ra. TOK OC K. As in xvi. 9, n so here the effect of the judgment is only to harden the hearts of the heathen nations. This attitude of theirs stands in contrast with that of the Jews in xi. 13.

o+ftpo. Here only in our author. It stands last like 1KD in Hebrew, not only here but elsewhere in the N. T. Cf. Matt. ii. 10, xxvi. 22; Mark xvi. 4, etc But in all such cases follows immediately after the adjective it qualifies, whereas here, as occasionally in the case of the Hebrew 1KB, the adjective and adverb are sundered.

CHAPTER XVII. x. Contents and Authorship.

This chapter begins with a promise on the part of an angel to the Seer to show him " the judgment of the Great Harlot, 1 but throughout the chapter this subject is not referred to save once (in xvii. 16), and alike the vision in xvii. 3 b-6 and its interpretation by the angel are concerned with the Beast, which according to the present form of the text symbolizes the demonic Nero, or Nero returning from the abyss to lead the Parthian powers against Rome. The judgment of the Great Harlot is given at length in xviii.

But if we are to give the subject the fuller treatment it demands, we soon recognize that xvii. cannot be treated apart from xviii. Thus in xvii. i an angel summoned the Seer to show him " the judgment of the Great Harlot," and transported him in the spirit (xvii. 3) to the wilderness, where he had a vision of the woman and of the scarlet Beast, whereon she sat, with its seven heads and ten horns. Now the woman was magnificently arrayed in purple and scarlet and adorned with gold and precious stones, and on her forehead she bore the name of Babylon, the mother of fornication and abomination, and she was drunken with the blood of Christian martyrs (xvii. 4-6). And when the Seer was filled with amazement at what he saw, the angel turned aside from his original purpose of showing him the judgment of the Great Harlot, and proceeded to explain the hidden meaning of the woman and the Beast with the seven heads and ten horns. The Beast, said the angel, " was and is not and is about to come up out of the abyss and goeth to destruction," and all the faithless upon earth shall marvel at his return after his death (xvii. 7-8), but they that are wise will not do so; for they will see that the seven heads are seven kings, of whom the sixth is at present reigning. This sixth would in due course be succeeded by the seventh, who would reign but a short time. And on the death of the seventh king would follow an eighth, who was in reality the Beast and yet he would not be the eighth king, since he was actually one of the seven (xvii. 9-11). (The Beast is clearly here the demonic Nero returning to earth from the abyss.)

So much for the seven heads. As for the ten horns, these are ten subordinate kings who will shortly come into their royal authority, and with one accord will, through the ordinance of

God, place all their power at the disposal of the Beast, and the Beast and these kings will hate the Harlot, and destroy her by fire (xvii. 12-13, X 7 J 6)- And having destroyed the Harlot they will go to war with the Lamb, but they will be overcome by the Lamb and His followers (xvii. 14, a conquest implied by xix. 13). Now the Harlot is none other than the city Rome (xvii. 18), whose doom is described in the vision that follows.

So much for the thought of the chapter as it stands. But the order of events is strange and unexpected. Though the Seer has promised in xvii. i a vision of the judgment of the Great Harlot, in all the verses that follow there is not a reference to this subject save in xvii. 16. The promise, in fact, is not redeemed till xviii., for the single mention of this judgment in xvii. 16 cannot be regarded as a fulfilment of it xviii. is necessarily introduced by the technical phrase xcro ravra ct8ov, since other weighty subjects have intervened between xvii. i and its fulfilment in xviii.

The irregular character of this chapter prepares us for the conclusion which a detailed study of it makes manifest, i. e. that our author is here using sources which for convenience sake are here designated as A and B. A= i c-2, 3 b-6 a, 7, 18, and some clauses in 8-10. B is fragmentary: 11-13, 17, 16 (see 5). The order of the words in A is Semitic, but not in B, and whereas the diction and idiom in both show indubitable traces of our author's hand, they just as indubitably contain idioms which are against his usage (3). Again, though the thought underlying present form of the chapter is that of our author, even the most superficial criticism makes it clear that this thought is superinduced, and that the meaning of the symbol "the Beast" has been transformed by additions to the text. Thus in A the Beast symbolized the Roman Empire, a meaning which still survives in xvii. 3, whereas in B it symbolized the living Nero returning from the East at the head of the Parthian kings in order to destroy Rome (4). By certain additions in xvii. 8, 11 the Beast has come to symbolize Nero redivivus or the demonic Nero coming up from the abyss an expectation prevalent from 90 A. D. onwards in many Christian communities.

There are certain dislocations of the text Thus xvii. 17 should be transposed before xvii. 16, and xviI 14 an addition of our author should be placed after xvii. 16, since it deals with the destruction of the Beast and his Parthian allies, who in xvii. 17, 16 have already destroyed Rome. There are two glosses, one in xvii. 9, which gives an alternative and wrong interpretation of the seven heads in xvii. 9, and another in xvii. 15, which was originally a marginal gloss on CTTL vsarwv in xvii. i and has got wrongly thrust into its present position (4).

6 THE REVELATION OF ST. JOHN XVIL fi 3.

In the Introd. to xviii. we shall find grounds for regarding A and xviii. as derived from one and the same source.

2. The order of the Words.

So far as the order of the words goes, this chapter falls into two parts, xvii. i-io is Hebraic as to order. Thus the verb precedes the object three times in xvii. 7, twice in xvii. 3, and once in xvii. i, 6. In xvii. 8 the verb precedes the subject twice, and once in xvii, i and 2. In xvii. 4-5 there are only substantive sentences.

In xvii. 11-17 the order is decidedly non-Semitic. Only once, i. e. in xvii. 17, does the verb precede the subject, whereas the object, and also the subject where expressed, precede the verb twice in each of the verses xvii. 12, 13, 16 (i. e. six times in three verses). Again, in each of xvii. 14, 16, 17 the order subj. vb. obj. occurs once, and in each of xvii. 14, 15 the order subj. and vb. It is true that in some of these cases the order is quite good Semitic, inasmuch as its unusualness serves to mark emphasis, opposition, or the like: but in respect of order xvii. 11-17 is, as a whole, non-Semitic and differs in this respect from xvii. i-io. Such a fact can hardly be accidental, and must be accounted for. The linguistic character of xvii. 11-17 is almost without parallel in the rest of the book save in xi. 1-13, which on these and other grounds we were obliged to attribute to a Greek or Aramaic source (see i. p. 270 sqq.). Any theory as to the authorship of xvii. should account for these facts. So far as these facts go we are predisposed to assign xvii. i-io and xvii. 11-17 (or the original forms of these; for they exhibit undoubted marks of revision, as we shall see presently) to different sources, the latter apparently to a Greek source.

3. The diction and idiom of this Chapter show manifest traces of the hand of our author (in the way of revision, as we shall see later), but they are frequently against his usage.

(a) Traces of the hand of our author, especially in xvii. 1-9, 14 (which verse is wholly from his hand). not 4jx6ck. Seifw in xvii. i, recurs in xxi. 9: indeed every word and phrase of xvii. i are from our author. Thus els 1 is his universal usage. On Xlywk and Scijw roi see iv. i n. In xvii. 3, dmlj-TTK up. ati recurs in xxi. 10. The constructions xvii. i 1 and Kootjjj n m (hqptok in xvii. 3 1 If, as we shall seek to prove, part of xvii. i has come from a source, then the form of the phrase raflijju Tji 6ri MTUV ToxAfiy seems to come from our author; for the phrase is clearly derived from Jer. li. (xxviii.) 13, and since gabijfffftu is never used as a translation of jar which is in the original here, are also his idiom (see iv. 2, note). mpi0cpxi)fi4inf c. ace. xvii. 4 (see iii. 5, note); also tol T U TWTTOK afrrijs, xvii. 5 (see vii. 3 n.); also ol Karoikourrcs irl TTJ YTJS, xvii. 8 1 (see i. p. 336, and contrast ol KatoikogitCS iv yi v, xvii. 2); also fy nal OUK ipi-ir ical UXXci dwipaikeik. fiirdyci and OTI K. irdpecmu in xvii. 8; c. ao tar (cf. xiii. 18) in xvii. 9; ft ty. law and Kal cis dmsXeiaf fadyei in xvii. u, and otrircf ("=01) in xvii. 12. xvii. 14 is wholly from his hand: with osroi. wic crci afrrou's cf. xiii. 7, which is his; with nupio. pcunxtai cf. xix. 16 while marcs is often used by him. In xvii. 16 we have an instance of an idiom used by our author; i. e. 4)pi jmjicvi)i iroi aouoik abrf v: cf. xii. 15, xxi. 5. In xvii. 17 with rcxccrorjcrorrai cf. x. 7, xv. 8, xx. 3, 5, 7.

(b) Idiom and diction against his usage. In xvii. 2, oi KOTOI-KOUKTCS TTJK yfjK conflicts with the universal usage of our author: see vol. i. p. 336, and note on xi. 10. yfy. orra opoparo, xvii. 3 (3) elsewhere c. gen. See n. on xvii. 3. In xvii. 8 ylypairrai tirl TO pi0Xtoy is against his usage; for in this phrase we have always ypanft(ro(u iv T 3t io) elsewhere: cf. (i. 3) xiii. 8, xx. 12, xxi. 27 xxii. 1 8, 19. In different phrases ypcu ctk CTTI cum ace. is found: cf. li. 1 7, CTTI TJJV frr toi. ycypaxxevov: iii. 1 2, ypdifw far avrov TO dvoua: cf. also xix. 1 6. The order in aorok Set is against his usage, xvn. 10 elsewhere ci precedes: cf. x. n, xx. 3, xi. 5: IK TWK iirrd, xvii. n elsewhere in Apoc. always else: cf. v. 5, vi. i (to), vii. 13, ix. 13, xiii. 3, xv. 7, xvii. i, xxi. 9.

In xvn. 8, which like xiii. 8 is a rendering of the same Hebrew source, the split relative is not reproduced in the Greek, though it is in xiii. 8. In xvii. 15 ou is used, though our author uses OTTOV always elsewhere (but this verse is a gloss on xvii. i). yi p in xvii. 13, 1 7 is not found elsewhere in the Apoc., and the form ot the enumeration in xvii. 15 is not that of our author. Here 0 X01 is substituted for Aaoi: see note in loc. Finally, in xvii. 17 axpi is followed by the indicative (by the subjunctive in inferior MSS) but elsewhere in our author by the subjunctive: see ii. 25, note.

From (b) we see that this chapter exhibits many constructions, which are against our author's usage elsewhere in the Apocalypse.

On the other hand, (a) just as decidedly exhibits his handiwork. Since the thought underlying the present form of the text is that of our author, the obvious hypothesis is that he is making use of sources, which he revises and recasts to suit his (as in the LXX) would be the natural rendering. But our author could not use this latter participle, since it is reserved by him for dwellers in heaven; see note on xvii. I. Hence we have Kafantinfl M vddrow instead possibly of KarcurkTjvqforp ftrl ddrwi.

1 Since this verse has been recast by our author, this form of this phrase instead of that in xvii. 2 may be due to him.

own purpose. In other words, the evidence of this section tends to prove that not only is xvii. 11-17 based on a source as we inferred in 2, but also xvii. -0, 18.

Further research will define more closely the extent and character of these sources. But first of all we must show that the conclusions provisionally arrived at from the form of the text are confirmed by the subject-matter. Hence we shall now proceed to prove that the chapter as it stands is of a composite nature.

4. The text is deranged and composite being based on two Sources.

The text is deranged, however we may account for it. For whereas in xvii 7 the angel promises to disclose the mystery of the woman and the Beast (which the Seer had already seen in xvii. 3) and in this order, he at once proceeds to tell the mystery of the Beast, and there is no mention of the woman till xvii. 18. Hence the natural position of xvii. 18 is immediately after xvii. 7. Again, xvii. 17, which gives the explanation of xvii. 13, can hardly have been read unless in immediate connection with xvii. 13: i. e. 13, "These have one mind, and they give their power and authority unto the beast. 17. For God did put into their hearts to do His mind and to come to one mind, and to give their kingdom unto the oeast," etc.

The chapter is also composite. We have already seen in 3 that whereas certain parts of the chapter show clear traces of the hand of John, the phraseology of certain other parts is decidedly against his usage. We have also seen in 2 that the order of the words in xvil i-io is Semitic, whereas that in xvii. 11-17 is not so. Now, if with these facts we combine the further one that, whereas xvii. i-io culminates in a prediction of the death of Titus (xvil 10), the other (xvii. 11-17) culminates in a prediction of the destruction of the Harlot City (xvii. 16), we can hardly evade the conclusion that behind these two sections there were two independent sources. 1 But there is another indication of the independence of these two sections. In xvii. 3, 7 the Beast can only be the Roman Empire, whereas originally in xvil 11-13, J 7 l6 the Beast was not the Roman Empire (as originally in xvii. 3-10), but the living Nero returning from the East at the head of the Parthian kings.

That our author, therefore, has laid two sources under contribution is to be concluded from the above phenomena, in the first of which the Beast represented the Roman Empire, 1 I have thus on largely independent grounds arrived at the same conclusions as Wellhausen (Analyst, 26-29) on the original sources of this chapter.
whereas in the second it represented the living Nero returning from the East at the head of the Parthian hosts (cf. xvi. 12).

To the above evidence of the compositeness of this chapter we might add the twofold explanation of the seven heads in xvii. 9-10 as symbolizing seven hills and seven kings: the glaring contradiction between xvii. 16, where the ten horns are represented as God's agents in destroying Rome, although they had themselves been already destroyed by the Lamb and His followers in xvii. 14, and the belated gloss in xvii. 15, which has no raison detre in its present position but was obviously added by a stupid scribe originally in the margin opposite xvii. i as an explanation of TTS iropvrjs. T S Ka iev s ri 5. The two Sources A and B, and their dates.

In the determination of these two sources I agree on the whole with Wellhausen. 2 A consists, according to this scholar, of 3 (with the exception of the phrase " and ten horns ")-4, 6 b-7 (with the exception of "and the ten horns"), 9 (excluding all but the words "the seven heads"), 10 (omitting the initial "and"). He thinks that 18 may have originally stood after 7 but was omitted by the redactor, who, however, out of a feeling of conscientiousness added it at the close of B! B consists, he holds, of 11-13, 1 6 (omitting "and the ten horns which thou sawest and the beast"), 17. A and B were bound together by a redactor and revised. In A, 6 is a Christian addition, and in B 14. xvii. 1-3 may, with the exception of xvii. i a, have belonged either to A or B.

I am unable to accept Wellhausen's hypothesis in all its details, but, as we have already seen (2, 3), the evidence of the order of the words and to some extent the idioms point to two sources, and these, like Wellhausen, I designate as A and B.

(a) A consisted originally of i c (beginning with TO Kptxa r)s iropvys.,)-2, 3 b (icai ciow.)-6 (om. icai eic. Iicrov), 7, 1 8, 8 (om. rp KOI OVK. vrrayet which addition has displaced a clause: om. also ore fy.-irapccnvu), 9 (om. wfic. cro iav and CTTTOL. avrcov), 10 (om. the first ctt).

In this oracle the beast is the Roman Empire, its seven heads are the Roman emperors, five of whom belong to the past, one is,., Vespasian, whereas the seventh, Titus, as the 1 This, however, is no doubt due to an accidental displacement. When it is read after 11-13, 7t J 6 this contradiction disappears. In the text as it stands the demonic Nero reluming from the abyss is the Antichrist, and therefore must be destroyed by the Christ.

1 Bouset regards xvii. 1-7, 9-11, 15-18 as an original Jewish source of Vespasian's time, while he assigns xvii. 8, 12-14 and certain clauses in 6, 9, 1 1 to the last editor of the Apocalypse.

destroyer of Jerusalem, would speedily perish. The date is thus fixed and the authorship may have been Jewish Christian.

(V) B = 11 (om. rjv ical owe mv ical and ical cts a7rua. tav wrayci), 12 13,17,16. In this second oracle the Beast is Nero returning from the East, and not the Roman Empire as in A. The order of the words, as we have shown (2), differs in B from that in A. This source is fragmentary. Preceding ver. 11 there must have been some account of the seven heads, but not that in A, since it identified the Beast with the Roman Empire and not with Nero. 1 Since the eighth is spoken of, . Nero returning from the East, we may conclude with great probability that it was written during the reign of Titus. The oracle may be regarded as written by a Jew; for whereas the hatred of the Jews was fierce against Rome in the time of Vespasian and Titus, it was not so on the part of the Christians. The Christians, moreover, could not have had any sympathy with Nero. Their expectation is best expressed in the addition of John, i. e. ver. 14, where Nero and his allies attack the Lamb.

We have already observed that 15 was originally a marginal gloss on ver. i, rijs iropvrp. fcrt vfiaroiv. Ver. 14 is clearly from the hand of John, 16 manifestly stood originally after 17.

6. Our authors editing of A and B and the new meaning given thereby to the whole.

Now that we have determined the extent of A and B, we have next to show the use our author made of them. First of all, the introductory words in xvii. i, ical iAlc? els c. Acvpo CD croi, are clearly from his hand. Then follow the woids from A, TO icpiia. rip iropvtw avrijs, which form the title of xviii. But though iropvrp is preceded by the article another fact pointing to a source the Harlot has not been mentioned as yet The original vision of the Harlot consisted of the source A, in which the Beast was the Roman Empire on which the woman (Rome) was seated. This source our author introduces by 3 Kal airrjvcykcv AC cfe ipijfjlOv cv nrcuAart. In 3 b 7 he makes no change save by the insertion (?) of ical iccpara Scvca in 3, in order to prepare for B (i. e. 11-13, 7i 6) an d by the addition of the clause 6 b ical IK rov aifi, aro. Iiprov. In 8-1 o he has recast the text. For the original form of 8 see the note in loc. (p. 67 sq.). His additions, ty al ov mv. virayci and OTI ty. fl-apconrat, transform the meaning of the verse, which, though it originally identified the Beast with the Roman Empire, signifies in its present form the demonic Nero returning from the abyss.

1 The Beast is the supporter of the woman, i. e. Rome (xvii. 3), in A, whereas in B the Beast is the destroyer of Rome, rvii. 12, 16.

In 9, 8c vov9. ro av is from his hand, while Jwra piy. avrcuv ai is clearly the gloss of an ignorant scribe. Ver. 18, which originally stood in A after 7, was transposed to its present position in order to introduce the great chapter xviii. on the doom of Rome.

Having utilized A our author now proceeds to incorporate B of which only 11-13, X 7i J 6 survives in our author's work. The introduction, as we have already pointed out (5 (3)), has been omitted and its place is now taken by 10, which belongs to A. Two clauses have been introduced by our author into u, i. e. 8 j)v Kal OVK lmv and al ct? atrcoxctav vrrayet. By their introduction the expectation of a living Nero returning from the East at the head of the Parthians is transformed into an expectation of a demonic Nero, as in xvii. 8. 12-13 are apparently as they stood in the original oracle, but 14-15 had no place there. 15 is, aft we have elsewhere observed, a gloss, which stood originally in the margin opposite ver. i (r s iropvrjs. brl vsdrtov), while 14 comes trom our author's hand; but, since it could only properly follow 16, as it deals with the destruction of the Beast and his Parthian allies, who in 16 destroy Rome, it has most probably got displaced. Thus 11-17 should be read in the following order: 11-13, J 7 I 14-

Thus by his editorial changes and additions our author has transformed the original meaning of his sources except in ver. 3, where the Beast is still the Roman Empire. Throughout the rest of the chapter, however, the Beast has become none other than the demonic Nero.

7. A (= xvii. i c-2, 3 b-6, 7, 18, and certain clauses in 8-10) was probably derived from the same source as xviii.

See Introd. to xviii. 7.

8. A, though found by our author in a Greek form, was most probably translated from a Hebrew source.

In 6, 3 I have shown that, although there are indubitable signs of our author's revision of A, yet some idioms and constructions survive, which are contrary to his usage such as ol jcarotkOvvrc? T V yjfv (xvii. 2), ycfunra ydiara (xvii. 3), ycyWMrrai frl rd pifixlov (xvii. 8). It thus appears that the Greek form of A is not due to our author.

But, further, there are signs that A was originally written in Hebrew. Thus, if iropyftv is the original text in xvii. 5, the context (8cxvyuu rwi) suggests that we should here have not "harlots" but "harlotry." This, as I have shown in the note in loc. could have arisen from a misreading of JTOT (- harlotry) as nfof = " harlots."

But the strongest evidence is that found in ver. 8, which is a doublet of xih. 3, 8. These two passages cannot, so far as I can discover, be explained except as independent

Greek renderings of one and the same Hebrew original, the Greek rendering of xiii. 3, 8 being that of our author and the Greek of xviii. 8 being that of some unknown scholar. This question is fully dealt with in the Introd. to xiii. 4, vol. i. p. 337.

1. KCU fj 0 K cts K TUP JITT AyywK TWK C KTWH TS lirrd 4idxa, xal Adxrjo-ek JWT IJAOU Xlyw Acupo, Bei u aoi TO Kpipa

TTJS 1To'plt)S TTJS tcy XT) TTJS Ka6l) Umf)S fal dsd-TUP TTOXXWK, 8. pco fjs inspkCoaak ol paaixcis TTJS yijs, xal p, cOuor0T)aaf ol

KatOlkOUKTCS iv ytjK ilc TOO OIKOU TTJS ITOppCias auTTJS.

1. ct. Ayyuk. One of the angels of the Bowls acts as the angel of interpretation. The words al rjxS v ets. 8ct a o-ot recur in xxi. 9. On Aax orc ftcr cA, oii A. cyav see iv. i n. 3c a oroi has already occurred in iv. i; Scvpo, as we have seen, recurs in xxi. 9.

TO Kpijia TTJS ir6pnr s. iropraias au-rrjs. These words form the title that should be prefixed to chap, xviii. They prepare us for a vision of the judgment of the Great Harlot, but there is none such in xvii. 3-18: only a prediction of it in xvii. 16. But in xviii. we have an elaborate vision of this judgment, and it is therefore to this chapter that these words form a title. And lest there should be any doubt on this head we find that the greater part of the title xvii. 2 is repeated in xviii. 3, though the order of the clauses is reversed and the diction slightly changed, and that the words TO Kpipa. reappear as y piw in reference to her in xviii. 10. Cf. also xviii. 8, 20. But since the Great Harlot has not hitherto been mentioned, another vision is necessary to her identification. In this vision (xvii. 3-6) she appears riding the Beast with seven heads and ten horns elements which are duly interpreted in xvii. 9, 12.

TO Kpipa TTJS Tro'pinris. The Harlot is the city of Rome. This word is applied to Nineveh by Nahum (iii. 4), and to Tyre by Isaiah (xxiii. 16, 17). In 5 it is named Babylon. The doom of Babylon has already been pronounced twice, xiv. 8, xvi. 19. Rome is already known by this name in i Pet v. 13; 2 Bar. lxvii. 7, M The King of Babylon will arise who has now destroyed Zion"; and the Sibylline Oracles, v. 143, 159.

TTJS Ka6f fumr)s tiri dsdrw iroxX K. This is an independent translation of Jer. li. (LXX xxviii.) 13, D3i DD Sy T03P. The LXX has here Jcatcurfcivoiwac (jcarcurjc-tjvoucra, Q) e " vscuri iroaAois. Karaa-Krjvovv or oncrjvovv is the natural rendering of pt? here, but our author reserves this word for dwellers in heaven: cf. vii. 15, xii. 12, xiii. 6. Rome cannot be rightly described as " sitting on many waters," but the description of Babylon, which stood for the personification of wickedness in the O. T., is here simply taken over. The idea of security may underlie the phrase: Babylon felt safe owing to the many waters on which it was situated the Euphrates which flowed through it and the morasses and canals by which it was surrounded (see Cornill on Jer. li. 13). Vet this fact that Rome did not sit on many waters was a difficulty to a later writer and led to the gloss in xvii. 15, that the many waters are many peoples. Bousset thinks that a still older tradition lies behind this figure of a woman seated on many waters, and compares Sibyll. Or. iii. 75-77, v. 18, viii. 200. Gunkel (Schopfungi 361) finds in the "many waters" a reference to the abyss which was the dwelling of Tiamat. But, however this may be, there was no consciousness of the Babylonian myth in the mind of the writer.

2. Mpnuvav ol poaixcis TTJS yi)f. Cf. xviii. 3, 9 for the recurrence of this diction. The iropveia of which the kings of the earth are guilty is set down to the account of all the nations in xiv. 8. They have all shared in the vices and idolatries of Rome. With pc6ucr9i)ow cf. Jer. xxviii. (li.) 7, irorrjptov p xro, v Ba? vaav ev x l P fcupiov, piovvkOv iraxrav rrjv yfjv. It points to the result of TTCTTOTIKCV in xiv. 8: cf. also xviii. 3. ol Katoncoorrcs TTJI YT)K. On this construction, found here only, see note on xi. 10, and 4 of the Introd. to xiii., vol. L p. 336. On ouou iropfeios cf. xiv. 8, xviii. 3. We should observe that the relative construction is broken off in the sentence, ca! tptovaorjo-av. avtJTs. This is good Hebrew. It is also good Greek: see W.-M. sect. xxii. p. 186.

It is noteworthy that in the two clauses LLC fa ciropvevaav. yijs and KOI ifieovororjo-av. avrfjs of this verse and in xviii. 3, the same thought and largely the same language recur, but in the reverse order.

3. Kal dtn eykev fie els 2pt fioi cv irkeupcm. xal ciSok yupaiica irrd xal K para

This clause introduces a new vision. See note on iv. 2. The Seer has the vision of Babylon in the wilderness: of the Heavenly Jerusalem from a lofty mountain top, xxi. 10, where see note. The contrast is significant. Many scholars think that the wilderness as the scene of the vision was suggested by Isa. xxi. i, where to the vision of the fall of Babylon is affixed the heading, u The oracle of the wilderness of the sea " (Dpaid fctep). Here the LXX has simply TO opam rfc iprjuov.

yuyaiita. im Oijpiok tcrficjciyor. The omission of the article before nov points to an independent vision here. The Beast is undoubtedly the Roman Empire. On its power the Harlot reposes. The scarlet colour indicates the luxury and ostentatious magnificence of the empire, and refers probably not to the Beast itself but to its covering. Swete quotes Juv. iii. 283 sq., "Cavet hunc, quern coccina laena Vitari iubet et comiturn longissimus ordo." The word is a rendering in the LXX of jfon, ny in, JB, Vwa, w njfon or njfon JB.

In this vision of the Harlot we may have an indirect contrast to the woman clothed with the sun in xii. 1-6. There is no real contradiction between the description of the woman in i as sitting on many waters and here sitting on the beast. The former is a traditional epithet of Babylon used descriptively by the angel, the latter represents the actual appearance in the vision.

ylpotra 6y6 ara pxacr rjfuds. The construction is Kara cnwrtv. In xiii. i names of blasphemy are only on the seven heads, f. e. the seven deified emperors. Here they cover the entire body, and may refer to the innumerable deities of her own and subject countries which Rome recognized, ycictv c. ace. once in xvii. 4, but always elsewhere in Apoc. c. gen. iv. 6, 8, v. 8, xv. 7, xvii. 4 d, xxi. 9.

ix"" Kc axds irrdl Probably the original text On the jcc aaa? cirra see note on xiii. i.

4. ircpipcpxi) ilit). papyapitaif. Almost the same phrase recurs in xviii. 16.

iroptupour ica! KKKIVOV. "Purple and scarlet." These colours symbolize the luxury and splendour of imperial Rome. The two colours are nearly allied, for the x-isSa KOKKIVTJV of Matt, xxvii. 28 is called iropfrvpa in Mark xv. 17, 20, and liariov iropfapovv in John xix. 2, 5. But the colours are distinct. See Ex. xxv. 4, xxvi. i.

Kcxpuawfutt) xp uo up Kttl Xiou Tifjluo. Ai o Tifjiita is generally said to depend on KCXPOTUACIT? by a zeugma, "from uhirh the reader must mentally supply some such participle as KCKOO- ! " (Swete). But xpvcrovv appears to be used in a loose way in the LXX as = "to cover or adorn"; for xpvcroiv xpwiw (2 Chron iii. 10), Karaxpvvovv xp V(rt V (x- x- JI J 3 2 Chron. iii. 4, ix. 17), ireHXpvcrow XP VO1 V (1 Kingsx. 18) are renderings of nex (= to overlay) when followed by ant. Similarly xwow XP VO1 V of nn followed by nnj in 2 Chron. iii. 7, 8. When followed by ntO it is actually rendered Karaxa Kwp.(va xa Kcp in 2 Chron. iv. 9, and when followed immediately by mp p in 2 Chron w 6, by fcooyxciv. Hence we should render Kcxpucrcducvi? here by "covered."

. ical fiapyapitOis. Cf. T. Jud. xiii. 5, KCU CKOCT fjuprtv avryv cv xpwup ral ftapyopirats. These words are said of the father of Bathshua who so adorned her in order to seduce Judah.

fxowra wrijpiok xpucrogr fr rfi x ci pl HJ- These words are modelled on Jer. xxviil (li.) 7, iroryptov xpwavv Ba3v ov lv x tpl Kvpiov y pevrkOv irarav ryv yfjv airo rov OIPOV avrty? cirtbcrav 20n;.

y fioK fftcxirypdrttf xal ii fticdoapra. Here ical ra faaoapra is either to be taken with R. V. as " even the unclean things of her fornication," or as governed by CXOOTO, just as the words that follow KOL ial TO fjlcrwnrov are dependent on this participle. Cf. Cebes, Tab. V., 6p s ovv irapa TVJV irvxijv Opovov nva jccticvov Kara rov TOITOV. lf ov Kaorjrat. yvn, ircirxeuryyicii; TW i Kai Trt av atvoxcvt;, 17 v TJ? X CC P X ct OT piov rt; 6pa, d Xa rt9 ccrriv avnj; Zfrjv A-rrdrrj icaactrai, (Ttv, Travra? rovs Trxavaxra. etra Tt irparrei avn;; TOVS cunropcuoi ovs is TOV irorifci T V atrr s Bvvap. iv. TOVTO 82 ri OTt ro TTOTOV; irxavos, Kal! yvoia (from Jerram's text).

5. xal m T fa ruirok afitTj? OKOfia Ycypa)i yok. Roman harlots wore a label with their names on their brows: cf. Seneca, Controv. i. 2 (quoted by Wetstein), "Stetisti puella in lupanari. stetisti cum meretricibus. nomen tuum pependit a fronte"; Juv. vi. 122 sq., "Tune nuda papillis Constitit auratis titulum mentita Lyciscae."

(luar pioK. This word indicates that the following name is not to be taken literally, but to be interpreted irycvAariiccus (xi. 8). This can be done only by the initiated. Babylon is the mystical name for Rome. Many scholars take it as part of the inscription.

i Ti)p TUP t iropvv t- As we see from the critical note, the Vg. and Prim, read iropvuov, i. e. vopvtuav. This is not improbably the original reading. At all events it forms an excellent parallel to ?8e iwiatw. If the text is derived from a Hebrew source, then iropvw nfof, which is a wrong punctuation for DUT siropvcias. 1 Thus Rome is the mother of harlotry and the world's idolatries. With this statement we might compare Tacitus, Ann. xv. 44, where he speaks of Rome as the city " quo cuncta undique atrocia aut pudenda confluunt celebranturque."

6. Nat clsop i4 K yupaixa pcououtrap IK TOO a? p, aros TWK dyiw xai IK TOU atfjiatOS TUK fiapnsp p Ifjcrou.

The text refers to the Neronic persecution described so vividly by Tac. Ann. xv. 44, "Igitur primum correpti qui fatebantur, deinde indicio eorum multitude ingens haud perinde in crimine incendii quam odio humani generis convicti sunt. Et pereuntibus addita ludibria, ut ferarum tergis contecti laniatu canum 1 It is noteworthy that Wellhausen mistranslates ropvuv as "harlotries." It was a right instinct, however, that led him to this mistranslation. VOL. IL 5 interirent aut crucibus affix!, aut flammandi, atque ubi defecisset dies, in usum nocturni luminis urerentur." This verse, either in part or as a whole, is from the hand of our author, who thus gives a Christian character to an originally Jewish source and transforms an oracle of Vespasian's date into a prophecy of the destruction of Rome in the last days (see Introd. 5).

pcououow iic TOU atfiaros. This conception of a nation drunk, not with wine but with blood, was familiar to the literature of the ancient world. Thus Josephus (Bell. v. 8. 2) writes of his infatuated countrymen besieged by the Romans: In yap irapyv ioUiv IK roy Si ocriw KO. KWV KOI TO Tijs iroxccos alpa iriveiv. The metaphor is also found in a fragment of Euripides preserved in Philo, Le. Alkg. iii. 71, t Trxr S-rjtL JLOV irivowra iccxaivov alat: in Cic. Phil. ii. 29, " gustaras civilem sanguinem vel potius exsor-bueras"; Suet. Tib. 59, "Fastidit vinum quia jam sitit iste cruorem: Tarn bibit mine avide quam bibit ante merum," and in a form more closely related to our text in Plin. H. N. xiv. 22, 28, "(Antonius) ebrius jam sanguine civium." But in the LXX we find the best analogies: cf. Isa. xxxiv. 5, cueovcroy. rj uaxupa fiov, xxxiv. 7, Aeflvcrflijererai fj yrj airb rov atfuito?: also li. 21; Jer. xxvi. (xlvi.) 10.

ical K TOU atparos T f paptupw lijcrou. This clause is regarded by the majority of critics as an addition to the original Jewish source. If it is from the hand of our author, his intention seems to have been to give his source a Christian character, though this was hardly necessary when once the source was incorporated in his work. If the aytot are Christian saints, the two clauses are tautologous. The ayios who is martyred is of necessity a ftaprw. On this word see note on ii. 13. It is possible, but improbable, that the Syioi represent the Jewish martyrs who fell in the war of 66-70. This was the meaning of the clause in the original source.

7. xal loaripaaa IK aurf K 6aup, a ply a. ical ctwp pot 6 p am TO julUor ftyycxos Aia TL 0auJLaoras; fyw lp am TO julUorrjpioy-njs Kal TOU Oi)piou TOU paordlokTOS a. vrr v, TOU? x OKT S " 5 urd KOI TCI olxa K pata. The Seer is naturally astonished at the fearful vision he has just seen, just as the inhabitants of the earth will be astonished when they see the reality, xvii. 8. In xvii. 1-2 he was promised a vision of the judgment of the Great Harlot. This vision is given in xviii., but since the Great Harlot had not heretofore been mentioned, the mystery of the Great Harlot is beheld by the Seer in a vision, xvii. 3-6, and interpreted in xvii. 18, which originally followed on xvii. 7. See Introd. to this Chap. 6.

For a linguistic parallel to ro fivtrr ptov r s ywaiks cf. i. 20; and for a like dialogue between the angel and the Seer, cf vii.

13-14. We should observe here that the angel promises an interpretation of the woman and the Beast with seven heads and ten horns, and in this order. But the mystery of the woman is not explained till xvii. 18, and the angel at once proceeds to set forth the meaning of the Beast. Our author is here using sources, and has freely recast them to suit his own purpose. In our text the Beast is Nero redtvivus, but in the sources used by our author we have seen that this was not so (see Introd. 4). In the source behind xvii. 3-10 the Beast was originally the Roman Empire, as it still is in xvii. 3 (see note in loc. In the second source, xvii. 11-17, 1 e Beast was obviously Nero returning from the East at the head of the Parthian kings in order to destroy Rome. But our text as it stands represents the expectation of Nero returning as a demonic king from the abyss. This interpretation is indubitably set forth in xvii. 8, which is a recast of the older tradition identifying the Beast with the Empire, and in xvii. 14 which comes directly from our author.

8-18. An interpretation of the vision, in the course of which the older materials of the source are recast with additions in order to depict the expectation of the Neronic Antichrist who was to come up from the abyss.

8. T 6r)pioK 8 ciBcs V lca r " K cortf ical plxXci dkdpaikCif In rr)s PUOTOTOU, ical els Trtfxciap ftirdyci ical Oaufiaao crorrai ot KOTOI-KOUITCS lirl rrjs Y)? " Y YP airrai OKOACL tin T 0i Xiok TTJS IWTJS ir Katapoxtjs Koajiou, pxcirowui TO Srjpioy OTI JJK ical ouic jfartr ical irdpcorai.

Thus the verse ran originally: TO Orjptov 8 c78c9. (original lost) ical Oavfjiao-Orjo-ovtoi ot KaroicovvtCS cirl njs yiys, v ov yey-pairrat TO ovoia CTTI TO fiifixlov nys forjs airo Kara ox? KOCTAOV,)8Xe7rdvtcov TO Ovipiov. In the original form of this verse the Beast symbolized the Empire, as it still does in xvii. 3, and in xiii. 3-10 originally. But here our author has omitted the description of the Beast which came after c78c, and substituted rjv a! ov COTIV. virayei, and again after A. rdvToi TO wov added OTI fy. irdpcorat in the place of quite a different clause that stood in the source, as we shall see presently.

But not only has some description of the Beast at the beginning of this verse been displaced by the additions of our author, but something has also been lost or displaced at the close of the verse by another of his additions. For, as it stands, 8 simply states that the faithless inhabitants of the earth shall marvel when they behold the Beast. But there is nothing surprising in this fact; for the Seer marvels in the preceding verse. Hence, since the context implies that they will do something which would be the natural outcome of their ungodliness, we conclude that a clause to the effect that they would worship him has been dislodged by the addition " which was and is not and shall come." Now, if we turn to xiii. 3, 8 we find the very clause we are in search of, KCU vpoo-Kvmfo-ownv avrbv iravres. When this clause is restored, the mystery of the beast in the source is sufficiently disclosed. The Beast is clearly the Roman Empire. It is on the Beast, i. e. the Empire, that the woman, i. e. Rome, is seated. But the changes introduced by our author have transformed the significance of the Beast. The Beast now means the demonic Nero returning from the abyss, and it is clearly the intention of our author that 1 1 should be taken in this sense.

The Beast is now the Neronic Antichrist coming up from the abyss, as in xiii. 3, 12, 14. In these passages he is represented as the hellish antitype of Christ. In ore rjv KOI owe w cu Trdpearai there is a parody of the divine name 6 v cat 6 ty KOI 6 tpxofj-tvo? in i. 4, 8, iv. 8, while the owe tmv and the parallel descriptions, ws r Q. ypnp efe Odvatov, xiii. 3, and 69 fy 1 ity wxrjyrjv rfj? iia aipa xiii. 14, are intended to allude to the death of Christ In the Introd. to xiii., vol. i. p. 337, I have, I think, proved that this verse is a doublet of xiii. 3, 8 and that both are Greek versions of the same Hebrew original. Since xvii. 8 in some form belonged to xvii. 3-10, it is from this Hebrew source that xiii. 3, 8 is derived. When our author incorporated his Greek version of this source in xiii. 3, 8 he added rov apvcov rov r ayAevov. Bousset is of opinion that a redactor in close dependence on xiii. 8, or the same writer who wrote

xiii. (in the opinion of Bousset our author), composed xvii. 8; but all the evidence when closely examined points in a different direction.

pxcwrfitw where we expect fixitrovrts may be due to v, or to a not unnatural rendering of 9-10. oc 6 rous iyuv cro+io at lirra icc+axal lirra on ik, Sirou Vj yuri) K 0T)Tiu ITT arv. 1O. KCU aaixcis fard ctcrik ol irtrn lircaw, A cts lanr, 6 axXos oihr 4jx6ck, xai OTOK 9. Sc 6 KOUS Krx. = u here is needed the intelligence which is wisdom. 11 It relates to what follows, as in xiii. 18, and comes from the hand of our author.

3pr. ojrwk icai. This is an obvious addition to the text, but it appears to be a very ancient one and may have gone back to the Johannine school, as its Hebraic character shows: . rov. avrwv. Bousset (p. 416) suggests that our author himself made this addition, when he found that he could discover no historical interpretation of xvii. 10-11. This addition, however, is wholly unsuitable; for the seven heads do not belong to the woman (i. e. Rome) but to the Beast. But the gloss interprets the heads as if they were an adjunct of the woman, whereas they belong to the Beast. This absolute misconception of the text is fatal to the genuineness of these words. Again our author in the genuine sections uses Koftprloi only in the participle (see note on iii. 21) and Kaofaw in the finite tenses and infinitive. But there is another objection; for it is clear that, of the two conflicting explanations given in immediate connection, only one can stand in this case the latter. The idea conveyed of the gloss was a familiar one. "The city of seven hills" was a familiar expression in classical writers: cf. Horace, Carm. Sec. 7, "Di, quibus septem placuere colles"; Virg. Aen. vi. 782, "Septemque una sibi muro circumdabit arces," Georg. ii. 534; Martial, iv. 64, "septem dominos montes"; Cicero, Ad Att. vi. 5, TTC05 faroao ov: Propertius, iii. 10. See Wetstein in loc.

10. pocnxcif iirrd x rrx. For facriaci? as applied to Roman emperors see i Pet. ii. 13, 17; i Tim. ii. 2. We have here a very clear intimation of the date of this source. Five emperors have already fallen, one is, and another is yet to come. This source was probably written, therefore, under the sixth emperor. Before we can ascertain who this emperor was, we must decide whether we shall include or exclude in our reckoning Galba, Otho, and Vitellius, and with what emperor we shall begin. First of all we may safely exclude the above three emperors from our consideration. Suetonius (Vesp. i.) describes their reigns as "rebellio trium principum." Next, though Suetonius, Josephus, and 4 Ezra xi. 12, 13, xii. 14, 15 (see Box, p. 262 sq.), begin with Caesar, it seems clear here that our text begins with Augustus, as does Tacitus. The first five emperors are Augustus, Tiberius, Caligula, Claudius, Nero. The emperor who "is" is Vespasian, 69-79 A. D., and the one who "is not yet come," Titus, 79-81. Titus thus fulfilled the prediction, orav 3M0 axiyov fcra.

ow? X0Tj oxiyok KT. The ground for this expectation is most probably that assigned by Wellhausen (Analyse, 28). "Titus is assumed to be the coming seventh and last: he as the destroyer of Jerusalem will be overtaken by vengeance after a short reign." 8

But what are we to make of this reckoning in its present 1 On the order of the numerals see note on viii. 2. When the gloss 09. tor adr r cat was incorporated in the text, Irrd was of necessity added 9 Another explanation of this prophecy is that the writer of this source knew of the hopeless condition of Titus' health: cf. Suetonius,

Titus, 7; Dio Ca. i S, Ixvi. 26. 2; Plutarch, DC tuenda sanitate praecepta, c. 3, p. 123 D (quoted from Bousset). Another is that there was a traditional view that the empire must have seven emperors before its destruction. As the sixth was now living, the Seer necessarily predicts a seventh.

context? Our author has taken over this source and that which follows, but he is writing in the reign of Domitian. If he took xvii. 10 seriously, Domitian must have been for him the sixth emperor, and he could only have justified this view, as Bousset points put (p. 416), by a very artificial method of reckoning, i. e. by beginning with Galba, the successor of Nero: Galba, Otho, Vitellius, Vespasian, Titus, Domitian. But we may safely reject this reckoning as impossible, and assume that here, as frequently elsewhere, our author has taken over material that in some one or more respects served his purpose, though in others it was unsuitable. Owing to its unintelligibleness from the historic point of view, some scribe added a geographical explanation in xvii. 9.

11-17. On the source behind these verses see Introd. 5.

11. KCU T Otjptoy, 6 4jf PC a! OUK ftm?, ical afiros oysofe OTIK KOU IK rv inrd lornr, xal els AirisXciap dirdyci.

This verse presents some difficulty. We have already sought to show (Introd. 4-5) that xvii. 11-17 is a new source used by our author, referring to the return of Nero from the East at the head of the Parthian kings. Only the latter part of this source is preserved in our text, and this is edited and brought up to date by the addition of 8 ty KCU. owe corn and al cfc atrdiaciar virayci in xvii. u (see similar addition in xvii. 8), and other changes subsequently. In the original source the Beast was the living Nero returning from the East: in our text the Beast has become Nero redivivus, as in xvii. 8. This is the view accepted by such scholars as Ewald, De Wette, Hilgenfeld, Vischer, Volter, Spitta, Holtzmann, Weizsacker, Bousset. On the other hand, it has been maintained recently by J. Weiss and Swete and Moffatt that the Beast is to be identified with Domitian. Moffatt regards this verse as "a parenthesis added by John to bring the source up to date. since the death of Titus had not been followed by the appearance of the Nero-antichrist". " Domitian, the eighth emperor, under whom he writes, is identified with the true Neronic genius of the empire." (Cf. Eus. H. E. iii. 20; Tert. Apol 5: "portio Neronis de crudelitate." De Pallio, 4, Subneronem. To these we might add Juv. iv. 37 sq., "Calvo serviret Roma Neroni"; Mart. xi. 33, etc. Moffatt seeks to explain the words cv TWV rr by showing that Domitian was closely associated with the imperial power already (Tac. Hist. iii. 84, iv. 2, 3; cf. Jos. Bell. iv. u. 4, etc.), and points out that whereas it was said of the Neronic Antichrist in xvii 8, dpofruvctv c TI S ? ucrrou, no such expression is used here. Thus Moffatt recognizes the true Nero redivivus in xvii. 8, 14, and a second Nero in the person of Domitian in xvii. n, and maintains that they are not to be identified. That the juxta- 11-12. TEN HORNS = THE PARTHIAN KINGS l position of Domitian as a second Nero and Nero rcdivivus is awkward, Moffatt admits, but says it is "inevitable under the circumstances. 11 But his arguments are unconvincing. The 6 ty icai OVK Irtiv taken together with c rgv find admits of only one interpretation. The person so described " was and is not" (rjv KOL OVK corn?). But Domitian Ivnv. Of him our author cannot say OVK cortv. Moreover, the pre-existence ascribed to Domitian in ty is also inexplicable. Nor can he in any intelligible sense be described as c rov cnra. Finally, if we interpret xvii. 12-17 of tne Parthian invasion, there is no ground in comparative religion or history for representing Domitian as in any sense its leader. The addition of KCU xcxXct foaflafaur CK TTS afivo-ftov is here wholly unnecessary. 6 ty KCU OVK cortv has the same force as the like expressions in xiii. 3, 12, 14.

cis AmsXciap uirdyei. The issue of the impending conflict is certain. The Antichrist, though he thinks he is accomplishing his own purposes, is accomplishing the purposes of God, and is all the time marching to his own destruction, which is also the purpose of God.

12-13, 17-16, 14. The destruction of Rome by Nero rcdivivus and his Parthian allies (12-13, 7 J 6) an the destruction of the latter by the Lamb (14).

12. KCU rd cwica K para ciBcs o ica 3acrixci claik, OITIPCS ouirw cxapo, dxXd 4 ounay u s paatxcis ftta pav ik ficrd TOU Ovjpiou.

The kings are symbolized by the horns, and are thus differentiated from the emperors who are symbolized by the heads of the Beast. Who are these kings? Various answers have been given, i. They are said to be unknown powers belonging to the future which as confederates of the returning emperor will arise and overthrow Rome (Weizsacker and Holtzmann). Swete's interpretation belongs partly to this class. "The ten kings. represent forces which arising out of the empire itself. would turn their arms against Rome and bring about her downfall." 2. The governors of the senatorial provinces who held office for a year (uai wpav). So Ewald, Volkmar, Hilgenfeld, Hausrath, Mommsen, B. Weiss, Briggs, Selwyn. Bousset states that the expressions TTJV Wui ecu TTV c(owiav avrtav rep Gypi Siso'acriv, xvii. 13, and the parallels in xvii. 17 are against this view; but this is not necessarily so. These governors possessed a certain delegated authority (to? foo-iaels), and only for a year (juav pav). But again this interpretation has not the support of xvi. 12 or of the universal expectation that was then current in the East and in the Roman Empire. The phrase oovvai rrjv (3atL iav avtv rp Orjpiu shows that these have actual kingdoms, and so the text could not apply to Roman officials. 3. The

Parthian satraps (Eichhorn, De Wette, Bleek, Bousset, J. Weiss, Wellhausen, Scott, Moffatt). According to xvi. 12, the Parthians had several kings or satraps. It is stated that there were as many as fourteen, but the number ten here is not to be pressed. According to the current belief of the generation that followed the death of Nero, it was held that Nero had escaped to the East, and that he would return against Rome at the head of the Parthian hosts. That this belief was taken seriously is proved by the fact that three pretenders appeared between 69-88 A. D. under Nero's name as claimants of the imperial throne. For the evidence see App. to this chapter (p. 80). Since this belief had firmly established itself both in the Gentile and Hellenistic Jewish worlds within the first decade after Nero's death, since, further, it is attested actually in our text in xvi. 12, there can be little doubt that the source in xvii. 12-17 is to be explained thereby. But in the present context, in which Nero is a demon from the abyss, it is possible that these kings are, as Bousset suggests, regarded by our Seer as demonic powers.

Cf. Dan. vii. 24, ical ra Sca fccpara avrov Sew ouiru exapop. These words referring to the Parthian satraps are intelligible from the standpoint of the world empire of Rome. They hold a quasi-kingly power (us acria r j) for a brief span (utav fyav), since the Antichrist's power will speedily be brought to an end.

13. OUTOI fuav ykwitjk fx U(rik K u T? JK Sufajuy ical ouaiay ofa-uk TW Orjpiy Sitwik. The Greek structure of this verse is still more manifest than that which precedes.

(liar ykwp)K fyovw a g d Greek idiom. Cf. Thuc. ii. 86, fjLrjv fyovres. prj cffaitrciv, Herod, i. 207; ii. 56, etc.

The unanimity of the Parthian kings is ex)lamed in xvii. 17.

15. ical ctirck fioi Ta usara ctcs, ou iropmfj Kc 0i)rai, Xaol ical oi tivlv ical conf) xal yxucnrai.

This is a gloss explanatory of xvii. i, where the Harlot City is said to sit ri vsaruv TroxAwf. But since it was not Rome but the literal Babylon that was so situated, the glosser, after the analogy of Isa. viii. 7, Jer. xlvii. 2, interprets the many waters here as referring to the peoples over which Rome ruled. In xvii. i the phrase fal vsdrwv iroaXv is simply taken over from Jer. See note in loc. The style is not that of our author. He never uses ov but oirou: cf. ii. 13 (Hs xi. 8, xii. 6, 14, xx. 10. Nor is the enumeration Aool icra. that of our author. See note on v. 9. He uses u ai instead of 0 X01. Again we should expect gadget in our author and not ica rai. See note on 9 and on ill 21.

XVH. 17, 16. ROME TO BE DESTROYED BY FIRE 73 17. 6 yap 0C? ISttitcK els TS Kopftios arv norfjcrai v aujou, ical iroujcrat LLUW yk 5p)M ical Soupai rtji TW Otjpup, axpi Tcxea aoitai oi Xtfyoi TOU Ocou.

This verse explains the remarkable unanimity of these kings. It was due to God, not to any mere earthly policy, and it would last till the oracles of the prophets regarding Rome were accomplished, and the Antichrist and the kings met in the last great battle with the Lamb, xvii. 14. Even the wrath of men is made to praise Him. There is no real dualism in the universe. The very powers of evil ultimately subserve the purposes of God and are then destroyed. (Cf. xvii. 14.) Since the Beast, which in the source meant the living Nero returning from the East at the head of the Parthians, has become in our author the demonic Nero, it is probable that his attendant hosts are also to be regarded as of demonic origin.

jfbwkCK els TC S napios drrwk. For this Hebraism (JTU 3awtf) cf. Neh. vii. 5. There is a closely related idiom in Jer. xxxi. (xxxviii.) 33; i Thess. iv. 8; Heb. viii. 10.

ical iroivjcrai fuw yytfpi)?. I have, with Alford, bracketed this clause as an early gloss from xvii. 13. It is superfluous after irotrjfral rrjv yv fjl-rjv avrovy which is really explained by ical Sowcu jcra.

rcxcao aorrai oi 5yoi TOU Oeou. In their present context these prophecies must relate not only to the destruction of Rome by Nero and the Parthians as in the source, but to the overthrow of the power of the Beast and his Parthian allies.

16. Kai T tclpara ciScs ical r 0rjpwk, OUTOI punfjeroimrik T P irop T)K, ical jpr)fuf KV)K iroiqaoiurii aurrjk ical yufim K, ical rd adpicas autTJs dyorrcu, ical aur y Karaicaucrouaik iv mipt.

I have restored this verse to the place which it had originally in the source and in our author, i. e. after xvii. 17, which in its turn followed immediately on xvii. 13.

The Harlot City was to be destroyed by the forces of evil themselves. As the Beast is demonic and the horns are conceived as part of him, these kings appear also to have a demonic character in their present context.

The author of this source must have had Ezek. xxiii. 25-29 before him, but not the LXX. He reproduces the thought but not the form of the Hebrew. Thus fittnprovcrty rrjv iroprqv is a free rendering of xxiii. 29, Htofco- JVik 1GW, which the LXX translates literally. Next with P WXCKIV voufaowriv amjv ical yvfjurfv cf. xxiii. 26,-pjQ-nk TWPDrri (immwrw crc rcv itaturfuy crov, and xxiii. 29, Dny Itttjn 1XT4 3 np). With amp KatCLKCLvvowlv Iv itvpi cf. xxiii. 25, fi K3 3 n. All these statements are made by Ezekiel with regard to Jerusalem, which at one moment is spoken of as a woman stripped of her garments and left naked, and at another as a city burnt with fire. The writer here uses the same figures of Rome.

noufjoroikn?. For construction, see Introd. 3, p.

TS r pitai afi-rfjs +frywtu: cf. xix. 18, Ps. xxvii. 2, rov ayclv TOS crapfcas AOV. Mlc. iii. 3, fcarc ayov ra? ordpicas rov Xaou iov: 2 Kings IX. 36, xara dyovrat ol KUIC? ras erapkas UfaSea 0-apfcc? denotes the fleshy parts of the body.

naroicaucjouaik fr irupi: cf. xviii. 8; Jer. vii. 31; Nah. iii 15. These words can only refer to the city whom the woman represents. Death by fire was not the punishment of the harlot, unless she were a priest's daughter: cf. Lev. xxi. 9.

14. OUTOI JICT TOO Aptaou iroxcp, aouotk,

KCU TO dpploK Klk acl QUTOUS, 8n itupios icupiwk Ivrlv KOI paaixcds f3arixi, Kai ol ficr autoo icxtjtol Kal K CKTOL ical iriarou

This verse is manifestly added by our author to the source he is using. But this verse could not have been inserted in its present position by our author; for it treats of the destruction of the forces appointed by God for Rome's destruction, which they effect in 16. In xvii. 17, 16, according to the MSS text, the ten horns and the Beast are represented as executing a divine judgment on the Harlot City and as destroying Rome after they had already themselves been destroyed (xvii. 14). Hence this verse belongs rightly after 16. I have restored it accordingly. With yxcra rov apvlov TroxcAijcrovo-iv. vikijcrct avrovs compare xiil. 7, which is from his hand. For Kvpto?. fao-ixcw cf. xix. 16. The subject of this vision, i. e. the Parthian kings and their destruction (12-13, 17, 16, 14), has been in part referred to in xvi. 12, and is regarded as already accomplished in xix. 13, where the words ircptj3c Xi?i, cvo? iumov fcjsaj.j. eiov aium speak of the vesture of the Divine Warrior as already dipped in blood (i. c, in that of the Parthian kings) before the Messianic campaign against the kings of the earth in xix. 11-21.

The concluding line describes the armies who followed the Lamb, . "the called, elect, and faithful." That these should crush hostile nations we leam from ii. 26, 27, and their descent from heaven to do so is seen in a vision in xix. 14. Hence they are a martyr host of warriors. It was a well-known Jewish expectation that the righteous would take part in the destruction of the wicked: cf. i Enoch xxxviii. 5, xc. 19, xci. 12 for the period of the sword, when the wicked are given into the hands of the righteous, op. cit xcv. 7, xcvi. i, xcviii. 12, xcix. 4, 6; Wisd. iii. 8. The martyrs are not here engaged on a mission of revenge, but in the fulfilment of a righteous retribution.

XVH. 14, 18. J THE LAMB CONQUERS THE PARTHIANS 75 In xv. 4 the vision which is in reality a prophecy shows that the thought of revenge has wholly passed from the minds of the glorified martyrs. But the nations there referred to are those that are contemporary with the Millennial Reign. See the third note further on.

itrfpvos Kupiw. paffixlup. This title recurs in xix. 16. In both instances it is used of the Son. The combination of these titles as applied to God is found first in i Enoch ix. 4,6 dco?

TQV 0CO1 KOI (6) KVplOS TO)V KVuw KOI 6 JttcTlactis TO)V fta(Tl Cv6vt(i)V.

(So the two Greek versions in Syncellus, whereas the Ethiopia implies ? ariaew for feo-iacvovrwv.) It is worth observing that i Tim. vi. 15 has fao-tacv? TWV fturtacvoirctii. These titles occur often separately as applied to God, tcvpiog rwy Kvpiwv, Deut x. 17; 6 frurtacvs rcuv facna. cw: i Enoch Ixiii. 4, Ixxxiv. 2; 2 Mace. xiii. 4. See Bousset's Rel. d. Judenthums, 306.

The use of such titles in reference to Marduk in Babylonian literature is noted by Zimmern, K. A. T 373 sq., 390. Marduk is actually named "Lord of Lords, King of Kings." "King of Kings " was a designation of the Babylonian and Persian kings: cf. Ezek. xxvi. 7; Ezra vii. 12; Dan. ii. 37: of the Egyptian kings, Diod. Sic. i. 55. 7, Jacriaevs fruriacaw al Sccrirons Sccrirorcov Sccrowis. But this title is far outbid by those given to Dom-itian: "Dominus et deus noster." Suet. Domit. 13: cf. Mart, v. 8.

ol per aurou K TJTO KT. K Tjrdi and ecaccrot occur only here in the Apocalypse. We are to understand iroacuto-ovcrivand vunprovcnv from what precedes. The followers of the Lamb who have been called and chosen will manifest their loyalty and share in the Lamb's victory (cf. xii. n). According to this context those who answer the call are elected and prove their loyalty: cf. 2 Pet. i. IO, oirovscurare ? c? atav vfuuv ryv K r)rw KCU cicaoy v woultrotu. But these loyal followers of the Lamb belong already to the heavenly hosts; for they accompany Him from heaven: cf. xix. 14. They are called irurrot as their Leader is called IWTOS (i. 5).

18. Kal yuk i r v ctscs niv tj ir Xis pey Xi)? x oora paorixciav im TOP fturi iuv TYJ? yijs.

Our author knows at last the interpretation of the chief figure in the vision. The woman is the city Rome, the empress of the entire world.

This verse belonged to the source A: see Introd. to Chap., 5, and had its place immediately after xvii. 7, but was transferred to its present position in order to introduce the great chapter of the downfall of Rome.

On the phrase 7 iroats i? ftcyoai;, S ee note on xl 9.

ADDITIONAL NOTE ON XVH.

The Antichrist Bcliar? and Neronic Myths and their ultimate Fusion in early Christian Literature.

This question bristles with problems. Many of these, it is true, have been solved and others are on the way to solution. Nevertheless, many lie still in the background and have not as yet yielded up their secret to research. The chief workers in this field have been Gunkel and Bousset. While the services of the former have been at times brilliant, they have at the same time showed a lack of sound judgment In the latter respect Bousset in his Antichrist Legend (translated from the German, 1896) and in the Offenbarungjohanni 1906, has made an admirable contribution, and proved that outside Daniel and Revelation there was an independent tradition of the Antichrist myth coming down from ancient times and diffused through many lands. A study of such articles as Creation, Dragon, Leviathan, Serpent in the Encyc. Biblica will show that the Creation Story passed through a long development within the domain of Hebrew and Jewi3h thought, and further study proves that such an expression as "the great dragon, the ancient serpent, who is called the Devil and Satan " (Rev. xil 9), finds one of its sources ultimately in the myth that underlies the Creation story. But the present study cannot take account of the manifold traces of this development discoverable in the O. T. (see Gunkel, Schbpfung und Chaos a book full of suggestion, but in many of its conclusions, especially as regards Revelation, demonstrably wrong). It must be strictly limited to the ideas of the Antichrist and kindred conceptions that prevailed within Judaism and Christianity from 200 B. C. to 100 A. D. or thereabouts.

In a study of the present subject in 1900 (see Ascension of Isaiah pp. li-lxxiii) I pointed out that, whilst Bousset's and Gunkel's works (above cited) were most helpful and stimulating in many directions, they did not deal satisfactorily with the relations of Beliar and the Antichrist, and that their account of the fusion of the latter with the Neronic legend was wanting in lucidity and consistency. This defect Bousset has from his own standpoint partially remedied in Rel d. Judentums im Neutest. Zeitalter, 1906, and his article on "Antichrist" in Hastings' Encyc. of Religion and Ethics i. 578 sqq. Here he has vastly improved on his earlier studies, and removed many of the defects to which I took objection in 1900. But, notwithstanding these advances on Bousset's part, I feel constrained to republish here the main part 1 This is the form that Belial takes in Jubilees, Testaments XII Patriarchs, the Sibylline Oracles, Martyrdom of Isaiah.

XVEL ADDITIONAL NOTE ON XVII. JJ of my study of 1900 with such additions and improvements as the work of the intervening years has naturally brought with them.

If we can succeed in establishing with approximate accuracy the dates when the Antichrist, Behar, and Neronic myths originated and became fused together, we acquire means for determining the dates of the fragments of such myths as have secured an entrance into the work of our author.

The aim, therefore, of the present note is to touch briefly on the history of the Antichrist, Beliar, and Neronic myths, before the fusion of any one of them with another, or of each with all: and next to give the passages from Jewish and Christian literature where such fusion is attested and their approximate dates. Thus I shall deal with I. The independent development of the Antichrist, Beliar, and Neronic myths.

II. The fusion oj the Antichrist myth with that of Beliar, and subsequently and independently with the AJeronic myth. III. The fusion oj all these myths together.

I. The independent development of the Antichrist, Beliar, and Neronic myths.

L The Antichrist myth. The term " Antichrist" is comparatively late though the idea signified by it is early. Thus it is not attested till far on in the first century of our era; for it is found in the N. T. only in the Johannine Epistles i John ii. 18, 22, iv. 3; 2 John 7. The idea, however, can be traced back to the second century B. C., and appears first in the Book of Daniel. This conception takes two forms: (a) the individual Antichrist, and (4) the collective Antichrist.

(a) A God-opposing individual. In Daniel we find the individual Antichrist (the king of the North, xi. 40) appearing at the head of mighty armies, with which he crushes certain nations and preserves others, persecutes the saints (vii. 25), putting numbers of them to death (viii. 10), sets up in the Temple "the abomination that maketh desolate " (i. e. the heathen altar over the altar of burnt-offering, viii. 13, ix. 27, xi. 31, xii. n), "magnifies himself above every god " (xi. 36: cf. 2 Thess. ii. 4), and after a reign of three and a half years (vii. 25 sq.) meets his end (xi. 45). The historical figure here referred to was Antiochus iv. Epiphanes (i. e. (God) made manifest). The idea, which may in part have existed already and which became impersonated in Antiochus disassociated itself from the historical figure of Antiochus, and through its enlargement and enrichment in the Book of Daniel established itself as a permanent expectation in Judaism. ID the 78 THE REVELATION OF ST. JOHN XVII.

earliest literature, therefore, where the idea appears, it implies a being of human origin (though claiming divine prerogatives), whereas Beliar, who came subsequently to be identified with the Antichrist, was originally a superhuman or Satanic being.

The next historical character to whom epithets belonging to the Antichrist are applied, is Pompey the Great, who committed the unpardonable act of profaning the Temple by entering the Holy of Holies after his conquest of Jerusalem. Thus in the Pss. of Solomon (70-40 B. C.), Pompey is called " the Dragon" (6 Spofcw, ii. 29). There may be here an unconscious allusion to the Dragon myth (see Cheyne's art. " Dragon " in the Encyc. Bib. i.). He is described as "the sinner, 1 ii. i (6dfiapruao?), the personification of sin (cf. 2 Thess. ii. 3, 6 av owros r so the inferior Uncials): " the lawless one," xvii. 13 an attribute of Beliar (cf. 2 Thess. ii. 3, 6 avbpuiros KB). But since his soldiers are designated " the lawless ones (xvii. 20, 01 avouot), the epithet may mean no more than heathen, as in i Cor. ix. 21; 2 Cor. vi. 14; Acts ii. 23. The epithet "lawless," if technically used, is proper to the Beliar myth.

This expectation may have been influenced by the action of the emperor Caligula (37-41 A. D.), when he ordered the governor Petronius to erect his statue in the Temple. If he had persisted in this act of profanation, the Jews would undoubtedly have regarded it as a fulfilment of the prediction of the setting up of" the abomination of desolation " in the Temple. This phrase was, as we are aware, first applied to the heathen altar set up by Antiochus in the Temple (i Mace. i. 54), and probably also to the image of Olympian Zeus beside it (cf. Taanith iv. 6). Bousset suggests that "the ever recurring expectation of later times, that Antichrist would take his place in the Temple of Jerusalem, dates. from this period."

The next reference to the Antichrist is to be found in 2 Bar. xxxvl 5, xxxix. 3, xl. i, 2, according to which the head of the Roman Empire was to be brought before the Messiah and destroyed, and still another in 4 Ezra v. 6, where the reign of the Antichrist is foretold: " Et regnabit quern non sperant, qui inhabitant super terram."

(b) A God-opposing power or the collective Antichrist. So far we have cited our authorities as testifying to a single individual Antichrist. But with the expectation of an individual Antichrist that of a collective Antichrist, (a) secular, or (J) religious, is often involved.

(a) Thus in Dan. vii. 7 sqq., 19 sqq. the Fourth Empire (i. e. the Greek or Macedonian) is the collective Antichrist The identity of the Seleucidae or Greek rulers of Syria with the Fourth Kingdom appears in the Sibylline Oracles, iii. 388-400 (before 140 B. C.). But at the close of the first cent. B. C. or the beginning of the first cent. A. D. the prophecy of Daniel was reinterpreted, and, since Syria had now ceased to be a world power, the Fourth Empire was identified with the new world power Rome. This is first seen in the Assumption of Moses (7-30 A. D.), where the overthrow of Rome by Israel is predicted: x. 8. "Then thou, O Israel, shalt be happy, And thou shalt go up against the eagle, And its neck and wings shall be destroyed." l

Lest his contemporaries should misunderstand Dan. vil 17-19, 23 sqq. as referring to the Greek Empire, the Seer in 4 Ezra xii. 1 1-i 2 expressly states that this passage refers to the Roman Empire. This is the universal view of the first century A. D. Cf, 2 Bar. xxxvi.-xl.; 4 Ezra v. 3-4, xi. 40 sqq. It is attested in the N. T.: see the Little Jewish Apocalypse incorporated in Mark xiii. (especially 14 = Matt. xxiv. 15 = Luke xxi. 20), and in the sources behind xiii. i-io (see 8 in the Introd. to xiii.), xvii. 3-10, where it is symbolized by the Beast in our Apocalypse. But in our text the meaning of the symbol has been changed: it stands only in part for the Roman Empire, but mainly for Nero redivivus, the demonic Antichrist coming up from the abyss, in xiii. 3 and similarly in xvil i-io; but the original meaning of the symbol still survives in xiii. 1-2, xvii. 3. In the Ep. Barn. iv. 4-5 (100-120 A. D.) the Fourth Kingdom is Rome: so also in Hippolytus (220 A. D.), and in the Talmud Aboda

The collective Antichrist of a religious origin. In the Johannine Epistles of the N. T. (i John ii. 18, 22, iv. 3; 2 John 7) the Antichrist is the collective name for the false teachers who have gone forth from the bosom of the Church as deceivers (irxdvoi). This conception is not to be confounded with that of pseudo-Christ (cvsoxpurro?) of Matt. xxiv. 24; Mark xiii. 22. The individual Antichrist of the religious type is probably referred to in John v. 43, "If another shall come in his own name, him ye will receive."

Again the original source lying behind xiii. 11-14, 16-17 1 Here the words " its neck and wings " have been transposed from line 2. The transmitted text runs:

"And thou shalt go up against (i. e. iy nsjn) the necks and wings of the Andtney shall be destroyed"

(where " implebuntur " of the MS=ruvrex cr (wrot, which should have been rendered "delebuntur" here). We have here an early form of the Eagle Vision such as we find in 4 Ezra xi, was a Jewish Apocalypse directed against the individual Antichrist in the form of the False Prophet (see Introd. to Chap. xiii. 8, vol. i. pp. 342-344). In our text it has been transformed into a collective Antichrist, i. e. the heathen imperial priesthood, and designated the second Beast in subordination to the first in xiii. i-10. Originally this Antichrist was conceived as independent and without any Antichrist beside him.

ii. In the O. T. Beliar does not appear as a proper name (see " Beliar " in the Bible Dictionaries). Beliar first attains to personality in the second century B. C. Thus, according to the Test. XII Patriarchs, Beliar rules over souls that are constantly disturbed (T. Dan iv. 7), or which yield to the evil inclinations (T. Ash. i. 8), but flees from those that keep the law (T. Dan v. i). The Messiah will make war on Beliar and take from him the souls he had led captive (T. Dan v. 10), and Beliar will be bound (T. Levi xviii. 12), and cast into the fire (T. Jud. xxv. 3), and the spirits subject to him will be punished (T. Levi iii. 3). This conception is very like that of Satan a fact which becomes clearer still in Jubilees i. 20, where Beliar (like Satan: cf. i Chron. xxi. i; i Enoch xl. 7; Rev. xii. 10) is said to be the accuser of the faithful before God. This identification of Beliar and Satan appears in the Christian pseudepi-graph, The Questions of Bartholomew (ed. Bonwetsch, 1897), iv. 25. In 2 Cor. vi. 15, Beliar seems a synonym for Satan. Hence we may conclude that towards the close of the second century B. C. Beliar was regarded as a Satanic spirit, and as naught else, until the Beliar myth coalesced with that of the Antichrist.

iii. The Neronic myth in its earliest form. Here our task is simply to show that soon after the death of Nero the myth became current that (a) Nero had not really died, but was still living; and (b) that he would soon return from this far East to take vengeance on Rome.

(a) When Nero with the help of a freedman committed suicide and was cremated (Suet Nero, 49), so great was the public joy that the people thronged the streets in holiday attire (op. cit. 57). All, however, did not share in the belief of Nero's death. Thus Tacitus (Hist. ii. 8) writes that there were many who pretended and believed that he was still alive; and Suetonius (Nero, 57) declares that edicts were issued in his name as though he were fetill alive and would return speedily to destroy his enemies. As early as 69 A. D. an impostor appeared under his name and headed a rebellion against Rome (Tac. Hist. ii. 8, 9).

(o) That Nero had taken refuge in the East probably formed a constituent of the myth from the outset a point on which evidence will be furnished later. Predictions had been made during Nero's lifetime that the East would be the scene of his future greatness: some of these represented Jerusalem as the seat of his empire; others promised him the sovereignty of the world (Suet. Nero 40). Probably such vaticinations as these, combined with the fact that Nero had already established friendly relations with the Parthian king Vplogeses i. (Suet Nero, 57), led Nero, as the end drew nigh, to think of fleeing to the Parthians (op. cit. 47).

In conformity with this expectation we find that a second pseudo-Nero appeared under Titus on the Euphrates, about 80 A. D., and was recognized by the Parthian king Artabanus (Zonaras, xi. 18). Finally, about 88 A. D. a third pretender came forward among the Parthians and all but succeeded in hurling Parthia against Rome (Tac. Hist. i. 2; Suet. Ncro 57). This Nero myth, thus firmly rooted in the Gentile world, passed over to the Jewish. The Jewish source, lying behind Rev. xvii. 12-17 (i. e. xvii. n, 12-13, J 7 6) an(written probably in the reign of Titus, embodies this expectation and predicts the destruction of Rome by the Parthians under the leadership of Nero, who is there called "the beast" This expectation of a Parthian invasion of the West is explicitly stated in xvi. 12. With these passages Rev. ix. 13-21 should be compared, though here we have a demonic form of the myth. The Sibylline Oracles, v. 143-148 (71-74 A. D. so Zahn and Bousset), prove that this myth had established itself in the eschatology of Hellenistic Judaism. According to the passage just referred to, the flight of Nero from Rome to the Parthians is mentioned, and in v. 361-364 his return to destroy Rome. Early in the next decade we find other testimonies to the prevalence of this myth: see Sibyl). Or. iv. 119-122, where Nero is described as a fugitive to Parthia, and iv. 137-139 where he is described as returning to assail the West at the head of a vast host It is possible that the statement in the Talmud (Yoma, 10), to the effect that Rome would be destroyed by the Persians, is an echo of this early expectation.

II. The fusion of the Antichrist myth (i.) with that of Beliar before jo A. D.; and (ii.) independently with that of Nero redivivus, 88-100 A. D.

i. As a result of this fusion the Antichrist is regarded as (a) a God-opposing man armed with miraculous powers this appears to have been effected on Christian soil before 50 A. D.; (b) a purely Satanic power before 70 A. D.

(a) 2 Thess. ii. 1-12, according to the usual interpretation, presents an indubitable instance of this fusion. Thus, on the one hand, we have Beliar. "The man of lawlessness"

VOL. II. 6 (6 avopwiros TI S Avouas) is all but certainly a translation of Beliar; for ivoiifia is the LXX rendering of it in Deut. xv. 9, and voua in 2 Kings xxii. 5, and vapdvofio is frequently found as its equivalent, when it is used as an epithet: Deut. xiii. 13; Judg. xix. 22, xx. 13; 2 Kings xvi. 7, etc.

In the next place it is Beliar appearing as the Antichrist; for the words " he that opposeth himself. against all that is called God" (6 dkrucctmcyos. evl iraira Acyoxcvov 0cdv) form an excellent definition of the Antichrist Since 2 Thess. is now generally (and certainly by the present writer) regarded as an authentic writing of St. Paul, we have here the earliest evidence for the fusion of these ideas (arc. 50 A. D.), and also for the humanization of the Beliar myth through its fusion with that of the Antichrist for hitherto Beliar had been conceived as a Satanic or superhuman being. The Antichrist thus comes to be conceived as a God-opposing man armed with Satanic powers.

We should next observe that in 2 Thess. ii. 1-12 the myth appears to have a purely religious significance and not apolitical one, as in Rev. xiii. i-io, xvii. Thus in 2 Thess. ii. 6, 7 the Roman Empire is referred to as the power which checks the manifestation of the Antichrist, whereas in Rev. xiii. i-io it is the Roman Empire that stood originally in the source of this passage and that still stands in the background as the Antichrist, while the demonic Nero stands in the foreground as this being. In no case could 2 Thess. ii. 1-12 have been written after 70 A. D. This section is a Christian transformation of a current Judaistic myth.

Another phase of this expectation appears in Rev. xiii. 11-17. In the source of this passage the Antichrist was conceived similarly to that in 2 Thess. ii. But by our author this conception was recast and interpreted of the priesthood, which was attached to the cultus of the Caesars, and had the chief seat of its activities in the province of Asia. This Antichrist in our author symbolized by the second Beast is a false teacher and prophet. Hence this conception is akin to that which prevails in the Johannine Epistles: i John ii. 18, 22, iv. 3; 2 John 7. Though both in the Epistles and Rev. xiii. 11-17 the Antichrist is human, in the latter passage he is armed with Satanic powers and " deceiveth them that dwell on the earth by reason of the signs which it was given him to do in the sight of the beast" (xiii. 14). His task is to make the inhabitants of the earth worship the first Beast (i. e. the Beliar Nero), whose death-stroke had been healed (xiii. 12). This subordinate Antichrist is designated as "the false prophet" in xvi. 13, xix. 20, xx. 10. Thus a conception which had originally grown up in Jewish and Christian circles, and, referring to a Jewish Antichrist, had a purely religious significance, was recast by our author and reinterpreted of a heathen corporation, the Imperial priesthood, which was in part religious and in part political in its aims.

Sibylline Or. ii. 167 sq. (circ. 200 A. D.) should probably be cited under this head, where it is said that Beliar will come and work many portents before men.

() The Beliar Antichrist=a purely Satanic power before JO A. D. (or jo A. D.).

This stage of the myth is attested in Rev. xi. 7, where as the Beast from the abyss he makes war with and kills the witnesses. The Antichrist in this passage makes his advent in Jerusalem (xi. 8), and therefore before 70 A. D. This phase of the myth was originally independent of that which appears in Rev. xiii. and XVH., where it has been fused together with the Neronic myth. But in its present context in xi. it is treated as identical with the conception in xiii. and xvii. and is used proleptically in reference to it.

We should probably not be wrong in recognizing in the Assumption of Moses x. i, 2 an instance of this compound conception.

1. "And then His kingdom shall appear throughout all His creation,

And then Satan shall be no more, And sorrow shall depart with him.

2. Then the hands of the angel shall be filled Who has been appointed chief,

And he shall forthwith avenge them of their adversaries."

If this passage comes rightly under this head, then the fusion of the ideas of Beliar and Antichrist must be anterior to 30 A. D.

ii. Fusion of the Antichrist myth with that of the Nero redwivus. This fusion could not have taken place before the first half of Domitian's reign, when the last Neronic pretender appeared. As soon, however, as the hope of the return of the living Nero could no longer be entertained, the way was prepared for this transformation of the myth. The living Nero was no longer expected, but Nero restored to life from the abyss. This expectation appears in Rev. xiii., xvil But it is questionable if this classification is right, and the very much conflated conceptions of the Antichrist in these chapters had best been reckoned under III. The simple Neronic myth needs some infusion of the Beliar myth in order to develop the expectation of Nero redivivus or Nero as a demonic power.

III. Fusion of the Antichrist Beliar-, and Neronic myths in various degrees and forms.

From this fusion the myth emerges in three forms, which owe their diversity in the main to the three variations of the Neronic myth which enter into and affect the combination. These are: (i.) Incarnation of Beliar as the Antichrist in Nero still conceived as alive. The Antichrist has here a political significance, and is human, (ii.) Incarnation of Beliar in the form of the dead Nero. The Antichrist is here a Satanic being, (iii.) Incarnation of Beliar as the Antichrist in Nero redwivus.

(i.) Incarnation of Beliar as the Antichrist in Nero still conceived as living before 90 A. D. We have seen above from documentary evidence that before 80 A. D. the myth had gained wide circulation both among Gentiles and Jews, that Nero was still living in the East, and would speedily return to avenge himself on Rome. We have further seen that long before 80 A. D. the minds of both Jews and Christians were familiar with the expectation of the Antichrist pure and simple, and of the Antichrist possessing the attributes of Beliar or Satan, and so denoting a God-opposing man armed with miraculous powers, or a truly Satanic being. So strong was the tendency of such mythical currents to merge in a common stream that it is not surprising to find this coalescence achieved in Sibyll. Or. iii. 63-74. This passage is unhappily of uncertain date, though no doubt before 90 A. D., since Nero is still regarded as alive. Its significance, however, cannot be mistaken. Beliar comes as Antichrist and is descended from Augustus (c c Sejgocmpwv). That this descendant of Augustus is Nero there seems no room for doubt. The lines are: fc Sc arri7vov i? ct Bcatap Acron-urlcy at f onjcrci f opcaiy ityos, onprct 2 0a arrav..

Kal vcfcvas ar orci ical onjiara iroxXa irouprci.

AAV diroray icy Koto 0cov vcxcurcixriv atreixat,

Kal Swaus Xoyeovra otstaros cis yalav jcat Bcxtap 4A. c ct jcat utrcp tciaovs dvlpunrov?

nukrac, 3rot TOVTW trurrtv cvciroii ravro.

It is possible, however, that the Scjsao-nvot are the inhabitants of Sefoonj, i. e. Samaria. In that case the text would come under II. i. (b).

ii. Incarnation of Beliar as Antichrist in the form of the dead Nero. In due time the belief that Nero was still alive in the East began to die. The time of its extinction must naturally have varied according to temperament and locality. It is accordingly difficult to assign definite dates. Since, however, the latest pretender to the Neronic role came forward in 88 A. D., we may not unreasonably infer that from that year the belief began to lose its grip on the common folk, and to decline steadily till it finally disappeared. No doubt during the next twenty years or more it crops up sporadically, but even during that period its place has been taken by two rival and stronger forms of the same myth.

These new forms may have already been evolved in the later yean of Vespasian. At all events they are not later than 90-100 A. D. Now that the belief that Nero was still alive had already been abandoned, there were two courses of development open for this myth, in case the Neronic element was still to be retained. Either Beliar must come in the form of the dead Nero, or Nero must be recalled to life by a Satanic miracle as in (iii.). The first course is adopted by the writer of the Ascension of Isaiah, the second by our author in xiii., xvii. The passage in the Ascension, iv. 2-4, is as follows:

"And after (the age) is fulfilled, Beliar, the great ruler, the king of this world, will descend, who hath ruled it since it came into being; yea he will descend from his firmament in the likeness of a man, a lawless king, the slayer of his mother, who himself (even) this king 3. Will persecute the plant which the Twelve Apostles of the Beloved have planted. Of the Twelve one will be delivered into his hand. 4. This ruler in the form of that king will come, and there will come with him all the powers of this world," etc.

(iii.) Incarnation of Jfeliar as the Antichrist in Nero redivivus. The chief authority attesting this expectation is Rev. xiii., xvii. in their present form as they left our author's hand. But we shall first deal shortly with others in the Sibylline Oracles. In Sibyll. Or. v. 28-34 (written in the reign of Hadrian) the description of the Antichrist involves all the above elements. Thus it is Nero redivivus that is described; for the author of the lines is writing two generations after Nero's death. In the next place he is called in semi-mythological language " the serpent" (herein we have the Beliar element), and finally he makes himself equal to God. The lines bearing on our subject are v. 28-29, 33-34- ircm Korra 8 OTIS KCXUTV Xa c, KOtpavos IOTCU,

Scivo? cw is.

dxX (otai ical aurros oaouos ctra brafcov 0cp avrdv.

v. 214-227 belongs more clearly to this division. According to this passage, Nero is to return aloft, upborne by the Fates. His achievements are portrayed in 219-225. In Book viii., of which lineji 4-429 belong to the close of the second century, the various myths have so thoroughly coalesced that Nero is no longer regarded as a man but as a Satanic monster. He has become the Dragon (viii. 88, irop vpcd T 8poxov), and assumed the monster's form (157, 0i pa It is needless here to pursue the ramifications of this myth further in this and later literature than to state, that so thoroughly did the Neronic element in the composite Antichrist conception gain the upper hand in the East, that in Armenian the word Nero became and remains the equivalent for Antichrist.

We shall now return to the most important testimonies of this subject, i. e. in Rev. xiii., xvii. We need not here deal with them in detail, since they are fully discussed already. Here we have the most vigorous and illuminating conception of the Antichrist in all literature, although, as we have seen in our study of these chapters, our author was to a considerable extent indebted to existing sources in their composition. But though the elements of the Antichrist were drawn for the most part from disparate sources, the result is no mere mosaic, no laboured syncretism of conflicting traits, but a marvellous portrait of the great God-opposing power that should hereafter arise, who was to exalt might above right, and attempt, successfully or unsuccessfully for the time, to seize the sovereignty of the world, backed by hosts of intellectual workers, 1 who would uphold his pretensions, justify all his actions, and enforce his political aims by an economic warfare, which menaced with destruction all that did not bow down to his arrogant and godless claims. And though the justness of this forecast is clear to the student who approaches the subject with some insight, and to all students who approach it with the experience of the present world war, we find that as late as 1908, Bousset in his article on the "Antichrist" in Hastings' Encyclopedia of Religion and Ethics writes as follows: " The interest in the (Antichrist) legend. is now to be found only among the lower classes of the Christian community, among sects, eccentric individuals, and fanatics."

No great prophecy receives its full and final fulfilment in any single event or series of events. In fact, it may not be fulfilled at all in regard to the object against which it was primarily delivered by the prophet or Seer. But, if it is the expression of a great moral and spiritual truth, it will of a surety be fulfilled at sundry times and in divers manners and in varying degrees of completeness. The present attitude of the Central Powers of Europe on this question of might against right, of Caesarism against religion, of the state against God, is the greatest fulfilment that the Johannine prophecy in xiii. has as yet received. Even the very indefiniteness regarding the chief Antichrist in xiii. is reproduced in the present upheaval of 1 This is the second Beast in xiii. the false prophet 9 The measures described in xiii. 16-17, evil powers. In xiii. the Antichrist is conceived as a single individual, i. e. the demonic Nero; but, even so, behind him stands the Roman Empire, which is one with him in character and purpose, and is itself the Fourth Kingdom or the Kingdom of the Antichrist in fact, the Antichrist itself. So in regard to the present war, it is difficult to determine whether the Kaiser or his people can advance the best claims to the title of a modern Antichrist If he is a present-day representative of the Antichrist, so just as surely is the empire behind him, for it is one in spirit and purpose with its leader whether regarded from its military side, its intellectual, or its industrial. They are in a degree far transcending that of ancient Rome " those who are destroying the earth" (Rev. xi. 18).

CHAPTER XVIII. i. The Contents and Character of this Chapter.

This chapter, which deals with the doom of Rome, opens with a prophetic prelude, in which the Seer looks far forward and sees the destruction of Rome as already accomplished, and the earth's proud capital as the haunt of every unclean thing both demonic and belonging to this world. 1 This prelude, described as an angelic utterance from heaven (1-3), is proleptic, since in the rest of the chapter various stages in the actual destruction are described.

In 4-8 there follows another voice addressed to the faithful (4-5) and to the ministers of God's wrath, 8 who were assembled for the destruction of Rome.

We now come to the three threnodies pronounced respectively over burning Rome by the kings (9-10), by the merchant princes of the earth (11-13, 15-16), and by the shipowners and sailors of all the world (17-19). Each in turn bewail the doom of the great city in whose wantonness and luxury and wealth they had all shared.

The chapter closes with a song of doom preluded by a symbolic action on the part of a strong angel. This dirge is uttered by the Seer who wrote the Oracle, which John has utilized here for his own purposes. At its close he has added 20, 23 f-24, in which he appeals to heaven and to the martyrs, 1 As John had not the opportunity of revising his great Apocalyse, several traces of the expectations belonging to the Vespanianic period survive in this Jewish source. According to John's own view, the smoke of Rome was to go up till the world's end (xix. 3), but not so in this source (xviii. 2).

8 Another element testifying to the origin of the source in Vespanian's time. The faithful had all been removed from the earth at the close of xiii.

8 In the original source Nero and the Parthians.

apostles and prophets already there, to rejoice over the destruction of Rome. This appeal is answered in xix. This last part of the chapter was evidently found by our author in a very confused condition. It should be read as follows (as we have shown in 6): 21, 14, 22 tbcd, 23, 22 h, 23, 20, 23, 24.

As we have already stated, John has here used a source belonging to the Vespasianic period, and written soon after the destruction of Jerusalem. It was apparently written originally in Hebrew, and found by John in a Greek translation. The grounds for these statements are given in the sections that follow. To the same Vespasianic source xvii. i b 7, 18, 8-10 (in part) originally belonged.

2. The Diction Idiom, and Style of xviii. 2-23 is not that of our author.

The style of this chapter has none of our author's characteristic abnormal constructions (see 2). It has, on the other hand, constructions which are wholly against his usage (see 3). This chapter contains a great many airo Acyducva so far as the rest of the N. T. is concerned (see footnote on i), and also peculiar usages of certain words (see 5) not only unknown in the rest of the N. T. and the LXX, but almost unknown elsewhere. The style is most carefully elaborated, and in this respect different from that of our author. Our author is, of course, a stylist, but with him style is a wholly secondary consideration. His theme had wholly gained possession of him, and being the greatest of all themes it naturally expresses itself in great and noble words. But the writer of xviii. 2-23 is no less conscious of the claims of form than he is of the subject-matter of his vision. He is a conscious stylist. Moreover, the order of his words is less Semitic than that of any other chapter in the Apocalypse from our author's hand. Thus the verb frequently follows after the subject or the object, or both combined: cf. 3, 7, 8, n, 14, 15, 17. In xvii. i-2, 3 b-7, 8-10, the earlier part of this source, the order is Semitic, but this seems owing to the revision it has undergone at the hands of our author before he incorporated it in his text

Finally, this source has influenced our author (see 7).

i. Diction. The source begins with 2. It is introduced by i, every phrase of which is from our author. Thus xrra ravra ctsov is a characteristic phrase: ctSov A o? Jyycaov Karafatwra IK rov ovpavov is found in x. i and again in xx. i. On c ovra i ova-iav cf. ix. 3, xvi. 9, xx. 6; and on tyuturorj IK ris 80 7? avrov, cf. XXI. 23, ij yap a rov tfcov c uturey avrrjv. The style of 2-23 is not that of our author, nor the diction nor the idiom.

The diction is in the main different. I have added a list of phrases and clauses common to xviii. and the rest of the book. Now from this list must be withdrawn those given under 20, 23, 24, since either originally or in their present form they are from our authors hand. Next, those given under 3 b, 10, 16 are repeated from the earlier part of the same source, xvii. i-io, but not found elsewhere in the Book. Again, this old Vespasianic source has not unnaturally influenced our author's diction: hence the clauses given in 2, 3 are the source of xiv. 8, and the rare use of PVO-O-WOV in 12 appears to be the source of our author's use of it in xix. 8, 14. Thus the clauses with a diction akin to that in our author are those given under 4 (8), 9, 21 (below). But the clauses which in these verses are common to this source and our author are not distinctive. On the other hand, xviii. has a large number of airaf Acyoicva, so far as the rest of our author and the N. T. are concerned. 1 2. eirccrcp, circorci Bapuxf pcyiixi): cf. xiv. 8, which, however, appears to be borrowed from this source.

3. IK. TOU otpou TOU Ouftou Ttjs iroppcias aurijs irciroriieci irdlira T cott) the source of xiv. 8. ot jjaaixeis-rijs yrjs per afrrijt ra?: cf. 9, xvii. 2, where the clause has already occurred.

4. TJicouaa axXtjy upf)? C K TOU opapou Xlyoucraf: cf. X. 4, 8, xi. 12, xiv. 2, etc.

8. 8ia TOUTO: cf. vii. i5, xii. 12. friruplicataicau9 rctai: cf. xvii. 16.

9. Kityoirai ev aurfj: cf. i. 7.

10. i iroxis Vj pcydxi): cf. 1 6, 19, xvii. 1 8 all belonging to the same source.

18. Puomrou: cf. 16, xix. 8, 14, where this use of fowuw as a noun appears derived from the use in this source.

16. ircpij3 pxi)fi, linr). fiapyapitfl: repeated with slight variations from xvii. 4 both belonging to the same source.

17. ftrnjcrat. Our author would have used Icrrao aak or o-ay. See vol. i. p. 272.

20. o4 patkou: cf. xii. 12. oupa Our author uses this word in the sing, ot ayioi K. ol Airovroxoi xal ol irpo fjrai. The order is unusual: contrast xi. 18, xviii. 24. frpipci: cf. xvi. 6.

21. cts (cf. viii. 13, xix. 17) ayyexos laxupds: cf. v. 2, x. i. els: very frequent. 06 id cdp 0 2rt: cf. 22, 24, xii. 8, xiv. 5.

28. tirxan Oqaai irrfmra rd lonfj: cf. xx. 3, 8, xii. 9, xiii. 14.

1 Thus we have 0vxain in xviii. 2: orn oi in xviii. 3 (cf. arpixidw in 7, 9, also AT. Xry), irxuxrarc, and Atrxfi and 8it ow as nouns in 6, npikov t OIHVOV, Ae dvrtyor, fmpftdpov in 12, and in the same verse K OK K Lvov as a noun (cf. 1 6, xvu. 4), KUfvfjiwijiov, Afjlufunf, ffcpl8a uf ficsuv, ffwpruv in this sense in 13, (hrdpa, Xtirapd in 14, ropfvpodr as a noun in 16 (xvii. 4), i (in this sense) in 17, Tifunrrrot in 19, ptxirov, dpfitfifiart in 21, 22.

4. irpo4 T)TK xai dyiw: cf. xi. 18. lv+ayptvw: cf. v. 6, 9, 12, vi. 9, xiii. 8.

2. The style of xviii. 2-23 exhibits none of the abnormal constructions 1 so frequent in our author, is far more normal than that of our author, and is comparatively good Greek. In fact the writer of this source was a conscious stylist 3. Whilst this source has none of our author's characteristic abnormal constructions, it contains constructions which are wholly against his usage. Thus ovat cum nom. in 10, 16, 19, whereas it appears in our author only cum ace. iv urxypf wvjj in 2 is both as regards the epithet and the order in this phrase unexampled in our author (see note in he.), avrfp ol diaprtcu in 5 is an example of the unemphatic position of avros not elsewhere in our author save in one Uncial (A) in xxi. 3 (see vol. ii. p. 208, footnote). Kpdfav v. aifl in 2 is against our author's usage, who never inserts the iv here: cf. vi. 10, vii. 2, 10, x. 3, xix. 17. In xviii. 4 the order TWV iraipywv avr s tva piy Xafyrc (ACQ) is unparalleled in our author. Hence some later authorities transpose c r. ir rjygv avrfjs after d3r T. Again, rj ACyoa.7 iroais in 21 is unparalleled in our author in this phrase (see note in loc.). The attraction of the relative in xviii. 6, Trorqptcp 5 ckcpoo-cv, is against his usage: cf. L 20. Even the title of Babylon in xviii. 10, rj iroats rj lo-xypa-, is against our author's use, who calls it rj icyaai? in xiv. 8, xvi. 19, a title which appears also in this source in xvii. 5, xviii. 2, 10, 21. Finally, in xviii. 7 we find Kaojjp. au. where our author would have used Ko0t a: see note on iii. 2 1; and ov , xviii. 14, with cvpijerovo-iv, where he would use cvpoxriv.

4. The accumulation of participles is a frequent characteristic of this source without any real parallel in the rest of the Book. Thus in xviii. 9-10 we have 01. iropvcwraitc? KOL OTwyvwuravres orav JAorctfcriv. arro pakpoocv ccmKorc?. Xcyokrcf, all dependent on the subject of the principal verb. In 15, 01 Traoimo-avtCS. icaatovrcs teal ircv0oi)itC9, Acyovrc?, similarly dependent on the subject of the principal verb: in 1 8, 7TOVT 5. AcyoKTC?: in 19, fcaatoKTCS Kal 1T V60VVT S 9 Xcyorrc?. The same accumulation of participles is to be found in the earlier fragment of this source, i. e. xvii. i c-2, 3 b 7, 18, 8-10. Thus in xvii. 3 we have

ywalica ica Acn brl Orjpiov. fyw: in 4, 7repi3eft r fj, VT). KCLL jccxpwrcuLLcvty. i avra.: in 7, rov 3ao-T(i ovtos y rov? X OVTO?: in 8, ol arot-KOVVTC?. SActTOVrcDI.

5. The use of neuter adjectives in the sing, as nouns is 1 Thus the syntax is carefully observed as regards gender and number. Even X ywv (Xtyorret, etc.) always agrees with the noun on which it depends; contrast our author's use: i. n, iv. I, v. 12, 13, iz. 14, z. 8 (i), xi. I, 15, xiv. 7, xix. I, 6.

-8. J A HEBREW SOURCE pi characteristic of this source: i. e. Jiwivov = " fine linen " in xviii. 12, 16. This usage occurs only once in the LXX in Dan. x. 5. Occasionally ra jwcva is used in this sense in the LXX. Similarly iropfvpovv in xvii. 4, xviii. 16, KOKKLVOV in xvii. 4, xviii. 12, 16, o-ipifcov, xviii. 12, and Siiraoui in xviii. 6, are used as nouns, although, save in the case of (npi ov and 8 raow, such a use of these words in the sing, seems unattested elsewhere. cripikov is found in Arrian and Strabo as a noun, and SLTT OVV appears to be used similarly in the LXX in Ex. xxii. 7, 9. For certain adjectives employed in this way in the rest of the N. T. see Robertson, Gram. 653 sq., who, however, as the rest of the N. T. grammarians, fails to notice most of the above words.

6. The order of this source is less Semitic than that of our author: see above.

7. This source appears to have influenced our author. As regards xviii. 2-23, it has become clear that it is not our author's production, as we have found also with regard to xvii. i c-2, 3 b-7, 18, 8-10. Now this source, dating from the time of Vespasian, had been in our author's hands and was apparently laid under contribution by him. Thus xiv. 8 is composed simply of xviii. 2 b, 3 put together. Again our author's peculiar use of PVCTO-LVQV in xix. 8, 14 as a noun appears due to this same use in xviii. 12, 16 (see 5. above). The fact that this use of ? iwivov is characteristic of this source and borrowed by our author gains support by its use of iropfyvpovv (xvii. 4, xviii. 16), KOKKLVOV (xvii. 4, xviii. 12, 16), o-iplKov (xviii. 12), and WAo9v (xviii. 6) as nouns, although, save in the case of the npikov and Sitraovi, such a use seems unattested elsewhere. 8i? r a and ra KOKKWO, are found elsewhere. Since, therefore, our author appears to have been influenced by this source in the above respects, it is possible that he may have been also influenced by it in his use of urxvpo?, which occurs 4 times in xviii. and 5 times in the rest of our author. Three of these five times it occurs in the phrase ayyexos icrxvxfc found also in xviii. 21. But OVK. crt, which is 6 times in xviii., occurs 9 times in the rest of our author and belongs to his vocabulary. His use of Sta rovro, vii. 15, xii. 12, is not to be traced to xviii. 8, seeing that it is a very common phrase, being found 15 times in the Johannine Gospel and 3 times in the Epistles.

3. The Greek appears to be a translation from a Hebrew source.

The evidence for the hypothesis is not conclusive. It will be found in the notes on 8, 19, 22 in connection with the words and phrases vmos 9 e TIS Ttfuotryros, and nova-new. The use of in 3 may suggest n = "wealth."

4. The text has suffered great dislocations in some degree comparable to those in xxti. Translation of xviii. 21-24 in its reconstructed order.

One of these dislocations that of 14 was observed by early scholars like Beza and Vitringa, which they restore after 23. But the present writer thinks that 14 should be read immediately after 21: 20 he finds is also out of place. It should be replaced after 23. The various elements of 22-23 nave been disarranged, as is shown in the notes.

21-24 should be read in the following order: 21,14, 2 2-, 23 cd, 99-h 4 9 ab in f 9 A 22 23 i 3 Z 4 21. And a strong angel took up a stone as it were a great millstone. and cast it into the sea, saying:

"Thus with violence shall be cast down, Babylon the great city, And shall no more be found.

(The Seer's dirge over Babylon.) 14. And the fruits which thy soul lusted after
Are gone from thee: And all the dainties and the splendours
Are perished from thee. And men shall find them no more at all.
22-. And the voice of the harpers and singers
Shall be heard no more in thee, And the voice of the fluteplayers and trumpeters
Shall be heard no more in thee.
23. And the voice of the bridegroom and the bride
Shall be heard no more in thee: 22 ef. And no craftsman of whatsoever craft
Shall be found any more in thee:
And the voice of the millstone
Shall be heard no more in thee: 23 th. And the light of the lamp
Shall shine no more in thee.

(The Seer's appeal to heaven and its inhabitants to rejoice over the doom of Rome.) 20. Rejoice over her, thou heaven,

And ye saints and ye apostles and ye prophets; For God hath judged your judgment upon her; 23. For with her sorcery had all the nations been deceived: 24. And in her was found the blood of the prophets and saints And of all that had been slain upon the earth."

5. xviii. was written in the time of Vespasian This statement can be proved by means of 2, 4, 6-8.

(a) For first of all 2 presupposes the fires of Rome to have been long extinct, and its ruins to have become the abode of every unclean spirit, bird, and beast. Now such a supposition even in a vision was not possible for the Seer writing in 95 A. D. He was then looking forward to the destruction of Rome as one of the last great acts in the judgment of the world. Moreover, the fires which should consume Rome, xviii. 9,15, 18, were never, so long as the earth lasted, to be extinguished, xix. 3. Hence, however we explain xviii. 2, it was written at an earlier date than the Apocalypse as a whole. But, whereas the prophecy in 2 is merely proleptic and therefore not at variance with xviii. 8, 15, 18, it is really irreconcilable with xix. 3, which declares that the smoke of Rome's ruins will go up till the world's end. The former gives the expectation of a Jewish Seer in Vespasian's time, the latter that of our author John in 95 A. D.

(b) In the note on 4 I have shown that the presupposition underlying it runs counter to the expectation of our Seer, that after chap. xiii. all the faithful had been put to death. But in this verse a considerable body of the faithful is presumed to be actually present in Rome. Such a presumption would be justifiable in Vespasian's time after the fall of Jerusalem, to which period xviii. can most reasonably be assigned.

(c) In 6-8 the same Vespasianic standpoint is transparent. We have such an expectation here as would be naturally entertained by a zealous Jew after the destruction of Jerusalem.

6. xviii. preserved in a corrupt condition and adapted by our author to his own purpose.

The dislocation of 14 and 20 and of several clauses in 21-24 from their original contexts shows how profoundly the original source has suffered (see 4). There is no reason to suppose that these dislocations were due to our author. Either they were already present in his source, or they are due to accidental disarrangement subsequently. It should be borne in mind that, if the present writer's hypothesis is sound as to the death of John when he had completed xx. 3, we are to regard i.-xx. 3 as never having undergone a final revision at his hands. In fact we have in i.-xx. 3, the first sketch of a great work, portions of which 1 On a variety of grounds Sabatier, Rauch, Spitta, Weyland, Bousset, J. Weiss, Wellhausen, and Moflatt accept the Vespasianic date of xviii.

have been most carefully worked out from the visions of many years, while others show not a few inequalities and inconsistencies that a final revision would have removed.

As regards the corruptions in the text we have already (3) sought to explain those in 8, 19, 22 by means of a Hebrew background. The ungrammatical clause (KOI Zmrw KT.) in 13 is merely a gloss. 23, if it belonged to the original source, is at all events in its wrong context where it stands. 24 is from the hand of John as well as the phrase KOL ol dirooroaot in 20.

7. ocvtii. and xvii. c-2, j 6-, ?, 8-10 are a Greek translation of one and the same Hebrew source.

We have already come to the conclusion that xvii. i c-2,3 b-7,18, 8-10, and xviii. 2-24 are of a Vespasianic date, and that the Greek of these sections is apparently a translation (not made but revised by John) from a Hebrew original. Since xvii. i c-2, 3 b-7, 18, 8-10, and xviii. 2-23, which are closely connected by their peculiar and in some respects unique diction, deal with the same subject and belong to the same date, we conclude that they are from the same hand. The former served as an introduction to the latter, xvii. I gives the title of xviii. TO fcpipa ri s iropviys rijs Acyaai?? ri K00i? ficv79 CTrt vsarov iroaAujf. Next, xvii. 2 (AC0 qs ctropvcvcrav oi faurtxci? T? Js 777 KOI Ovcrorja-av ol jcarotkoiwcs rrjv yrjv cc rov otvov rijs iropieia? avrijs) is repeated in substance and in part verbally in xviii. 3, CK rov olvov rov Ovpov ri s u-oppetas airrijs ireirotikcv travra ra tory, and 23, V r apAaici? crov (Trxavrjorjo-a iravra ra Wvt. Next, clauses from xvii. 4 (7rcpi c? A. i? p, cn? irop- fopoVV l KOLL KOKKIVOV, KOL KC OVOCOflcn; XDVCTla) KO. I Xt O) rtfllcl) KOL iapyaptrats) are repeated almost word for word in xviii. 16,17 ircpi-fic3 r p. cvr. 7roptvpovv KOL KOKKLVOV KOL K XpvtWfjltvrj. XLOu rtuo) Kal fiapyapirrf. Again, ironypiov. iv ry ipl aur s yipjov Scxvyiarcdv in xvii. 4 is recalled by cv ry iroriyptw oi ckcpao-ev in xviii. 6; Baj3vao? fieyaxi; in xvii. 5 by a kindred clause in xviii. 10; and 17 Troats 17 yaxrj in xvii. 18 by the same phrase in xviii. 10, 16, 19.

Hence xvii. i c-2, 3 b-7, 18, 8-10, and xviii. appear to be derived from one and the same Hebrew source. 2 With this he has combined another source, xvii. 11-13, J

7 16 which foretold the destruction of Rome by Nero and the Parthians. xvii. 2 gives the title of the Vision in xviii., t. e. the Doom of Rome; this judgment is preceded by a vision of Rome before its overthrow in 1 It is important to observe that ropfvpow used as a noun seems to occur only in xvii. 4 and xviii. 16, that K KKWOV is used as a noun in the sing, in xvii. 4 b, xviii. 12, 16 a most rare use, though it is found in the LXX and elsewhere as a noun in the plural. See 2. 5 above.

9 The order of the words in xviii. while in the main Semitic, is not as decidedly so as in xvii. i-2, 3 b-;, 18, 8-ia The latter has been thoroughly revised by our author.

xvii. 3-7, 18, 8-10, and by a prophecy of the coming destruction of Rome by fire at the hands of Nero and the Parthians, i. e. xvii. 12-13, 7 16- I s not tin we come to xviii. that the promise of the Angel of the Bowls in xvii. i, ct i crot rd icpcxa TIS Wpinjs, is fulfilled, xviii. is a vision of Rome's doom, which sforetold in xvii. 16.

1-8. The proclamation of the doom of Babylon by the first angel. This proclamation is proleptic. The angel's words regard Rome's doom as already accomplished far in the past.

From 2 cde it appears that the fires that consumed it have long since been quenched, and that it has become the abode of unclean birds and demons. See the note on these clauses below.

1. axXoy ayyexoc. This angel is distinguished from the angel mentioned in xvii. i, 7, who is the angelus intcrfres.

4 yrj c wtiffov) K Trjg W t s ofrrou. This is a direct rendering of Ezek. xliii. 2, HODD nvtfn pun, where the LXX has 17 79 v us eyyos aaro TI S So' s. Here the Targum has KJHK VTO mru. Thus the brightness of God's glory is heie attributed to an angel. See fuither on this "brightness" in note on xxi. 23. On this use ot c = "by reason of, 1 " cf. viii. 13, xvi. n.

2. ikpoiep lv ix u P + The diction in this phrase is unexampled in our author: the order is most exceptional. See note on x. 3.

lirco-ck circacp Bapuxup YJ facydxt. This clause has already occurred in xiv. 8 (see note). The Greek here, with the exception of the epithet, is an independent rendering of Isa. xxi. 9.

2 cde. These three clauses are to be taken proleptically in reference to 9, 15, 18: otherwise they occasion difficulty; for in 9, 15, 18, Rome is seen in the Seer's vision to be consumed by fire: whereas these clauses presuppose the fires of Rome to have been long extinct, and the ruins to have become the hold of unclean birds and demons, xiv. n refers not to the city Rome, but to the eternal torment of the worshippers of the Beast in the next world On the other hand it is impossible to reconcile 2 cda with xix. 3, which represents the smoke of her burning as going up for ever and ever, i. e. to the end of the world. This last is our author's own expectation. Here that of his source conflicts with it: see In trod, to this Chap., 5.

fylccro Katoneijt piop SaifjiokUJi. fjl fiicnr)p Kou: cf. Isa. xiii. 21-22 (Sattdvui? 6pxrjorjtovtai); Jer. li. 31, "Babylon shall become. a dwelling for jackals"; i Bar. iv. 35, jcaroiki? crcrcu viro 8aiu, ovtw. In Isa. xxxiv. u, I3 b, 14-15, Jer. 1. 39, there is a list of unclean birds and beasts that are to inhabit Edom or Babylon given: cf. Zeph ii. 14. The SaiAovta are the D"Y, or more probably the DTyfc (Isa. xiii. 21, xxxiv. 14).

opyfou dxaodprou: cf. Deut. xiv. 12-19.

8. The nations as a whole, the rulers of the earth and its merchants, were involved in the sin of Rome.

IK rod otrou rou Oupou TTJS iroppciot afrrijs. I have here with much hesitation bracketed rov Ovftov, although it has the support of the best MSS. But the extraordinary diversity among the authorities points to some corruption in the above text. See notes on xiv. 8, xvii. 2. In the latter passage we have an exact parallel to xviii. 3 for 3 (cf. 23 on lv rjj fappakiq, rou evXanf-Orprav irdvra, ra ZOvrj) corresponds to Iptovo-Oirja-av ol fcarotkOvrrcs T. yvfv IK rov oivov Tijs iropvctas avrij. 3 b corresponds almost verbatim with xvii. 2 a, p. tff rjs ftrdpvcwav ol Scurixctf rijs yi.

ol paaixeis TIJS yijs. Their lamentation over Rome is given in 9-20, as that of the merchants in 11-13, 15-16.

imrriktv. This reading, supported by a few cursives, appears to be the true one, though in the cursives only a happy conjecture. It explains the impossible readings of ttaCQ. It is also required by the context: otherwise Rome is represented only as passively evil. Wirrwkav though originating in a scribal error seemed to derive support from CTTCO-CI. As Babylon fell, so did the nations.

ol cpiropoi TTJS YY)S. This phrase, which is peculiar to this chapter in the N. T. (cf. n, 15, 23), is significant. All the merchants of the world are involved in the overthrow of Rome. The long list of merchants who traded with Tyre, according to Ezek. xxvii. 9-25, was in the mind of our author.

IK. a(rrrjs Trxoutrjo-OK: cf. 15.

TTJS owpcws = " wealth " a meaning which is found also in the LXX of Deut. viii. 17, Ruth iv. n, where Swau? is a rendering of! Tl. In Isa. Ixi. 6 it is rendered by TXVS=" wealth." This meaning is to be found in Xen. Cyr. vii. 4. 34, etc., 2 Cor. viil 3, and the Papyri.

TOO crrp ous auttjs = "of her wantonness." Here and in 2 Kings xix. 28. Cf. rrprjvt v in 9, and Karaorpqvt v rov Xptorov, " to wax wanton against the restrictions prescribed by Christ," in i Tim. v. ii.

4-8. The second voice, which comes from heaven itself. 4-5 are addressed to the faithful, and 6-8 to the ministers of God's wrath who were seen by the Seer to be assembling for the work of destruction.

4. No justifiable meaning can be attached to this verse as it stands. As we have repeatedly seen heretofore (cf. also ver. 20), the presupposition of the Seer is that after xiii. all the faithful had been put to death. In xv. 2-4 the army of martyrs is seen in its completeness in a vision before the throne of God, while the Seven Bowls are poured down on a wholly heathen world. In the present verse, therefore, indeed in the present chapter, we have a document that belongs, as a large body of modern scholars have recognized, to the time of Vespasian. This oracle dealt with the destruction of Rome. Vblter (Offenbarung Jbhannis, 1904), J. Weiss and Erbes ascribe this oracle to a Christian source written respectively about 60, 70 and 80 A. D. On the other hand, Vischer, Schoen, Weyland, Spitta trace it, and rightly in the opinion of the present writer, to a Jewish source. Whether Jewish or Christian originally, it is partially adapted to its present context by the mention of the "apostles" in 20, and by the addition of 24.

ox T)K 4wfT)K. The words that follow 6 Aaos fiov seem to suggest that it is God that speaks. But 5 is against this conclusion. Cf. xvi. i for a like difficulty. It may, however, be Christ that speaks.

i lx6arc autTJs 6 Xals pou. These words appear to be a reproduction of Jer. li. (xxviii.) 45, y fldtao K. Since they are not found in ABQ of the LXX and in Q are rendered by J c 0crc K ACO-OV avri s Xaos JAOV, this clause seems to have been translated directly from the Hebrew, and independently of the LXX.

There are, it is true, many parallels in the O. T. to the above clause in-our text Cf. Jer. xxvii. (I.) 8, cwroaAotpioifliytc c ACO-OV Bajgiauwo?. cai c ca0arc: xxviii (li.) 6, favycre CK icaov Ba? i Auvos, cat dvacrojfere cxacrro? rrjv i xv avrov KOL py atropi rc cv TQ a8ikiq. avtrjs: Isa. xlviil. 20, 2 ca0c IK Ba vatovo?: Hi. u, diroon-c, atrdotitTc, A0atC iktwtv. c ea0at CK jl rov avrrjs: cf. also 2 Bar. ii. i, "Retire from this city "; Matt. xxiv. 16, TOT 01 Iv rg lovup cvycrokrav TTI ra oprj. The last quotation belongs to the Little Apocalypse, and refers, of course, to Jerusalem.

niiitoikUi at)TC rais Vjfiaptias: cf. Eph. v. II, p. rj TWKOIV-OV IT T. Cpyois. T. CTKOTOVS. I Tim. V. 22, fh8c KOlfctfvCt iAapruus daAorptat?. These words deal with the guilt of sharing in the sin of Rome, as the words that follow deal with the punishment that such guilt must entail.

K TUP tr riy)v aurrjs, " some of her plagues."

5. iko r fa rav. dxpi T. ofipapou. These words are, apparently, a reminiscence of Jer. li. 9, ne? D D Dtrn y. If so, then evoaA fyo-av is simply to be rendered (as in the A. V. and R. V. and the Vulg., pervenerunt) "have reached." This rendering of W is very rare, see Lam. ii. 2 and Zech. xiv. 5, "coaAi?0iprctu (JTJP) fripayf; 6otcov a? Iaro9, but the meaning belonging to this Hebrew verb is clearly the one required by our context. We might also compare with Our text I Esdr. viii. 72, at 8c ayvtutu rfiuiv vrrcpi cyicav ecus rov ovpavov: cf. Ezra ix. 6; also 4 Ezra xi. 43, "Et ascendit con-tumelia tua ad altissimum et superbia tua ad fortem." If this VOL. ii. 7 rendering is right, then we are not to attempt to render Kox rj(hirav ra. as " have grown together into such a mass as to reach the heaven." It would be extraordinary if God was not mindful of the sins of Rome (s b) till they pressed in a mass against the roof of heaven. To such an extravagant conception the parallelism KOI CAV AOVCVO-CV 6 0eos ra abuajfiara avrrj would form a singular anticlimax a piece of sheer bathos. Hence we infer that tkokxrjorjo-av is here = IJPJii, and that the rendering is independent of the LXX in Jer. li. (xxviii.) 9, jjyyifccv cfc ovpavov TO fcptxa avr s. The rendering of the two Syriac Versions here is very infelicitous, i. e. "have cleaved to. 11 This rendering of jcoaAoo-ftu is found once more in the Syriac Versions, namely, in Luke x. n, but there it is very felicitous.

On the other hand, it must be conceded that KoxXao-Oai is the general rendering of pyi in the LXX. If it presupposes this Hebrew word here, then our text is not a reminiscence of Jer. li 9. But even so, the context is against the meaning belonging to p21. Such a passage as i Bar. i. 20, lko rjorj cfc ypas ra gaga al rj apci, does not support our text in the sense of " cleave unto." Even in this passage of Baruch evoaArjfli probably presupposes a corrupt Hebrew text. See Whitehouse in Charles, The Apoc. and Pseud, i. 578, and Kneucker in loc. The Syriac Version of Baruch =

Kani (= et pervenerunt), while the Greek = pjirn. Dan. ix. n, with which i Bar. i. is-ii. 17 is closely related, supports the former.

awjs at papriai. On this vernacular use of the genitive of avrds see notes on ii. 2, 19, and in vol. ii. 208, footnote.

fipT)p icurci 6 dec's KT. Cf. xvi. 19, Ba? vaW jj p. cyd rj nfarori iviinriov TOV Ocov.

6. In its present context this verse is to be taken as addressed to Nero redivivus and the hosts that followed him: cf. xvii. 11-17. But it is not to be forgotten that already Rome has for the most part been destroyed in xvi. 19 by a great earthquake, and its entire destruction by fire foretold in xvii. 16. The present chapter, taken by itself, shows no consciousness of the first of these judgments. But the destruction of Rome by fire is proclaimed in xviii. 8, 9, 15. Hence the description of the final overthrow of Rome in xviii. 21 must be taken as purely figurative.

dirrfsotc afrrfj 6s KCU aur dirwicck KT., i. e. deal out to her the same measure that she dealt to others. Cf. Jer. xxvii. (1.) 29, vra-irosorc avr Kara ra cpya avrijs' jcara iravra ora ciroujcrcv iroti rat avr: 15. iicsiicittC cir avrijv icadus taotiorcv, Trot o-arc avrjj: Ps. CXXXVi. 8, xacapto? os dkra7ro3ukrci (rot TO avtavosofjid rov ayra-fl-fsuicas rjf y. On this principle of lex talionis see the notes in my edition of Jubilees on iv. 31, xlviii. 14.

ftiirxa: cf. Isa. xl. 2, ese aro cv ctpos tevpiov

Stirxa ra dfuzpn Liara avr s: Jer. xvi. 1 8, airatrosucra). Strrxa? TO icaiaas aurav. Stirxouv 8i7rxa is an extraordinary expression. Cf. Aesch. Agamem. 537, Stirxa 8 crto-av Ilptailsa

But in Aeschylus the Swrxoijs is used purely as an adjective, whereas in our text it is a noun. For this use cf. Ex. xxii. 3, 6, 8. In the first passage we have Sitrxa in the LXX (DW), in the second TO (?) Swrxow, and in the third i. e. cwrotMTCi owXow TW irxiyo-tov. Cf. also Zech. ix. 12, Iv TW irotT)piw icrx.: cf. xiv. 8, xvii. 4. This cup is the cup of the wrath of (Jod. Cf. 2 Bar. xiii. 8, in which the Romans also are addressed.

"Ye who have drunken the strained wine Drink ye albo of its dregs, The judgment of the Lofty One Who has no respect of persons."

7. In this verse it is a question whether the speaker is a heavenly being or the Seer who wrote this vision.

Sao. Tocroutoy. The torment and grief (or " misfortune ") of Rome are to be proportionate to her self-glorification and wantonness. Cf. Isa. iii 16, 17, avff wv v Orja-av at 0vyarepcs eioi. KOI Tair iiuMT i 6 0eos ap ovottts 0vyatejpas SCKOV: Prov. xxix. 23, u? pis av8pa Ttttrctvoi: Luke xiv. n, etc. On the probability that Trcvflos, which occurs twice in this verse, is to be rendered " misfortune " or " calamity," or that it is a translation of a corrupt form in the Hebrew original, see note on ver. 8.

STI lv TJJ icapsia aurfjs Xeyci. isw These lines repro duce freely Isa. xlvn. 7, 8,. mm HMK D j6 nptfm y iw jn dn n3D n x vb. raa n n-jjpnn. But the LXX is not followed, which here gives ctiras EU rov alum ap owra. fj Xeyoixra cv rfj Kapsta avrijs. ov yvwtrofjlcu op avciav. We should observe that for ico xat we should expect Kaflifw (see note on iii. 21) if this chapter were from the hand of our author. As a parallel to our text, the boast of Tyre in Ezek. xxvni. 2 should be compared and also the self-glorification attributed to Rome in 2 Bar. xii. 3.

8. Because of (on. a rovro) Rome's pride and self-confidence she shall be overthrown suddenly.

lv p, i pcpa ouaik. Isa. xlvii. still influences our writer; for these words are derived from the Massoretic ver. 9, where the LXX (B) renders qt. hrl rt tv rfi opfuuctp o-ov. But NA etc. agree with Mass. It is noteworthy that cfc is postpositive in ix. 12, 13, but prepositive in viii. 13, xvii. 12, 13, 17, xvhl 8, 10, 16, 19, xix. 17.

t Odlvatos Kal irfroos ital Xipfe f. We might compare vl 8. It must be confessed that ircplo? (" mourning ") cannot with any justice be reckoned under the category of plagues. But first of all the presence of Atid? suggests that Qdvato? here as in vi. 8 and frequently in the O. T. = "QT, " pestilence." In that case the natural order would be XIAOS K. Oavaros K. ircvoos. Now returning to ircvflos, it is possible that it should be rendered here according to a rare meaning by "calamity," "misfortune" (cf. Pindar, Isth. vl (vii.) 51, erxw Sc TTO OS ov ardv: Herod, iii. 14). If so, we should translate "famine and pestilence and misfortune." But the error may be due to a corruption in the Semitic original. Thus ir VOos = 3K, corrupt for?3n. If this is right, we obtain an excellent sense "famine and pestilence and destruction." The approach of the Parthians from the East under Nero would cut off food supplies from Rome and lead to famine, in the train of which pestilence would soon follow. The third plague would then prepare for the destruction of Rome by fire. Or, since the writer has, as has been shown on 7, borrowed freely from Isa. xlvii. 7, 8, it is possible that 73K (= irw0o?) may be a corruption of 3P in Isa. xlvii. 8 "famine and pestilence and loss of children." But the former restoration is to be preferred.

jr irupi Katakouo o-rnu. The judgment of Rome by fire, which according to xvii. 16 is to be executed by Nero and the Parthian kings, is here declared to come from God in the first instance. On the judgment by fire cf. Jer. I. 32, li. 25, 30, 32, urxups 4 Ocs 6 Kpiyos afrnj?. The translator of this chapter is fond of the word compos = cf. 2, 10, 21. Outside this chapter it occurs only five times in the Apocalypse: cf. Jer. xxvii. (1.) 34, 6 AvrpovLLCvo? avrous ixypos. Kpia-tv jcpivci irpos rov? aittstcovs autov. This Kptva? points to the fact that the decree of judgment has already been passed on Rome.

9-19. The dirge chanted over the conflagration of Rome by the kings, 9-10, by the merchant princes of the earth, 11-16, and the shipowners and sailors of the world, 17-19. The author is influenced by the doom song pronounced by Ezekiel over Tyre, Ezek. xxvi.-xxviii.

9-10. Cf. Ezek. xxvl 16-17, where the princes of the sea mourn over Tyre.

KXaifoomu KOI K rorau lirl aorfj: cf. 2 Sam. i. 12, tatyrairo. Kal cjcaavarav. cvt. Hence our text " shall weep and mourn over " (=? y ndDi 133 1). See also u, 15, 19.

ol pao-txcis TT)S Y)?: vi- 1 S (see note), xvii. 2, 18, xviii. 3. These kings are the heads of the heathen nations. Foremost amongst them are princes subject to or in alliance with 9-11. DIRGE OF KINGS AND MERCHANTS IOI

Rome; for, as the next clause shows, they have been deeply affected by her influence. They are distinct from the Parthian kings who destroy Rome, xvii. 16.

ol per ofavjs iroppcriaaircs: cf. xvii. 2, xviii. 3. rrpv)vu cravtCf. They too had lived wantonly like Rome: cf. 3.

ovan pxfirwaik. afrrijs. This clause recurs in 18.

rijs iruptfactts. The prophecy of Rome's destruction by fire is dwelt on again and again: cf. xvii. 16, xviii. 8, 18.

10. dir ftakplock: cf. 15 (see note), 17; Matt. xxvi. 58; Mark v. 6, viii. 3, etc.

Sia-r toffop. afrrijs. This phrase recurs in 15.

ofial oual insXis KT. This construction is not found in the N. T. except in Luke vi. 25; but it occurs frequently in the LXX: cf. Isa. v. 8, n, 20, 21, 22; Hab. ii. 6, 12, 19; Zeph. ii. 5; Amos v. 18, where the R. V. rightly renders: " woe unto." Hence the rendering here, as in these passages, should be, "Woe, woe to the great city." The construction suggests the writer's acquaintance with the LXX. Our author's construction is ovai with the dat.: cf. viii. 13.

u Spa: cf. 8, 16, 19.

11-16. The merchants of the earth take up their dirge over Rome.

11. ot iffjiiropoi TTJS yfjs. In Ezek. xxvii. 12-24 the various nations that had commercial relations with Tyre are enumerated.

KXaiouaic KCU ire 6oc(rif ir aurfj: cf. 9, 15, 19; Mark xvi. 10; Luke vi. 25; Jas. iv. 9. This combination is found in Neh. i.4- y6fiop = ship's freight or cargo: cf. Acts xxi. 3. The vastness of the commerce of Rome may be inferred from the following passages, which are all taken from Wetstem; Galen, DC Antidot, i. 4, v CP "Pwwy jcaroucoyiev, ci? r)v c atrawcuv raw iovwv naff cfcaorov ivlavrov c ifcvowrai iraATroxXa. eis rjv ra iravra o cy rjk Ka a 8ia iravro? crovs: Pliny, H. N. vi. 26, "Minima computa-tione millies centena millia sestertium annis omnibus In(lia et Seres peninsulaque ilia imperio nostro adimunt": Anstides, In Rom.) p. 2OO, aycrcu K? ran?9 v 5 ical Oa dmrj y ocra wpat fvowri, ical xpa Kacrrai epovcrt, jcai Troraiot, cat Xinvac, ical rc vat "EXXi vcov Kat)3apj9apav OOTC ci ri9 ravra irdvra cn-isci?)9ovxoiro, Set avrov fj iraorav eicrcx orra rrjv oikovfjitvrjv ovroi 0cacracr0at, 17 iv rjj TQ Tr6X. i ycvdLtcvov. rocravrat 8c OL LKVOVVTCLI 8cvpo KOII- ougrai irapa vdvnw oxicase?, va Tracrav iev opav, Tracrav 8c f6Lvo-irwpoy ircptrpomv, aior iotcevat TTJV iroxiv KOIVW Ttvt T S yi s cpyaarnyptu. dprovs xev dir 'Ivswy, ft)3ovxci 8c Kat raw cvsaixovwv Apa 3i)V rorovrov9 op tv eoriv, Sore cuca ciy yvfiva TO XOITTOV rot? cvet Xcxcu ac ra Scvspa.;. Eo ras 8 al Ba? yxavw5, KOI rovs cic T S jfrckctva fiapfiidpov icocrAOv?. Ilakra cyravla (rvAirtirrec, ifjaroplaij pavraxtai, ycwpytcu, ieraaAo)? Ka0aprif, TC V(U OTTOO-CU cicri re KCU ycycmvrcu, irarra ocra ycvrarai cat 0vcrat. o rt 8 av x, cvravoa IH ri5, OVK 4m raj? ycvoAcvwv 17 ytyvofjlWtov. In the Talmud, (?. 49 b, it is stated that "Ten measures of wealth came down into the world: Rome received nine, and all the world one."

Since 23 cannot stand in its present context, it may originally have stood after u a, and so this verse may have run as follows: 11 " And the merchants of the earth weep and mourn over her, 23 6 For thy merchants were the princes of the earth, n b For no man buyeth their merchandise any more."

13-13. These two verses give a list of the articles imported by Rome from all quarters of the world. Holtzmann has recognized that the first four articles mentioned (i. e. precious stones) harmonize rhythmically with the next four, consisting of costly garments. But further examination of the passage shows that it consists, according to the present text, of nine lines. That the first four of these consist of two couplets there can be no doubt, but great difficulty attaches to the method of dealing with the remaining five lines. If they are to be retained as they stand, it might be best to regard them as consisting of a tristich and a distich:

"And cinnamon and spice and incense, And ointment and frankincense and wine, And oil and fine flour and wheat: And beasts and sheep and horses And chariots and slaves and souls of men."

But it is probable that the words I have bracketed are an interpolation; for (i) their syntax genitives where there ought to be accusatives is wholly anomalous. It is without a real parallel in the abnormal style of our author, and is still more at variance with the much more grammatical style of this chapter, which, as we have elsewhere seen, comes from an independent sou ice. (2) The same ideas are repeated in immediate proximity undtt different forms; for "slaves" and "souls of men" are here synonymous. imjKY), as is shown in the notes on 13 = draught cattle, i. e. horses, asses, etc., and thus the mention of horses separately, as in the present text, is wholly gratuitous. Now, if we excise as a gloss, which has crept in from the margin, the words "and horses and chariots and slaves," we get rid of the anomalous syntax, and of the meaningless repetitions in the last line, and recover the original text of 12-13, consisting of four stanzas of two lines each. The last stanza then would be:

"And oil and fine flour and wheat, And beasts and sheep and souls of men."

The dramatic forcibleness of what seems at first a purely prosaic list of imports is in the highest degree impressive, closing as it does in the climax

"And beasts and sheep and souls of men."

12. On the various articles mentioned in 12-13 the Bible Dictionaries should be consulted. Most of them are to be found in the imports of Tyre: Ezek. xxvii. 12-24, . gold, silver, precious stones, fine linen, purple, brass, iron, all spices, oil, wheat, cattle, sheep, horses, and the souls of men.

f3uomfou: cf. xix. 8.

aipikou (so the uncials. The usual form is cnpikov). This word (= "silk") is a a? r. Acy. in Biblical Greek, but it was used frequently by Greek writers after Alexander's time. How commonly it was used in Rome about 70 A. D. may be inferred from the words of Josephus (BJ. vii. 5. 4), who describes the triumphant army of Vespasian and Titus as being clothed iv ical irav u w GUIPO?. The construction here changes and is governed directly by tyopa ei. This change may be due not to a slip on the part of the translator, but to a right rendering of his text. The ovsets dyopafci is to be taken closely with irav fuaov (= Jjri3. B K rup 6) = "no one buyeth any thyine wood." Hence Kal irav v w dvwov should be rendered "or any thyine wood " and not as in the A. V. and R. V. " and all thyine wood." Of course it is possible that the translator ought to have rendered iravros v ov, but, so far as the Hebrew before him went, the ace. was not only a possible but probably the right rendering.

0uikOK. This wood most probably came from Thuia arti-culata, a tree which grew in N. Africa. It was known to the Greeks as Ova, Ovov, or 0vio, to the Romans as citrus. It was much used in the making of costly tables: cf. Martial, xiv. 87, "Mensa citrea." Seneca (quoted by Swete from Mayor on Juv. i. 137) had (according to Dio, Ixi. 10. 3) 300 such tables with ivory feet.

Ae dn-ikOK. Ivory was largely used, as Swete states, by wealthy Romans in the decoration of furniture, quoting Juv. xi. 1 20 sqq.

13. wvdpu kqv. In the O. T. cinnamon appears thrice among aromatic spices. It is the Cassia tignea and was imported, as it still is, from China. It was much used in Rome, as we can infer from Plautus, Propertius, Lucan, Martial.

fyufioy. This perfumed unguent was derived from a shrub of Eastern origin (Virg. Eel. iv. 25, "Assyrium vulgo nascetur amomum"). It was well known at Rome: Mart. viii. 77: "Si sapis, Assyrio semper tibi crinis amomo splendeat": Statius Silv. i. 113: " Nee pingui crinem deducere amomo cessavit" (quoted by Wetstein). Theophrastus, ix. 7, is uncertain whether it was derived from Media or India. Pliny, H. N. xii. 28, mentions this costly unguent for the hair.

Oufudfaro. See v. 8, Xifjakos: cf. viii. 3.

crcpisaxik (= nte). This word, meaning fine flour, is not found elsewhere in the N. T. though frequent in the LXX. Pliny, H. N. xiii. 21, refers to it: "Similago ex tritico fit lauda-tissimo."

OITOP. Egypt was the granary of Rome.

KT KI). This word generally means flocks and herds, but it can also mean draught cattle or beasts for riding: hence horses or asses: cf. Luke x. 34; Acts xxiii. 24. That KTJ OS could mean "a horse" is to be inferred also from Gen. viii. 19, where the Hebrew is BW, which clearly the Greek translators read as BO"J ("horse"), and from Num. xvi. 32, where the translators again read fcbi instead of B O"i (= " substance "). From these facts we conclude that Kryrtj means all kinds of cattle for draught or riding. Hence there is no real need for the word unniw which follows, as it is already included in icnjn. Horses are mentioned among the imports of Tyre in Ezek. xxvii. 13 sq.

KCH itnrwk. owjidtw. I have already given in the introductory note on 12-13 the grounds on which these words are to be excised as an interpolation. The absolutely anomalous genitive here is, so far as I am aware, universally explained by inserting yoAov before it. Thus Holtzmann and Bousset remark here that as in 12 the gen. passes over into the ace., so here the ace. returns again into the gen. But, as I have shown on 12, the ace. can not only be accounted for, but probably justified: whereas nothing can justify the present genitives between a series of accusatives preceding and an ace. following. They are therefore to be regarded as an interpolation.

fcfcwk. The c7 came, according to Quintilian (i. 5. 5), from Gaul and was a vehicle with four wheels (Isid. Etym. xx. 12). Cicero used it, and apparently it became fashionable at Rome.

arifiato. This word is used to translate ntecO (" souls ") in the LXX of Gen. xxxvi. 6. It is also used elsewhere in the LXX in the sense of " slaves ": cf. Gen. xxxiv. 29; Tob. x. 11 (o-wiara feat Krqvrj); Bel 32 (Theod.), Suo cruyuira KOL vo irpofara: 2 Mace.

viii. 11. This non-Attic usage of the word arose apparently in Egypt, as the Papyri show, and later established itself in Greek generally. Hence a slave dealer is called a crwAatefwropos and a slave house cnoAarorpo cioi.

ijruxs di Opcirwk. This phrase is borrowed from Ezek. XXVli. 13, oftroi cvctTopcuorro rot Iv iw ai? dv0pu7rav (D 1K WStt). The phrase occurs also in i Chron. v. 21, but there it does not mean slaves as here.

14. This verse, as Vitringa, and in modern times Ewald (2nd ed.), Volkmar, B. Weiss, and Mofiatt have recognized, is here out of place. These scholars have restored it after 23 d, but the present writer is of opinion that it originally stood after 21, where he has restored it m this edition.

15. This verse resumes the dirge of the merchants over Rome, from which the writer had turned aside to describe the nature and extent of their commerce with Rome.

ol cfjiiropoi Tourwy i. e. the merchants who dealt in the merchandise mentioned in 12-13: cf. 23. This phrase in itself, as B. Weiss observes, unconditionally excludes the presence of 14 where it stands in the text.

ot irxourrjcrakT S ir aurrjs: cf. 3, 19.

dird pakprfocy ar crorrai: cf. 10, airb utcucpoflcv cmjkarcs: 17, diro Attkooflcv ccrrqo-av.

Sid TOK 4pok TOO Paoxmcrfiou aurrjs. This phrase has already occurred in 10. xxaiorrcs K. irepooutrcs: cf. 9, n, 19.

16. On this construction of ouai see note on 10. 4 irlxif cf. 10, 19, xvii. 18. T) ircpi0cpxT) Uinr) irop+upoui KCU Repeated from xvii. 4. Kcxpuaiuficmrj xp U(r "! ty, Repeated from xvii. 4. pi po, pt fjuu6rj. Repeated in 19. A corresponding clause in the dirge of the kings is found in 10.

17-19. Dirge of the seafolk. Cf. Ezek. xxvii. 28-29 on Tyre.

17. KupcpmfjTi)s. This word means "shipmaster" or captain as distinct from vavicxiypos = " shipowner." In Acts xxvii. n we have T j Kvpcpvrjtrj Kal TW pavfcai? pa = " the captain and the shipowner." Cf. Plutarch, Moralia 807 B, vavras lev cfcxeycrai Kv3cpv ns Kal Kv3fpvtqtrjv vavk rjpo: Artemidorus, i. 37, apx t Sc. irpwpcai? 6 KvjsepviTTs, KvbcpntjTorv S 6 vavicaipos. The word mfaprrrnp is a rendering of pah in Ezek. xxvii. 8, 27, 28, where it means "pilots." In Jon. i. 6 it means "a sailor," for the captain is called?3hn an, or "chief of the sailors."

6 irl Tirok irxlup = "Every one that saileth any whither" (R. V.). Cf. Acts xxvii. 2, iraeiv efe TOUS Kara T7v Acrtav r irov?. But the expression is a strange one, and there is much to be said for Nestle's (Textual Criticism of the N. T., p. 168) correction of TOTTOV into TTOTOV, i. itoitov. At all events Primasius supports this emendation: " omnis super mare navigans."

Scroi-rt v Odxourarcu pydtorrai, " gain their living by the sea " (R. V.), lit. " work the sea." This is good classical Greek. Thus Hesiod (Theog. 440) has ot y avkrjv Svnrcp. fc ov pya ovrcu: Dion. Hal. A. Hi. 46, TTJV avrrp ctpyo cro. Qaxacra-av: Appian, Pun p. 2, rrjy Odxavvav. cpyo oficyot. For abundant illustrations of this idiom, see Wetstem in loc. What the Hebrew equivalent of the clause is is uncertain: possibly

DVrnk DnndH = " who trade on the sea": cf. Gen. xxxiv. 10, 21, T- v xlii. 34. The corresponding phrase epyafco-0ai r v-yrjv is also good Greek and likewise good Hebrew: cf. Gen. li. 5, 15, iii. 23, iv. 2; but the verb used in this connection lay would not serve for the clause in our text.

ir fjiakp60 K cforrjcrak. Cf. 10, 15.

18. px irorrcs TOP Kairko? TTJS irupwaews adrrjs. This is the exact equivalent of the orav. avris clause in 9.

18-19. The last clause of 18 and the first clause of 19 are dependent on Ezek. xxvii. 30-32. Thus rk 6iota rjj v6 ci TQ ficyaxg recalls Ezekieps words with regard to Tyre, xxvii. 32, "who is like unto Tyre?" Here ito is rendered in the LXX by T ounrep Tvpos; Next, 3a ov x w W ra icc axas avrwv is from xxvii. 30, "They shall cast up dust upon their heads " (DrpEten y "ibV vj). Here the LXX presupposes quite a different and corrupt text (ri0i (roi; o-iv ITTL TVJV xcfaxrjv avruv yvjv Kal oirosov orptotrovrat). The same Hebrew clause is found in Josh. vii. 6 and Lam. ii. 10. In the former passage the LXX renders it almost as in our text. Even Kpa av KXaiovrcs Kal irevoowtc seems to be suggested by Ezek. xxvii. 30, 31, "they shall cry" (LXX Keicp okrai). "they shall weep" (LXX A only fcxavo-ovrat). But the combination fcaotwrcs al Trcvtfowtcs has already occurred in the text in 11, 15.

odal Vj ir Kis. See note on 10.

irxoifar)crai. Cf. 3, 15.

t In rfjs Tip, i(TT)Tos aurqs STI fjiift csp jptjp56T) f. The text is here corrupt This becomes apparent, if we compare the corresponding clauses in the woes pronounced by the kings in 10, OTI u wp vj 6 v y Kpicris rov, and by the merchants in 16, on p. uj. upp yprhJLvor) 6 TOO-QVTOS irxovros. These parallel clauses lead us to expect a definite subject to be added after p-rj Orj in 19 as there is after the verbs in 10, 16. Now we discover in the corrupt phrase IK.-rijs Ttyuot Tos avri s, the subject needed for i)piflw, a0i7, f. e. TIIIOTT;? avr. Thus the final clause of the text should run: on u woi rjprjjjuoorj T) TiAiorijs avtys. Thus this clause is brought into line with the corresponding clauses in 10, 16, and the woe pronounced by the seafolk falls naturally into three lines as the woe of the kings in 10.

"Woe, woe unto the great city,

Wherein were made rich all that had their ships at sea; For in one hour are her precious things laid waste."

The corruption can be explained best through the Hebrew. The original-aj n DP3 nrw Piyp3 "3. The corruption could have arisen through an accidental doubling of the D (hence njtag) and the subsequent transposition of roind before 3 in order to give some intelligible sense to the passage. Hence DP3 nn njjBa a rano the source of our corrupt text 21-24. This section, embracing as it does 14 and ao, consists of a song of doom preluded by a symbolic action, the original idea of which is derived from Jer. li. 63, 64. This dirge is not put in the mouth of some particular class. The speaker is the Seer who wrote the original oracle, which has been utilized here by our author. Some attempts here have been made to adapt it to its new context. Thus the insertion of the phrase KOI ol atrooroxot in 20 is due to our author, and most probably the last clause of 23 and the whole of 24. The penultimate clause of 23 is either a gloss or should probably be restored after the first clause in n. A line has probably been lost in 22.

21. Kal f pcv cis oyyexos io up6s KT. Here as in v. 2, x. I we have the phrase ayy. lrxvpos. The writer had Jer. li. 63, 64 in his mind: " And it shall be, when them hast made an end of reading this book, that thou shalt bind a stone to it, and cast it into the midst of the Euphrates: and thou shalt say, Thus shall Babylon sink and shall not

rise again." There may also be a reminiscence of Ezekiel's words with regard to Tyre, xxvi. 21. Cf. also Or. Sib. v. 158 sqq., on the destruction of Babylon by a great star.

Xiook 6s jufxiiw piyav. The particle os shows that it is not a millstone that is referred to here, but that what the Seer saw in the vision recalled the idea of such a stone. The stone was probably the ivxos octtos, seeing it is defined as fteyas. To turn such a stone an ass was needed.

OUTOS 6pfi cm P T 0T)(T Tu. It is not quite clear what opfjujfjlatL means here. It is rendered by Weizsacker and Swete "with a rush": cf. Deut. (LXX) xxviii. 49; i Mace. vi. 33. This rendering is in keeping with the symbol of the boulder hurled down into the sea, but it is not in keeping with the thing symbolized the destruction of Rome by fire by Nero and the Parthians. The rendering of the A. V. and Holtzmann, " with violence," suits the figure, but how it can be justified is not clear.

Perhaps op 7fp. a has here the meaning which belongs to it in the LXX in Hos. v. 10 (also in Symm.), Amos i. n, Hab. iii. 8, i. e. " indignation "- may. This would suit the attitude alike of heaven and the Parthian hosts towards Rome. But the matter is uncertain.

jwydxij irfxif. The order of the words as regards this particular adjective is not that of our author (see note on xvi. i) nor of the rest of the source here used by him.

ou p?) cflpcgjj n. Cf. Ezek. xxvi. 21 in reference to Tyre.

14. This verse forms the opening stanza of the Seer's dirge over Rome. It consists of four stanzas of four lines each. These four stanzas are followed by two stanzas of three lines each. The text has suffered owing to one or perhaps two disturbing glosses and the loss of a line in the second stanza.

frirwpa ripe fruit. This word, like the Hebrew pp, means first late summer or autumn, and next the fruits that then ripen. Cf. Jer. xl. io y 12. The phrase? ou TTJS taioupias TTJS +UXTJS is a literal rendering of Bta JW (cf. Deut. xn. 15, 20, 21, xiv. 26, Hebrew and LXX). The unemphatic or vernacular use of rou here should be observed. That rov is unemphatic is shown independently by its absence from the parallel verse. rov follows ITOX??? in the LXX.

T Xiiropd. This phrase denotes the things that belong to a rich and sumptuous mode of life. Possibly food is specially referred to here. At all events Anrapos is, in the few cases where it occurs in the LXX, a rendering of jotr, which primarily and generally means oil or fat. It is used in Ezek. xvi. 13, Prov. xxi. 17, as a sign of luxury, and refers undoubtedly to rich food. Cf. also Isa. xxx. 23.

T Xajnrpd. It is difficult to assign a definite meaning to this phrase. Probably it indicates the well-ordered magnificence in which the " pride of life" exhibits itself. Perhaps we might render " the splendours."

ica! ofc n. efiprjaoucrtk. There can hardly be a doubt as to this clause being a gloss. Without it the stanza consists of four lines, as do the three succeeding stanzas. See In trod, to this Chap., 4. We should observe that our author uses ov XT; with the aorist subjunctive.

82-98. These verses have suffered severely in the course of transmission. We have already seen that 20 (see p. 92) should be restored after 23 b. After a dirge of four stanzas of four lines each (=14, 22, 23") the Seer in the original source calls upon heaven and the saints on earth to rejoice over the doom of Roma. But this is not all.

In 22 there has been a loss of some words, while in 23 there is an addition to the text which is not only meaningless but is also against the structure of the stanza.

22. This verse consists of two stanzas of four lines each. But the second line of the first stanza and one of the words of the third line haye been lost. These losses can, however, easily be restored. It is obvious, from a comparison of the remaining stanzas, that OVT) Ki0aposai KCU fiova-ikvv KCU avxiTuv icat o-axirio-Ttov is too long: in fact these words are but the relics of three lines, and the whole stanza is to be read as follows:

Kioapusp Kal ou fjrf) dkouaofj lv orol itai4w auxrjtWK KCU craxirunw ou pi) Kour0fj iv rol CTU

The omission may have been due to a lazy scribe, who failed to see that he was transcribing verse, and thought that the sense was not affected by his compression of the text. The student of MSS is not unacquainted with such arbitrary proceedings.

4w Kiflapwsuk KCU t jj. ourikwir t = " the voice of the harpers and singers." The writer had Ezekiel's words against Tyre (xxvi. 13) in his mind:

"I will cause the noise of the songs to cease And the sound of thy harps shall be no more heard."

He adopted the words " shall be no more heard," and instead of speaking of " harps " changes this word into " harpers " and "songs" into "singers," though as we shall see presently the text used by the Greek translator may have been corrupt here. Thus the first two lines would be somewhat as follows:

while the next two lines would speak similarly of the fluteplayers and trumpeters.

But to return to ULOOTUCWV, it will be seen that I have rendered it " singers " on the strength of the context (i. e. that we must here have a specific and not a generic term) and of Ezek. xxvi. 13 (quoted above). Now in classical Greek IOWIKOS never appears to mean "a singer," nor in later Greek, unless it is a translation from the Hebrew It has been thought by some scholars that in i Mace. ix. 39, 41, 6 ios t TJ 6cv Kal 04 txoi avrov. fiera Tvpirawv at fjlowrikv Kal otrxwv TroxXtov. icai flcrccrrpctyty. fwvrj ftowucujy avruv ets Opfjvov, the word fwwo-iicwv may mean " singers "; but the fact that it stands between rvuravw and otrxwv does not favour this view. Cf. Gen. xxxi. 27, xera tovo-ikcov (D W) al In i Esdr. iv. 63 the meaning is uncertain: ci0avi oito fjlova-LKtdv (= " songs" or "musical instruments") cal But cf. v. 2, 59, Dan. iii. 5, 7, 10, 15, where it =" musical instruments," or "music." However, if it be conceded that the word in some of these passages means "singers," then this otherwise unattested meaning, appearing as it does in translations from the Hebrew, is in some way due to the Hebrew text. Only in one case does Aowrucds appear as =" a singer," in a passage which none of the commentators has noticed, i. e. T. Jud. xxiil. 2, TOS tfvyarcoas vp. wv AOWMCGLS juu S fuxrta? 7rot7a-ct. Here the Greek is a translation from the Hebrew, and even here the rendering "minstrels" would accord better alike with the context and the etymology than "singers." 1 In other passages in the LXX nowika = "songs." Cf. Gen. xxxi. 27; Ezek. xxvi. 13; Sir. xxii. 6, xxxv. 3, 5, 6, xliv. 5, xlix. i. From this examination of the word it follows that Aouo-ikwv means either " song " or " music," but never save in T. Jud. xxiii. 2 does it mean " singer " or rather " minstrel." And yet our text makes the meaning of " singers " indispensable. Hence we conclude either that AOVO-LKUJV here = " singers," a meaning difficult to justify, or that it is an error due to a corruption in the source. That is, fuihr coi = D VB, corrupt for Dn = " singers." The rendering "minstrels" (R. V.) is here inadmissible; for we cannot have a generic term such as " minstrel " occurring in the midst of a list of specific terms.

adxTjtup. The fluteplayer (tibicen) was in much request on the Roman stage, and at Roman festivities as well as at funerals.

aoxmoruk. The trumpeter (tubicen) had his part in the Roman games, in the theatre and at funerals.

aa e h-28. The order of these verses seems to be wrong. We should expect that the dirge, having begun with the luxuries of life and dwelt on their being brought to an end, would proceed in due gradation to the destruction of the barest necessities of life. And this expectation is confirmed by Jer. xxv. 10, which the Seer had in his mind: " I will take from them the voice of mirth and the voice of gladness, the voice of the bridegroom and the voice of the bride, the sound of the millstones and the light of the candle." If this view is right, as the present writer believes, we should rearrange as follows:

And the voice of the bridegroom and the bride Shall be heard no more in thee: 1 Observe that in Eccles. ii. 8 nnsn on? is rendered by the jral pdoifrar, and not by uowruofc xal ftowurdr, which would mean "male and female minstrels."

8S 6 11. And no craftsman of whatsoever craft Shall be found any more in thee.

And the voice of the millstone

Shall be heard no more in thee: 88. And the light of the lamp

Shall shine no more in thee.

Thus the rejoicings attendant on marriage would no more be known; the arts of civilized life would come to an end; the familiar sounds of the household mill to be heard in every hamlet would be no more heard, and the light of every lamp would be extinguished. It will be observed that by this rearrangement our text reproduces the order in Jer. xxv. 10.

23 C 4w KU i4iou Kal PUJJL TIS. See the quotation from Jer. xxv. 10 given above. Cf. also vii. 34, xvi. 9, xxxin. u.

2- TCXVITTIS KT. This line would embrace skilled workers in every kind of material.

topj) puxou (= DVn ip, Jer. xxv. 10). It will be observed that for tfxavri fiv ov the LXX reads 6rp. rjv p. vpov, presupposing rn fjip.

23 ftb. 4s Xrixvou (= " 3 "tf i Jer. xxv. 10). At this stage the Seer is not thinking of the brilliant lights and torches borne by slaves as they escorted the wealthy Romans to their homes, but simply anticipating the hour when all lights even the meanest will be extinguished for ever.

20. Restored to its rightful place at the close of the writer's dirge over Rome, this appeal to heaven and the saints to rejoice over its destruction is most appropriate, and forms a fitting introduction to xix., which contains the heavenly response, whereas this apostrophe, standing as it does in the MSS, comes in most awkwardly between two descriptive passages as Moffatt has already recognized. The whole verse is to be ascribed to John: Moflatt assigns it to the hand of a Christian editor.

There are, it is true, some difficulties in the style. Thus from xi. 18, xviii. 24, we should expect ot Trpo rai. at ol aytot. But the fuller phrase here, 01 aytot K. ot drrooroxot K. ot irpo rai, may account for the difference of order. Again, fcptAa seems here to have the sense of lawsuit or case a meaning not found elsewhere in our author: cf. xvii. i, xix. 2, where it = sentence, judgment. But even here it can bear the latter meaning: " God hath judged your judgment (i. e. the judgment due to you) upon her." On the other hand, cvpatveo-0ot belongs to the diction of our author: cf. xii. 12, and the use of the singular oupavos is characteristically that of John. Hence 30 is from the hand of John: likewise 2-24.

This call of the Seer to heaven and its inhabitants to rejoice over the accomplished doom of Rome is formed of two tristichs: 20, 23 f-24.

etyptukou. Modelled apparently on Jer. li. 48 (233 ty rn DDP), which is not found in the LXX.

ol fty 101 KCU ol Airrffrroxoi xal ol irpo+fjrai: cf. xvi. 6. These must be the blessed in heaven martyrs, apostles, and prophets: cf. xii. 12, where those addressed are the angelic hosts.

cxpircc T Kpipo, d MK afrrijs = "hath judged your case against her" (lit. "at her cost"). This phrase is found in Lam. iii. 59, B9PO ntpd "judge Thou my cause." With the idiom l avns cf. Ps. cxix. 84 (LXX), but here the present Hebrew text has 3 and not jp. Or, as is suggested above, may here be taken in the sense of judgment. rjs is probably to be taken as the equivalent of atO: cf. xix. 2; 2 Kings ix. 7.

23. Srt ol cfiiropoi o ou fljcrak ot pcyiorakCS TTJS "H- This line, which is based on Isa. xxiii. 8, ptr-naaa. Dnp rnnb where the LXX has ol cftiropoi av-rfjs. a orre?-riys yj s. But in its present context there is no place for this line, being against the parallelism. It is also meaningless. There is no ground for saying that God destroyed Rome because its merchants were the great ones of the earth. The real reason is given by the next OTL clause. It is possible that this line may be a fragmentary survival of the original ending of the source used by our author. Perhaps it should be read immediately after the first clause in n, " and the merchants of the earth for thy merchants were the princes of the earth weep," etc. This would be analogous to the descriptive clause added in 9 after the phrase "the kings of the earth."

23 f-24. This stanza, consisting of three lines, gives the grounds for the destruction of Rome: her leading astray of the nations by her sorcery, and her bloodguiltiness in respect of the prophets and saints and of all the righteous, who had been slain by her throughout the world.

23 f. on CK Tip 4apfjltuua f aou f irxan oxii vdvra, r comr): cf. 3. The o-ou is here corrupt for avr s. The corruption can be explained by the dislocation of the text and the influence of the preceding occurrences of the second personal pronoun. lv rfj KT. Cf. Nab. iii. 4, where Nineveh is called "the mistress of witchcrafts (yovicvi; opAoicon), that selleth nations through her whoredoms and families through her witchcrafts." Cf. also Isa. xlvii. 12, where analogous charges are brought against Babylon.

24. While there is some doubt as to the provenance of 23 (i. e. the first line of the closing stanza), there can be none as to that of the last two lines. The irpo rtu KOL ayioi are the Christian prophets and saints, and the subject of the last line is

the universal martyrdom of the Christians apprehended by our author and regarded as accomplished at the close of xiii.

irpo4T)Ty ita! YIWK. See note on xvi. 6, xviii. 20.

atpa irpo+Tjtwi icrx.: cf. Ezek. xxiv. 6, u 71-0X19 aiuurrcov: Jer. li. (LXX, xxviii.) 35, TO atxa JLOV CTTI TOUS Karoikoviras XaaSatow, cpet Icpovcraaifu In Matt. xxii. 35 a like charge is brought against Jerusalem: OTTWS c vias vov alza oy aiov K)(yvv6p. cvov ri rijs yijs. The Seer here is not thinking only of the martyrs under the Neronian persecution, nor yet of such as had already fallen under Domitian (see list of passages referring to this persecution in Lightfoot, Ef. Clem. i. 104-115) at the time of writing; he is rather from the standpoint of the Seer looking back on the universal martyrdom of the Christian Church as a fact already accomplished. The diction used TTOLVTWV rv fo-tayfjicvuv rt rfp yvjs shows that it is of the martyrs that our author is thinking; for o- a u has this connotation in our author's language: cf. v. 6, 9, 12, vi. 9, xiii. 8. xiii. 3 is no exception, for the Beast is therein caricaturing the Lamb. On the other hand, in vi. 4 r o a is used in a more special sense.

CHAPTER XIX. i. Its Import.

No real difficulty emerges in this chapter either as regards its authorship or its relation to the chapters that precede and follow it. There can be no question as to the Johannine authorship of xix. i-8 a, 9, 11-21 from the standpoint of its style and diction (2), and there can be no doubt as to the relevancy and indis-pensableness of its subject-matter (4). Alike from its form and substance it receives unequivocal attestation.

The chapter opens with the response (1-3) that the heavenly hosts make to the appeal of the Seer in xviii. 20, who thunder forth as with the mighty voice of a great multitude their exultation over the destruction of the Harlot City and God's avenging of the saints which she had slain. The theme is taken up afresh by the Elders and the Living Creatures and by the angel of the altar of incense, 4, xvi. 5 b-7. The echoes of the closing words of this anthem have hardly ceased to reverberate, when at the summons of a voice from the throne (5) the glorified host of martyrs burst forth with, as it were, the voice of many waters and the voice of mighty thunderings into glad thanksgivings (6-7),

VOL. II.- 8 for that now at length the Lord God Omnipotent reigneth upon the earth and the advent of the kingdom of Christ is at hand. Thus, whereas the angels rejoice over the vindication of divine justice, the martyred host rejoice in that the kingdom of Christ is at hand with fresh stores of mercy and salvation for the sons of men (cf. xv. 4).

At this stage we should have expected a vision bearing on the destruction of the Parthian kings, mention of which was made proleptically in xvii. 14 (see 4 ad fin.); but this vision may have been displaced by the interpolation g-io (see 2). 1

Now that the Harlot City (and the Parthian kings) have been destroyed, there remains only the execution of judgment on the kings of the earth who had shared in the spiritual fornication and abominations of Rome (11-21). These are slain with the sword that proceeded out of the mouth of the Word of God, and the Beast and the False Prophet that deceived them were cast into the lake of fire.

2. The Diction and Idiom.

There can be no doubt whatever that xix. 1-8, 11-21 comes from the hand of our author. Alike (a) the diction and (b) the idioms are his, as is shown fully in the notes on the various verses, but it will not be unhelpful to show in the case of a few verses how intimately every verse is bound up with what precedes.

(a) Diction. 1. jiera Toura tjicouo-a. Frequent in our author.

twv pcydxi)?: cf. i. 15, vi. i, 6, ix. 9, etc. fteyas is the adjective generally connected with wq: see xvi. i, note.

oxxou iroxXou. Xeyovrwy: cf. vii. 9. 6 o iroa. vs. COTOJTC?. Observe the same construction Kara awco-tv. ownjpia xal 4 a "at 4 Wwus TOU Ocou p?: cf. iv. n, v. 12, vn. 10, xii. 10.

8. dxT)Oiml ical Siitaiai at xpiaeis aurou: cf. xv. 3.

frri tkpivev tv ir6pyi y T P pcy Xi)i: cf. xvii. i; also 5, 16. TJTIS c Ocipck rf)v yrjK: cf. xi. 18. iv rg iropkcia afirrjs: cf. xiv. 8, xvii. 2, xviii. 3. Jestittjai T atpa. In: cf. vi. 10.

8. xal 6 KOTTV S dhi) vafiaiv i irrx.: cf. xiv. n (xviii. 9, 18).

4. Jireaak ot irp apurepoi ol CIK. Wavapcs: cf. iv. 10, v. 8, xi. 16. Sraaay ol irpeapotcpoi. Kal irpocrcki nr)rak: cf. xi. 16. T. naov))i u lirl T. 0p K: see note on iv. 2.

XVI. 6 b-7. See notes on p. 120 sqq.

XIX. 5. furi) dird TOU 0p6rou 1 KBtv: cf. xvi. 17 for the more usual order, ol Souxot afrrou. jieydxoi: almost a verbal reproduction of xi. 18, though with a limitation of meaning.

1 8 b is a gloss and 9 b-io an interpolation (see notes m loc., which may have displaced a vision of the destruction of the Parthian kings and their hosts by the Lamb and the glorified martyrs. See 4, adfinem.

6. 69 ttivv fyxou iroxXou: see note on I. 6s iroxXui: cf. i. 15, xiv. 2. ws w V Ppon-ftp: cf. vi. i. lpuri-Xeuorey Kupios 6 Oca's, o irairokpdtttp: cf. xi. 1 7, ei apiarrovbicy croc, Kvpic, 6 0cos, 6 iraiTOKparwp. art. ? acrtxcwas.

7. Bftfcropek iv Soiak: see note on xi. 13. fjxOck 6 ydpos: cf. xi. 1 8 for same use of verb. Toipacrci lavrfiv: cf. xxi. 2, qroi-fiao-fjLtyrjv a? vvptr v, also ix. 7, 15, xvi. 12.

8. irepipdxi)Tiu piwikOH: cf. for construction vii. 9, 13, x. i. O h-10. See notes in he.

11. irurros K. dxtjoi s: cf. xxii. 6. iroxcpci: only used outside our author once in the N. T., whereas he uses it six times. Id. ol tyoaxpol afrou s Xo irupfc: repeated from i. 14: K. afrris a gloss, though the diction is Johannine.

14. T orrpatcupata: cf. ix. 16. cvocuiilroi PUOXTIHOK i 1 cf. i. 13, xv. 6.

15. CK rog orfyajos elciropeuenu jtap aia cia: cf. 21, i. 16, ii. 12. Troipaici aurous iv pdpsw atsrjp: cf. ii. 27, xii. 5.

T. XIJKK TOU otwu T. 0ujiou nrx.: cf. xiv. 19-20, T. Xiyvov T. T. O QV. KOI ctranfjfci vj Arpos.

16. pcunxeos paaix uk Krx.: cf. xvii. 14.

17. 2 cpa ck 4wi ficydxn: see note on xiv. 15. IK fxcoroupam fjlari: cf. viii. 1 3, J v. 6.

18. x l PX w: cf- v i I S- (Xcub puk. fji Yc Xwk: cf. xiii. 16.

19. T. paaixcis T. yf)s: cf. vi. 15 (xvi. 14), xxi. 24. T. Tr5Xefiok fierd: cf. xvi. 14, 1 6, xx. 8.

20. 6 +eusotrpo4T)TT s: cf. xvi. 13, xx. 10. 6 iroivjaas T ot jicia: cf. xni. 13, 14. firxdnqack m-X.: cf. xiii. 14, xx. 3, etc.

xip a YH La T jpiou: cf. xiv. n, xx. 4 (xvl 2, note). T. cu a: cf. xiii. 14, xiv. 9; see note on vii. 11. etc T. Xtjmji T. irups. Ociw: cf. xx. 10, xxl 8.

21. TJJ of aif. cx0ou0j) in r. ar patos afirou: see on (6) Idiom. There are no idoms against our author's usage, while those that follow are characteristic of him.

1. ws 4w K: cf. passim. oxxou. Xcytwi: cf. vii. 9.

2. Y)TIS = in 2: cf. i. 12, xii. 13, xvii. 12. eiict)(w rd atjia. IK: cf. vi. 10.

1 ptofflvov is used as a noun only once in the LXX in the sing., Dan. x. 5; in the plural hi the LXX in Dan. z. 5 b, xii. 6, 7; Isa. iii. 23: but in our author only in sing.; cf. zix. 8 ab, 14, xviii. 12, 1 6. This use of adjectives as nouns in the sing, is characteristic of the writer of xviii. Thus he uses pfoffivos as a noun in 12, 16, ro upoqx as a noun in 16, and in zvil 4 which is from the same source, whereas the Fourth Gospel uses it as an adj. (cf. six. 2, 5), K KKWW as a noun (rare except in plural) in 12, 16 and in xvii. 4, but as an adj. in xvii. 3. I do not know of any other instances of Topjvpovr as a noun, fftpucbv in 12; here only in Biblical Greek, though used by Plutarch, Strabo, etc.

4. Trpocrekifnrjcrar T 0e: see note on vil 11.

T Kaoqpfap 4m T 6p5yp: see note on iv. 2. ol juicpoi nal ol feydxoi: cf. xi. 18.

5. aircirc T 6e: a Hebraism; see note in loc.

6. s tu p 5xxou. Xcyo'irtti: see note on i. 8. is40i) aurjj fra: cf. ix. 5.

11. 6 ica cios ir a Tfc: see note on iv. 2. 18. im r. K faxf)K afirou: cf. x. i, xiv. 14 (see Introd. to xiv. 3).

13. ircpipcpxi)p yos a participle used as a finite verb: see note on iv. 7, vol. i. p. 104.

14. aurw ty iinrois. The dat. after brt here seems due to avrw: cf. our author's usage where Kaorjpwov is followed by gen. in 1 8, 19, 21, and where ica0i?Acvu is followed by dat.: iv. 9, v. 13, vii. 10, etc.

15. iroiparci: here used as equivalent to " will break ": see note on ii. 27.

16. lirl I K jitjpoy. ycypafifuKo: cf. iii. 12, ypdifho lif

TO OVOFjM.

18. Ka6i)fi up ITT aujw: cf. 19, 21: see note on iv. 2. 2O. irpoakUKourras T. cu a: see note on vii. 1 1.

3. xix. tf-io an Interpolation. See note in loc.

4. 7 Structure of the Book requires xix. 1-4, xvi. xix. j-, f, 1-2 1.

xix. 1-4, xvi. 5 b-7, xix. 5-8 is the heavenly response to the Seer's appeal in xviii. 20. 9 contains the fourth of the seven beatitudes. The contents of xix. 11-21, which have already been proleptically described in xiv. 14, 18-20, xvi. 14, 16, are here seen in their due chronological connection, as the necessary prelude to XX.-XXH. The kings of the earth, who had shared in the idolatries and abominations of Rome, here meet with just doom, while the Beast and the False Prophet are cast down into the lake of fire. Only one more event must intervene before the advent of the heavenly Jerusalem, and this the chaining of Satan is witnessed in xx. 1-3.

There appears, however, to be a lacuna in this chapter. Where the interpolation (9-10) stands we should expect a vision relating to the destruction of the Parthian kings. In xviii. we have the vision of the destruction of the Harlot City which had in an earlier chapter been spoken of proleptically as though already accomplished: cf. xiv. 8. In xix. 11-21 we have a vision of the destruction of the kings of the earth and the final doom of the Beast and the False Prophet in their due chronological sequence, save in one respect, and this is, that after the destruction of Rome and before the destruction of the kings of the earth there ought to be a vision of the destruction of the Parthian kings a destruction that has already been referred to proleptically in xvii. 14 (see 12-13, 17, 16, 14). A short vision to this effect may have been displaced by the interpolation xix. 9 b-io.

5. The Method of our author elsewhere in this Book is observed here.

In xix. 1-8 our author pursues the method already familiar to us in preceding chapters, in accordance with which over against a vision of the tribulation of the faithful is set one of their deliverance and triumph, or over against a vision of coming judgment on the enemies of Christ is set one of the ultimate blessedness of the redeemed.

Thus xix. 1-4, xvi. 5 7, xix. 5-8, which sets forth the joy of the angels on the dooms just executed on Rome and the joy of the glorified martyrs on the impending advent of the kingdom, is not only a heavenly response to the appeal of the Seer in xviii. 20, but the counterpart we expect of the dread judgments culminating in xvii.-xviii. With this notable contrast we might compare earlier analogous contrasts on this Book. Thus xv. 2-3, which comes in reality immediately after xui. (since xiv. is entirely proleptic), brings out the glaring contrast between the universal martyrdom of the faithful in xiii. and the blessed inheritance on which they entered forthwith in heaven itself. Also in xiv. 1-5 we have a parallel to xv. 2-3 in contrast to xiii., where the visions were of such a nature as to daunt the faith-fullest heart, as they foretold the destruction of all God's servants. In like manner xi. 14-18 comes in as a contrast to the tribulations depicted in xi. 1-13 and the still darker visions that follow in xii.-xiii., claiming as it does that already, however great may appear the triumph of the Antichrist, it is but a passing one, and that the issues of the strife are already made known to the hosts of heaven. Once more, after the account of the Seals is placed the vision of the great multitude in heaven, vii. 9-17.

On every ground, therefore, whether we regard the diction, the idioms, the due development of events in the Book, or the method pursued in this chapter, we conclude that it is the undoubted product of his pen.

1-8. Thanksgivings in heaven. The closing appeal in xviii. 20 to heaven to rejoice in that God had judged the great Harlot

City is answered by an exultant anthem voiced by a great multitude of angels (1-3) which is closed by the four and twenty Elders and the Cherubim with the response, "Amen, alleluia" (4-5). They had already voiced their thanksgivings in two anthems on the same subjects in xi. 15-18. Hence here they simply give utterance to their approval of the theme of the angels' song. And whereas a voice from earth summoned the heavenly hosts to the duty of thanksgiving in that the doom of the Harlot City is already accomplished in 1-5, now in 6-8 a voice from the throne summons the glorified martyrs in heaven to the glad service of thanksgiving, whereupon there arose as it were the voice of a great multitude and of many waters and of mighty thunderings proclaiming that the Lord God Omnipotent had become King, and that the advent of the heavenly Jerusalem was at hand. It is fitting that the last song in the Apocalypse should come from the lips of the martyrs.

1. The thanksgiving in this verse has been explained by some interpreters as coming from the glorified martyrs, as in: i. 10-12; but the context and our author's usage is against this interpretation. The context is against it; for the faithful, who appear to embrace only the glorified martyrs, do not offer their thanksgiving till 6-8. Further, our author's usage is against it In such a series of thanksgivings those of the angels could not be omitted, and, if the alleluia in i is ascribed to the glorified martyrs, then we have such an omission, while in 6-8 there would then be a duplication of the praises of the martyrs. Furthermore (see notes on iv. 4, v. n), if any reference to the angels' thanksgiving is made in our text, it must come in i; for the mention of the Elders and the Living Creatures (and in this order) in 4 shows that the Seer is beginning his description with the outer ranks of the heavenly beings and proceeding inwards towards the throne. Thus, as in vii. n, we have first angels, then the Elders, then the Living Creatures.

If the same order were observed as in vii. 9-11, we should have 6-8 before 1-5: in other words, the thanksgivings of men, then of angels, then of the Elders, and finally of the Living Creatures. But the order is otherwise here, and the change is instructive. Whereas in an earlier chapter, vi. 10, the cry of the faithful was for vengeance on their persecutors, here (cf. xv. 4) their sole theme of thanksgiving is that now at last " the Lord God Omnipotent reigneth," and that " the marriage of the Lamb is come." This prepares the reader for what is to follow in the speedy removal (in xix. 11-21) of all that prevents the advent of the heavenly Jerusalem. Hence 6-8 comes rightly at the close of 1-5. On the other hand, it is noteworthy that in 1-5 the theme of the angels' song is one of profound thanksgiving for

XIX. 1-8. THANKSGIVING IN HEAVEN lip
God's righteous judgment of Rome and His avenging of the blood of the martyrs. This thanksgiving follows naturally and immediately in response to the appeal in xviii. 20.

6s fwfv icyci t)K. With ws on v cf. i. 15 (v. 11), vl I, 6, ix. 9, xiv. 2, xix. 6. mcyox is the usual adjective our author connects with wvi (see xvi. i, note). With cgaou roaAov, cf. vii. 9. Xcy rruk. A construction KCLTO, crvvco-tv with o ov exactly as we find it in vii. 9 ox os. TTWTCS. "AXXi)Xouidl As this word is a transliteration of ft 7? n, the 17, where we should have c, is strange. The same irregularity is to be found in r 0o-77jlavei, which according to Dalman (Gram. p. 152, note 3), Delitzsch, and others is derived from Dipt? na. This transliteration came into use before the Christian era amongst Hellenistic Jews, as Swete remarks, since it is found in 3 Mace. vii. 13; Tob. xiii. 18. In the LXX it is found frequently at the beginning and end of certain Pss.: see Swete, Intr. to O. T. in Greek, p. 250.

f cwnjpia Kal Vj S a ical 4 Sifpapis TOW 6cou 1 i v. In xii. 10 we find 17 T(njpia and fj Swaus conjoined, and in iv. n, vii. 12, fj Sofa and Swaxts (also in v. 12, but in the reverse order): in vii. 10, 17 croj-npta alone. This construction ij o-omjxa. rov

Q OV VHMOV has already occurred in xii. 10, the more usual being that which is found in L 6 (avruj fj Sofa), vil 10.

2. dxvjoi al xal Siicaiai at Kpiarcis afoou. This clause has, it we have concluded rightly, been reproduced in xvi. 7, which belongs to a dislocated passage, i. e. xvi. 5-7. A distant parallel occurs in xv. 3, KCUCU KCU darjvai at 6Sot a-ov. These words define the reason for this hymn of praise the righteousness of God's judgments as exemplified in the destruction of the Harlot City.

on! KPIKCK TV ir6pyi v T K fccy(2XT)ir. This clause is a justification of the preceding on clause. It recalls xvii. i, TO Kptm TTJ T S icyoxis. On Kptvcv cf. xviii. 8, 20, and on-rijs. ficyox s cf. xvii. I, 5, 15, 16.

tjris 2f0 ip K r? K yr v: cf. xi. 18, Sux cipai TOVS Sta cpovras ryv yjjvy and the note thereon. The pronoun ijfrts appears here to be simply the equivalent of jf. It definitely determines who the Harlot is. For this usage of ooms see note on xi. 8. Iv Tfj iropvci T afirqs. This is the first charge brought against Rome. It has corrupted the whole earth, cf. xiv. 8, xvil 2, xviii. 3. The second charge is that stated in the words 4jciki)oii T atpa Tr Souxwk rrx. These words recall the complaint of the martyrs in

Vi. 10, OU. fckCls TO ttlio UUOV IK TWV KtttOilcOVFTWV M T S 7V and now recognize the consummation of divine justice: cf. xi. 18. The idiom itself is found in 2 Kings ix. 7, TGI aiiata TOW Sovxuv tov.

Cf. also Deut. xxxii. 43. TWK Soifxw afrrou recalls xviii. 24 the prophets and saints.

3. Kal Seutcpok ctpv Kay. "And a second time they say." The second utterance or antistrophe from the lips of the same multitude consists not only of the word oxX Xouta, but also of the words that follow KU o icatrvos. auovcov. These words correspond to the tetrastich that follows the first oaXqaovta in 1-2.

icol 6 Kaws aurris KT. This clause recalls xviii. 8 (v mpl Karafcavtfiprctai) and xviii. 9, 18 (rov KO. TTVOV TI S irvDicrci? airrijs). Cf. also xiv. II, Kal 6 Ka-nros rov fturavuriov avrcov ci? auovas aiuvav dpa? atw. The cat is not to be taken here as a mere conjunction. We can only secure the right meaning of the clause that follows if KCU is taken as a Hebraism: j. e. " Hallelujah; for the smoke thereof goeth up for ever and ever." This clause therefore is a circumstantial clause introduced by icot (= 1) and gives a statement of the concomitant conditions, which justify the action denoted by the principal verb (nn n). See Oxford Hebrew Diet. p. 253.

els-rods alums TWK alow. This expression is equivalent here to 1000 years. For, since the advent of the Millennial Kingdom is already at hand, and since the earth is to be destroyed at its close, it follows that even the smoking ruins of Rome will cease to exist at that date. Contrast this meaning with that which it bears in xxii. 5, where it denotes eternity.

4. Now that the angelic hosts have sung their two paeans of triumph, the Elders and the Living Creatures too take their share in the praises of heaven with the words, Axijv, AAX Xovto, followed by xvi. 5 b-7, which belongs here.

In iv. 8, n, xi. 15-18 the Cherubim and the Elders offer their praises independently; in v. 9 together, as in the verse before us; in v. 14 the Cherubim pronounce the "amen" at the close of the doxology of all creation. In the present text both orders unite together (as in v. 9) in singing the antistrophe (consisting like the strophe i b-2 of two stanzas of three lines each), 3, xvi. s b-7.

irpoacku'ttpah TW 0ew. Our author uses the dative when speaking of the highest form of worship: see note on vii. n. TW Ka0. m TW 0p6jw also a characteristic usage of our author: see note on iv. 2.

, XXi)Xouid. These words form the close of Ps. cvi. 48, tpk, where they are rendered in the LXX by ycrotro, ycvoiro. Cf. also Neh. v. 13.

XVI. 5 b-7. These verses, which in the MSS follow after xvi. 5, do not belong to xvi., but have in this edition been restored to their original context after xix. 4. Either what originally followed was lost (loss in xvi. 10), or else it was deliberately removed by the Johannine editor and these verses substituted in their stead.

(1) The first ground for regarding these verses as an interpolation in their present context is that they limit the incidence of the Third Plague and probably that of the Second to the adherents of the Roman Empire. But, if the Second and Third Plagues are studied apart from these verses, the fact that. their incidence is universal for sea and land cannot be questioned any more than that of the Fourth Plague, the Sixth, and the Seventh. We have already seen that the First also affects all the earth. Hence all the Bowls are universal in their incidence save the Fifth, just as all the Seals are likewise universal save the Fifth.

(2) The main point of these verses was not understood by the Johannine editor. Rightly understood they mean: God is righteous, inasmuch as He has made those who shed the blood of the prophets and saints to shed each other's blood (alia avrofc Scsufcas irf. lv, xvi. 6 b) and stirred up the kings of the East against the great Harlot City Rome to destroy it, and eat her flesh (TOLS o-apkas avrrjs fdyovtu, xvii. 16). Now this judgment of Rome is not referred to till we come to the vision in xvii. 12-13, 17, 16: hence xvi. 5 b-7 cannot rightly occur till after xvii., nor in fact till after xviii., which describes the destruction of Rome.

(3) Since xvi. 5 b-7 does not belong to xvi. and cannot justly be used till after xviii., we have two further points to determine: i. e. (a) Are these verses from our author; and, if so, (b) what was their original context?

(a) The passage is genuine. In xvi. 5 on 6 v al 6 v cf. xi. 17 (.): on ocrios as applied to God cf. xv. 4, on- ftovos oono?: on ravra? Kxvas cf. vi. IO, xix. 2. 6. On atia dyuav. nyxx Trtov cf. xi. 18, xviii. 24, xix. 2: on a ioi cicriv cf. iii. 4 and xiv. 5 for exactly the same asyndetic construction. 7. On icvptc 6 0cos, 6 Travrojcparcdp cf. i. 8, iv. 8, xi. 17, xv. 3, xix. 6, xxl 22. Here we should observe that the divine title in 5 and this title in 7 are already conjoined in xi. 17: on Xrjowal K. Sucouu a! fcpurct? crov cf. xix. 2 where the words recur exactly as here; also in xv. 3 (in reverse order).

Thus the passage is undoubtedly Johannine.

(b) All the evidence is in favour of restoring it immediately after cuArjaovta in xix. 4. Thus we have: first two stanzas of three lines each, xix. i b-2, followed by one of two in xix. 3, and parallel with these two other stanzas of three lines each in xix. 4, xvi. 5 b-6 followed by another of two in xvi. 7. The structure is thus perfectly symmetrical.

The Song of the Angels.

1 b. AXXijxoui

Kal 4 a Kal Suvapif TOU 6cou 8. OTI dxT)Oikal ital Bucaiai at Kpurcis adrou

Ori cvpiiw TV trlppi)? ity jwydxt) Hri fyocipci TV YV cv-rfj iropwia amis, Kal c csikT)rcf T atfia TK Souxw aurou C K auTTJS.

8. Koi BcisTCpor ctptjitak

AXXi Xouid-Kal 6 Kairris afittjs drnpatkCi civ Tod atopa of the Elders and the Cherubim.

4. Arfr, XXt)Xouid-XVI. 5 b. Auccuo el, 6 fiy ital 6 J K Sri Taura citpiyas-

Ori atjio dyiw Kal Kal atua adroif ctw.

7. Kal ijKOuaa TOU Oucnaomipiou Nat, Kiipic, 6 06 6 irak

Kal Sinatat at Kpurcis aou.

At first sight it might appear an objection that this doxology is addressed directly to God, whereas the doxology in xix. i b-2 is not so directed, but God is spoken of in the third person. But this objection is groundless; for in iv. 8 the doxology speaks of God in the third person, whereas that which follows in iv. 1 1 is addressed directly to God. The same change of persons is found in the two thanksgivings in connection with the Lamb in v. 9-10 and v. 12. Here also the Elders and the Cherubim join together, as in v. 9, in this great anthem of praise. Again it is noteworthy that the doxologies of the twenty-four Elders are always elsewhere in our author (cf. iv. n, v. 9, xi. 17) addressed directly to God, just as they are above in xix. 4, xvi. 5 b-6. Thus what at first sight appears to be an objection turns out to be evidence in favour of the above restoration.

(4) The reader will recognize at a glance the similarity of construction between the doxology in xix. 1-2 and that of the Elders and Living Creatures in xix. 4, xvi. 5 b-6, both of which consist of two stanzas of three lines each, and that in each case these stanzas are followed by one of two lines. They both also deal with the same subject thanksgiving over the fall of Rome.

XVI. 6 b. 6 P nal 6 fy. See note on i. 4.

feu. Cf. xv. 5. So the best authorities: "holy" in apposition to Sfcaioc. If with P we read 6 00-105 the phrase is to be taken as a vocative, "Thou Holy One." It represents God as faithful in His relation to men. See Trench (Synon p. 316) on the relation of Stwos and oo-toc in Classical Greek. On this attribute of God cf. i Enoch i. 2, 3, x. i, xiv. i, xxv. 3, xxxvii. 2, cxxxiv. i, xcii. 2, xciii. n, xcviii. 6, civ. g.

6. alfia. x a Cf. Ps. lxxix. 3.

YUW xai irpo Tjtwk. We should expect the reverse order: cf. xviii. 24, xxii. g.

atpa aurois Suicas irtlv. This expression has a technical sense in the O. T. and later books. Thus in Isa. xlix. 26 we haves"I will feed them that oppress thee with their own flesh, and they shall be drunken with their own blood." In that time " no man spareth his own brother " (Isa. ix. 19). This is the so-called Period of the Sword: cf. Ezek. xxxviii. 21," I will call for a sword against him. every man's sword shall be against his brother"; Hag. ii. 22, "I will destroy the strength of the kingdoms. everyone by the sword of his brother"; Zcch. xiv. 13; i Enoch xxxviii. 5, xcviii. i2, xcix. 4, 6; Jub. xxiii. 19; 2 Bar. xlviii. 32, lxx. 6-7; Mark xiii. 8. Thus the meaning of the clause in our text is that God would cause internecine war to arise amongst the Antichristian nations, i. e. between Rome and the nations of the East; for the latter, as the Seer has already testified in xvii. 12-i3i i? i i6 would invade the West and destroy

Rome. But the Johannine editor was wholly ignorant of the force of these words and took them in a literal and material sense: As Rome had shed the blood of the saints, so it should drink actual blood! whereas they mean that the doom pronounced by God on those who had martyred the prophets and the saints would be that they should fall by each other's hands, and thus they should eat each other's flesh (xvii. 16) and drink each other's blood (xvi. 6). We should observe that the two ideas in Isa. xlix. 26 are thus adopted by our author. irciv=irtciv: cf. Blass, Gram. 23.

(LOL CUTIK. Contrast the use of this phrase in iii. 4, and for the absence of the copula xiv. 5.

7. tjicoucra TOO Ouaicumjpiou X yoiro. This clause must be taken in connection with the statements made in reference to this altar, i. e. the altar of incense in the preceding chapters. In vi. 10 the souls of the martyrs are represented as beneath this altar, and from thence their prayers go forth to God. In viii. 3-4 the prayers of all the saints that are still upon earth are offered up upon it. In ix. 13 this altar first appears in con- nection with judgment, where it is conceived as initiating the second Woe by ordering the four angels of punishment to be let loose. In xiv. 18, which represents a period chronologically later, i. e. when the roll of the martyrs is complete, an angel goes forth from this altar and delivers to the Son of Man the divine command to undertake the judgment of the earth. In the present passage the altar confirms the doxologies just uttered (vai), and declares that in the destruction of Rome the truth and righteousness of God are vindicated. Thus at last the prayers of the martyrs and of the saints are fulfilled.

XTX. 6. w Aird TOU Oplpou. This voice directed to God's servants in heaven (i. e. the martyrs) seems to be that of one of the Cherubim or of the Elders, and not of an angel, since the two first orders were the nearest to the throne. In no case should the voice be ascribed to Christ, as in that case we should have not T5 0cj i7buiv in the words that follow, but r5 0cp xov, as in iii. 12.

aircitc T 6c K (-titOO n). aivciv takes the ace elsewhere in the N. T. and all but universally in the LXX. In the half-dozen or more of cases where aivciv takes the dative in the LXX, we can explain it in i Chron. xvi 36, xxiii. 5, 2 Chron. xx. 19 as a reproduction of the Hebrew idiom mn n or mn rrnn. Still more remarkable is the careful following of the text in Ezra iii. 10, where aivilv takes the ace. as Wn does in the Hebrew, and in iii ii, where alvclv r vp p is a rendering of rnnb 5n. In 2 Chron. v. 13, aivclv r K. is a translation of " rmn; also in vii. 3. Hence it is not improbable that this Hebrew idiom was in the mind of our author when he wrote, aivcirc ra 0c ijp? v. The dative is also found in Pss. Sol. v. i, afcccro ra ovdiart o-ov.

aifcirc. irdrres ol Souxoi adrou, ical ol 4o0ou i KOi afrov, ol xal ot ficydxoi. Cf. XI. 18, roi? Souxot? erov Kal rous o-fovzcvovs TO ovofui o-ov, TOVS mifcpovs ical TOVS ficyaaovs. First of all, our text is influenced by Ps. cxxxv. i, mrp nay. rmn (LXX, aiv it. oouxot Kvpiov), and 20, mn NT (LXX, 01 fofiovfjiwoi rov icvptov). In the usage of our author the phrase Sovaot (rov 0 ov) represents the most notable servants of God the Christian prophets (cf. i. i, x. 7, xi. 18, xxii. 6) and martyrs (cf. vii. 3, xix. 2), and the servants of God generally in ii. 20, xxii. 3. The context therefore must decide its special significance in each case.

We have next to discover who these servants of God are. They can hardly be said to compose the Church universal; for (i) the presupposition of xviii. 20, cfrxuvov. ovpavc, is that only those who are in heaven should take part in the thanksgivings over the fall of Rome. (2) The words, further, wvq A

TOV Opovov, have the same implication. They are addressed to those in heaven. If the voice were addressed to those on earth we shall expect cwj? IK TOV ovpavov: cf. x. 4, 8, xi. 12, xiv. 2,13, xviii. 4 In xxi. 3 God tabernacles with men = hence this phrase has not the same significance there that it has in the earlier chapters. (3) We have found that all the faithful had been removed from the earth after chap. xiii.

Thus since the divine command is issued only to the servants (Sovxoi) of God in heaven, these can only be the glorified martyrs, who have already been described as " a mighty multitude which no man could number" in vil 9. The martyrs have already been so designated in vii. 3, xix. 2. It is used elsewhere also of the Christian prophets, and also of God's servants generally (see above).

So much then appears clear. The anthems of thanksgiving in xix. 1-8 are sung only by those actually in heaven angels and glorified martyrs. We have now to deal with the further description of the latter, which is given in the next line.

KCU ot 4opou jl KOi OUTO, ol fjiikpol Kdt ot pcydxoi. If we accept the KU (with AQ min 01 " vg. syr. 1 a Prim.) we must render it as "even"; for there is no question here of two distinct classes of the faithful in heaven: there are only the martyrs. The martyrs are described here as ol Sovxoi avrov, as in the angels' song in 2. This being so, the phrase KCU ot topovp voi avrov is not a strong one as descriptive of the martyrs. KU ol o?. avrov. Acyaa. oi appears to be derived from Ps. cxiv. 13 (cxiii. 21) originally. The phrase ol fopovfjicvot TO ovopa o-ov bears another meaning in xi. 18. There the whole body of the faithful are referred to; xi. i8 d refers to the events subsequent to the final judgment, and to all the orders of the faithful who then enter into the everlasting Kingdom of God. Hence a! ol o3ov-ftcvoi TO ovoutd o-ov denotes a class of the faithful quite distinct from the other classes there enumerated. But in the present context only one class is mentioned, i. e. that of the martyrs.

6. Response of the martyr host to the divine command.

s +uri)i QX OU iroxXou. See note on ver. i. s fri)? ASdruk iroxXwh: cf. i. 15, xiv. 2. 6s tytvty ppomry ivyupv: cf. vi. i (x. 3). Xcy mjk. This is the best attested reading (AP and many cursives). Presumably our author took it in immediate connection with Spovrwv. Cf. like irregularities in iv. i, OVT). Aeyav: in ix. 13, av v. Xeyovro. Afyovrcs (Q and many cursives) is, though parallels in our author's use (cf. v. ii, xiv. 6-7) could be adduced, probably a correction.

Sri ipoacXtihjf r. xaipttfici KOI dyoxXiwficK. For the same connection of ideas cf. Ps. xcvii. i pgn n "pd mrr (xcvi. i, acrixcvrcv, dyaxAubrcrai 17 y). With ifiar WT v: cf.

xi. 15 17- With the destruction of Rome the reign of God is established on earth. Cf. Pss. Sol. ii. 34, 36, v. ax, 22, xvii. 4 389 5 X where the like thought of the kingship of God prevails. This is the second great stage in the destruction of evil in the universe. The first was achieved when Satan was cast down from heaven (chap. xii.).

Kupios o Ocos 6 iratrokprftup. A favourite designation of God in our author. Cf. i. 8, iv. 8, xi. 17, xv. 3, xvi. 7, xxi. 22. Against (A i, 49, 95 al. me. arm.) other authorities add wuw after 0co9 owing to the influence of i, 5. But this is against the usage of our author in this phrase, and the context itself is against its insertion. When 6 iravrokparup does not immediately follow, as in iv. 11, we have 6 Kvptos cal 6 0cos twv, where Dr. DArcy suggests there may be a reference to the blasphemous title assumed by Domitian, "Dominus et Deus noster."

7. x a P u) f l KC " AyaxXiwfiik. For the same combination cf. Matt v. 12, xatpcTC ai ayoaAtacrdc. ayaaAiav is found in the N. T. only here and in Luke i. 47. Elsewhere in the N. T. and in the LXX the middle form is used. The classical form is ayoxAoicu.

fetoopci iv S6 ak. See note on xi. 13.

Jjx0 K 6 ydjaos TOO Apiaou. rjxOtv is used prolep'caliy in xi. 18, but not to the same extent here; for Rome is already overthrown: the impenitent nations, the Beast and the False Prophet are on the eve of being cast into the lake of fire, the Millennial Kingdom on the eve of being set up, and the heavenly Jerusalem the bride of coming down from heaven. In fact, 3A0C? refers here to the time just preceding the advent of the Millennial Kingdom, whereas in xi. 18 to the period that follows on its close. Cf. xiv. 7, 15, where it also occurs.

6 yd us TOU Apriou. As God in the O. T. is the Bridegroom of Israel (cf. Hos. ii. 16; Isa. liv. 6; Ezek. xvi. 7 sq.), in the N. T. this symbolism is transferred to Christ and the Church, which in our author is symbolized by the heavenly and the New Jerusalem: cf. xxi. 9-10, xxii. 17, xxi. 2. This figure of marriage denotes the intimate and indissoluble communion of Christ with the community which He has purchased with His own blood (v. 6, 9, vii. 17, xiv. i). This communion is reached first in its fulness by the martyrs who reign with Christ for 1000 years in the Holy City, which comes down from heaven, and are yet in a mysterious way identified with the Holy City xxi. 9, xxii. 17, i. e. the Church, the Bride of Christ The Gentiles converted during these 1000 years belong also to the Church. When the New (nawy) Jerusalem descends in xxi. 2 after the final judgment and the creation of a new heaven and a new earth, has become a symbol for the Church Universal It is worth observing that the heavenly (or New?) Jerusalem is symbolized by a woman in 4 Ezra ix. 38 sqq., x. 25-50.

But to return to the term yazos, we meet with the above symbolism in other parts of the N. T. Thus the marriage feast (yopot) is made by the king for His Son in Matt. xxii. 3 sqq.; the bride chamber is mentioned Matt. xxii. 10 (wx ov), and the wedding garment (ifvsiyta yauv), xxii. 11; the sons of the bride-chamber, Mark ii. 19; the bridegroom (WA IO?), Mark ii. 19, Matt. xxv. i; and his friends (John iii. 29) and the bride (v p rj) in Matt. xxv. i (D). In 2 Cor. xi. 2 the same symbolism occurs, rjpfjlorlfjit V yap tyias m dvspl irap0cyov dyv v iraparnjrai rp Xptcrru: Eph. V. 25, 32, otavspc?, dyavarc rat ywaticas, KO0a? KOI 6 Xptoros rfyd-mjcrcv TJJV ikK r)riav. TO xvcrr piov rovro Ltcya coriv, tya 8e Aeyw ci9 Xpurrov Kai cfc rijfv KK r (riav.

1 yukf) autoo. Here yvn is used as equivalent to ij uctvi?-orcvLiln? (= nbn p), as in Deut. xxii. 23; Matt. i. 20. In xxi. 9 of our text the rrjv ywaika appears to be a gloss.

Toipcurck iavrfiv. A favourite word in our author (ix. 7, 15, xii. 6, xvi. 12, xxi. 2 (viii. 6)). Only the destruction of the Anti-christian kings and nations, the casting of the Beast and the False Prophet into the lake of fire (xix. 11-21), and the chaining of Satan in the abyss (xx. 1-3) must intervene before the actual bridal, before the full spiritual communion of Christ and His Church is accomplished in the descent of the Holy City in xxi. 9 sqq.

8. KCU t60i) ofrrfj tm irepifkXtirai 9isovikOK = " And it had been given unto her that she should array herself in fine linen." This privilege was already accorded to the martyr Church in vi. ii. ircpt? oaAcrOai ftwtvov, iurna, oroxas are favourite expressions in our author: cf. iii. 18, vii. 9, 13, x. i, xviii. 16, etc. Our author uses also the phrase cv8ucrOu Jiwivov: cf. 14, xv. 6 (?). In the words tiofoj avrjj Iva. n-cpt oxirai tcrx, and in the preceding clause rotiao-ev cavn v, we have presented God's part and man's part in the work of redemption: cf. Phil. ii. 12-13, Tyy zvrov (rwripiav icatepyafcerflc, cos yap COTIV 6 fapya cv vp. lv Ktil TO Icaetv Kal TO cpyciv. The words KOI cfetfi?. fcatiapdv could be taken as part of the martyrs' song. But both the context and the parallelism are in favour of regarding them as a remark of the Seer.

pucnriw: cf. 14, xviii. 12. Here used as a noun, as in Dan. (LXX) x. 5. On the meaning of this "fine linen" see note on iii. 5, vi. ii, vol. i. p. 184 sq.

Xoftirpok naoopov: cf. xv. 6. The vesture of the saints stands out in strong contrast with that of the Harlot in xvil 4, xviii. 16.

TO yip puww T Butausjacrra TMK dywak 6rnv. This is regarded by some scholars as the close of the anthem: if so, it is a prosai? one. Of course it might be urged that it does not come from the heavenly choir, but is an explanation of the Seer himself, as the preceding clause itself appears to be. But this can hardly be maintained. As we have seen in the note on xiv. 13, the righteous acts (so Sucaictfuira: cf. xv. 4; Rom. v. 18; i Bar. ii. 19) of the saints are regarded by our author as the manifestation of the inner life and as practically identical with character the character a man takes with him when he leaves this life. Neither his righteous acts nor his character are to be regarded as the garment of the soul of the martyrs; for, though they had already this character they are described as without such garments for a time, even in heaven: see vi. n. As a fitting clothing of the souls of the martyrs, God assigns them spiritual bodies, vi. n (see note), which in iii. 5 (see note) and here are described as white garments or shining pure garments. The individuals also who compose the Church or Bride at this period are the martyrs. If this view is right, then 8 b is a gloss. In a limited sense it is a correct gloss, since the spiritual bodies will be in keeping with the character or righteous acts of the saints.

Alford regards the entire verse as an explanation of the Seer. But the objections to 8 b hold nevertheless.

9 b-lo. This passage, which is in part a doublet of xxii. 8-9 but rewritten and given quite a different meaning, is bracketed as an interpolation.

1. The clause ovrot ol Xoyot 01 axrjoivol TOV Ocoii ctcrfv (9) IS rather inept here, seeing that the words referred to are the triumphant songs of the angels and martyrs in

heaven. In xxii. 6, on the other hand, they are full of significance, coming in as they do at the close of the Book and giving it a solemn attestation. In xxi. 5 the authenticity of the phrase can hardly be maintained.

2. xix. 10 is in part a doublet of xxii. 8-9. This fact in itself is only of importance when combined with others.

3. xix. 10 is rewritten from xxii. 8-9 by the editor and given a less general meaning. In xxii. 8-9 the angel is a fellow-servant of the prophets and of all Christians. In xix. zo he is a fellow-servant only of the prophets and those endowed with the prophetic spirit 4. If xix. 10 were original, the action of the Seer in xxii. 8-9, in again prostrating himself before the angel, would be incomprehensible. But if xix. 10 is an interpolation, then xxii. 8-9 is intelligible and in its right context at the close of the Book.

5. Trpoo-KvvtJvai avru (10) is not used elsewhere in our author of simple homage or even of a fynjo-Kefo rov dyycxuv (Col. ii. 18), but only of divine worship (see note on vii. n). We should, if this phrase were from our author's hand, have irpoo-Kwfjo-ai avrov. In xxii. 8 no such breach of our author's usage is committed.

The above difficulties are against the direct authorship of the Seer. The most natural hypothesis as to their insertion Jbere is x that they were inserted by the disciple who edited thewhole, work, who, though he repeats some clauses from John's own hand, supplements them with others from his own. This hypothesis would explain the misuse of the phrase Trpoa-Kwrja-ai avru in this context, and the addition of the final clause jj yap fjmprvpia It)rov icrriv TO irvcvfui-riys irpo iretas. For this clause gives the preceding one, TWV CXOVTW rrjv paptvpiav Iiyo-ov, a new meaning. In itself the latter means the whole body of believers generally, but when the last clause of 10 is added it means the limited body of Christian prophets. By this gloss the exact parallelism of xix. 9-10 with xxii. 8-9 is destroyed, for there the angel represents himself as the servant of the prophets and the whole Christian community.

9. Kat X yci u. oi rpdtyoy Mcutdpioi ot els TO Sciirroi TOO ydpou TOO dpkloO KCKXTIfuPOl.

This beatitude is the fourth of our author's seven beatitudes. But there is a difficulty in KCfcxqpcvoi; for throughout the Millennial Reign all men alike are "called" to share in the kingdom: cf. xiv. 7, xv. 4, xxii. 17. There is no blessedness in being called (cf. Luke xiv. 24, ovscls. T. KCKXiyAeywv ycucrcrai iov rov Sctnrov), unless a man accepts the call and is found faithful is " chosen " XCKTOS and found faithful Trurros (cf. xvii. 14). The words of our Lord can hardly have been unknown to our Seer; iroxXoi yap cio-iv icxirot, oaiyoi c ctcxckroi (Matt xx. 16, xxii. 14). But KCfcxqxlyot has not this technical meaning here, but simply that of " invited." Here, as in Matt xxii. 2 sq., the guests and the Bride are one and the same. But, though the guests or the faithful might (as Israel in the O. T. in relation to Yahweh) be rightly designated the Bride, as, for example, in xxi. 9 (cf. Eph. v. 27), at the beginning of the Millennial Kingdom, since the words Bridegroom and Bride symbolize the close relation between Christ and the Church at all times, yet the realization of the things so symbolized is always partial and imperfect till the number of the saints is complete. Hence not till then has the time come for the Wedding Feast and for the Bride to become the Wife of the Lamb. It is to this feast, therefore, that the faithful are "invited"; and all such as are then invited naturally accept, for they are all saints. So the writer of 4 Ezra ii. 38-41 rightly connects the Marriage Supper and the completion of the roll of the saints: " Videte numerum signatorum in convivio Domini. VOL. n. 9

Qui se de umbra saeculi transtulerunt, splendidas tunicas a Domino acceperunt. Recipe, Sion, numerum tuum. Filiorum tuorum. plenus est numerus. populus tuus, qui vocatus est ab initio." As Dalman (Words of Jesus, 118 sq.) points out, KCJtaijtcvot-= DJBttd: cf. Babba Bathra, 75 b: "those who are invited go up to the Jerusalem of the age to come"; Midr. Tehill. i4 7, where Jacob is "invited to the heavenly banquet" (rntyd!???) With the beatitude in our text cf. fta aptos OOTIS aycrcu aprov cv rfj Wiaeip rov Qtov (Luke xiv. 15).

K fc Tj Kou Koactv always means " to name " in our author except here and in xvii. 14, where the meaning our author attaches to K rjroi is seen from its context: ica roi u e ca Jcrol got vurrol Here these three epithets refer to the same persons.

ootot ot Xrfyoi 01 dxijoiral TOO Oeou clvlv. See i in the note on 9 b-io.

10. lircra cpirpooroc? TUV iroswy aurou: cf. xxii. 8. nwretv followed immediately by such phrases as irpos r. irosat, i. 17, cvam-to?, iv. 10, v. 8, vii. n, cvi ra irpora7ra, xi. 16, is used of the divine worship of God or the Lamb. Hence in cuwa Zpxrpoo-Otv r. irosuv avrov the same worship seems implied. It is strange that the phrase vpocrkvveiv Zfjurpotrbev is used simply of homage. See note on xxii. 8.

irfmxrkUKT)orai aurw. On this usage (contrary to that of our author) see 5 in the note on 9 b-io and vii. n note.

opo fi. dscx oik orou. See xxii. 9, where these words occur in their right context.

TUP IXVTWV iv fjiaprupiap "itjaou. This phrase is found already in xii. 17. It is certainly in the phraseology of our author. Cf. vi. 9, T V fmLprvpiav fy cl oi, and i. 2, 9, xx. 4, where we have the phrase fj naprvpia I o-ov. In TTV paprvpiav Irjo-ov the question arises whether we have in Iro-oi) the subjective or objective genitive, i. e. the testimony borne by Jesus, or the testimony which men bear to Jesus. The former, according to i. 2, xii. 17, means the sum of the revelation made by him, and should naturally be the meaning of the phrase here. But the words that follow, 17 yap xaprvpta Irjcrov rx, require us to make them mean "the witness to Jesus." Hence it follows that the yap is here to be taken in an explanatory sense: "now the witness to Jesus is the spirit of prophecy." Thus the angel declares that he is the fellow-servant of John, and of those who share with him the prophetic spirit. This is not the meaning of the parallel passage in xxii. 10.

There is, however, the possibility that 17 yap fuiprvpia. may have been a marginal gloss on rjv liprov, which was subsequently incorporated in the text. It certainly comes in very awkwardly after ru 0ecp It should have preceded it If this clause was a gloss, then the words crwsouxos rov ctu KCU row d8cx av. Irjaov and XXll 9 would be practically equivalent in meaning. Even so, many of the objections to the originality of xix. 9 b-io still remain.

11-81. Cf. xiv. 14, 18-20, and xvi. 13-16 for proleptic accounts of this destruction of the kings and the nations by Christ and His angels. See note on 14. 11-21 deals with the victory of Christ and His angels over the Beast, the False Prophet, and the kings of the earth. With this victory of the Messiah cf. i Enoch Ixii. 2; 2 Bar. xxxix.-xl.,

Ixxii.; 4 Ezra xii. 32, xiil 38. This destruction of the remaining active foes of the Messianic Kingdom comes in here of necessity after that judgment has been executed on Rome and before the inauguration of the Millennial reign. This corresponds to the judgment of the Sword at the beginning of the Messianic Kingdom in i Enoch 1. 2, xc. 19, xci. 12, xcv. 7, xcvi. i, xcviii. 12. Though the destruction of the Parthian kings is foretold proleptically in xvii. 14, it is nowhere subsequently described.

11. ctoK rbv oupavoy i vtwyn. ov: cf. Ezek. i. I, KOLL avctpx rov 01 ovpavoii 2 Bar. xxn. i; 3 Mace. vi. 18; Matt. iii. 16; John i. 51, o ft(roc TOV ovpavov avttayora.

As we learn from what follows, it is only the nations that are hostile to Christ that are to be destroyed. For the attitude of Judaism to the Gentiles in the O. T. and Apocryphal and Apocalyptic literature, see my Eschatology, 165, 246, 296, 297, 332, 361, also Sibyll. Or. iii. 740; Tob. xiii. n, xiv. 6 sq.; Test. XII. Patr. (see Index, p. 242, in my edition), and Volz, Judiscke Eschatologie, 322-325.

ZTTTTOS Xeunos nal 6 Kaovfficros Iw auroy: repeated from vi. 2, but the two riders are quite distinct. Here there is no question as to the personality of the present Rider. He is the Messiah "the Word of God." The very epithets that are applied to Him have occurred before in the same connection: cf. iii. 14, oioprv? 6 iriotos KOL dai?0ivos. See also i. 5, iii. 7. This same combination of epithets is used by Chnst (the Logos) in xxii. 6, ovrot oi Adyoi TTwnroi ical dxijvoi. For this combination of epithets cf. also 3 Mace. ii. n. The Messiah as a man of war appears in Pss Sol. xvii. 23-27; Philo, De Praem. et Poena y 16, arparapx v KOL iroaextuv 0vr). cipokrcrat.

iv Bikcuooufty Kpirci icai itoxcjici. This description of the righteousness of the Messiah is brought forward very distinctively in Isa. xi. 3 sq.: " He shall not judge after the sight of his eyes. 4. but with righteousness shall he judge (p wa DBKl) the poor, and reprove with equity the meek of the earth. 5. And righteousness shall be the girdle of his loins and faithfulness the girdle of his reins." In i Enoch he is designated as " the Righteous One"

(xxxviii. 2), "the Righteous and Elect One" (liii. 6), "the Elect One of righteousness and faith " (xxxix. 6). Cf. also Pss. Sol. xvil 31, Kptvtl. cflin; iv o-o i Stjcatocrunys avrov: also in 35 he is described as a 0ocriacvs Sucaios icai 5a ro? wro Otov: cf. also 36, 41: Ps. xcvl 13; Acts xvii. 31.

12. ot te 6 6axpol atari fa +Xft mipfo. Repeated from L 14: cf. ii. 18.

lirl r. Kc+axV 061-08 Siasiffiata woxXd. Here as always, except in xil i, our author uses M r. icc oxiv and not ewi r. jcc oxi??. See note on Introd. to xii., vol. i. p. 300 sq. As King of kings (16) the Messiah wears many diadems. The Dragon (xil 3) and the Beast (xiii. i) wear respectively seven and ten. According to z Mace. xi. 13, Ptolemy wore two diadems on entering Antioch one for Egypt and one for Asia.

19 C. fyttf oropa ycypapfllfop o odels oftcr ci i9) adrfc. Though the diction is Johannine (on 1 V y y oa f t A t vov c l6 and with ft ovscts olsev cf. ii. 17) this clause appears to be inter-polated. The objections are three. First, there is a break in the thought. We should not expect a reference to the name here in the midst of a description of the person and dress. Moreover, the statement that no one knows His name save Himself is flatly contradicted in the next verse (i3 b), where the words icai K K Tjrai TO ovopja avrov O Acfyos rov Ocov cannot be explained away (see note in loc.). Finally, by the omission of this clause the parallelism is restored.

19. ol Be Waxpol aftrou 6s +X6 irupi, Kal irl-rt v Ke ax9 K adrou BiabVjfata 13. icai ircpipepxirj Kos Ifidrto c 3a JL K

Kal K K v)Tai TO Sropa a rou O A5yos TOU 6cou. The interpolated line may have originated in a marginal gloss. We have now to inquire what meaning can be attached to this gloss. Some interpreters have thought the unknown designation to be 6 icuptos, Phil ii. n; others (as Ewald and Volkmar) have taken it to be the tetragrammaton; others a really mysterious name known only to Christ Himself, comparing ii. 17, 5vopa KO. I. VOV yeypaAucyoy ft oftsci? otSev ct fj j 6 Aai avav, and iii. 12. As regards this last interpretation scholars are again divided. Swete is of opinion that all created beings are excluded from the knowledge of this name. Alford thinks that the knowledge of this name is withheld till the final and complete union of Christ and His Church. In favour of this view we might compare Asc. Isa. ix. 5: "This is. the Lord Christ, who will be called Jesus in the world, but His name thou canst not hear till thou hast ascended out of thy body." Others, as Bousset, that this knowledge is withheld because of the power that attaches to such knowledge. The Messiah alone has a name which carries with it power over heaven and earthy and as no one knows this name but Him, so He is the sole possessor of the power bound up with the name. This last interpretation belongs undoubtedly to the reign of magic, and is found among the Gnostics. This idea underlies Gen. xxxii. 29 and Judg. xiii. 17 sq. It was a very widespread idea among many ancient nations that the man who knew the name of a god or a demon possessed certain powers over him. Hence the name was concealed: cf. Heit-miiller, Im Namen Jesu, 162 sqq.; Giesebrecht, Gottesname, 23, 45, 100 (the last reference is from Gunkel's Genesis, p. 362; Jevons, Introd. Hist. Religion, p. 361).

6 odscls rrx.: cf. ii. 17, Hi. 12.

18. Kal irefhpepxf) ilfos ipd-nof Pcpappfrop azpari. This clause has created no little difficulty. But, if we hold fast to the following facts, the difficulty can be surmounted. The first is that in the leader of the heavenly hosts we have to do not with the Slain One, but the Slayer. The Word of God has come to execute divine judgment. Hence the idea that the blood on His Vesture is His own (cf. L 5, v. 9, vii. 14, xii. n) cannot be entertained. When our author wishes to express a thought of this nature, he speaks of the dpvtov. d co-cxxyficvov (v. 6). Now this being so, how are we to explain the iuumo? fcfaxicw aturn? In whose blood is the vesture of the Divine Warrior dipped? If it is not His Own, no more is it that of the kings of the earth and their armies (15, 18); for the judgment of the sword as regards these has not yet begun, and the garments of the heavenly armies are still white and pure (14). A comparison with Isa. Ixiii. 1-3 which passage is in the mind of our author confirms this conclusion: " Who is this that cometh from Edom, with red garments from Bozrah?. 2. Wherefore art thou red in thine apparel, and thy garments like him that treadeth in the winefat? 3. I have trodden the winepress alone. yea, I trod them in my anger. and their lifeblood is sprinkled upon my garments." Here the redness of the garments is due to the blood of those who have already been slain, exactly as in our text Since, therefore, the redness of the vesture in 13 is not due to the warfare in 11-21, there remains only one other possible explanation, and this is that the blood on His vesture is that of the Parthian kings and their armies, whom He had already

destroyed, and whose destruction had already been pro-leptically prophesied in xvii. 14. In this strife He was supported by the glorified martyrs (ol ACT avrov K ijrol al fcxcfcrot icrx.).

Ifidrtok pcpapjupor azfum. These words are freely based on Isa. Ixiii. 3, Hn V DTOO n (= "and their blood is sprinkled on my garments 11). Here fcfappcrov (AQ, etc.) is to be accepted and not ptpavrwrAevov, Ippaiwov, or the other variants from buvco and pavri ci; for, whereas both these latter verbs are used in the LXX to render n?3 (the Hebrew verb in Isa. Ixiii. 3), and whereas Aquila and Symmachus do render it by pavrtfu in Isa. Ixiii. 3, but no translator ever renders it by fcwrrco, it follows that, though there were possible grounds for changing ? c3a J itcvoj into IppaAAcpov, there were none for changing cppa.icw into P ftafifjltvov from the standpoint of Isa. Ixiii. 3, whence the idea was derived. Our author thus deals freely with Isa. Ixiii 3. That such a free reproduction was not unknown in Judaism we might infer from the late Palestinian Targum on Gen. xlix. n, which recounts the victory of the Messiah over His enemies: " How beauteous is the king Messiah, who is about to arise from the house of Judah. He hath bound his loins and gone forth to war against those that hate him: kings and princes shall be slain: he will make red the rivers with the blood of their slain. his garments will be dipped in blood (nb1 n pjyiyo TO3). 11 teal K t Tai TO oyopa aftrou O Ayos TOO 0cou. This line has been taken by Volter, Spitta, Hilgenfeld, Bousset, and others to be the addition of a scribe or reviser. Now it is manifest that either 12 (fyw OVOJM. o ovsct? otSci icrx.) or the present clause must be of this nature. But, whereas we found that 12 was open to serious objections on various contextual grounds, no objection of such a nature can be brought against the present clause, which accordingly comes from the hand of our author. We have here another of the numerous instances of community of diction between the Apocalypse and the Fourth Gospel, in many of which there is no community of meaning. For the Logos here is a Warrior, and our text reminds us of Wisd. xviii. 4-25, especially of xviii. 15, 6 TravrosiwAos a-ov Aoyoe av ovpavaw CK Opovw patrtxeudV diroroxo? Troaeuoriys ets ACOW TTS Ac0pias jj aro yi s i os 6 v TTJV awirokpirov cirtrayiv crov (frcpw. We might compare also the later Jewish conception, "i NO and 6 Xoyos TOU 0 ou in Heb. iv. 12. Although the ideas underlying the words are different, in the latter passage this word is said to be "sharper than any two-edged sword."

14. teal ri otpatcojxata KT. To 14 conjoined with i6 b we have remarkable parallels in xvii. 14, but there the enemies of the Lamb are the Parthian kings, who are also referred to in xvi. 12. Here we have a conflict on a larger scale, as in xiv. 14, 18-20, xvi. 13-16. See notes on xiv. 14, 18-20, xvi. 12-16, xvii. 14.

A study of the chief passages (ii. 26-27, xiv. 14, 18-20, xvi. 12-16, xvii. 14, xviii., xix. 11-21) dealing with the destruction of the world powers helps us to understand the expectations of the Seer as to (a) the order in which the world powers were to be destroyed before the Millennium, and (b) the nature of the heavenly armies which destroyed these powers.

(a) The destruction of Rome was to come first, next that of the Parthians, and finally that of the remaining hostile powers. In xiv. 8-11 the destruction of Rome is foretold, followed immediately (for xiv. 12-13 belongs after xiii. 15 or 18) by that of the hostile nations, xiv. 14, 18-20. The same sequence of events is found in xviii. (the destruction of Rome) and xix. 11-21 (that of the hostile nations). But the sequence of events can be determined more definitely. Thus in xvi. 12 the forces led by the Parthian kings are clearly distinguished from those of the remaining hostile nations in xvi. 13-16; and that these two divisions of the hostile heathen world, which survived the destruction of Rome, were to be separately destroyed, we infer from xvii. 14, according to which, immediately after the destruction of Rome, Christ and His armies would destroy its destroyers, i. e. the Parthians.

(b) The heavenly armies were to be composed of angels and (in certain cases if not in alt) of the glorified martyrs. The armies of the Word of God are described in xix. 14 (TO. orparevuara ra c? nj ovpavu. e wnrots Xcwcot?). In xiv. 14,18-20 the presence of these heavenly horsemen is presupposed in xiv. 20 (axpt TV Xoaivwi r. (Wow). So far as these passages go, we should conclude that the heavenly armies were composed of angels only. But this is not so. Quite clearly in xvii. 14 it is stated that the armies of the Lamb will be " the called and elect and faithful," a description which cannot be applied to angels. Now since this war of the Lamb on the Parthians is subsequent to the destruction of Rome, and therefore to the universal martyrdom of the faithful, it follows that this army is composed of the glorified martyrs, who had come down from heaven with Christ for that purpose. That they should share in this task we have already learnt from ii. 27, where of the individual martyr (6 vucaw) it is stated irotfiaici avrovs v paJp rt8i? p, the very words, which in xix. 15 are used of Christ Himself. That the martyrs take part in the judgment of all the hostile nations cannot be affirmed in so many words, though the comparison of irotxavci jcrx. in both ii. 27 and xix. 15 points probably to this conclusion. Moreover, the comparison of xvii. 14 (where Christ is called Kvpios jcvpiw icai feo-iaev? facrtacw, and His army is composed of glorified martyrs) and of xix. 14 where His followers are the armies of heaven and His name isfao-txcvs fturiaew. jcvpio? Kvpiw (i6 b), may point in the same direction.

Some of the chief expectations of our Seer relative to the judgment of the hostile nations may be briefly summarized as follows.

The Parthian kings are referred to in xvi. 12, xvii. 12-13, T 7 16, and their destruction by the Lamb and the glorified martyis in xvii. 14-. The other hostile kings of the world are mentioned: their gathering to Armageddon in xvi. 13-16, and their destruction by One like a son of man, xiv. 14, 18-20, by the Word of God with the armies of heaven in xix. 11-21. In these last two passages the Divine Leader is said to tread the winepress of the wiath of God (xiv. 19, xix. 15) Finally, at the close of the Millennial Kingdom there is the destruction of the unrepentant nations by fire sent down from heaven, xx. 7-10.

For the idea of armies in heaven cf. Test. Levi in. 3; 2 Enoch xvii.; 2 Esdr. xix. 6, crot irpoo-Kwovcriv al orparctdi TWV ovpavctv (where the armies are the stars); Matt xxvi. 53.

The heavenly armies, which are not definitely mentioned in the parallel account (xiv. 14, 18-20) but are implied in the words axpi raw x uv v 2Wui, have descended with Christ from heaven. In ii. 27 (see note), xvii. 14 (see notes) they appear to be the faithful: in ii. 27 the foes they destroy are the hostile nations generally: in xvii. 14 the Parthian kings.

Befcuji oi u(1 OK Xeuicov. For the phrase cf. i. 13, xv. 6.

15. In i5 abc are combined thoughts and words which are drawn from Isa. xi. 4 and Ps. ii. 9. But this combination is already found in Pss. Sol.

xvii. 26. CKrpiifai, VTT prjfav av ajlaprw tt)v os (Tfccui; iccpaACU)?, v pa?8a (risipa oiwrpurat irarrav V7rorrariv avrtuv 27. oxotfpcocrcu. tiovrj trapdvofla v Xdyu orojiaros avrov.

39. irar ci yap yfjv TW Xoya rov otOiaro? avrov.

nal IK TOU atopa-ros aurou Kiropcucrai pop aia 6 cia: cf. i. 16, ii. 12.

Iva iv afirfj irarc ra c6mr). From Isa. xi. 4, KOI Trard ct yr Tp Xoyu) rov OTOACLTOS avrov, jcat v Trvcvxari 8ta c Xccov diicxc? da-cjs, cf. Pss. Sol. xvii. 26-27, 39 (quoted above). Wisd. xviii. 22, ivlKTjo-f. rov QX OV OVK Itr vi rov o ofiaro ov 6VXv cvcpycta daXa Xdyp rov Koxa ovra vtrcrav: i Enoch Ixii. 2, "The word of his mouth slays all the sinners." All these passages imply that the sword that proceeds out of the mouth of the Messiah is simply a figure for forensic or judicial condemnation.

it a! aoros mufaapci aurous iv f dps aieTjp: cf. ii. 27 (see note), xii. 5. From Ps. ii. 9. The avros in this and the next clause is emphatic. Neither here nor in ii. 27, xii. 5 has iroi-fuuvcik a favourable meaning.

In these three passages it connotes punishment and destruction. Contrast, on the other hand, its meaning in vii. 17. See note on ii. 27. Hence render "break them with an iron rod. 1 ical auros irarci T H XIJKOK mx. Here, though accompanied by hosts of angelic warriors, the action of the Messiah alone is dwelt upon, just as in xiv. 19 sq. and in similar words. Only here and in xiv. 19-20 is the Xippos of divine judgment spoken of in our author. The two ideas of the winepress (xiv. 19) and the cup of wrath (xiv. 10) are here combined, and mean that from the winepress trodden by Christ flows the wine of the wrath of God, of which his enemies are to be made to drink. It is a case of mixed metaphors.

16. Im TO tjubrioi KU Ivl TOK pipo? aurou KT. Of this text there is no satisfactory explanation. Diisterdieck, B. Weiss, and Holtzmann think that the title is inscribed on the girdle; Swete, that " it is displayed on His habit where it falls over the thigh "; Grotius imagines a sword on the hilt of which the name was inscribed. Wellhausen, recognizing the unintelligibleness of the text, proposes l-mrov instead of ip. ari. ov and makes the avrov refer to the Mnrov. Horses were branded on the thigh amongst the Greeks: see Wetstein in loc. But the idea of such an inscription on a horse cannot be entertained. If, therefore, we are to gain any satisfactory meaning here, we can only do so by following our chief Uncial A, Cassiodorus, and some Ethiop. MSS, which omit the words I have bracketed above. If A is right, the chief Synac Version (s 1) would probably be the first stage in the interpolation of the text; for s 1 here places the two phrases rl TO iitttwv aurov and ciri T. firjpov avrov side by side without the conneuing cat. Thus the first phrase would appear to have originated in a marginal gloss owing to 13 (ircu? e? A. i;Acio Ipanov ra.). The final stage in the corruption of the text is that which all the remaining authorities attest. At this stage the first avrov is omitted and the cat inserted.

Our text now runs rl r. pypov avrov. For the occasional appearance of names and inscriptions on the thighs of statues we have evidence in Greek and Roman authors (see Wetstein from whom these quotations are derived). Thus in Cicero, Verr. iv. 43, we find: " Signum Apollinis pulcherrimum, cujus in femore literulis minutis argenteis nomen Myronis erat inscriptum." Also in Pausanias, Eliac. extr., TO dva ia. Avfyos cucwv. cacyctov Sc r avro ycypaiieiov 6ri TOV prjpov: "Justinus (4 cent. A. D.?), xv. 4, 5: Figura anchorae, quae in femore Seleuci nata cum ipso parvulo fuit. 9. Originis ejus argumentum etiam in posteris mansit, siquidem filii nepotesque ejus anchoram in femore veluti notam generis naturalem habuere."

The Seer sees in the vision the Divine Warrior and His heavenly horsemen not halting but sweeping downward from heaven and onward against the serried armies of the Beast, False Prophet, and the kings of the earth, and, as they thunder along, their garments stream behind them, and so on the thigh of the Leader is disclosed the name: " King of kings and Lord of lords."

0aaixcfc fwixfoy nrx. See note on xvii. 14.

17-91. An angelic summons to all the birds of prey to hasten to the scene of slaughter of all the mighty of the earth. The overthrow and final doom of the Beast and the False Prophet.

17. w (cf. viii. 13) dyycxop iorura iv T Xu. What was the original idea underlying this phrase is unknown. It is generally explained that the angel took this central position in mid heaven in order to deliver from thence his message of victory and his summons to the birds of prey.

KCU ftcpascp JW TJ pcyrfxj). See note on xiv. 15.

Xlyw iracri TOIS ftpploi? TOIS irctOfuifus lv p, caoupamijp, ati (cf. viii. 13, xiv. 6) ACUTC owdxo 1) els T SCIITKOK. roc 0cou. 18. fra jh yy)Te adpicas ftaaixlup. ical orrfpicas la upcjv. This passage is clearly based on Ezek. xxxix. 17, where the LXX reads ctirov wavrl 6pvcu irercivwv.)vol Otft icai cp ecrdc. CTTI TTJV Ovcrtav fiov. KU aycr c. 18. icpca yiyttiTwv. KCU atma dp ovrui. 2O. xal. ITTTTOV KCU avaBdrtjv. It is obvious, however, that our author is giving an independent rendering of the Hebrew: observe Scirre auvax Tc (ibDKPl 1 3) with (r KOI cpxco-fc, and tor vpoiv in our text with-ytyttvrwv, and it K. TWV Ka xevwv TT avrwv with ITHTOV Kal avapdtvjv in Ezek. xxxix. 20.

Our author here borrows his imagery from the slaughter wrought by God in Ezek. xxxix., and yet the final overthrow of Gog and Magog in our author is adjourned to the close of the Millennial reign in our author.

Td Sctiryoy T)Uya TOO 0cou. See Gressmann, Ursprung der Isratlit. Jud. Eschatologie, 136-141.

18. TUP KaorjfuKUK ir a6rwp. Here the reading avrwv (PQ min fere oxn11) is to be followed. A with two cursives and K read respectively avrovs and avrois which are both corrupt. Cf. 19, 21. Xcuolpwf TC KCU Souxup. See note on xiii. 16. p. titpwk Kal pcydxuk. See note on xiii. 16.

19-21. The Beast, the False Prophet, and the kings of the earth overthrown and cast into the lake of fire.

19. T OTjpiop i. e. Nero-antichrist. See xi. 7 (note), xiii. 3 (note on various stages of the Neronic myth).

TOUS poaixeis TTJS yrjs: cf. xiv. 14, 18-20 (though not here specifically mentioned), xvi. 14 (note), xvii. 2,18, xviii. 3. These are to be carefully distinguished from the Parthian kings, xvi. 12, xvii. 12-13, X 7i I who are destroyed by the Lamb (and the glorified martyrs). See also note on 14 above.

T crrpatcisjjtata aurwk. For avrov A and a few cursives read autow. This is perhaps right. Though they are the subjects of the kings, they are the armies of the Beast.

aukTjyjum iroujaai T? irlxcjiop. For the diction cf. xvi. 14, 16, xx, 8.

TOU irrpcrrcifpatos aurou. Though the heavenly army is described in the plural as orparcviara, it is here very significantly described as a single host While the opposing hosts of evil are moved by a variety of conflicting aims, the heavenly host is actuated by one only.

SO. With the Beast and the False Prophet we might compare Ahnman and Azi-Dahaka in the Zend religion, which influenced Judaism from the East. Cf. De la Saussaye, Lehrb. d. Rcligions-gcschichte, ii. 206 (ii. 226 in 3rd ed.): "Zuletzt bleibt noch der Kampf zwischen himmlischen und hollischen Geistern iibrig. Alle Ameshas Spentas ringen da mit ihren teuflischen Gegen-geschopfen und vernichten sie ganzlich: Ahriman selbst und die Schlange Azhi zu bandigen, wird die Sache Mazda's und Sraosha's sein. Als Pnester erheben sich die beiden Cotter, mit Gebet und Gebetschnur liberwaltigen sie die Bosen und sturzen sie und ihr Versteck in den gluhenden Strom. Dann ist die Weu vollkommen rein, das Universum nur von Mazda's Wesen erfullt, und alles, was lebt, geht in die Unsterblichkeit und himmlische Vollkommenheit ein (Bahman Yasht, 43; Bundehesh, 30)." See also Bbklen, Die Verwandschaft d. jud.-chnstichen mit der parsischen Eschatologie, 127 sqq.

tmtooi). The Attic form of this verb is irufro, but in late Attic 7na o is also found. The classical meaning was to press, weigh down, stifle, etc. But its later meaning, as here, is to seize, lay hold of. Triafw, which occurs only here in our author, is a favourite word in the Fourth Gospel, being found there eight times and only four times throughout the rest of the N. T. (one of these being in Luke vi. 38, where it retains the ancient classical form and meaning).

6 i u8oirpoftJTT)s. See xiii. n sqq. notes, xvi. 13, xx. 10. The False Prophet represented the priesthood of the Imperial cult, which practised all kinds of magic and imposture to beguile men to worship the Beast.

irx nr)rci rods Xafmrras TO xdpay a KT. Only those who had received this mark were an easy prey to the False Prophet. On the TO x payxa see note on xiii. 16: cf. xiv. g sqq., xvi. 2 (note), xx. 4.

irpooxupoufras T K elicova auroc. Though weakly attested 28, 39), this seems to be the right reading: see note on vii. n. Possibly the dative is right. In that case the text would mean that divine worship was actually offered to the image.

TV Xiim)? TOU Trope's: cf. xx. 10, xxi. 8. On this final abode of punishment for Satan, the Beast, the False Prophet, and wicked men, see note on ix. i.

T? IS Kaiofunfp lv Ocup. The genitive here can only be explained as a slip on the part of the writer. Contrast xxl 8 rjj Xlfivy rjj

UOACIT?.- On iv 0c i in this conjunction cf. xiv. 10, xx. 10, xxi. 8.

91. ol Xoiirol dirckrdi Tjirair rrx., . the kings of the earth and their armies. These kings and their armies had been affected by the Caesar-worship: cf. xiv. 9 sq. They were not, like the Beast and the False Prophet, cast forthwith into Gehenna. Their physical life was destroyed by the sword, i. e. by the sword of the Word of God (cf.

ver. 15), and their spirits no doubt consigned tc Hades. In the judgment all the dead are raised (xx. 12), and then death and Hades and all the wicked are cast into the lake of fire (xx. 14-15). In the Test, of Hezekiah a work incorporated in the Ascension of Isaiah, i. e. iii. i3 b-iv. 18, and written before 100 A. D. a different sequence is anticipated: Asc. Isa. iv. 14, "The Lord will come with His angels and with the armies of the holy ones from the seventh heaven. and He will drag Beliar (i. e. the Antichrist) into Gehenna and also his armies"

m rra r oprca x P T 1 I (ra i f KT Cf. 17 sq.; also i Enoch xlvl 4-6.

CHAPTER XX. 1-3. INTRODUCTION.

i. Contents. Now that Rome has fallen (xviii.), the hostile nations been destroyed, and the two Beasts cast into the lake of fire (xix. 19-20), there remains no obstacle to the manifestation of the kingdom save the presence of Satan still on earth. Hence to his activities an end is put by his being cast down into the abyss and chained there for 1000 years (xx. 1-3). The destinies of Satan are determined by the chief events in the life of Christ. In xii. Satan's expulsion from heaven is connected with the birth and ascension of Christ. On the earth, as he had only a short time, he raged furiously against Christ's followers, but on Christ's Second Advent and His overthrow of Satan's agents, Satan too is cast down from the earth into the abyss and the Millennial Kingdom established. At the close of this kingdom Satan is loosed from the abyss and finally conquered and cast into the lake of fire, and the new heaven and the new earth appear, wherein is the joint throne of God and the Lamb.

That xx. 1-3 comes from our author's hand there can be no doubt, as the diction and idiom prove.

2. Diction and idiom.

1. ctsok ayycxoi KaropaikOira K TOU ofiparou. The whole clause has already occurred in x. i, xviil i, and the last four words also in iii. 12, xvi 21, xxi. 2, 10.

T K itxiir Ttjs dfliwou: cf. ix. I.

XX. 1-0. DRAGON BOUND FOR IOOO YEARS 14!

9. rd? Sfxlicorra 6 fyi? 6 pxaio. The same words in the same characteristic and anomalous construction have already occurred in xii. 9. us forii Aidffoxot KU 6 Zararos. Cf. i. 9, 6 KoaovACVOS Aiaj3oxo? Kal 6 Saravas.

c8i)rcp autK Cf. ix. 14, cftc cvovs.

8. 2pa H autK cts rf)r apuacroy. For this use of cf. ii. 10, viii. 5, 7, 8, xii. 9, xix. 20, etc.

ftcxcure?: cf lii. 7, 8, xi. 6, xxi. 25. times elsewhere in our author. irdrw: cf. vi. 8. fra irxamjcrg 3ri rd cbmrj: cf. xiii. 14, xii. 9. XP 1 w; w su h a use: cf. 5, vii. 3, xv. 8. rexcaefj: cf. 5, 7, x. 7, xv. i, 8.

3. Order of words. Wholly Semitic.

1-8. The binding of the Dragon in the abyss for 1000 years.

1. Kal etsok. See note on iv. i.

TV itxci? Ti)s 0iwou. See notes on L 18, ix. i. The abyss is regarded only as a temporary abode of punishment. Satan is finally cast into the lake of fire, xx 10.

oxuo-if lacydxT)!. ua. vri? seems to be used here to denote a chain or bond by which the body is bound. In Mark v. 4 and frequently elsewhere it signifies hand fetters as opposed to ircu. See note of Lightfoot on Phil, p. 8.

irl T(V X P a- I 1S h ar d to explain the use of lirf here. The best parallel is to be found in v. i, rl rrjv c tav. ptftxiav. But in this latter case the idea implied is that the book is lying on the palm of the hand. It is perhaps best to regard the present instance as a loose use of evi, which does not admit of any exact explanation. It is practically here equivalent to (cf. i. 1 6 with i. 20), and indeed v is read here by 38 syr. L 2. Another difficult use of fcr but with the dative, occurs in xxii. 16, where, however, the best authorities have iv.

2. rd? Bpdkorra, 6 0 15 6 dpxaios. For a like anacolouthon cf. i. 5. See note on xii. 9 on the identification of the old serpent and the devil. Gunkel on Gen. 8 iii. i maintains that the text there implies that originally the serpent was an evil demon hostile to God and man and possessing a snakelike form. He further points out in support of this view that in 2 Kings xviii. 4 divine worship is offered to a snakelike form by the faithless Israelites, and that heathen gods and demons were frequently so conceived in the ancient world.

ftrjcrci outy x ia fa)- This idea of binding the powers of evil in prison for an undefined period is already found in Isa. xxiv. 2 2, and of their final judgment in xxiv. 23. These powers consist of the host of heaven and the kings of the earth This idea of the angels and the kings of the earth being judged together reappears in i Enoch liii. 4 lw. 5, and the idea of the binding of the fallen angels in a place of temporary punishment till the day of the final judgment is found in i Enoch xviii. 12-16, zix. 1-2, xxi. 1-6, from which the final place of their punishment an abyss of fire is carefully distinguished, x. 13-15, xviii. 11, xxi. 7-10, liv. 6, xc. 24-25. Their leader Azazel is bound in a place by himself (x. 4-5) as a preliminary punishment, but at the final judgment is to be cast into a place of everlasting punishment (x. 6). In nearly all cases the evil spirits are spoken of in i Enoch as being " bound " in a preliminary place of punishment, just as in Isa. xxiv. 22 and in our text.

In the Zend religion the same idea is found. According to the Bundehesh iii. 26 (cf. xiii. 77) the evil serpent Azi-Dahaka was smitten by Thraetaona and fettered in the mountain Dama-vand for 9000 years, S. B. E. iv. 9 (note), 226, 245 sq., v. 234, 397, xviii. no, 201, etc. He was released by Ahriman, S.13. E. v. 233-235, and reigned for 1000 years, v. 150, xxiv. 103, but was slain by Sam or Keresasp, v. 235. After the renovation of the world there would be no Azi-Dahlka, xviii. 118. But, since these Iranic myths belong to various periods before and after the Christian era, there is no ground for tracing any direct connection.

Xixio 2n). Before the year 100 B. C. it was generally believed in Judaism that the Messianic Kingdom would last forever on the present earth. Sometimes the conception was universahstic in character, especially in the greater prophets of the O. T., as Jeremiah, the Second Isaiah, Jonah, Malachi; but in others, as in Ezekiel, Haggai, Zechariah, Joel, it was particularistic. The idea of the everlastmgness of this kingdom on earth persisted, as we have above said, till about 100 B. C. For such it appears to be in i Enoch Ixxxiii.-xc., vi.-xxxvi., but by the date just mentioned the earth had come to be regarded in Judaism as wholly unfit for the manifestation of this kingdom except in a temporary character. The dualism which had begun to affect the religious forecasts of religious thinkers in the 2nd cent. B. C. succeeded in leavening wholly their expectations in the ist. As a consequence of this breach between the things of earth and the things of heaven, the writers of this century were forced to entertain new conceptions of the kingdom. Hence in i Enoch xci.-civ., Pss. Sol. i.-xvi., the Messianic Kingdom is declared to be of temporary duration on the present earth, and the goal of the risen righteous to be not this transitory kingdom, but heaven itself after the final judgment, which from this period forwards was conceived of as taking place not at the beginning, but at the close of the Messianic Kingdom. Thus it is that the Millennium in our text, as in 2 Baruch and 4 Ezra, is really a late and attenuated form of the old Jewish expectation of an eternal Messianic Kingdom on the present earth. For a fuller treat- ment of this question the reader can consult my Eschat-ology pp. 103, 106-108, no sq., 113-116, 219 sq., 223, 248, 250 sq.

We have next to consider the duration of this kingdom. Apparently nowhere in earlier or contemporary literature is the duration of 1000 years assigned to the Messianic Kingdom save here. Its duration is not defined in i Enoch xci.-civ.; Pss. Sol. xi. i sqq.; Sibyll. Or. in. 1-62; Jubilees xxiii. 27-29; Assumption of Moses x. 7; 2 Bar. xxix. 4-xxx. i, xxxix. 7, xl. 3, lxxii. 2-4; 4 Ezra xiii. 32, 36. In 4 Ezra vii. 28 it is definitely said to last 400 years.

3. j3axcy aurok cts r. afiutnrov ical cicxeiarei. On the a? wcros see ix. T, note.

cicxciorci xal iafypdyurev tadw aurou, i. e. closed the abyss and sealed it over him. Our text recalls the Prayer of Manasseh, 2-4, and the two passages are distantly connected, though our Seer has no thought of this passage nor of the myth that it presupposes.

For, whereas it is a literal Satan overcome by an angel that is presupposed in our text, it is a mythological monster that is overcome by God in the Prayer of Manasseh. What was originally a mythological idea concerning the uprising of the Chaos monster (i. e. the sea) against God at the world's beginning, had long ere our Seer's time been transformed into an eschatological expectation, i. e. the rebellion of Satan against God at the world's close, and his being cast into the abyss. The mythological idea is quite clearly set forth in the above-mentioned Prayer of Manasseh: 6 irotijcra? rov ovpavov KOL ri v yfjv rvv iravrl r3 Kocrxa) OLVTOV, 6 Tresijcras rrjv Od a. rcrav TO A. dya rov TrpocrrayAaro? crov, 6 icxcuras rrjv apwov KOI o- payicraAcvos avrrjv TS jo3cp(p KOI v8d a) ovdxart (rov.

irxa cn en ri tonfj. As he had done before: cf. xiii. 14, xvi. 13. See also xii. 9. As these words point to the future, they imply that there would still be heathen nations after the Messianic judgment executed in xix. 19-21. Now that Satan's chief agents, the Beast and the False Prophet, were cast into the lake of fire and Satan himself bound in the abyss, the time for the Millennial reign has arrived and for the evangelization of the surviving heathen nations: see xiv. 7, xv. 4, xxii. 17. The astonishing part in our Seer's forecast is that the preaching of the Gospel during the Millennium will only in part be successful, though the active impersonations of evil have been wholly removed from the earth for this period. The implication is that each man carries in his own bosom the possibilities of his own heaven and his own hell.

4-XXII. THE TEXT INCOHERENT AND SELF-OONTBJLDIOTOBY AS IT STANDS.

4-XXIX. These chapters have hitherto been a constant source of insurmountable difficulty to the exegete. They are full of confusion and contradiction if the text is honestly dealt with. And yet the Apocalypse exhibits, except in a few passages, and especially in chap, xviii., a structural unity and a steady development of thought from the first chapter to the close of xx. 3. Now this is just what we should expect in an Apocalypse which is designed to be a philosophy of history and religion from the standpoint of the author. It was a combination of vision and reflection. Though the book of a prophet did not necessarily show any structural unity or steady development of thought, it was far otherwise with the apocalyptist, in whose writings such characteristics were indispensable. While the ordinary man saw only the outside of things in all their incoherence and isolation, the apocalyptist sought to get behind the surface and penetrate to the essence of events, the spiritual motives and purposes that underlay and gave them their real significance in fact, to lay bare their origin, course, and consummation. It was thus, in short, a Semitic philosophy of religion, and as such it was ever asking Whence? Wherefore? Whither? Apocalyptic, and not prophecy, was the first to grasp the great idea that all history, alike human, cosmological, and spiritual, is a unity a unity following naturally as a corollary of the unity of God preached by the prophets.

I have emphasized these two points structural unity and orderly development of thought to the final consummation of all things as pre-eminently the characteristics of apocalyptic and not of prophecy or of any other form of writing in the Bible. This being so, we are all the more astonished that the three closing chapters of the Apocalypse are all but wholly wanting in these characteristics, and so far from advancing steadily to the consummation that all the preceding chapters postulate exhibit many incoherencies and self-contradictory elements.

To some of these I drew attention in my first edition of the Book of Enoch in 1893, where on p. 45 I wrote as follows: "We have here (i. e. Rev. xxi. i, 2) a new heaven and a new earth, and a New Jerusalem coming down from heaven: yet in xxii. 15 all classes of sinners are said to be without the gates of the city. But if there were a new earth this would be impossible." This is only one of the many difficulties that confront the serious student of these chapters. Now to make the problem before us clear it will be best to deal shortly with a few of the passages which make it impossible for us to accept the text as it stands.

1. In xx. 7-10, after the close of the Millennial Kingdom, Satan is loosed, and the heathen nations (Gog and Magog), which have refused to accept the Christian faith, march against Jerusalem and the camp of the saints, but ar? destroyed by fire from heaven. Satan also is cast finally into the lake of fire and brimstone, to be tormented there for ever and ever. Thus the prime source of evil and his deluded followers (Gog and Magog) are removed finally from the world, and their power to influence the world for evil nadt impossible for ever.

2. In xx. 11-15 the old earth and the old heaven are given over to annihilation. Then the final judgment takes place, and all the dead are judged according to their works, and death and Hades are cast into the lake of fire, together with all those whose names are not found written in the book of life. At this stage we have arrived at the final condemnation and destruction of all evil, together with the destruction of death if self.

3. Now that all evil and death itself are cast into the lake of fire, the new heaven and the new earth come into being, and the New Jerusalem comes down from heaven, and God Himself dwells with men (xxi. 1-4).

is clear from this passage that we have arrived at the closing scene of the great world struggle between good and evil, and that henceforth there can be neither sin, nor crying, nor pain, nor death any more. In fact, there can be no place at all for these in the universe of God the new heaven and the new earth, and the New Jerusalem that cometh down from God to the new earth.

The conclusion just arrived at is inevitable, if there is a steady development in the visions of the Seer. Now since such a development is manifest in chaps, i.-xx. 3, when certain verses and glosses are excised and a few disarrangements of the text set right expecially in xviii we naturally conclude that our author will not lightly fall into contradictions, even of a minor sort, in the last three chapters. But unhappily this is not our experience as we study them; and at last we stand aghast at the hopeless mental confusion which dominates the present structure of these chapters, and are compelled to ask if they can possibly come from his hand, and, in case they do, to ask further, if they have been preserved as they left his hand. But we must first justify the above statement, though we shall adduce here only the main contradictions in these chapters.

i. Inasmuch as according to our text the New Jerusalem does not come down from heaven till Satan is bound for ever in the lake of fire, and all sin and death itself are at an end, and the place of the old world has been taken by a new and glorious

VOL. H. 10 world, wherein there is neither spot nor blemish nor any such thing, how is ft that we are told that, outside the gates of the Holy City which has come down from God to the new earth, there are " the dogs and the sorcerers, and the fornicators, and the murderers, and the idolaters, and every one that loveth and maketh a lie" (xxii. 15)? A greater contradiction in thought and statement is hardly conceivable. But, if this statement were made in connection with the Millennial Kingdom which was to be established before the Final Judgment, everything would be intelligible.

2. Again, since the new earth is inhabited only by the blessed, on whom the second death could have no effect, and since these are all righteous, and God Himself tabernacles among them, how is it that in xxii. 2 the leaves of the tree of life are said to be for the healing of the nations? This statement can have no meaning unless it applies to the period of the Millennial Kingdom. During Christ's reign of 1000 years the surviving nations have still a further period of grace accorded to them. This evangelizing of the nations during this period has already been proclaimed in xiv. 6-7, xv. 4. It is thrice elsewhere referred to in the last two chapters, i. e. xxi. 24, xxii. 14, 17.

3. Only on the supposition that the Millennial Kingdom is still in existence can we explain xxi. 24-27:

"And the nations shall walk by the light thereof: And the kings of the earth do bring their glory into it. And the gates thereof shall not be shut day or night 1

And they shall bring the glory and the honour of the nations into it: And there shall not enter into it anything unclean, or he that maketh an abomination or a lie; But only they which are written in the book of life of the Lamb."

Now from the above contradictions the solution of which is in part already suggested it follows either that (a) a consideiable part of xx.-xxii. is not from the hand of our author, or that, (b) if it is from his hand, it is disarranged.

Now the first solution (a) is that adopted by most of the leading German scholars of the past thirty years. Thus while Volter (Die Offenbarung Johannis, 1904), Weyland (Omverkings-en Cohipilatie-Hypothesen toegepast op de Apocalypse van Johannes 1908), and J. Weiss (Die Offtnb. des Johannis, 1908) assume that xx.-xxii. is derived from three diflerent sources, and Spitta (Die Offenb. des Johannes 1889) finds traces of four authors, 1 A necessary emendation. The corruption in the text arose from the present disorder, and the influence of xxii. 5, "and there shall be no more night where this clause is wholly justifiable.

XX. 4-XXtt. FROM JOHNS HAND BUT IN DISORDER 147

Erbes (Die Offenb. Johannis, 1891) and, on the whole, Bousset (1906), are content with two. Bousset, in fact, regards xx.-xxii. as the work of our author, with the exception of the fragment xxi. 9-xxii. 5.

But, even though for the time being we accepted as a working hypothesis any one of the theories of these scholars based on a plurality of authorship, we have still two insuperable difficulties to face, (a) The first of these is that the more closely we study i.-xx. j, the more convinced we become of the structural unity of these chapters a fact which does not exclude the occasional use and adaptation of sources and the clear and masterly development in thought, working up steadily to a climax. This being so, how is it that xx.-xxii. shows no such orderly development but rather a chaos of conflicting conceptions f (?) But the second difficulty is still greater. The hypotheses of the above scholars, with the partial exception of Bousset, break down hopelessly in the face of the general linguistic unity of xx.-xxii. In fact, these scholars had failed to make a thorough study of the style, vocabulary, and grammar of the Apocalypse. Bousset, it is true, has done much to compensate for the deficiencies of his predecessors in this field, but a deeper study of his materials would have precluded his assuming the existence of xxi. 9-xxii. 5 as an independent source, seeing that it is internally self-contradictory and that yet linguistically it is from the hand of our author. To the conclusion, in fact, that, with the exception of a few verses, chaps. xx.-xxii. are from the same hand to which we owe the bulk of the preceding chapters, a close and prolonged study has slowly but irresistibly brought me. If, then, this is so, we must conclude that the text in xx.-xxii. is disarranged in an astonishing degree and does not at present 'stand in the orderly sequence originally designed by our author.

To what cause, we must now ask, is this almost incredible disorder due? It cannot be accounted for by accidental transpositions of the text in the MSS a phenomenon with which the students of MSS in every ancient language are familiar. For no accident could explain the intolerable confusion of the text in xx. 4-xxii., and apparently the only hypothesis that can account for it is that which a comprehensive study of the facts forced upon me in the beginning of 1914, and this is thai John died either as a martyr or by a natural death, when he had completed i.-xx. 3 of his work, and that the materials for its completion, which were for the most fart ready in a series of independent documents, were put together by a faithful but unintelligent disciple in the order which he thought right.

This hypothesis we shall now proceed to establish by adequate proofs.

1. First of all it is a matter beyond dispute that xxii. 15, xxi. 27, which state that outside the gates of the Heavenly Jerusalem evil in every form exists, but that it can in no wise pass within the gates of the Holy City, prove that the Heavenly Jerusalem here referred to was to descend before the disappearance of the first earth and the first heaven and the final judgment described in xx. 11-15. A kindred expectation is found in 4 Ezra vii. 26-28, where the Heavenly Jerusalem, 1 the Messiah, and those who had been translated to heaven without seeing death, are to be manifested together on the earth for 400 years. The same view appears in the same work in xiii. 32-36. In this latter passage evil in every form exists outside the Heavenly City.

From later Jewish sources we are familiar with the connection of the rebuilt Jerusalem and the temporary reign of the Messiah. The advent of the Messiah determines the hour when the Temple and therefore Jerusalem should be rebuilt (Shemoth rab. c. 31). According to the Targum on Isa. liii. 5 (cf. Bammidbar rab. c. 13) the Messiah Himself was to build it.

From the above facts we conclude that in our author the account of the Heavenly Jerusalem (xxi. 9 xxii. 2, 14-15, 17) should have followed immediately on xx. 3 as the seat of the Messiah's Kingdom.

2. Verses xxi. 24-26, xxii. 2, 14-15, 17 assume that the nations are still upon earth, that the gospel is preached to them afresh from the Heavenly Jerusalem, that they are healed thereby of their spiritual evils, their sins washed away, that they can enter the Heavenly City and eat of the tree of life which was therein. And to this salvation they are bidden of the Spirit and the Heavenly Jerusalem (i. e. the bride, xxii. 17).

Now this expectation is derived from the Old Testament In Zech. xiv. 16 sqq., when the blessed era sets in, the nations are to go up yearly to keep the Feast of Tabernacles at Jerusalem. In Tob. xiv. 6 the conversion of the Gentiles is to synchronize with the rebuilding of Jerusalem in a fashion far transcending all that Seer or prophet had hitherto dreamt of when its gates should be " builded with sapphire and emerald," and all its walls "with precious stones," and its streets "paved with carbuncle and stones of Ophir" (xiii. 16-17). Similarly in i Enoch (161 B. C.) we find it prophesied that the conversion of the surviving Gentiles would follow on the setting up of the Holy City, which was to be done by none other than God Himself. Next, in the Test. XII Patriarchs the conversion of 1 Box, it is true, regards vii. 26, which tells of the manifestation of the Heavenly Jerusalem, as an interpolation; but the evidence of our text and later Judaism supports the connection of the Messiah and the Holy City.

XX. 4-XXIL GROUNDS FOR THIS CONCLUSION 149 the Gentiles is associated with the advent of the Messiah, T. Levi xviii. 9, T. Jud. xxiv. 5, and that of the New Jerusalem in T. Dan v. 12. Like expectations are expressed in the Sibyll. Or. iii. 751-59, 767-95; i Enoch xlviii. 4 (where the Messiah is described as the light of the Gentiles); Pss. Sol. xvii. 27, 32.

Thus in many books in Judaism the hope is entertained, as in our text, that the Gentiles would turn to the worship of the true God, when either the earthly Jerusalem was rebuilt or a Heavenly Jerusalem set up on earth, or when the Messiah established His Kingdom upon the earth. It is true that Judaism associated this expectation with the First Advent of the Messiah; for it looked for no second. But in Christianity it was different. What had not been realized on the First Advent of Christ is, according to many a Christian prophet and Seer, as also to our author, to be realized in a far higher degree when Christ came the second time in glory.

That the conversion of the heathen nations in our text, therefore, was to be accomplished in connection with the Heavenly City, which as the seat of the Millennial Kingdom was to descend on the earth before the Final Judgment, needs no further demonstration.

3. The facts just stated in the preceding paragraph, that the Gentiles shall still be upon the earth on the advent of the Heavenly City, and have a right to enter therein, are already postulated in the earlier chapters of the Apocalypse. Thus in xv. 4 we read in the song sung by the triumphant martyrs before the throne of God

"Who shall not fear, O Lord, And glorify Thy name? For Thou alone art holy; For all the nations shall come And worship before Thee; For Thy righteous acts shall have been made manifest."

Again, in xiv. 6-7 the Seer recounts a vision in which he hears an angel proclaiming the coming evangelization of the nations of the world: 1 " And I saw another angel flying in mid heaven, having an eternal gospel to proclaim unto them that dwell on the earth, and unto every nation and tribe and tongue and people, saying with a great voice, 1 A somewhat analogous expectation is found in I Cor. xv. 23-28, where we have an account of the Messianic Kingdom. This kingdom is heralded by the resurrection of Christ: it is apparently established on Christ's (second) Advent with the risen righteous (23). Then follows the reign of Christ, in the course of which every evil power is overthrown (24 28). Then comes the end (the general resurrection, final judgment, the destruction of the old world and the creation of the new).

Fear God and give Him glory;
For the hour of His judgment is come:
And worship Him that made the heaven and the earth
And the sea and fountains of waters."

Now, according to the present form of the text of the last three chapters of our booh, these prophecies, which definitely foretell the evangelization of the nations of the world and their acceptance of the Gospel preached, remain wholly unfulfilled. In fact, according to the present text, the nations are simply annihilated before the advent of the Heavenly City. On the other hand, it the account of the Heavenly Jerusalem as given in xxi. 9 to xxu. 2, 14-15, 17 is restored immediately after xx. 3, then these prophecies are fulfilled; for the nations, according to this account, walk by the light thereof, and the kings of the earth do bring their glory into it, and yet outside its gates there is still evil of every kind.

4. Again, in xi. 15 we read
"The Kingdom of the world is become the Kingdom of our
Lord and of His Christ, And He shall reign for ever and ever."

These words quite clearly assume that the rule of God and Christ will be extended over the whole world of the nations. But, as the text at present stands, not a single nation is mentioned as being brought beneath its sway, while in the verses (xx. 9-10) that precede the description of the Final Judgment (KX. 11-15) we are led to infer that they are wholly destroyed by fire from heaven. That is one way of establishing authority over the neutral or hostile nations, but it is not God's way. We have only to read chaps, xxi.-xxii., which deal ostensibly with events occurring only after the absolute destruction of all the nations and of the first heaven and the first earth, when we discover the nations, that had presumably passed out of existence, going up in pilgrimage to the Heavenly Jerusalem, each under its own king, passing within its blessed portals, bringing their glory and honour into it, receiving spiritual healing in the Holy City, and assimilating the divine truths that make them heirs to immortality, that is, eating of the tree of life. That all the nations do not avail themselves of these privileges is plainly asserted in the text; for outside the gates are sorcerers and whoremongers and idolaters and whosoever loveth and maketh a lie.

On this ground again we must transpose the description of the Holy City before the Final Judgment, and regard it as the seat of the Millennial Kingdom.

5. The city that is spiritually designated Sodom and Egypt (xl 8) cannot be called " the beloved city " as in xx. 9, nor can

XX. 4-XXII. GROUNDS FOR THIS CONCLUSION 15!

it become the seat of the Millennial Kingdom. Much less can the ruins of such a polluted city become the abode of Christ and of the risen martyrs come down from heaven to reign with Him for a thousand years.

6. Again, as we study xxi.-xxii. we discover that there are in reality two descriptions of the Heavenly City, and not one, as has hitherto been universally assumed. The Seer has two distinct visions, and they deal not with one and the same city, but with two quite distinct cities. The first (xxi. 9 to xxii. 2, 14-15, 17) presupposes the existence of the present earth. Thus the Seer tells how the angel, that had showed him the destruction of the great world-capital Rome in xvii., came again to him and carried him off to a great high mountain to show him the Heavenly City that was to take the place of Rome as the metropolis of the world. The very first words of the vision presuppose the coexistence of the Heavenly Jerusalem and the present earth. This city the Seer beheld coming down from heaven to earth (i. e. the first heaven and the first earth). It becomes the great spiritual centre of the world. The nations flock up to it from every side to share in its spiritual blessings, its gates are open day and night, and yet none of the evil individuals or nations that are without may enter into it (xxi. 24-27).

It is manifest that since sin, and therefore death, prevail outside the gates of the Heavenly City, the present order of things still prevails, the first heaven and the first earth are still in being.

But there is another Heavenly City (xxi. 1-4, xxii. 3-5) described by our author, quite distinct from that just dealt with. The angel in xxi. 9 has apparently had no direct part in mediating this new vision. The vision, just as those in xx. 1-3, 11-15, xxi. i, seems to be independent of any angelic agency. With regard to this Heavenly City there can be no question a to the hour of its manifestation. The very first words of the text imply that the vision of the Seer has outleapt the bounds oi time, when the former heaven and earth have vanished for ever. This second Heavenly City does not appear till the first heaven and the first earth have vanished and their place been taken by the new heaven and the new earth. Hence as distinguished from the first Heavenly City, it is designated " new," . icoun, that is, of a new sort or quality as distinct from the first, just as the second heaven and the second earth are themselves described as " new " (KCUVOS and iccun?). This epithet is never applied to the Heavenly City described at such length in xxi. 9-xxii. 2, 14-15, 17. Sin, of course, no longer exists in this new world. Hence there is no more crying, nor mourning, nor pain, nor curse, nor death (xxi. 4 abc, xxii. 3), though round about the first Heavenly City close even to its very gates sin in every form and death did exist, and even within its stately walls sorrow for sin and repentance were never absent, for the nations of the earth flocked to it from every side to be healed of their spiritual ills and infirmities (xxi. 24-26, xxii. 2).

7. It is finally to be observed that, since the earthly Jerusalem was in ruins, and never in the opinion of the Seer to be rebuilt, a new city was of necessity to take its place as the seat of Christ's Kingdom and the abode of the blessed martyrs, who were to come down from heaven to reign for a thousand years with Him. Since this new city was to be the abode of Christ on His Second Advent from heaven, and of the martyrs coming down from heaven with Him in their glorified bodies, it follows that the new city must be from heaven also, if it was to be a fit abode for its inhabitants from heaven. Even as early as 161 B. C. (as we have already mentioned above), we have a like expectation in i Enoch xc. 28-38, where it is said in the vision that God Himself set up the New Jerusalem, to be the abode of the Messiah and the transformed and glorified Israel. A like expectation is attested in a work almost contemporary with our author, i. e. 4 Ezra, as we have already shown.

8. To the revision of John's literary executor we may probably ascribe the non-Johannine combinations r. Kayxevov lif avrov in xx. n, where, though only A and some cursives attest this reading, they are to be followed; 6 jcatf cyos cvi r. Gpovov in xxi. 5, where, since every MS is wrong, the error must go back to the editor; row ircirca, KigrA iiv. KCU oirtvc? 0 irxxrcieunpray in xx. 4, where the oinves is thrust in against John's usage (see i. 5, note). Possibly the normal construction r. Aixvg rfj KCUOACVT? irvpl Kal 0cip in xxi. 8 may be due to him: contrast that in xix. 20. Again in xxi. 6 instead of rj Suwrri Soxra the Johannine idiom is rjJ Swranri Suxrco avrj (see note in loc.).

From the above facts the conclusion is inevitable that after xx. 3 our author had intended to add a description of the Heavenly Jerusalem that was to come down from heaven to earth and be the habitation of Christ and the martyrs that accompanied Him from heaven in their glorified bodies: and also that this very description has been preserved in certain sections of xxi.-xxii.

We have next to determine the extent of this description. Now even the cursory reader will observe that there are two accounts of the Heavenly Jerusalem in these chapters, which have been rudely thrust together by the Seer's literary executor. 1 A

1 We might compare 2 Corinthians, which is now recognized by the learned world as consisting of two mutilated Epistles of St. Paul edited together as one, the last four chapters belonging to the earlier Epistle. In Cicero's letters Professor Purser shows that in several cases exactly the same phenomenon may be found.

close study of these chapters will show that the section xxi. 9-xxii. 2 constitutes a unity, though incomplete in itself, as we shall see presently, and gives a description of the Heavenly Jerusalem that was to be the centre of the Millennial Kingdom. Two further fragments of this description are to be found in xxii. 14-15 and 17. This description fits in perfectly with the conditions of the Millennial reign of Christ and the martyrs for a thousand years. It is conceived of as a period of beneficent rule and evangelizing effort in regard to the surviving nations who visit the Heavenly Jerusalem and bring all their glory and honour into it. Wickedness, of course, still exists without it, but nothing that is unclean, nor any liar or abominable person, is permitted to enter into it (xxii. 15, xxi. 27).

So far the first description. But what are we to make of the second, which begins with xxi. i? Only the disjecta membra of this description remain. Two fragments of it are recoverable in xxi. 1-4 and xxii. 3-5. These should be read together, as the first clause of xxii. 3 forms the fourth line of the stanza, the first three lines of which are preserved in xxi. 4 bc. In this second description the former heaven and earth have passed away for ever, with all the sin and sorrow and pain that prevailed on the former earth. Death itself shall be no more throughout the new heaven and the new earth and the New Jerusalem (xxi. 4). And whereas in the Heavenly Jerusalem that came down from God for the Millennial Kingdom the saints who had been martyred reigned only a thousand years, in the later New Jerusalem they are to reign for ever and ever (xxii. 5). It is noteworthy that even the very diction of xxi. 1-4 and of xxii. 3-5 testifies to the fact that they form part of one and the same poem. Thus owe rru? ri, which occurs three times in xxi. i 4 1, recurs twice in xxii. 3 5 (contrast xxi. 26) and not elsewhere throughout our author. OVK. ri occurs nine times in connection with other verbs. Thus while OVK lorai 2rt is confined to xxi. i-4 abo, xxii. 3-5, it is to be observed that OVK. n is characteristic of our author in the N. T., since outside our author it occurs in the N. T. only six times and twice of these in quotations.

We have now dealt with the chief difficulties in xx.-xxii. There are, of course, many of a subordinate nature affecting the original order of the text in xxii., but they are treated shortly in the introductions to the various sections of the rearranged translation that follows. Chaps, xx.-xxii. should provisionally be read in the following order: xx. 1-3. Vision of the chaining of Satan for a thousand years.

xxi. 9-xxii. 2, 14-15, 17. Vision of the Heavenly Jerusalem 154 THE REVELA-TION OF ST. JOHN XXL9-XXH. fi.

which comes down to be the abode of Christ and the glorified martyrs, and the centre of a new evangelization of the nations for a thousand years.

xx. 4-6. Vision of the glorified martyrs who reign with Christ for a thousand years.

xx. 7-10. Vision of the loosing of Satan, and the attack of Gog and Magog on the Beloved City; of the destruction of Gog and Magog, and the casting of Satan into the lake of fire.

xx. 11-15. Vision of the great white throne; of the vanishing of the former heaven and earth; of the judgment of the dead, and of the casting of death and Hades into the lake of fire.

xxi. 5, 4 d, 5 b, i-4 abc, xxii. 3-5. The outworn world has vanished: God creates a new world. Vision of the new heaven and the new earth: of the New Jerusalem descending from God to the new earth, in which the saints are to reign for ever.

xxi. s c 6 b-8. Admonition of God conveyed through the Seei to his contemporaries.

xxii. 6-7, 18 16, 13, 12, 10. Declaration of Christ as to the truth of the words of the Seer; His assurance of His almighty power and His speedy advent; and His command to the Seer to publish the prophecy: for the time is at hand.

xxii. 8-9, 20. John's testimony and closing words regarding Christ. 1 xxii. 21. The closing benediction.

VISION OF THE HEAVENLY JERUSALEM.

. 9-XXII. 2, 14-15, 17: Vision of the Heavenly Jerusalem coming down from heaven to be the abode of Christ and of the glorified martyrs, who are to reign with Him for 1000 years, and to be the centre of a new evangelization of the nations.

This vision forms (I.) an integral part of the Book, and (II.) is from the hand of the Seer. Since the question has already been discussed (see pp 144-154) we shall sum up shortly the evidence for the above statements.

I. The vision forms an integral part of the Book.

1. There must be a fitting seat on earth for the kingdom of Christ during the Millennial reign with the glorified martyrs in their heavenly bodies. This city while obviously supramundane, as befitting Christ and the glorified saints, must yet be accessible to the actual dwellers on the earth, as in fact it is: cf. xxi. 24-27, xxii. 14-15 I 7- 2. Such a kingdom or centre of the evangelization of the heathen nations is clearly foretold in xv. 3-4, and implied in v. 10,

XXI. 9-XXII. 3. J VISION OF HEAVENLY JERUSALEM 155 xiv. 7. Without such a kingdom there would be a lacuna in the Book.

3. As one of the angels of the Seven Bowls showed the doomed city of the Antichrist to the Seer (xvii.-xviii.), so the same angel, or one of the same Seven, shows him the blessed city of the Christ (xxi. 9).

Thus so far as the subject-matter goes, the presence of this vision is indispensable.

II. It is from the hand of the Seer. Full evidence of this statement is given in the notes, but sufficient evidence will here be adduced to establish this point i. First, as to diction.

XXT. 9. KU fljxOev. Scigw croi agrees exactly with xvii. i. With +idxas TUP ycfjrfpraip TWP irr irxT)yp cf. xv. 7. r. pup r T. yupalica TOU dppiou is prepared for in xix. 7-8.

10. dmjpcyiccp. irpciffum. So also in xvii. 3. T JP irlxip T. Ay tap lepu(raxr)fi: of. xxi. 2. ttataffaipothrap T. oupapou dir6 T. 0eou: cf. iii. 12, x. I, xxi. 2, etc. fyouaap T. 86 ap TOU Ocou (also in 23): cf. xv. 8.

11. fc Xt0u Ucnribt: cf. iv. 3, op. ous. A o cwist. Now we know (see vol. i. p. 36) that our author several times uses 3MH09 as the equivalent of ws. KpuoraxXilopm: cf. iv. 6, 6Aota 13. dv dmtoxfjs: cf. vii. 2, xvi. 12. 15. 6 Xaxwv ftct jfiog: cf. xvii. i.

18. flday (vaxos, 21): cf. vdxtvo?, iv. 6, xv. 2.

22. Observe the divine title so frequent in our Book.

23. 06 xpciap jfxci: cf. iii. 1 7, xxii. 5. taipuanp: cf. i. 16, viii. 1 2. 84. irepiirat aouaip: cf. ii. I, iii. 4, xvi. 15.

26. T?)P 6 ap it air. rijufjp: cf. iv. 9, IT, V. 12, 13.

27. ycypapplpoi, Iv T. j3i0Xib rfjs Junjs: cf. xx. 12, 15. TOIP 3Scxuy jla (cf. xxi. 8) ital 4 usos: cf. XKII. 15.

XXII. 1. Xaiirp6p: cf. xv. 6, xix. 8. irotaprfp. 69 icpuv TaxXop: cf. iv. 6, axacrcra. ofuna fcpvcrraxXa), and see above on xxi. 10. iinropeurfficpop IK T. Oprfpou: cf. iv. 5.

14. irxupoprcs T. oroxois ad-rup. So vii. 14. gouo-ia a favourite Johannine word though here used with a slightly different meaning.

15. apfiaicol. clbuxoxdrpai. For the same list of four see xxi. 8, though in a different order.

17. ptff frt: cf. xxi. 2, 9. ep X ou: cf. vi. i. Si m: cf. xxi. 6. flwp t)s Swpcdp: cf. xxi. 6.

2. Technical use of idioms.

(a) Anomalous constructions: cf. xxi. 9, idxa TUP ycp6prtp. 14. T Teixos.? X K. (b) Participle = finite verb, CX P= x, xxi. 12, 14: cf. iv. i, etc. (c) Delicate distinction of our author preserved between tfswp wrjs and JXop Jwrjs in xxii. 14, 17. This distinction is not made, so far as I am aware, in any other book before 100 A. D.: cf. vii. 17, xxi. 6 on vswp frnfc, and ii. 7 (note) on (v ov w s. () Observe how the difficult phrase 6 t xrr?)p odtvjs ftjioios. Xify Idamsi (xxi. n) is explained by the clause in iv. 3, 6 KOJICVOS oioios. Xflty UOTI (see note on xxi. n). ( ) The use of t and opoios as equivalents: cf. xxi. n, 18, where OLUKOS is used in this sense, and xxi. n, 21, xxii. i, where s is so used. Observe also that whereas we have ffstip twjs 8 pclv in xxii. 17, we find iou UCLTOS TTJS IWTJS fopedi in xxi. 6 a fact which points to xxi. 6 having been written subsequently to xxii. 17. () The order observed by our author as to numerals but nowhere else rigidly observed, is attested in every instance in this vision. Thus our author also places Scoscica after its noun when the noun is otherwise unqualified: SO also in xxi. 12 ( ), 7rv. was Swscco, ayycxov? Swscfca, and Kapvovs Swseica, xxii. 2; but before it when the noun has a dependent genitive: so also in xxi. 12, Suscjca 6vofidra raw Scoscmi dirootoxuv. Finally, when the subject of a clause consists of Sucfca preceded by the article and followed by a noun, and the same numeral recurs in the predicate with a noun, the Solera precedes the noun. So also in xxi. 21,0! Suscica Tnawpc? Swscxa IMLpyaplrai. See note on viii. 2.

XXT. 9-81. An angel of the Seven Bowls shows to the Seer the Heavenly Jerusalem which is to be the seat of the Millennial Kingdom.

9. KU fjxOc?. 4i Xos. Repeated from xvii. i. irfxa? TUP yfp KTWK. This is certainly an extraordinary construction even in our author. It is best, perhaps, to explain it as an oversight KU A Xi)(rek. i ooi. Repeated from xvii. i.

-rt v rip l" TV Y UKC " Ka T0 " Ap iou. The phrase in brackets is with Bousset to be excised. It can be explained as a marginal gloss on r. VV TJV based on xix. 7. The great variaiion in the MSS points to this phrase being an intrusion.

10. KCU mfji yic6 pc iv iritufmm. This clause has already occurred in xvii. 3, and the phrase that follows here, cvi opo? firyo, suggests the present earth just as explicitly as does ei? tprjfjlov in xvii. 3. The implication is that the present earth and the Heavenly Jerusalem would coexist. But there is no such implication in regard to the New Jerusalem. The former heaven and earth have already vanished (xxi. i). Ezek. xl. appears to have been in the mind of our author when he committed this vision to writing. 10 is practically an echo of Ezek. xl. 2, "In the visions of God

brought he me. and set me down upon a very high mountain." Here, as the LXX renders ijyayev ic? opao-et 0cov. ical c tccv uc bf opo? vifnrjkbv r ospa, our author has thought of the Hebrew only. On this very high mountain

XXT. 10. J VISION OF THE HEAVENLY JERUSALEM 157 (cf. Ezek. xvii. 22; Isa. ii. 2) stood what appeared to be the structure of a city.

There he met a man with a measuring line (Ezek. xl 3) wherewith he measured the Temple.

iirl opos plya ical 6i rr Xk. Paradise and a lofty mountain are associated together in i Enoch xxiv. sq., and again in Ixxxvil 3, and probably in Jub. iv. 26. But this association may go back to primitive times, when the mountain of God (Ezek. xxviii. 14, Ps. xlviii. 2) was associated with the glorified Jerusalem (Isa. ii. 2); see Oesterley, Evolution of Mess. Idea, p. 129 sqq.

TV irlxi? TV dyiaf lepoucrax p. If we compare this phrase with that in xxi. 2, which refers to the New Jerusalem which descends after the Judgment and the creation of the new heaven and the new earth, we observe that it is word for word the same save that the latter adds the significant word KCUVI V. This seems to imply that the Heavenly City is itself renewed or replaced by another.

But there are other questions which call for discussion in connection with this conception. We have four titles of this future abode of the blessed in our author: i. rj n-oais TOV 0cov fiov (iii. 12). 2. 17 Troxis rj ayia Icoovo-oa. mum? (xxi. 2.), or ij Kur) Icpovcraxi?A (iii. 12). 3. 17 iroats fj ayia Icpovcraa, i?A (xxl lo). 4. 6 irapascuros TOV Ocov iov (ii. 7). This list we can at once reduce to thiee by referring to iii. 12, where i and 2 are identified. Next, by comparing xxi. 10 and ii. 7, we are enabled to identify 3 and 4; for both these are the seat of the v ov ui s (cf. xxii. 2). We have now to consider in what relation does (a) ij irdxis 17 ayia Iep. (= 6 wapaseio-os TOV Qtov pov) stand to (fi) fj iroais 17 ayia lep. Kawri (= ij iro'Xis TOV 0 ov JAOV). Are they really different or are they identical? They are closely related in the mind of our author, but they are not identical, (a) The first, i. e. 17 iroats ij ayia lepovo-aai, is the seat of the Millennial Kingdom. It contains the tree of life (ii. 7, xxii. 2). At the close of the Millennial Kingdom and before the Final Judgment, when both the heaven and the earth vanish, its removal from the earth is presupposed together with Christ and the glorified martyrs. This removal from the earth is not expressly stated, but it is undoubtedly presupposed. There are analogous expectations in contemporary Judaism. Thus in 2 Bar. vl 6-10 it is said that even the sacred vessels of the Holy of Holies were removed by angels before the destruction of Jerusalem in 70 A. D. For an analogous account see 2 Macc. ii. 4-8. In 4 Ezra vi. 2-3, iii. 6, moreover, where the main source (S: see Box) identifies the heavenly and earthly Paradises, Paradise, which had been prepared by God before the creation of the world, was placed afterwards on the earth as Adam's abode, iii. 6, but with- drawn after Adam's fall (see Box on 4 Ezra, p. 197). Hence we might reasonably conclude that it is the same city the Holy City, Jerusalem that is spoken of in xxi. 10 sqq. and in xxi. 2, but that it has been transformed (jcaui?) in order to adapt it to the new heaven and the new earth. Further, in this connection we might remark that just as the Heavenly Jerusalem is associated with the manifestation of Christ on earth in our text, so also we find the same association in 4 Ezra vii. 26, xiii. 36. It is true that Box rejects both these passages as interpolations. But if it was believed that the heavenly Paradise had come down to earth to be Adam's abode, there could be no objection to the hope that the Heavenly City should come down to be the abode of the Messiah.

(ft) But, though the Holy City, Jerusalem, has been removed from the earth before the Final Judgment, when the former heaven and earth vanish into nothingness, this city is not to be absolutely identified with " the Holy City, New Jerusalem," which comes down from the new heaven to the new earth to be the everlasting abode of the blessed. This new city is either wholly new in every respect, or it is the former city transformed. It belongs to the new creation, xxi. 5 b. As opposed to the former Holy City, this Holy City is " new " (KCUVI;); that is, it is here contemplated not under aspects of time but of quality: it is new as set over against that which is in some respects materialistic, or outworn, or marred, or unfit.

In 0, as we have already remarked, there is an identification of 17 jcoivi? Itpovo-raxyfji (iii. 12) and rj Trdxis rov 0cov. It seems as if 3 is distinguished also in another respect from a. There is no mention of the presence of the tree of life in p, though this is a characteristic feature of a. But the tree of life is unnecessary in, since death itself is wholly at an end, xxi. 4 b, and the blessed live in the light of God's presence and reign for ever and ever, xxii. 5.

In the conception of the New Jerusalem our author has fused together i and 2 and discarded 4 (see above). But these ideas were originally very different, as the following notes will show.

i. The city of God. The idea of the heavenly city or the city of the gods, found in many nations of the ancient world, was taken over by Judaism.

The city of the gods was originally suggested by the heaven with the sun and moon and the twelve signs of the Zodiac and the twelve gates through which they were conceived to pass, on the north three gates, on the east three gates, on the south three gates, and on the west three gates. There was also the great Milky Way, which was conceived as the great street of the heavenly city.

It has been said that our author had before him the descrip- 10. VISION OF THE HEAVENLY JERUSALEM 159 tion of Ezekiel's city (Ezek. xlviii. 31 sqq.) with its twelve gates, three in each of the four walls, and that this description with the enumeration of the twelve precious stones in the high priest's breastplate (Ex. xxviii. 17 sqq., xxxix. 10 sqq.) was all that our author drew upon in the ideas and facts of the past for his own description of the Heavenly City. But our text itself refutes such a view. For the fact that in this city are twelve gates, 1 which are respectively composed of the twelve precious stones, sh ws that some of the ideas in our text go back ultimately to the heavenly city itself. There is some hint of this connection in i Enoch Ixxii. 2 sqq., Ixxv. 6, Ixxxii. 4 sqq., where there are said to be twelve portals in the heaven through which the sun, moon, and stars go forth at different seasons. The connection is here very slight, but the connection between these gates and the precious stones mentioned in our text recalls the fact that Philo (De Monarchic ii. 5: cf. Vita Mos. iii. 14) and Josephus (Ant. iii. 7. 7) interpret the twelve precious stones on the breastplate of the high priest of the signs of the Zodiac; and Kircher (Oedipus Aegyptiacus, 1653, 11. ii. 177 sq.) has shown that according to Egyptian and Arabian monuments these stones correspond to these signs.

The peculiar shape of the city, that it is equally long, broad, and high, may possibly be explained from this standpoint; for to the human vision the heaven appears to be of this character. We might here compare the Holy of-Holies in Solomon's Temple, which was a cube, being 20 cubits each way: cf. i Kings vi. 20.

But our author disassociates (see p. 167 sq.) the Heavenly Jerusalem from this ethnic conception of the city of the gods, which had impiessed itself slowly, and perhaps for the most part imperceptibly, on the Judaism of the past. As the stars were naturally compared with precious stones, and as we have just seen that a clear association between the signs of the Zodiac and certain precious stones was established before the Christian era, it is not improbable that in Isa. liv. 11-12, where the earthly Zion is referred to, we have traces of the heavenly city:

"Behold I will set thy bases in rubies, And thy foundations in sapphires. And I will make of jasper thy pinnacles, And thy gates of carbuncles, and all thy border of jewels"

(Box's translation); and also in Tob. xiil 16-18,

"And the gates of Jerusalem shall be builded with sapphire and emerald, 1 The Babylonians were already familiar with the idea of heavenly gates; ee Zimmern, KAT p. 619.

And all thy walls with precious stones. The towers of Jerusalem shall be builded with gold,

And their battlements with pure gold. The streets of Jerusalem shall be paved

With carbuncle and stones of Ophir, And the gates of Jerusalem shall utter hymns of gladness,

And all her houses shall say, Hallelujah."

In a much later work, Sibyll. Or. v. 420 sq., we find got iroaiv rjv e? rd0iprc 0cos, ravrrjv faipoT pav cwrrpcov re icat fj tov rj

Now from the contents of these passages it appears clear that we have to do not with the heavenly city of God, but with the earthly Jerusalem, and yet the descriptions reflect the characteristics of the heavenly city. 1 2. Paradise. Paradise 2 is very variously conceived at different times and in different writings. First of all the term is used of the Garden of Eden in Gen. ii.-iii. In the 2nd cent. B. C. it has become the abode of the righteous and elect after this life, and is called the Garden of Righteousness, or of the Righteous, or the Garden of Life, i Enoch Ix. 8, 23, Ixi. 12, and is situated at the ends of the earth, Ixv. 2, cvi. 8 (Ixxxix. 52), or on the N. VV, Ixx. 3, Ixxvii. 3, or to the east of the seven great mountains, xxxii. 1-2, xxiv. 1-4 sqq. In Test Levi xvni. 10, 2 Bar. li 10-n, 2 Enoch ix. i sqq., xlii. 2-4, Paradise does not become the abode of the righteous till the Advent of the Messiah or the last judgment, i Enoch xxii. In nearly all these passages it is the heavenly and not the earthly Paradise that is meant, or rather the earthly Paradise has assumed a heavenly character. In 2 Enoch viii. 1-6 the heavenly and earthly Paradises are mentioned in succession. The earthly Paradise was created on the third day, Jub. ii. 7, 2 Enoch xxx. i, whereas according to later Judaism the heavenly Paradise is described as existing before the world either actually or in the thought of God, Pesach. 54; Ned. 39".

In 4 Ezra (source S) the heavenly and the earthly Paradises are identified. This Paradise was prepared by God before the Creation as Adam's first abode, iii. 6 (cf.

2 Bar. iv. 3), but afterwards withdrawn from the earth and reserved for the righteous after the final Judgment. In this author Paradise has become identical with heaven and is set over against Gehenna, 4 Ezra 1 See Zimmern, KA T t p. 619; Gunkel, Zum Verstandniss des NT., p 48 sqq.; Bousset in loc.; Jeremias, Babylonisihcs im NT., p. 68.

The Talmudists are almost unanimous in maintaining that there was both a heavenly and an earthly Paradise. The Rabbis distinguish between Can and Eden. Thus Samuel bar Nahman declares that Adam dwelt only in the Can, whereas no mortal eye had ever seen Eden (Ber. 34).

XXL 10-11. VISION OF THE HEAVENLY JERUSALEM l6l vii. 36-38, 123. See Box, 4 Ezra, 195 sqq. But in 2 Bar. iv. 3 the two Paradises are distinguished apparently; for Adam did not live in the heavenly Paradise, but only enjoyed the vision of it before his fall.

3. The New Jerusalem. In the O. T. such passages as Isa. liv. ii sq., Ix. 10-14, Hag. ii. 7-9, Zech. ii. 1-5, refer only to the earthly Jerusalem, though in Isa. liv. this conception has been influenced by the conception of the city of God. In Tob. xiii. 1 6-1 8 this influence is still clearer, while in 2 Bar. iv. 2-4 the heavenly Jerusalem is definitely affirmed and distinguished from the earthly and likewise from Paradise. But it is an error to suppose, as some do, that it was only after the destruction of the earthly Jerusalem that the idea of the heavenly was evolved, for we find it clearly stated early in the second century B. C. in i Enoch xc. 29, where God Himself builds what is symbolically called " the New House " on the site of the earthly Jerusalem, which He had removed. In 2 Bar. iv. 3 the manifestation of this city is connected with the manifestation of God, just as in 4 Ezra vii. 26, xiii. 36 the heavenly Zion is to appear along with the Messiah, and in our own text the Holy City, Jerusalem, with Christ and the glorified martyrs. If the heavenly Paradise could appear on earth for Adam, it was only natural that the heavenly Jerusalem should appear on earth for Christ the Second and greater Adam. Finally, we should observe that the transference of the tree of life from Paradise to Jerusalem, i Enoch xxv. 4-5, implies the identification even at this early date of Paradise and Jerusalem: also in Test Dan v. 12, 11 And the saints shall rest in Eden (i. e. Paradise), And in the New Jerusalem shall the righteous rejoice."

. rou 6cou. For parallel phrases in our author see above, p. 155.

-rt v oogay TOU Ocou. See note on 23, xviii. i.

11. 6 4okrrf)p a6Ttjs = "the light thereof." This phrase is practically equivalent to that which immediately precedes, i. e. fyourrav TIJV 86 av Tov 0cov. The city is lighted up by the glory of God Himself, and this light was " like a most precious stone as it were a jasper (oiotos Xi0p Ttuoyrdrw, ws Xi0 icunrisi). o cixrrqp avrijs does not mean "the luminary thereof" and is not equivalent to 6 Xv vos avriys in 23, but is to be rendered as given above. This is clear when the words that follow 6ioios i6u. At0p iacnrtst are compared with iv. 3, where " He that sat on the throne " is described as being " to look upon like a jasper stone " (010109 A uwnrisi). Thus the light that pervades the Holy City is in colour like to that which flashes through the nimbus that surrounded the throne of God (iv. 3). Moreover, we are VOL. H. ii told that it is the glory of God that gives light to the city (xxi 23, 17 yap B6(a rov 0cov c

wrto-cv avrqv). This USC of axmyp light, is very rare. Cf. i Esdr. viii. 79. Thayer quotes Anthol n. 359 as another instance of this use.

12. fxouro- j? x. See p. 155 ad fin. The second Igovara is an ordinary participle.

TCIXO. Cf. 2 Enoch Ixv. 10, "And there shall be to them a great wall that cannot be broken down."

mixwyos StsScko. Twelve gates, as in the city of Ezekiel: cf. Ezek. xlviii. 30 sqq., corresponding to the Twelve Tribes. In i Enoch xxxni.-xxxv. there is a similar distribution of the gates of heaven whence the stars issue. In Classical Greek irvxcov meant a gatehouse, gatetower, or porch, and was, therefore, distinct from irvxy. It has this meaning in Acts xii. 13, TV 6vpav TOV 7riaoio: cf. ibid. xii. 14; Matt. xxvi. 71. But it came in late Greek (see the LXX) to mean simply a large gate: cf. Luke xvi. 20; Acts x. 17, xiv. 13. It is in this sense that it appears to be used by our author in all eleven times. This is clear from xxi. 21, ot 8o8cica Trvawves Soiscca lapyaptrat. He does not use rv vj. In the LXX irvxuv is often used as a rendering of nna and sometimes of "IK, while Truxiy very often renders "i K and sometimes nna. Hence it is no guide here. It is noteworthy that whereas the Fourth Gospel does not use irvxcov or irvai?, it employs Ovpa many times in the same sense (x. x 2 7 9 xvni. 16, xx. 19), as does our author (in. 8, 20, iv. i).

dyyous ScsScica. Cf. Isa. Ixii. 6, "I have set watchmen upon thy walls, O Jerusalem."

fsjj, ata iriycypapjuia KT. The twelve gates are entrusted respectively to the Twelve Tribes, and the names of the latter inscribed respectively on these gates, as in Ezek. xlviii. 31, "The gates of the city (LXX, Trvaxu-rifc wdxcws) shall be after the names of the tribes of Israel." If the gates bear the names of the Twelve Tribes, the names of the Twelve Apostles (14) are engraven on the foundations. Thereby the Seer maintains the continuity of the O. T. and the Christian Church.

13. The order of the points of the compass in this verse are E. N. S. W., whereas in Num. ii. 3 sqq. it is E. S. W. N. and in Ezek. xlviii. N. E. S. W. How the gates were respectively inscribed we have no means of determining.

14. TCIXOS. 2x w "- See above, p. 155 ad fin. Ocpextous Swscica Since there are twelve gates, the wall surrounding the City is divided into twelve sections, each section of which rests upon a single foundation stone. These twelve foundation stones consist of twelve precious stones, which are enumerated in 19 sq., and form apparently an unbroken and continuous basement.

XXI. 14-16. VISION OF THE HEAVENLY JERUSALEM 163 to OTUP feftcita jiara T. WCKCL Airoarrixw. Elsewhere in the N. T. we have a similar combination of the Christian and Jewish Churches. In Matt. xix. 28, Kaoijo-co-Oc KOI vuw hrl Oci8cfca Opovovs Kptpoircs ras Scoscica vaas rov IcrpaiX, which may contain a reminiscence of T. Jud. xxv. i. A remote parallel is to be found in Eph. ii. 20, ciroucosoM70cvrc? evt r3 foicxup ran atTOOToatdV KCU TTpo IJTW, 5ltO CLKpoytdVloLLOV CLVTOV XpuTTOV ll CTOV.

In Eph. the whole spiritual Church is the theme of St. Paul: here it is only the foundations of the wall that encircles the Holy City. We have really a nearer parallel in Heb. xi. 10, cse-

X TO yap Ttyv TOVS 0 Aea. touS tyowTOLV 7Toa. IV, TC lttys. 6 0COS.

TWK Swscka Airoorlxuf. The Twelve are here referred to as a corporate body, and there is no hint as to its exact composition. "The absence of Paul's name," as Moffatt remarks, "is no more significant than the failure to emphasize that of Peter."

16. This and some of the verses that follow have been suggested by Ezek. xl. 3 sqq. The measuring in each case has to do with the respective ideal cities of the O. T. prophet and the N. T. Seer, and not as in xi. 2, where the actual Jerusalem is referred to. The act of measuring here has none of the meanings given in the note on xi. i. The measures are given to the Seer in order to elucidate the vision.

16. ir4 i Tcrpdyupos. Babylon, according to Herodotus (L 178), was a square (rctpaywvos), each side of the square being 120 stades. The Greeks regarded the square as a symbol for perfection: cf. Simonides in Plato's Prot 344 A, flvbp ya06v, X prl re Kal TTOcrt KCLL voo Tcrpaycwov, avcv j6yov rcrvyftepov, Xaxcirov dxa0eus: Aristotle, Rhet. iii. II. 2, rov ayaoov avspa avai rcrpaycovov: cf. Eth. Nic. i. 10, II, dyatfos a ijo: Kal rcrpaycovos avcv oyov. xcirai = " stood." Cf. iv. 2; Jer. xxiv. i, Svo Kaxa ovs. Kcixevovs (DH ID): John ii. 6, xix. 29.

firl orasious Subcka xtxidsu. This reading, which is that of AQ and most of the cursives, is very difficult. Ivl oratovs is in itself the usual classical construction, but the genitive (so KP) also is found: see Thuc. ii. 90; Xen. Cyr. ii. 4. 2, cycwro TO icvfuTrov lirl Tpia. KotLtov. TO Si Sd os c 1 cicarof. But how, if we adopt the oraw, are we to explain Soica x ascoc? Winer (p. 244 n.) describes it as a genitive of quality and compares irqxw (see Blass, p. 99, n. i) in the next line. But the cases are not analogous. If it is original, it is perhaps to be rendered "to the length of furlongs of the amount of 12,000." Possibly, however, orafovs is a primitive error and P have rightly emended the text: rl oraw 8. x- a "at 12,000 furlongs." Cf. xiv. 20, dird orastcuv x L Muv aicocruiiv.

S SScka x fbw. 1 2,000 stades nearly 1500 miles. This is either the length of one side of the square or of the four sides combined, but the words that follow are in favour of the former view. These huge figures are not, of course, to be taken literally. Our Seer is using the language of symbolism. When dealing with the subject of Paradise later Jewish writers make statements of a kindred nature. Amongst the more moderate computations is that found in Sibyll. Or. v. 251 (88-130 A. D.): 3, pi Si KOI lotnys reives ftcya jcvicaakrawc? v rocr detpoKTOi pi icai vc coiv iptficwwv.

Here the circumference of the city would be about 280 miles.

A larger estimate (quoted from Wetstein) appears in the Shir R. vii. 5, where it is said that Jerusalem would be enlarged till it reached the gates of Damascus, and exalted till it reached the throne of God (ix. i). In the Baba Bathra, 75, its height is defined as twelve miles. But the imagination is wholly baffled by the amazing figures in Taanith, 10, where the whole world is declared to be the sixtieth part of the Garden, and the Garden the sixtieth part of Eden.

17. licatOK TccrcrcpdkOira Tfoadpwy TTT XWK. This wall of 144 cubits is wholly out of proportion in view of the gigantic magnitude of the City. It cannot rightly be described as icya ca! v lrq 6v in connection with the City, and so it may be either a fragmentary and now unintelligible survival of some archaic element, or else merely a poetical detail, and without symbolic significance. But if we might take the

wall as an outer line of defence distinct from the City, then it could well serve as a defence against the entrance of the wicked and unclean (xxi. 27, xxii. 15).

jj rpok d pwirou 6 icrtth YYOU. The measures used by the angel are those in common use amongst mankind. This is not unreasonable, since both angels and men are fellow-servants of God (xix. 10, xxii. 9).

18-XXH. 2. This section is in verse, and deals with the appearance and character of the City.

18-21. The materials of which the city is constructed.

18. if6fi, if ais. looms. cvswppris found only here and in Joseph. Ant. xv. 9. 6 (fj 8c frsdMcris 5rov rjv cj8oa. Xcro Kara rr Oaxafrcrr Siaicocrtov? iro3a?), and in a pre-Christian inscription, ryv cv5dfii7riv TOV refjlcvow: (Dittenberger's Sylloge Inscnpt. Grace 583, 31, quoted from Moffatt), appears to mean materials or fabric. Thus not only was the radiance that came forth from Him that sat on the throne (iv. 3) of a jasper hue, and likewise that of the whole atmosphere of the Holy City (xxi. n), but the wall itself was constructed of jasper. This structure of jasper was based on twelve precious stones, each of which formed one-twelfth of the entire foundation (cf. 12, 19).

XXI. 18-10. VISION OF THE HEAVENLY JERUSALEM 1 65 xpixrioi naoap K irrx. The city itself was composed of transparent gold.

10. The twelve precious stones which compose the twelve foundations of the wall correspond on the whole to those that were set in gold on the high priest's breastplate in Ex. xxviii. 17-20, xxxix. 10-13 (cf. also Ezek. xxviii. 13 on the dress of the King of Tyre, where, however, in the Hebrew only nine stones are mentioned though twelve are given in the LXX).

Whereas, according to Ex. xxviii. 17 sqq., the names of the Twelve Tribes were written on the twelve stones on the high priest's breastplate, in our text the names of the Twelve Tribes are written, as in Ezek. xlviii. 31, on the twelve gates; but it is the names of the Twelve Apostles that are written on the twelve precious stones which form the foundations of the wall of the City. By means of xxi. 13, where the order in which the angel measured the four sides of the city (i. e. E. N. S. W.), and xxi. 19-20, where the twelve stones are enumerated, we are able to discover the probable order in which these foundations were laid. This order has nothing whatever to do with the order given in Ex. xxviii. 17 sqq., as Myers, Encyc. Bib. iv. 481 1, and Bousset, following the same principle in his commentary, assume; nor is it to be explained from any accidental inversion or misreading of the twelve stones arranged in four lines, each line containing three stones. Bousset's explanation is as follows. Our author read the second three stones in Ex. xxviii. 17 sq. before the first three, and the fourth three before the third three, and thus arrived at the following order: I. avopa rcl7n ipos taoirts II. crdpsiov Towdfciov oyzapa-yso?

III. xpucroaido? JrpvaXiov 6vv iov IV. Xcyvptov d ariys aAC0vrro.

Next, he or his source had read the stones in I. and II. from right to left, and in III. and IV. from left to right. Now, only in the last resort could such a complicated hypothesis in itself a confession of failure be accepted.

While rejecting such an hypothesis, it is advisable to state the actual relations between our text and Ex. xxviii. 17-20. i. Our author has not followed the LXX of

Ex. xxviii. 17 sqq., seeing that his list differs in the renderings of four of the Hebrew words. 2. Our author's list presupposes a transposition of the sixth and twelfth stones, i. e. the D? rp (= TOTTOOV) and HOB (= tao-TTis). This was probably the original Hebrew order (see Encyc. Bib. iv. 4810). 3. It is not credible that, using as he did the Hebrew text first hand, he should accidentally invert the order of the first and second rows and of the third and fourtli,

THE REVELATION OF ST. JOHN XXI. 10.

and in addition read the first pair of rows from right to left and the second pair from left to right. In short, the order of the stones in our text cannot be explained from the order in Ex. xxviii. 17-20. We have now to discover the grounds which gave rise to the difference in order between our text and Ex. xxviii. 17-20. First of all let us arrange the list of stones in 19-20 in conjunction with the sides of the city as they were measured by the angel.

Now whereas in Num. ii. the tribes are arranged in a square, the sides of which look E. S. W. N., and the gates of the Holy City in Ezek. xlviii which bear the names of the Tribes are enumerated in the order N. E. S. W., we are tempted to ask why does the angel adopt an apparently capricious order and measure the sides of the Holy City E. N. S. W.? I know of no certain explanation, but it is possible that we may discover some ground for it, if we take the reconstructed list of the Tribes in vii. 5-8 and combine it with xxi. 13. As a result of this combination we have the following result:

Manasseh.
Naphtali.
Atsher.
Zebulun. I Issachar.
Levi.
Simeon.
Reuben.
-Judah.
Gad. Benjamin. Joseph.

In this diagram we see that the six sons of Leah, i. e. Judah, Reuben, Simeon, Levi, Issachar, Zebulun (see vol. i. p. 208), are arranged along the E. and N. Immediately adjoining the children of Leah come the children of Rachel in our author's list, Joseph and Benjamin (see i. 208), and since the S. was preferred to the W. among the Jews, and the angel measures the city in the order E. N. S. W. (xxi. 13), these two must be arranged along the S. Next (see i. 208) come the sons of Leah's handmaid, i. e. Gad and Assher. These take the next position of honour, i. e. S. W. S. and W. S. W.

XXI. 19. VISION OF THE HEAVENLY JERUSALEM 167

This solution of the difficulties of vii. 5-8, xxi. 13, 19-20 has this recommendation, that it explains all three passages as part of one coherent conception. If it is rejected, some other explanation must be discovered, else the direction pursued by the angel in measuring the walls E. N. S. W. is highly capricious.

The angel measures the walls in the order E. N. S. W. Now, let us take the twelve stones enumerated in 19-20 and beginning with the S. E. corner place the first three on., which the angel measured first, the second three on N., which the angel measured next, the third three on S., which the angel measured next, and the fourth three on W., as is done below. But it is not till we combine these data with the following fact that we arrive at the solution of the problem. This fact is that, according to Kircher's Oedipus Aegyptiacus) n. ii. 177 sq. (1653), eac f h e twelve precious stones 1 in our text is connected respectively with one of the twelve signs of the Zodiac on Egyptian and Arabian monuments. That this connection was already recognized by the Jews we learn from the express statements of Philo and Josephus (see references in note, p. 159). The following table (from Kircher) gives the connections between the signs and the precious stones: 1. The Ram the amethyst 2. The Bull the hyacinth.

3. The Twins the chrysoprase.
4. The Crab the topaz.
5. The Lion the beryl.
6. The Virgin the chrysolite.
7. The Balance the sardius.
8. The Scorpion the sardonyx.
9. The Archer the smaragdus. 10. The Goat the chalcedon.
n. The Water-carrier the sapphire. 12. The Fishes the jasper.

In the diagram that follows I have placed the precious stones in the order suggested by our text in 13, 19-20 and added the signs of the Zodiac with which they were respectively connected. Now, if we read the signs of the Zodiac as there given in the order prescribed in 19-20 we arrive at the following result. The sins or constellations are given in a certain order y and that exactly the reverse order of the actual path of the sun through the signs. Thus we have the Fishes, Water-carrier, Goat, Archer, Scorpion, Balance, Virgin, Lion, Crab, Twins, Bull, Ram; for the order to be followed is that given in xxi. 13, i. e. E. N. S. W. But in the apparent movement of the sun, the sun is said when 1 In Pliny's H. N. zxxiii. the definite number twelve is connected with precious stones.

THE REVELATION OF ST. JOHN XXL 19.

crossing the equator towards the north to be at the first point of the Ram, thirty days later it enters the Bull, and so on through the Twins, Crab, Lion, etc., till it reaches the Fishes. Now this cannot be an accident. The conclusion that our author is acquainted with these current beliefs as to the connection of the twelve precious stones with the signs of the Zodiac, and the sun's progress through the signs of the Zodiac cannot in the face of the above facts be questioned, while the further fact that he gives the stones in exactly the reverse order to that required by astronomical science, shows that he regards the Holy City which he describes as having nothing to do with the ethnic speculations of his own and past ages regarding the city of the gods. Thus he deliberately disconnects the Holy City with the city of the gods, in which the twelve gates were connected with the twelve precious stones and the signs of the Zodiac, (i) by connecting the gates of the Holy City with the names of the Twelve Tribes, and by representing each gate as composed of a single pearl, and (2) by using the twelve precious stones in an ornamental sense and describing them as engraved with the names of the Twelve Apostles.

Table giving the stones of the foundations in their probable order and their probable equivalents in Ex. xocviii. 77-20.

ffop 6vvt (rawafair
Balance. I
Scorpion.
Archer.
tariof (dxdyifrt in LXX = tofl, U Bull. J tfptor in LXX ori), Twins.
Crab.
in Goat.
(Mpf I Water-carrier.
Fish.
Lion, Virgin.

XXI. 19-2O. VISION OF THE HEAVENLY JERUSALEM 169 In the above diagram it will be observed that our author has rendered the Hebrew words 1D3, rvTBB, D5?7, and UP respectively by x a C7 7 v rap6w, xpvcrotrpacros, and vakivoos, whereas the LXX in Ex. xxviii. 17-20 renders them respectively by av6pa(, TOTrafiov, Xtyvpiov, a a-nys. Of the twelve stones enumerated in our text l three have already been mentioned, the lao-Tris, oyiapaysos, and crapstov in iv. 3, while vcuaytfos is implied in ix. 17. tacrms. This was probably of a green or emerald colour. See iv. 3.

rdir4cipos This stone "is identified (Theophr. 37; cf. 55, Knaves o-Kvorfa and Pliny, H. N. xxxvii. 120) with the opaque blue c lapis lazuli of Turkestan " (Encyc. Bib. iv. 4805).

xaxKtjswk. This word occurs only here in Biblical Gieek. This gem is taken to be of a green colour (= a copper silicate), and as we have seen already is substituted for avopa (a red garnet) in the LXX.

crpdpayos. See note on iv. 3.

20. aapovug (= the mos). If we may identify this stone with the topaz, it was, according to Strabo (770), translucent and golden coloured (xpvo-o 8es d7rorrtxJov lyyo?) or yellow green; according to Pliny (H. N. xxxvii. 8), yellow green (e virenti genere). The LXX renders mca by rotrafrov in Ex. xxviii. 17-20. But the crapsoivf was properly a variety of the ow(in which the white background was variegated by layers of red or brown (Pliny, h. W. xxxvii. 23) But what is the Hebrew? adpiof. See iv. 3 (n.).

Xpucrfxioos (= B nn). This gold stone is hard to identify: it may be golden yellow and opaque i. e. yellow jasper or yellow serpentine: or it may be golden yellow and translucent (see Encyc. Bib. iv. 4807). These stones are described by Pliny, H. N. xxxvii. 42, as "aureo fulgore translucentes."

pvjpuxXos (= Dnt?). This is thought to be the malachite by My res in the Encyc. Bib. iv. 4808, " with its wavy. bands and cloudy patches of light vivid and dark green." In Ex. xxvii. 20, xxxix. 13, DW is rendered 1 The identification of the Greek with the Hebrew names for these precious stones is in several cases purely hypothetical. This is in part due to the confusion of the order in the Massoretic. Although the same order in the four rows on the high priest's breastplate is given in Ex. xxviii. 17-20 and xxxix. 10-13 both in the Massoretic and the LXX respectively, yet the LXX implies a transposition of TO and ow. But the confusion is further aggravated by the two accounts in Josephus, Ant. iii. 7. 5 and Bell. v. 5, 7, which differ from each other as to the order of the stones in the third and fourth rows, and while the first account gives for the fiist stone in the first row ffap86w, the second gives adpdiov. Since Josephus states (Ant. iii. 7. 5) that the names of the Twelve Tribes were engraven on the stones, each stone having the honour of a name in the order in which they were born, this con-fuuon is all the more disturbing.

See under raps6w(above.

This word, which does not occur in the LXX, which has Aiyupiov, is the Greek equivalent of Dt It was prob- ably of a greenish yellow colour. According to Pliny, fl. N. xxxvii. 20, it was like the beryl but paler: " vicinum genus huic (beryllo) est pallidius, et a quibusdam proprii generis existimatur vocaturque chrysoprasus."

ddiuihos (. US?, where LXX has x T1 7 s)- According to Pliny, H. N. xxxvii. 41, it was of a violet colour, resembling the amethyst but less bright: "ille emicans in amethysto fulgor violaceus dilutus est in hyacintho."

dplouoros (. no! n) a transparent purple quartz.

31. ot Swscica iruxuccs. jiapyapitai. Cf. Sanh. IOO H: " Rabbi Jochanan sat one day and preached: One day will the Holy One blessed be He bring precious stones and pearls thirty cubits long by thirty cubits broad and excavate (openings) in them of ten cubits (in breadth and) twenty cubits in height, and they shall stand in the gates of Jerusalem ": cf. also Baba Bathra 75 b. AK et Macros. This is a " barbaric " construction: cf. Matt. xxvi. 22, etc. For this distributive use of vd cf. iv. 8, John ii. 6; but the aia is here an adverb, not a preposition. In Kaff ct? in Mark xiv. 19, Rom. xii. 5 the Kara is an adverb also (Robertson, pp. 460, 555). A somewhat parallel construction is found in Eph. v. 33, Kaff Iva ocacrros (Blass, p. 179). irxarcia. Probably to be taken generically " the streets," as uaov on? s in xxii. 2. XP UO " 1 "aoaplf. The whole city is described as "pure gold" in ver. 18. ws Jaxos Siauyifc. This may be rendered either " transparent as glass " or " as it were transparent glass." The latter is decidedly weak, but either is admissible: cf. i. 14, iv. 6, ix. 9, xv. 2, xxii. i. Siavyifc is found only here in the N. T. and not at all in the LXX. It occurs in Philo, Lucian, Plutarch, Apollonius Rhodius.

22. In the Holy City there would be no temple (see note on vii. 15), nor ark of the covenant the restoration of which was so eagerly looked for by the Jews; for that the Lord God would be the Temple thereof and the Lamb the Ark of the Covenant thereof. The absolute destruction of the earthly temple was foretold by our Lord, Mark xiii. 2; John iv. 21; but even the heavenly temple so often referred to in the earlier chapters would have no place as the Heavenly Jerusalem. This verse like those which precede and follow it was originally a tristich, but some words have been lost after cat TO apvtov. Not improbably the missing words are to be recovered from xi. 19, and thus the last two lines may have run yap jcvptos, 6 0co? 6 TravtOKparup, KOOS avn Ktu TO pviov rj Ktpwtos ri s a0i jci7? avrrjs.

The temple that was in the first heaven will disappear (cf. vii. 15, xi. 19). God Himself is henceforth the only Temple, and Christ the Ark of the Covenant. By this restoration the complete parallelism between 22 and 23 is restored. In vii. 9-16 the vision is concerned with the martyr host before the throne of God in heaven, still incomplete and still growing with fresh accessions from the great tribulation on the earth. This host serve God day and night in the temple in heaven, but this temple has no part in the Heavenly Jerusalem: still less in the New; for it belongs to the former things that have passed away (xxi. 4). See note on xxi. 3. In the Ep. Barn. xvi. the idea of anything but a spiritual temple is looked upon with disfavour. Man, when redeemed, forms the habitation of God "a spiritual temple built up to the Lord " (TricvAanicos vaos oucosoftovievos TO

Our restoration of the missing words 17 Kt? ciro9 TJJS avrifc is confirmed by Jer. iii. 16, where it is prophesied that on the advent of the kingdom of God " the ark of the covenant of the Lord " (mm ma jn) should no longer be thought of nor needed nor restored. That the Jews of the century before the Christian era expected the restoration of the ark on the advent of the kingdom is clear from 2 Mace, iu 4 sqq, where it is told that the ark had not been destroyed but had been hidden by Jeremiah on Mount Nebo with a view to its safe keeping. That this belief was current in the first century A. D. is to be inferred from 2 Bar. vi. 7-9, where the ark and certain other holy things belonging to the first temple are said to have been hidden by angels in the earth till the Messianic kingdom was established. That this expectation persisted long afterwards in Judaism we learn from Bammidbar rabba 15. For another kindred legend see Yoma, 54. Against such materialistic expectations our author declares boldly that there will be no restoration of the ark of the covenant, for that its place was taken by the Lamb.

1 88. With the whole verse cf. Isa. Ix. 19 sqq., KU OVK rrai o-oi crt 6 17X109 cis as fjp pas, ovbc avaroxrj o-exTJits amct roi rrjr VVKTO, dxX?0Tu crot Kvptos as aiviov. ov yap ovcrrrai 6 17X109 croc, KOI 17 tt Yprrj roi OVK cvXci ret, carat yap Kupids 0 01 fus alwviov. As in Isaiah the sun and moon do not cease to exist: their splendour is simply put to shame by the glory of God Himself: cf. Isa. xxiv. 23. Our author does not seem to have used the LXX here.

QXpiiavfy itov'ti Lovofoitfis crcx Kf)9 outfj: cf. xxii. 5; Isa. Ix. 19 sq. Here the glory of God see n, fyova-av 1 The ark was at all events a symbol of the divine presence. To the popular mind, however, it was more; it was conceived as the actual abode of Jahveh: cf. Num. x. 35, 36; 2 Sam. zv. 25.

TOW fcov (note) lights up the Heavenly City, and not the sun and moon as we see from the next clause, though these still give light to the world outside the City. Cf. Midrash Tillin, xxxvi. 2, "Neque in mundo futuro necesse habebunt lumen sol is interdiu, aut lunae noctu " (Wetstein).

4j S6 a TOO 0cog tyrfrurf P awJK: cf. 1 1, xviii. i. The " glory " of God manifests itself in light. This Sofa is probably the ft or brightness which went forth from the Shekinah or the glory (Kip) of God: cf. Targ. Jer. i on Ex. xxxiii. n, rk vr, and Jarg. Jon. on Ezek. xliii. 2, where we have " the brightness of His glory " (vr fcop). The brightness of Moses face Oldatn pjipk vr), according to Jarg. Jer. i on Ex. xxxiv. 29, was derived from the brightness of the glory of the Shekinah of Yahveh (1 KfljW "ipk VT p). This last expression will explain xviii. i, where it is said of an angel, 17 yrj tywturorj IK nys 8o 175 avrov: cf. xxi. 3, note.

ical 6 Xux" afi-rijs rft Apvlov. Here 6 AVXVOS avnjs is the predicate and corre- sponds to tyomo-cv avrrjv in the preceding line, just as TO dpvtov is the parallel to 17 Sofa TOV 0cov. There is no comparison here with the sun and moon as Bousset suggests.

84-87. The necessity of interpreting these verses with regard to the present earth and the nations surviving the advent of the Millennium has already been pointed out (see p. 146 sqq.). The evangelizing of the nations is already foretold in xiv. 7 by an angel flying in the midst of heaven, and the going up of the nations to worship God is proclaimed as an event of the future by the glorified martyrs in heaven (xv. 4). The Seer at last beholds in vision the fulfilment of these prophecies. Unless we explain xxi. g-xxii. 2, 14-15, 17 as the Heavenly City which was to come down from heaven to be the seat of the Millennial reign, then the prophecies in xiv. 7, xv. 3 remain unfulfilled.

The conversion of the Gentiles to Judaism was looked for by Zechariah, ii. T i, viii. 23, and the writer of Isa. Ixv.-lxvi.; Dan. vii. 14; Tob. xiii. n, xiv. 6; i Enoch x. 21, xc. 32 sqq.; Test. Levi xviii. 9; Test. Jud. xxv. 5; Test. Asher vii. 3; Test. Naph. viii. 4; Pss. Sol. xvii. 32; 4 Ezra xi. 46, amongst other Jewish writers. This expectation became a central truth of Christianity, but the conversion of the heathen nations is to be due, not to Judaism, but to Christianity.

84. This verse consists of a stanza of three lines, the second line of which is corrupt. The whole stanza is based on Isa. Ix. 3, ii not on the LXX of these verses, which runs as follows: iropcuaoptai ffaoixcif r WTI rou, rfi, ap, vponjri crov.

24-27. VISION OF THE HEAVENLY JERUSALEM 13 II. icat avoixorjo-ovrai, al iruxai crov Sia iravrcfe, filpas xai PUKTOS od KXciao aoirai ciaayayeif irpo"? ae Swauv lotw, KGU 0aoixtis avrcoi ayopwov.

The words in heavy type have their equivalents in our text, in 24-25, but our author has here rendered the Hebrew independently of the LXX. We might compare Pss. Sol. xvii. 34-35.

8ia TOU 4 irfc. Here a may be rendered "amidst 1 or " by."

25. plpas f ri yp oun ftrrai KCI f. The obelized clause was probably a marginal gloss originally, based on xxii. 5, which subsequently displaced the true text, Kal VVKTOS. In xxn. 5 the definite statement is made that there shall be no longer any night at all. That is what we should expect in the New Jerusalem and the new heaven and the new earth. But there are the following objections to this clause in its present context i. We should expect ij pas KO! WOTTO as in Isa. Ix. n, on which the text is confessedly based. 2. The parallelism is against it. 24-25 form a tristich occurring in the midst of a succession of tristichs, and the last line of this tristich is formed of 25. Hence instead of

Kal 01 TTuaaivcs avrjJc ov JJLT) icacicrflakriv rjntpas, vi(yap ow
TTCU CK l we should read
Kal ot 7rva. uves aurijs ov p, jj KXcwr akrtv i icpas KCU wicrbv.

3. We should then have the familiar phraseology of our author: cf. iv. 8, vii. 15, xx. 10.

It might, of course, be urged that the adverb licet justifies the clause in the present context by limiting the statement to the city itself. But this emphatic use of et implies clearly that day and night alternate as usual outside the City. What meaning is then to be attached to rjJitpas? Does this word denote the unbroken day that prevails within the City, or the usual period of light without it? The obelized clause introduces hopeless confusion into the context.

26. Based on Isa. be. n. See on 24: cf. also Ix. 5, "the wealth of the nations shall come unto thee." Here the LXX differs: Sri pcraftaxei el? ri iraovros Oaxdtrcnp KOI Mhuv KOI Acuoy. KOL rjfovo-tv o-ot dyeaai.

27. The unclean and the abominable and the liars are still on the earth, but, though the gates are open day and night, they cannot enter.

06 fi euroty. irar KOikov: cf. LXX of Isa. 111. I, ovccrt 0c? v a aov avtftir rjro ical OKaffapros; XXXV 8, ov M irap 0y cicct akaoaptos: also Ezek. xliv. 9. That our author is using the Hebrew text and not the LXX is evident here; for though faaoapros has already occurred four times, he does not use it here but KOIIOS. But there seems to be some primitive error in the text. Alike the passages in the O. T., of which our text is a reminiscence, and the following phrase TTOUM Kcxvyfux lead us to expect iras KOIVOS instead of irav KOIVOV. Moreover, the final clause ci AT) oi ycypaAAcpoi presupposes only persons to be mentioned here. If this is right, then we should render: " and there shall in no wise enter into it any that is unclean or that maketh an abomination or a lie." KOl-fa could represent was KOIVOS or irav iroiw plxuyfia. Contrast Babylon (xvii. 4) which was full of jsScxvyiata: cf. xxi. 8. iroiw. ijrcusos: and xxii. 15, ira?

lauv KU 7TOUOV fftvOOS.

ci pi) ol ycypajxpcvoi (= MirditDy 3). This construction, as I have pointed out above, implies that only persons should be mentioned in the two preceding lines: i. e., ov p. jj curcali? efc avrrjv TOS KOIVOS KOL Troiun po. vypa.

T pipxiw TTJS IWTJS TOO dppiou. See notes on iii. 5, xiil 8.

CHAPTER XXII.

1-2. The description of the Heavenly City that descends from heaven for the Millennial reign is continued in these verses The KCU ct ef mot points back to xxi. 9, 10, where the same phrase occurs. In this vision the spirit of the Seer is actually translated (cf. xvii. 3) to the Heavenly City, which is shown to him by an angel (cf. xvii. i). There is no such translation of the Seer's spirit in the vision of the New Jerusalem that is to descend from heaven after the Judgment and the creation of the new heaven and the new earth (xxi. 5 4 d, s b, 6 i-4 mbc, xxii. 3-5). This latter vision is part and parcel of the vision of the Judgment: cf. KCU ctSov in xxi i, 2 with the same phrase in xx. n, 12. In this vision there is no angelic intermediary. The Seer sees the great white throne and Him that sat thereon (xx. 11,12): he hears God proclaiming the end of the old world and the creation of the new (xxi. 5, 4, 51): he sees the new heaven and the new earth and the descent of the New Jerusalem, and hears a great voice from the throne declaring that God Himself will henceforth abide with men (xxi. 1-3).

1. ical 2Sci lk poi: cf. i. i, iv. i, and the preceding note.

irorapdi jjSaros Iwtjs. Has "the river of the water of life" the same spiritual significance as " the fountains (or (fountain)

XXH. 1-2. VISION OF THE HEAVENLY JERUSALEM of the waters (or water) of life" in vii. 17, xxi. 6 and "the water of life" in xxii. 17? It is probable, since the river goes forth from the throne of God, and " the fountains of the waters of life " may be conceived as forming the source of this river in the throne of God. But it is noteworthy that no spiritual significance is attached to this river here, whereas the tree of life (xxii. 2) is full of significance in this respect.

Whatever the relation of "the river of life" and "the fountains of the waters of life " may be in our author, their origin and meaning were originally different The idea of the river in the Heavenly City springs ultimately from the river in the Garden of Eden (Gen. ii. 10). The object of the river in Eden was simply to supply the garden richly with water. When, however, we come down to Ezekiel, we find that the river which flowed forth from beneath the Temple in the coming Kingdom of God was possessed of healing powers as regards the natural products of the earth (Ezek. xlvu. 8-T i). Zechariah (xiv. 8) speaks of these waters as issuing forth from Jerusalem eastward and westward, but attributes no transforming influence to them. Perhaps Ps. xlvi. 5 might be cited here, but both the text and its meaning are uncertain. Lastly, in 2 Enoch viii. 5 it is stated that the nver in Paradise in the third heaven flows from beneath the tree of life and divides into four streams of honey and milk and oil and wine. Thus so far as the O. T. and Judaistic literature down to 100 A. D. are concerned, this river in Paradise was not associated with any powers of spiritual transformation such as we find frequently with the phrase " fountain of life " or " water of life."

So far for "the river of the water of life." Turning now to the phrase "fountain of life," we find that this and analogous phrases had in Jewish literature a spiritual significance cf. Jer. ii. 13; Prov. x. n, xiii. 14, xiv. 27, xvi. 22; Ps. xxxvi. 10; i Enoch xcvi. 6 just as they have in our author.

Xapirpdr s KpuoraxXok. For AaATrpo's cf. xv. 6, xix. 8, xxii. 16, and with os KpvoraxXov cf. iv. 6, 6ioia. Kpvcrrd the two phrases being exact equivalents (see vol. i. p. 36).

2. JKiropeulpcioi: cf. Ezek. xlvii. I, KOI iov vsup cfciropcvcro virofcar(i0cy rov awplov KOLT dvaroxas: also 8; Zech. xiv. 8.

TOU Oprfrou TOU Ocog KU TOO apkiou. There is no difficulty in this conception nor is there any ground for regarding icat rov fyviov with the most recent German critics as an addition. This idea with regard to the Messiah is pre-Christian: cf. i Enoch Ii. 3, "And the Elect One shall in those days sit on My throne." Likewise the Elect One is described as sitting on " the throne of glory, xiv. 3, Iv. 4, and as sitting on the throne of His (i. e. God's) glory," Ixii. 3, 5 (cf. Ii. 3). Similarly the Lord of Spirits places the Elect One "on the throne of glory" (la. 8), " on the throne of His glory," Ixii. 2. This throne is called the Son of Man's throne, Ixix. 27, 29. Finally, it is to be observed that though the Lord of Spirits places the Elect One on the throne of glory in Ixi. 8, and he judges all men, yet in Ixi. 9, the praises of all are directed to the Lord of Spirits. On the other hand, in xxii. 3 of our text the phrase KOI rov fyvtov may be an addition, though there is no conclusive evidence for so regarding it.

iv prw TTJS irxarcias afrrijg. This phrase can be taken either with whatprecedes or with what follows, i. In the former case we are to translate as in the R. V. "he shewed me a nver. in the midst of the street thereof." The next sentence then proceeds: "And on this side of the river and on that." Here evrcudcv cat et0ev have a prepositional force as in Dan. xii. 5 (Theod.), els cvrcvtfcv TOV tc ovs rov trorafiov ("INV1 DDb6 nan): cf. ivfav Kal 6cv TI S Kijotov, Jnt6 rut nip, iri Jos. viii33. According to this view the river runs down the midst of the great heavenly way, and is flanked on either side by the trees of life. 2. But it is possible to take the passage differently and connect the words iv xeo-w TTJS wxareias aur s with what follows, and treat bratfc? KOL cktlocv as genuine adverbs (cf. Ezek. xlvii. 7, Mvopa TroxXa cr ofya tvqw Kal Ivfav (nr 1 HTD), and John xix. 18, irr v0cv Kai cvrtvow). The resulting construction is quite grammatical but the sense is unsatisfactory: " Between the street of the City and the river on either side of it was there the tree of life." These words presuppose that there was a space between the street and the river, and suggest that they ran side by side. There are two possible ways of conceiving the arrangement of the trees of life. Either these trees are arranged in two rows, one on either bank of the river (one row thus coming between the street and the river), or they are placed on either side of the space that lies between the street and the river. The unsymmetncal char-acter of 2. is certainly against it (rixor IWTJS. See note on xxii. 14. This expression is used here collectively. In Gen. i. n sq. py is used collectively. Hence our author departs here from the conception of a single tree of life as in Gen. h. 9, iii. 22; i Enoch xxiv. 4, xxv. 4-6 perhaps under the influence of Ezek. xlvii. 7, KOI I8ov fai rov Xcfaov? rov irorafjiov ocvpa iroaAa (31 Jy) cr o8pa KOI cv0cv, and 12, liri TOV xetaou? avrov cvocv KOI Zvocv irav (v ov 3pd)riAOV,. icat lorat 6 fcanros avraiv cis fyaicw Kal ij avaftatris avrcuv ctsvyiciav.

ITOIOUK napirods Bwscka. This is suggested by Ezek. xlvii. 12, which speaks of fresh fruit being produced every month.

itard fitJKa IK. CUTTOV dirosisou rov Kapirw aurou. This is a free rendering of Ezek. xlvil 12, na? Venn:?, where the LXX (AQ,

XXH. 3,14-15. VISION OF HEAVENLY JERUSALEM 177 other uncials omit-ting) has rijs jcanonros av fact which proves our author's independent use of the Hebrew text. The greater part of this verse is based on Ezek. xlvii. 12.

T u Xa TOO (rfxou its fapairciay rsv Wvv. Here again our author draws directly from Ezek. xlvii. 12, ncnnb np; p, which the LXX has rendered dvafacris afrrwv (-Dr6jt(?) ": cf. Ezek. xl. 6) cfc vyictav. The nations here are those that have survived the visitations in chap. xix. and are evangelized by the inhabitants of the Heavenly City.

14-15. This is the next fragment of the description of the Heavenly City which is to be the seat of the Millennial Kingdom. The persons referred to here are the nations who are contemporaries of this kingdom.

14. ol irxuwrcs rds crroxs aura?. See additional note on vi. ii, vol. i. p. 187 sq.

The phrase is the equivalent spiritually of ol VUCWPTCS. Each class alike has endured and overcome, and as access to the tree of life is here promised to those who have cleansed their robes, so in ii. 7 the right to eat of the tree of life is given to those who have overcome.

fro. jforai. ical. claraOumriif. On this combination of the future and subjunctive cf. in. 9. Iva is frequently followed by the future in our author: cf. vi. 4, n, viii. 3, ix. 5, xii. 6, xiii. 12, xiv. 13.

The icat here = "and so "; for the faithful must first enter the City before they can eat of the tree of life: " that they may have the right to the tree of life and so may enter, etc." To Iva COTCU? J e owta avrwv CTTI TO vaov T S 0)179 we have a remarkable parallel in i Enoch xxv. 4, ovscua crapf ova-lav c ci IWTJS. See note on ii. 7.

15. 2 w. There can be no question as to the meaning of this term here. Our author clearly states that outside the City or the gates of the City are all classes of sinners. We might compare Ps. ci. 7, "He that worketh deceit shall not dwell within my house." In the Pss. of Solomon xvii. 29 the writer declares of the Messiah:
"And he shall not suffer unrighteousness to lodge in their midst,
Nor shall there dwell with them any that knoweth wickedness."
Nay, more, like Joel iii. 17 (daAoycvcfc ov 8icacvvokru 81 avrijs ovfcert) the writer of this Psalm maintains the exclusion of the Gentiles in 31, "And the sojourner and the alien shall dwell with them no more." But in our author race distinctions are taken no VOL. H. 12 account of. Character alone is decisive of a man's fitness or unfitness.

ot Kites. If we compare this verse with xxi. 8 we observe that they are practically doublets. Thus the ot fappakol KOI ol Kdl ol Covets Kal ot eifiuxoaarpot as well as iras irotuv are repeated almost verbally in xxi. 8. To rot? Sciaot? u in xxi. 8 there is no equivalent, but we may reasonably infer with Swete that the KVVCS of the verse before us denote the same persons as the SexyyLtcpot? in xxi. 8. In other words, the persons referred to were either heathens or Jews stained with the abominable vice which excluded them from the Heavenly Jerusalem, the Spiritual Israel Anciently the word was used to denounce the moral impurities of heathen worship: cf. Deut. xxiil 18, "Thou shalt not bring the hire of a whore or the wages of a dog unto the house of the Lord thy God." Here "dog " is the technical term for a BHi?, or male prostitute, according to the inscription in the temple of Astarte at Larnaka. It was likewise employed by the Jews of the ist century A. D. to designate the heathen: cf. Matt. xv. 22 sq. In Phil. lii. 2 St. Paul applies the term to the Judaizing faction in the Christian Church (? A, cverc TOWS ows). See Lightfoot, who well paraphrases iii. 2-3: " We are the children, for we banquet on the spiritual feast which God has spread before us: they are the dogs, for they greedily devour the garbage of carnal ordinances, the very refuse of God's table."

On ol 4apfiaicoi. Kal ot clsoxoxdrpai see xxi. 8 (notes).

irfa tixw? Kal iroiuv t rcusos. Cf. xxi. 8, iran rot? irevsew. Unless we attach to iroiwv here the sense of doing with regard to a certain object or end, we should have an anticlimax in the phrase before us. The meaning then would be: " every one that loveth and maketh falsehood his systematic object." In this case 6 TTOIWV. would differ from 6 irpdo-a-w ji. The latter would mean simply "one who tells lies, 11 "one who practises lying," whereas the former would mean rather "one who lies deliberately with an object" (see Plato, Charmidts, 1621?, on this meaning of TTOICIV as distinguished from irpowccv). The iaow rcvso? denotes one who loves lying for its own sake. Here we might compare Rom. i. 32, ov AOVOV aura Troioiw axXa al (rvv v8okovriv rots irpdxrcrovcriv.

17. This is the last verse belonging to the description of the Heavenly Jerusalem, xxi. Q-xxii. 2, 14-15, 17. It cannot belong to any other section of the work. It deals with the evangelization of the heathen nations as foretold in xiv. 7, xv. 4, and implied in xi. 15.

This expectation is in harmony with most O. T. prophecies as in the Second Isaiah, Haggai, Zechariah, Daniel, and also in the Apocryphal literature in Sirach, i Enoch,

Testaments XII Patriarchs. See my Eschatology, and Wicks, The Doctrine of God (in the indexes of both).

T irkccfio. irvevfjla has many different meanings in our author, i. Either alone, as in xiii. 15, or with wijs appended, xii. ii, it simply means "life." 2. It means personalized living beings either (a) as angels, TO.-rrvtvpara rov 0cov, iii. i, iv. 5, v. 6: (b) as men, though in the passages that follow it is the spiritual element that is alone emphasized, iv irvcvuum, i. 10, iv. 2, xvii. 3,

XXi. IO, 6 0COS TOW TTVCVFjUJLTW TW TTpoffjTit)V t XXU. 6 I (f) ES UD- clean spirits or demons, irycviara dfcatfapra, xvi. 13, xviii. 2, wv. Satioviw, xvi. 14. 3. It means the Spirit of Christ. Thus in TO Tircfyia Xfyei, ii. 7, 11, 17, 29, iii. 6, 13, 22, xiv. 13 (where vat, Aeyci TO TTVCVIQ the utterance of the Seer answers like an echo the voice from heaven in xiv. i3 ab) it is the Spirit of Christ speaking through the Seer. For in all the Seven Letters the Speaker is Christ: cf. ii. i, 8, 12, etc. Similarly in the present passage, xxii. 17, it is the Spirit of Christ that is speaking through John. Thus the entire phrase TO irvwpa KOL y vvpfa means concretely " Christ and the Church in the Heavenly Jerusalem " that is the Church after the Second Advent, not before it: see next note. In such expressions of the prophet the human intermediary is wholly overlooked, and his utterance assigned directly to the Spirit, just as in the O. T. the prophet introduced his message with the words: "Thus saith the Lord." We might compare i Tim. iv. i, where TO TTVCVAO. pirus Xeyct means in concrete language: "a certain prophet says expressly": cf. Acts xxi. ii.

4 prfp+i). In xxi. 9 at the beginning of the description of the Heavenly Jerusalem this City is called rj vv rj: cf. xxl 2. Thus the term has a double meaning: it can denote either the Heavenly Jerusalem or its inhabitants, i. e. the Spiritual Israel, which is to be the Bride of Christ, just as Israel in the O. T. was conceived of as the Bride of Yahweh. It is as the Spiritual Israel, as the Church triumphant in the Heavenly Jerusalem, that the Bride evangelizes the earth afresh an evangelization which was promised in xiv. 7, xv. 4, and which, when it is accomplished, will make true in fact what was already declared as accomplished in the counsels of heaven in xi. 15, cycycro 17 oorixcta rov KOO-AOV TOV miMow jxwv Kal rov Xpurrov avrov. England can mean either a certain geographical expanse of country or the people who live in it See xix. 9 p. 129.

jfpxou. Cf. vi. i. This word seems to be taken universally as the reply of the Church to the voice of Jesus in ver. 12. But, as we have seen above, the Bride is the Heavenly Jerusalem or its blessed inhabitants in the Millennial Kingdom and not the

Church before the Advent Thus Christ has already come in this vision. Further, in line 17, there can be no question that cpxcrlco refers to the coming of him that is athirst to Christ. It is, therefore, only natural, apart wholly from the force of the term 1 WA I?, to take fy ov in 17 in the same sense: i. e. as the invitation of the Spirit of Christ, of the Heavenly Jerusalem, and of those who accepted the message, to the world of men that were still thirsting for life and truth or were willing to accept them. Cf. John vi. 35, 6 p oAcro? irpo? c ov p. rj TTCIVOOT, KOL 6 irtcrrcvcov cfc CAC ol py St o-ei trwirorc: vii. 37, lav rts, px r0a irpos p. c Kal Trtvcrw. Cf. the Didache, x. 6, in the post-Communion prayer of the Church.

"Let grace come And let this world go. Hosanna to the Son of David, If any one is holy, let him come If any one is not, let him repent Come, Lord (i. e.

We have here a spiritual adaptation of certain parts of our text. Here, since the Second Advent of Christ is still in the distance, the prayer " Come, Lord " can be taken eschatologically as well as spiritually.

leal 6 dkoowk KT. The call was to be taken up by such as heard it and repented. The hearer is to be regarded as one who heard and accepted. 6 SI OP pxr0u. Cf. Isa. Iv. i (KDirte D o5 D!); John vii. 37, lav TIS, cxcr0t irpos AC KOL TTIVCTOI. Cf. also xxi. 6 of our text.

JSwp IWTJS Stuped. The phrase recurs in xxi. 6 where it rightly has the article rov v aro? TT S 0117 8apcav a fact which points to xxi. 6 as really coming later in the text

CHAPTER XX. 4-15. i. Contents.

This section follows naturally on the elaborate description of the Heavenly Jerusalem, which had come down from heaven to be the abode of Christ and the glorified martyrs. After this vision we have another vision of the glorified martyrs who alone had part in the first resurrection (xx. 4-6). Then, at the close of the Millennial Kingdom, Satan is loosed and leads Gog and Magog to the assault of the Beloved City, whereupon follows their destruction by fire from heaven, and Satan is cast into the lake of fire (7-10). This section closes with a vision of the great white throne, before whose presence the former heaven and earth had vanished, of the raising of the righteous and wicked from the " treasuries " and from Sheol to be judged, and the casting of death and Hades into the lake of fire (11-15).

This section has suffered from a transposition of the text in 4. Most probaby 13 stood originally before 1 2. Glosses have been added at the close of 12 and 14, and the text tampered with in 13 on dogmatical grounds. 13 is meaningless as it stands. 4-15 with the above exceptions comes from the hand of John as we shall now show alike by its diction and idiom. That it forms an organic and indispensable element of the Book is obvious.

2. Diction.

4. t T. paprupiai 'lijaou icai Sia T. yw r. Ocog: cf. i. 2, 9, vi. 9, xii. ii. 06. T 0y)piok oufci T. cuW afirou: cf. xiv. 9. T x p a YI Jia T H Tttirok KCU lia T. x c P a: c f- x

Xcucrai jcrx.: cf. v. 10.

5. Zh rav= " came to life: cf. ii. 8 (xiii. 14). cf. xv. 8, xvii. 17, xx. 3.

6. 6 Scurcpos Odkaros: cf. ii. II, XXL 8. Upcis cuaouaik: cf. i. 6, v. 10.

7. CK TTJS 4uxaicfjs: cf. ii. 10 for phrase.

8. irxarijcrai ra?6: cf. xti. 9, xiii. 14 (xviii. 23), xix. 20, xx. 3, 10. K rats T acrapo-i yuiacus rfjs yi)S: cf. vii. I for the phrase. owayaycik adrous els T. insXejio: cf. xvi. 14 for the phrase.

10. 6 Sid0oxos 6 irxawy: cf. xii. 9, 6 Saravas 6 irxaiwy. PXT 0T cis T. Xip, it)i rou irup5s: cf. xix. 20, xx. 14, 15. Sirou KCU: cf. xi. 8. Paoxma aorrai: cf. ix. 5, xiv. 10. Vjplpas KOI KUKT S: cf. iv. 8, vii. 15, etc. cis T. aluyas T. auSfwy: cf. i. 6, 18, iv. 9, etc.

11. (tyuyek. KCU. odx cdp 6i: cf. xvi. 20, fyvyev ical. ovx cvptorjo-av. i iros o x cdp Oi) aurois: cf. xii. 8.

12. iorwras twmov T. 6p6 Hi: cf. vii. 9, rrorres evowrior r. Opovav, viii. 2, etc. Y c YP a f JL u f T0 s P pxiois: cf. L 3. cv avrg ycypaAxcia: xiii. 8, xx. 15, xxi. 27.

13. ikpiorjaap IKOOTOS Kard T cpya afrrwk. For ciccurros with plural verb cf. v. 8 (cf. John xvi. 32), and for Kara ra 14. lpxV)6r)rar cis T. Xifnr)K TOU irup s: cf. io, 15, xix. 20. 16. c6pc 6f). ycypa t ic tos cf. ill 2 for construction,

T. ptpxcftTjs IWTJS: cf. hi. 5, xxi. 27.

3. Idioms. 4. wpo9cicjnf)rar ri 9i piw: see note on vii. IT.

l irl T. x P 01: see n jte on xiii. 16, vii. 3.

6. XP 1 vnth su bj-: " 2 5 note v"- 4 xv etc- 6. liri Torfrwk. ofiic x l ouoriay: cf. ii. 26.

8. JK. aflrfik: cf. iii. 8, vii. 2, 9, ix. n, etc.

18. ic K="gave up 19 a Hebraism in this sense = ni In two cases the text abandons our author's idiom owing to the ignorance of the editor.

4. Abandonment of the author's idiom by insertion of oiwes by editor in row irarexcjcioAciwK. jcal oinvcs ov irpoo-fkvvtjo-av. See note on i. 5.

11. rov jcaftflcvov CTT! avrov: see note on iv. 2. Our author wrote fcr! avrov, but of our author's unique treatment of this phrase the editor of xxi. 4-xxii. was ignorant.

4-6. Vision of the glorified martyrs who reign with Christ for a thousand years.

4. The construction of this verse is difficult. Thus we have two clauses, ical cfcalurav r avrov?, Kal fcpfia isorj avrofc, intervening between ctsov and its accusative ra lvxfa. But not only is the construction irregular, but the sense is hopelessly uncertain from the standpoint of our author. For if we ask who are those who seat themselves on the thrones, no satisfactory answer can be given. It is not the glorified martyrs; for they are first referred to in the words ras rvx a r v 7r 7r ACKUTACVCOV. And yet from iii. 21, where it is said that the martyrs are to share the throne of Christ, we should expect them to be referred to here and to sit on the thrones as Christ's assessors. Somewhat in favour of this view is Christ's promise to His Apostles in Matt. xix. 28, icaftpreo-fc Kal vicfc evi 3o)8cfca 0povov. Likewise in Dan. vii. 9 (LXX Theod.), coeupow cox ore (orov, Theod.) Opovoi ercft rav, and vii. 26 (Theod.), TO Kpirypiov ikaoio-cv (LXX, rj icpuri? fca tlcrcrai), and vii. 22 (Theod.), icai TO Kplpja. (LXX, TTJV Kpuriv) 2Sa)KCv (+ roi9, LXX) aytot? (+ TOV, LXX), v!arrov, we have passages which not only speak of the function of judgment as assigned by the Most High to the saints, but appear to have suggested the clauses in our text. Cf. i Cor. vl 2 sq., ovic oisare ore o! aywn TOV Kovpov Kpivoixrw. art dyycxov? icpivovficr.

Thus owing both to the ungrammatical structure of the text and its unintelligibleness it is not improbable that tfpovovs, KOI ckaj0i(rav cv avrovs feat jcpcma 80 17 avrot; KOI was originally a marginal gloss based on Daniel, or rather that this passage has got displaced and should be restored after cat Ivl ryv x V a avro)v. By adopting the latter alternative, as the present editor has done, we restore sanity to the text by making it at once grammatical and intelligible, and recovering the lost parallelism of the passage:.

Kai cfto? T. +uxd T. ireirtxfkwrjjl wk Bid T. uaprupiai hjaou

Kal Bid T. Xrfyop TOU Ocou, ical ozrires od irpoatkunjaav rd 0T)pioK odse T. cikW adrou, ical o

Kal ct8oy Opovous Kal cxdoiaak fir xal Kpiua S6v) afirois.

This signifies that authority is now vested in the hands of the righteous, and not in those of the oppressors of the Church as aforetime.

TOP ir ircxckir 4, ckii, i. e. beheaded by the n-cxckw the instrument of capital punishment in republican Rome. Cf. Diod. Sic. xix. 101, pa?8tera9 rcaewc Kara TO irarpiov 20os. Joseph. Ant. xiv. 7. 4, SfuTrtciiy Se, ctriorcixavros avrj Uoptrrjiov dirojcrctvat AXc avspov TOV Aptaro ouxov, airiacramcvos TOV vcavarkw cirl rots TO irpurrov cis Pwwitovs Ifrifjlaptijfievok ra ircxcxct Sie p cratO. In vi. 9, xviii. 24 we find ccr ayievwv, the word used in connection with the Lamb that was sacrificed, v. 6, 9, 12, xiii. 8.

8i T. faptupiap itjaou xal Sid T. X4yop T. Oeoo. These phrases are found in the opposite order in i. 2, 9, vi. 9. Cf. xil n.

olrikcs ou irpoackunfjaak Krx. These had all suffered martyrdom according to xiii. 15. The clause gives a further definition of those who had been faithful unto death. To regard these as forming a second class of the faithful, i. e. the surviving faithful, is against the actual statement in xiii. 15, and the presuppositions that underlie xiv.-xix. (see pp. 4, 26, 40, 96 ad fin.) and also against the immediate context; for in that case we should have to attach two conflicting meanings to 2 i? cray which immediately follows: i. e. "lived again" and "continued to live" according as we connect it with the first class, the actual martyrs, or the second class, the confessors. Moreover, the opening words of 5, oi Xonroi row vcfcpow, clearly imply that the persons referred to in 4 were among the vtxpoi according to the usual phraseology.

otrikcs. This is probably an addition made by the disciple who edited these last chapters. See note on i. 5 b-6. By its omission we should recover our author's normal resolution of the participle into a finite verb, i. e. r. ircircxckio-pcvw. Kal ov irpoo-ckwi7(rav "who had been beheaded and had not worshipped."

irporckUKi)aak rd 6i)piof rrx. See vii. 1 1 n.

T X Y T- ptaw Kal M T. x 4 a- See xiii. 16 (.), vii. 3 (.).

li)rar, i. e. "came to life" (cf. ii. 8, xiii. 14; Rom. xiv. 9) in human parlance, though in their life in heaven they had been more truly alive than when they had been on earth. With this first resurrection or manifestation of the glorified martyrs in the Millennial Kingdom we should compare that of all the departed saints with Christ in i Thess. iv. 14-17, and that of certain saints who had been taken up alive into heaven in 4 Ezra vii. 28 (cf. vi. 26). This line resumes briefly the preceding eight lines.

Ipcurixcucrak perd TOU Xpurrou x TTJ. Cf. v. 10. The earliest authorities for the belief in a temporary kingdom of the Messiah are i Enoch xci.-civ. (xciii. 1-14, xci. 12-19), P SS- Sol. xi., xvii.; Sibyll. Or. iii. 1-62; Jub. xxiil 27-29, 31, TI; 2 Bar. xxx., xl 3, Ixxiv. 2, xii. 34; i Cor. xv. 23-28. The limits assigned to its duration are various. In 4 Ezra vii. 28 sq. this kingdom is to endure for four hundred years, and to come to a close with the death of the Messiah and ail His companions, and the world is to return to primeval silence a statement apparently without parallel for its explicitness in Jewish literature In 2 Bar. xxx., on the other hand, Christ returns in glory to heaven at the close of the Messianic reign. In 2 Enoch xxxii. 2-xxxiii. 2 there is a reference to a period of Sabbatic rest of a thousand years after the close of six thousand years of the world's history. Barnabas, Ep. xv. 2-8, accepts this view, and adds that the Son of God will appear at the close of the six thousand years to put an end to the reign of the Lawless one, to judge the wicked and to change the sun, moon, and stars. At the close of the Millennial period there will be the beginning of another world (oxXov KOO-AOV apx v). See my Eschatology, pp. 248, 250 sq., 270 sq., 301 sq., 330, etc. Weber 2, 373. The reckoning of a thousand years was based on a combination of Gen. L 2 and Ps. xc. 4 = 2 Pet iii. 8. From this it was concluded that as each day of creation stood for a world-day of a thousand years, so the history of the world would embrace a world-week of seven thousand years, six thousand years till the final judgment and a thousand years of blessedness and rest 5. ot Xoiirol TOP PCKPWK odk lltjaak. Therefore not even the righteous, who had died a peaceful death, have part in this first resurrection. We should observe that John, who must have been well acquainted with the traditional and current belief, that the righteous survivors would be blessed on the advent of the kingdom, deliberately ignores it This can only mean, as has been frequently shown in the preceding pages (see p. 183), that John held that there would be no righteous survivors on the advent of the kingdom. The traditional belief is attested in Dan. xii. 12; Pss. Sol. xvii. 50; Sibyll Or. iil 371; i Thess. iv. 17; i Cor. xv. 51-52; Asc. Isa. iv. 15.

aihrtj 4 dvdcmuris irpori). This must not be construed in a purely spiritual sense and taken to mean a death to sin and a new birth unto righteousness, i. The earliest expounders of the Apocalypse, such as Justin Martyr, Tertullian, Irenaeus, Hippolytus, and Victorinus, quite rightly take the words in a literal sense of an actual reign of Christ with the glorified martyrs on earth. The spiritualizing method which emanated from Alexandria put an end to all trustworthy exegesis of the Apocalypse, when adopted in its entirety with reference to the Apocalypse. The meaning assigned by the votaries of this method became wholly arbitrary, and every student found in the Apocalypse what he wished to find (see my Studies in the Apocalypse, 8, 9, 10, 12, 13, 14, 28, 30, 36, 38, 48, etc). The earliest expounders were right, as they were in close touch with the apostolic time.

2. Moreover, the Talmud, and other Jewish writings, and specially the Jewish Apocalypses, attest a literal reign and no other of the Messiah, so far as they deal with the question.

3. The context itself is wholly against taking the words in a spiritual sense; for (a) this resurrection is obviously the guerdon of martyrdom, and begins not with the beginning of the Christian life but after its earthly close, (b) As Alford rightly urges: "no legitimate treatment of it (.?. the text itself) will extort what is known as the spiritual interpretation now in fashion. If, in a passage where two resurrections are mentioned, where certain ryxu Ifrorav at the first, and the rest of the vc pot Zo-av only at the end of a specified period after the first, if in such a passage the first resurrection may be understood to mean spiritual rising with Christ, while the second means literal rising from the grave; then there is an end of all significance in language, and Scripture is wiped out as a definite testimony to anything." Hence attempts to revive the spiritualizing interpretation of the Millennial Kingdom are to be deplored from every standpoint

But since the first resurrection embraces only the glorified martyrs, who return to earth to share the Millennial Kingdom with Christ in the Jerusalem which comes down from heaven, it is different in character from the second. For only the faithful who had undergone martyrdom have part in it, whereas at the second resurrection the rest of the faithful and all the unfaithful rise to judgment As we shall see on xx. 12, these two classes appear before the great white throne, the former, as we must conclude, in their glorified spiritual bodies, and the latter simply as disembodied souls i. e. naked.

6. By meeting martyrdom on behalf of their faith the martyrs are admitted to share in the Millennial Kingdom, are not subject to the second death, and accordingly are exempt from the Judgment that is to follow on the close of the kingdom. Moreover, their priestly character in bringing the knowledge of

God and Christ to the nations during the Millennial Kingdom appears to be referred to in the expression Upcls rov 0cov al rov Xpurrov (see below).

paitdpios itat fiyiof. Majeapco? is used seven times in each case in connection with a beatitude cf. i. 3, xiv. 13, xvi. 15, xix. 9, xx. 6, xxii. 7, 14. Syios though of frequent occurrence is not used in this connection elsewhere in our author. Hence it is possible, as Wetstein suggests, that aytos refers to the blessed in their priestly capacity (tcpcis rov 0cov) and uacaptos in their kingly (jgao-iacverovow). The combination " blessed and holy" is found in Jub. ii. 23.

6 IX K plpos Iv. Cf. John xiii. 8, OVK fycis jtcpoe tcr cxov: also in xxi. 8 in a different form, TO xepos avrtitv, and xxii. 19.

firi Torfrwh. For lirt in this sense with the genitive cf. ii. 26 xi. 61 xiv. 18!

6 ocjrcpos Odwros. This death is defined in xxi. 8 (cf. Matt. x. 28). It is mentioned already in ii. 11 as a punishment, from which those, who are faithful to the end, are exempt In xx. 14 it is clearly an interpolation.

ofc jfxci cgoiaia?. Cf. ii. 26, vi. 8, ix. 3, etc.

tcpcis TOO 6cou KCU Tou Xpurtou. Cf. L 6,! cpet9 T(5 0 c3. Now it is to be observed that in i. 6 (see note in loc.), v. 10, and here the priesthood and the kingship of those whom John addressed are conjoined (in i Pet. ii. 9 they are combined in one expression, Wixctov Uparcvui). But it is further noteworthy that V. IO (oroito-as avrovs. 3acrta. ctay ical tcpei? xat fiari vovtiv 7rl T S y s) and the present passage connect the priesthood with a special period of kingship, i. e. that which they are to exercise in the Millennial Kingdom, and share with Christ (xx. 6) on the earth (v. 10). These facts suggest that the priestly offices of the blessed in the Millennial Kingdom have to do with the nations, who are to be evangelized during this period (xiv. 6-7, xv. 4), and this suggestion receives some support from xxii. 5 where, when the eternal reign of all the saints after the Judgment is mentioned (facriacwrovcriy cfc r. aumas r. aicavcoy), there is not the remotest reference to any special or other priesthood of the faithful paaixcifoouaif per aurou. The scene of this reign is given in the proleptic vision, v. 10, as tvl rq? yr s.

7-1O. Close of the Millennial Kingdom and of its evangelizing activities. Thereupon follow the loosing of Satan, the march of Gog and Magog all the faithless upon the earth against the Beloved City, their destruction by supernatural means, and the casting of Satan into the lake of fire. The Seer does not say what became of the Heavenly Jerusalem, but its withdrawal from the earth with Christ and the glorified martyrs before the

Judgment is presupposed, while its return to the new earth in a renewed form is definitely stated in xxi. 2. Since " the Beloved City " in xx. 9 is the Heavenly

Jerusalem, the saints referred to in the same verse include the risen martyrs and the converts from among the nations.

The same order of events appears in Sibyll. Or. iil 662-701, i. e. the advent of the Messiah, the establishment of His kingdom, the attack of the nations on Jerusalem, and the destruction of the invading hosts by God. In certain sections (A 1, A 8, A 8) of 2 Baruch (ist century A. D.; see my edition, pp. liii. sqq.) the writers look forward to a temporary Messianic kingdom preceded by the Messianic woes, a beneficent domination of the world by the Messiah preceded by the destruction of the antichristian powers, and of such heathen powers as had been in any way associated with them. In the Son of Man Vision in 4 Ezra xiii. the Messianic woes come first (xiii. 30-31), then the manifestation of the Messiah (xiii. 32), the assault of the heathen nations on the Messiah, and their destruction by Him, xiii. 33-34, and the manifestation of the Heavenly Jerusalem, xiii. 36. For yet another scheme of the last things see 4 Ezra iv. 5S-v. 13 vi. 11-28, vii. 26-44 (Box's edition, p. HI). According to a contemporary of our author, R. Eliezer ben Hyrkanos or R. Eliezer the Great, the woes of the Messiah were to come first, then the day of Gog and Magog, and then the Judgment. If we pass on to the Coptic Apocalypse of Elias (a Jewish work edited by a Christian, 2nd century A. D.) we find the order of events as follows: the destruction of Antichrist and his adherents, the advent of Christ with His saints, the creation of the new heaven and the new earth and the Millennial Kingdom! In the Hebrew Apocalypse of Elijah (3rd century A. D.) Gog and Magog appear after a Messianic reign of forty years. On their annihilation follow the Judgment and the descent of Jerusalem from heaven.

It will be observed that, though each of the works above cited differs in some respect from our text, in some respects they all agree with it It is obvious at a glance that our author here forsakes the apocalyptic style and adopts the prophetic. But he has already done so in, and in 9-10 he reverts to his apocalyptic style. Further, there are no grounds in this section itself for assuming a source, since there is not a single construction at variance with our author's style, though there are new phrases as might be expected in describing new events.

7. Xuftjattiu. Cf. vojjvat in 3 and the same verb in ix. 14 used in the same sense. IK T. uxaicvjs afrrou. Cf. ii. zo xviil 2 for the word 8. cxcuacrai (cf. iii. 12, vi. 2, 4, ix. 3, etc.) irxarijroi ra In 3 Satan was cast into the abyss, Iva. py irxavrjoy In ra 117.

to THIS Tfarapcri ywiais rrjs yfjs. Cf. vii. i where this phrase has already occurred.

TK rfcy itol Mayrfy. Three matters call for consideration here: i. The names. 2. The duplication of the invasion by and the judgment of the heathen nations, i. e. before and after the setting up of the Messianic Kingdom. 3. The comprehension of these terms in our text i. Magog first appears in Gen. x. 2 as a son of Japheth, but in the Mass, of Ezek. xxxviii. 2 Magog is represented as the land from which Gog came: i. e. " Gog of the land of Magog." The LXX (lire Fy ical ryv ffjv rov Maywy) and Peshitto, however, have " toward Gog and (+ toward, 1 Pesh.) the land of Magog," a reading which prepares the way for the later view current in Judaism, which conceived Gog and Magog to be two different leaders. In Ezek. xxxix. 6 Magog seems to be the name of a people. Gog is the foe whose invasion from the north had been prophesied by Jeremiah (iii.-vi.) and by Zephaniah (i. 7), but whose coming had hitherto been looked for in vain. The name Gog is undoubtedly ancient; for it is found in the Tel Amarna letters (1400 B. C.) in the form Gagaja as a designation of the northern nations. In Jubilees viii. 25 the land of Gog is mentioned. Gog is identified with the Scythians by Josephus (Ant. i. 6. i) and by the Chronicles of Jerachmeel (xxxi. 4). In Jub. vii. 19, ix. 8, Magog appears as a son of Japheth, as in Gen. x. 2. The same idea that underlies the LXX of Ezek. xxxviii. 2 is definitely set forth in Sibyll. Or. iil 512, 519: alal croi, Poy KOL TTOUCTW c i aia Mayor. "Y urros Scinyv eirtireu ct Ifoccri irxiyyiyv.

and 319 sq.: oioi croc, XtofkL r y ij8c Mayoiy ficarov ora Ai0t09rav iroraAoiv, irocrav aiaro? c c;(ua 8e fl.

By the second century B. C. this invasion of Palestine by the two peoples Gog and Magog was clearly expected.

2. The duplication of the attack on Jerusalem (see p. 46), i. e. before and after the establishment of the Messianic Kingdom and of the judgment on the heathen nations. The first attestation of this conception is, of course, in Ezek. xxxvii. 21-xxxix. In xxxvii. 21-28 the kingdom with the Messiah, the son of David, is established after the Captivity. Thereupon follows the final attack of the heathen natioas upon it in xxxviii.-ix. In the fragment, i Enoch Ivi. 5-8, we have a description of such an attack. In 4 Ezra xiii. 5, 8-9, 28-35 there is another account of this final assault of the heathen nations on the Messiah and on Mount Zion, or the Heavenly City, xiii. 35-36 (cf. 6), just as in our text.

In many of the authorities it is only the hostile heathen hosts that are destroyed: cf. Pss. Sol xvii 32; 2 Bar. Ixxii. 4; Tobit xiii. n, xiv. 6 sq.; Sanh. io5a; but in most Jewish writings after 100 A. D. a harsher view prevails as to the future destiny of all the Gentiles.

Gog and Magog are frequently mentioned in Rabbinic works. These nations march against God and the Messiah, Aboda-zara, 3 b. This war and the last judgment were to last twelve months according to the Rabbi Aqiba, Edujoth, ii. 10. Other references to Gog and Magog will be found in Ber. 7 and also in the Targ. Jer. on Num. xi. 26, where it is recorded that Medad prophesied: "In fine extremitatis dierum Gog et Magog et exercitus ejus ascendent contra Jerusalem, t per manus regis Messiae cadent, etseptem annis integris ignem accendent filii Israel ex eonim instrumentis bellicis " (cf. also Targ. Jon. in loc.). In the Targ. Jon. on Ex. xl. n, Num. xxiv. 17, Gog's armies are mentioned, and in the Targ. Jer. on Deut. xxxii. 39 and on Isa. xxxiii. 22. See Weber, Bousset, and Volz in loc.

3. The terms "Gog and Magog" comprehend all the faithless upon the earth. These are all destroyed by fire from heaven in 9. Hence the earth is left without inhabitant at the close of the Millennial Kingdom. Since the faithful at the close of the thousand years withdraw from the earth along with the Heavenly Jerusalem, there is no longer upon the earth any in whom is the breath of human life. At this point our Apocalypse agrees with 4 Ezra vii. 29-30, which declares that the world will revert " into the primeval silence. like as in the first beginnings, so that no man is left": cf. 2 Bar. iii. 7, "Shall the world return to its nature (of aforetime) and the age revert to primeval silence?"

cnikayaycik ad-rod? els TOP irlxcpor. This phrase has already occurred in xvi. 14.

K 6 ftpiojjlos ark s KT. On the Hebraism iii. 8, xiii. 8, 12, etc. On the metaphor o9 y 5tios rfc Qaxdo-oys, cf. Gen. xxii. 17; Jos. xi. 4; Judg. vii. 12, etc. The phrase 17 axxos rfc Oaxcnnrs has already occurred in a literal sense in xii. 18.

9. d jtjrak. Cf. i Enoch Ivi. 6 sq. where the Parthians and Medes are mentioned:

"And they shall go up and tread under foot the land of His elect ones.

But the city of My righteous shall be a hindrance to their horses. 9

Also Zech. xii. 3. dvaJovw is the word always used in connec- tion with the pilgrims going up to Jerusalem. We might compare the " Songs of the Ascents " the title of certain of the later Psalms sung by the pilgrims as they approached the Holy City. Cf. Ezek. xxxviii. 9, n, 16 of the going up of Gog to Jerusalem. Bousset and Gunkel explain the avtp-rjo-av of the march of Gog and Magog from the outlying periphery of the earth to the mountain of God lying in the centre of the earth.

firl ri irxdros TT)S yr. There are two ways of rendering these words, i. " Through the breadth of the earth." This phrase is found in the LXX of Hab. i. 6 (in connection with the march of the Chaldean army against Jerusalem) where it is a translation of p prnpp. 2. It is suggested that this phrase describes the goal, towards which Gog and Magog were marching, i. e. Jerusalem, which in Ezek. xxxviii. 12 is called the centre or navel of the earth. Wellhausen suggests that the Greek phrase before us = nine p (Ezek. xxxviii. n) and is actually identical with p n-fl3ld = fyufxixos-nfr yi s (xxxviii. 12).

JKiiicxcuffai. Here and in John x. 24 only in the N. T.

T V irapcfj oxV TUP Ayiwk. 1.0. the same as the Heavenly City. If the heathen nations had the daring to attack the supernatural Messiah and His elect (xvii. 14) it is not surprising that they should assault His city.

TV ir iv iv Y ai "l in l K- Tne " Hol Y City " is rightly here designated " the beloved." For a thousand years it has been the seat of Christ's Kingdom and the centre of the evangelizing efforts of the Church. Thus its record stands out in strong contrast with that of the earthly Jerusalem, which according to our author " is called spiritually Sodom and Egypt" (xi. 8). As such it rightly perished at the hands of the antichristian power of Rome. But far other is the destiny of "the beloved city." When Gog and Magog have been destroyed by fire and Satan cast down into the lake of fire, the Holy City, which had come down from heaven, is presupposed to be withdrawn from the sphere of the former heaven and the former earth, and after that it has itself been renewed (observe XXL 2, ify irdxiv TTJV aylav Icpovo-ox i icaimjr) to return from heaven from God to the new earth.

That an assault on Christ and the Holy City should be deemed an inconceivable event by a few scholars can only be due to their want of acquaintance not only with Jewish and Christian Apocalyptic but even with the text of our author. For in our author we find the Parthian kings making war upon the Lamb and the elect (xvii. 14), while in xix. 19 the kings of the earth and their armies levy war on Christ and His hosts from heaven (xix. 14). These passages refer to events at the initiation of the Millennial Kingdom. In 4 Ezra xiii., as in our text, the heathen nations (xiii. 5, 33, 34) assail the Messiah, who came flying with the clouds of heaven (xiii. 3) and brought with Him the Heavenly Jerusalem (xiii. 6, 35, 36), but with a flaming breath from His lips He burnt them all up so that there was nothing more to be seen of them " save only dust of ashes and smell of smoke" (xiii. 10-11, 38). We have here almost a perfect parallel to the account in our text from what was practically a contemporary Jewish source. For we have a supernatural Messiah, a Heavenly Jerusalem established on Mount Zion, an assault of the heathen nations, and their destruction by fire. There is, of course, one outstanding difference between the two accounts, i. e. that whereas these events are connected with the first advent of the Messiah in the Jewish document, they are incidents belonging to the second advent of Christ in the Christian Apocalypse.

Likewise in 4 Ezra xii. 32-34 we have a description of the Messiah destroying the heathen nations especially Rome. Similarly in 2 Bar. xl. i sq., Ixxii. 2 sqq. That He is a supernatural Messiah whom the nations have attacked is to be inferred from the description in 4 Ezra xiii. 3", 26, xiv. 9, and 2 Bar. xxx. i. We have already become familiar with this conception of the Messiah in i Enoch xxxvii.-lxxi.

icawptj irup IK. Tog oupayog. Cf. Ezek. xxxviii. 22, irvp at 0ctov jfyc a cv avrov (rov Twy) ical CTTI iravras rows ACT avrov: xxxix. 6, diroorcxo) irvp rt Pay, and the references given in the preceding note from 4 Ezra in exactly analogous circumstances: 2 Thess. i. 8, ii. 8; Asc. Is. iv. 18. So far as words go, a perfect parallel to fcarcii;. avtovs is found in 2 Kings i. 10.

Kartyayck afirou's. All the hosts of Gog and Magog are burnt up that is all the faithless upon the earth (see note 3 on 8 above). At the close of 10 we are left to infer that the Holy City has withdrawn with all the faithful from the earth. Thereupon follows the Judgment of the risen dead by God Himself, from whose presence the former outworn heaven and earth vanish into nothingness.

10. 6 u 0oxos 6 irxakuir. Cf. xii. 9, 6 Saravas 6 wxavv: xiii. 14 xix. 20. 40X 6i) els T K Xijutjv mrx. Cf. xix. 20. Sirou Kau Cf. xi. 8: also (for OTTOV without KOI) ii. 13, ovav. ct, xii. 6, 14. Cf. xvii. 9. 3curmcr64rorrai (cf. ix. 5, xiv. 10). t"jfupas xal yuicrls (cf. iv. 8, vii. 15, xii. 10, xiv. n). els rods alwyas ruv auSpw (i. 6, 18, iv. 9, 10, v. 13, vii. 12, x. 6, xi. 15, etc.).

11-16. Vision of the great white throne and of Him who sat thereon. Disappearance of the former heaven and earth. Judgment of the dead. Death and hell cast into the lake of fire. This vision consists of four stanzas of three lines each. This vision has suffered at the hands of interpolators.

11. ctok Optsfof jacyar. As distinct from those mentioned in iv. 4, xx. 4, this throne is designated tcyav. Moreover, whereas God has assessors seated on adjoining thrones in Dan. vii. 9, here He judges alone. With this line and the text which refers to God we might compare Isa. vi i, "I saw the Lord sitting upon a throne. and His train filled the temple." In our text there is not the same explicitness. God is referred to indeed under the unmistakable designation 6 KajKvos krl rov Opovov, but the place of the judgment is not specified. The latter is only natural; for before the judgment has taken place (12-15) the former heaven and earth have vanished into nothingness (i i 0). Hence the great white throne is conceived as the only thing (save the Heavenly Jerusalem which was to be renewed) that survives the annihilation of all that belongs to the first heaven and the first earth, and as situated somewhere in illimitable space. It is before this great white throne that the risen souls clothed in spiritual bodies and

unclothed, i. e. those of the righteous and of the wicked, appear. Since this throne was created before the world (Berisheth rab. i.), as the eternal place of God, it could well be conceived as surviving the world's annihilation. According to 4 Ezra vii. 33 also, " the Most High shall be revealed upon the throne of judgment" after the first world has disappeared (vii. 31; see p. 198). It was different, however, in earlier Apocalypses, where the Messianic Kingdom was everlasting on the present earth and was of necessity preceded by the Final Judgment. In such cases the Final Judgment took place upon the earth, and the throne of judgment was set up in Palestine, i Enoch xc. 20. In Joel iii. 2, 12, 14-16 and i Enoch liii. i the valley of Jehoshaphat is the scene of this judgment and the agents are the angels (Joel iii. 13).

The Final Judgment is reserved in our text for God Himself; but this Judgment has to do only with the dead, or rather those risen from the dead, both good and bad, whereas the judgment of the living va xiv. 14,18-20, xvii. 14, xix. 11-21, xx. 7-10 is committed wholly to Christ. In assigning the Final Judgment exclusively to the Father even in this limited form (see, however, xxii. 13, 12) our author stands apart from the doctrine presented in John V. 22, ovsc yap 6 Trarrjp Kpiv i ovscya, aaAa rrjv Kpurtv Tracrav Scscokcv T j vlq, and Matt. vii. 22, 23, xvi. 27, xxv. 31-46; Acts xvii. 31; 2 Cor. v. 10. Cf. i Enoch xlv. 3, Ixix. 27; 2 Bar. Ixxii. 2-6. On the other hand, God alone is mentioned in this relation in Matt. vi. 4, 6, 14, 15, 18, xviii. 35, while St. Paul sometimes ascribes the Final Judgment to God, Rom. xiv. 10, and sometimes to Christ, 2 Cor. v. 10.

XCUKSK This epithet may point to the absolute equity of the Judgment. Or since according to our text and 4 Ezra vii. 31 the first world and all that belongs to it have vanished, and according to 4 Ezra vil 41-42, "there is neither sun nor moon nor stars. neither shining nor brightness nor light, bat only the splendour of the glory of the Most High " (-frfy 1U5 VT), the throne of God is lighted up with the splendour of the Shekjnah, and hence it is the centre of light in the illimitable vastness of space. Whether this is so or not, it is the glory of God alone that lights up the universe. See note on r. 8o oy rov 0cov, XXL 10; also xxi. 23, note.

o3 TOO irpoorou tyuycv yij KU 6 oapai s. Cf. xvi 20. When we take this line in connection with that which follows, it is clear that there is here taught the literal vanishing of the former heaven and earth into nothingness. As I have shown in my Eschatology 127-128, the older doctrine in the O. T. was the eternity of the present order of things. This was the received view down to the 2nd century B. C. From the ist century B. C. onward in Judaism and Christianity, the transitoriness of the present heaven and earth was universally accepted. Cf. Mark xiii. 31, 6 ovpavos teal rj yfj irapexcvo-ovrat.

From the words before us we must conclude that before the Judgment began both heaven and earth had vanished into nothingness. This conclusion is of great importance when we come to deal with 13. That this was a contemporary Jewish doctrine we find from 2 Enoch Ixv. 6, " when all creation visible and invisible. shall end, then every man goes to the great judgment." See also 4 Ezra vil 31-36 (in the note on 13 below) where the same view is taught

Kai T6irof odx cdpkK) afrois. See xii. 8 n.

18. Since the verses that precede and follow 12 consist each of three lines, we naturally expect that 12 originally consisted of three lines also. When we examine the text we discover one or two disturbing glosses. When these are excised this verse is parallel in structure to that which precedes and that which follows it. But this verse should be transposed after 13, since it presupposes it.

rods Kcicpous, i. e. the rest of the dead who had no share in the first resurrection. Only the dead appear before the great white throne. As Christ had judged the quick in a series of judgments (see note on n), so God Himself judges all the dead save those who had pan in the first resurrection. From 11 taken in conjunction with 13 it is to be concluded that pur author has no thought here of a bodily resurrection save in the case of the righteous dead, who would naturally as in i Cor. xv. appear in their spiritual bodies. As regards the wicked, however, the case is different These would appear simply as disembodied souls "naked" in a spiritual environment without a body without the capacity for communication with or means of expres-VOL. n. 13 sion in that environment. Every wicked soul, therefore, would be thus shut up within itself and form its own hell even before it was cast into the lake of fire.

rods pcydxous KCU TOS juiepoife. Elsewhere our author writes TOVS fu pov at rovs uyc A. ov: cf. xi. 18, xiil 16, xix. 5, 1 8 (the usual order in the O. T.). But he may have here deliberately changed the order to emphasize the judgment which awaits the great ones of the earth, and which they so often escaped on earth. In the O. T. the order r. xcy. cat r. fuKpovs is found in Jonah iii. 5, but in i Sam. v. 9; Jer. vi. 13, xxxi. 34; Ps. cxv. 13 we have the usual order rov? ucpou? cat row Acyaaov?.

xal pi Xia JjroixoTio-ak. These books contain a record of all that men have done: cf. Dan. vii. 10, fi p ot tyoixorjouv: i Enoch 2 xc. 20, "The other took the sealed books and opened those books before the Lord of the Sheep "; 4 Ezra vi. 20, "The books shall be opened before the face of the firmament "; 2 Bar. xxiv. i, "Behold the days come and the books shall be opened in which are written the sins of all who have sinned"; Asc. Isa. ix. 22. On these books see my note on i Enoch 9 xlvii. 3, which deals with three distinct classes of heavenly books, two of which are mentioned in our text.

KU oxXo pipxiop jjroixor) 8 fcnv rfjs JWTJS. This book is the register of the righteous. Cf. i Enoch xlvii. 3, "The books of the living were opened before Him " (see note in loc.; also on iii. 5 of the present text). The explanatory clause looks like a gloss. Seeing that this book has already been mentioned with the article in iii. 5, xiii. 8, xvii. 8, such a clause is needless at all events. The relation of the book of life and the books is well stated by Alford. These "books and the book of life bore independent witness to the fact of men being or not being among the saved: the one by inference from the works recorded: the other by inscription or non-inscription of the name in the list. So the books could be as the vouchers for the book of life."

KOLT rd 2pyo am)?. This phrase is a mere tautology here. It is interpolated from 13, where it rightly occurs. If the dead are judged, e c row veypaxxeicov tv rots 2t? A. tw, that is the same thing as saying ckpiorjo-av fcocnro? Kara ra cpya avrstv (13).

13. This verse should be transferred before 12.

ical l8akcrt4 OAoawo f rois rcicpota rods xal 6 Orfrarof KOI 6 a8i)s ftaitak TOUS pcicpous TOUS Iv

Kal lkpiot)crak fcaoros itara r cpya afiroo.

This stanza betrays in its present form a hopeless confusion of thought, which can only be due to deliberate change of the text. The context cannot admit of a resurrection of the physical body from the sea seeing that the sea and everything pertaining to it 13. THE RIGHTEOUS WITH SPIRITUAL BODIES 195 had vanished. And yet this is the only natural meaning of 13. Hence, if 13 is original and we hold fast to the natural sense, z i b cannot be original. But the originality of iz b cannot be questioned, for xxi. 4 d, 5 presuppose it. Accordingly we must either interpret 13 in a wholly non-natural sense as defining not the place of departed souls but the means by which certain men perished, i. e. the sea, and 13 as giving the intermediate abode of all souls, which had died on sea or land, save only those of the martyrs. The general sense then would be: all souls together with their bodies even those lost at sea (13) are given up by Hades for judgment before the great white throne.

But it is only by a quite illegitimate tour deforce that such a meaning can be wrested from the words. 13 clearly presupposes the sea at once as existing and delivering up the bodies that had been engulfed in it, at the same time that Hades is represented as delivering up the souls that were in it. Body and soul would thus be reunited. The only natural meaning, then, of 13 is in conflict with the unmistakable statement in n b that sea is now non-existent, and with the presupposition that underlies the entire book, i. e. that the wicked rise as disembodied souls (see additional note on vi. 11). 1 Only the righteous are to possess 1 The doctrine of a bodily resurrection is consistently taught in I Enoch xxxvii.-lxxi. There the general resurrection takes place before the Judgment, while the former heaven and the foimer earth still subsist. In Izi. 5 we find an account of the resurrection of

"Those who had been destroyed by the desert, And those who had been devoured by the beasts, And those who had been devoured by the fish of the sea."

Here quite distinctly a physical resurrection is described. Further in the same work in li. I the body and soul are raised separately and reunited at the Final Judgment. In the case of the righteous a transformation of the physical body into a spiritual is presupposed in the rest of this section (Ixii. 15, 16).

"And in tho e days shall the earth also give back that which was entrusted to it,

And Sheol also shall give back that which it has received, And hell (= Abaddon) shall give back that which it owes."

Cf. also Ps.-Philo, dc Biblic. Antiquitatibus, iii. IO:

"Reddet infernus (= Hades) debitum suum, Et perditio (=Abaddon) restituet paratecen suam, Ut reddam unicuique secundum opera sua."

There is a remarkable parallelism here with our text (13). The doctrine of a physical resurrection is enforced dogmatically in 2 Bar. xlix.-li. and Sanh. 91. This was the orthodox Rabbinic belief, and it is expressed in the ancient Benediction (Ber. 6o b) still recited by the pious Jew every morning: "O my God, the soul which Thou gavest me is pure: Thou didst create it. and Thou wilt take it from me, but wilt restoie it unto me hereafter. Blessed art Thou, O Lord, who restores souls to dead bodies" (see Singer, Authorised Daily Prayer Book Hebrew and English, p. 5).

But this crass materialistic doctrine does not belong to the N. T. Such bodies, i. e. spiritual bodies. Finally, Sheol in our author is the abode, not of righteous but of wicked or indifferent souls. As we shall see presently, righteous souls (save those of the martyrs) were preserved in " the treasuries."

Hence we conclude that in Oaxtwa-a rove vocpous rofc fr avrjj there is a deliberate change of ra raACid into 17 0Acuro a in order to introduce the idea of a physical resurrection. These roActa (or "treasuries") contained the souls of the righteous (with the exception of the martyrs who were already in heaven), whereas ffip was the abode of the wicked souls. Thus we should have:

"And the treasuries gave up the dead that were in them, And death and Hades gave up the dead that were in them, And they were judged every man according to their works."

Our text thus, like the Pauline Epistles, teaches a resurrection of persons ("the dead" so called), not a resurrection of dead bodies even though in company with souls. The personality of the righteous is complete the soul clothed with a spiritual body: the personality of the unrighteous is incomplete the soul is without a body without the power of expressing itself or receiving impressions from without. Sin is ultimately self-destructive.

That such deliberate perversions of the text took place early probably in the 2nd century A. D. I shall show presently. In the meantime it is our task to prove that in apocalyptic circles, to which our author belonged, it was the accepted belief that the souls of the righteous were preserved in certain "treasuries." The word " treasuries " (in the Latin of 4 Ezra promptuaria, and in the Syriac of 4 Ezra and 2 Baruch P 1) clearly goes back to the Hebrew Dlttk, which is used also in the Talmud occasionally in this sense, and which in the Midr. rabba on Ecclesiastes iii. 21 (Weber 2, 338) is said to be placed in the heavenly height. These treasuries are first referred to in i Enoch c. 5, though not by name:

"And over all the righteous and holy He will appoint guardians from among the holy angels, To guard them as the apple of an eye, doctrine has no part in the Pauline Epistles, Hebrews, or in the Fourth Evangelist, nor does it find any countenance in our author, though it was enforced by many of the Fathers in the Christian Church from the 3rd century onward in opposition to Gnosticism, and other more legitimate doctrines within the Church on this question.

Until He makes an end of all wickedness and all sin, And though the righteous sleep a long sleep, they have nought to fear."

To these treasuries only the souls of the righteous were admitted. From this passage in i Enoch (early in the ist century B. C.) we come down to two Jewish works practically contemporary with our author, i. e. 2 Bar. and 4 Ezra. In 2 Bar. XXL 23, we have a remarkable confirmation of the above emendation of 13; for in xxi. 23 the angel of death is mentioned, then Sheol as the intermediate abode of wicked souls, and then the treasuries of the souls of the righteous. These treasuries are to be opened after the close of the Messianic Kingdom, 2 Bar. xxx. 2, and the souls of the righteous to come forth at the Final Judgment In 4 Ezra iv. 41-42 we find a second confirmation of the above restoration of 13.

"And he said unto me: Sheol and the treasuries of souls are like the womb: 42. For just as she who is in travail makes haste to escape the anguish of the travail; even so do these places hasten to deliver what has been entrusted to them from the beginning."

Here as Sheol (cf. viii. 53) is the abode of unrighteous souls, so the treasuries are the abode of righteous souls (cf. iv. 35, vii. 80). These treasuries were to restore the souls of the righteous at the Final Judgment, vii. 32, 95. These treasuries are likewise designated "habitations" (habitacula: cf. "mansions" or "abiding places," fjuovai, John xiv. 2) in vii. 85, 101, 121.

We have thus proved that towards the close of the ist century A. D. as well as earlier and later the souls of the righteous were conceived of as being guarded and at rest (cf. i Enoch c. 5; 4 Ezra vii. 95) in certain places called "treasuries," and that from these the souls of the righteous came forth at the Final Judgment

Such a conception as the above would suit pur text perfectly; for the Final Judgment has come, and since it is a judgment both of the righteous and the wicked, we exfect some reference to the former in our text. By the proposed restoration we recover this reference.

But the evidence in favour of this restoration is not yet complete. For an examination of our author's use of the word Sip shows that he uses it in a bad sense as the temporary abode of wicked souls. This is evident from the next verse (xx. 14), where it is said that death and Hades are cast down into the lake of fire. Hence 8ip bears no neutral complexion in our author. Had it done so, it would simply have vanished into nothingness like the earth (n b), but it is hurled into the abyss where Satan and his servants are tormented for ever and ever.

Thus, unless the text is restored as above suggested, there would only be a judgment of wicked souls, but by the above restoration we have a General Judgment of the righteous and the wicked.

It is significant that in 4 Ezra vii. 31-36 we find an analogous depravation of the text with a like object, that is, to introduce the idea of a physical resurrection. As might be expected, the thought of the text is thereby hopelessly confused. In vii. 31-36 we have a description in couplets of the new heaven and the new earth taking the place of the old which as corruptible had passed away.

31. "And it shall be that after seven days the Age, which is not yet awake, shall be aroused, And that which is corruptible shall perish."

32. And the treasuries shall restore those that were committed unto them.

33. And the Most High shall be revealed upon the throne of judgment 1

And compassion shall pass away And longsuffering shall disappear. 8 34. But judgment alone shall remain,

Truth shall stand and faithfulness flourish.

35. And recompense shall follow, And the reward be made manifest."

Box, following Kabisch, has through a strange misconception obelized 32 as an interpolation. But manifestly 32" is the intruder.

IS KCK. ilbwicak. Here Stsowu is used absolutely like jm = 1 Here a couplet has been displaced and another interpolated to introduce the idea of a physical resurrection.

32. " And the earth shall restore those that sleep in her, b. And the dust those that are at rest therein."

Seeing that the new world has already displaced the old in 31 this couplet is wholly at variance with the context Its aim is to assert the resurrection of the body, to rejoin the souls which come forth from the treasuries, 32. But since the treasuries are prepared for righteous souls only (cf iv. 35, vii. 80, 95; 2 Bar. xxi. 23, xxx. 2; I Enoch c. 5) the text would then teach only a resurrection of the righteous. But every couplet that follows proves that we have here a general resurrection. The lost couplet clearly spoke of Sheol giving up the souls of the wicked for judgment, as the treasuries in 32 yield up the souls of the righteous.

The Syriac here interpolates " And then cometh the end " against all the other versions.

9 The Syriac adds " And pity shall be afar off" against the Latin and the first Arabic versions. The Syr. is supported by the Eth. and Arab 8. The line appears to be a doublet

"to give up." It is not a classical use, nor so far as I am aware a Hellenistic one.

6 0dkatos KU 6 Si)s. As pointed out in the preceding note, 8179 can be here only the abode of unrighteous souls (as in i Enoch Ixiii. 10 xcix. H, ciii. 7; Pss. Sol. xiv. 6, xv. n), seeing that in the next verse it is cast into the lake of fire. Death and Hades have already been found together in i. 18 (.), vi. 8: also in Ps.-Philo, De Bibl Antiquitatibus. In the latter work the destruction of death and Hades are followed as in our text by the creation of a new heaven and a new earth.

"Et extinguetur mors,
Et infemus (= Hades) claudet os suum. Et erit terra alia et caelum aliud."

The alia and aliud here obviously go back to frepos which as distinguished from oaAo? involves a distinction in kind. While oaAos simply asserts the negation of identity, 2rcpos asserts the negation of likeness in kind. In 2 Ear. xxi. 23, when Sheol and the treasuries have yielded up the souls in them, the new world promised by God was to be manifested, xxi. 25. This accords with the order of events in our text, xx. 13, xxi. i. In 2 Enoch Ixv. TO it is said that "all corruptible things shall pass away, and there shall be eternal life."

c 4 Kpl0t aai IKOOTOS KCT T cpya aura?. Cf. ii. 23; Ps. xxviii. 4, Ixii. 13; Jcr. xvii. 10, Matt. x. 32, 33.

14-15. These two verses originally formed the concluding stanza of this section. The text as it stands is impossible. The statement OVTOS 6 tfdvaro? Sevrepos cartv, 17 Aimf)? rov irvpos can only be made in reference to human beings, who have undergone the first death, i. e. the physical one. Hence, if it belongs to the text, it does not do so in its present position. Here, though a number of cursives, the Sahidic Version and Primasius omit this line, the grounds for its rejection in its present position are not to be sought in textual evidence, since its intrusion is anterior to all such evidence. The real grounds for its rejection are that the statement is absolutely devoid of meaning. Even if death and Hades be regarded as persons, we cannot conceive (cf. Haussleiter, Die Lateinische Apocalypse 213) how the words 6 lavaro? 6 Scvrcpos can be applied to them. Moffatt suggests that this line was displaced from its original position after 15. There are, in fact, only these two alternatives. Either (i) the line is to be rejected as a gloss, and we must read as follows:

KCU 6 Odfaros icai 6 t)s tfi r Qi rav ci?-rt v Xi m f TOO irupo, (tat cl TIS oux up 8ij iv TJJ 0ipxu Ttjs IWTJS ycypajiplrof

Or (2) what appears here as the first and second lines must be read as the first, and what appears here as the third and fourth lines must be read as the second, and osros 6 0avaro 6 Scvrcpos COTIV, Mpvrj rov irvpos be read as the third. This latter arrangement is not free from serious objections. These are two. First, there does not appear any reasonable ground for the misplacement of the clause. In the next place, the clause in itself is an unmeaning mis-statement. The lake of fire is not the second death, but the second death is the lot of those who are cast into the lake of fire. The right definition of the second death is given in xxi. 8. The present writer, therefore, regards the clause as originally a marginal gloss drawn from xxi. 8 and subsequently incorporated into the text.

14. ip rj0T 7u els iv i Lrr v TOO irupfc. Cf. 10, xix. 20; Petr. Apoc. 8, ifavrj TIS rjv p. yd r) irerrkrjpwfjlCvr 3op(36pov Acyou cvou cv tjtrav avopunroi rives dirocrrpc ovrcs rrjv Sikcuorun? i.

OUTOS 6 Odmtos KT. See note above and cf. xxi. 8.

15. lv rfj pipxw TTJS IWTJS KT. Cf. xxi. 27, iii. 5, note. iv i Lvr v TOU irupfe. See note on ix. i on the significance of this phrase.

CHAPTER XXI. s, 4 d, S b, 6, 1-4, XXII. 3-5. INTRODUCTION.

The New Heaven the New Earth and the New Jerusalem with its blest inhabitants.

i. Now that all evil has been destroyed for ever, and all evil agents have been cast into the lake of fire, that the former heaven and earth have vanished, the final judgment brought to a close, and death and Hades destroyed, God creates a new heaven and a new earth, and summons into being the New Jerusalem. In this city, which would never know tears, nor grief, nor crying, nor any pain nor curse, God will dwell with men, and His throne, which is also that of the Lamb, will be in it, and His servants, whose character, as God's own possession, shall henceforth be blazoned on their brows, shall serve Him and they shall see His Face. And God will cause the light of His Face to shine upon them in perpetual benediction, and they shall reign for ever and ever.

That this section was written by our author is undeniable It forms the natural climax and the fitting dose to all that has gone before, and the nature of the blessedness of the new heaven and the new earth and the new city is in keeping with all that is foreshadowed in the earlier visions of the Seer. The diction and the idiom are our author's.

2. Diction.

4 d. T irpra dirijxOai: for this use of direxAft cf. ix. 12, xi. 14, xxi. i. irapea0c? v is used in this connection in Synoptics and St. Paul: cf. Mark xiii. 31 = Matt xxiv. 35 Luke xxi. 33; 2 Cor. v. 17, ra ap aia irapfjxOov.

5 b. Kaikd iroitt irdrra. These words summarize the action of God on the world. The faithful receive a new name, ii. 17, iii. 12; they sing a new song, v. 9, xiv. 3; and a new heaven, earth, and a new city are created to be their habitation, xxi. i, 2.

6. ylyovav. Cf. xvi. 17, fx vrj. Afyovcra Pfyovcv.

1. 6 irptos otiparos. For this position of wpwros cf. ii. 5. dirijxOai. See note on xxi. 4 d above.

2. T K irfxif T. dyiaf: cf. xxi. 10. icpouaax KCU K: cf. iii. 12. jcarajsaikouttak T. otipakou diro TOU 0cou: cf. iii. 12, xxi. 10. 4 TOl f iacr lmr)i 6s KO I K: cf. xix. 7.

3. turf)? pcyxi)s I TOU Oplrou: cf. xvi. 17, xix. 5. ncrjkisaci: cf. vii. 15, xii. 12, xiii. 6. auroi Xaol aurou IVOKTOI xal auras lorai Ocos autw: cf. xxi. 7.

4 Ab. axeiei xrx.: cf. vii. 17. OUK iforai In: cf. xxii. 3, 5. mspos: cf. xvi. 10, n.

XXTI. 3. OUK forai CTI: cf. xxi. 4. 6 0poyof TOU Ocou ical TOU dptaou: cf. xxii. i. ol SocXoi aurou Xarpcuaouo-ik: cf. vii. 15.

5. OUK? x oucri1 XP c ay TOS Xux w Krx.: cf. xxi. 23. paaixcu-aovau cts T. aiuras T. atcukWK: cf. xx. 4.

Idiom.

Johanninc: XXTT. 4.-rd okopa aurou M TWK U TWTTWK: see notes on vii. 3, xiii. 16.

6. oux? x ounk XP 61 0 XUNI: cf. iii. 17 for this extraordinary construction. moei fir afirous: a pure Hebraism: see note in he. Contrast construction in xviii. i, xxi. 23.

Non-Jokanninc: XXT. 5. 6 KO ICKOS M T Opow: see note on iv. 2.

God will Create the World afresh Heaven, Earth, and the Holy City. This New Jerusalem which is not created till after the Millennial Kingdom is always spoken of as belonging to the future (i. e. every verb is in the future): whereas the Jerusalem described in xxi. 9-xxii. 2, 14-15, 17 is described as already existing, though as yet in heaven.

gyt 5, 4 d, 5 b. God's Declaration at the close of the Final Judgment.

"The former things have passed away: Behold I make all things new."

We have already (see pp. 151-153) shown that xxi 1-4 and xxii. 3-5 belong together and form a description by the Seer of the New Jerusalem which is to be the eternal abode of the blessed. This poem consists of six stanzas, the first two of three lines each and the remaining four of four lines each. Next, since it is obvious that xxi. 4, 5 " do not really belong to what follows nor yet to what precedes in the present text, these dislocated lines, as representing the words of Him, from whose presence the former heaven and earth had vanished into nothingness, who has just judged the world (xx. 11-15), and who has cast all wickedness into the lake of fire, at once claim their rightful position as forming the close of the first creation and the beginning of the new.

6. KCU etirck 6 Kaftfjpcios fvifrw 6p6twt 4 d. TO, irpwra dirijxOak, 5 b. 18od Kaikd iroiu irdrra.

This restoration of the order of the text is supported by the remarkable parallel in 2 Cor. v. 17, ei T cv Xpiorw, Kaivrj KTIW TO. ap aia iran X0cv, ISov ycyovcv Kcuva. St. Paul here, it is true, refers to the new or spiritual creation of the individual. But in this respect man is a microcosm an epitome of the universe or the macrocosm.

5. Kol ciirck. The Speaker here as in i. 8, xvi. i, 17, is God Himself, and He speaks, not to the Seer hence no AOI is added as generally elsewhere in our author: cf. vii. 14, xvii. 7, xxi. 6, xxii. 6 but to the entire world of the blessed. The words are most probably conceived as pronounced from the great white throne at the close of the Final Judgment.

t iirl T 0p(W f. We have an error here traceable probably to the disciple of the Seer who edited xx. 4-xxii. When he makes an addition, he generally makes a mistake. Cf. xix. 10, irpocrfcwqcrai avrp, which should be avrov. We should, of course, have rl rov 0pow: see iv. 2, note.

The words 6 ical icvos eiri r. Opovov go back to xx. 1 1, where God is so described at the beginning of the Final Judgment. Now that character has attained finality and all men have entered on the issues of their conduct, and death and Hades have come to an end, He that sitteth on the throne makes the solemn pronouncement with regard to all that the past: ra vpura farijxBav. The first world and all that essentially belongs to it as distinct from the second and spiritual world have vanished for ever.

4. T npura dirf)X6af. With ra irpra cf. xxi. I, 6 yap irwro? oupavo? ical ij Trpwrrf yy airrj 0av. With fanj 0av cf. IX. 12, xi. 14, xxl i. That ra irpcora atnjxBav is to be taken immediately in connection with isov Kuva TTOIU Travra. is obvious in itself. But there is some external evidence that confirms the combination of 4 and 5; for, while it is recognized on all hands that Isa. xliii. 18, 19 was in the mind of our author here, we find on turning to this passage that the two main ideas in 4 and s b are already brought together (though in a more primitive and limited form), and set forth as a divine utterance as here: 18. fir) fiinfjfiov V T(. ra vptara eat ra dp aia fiy ruxXoyl ccr0c 19.!8ov cya iroio) KCUVO.

The two ideas are also brought together in 2 Cor. v. 17, ra apxata irapi)X0cv, isov ycyovcv fcaiva.

5 b. loi Kaipa, iroiw ir nra. On the idea of a new heaven and a new earth cf. Isa. Ixv. 17, Ixvi. 22; Ps. cii. 25-26: see note on xxii. i of our text. But in the current Apocalypses this idea was a familiar one. Thus in i Enoch xci. 16 (before 170 B. C.?) we find:

"The first heaven shall depart and pass away, And a new heaven shall appear "; in Ixxii. i (before no B. C.): "Till the new creation is accomplished which dureth till eternity"; in xlv. 4 (94-64 B. C.):

"And I will transform the heaven and make it an eternal blessing and light, And I will transform the earth and make it a blessing ";

Jub. i. 29 (before 107 A. D.): "From the day of the creation till the heavens and the earth are renewed"; also in 2 Bar. Ivii. 2 (before 70 A. D.):

"And belief in the coming judgment was then generated, And hope of the world that was to be renewed was then built up,

And the promise of the life that should come hereafter was implanted "; xliv. 12 (after 70 A. D.): "And the new world which does not turn to corruption those who depart to its blessedness "; xxxii. 6: " When the Mighty One will renew His creation"; 4 Ezra vii. 75: "Until those times come in which Thou shalt renew Thy creation." In the N. T. cf. Matt. xix. 28; Acts iii. 21; 2 Pet iil 13. The passage in Barnabas vi. 13 (Xcyct Si KVUO? I8oi n-otw ra rxara 09 ra irpura) has nothing in common with our text 6. ial Xlycr rptyof n osrot ol Xtfyoi wuml itai dxt)6ivot dpi?. As these words cannot be assigned to God, they are assigned to an angel. But if we accept this explanation we should here have an instance of bathos an error in style of which our author is never guilty. When God Himself declares in the hearing of the Seer that He recreates the world, His words do not require to be confirmed either directly or indirectly by any angel or archangel. The clause ovrot ol Xdyot. ix tvoi is repeated from xxii. 6, where it is full of significance in the mouth of Christ, ori may (i) introduce a statement or (2) give a reason. But it is not used in the first sense elsewhere in our author after ypcfyw, cf. ii. i, 8, 12, 18, iii. i, 7, 14, xiv. 13. Even if we take it in the second sense ("because") the bathos of the statement still remains unrelieved. Hence

5 appears to be an interpolation. That Christ should solemnly authenticate the truth of these visions in xxii. 6 is wholly fitting.

6. Kai ctir K oi lyyopai. Cf. xvi. 17. See note on xxi. 5 (English translation: see vol. ii. 443, note 3). An interpolation? If original, the words come from God or from the angelus interpret. The Seer hears God's first declaration: " Behold I make all things new," and following immediately thereupon the words: " They have become (new). 11 After this the Seer sees the new heaven and the new earth and the New Jerusalem (xxi. i-4 abo, xxii. 3-5). On the form ycyovav see Blass, Gram. p. 46.

XXT. I- 50, XXTT. 8-5. The vision of the new heaven and the new earth and the descent of the New Jerusalem adorned as a bride for her husband. God is to tabernacle with men, and never more is there to be grief or pain or tears or death, and all the faithful are to reign for ever and ever.

1. ctsok oopardf KCUKK nai ytjK iccun. On the meaning of fccupos as distinguished from rco? see iii. 12, note. On the new heaven and the new earth see the note on xxi. 4 above, p. 203. In Isa. Ixv. 17 the actual phrase used by our author is found: "For behold I create a new heaven and a new earth" (nenn pro onrrn DDtf rtia wa) where the LXX has forai yap 6 ovpavos KCUVOS icai 17 yi KOIVTJ. Wetstein quotes the Debarim rab. S. xi.: " Cum Moses ante obitum oraret, coelum et terra et omnis ordo creaturarum commotus est. Tune dixerunt: Fortasse adest tempus a Deo praestitutum, quo renovandus est orbis universus (id y n Bhnfc). Exivit autem vox dicens illud tempus nondum advenisse." See Volz, 296 sqq.; Bousset, Rel d. Judenth. 268 sq.

6 y P irpuros oupai s nal itrx. This disappearance of the first heaven and the first earth has already been referred to: cf. xx. i i b.

ical 4 Orfxaova odic? OTIK JTI. The earliest parallel to this statement is found in Test. Levi (109-106 B. C.), iv. i: "Now know that the Lord shall execute judgment upon the sons of men. Because when the rocks are being rent. and the waters dried up." Next in the Assumption of Moses, x. 6:

M And the sea shall retire into its abyss, And the fountains of waters shall 1 And the rivers shall dry up."

Also in Sibyll. Or. V. 159, 160, 447, mu 8 vcrrari xaipf TTOTC n-owof: viii. 236, woa-a 0aaarcra ou ert irxow 2 ft. All these passages point not wholly to any Semitic horror of the sea in itself, but in some degree perhaps unconsciously to its mythological connection with the Babylonian myth of the Creation, in which the sea is the water monster Tiamat, the special opponent of the gods. The omission of the sea by John may thus be owing to its evil associations, many traces of which survive in the O. T. See articles Dragon, Leviathan, Rahab, Serpent, in the Encyc. Biblica. A remarkable parallel in Plutarch's De hide et Osiride 7 should be observed. There the sea is regarded as an alien element in nature, fraught with destruction and disease: oa09 u rrjv 6d arrav IK irvpos fjyowrat Kal irapwpurfuvrjvy ov8 jutcpos oflw oroixeiov AAV daAotov ircptrroyaa 8ic 0opos KOI vora8cs.

2. TV irrfxik TTJK dyia lepouaaxfy K. airf v. This city is either wholly distinct from that described in XXL Q-xxil 2 the seat of the Millennial Kingdom or it is that city wholly transformed and hence described at. vr v: see xxi. 10, note. Since God re-creates all things, xxi. 5, the Holy City is either transformed or created afresh as

are the heaven and the earth. This city is clearly distinguished from that in xxi. g-xxil 2. In the latter the saints reign for a thousand years, and the tree of life stands in the street thereof in order that all who were worthy might eat thereof, that is, attain to immortality. But in this city there is no mention of the tree of life: it is not needed; for all its inhabitants are immortal (xxi. 4 b) and reign with God for ever and ever (xxii. 5). With this New Jerusalem we might compare Heb. xii. 22, Itpovo-axrjp. evovpavt: Gal. iv. 26, i? Si avo lepov-0-0X171: and Phil. iii. 20, iov yap TO iroxtrcvia Iv ovpavois

Karapaivoucrak IK TOO ofiparou dir6 TOU Ocou. Cf. iii. 1 2, xxi. 10. Totfiaaplitii 69 KOJI+TJK. Cf. xxi 9; Isa. xlix. 18, Ixi. 10. rf d pl a5rr). Cf. 2 Cor. xi. 2; Eph. v. 23. 8. +ttrijs xcyaXv) IK TOU Oplyou. The throne is that in xix. i x. The speaker is probably one of the Cherubim.

TOU 6cou 9K1)MS9Cl fcT auT

The word na? vi? here has nothing to do with the Tabernacle (pt? D). For in Jewish writings there is no expectation of the lestoration of the Tabernacle in the Heavenly Jerusalem. lu place is always taken by the Temple (cf. Weber 8, 375-77). But, since our author expressly states (xxi. 22) that there will be no Temple in the Holy City, that is to be the seat of the Millennial Kingdom, it follows that he could not have looked for a restored Tabernacle in the New Jerusalem which was to be the everlasting abode of the blessed. The word cr has already occurred twice. In xiii. 6 it means God's dwelling,. heaven, or rattier (?) " His Shekinah (see note in loc.). In xv. 5, where it is found a second time, we have seen that the text is either corrupt or interpolated; for 6 voos-n? owipi?? rot) taprvpiov cv r ofyxww is an intolerable, because an unintelligible, expression.

What, then, is the meaning of o-icinf here? The context appears certainly to favour the interpretation suggested by Dr. Taylor (Pirke Aboth p. 44). "The two (Shekinah and Memra) are brought together by St. John. 6 Adyo? rap ycro, KCU rajvaxrcv iv-fjp. lv (John i. 14). The word crmny and its derivatives are chosen on account of their assonance with the Hebrew to express the Shekinah and its dwelling with men-compare especially Rev. xxi. 3: 1 ov 17 o- rov Ocov icra rw foopwrrw icai OVOVUKTCI fter avrv." Even in xiii. 6, where our author is adapting to a new situation an earlier source, the probability is that he gives a new meaning to the phrase rrjv o-Kyvyv avrov, i. e. " His Shekinah."

Moreover, in Lev. xxvi. n we have a confirmation of the above view. Here the Targum regards the Tabernacle simply as the manifestation of the divine presence. The Hebrew (nrtti DDara aptd) " I will set my tabernacle among them " LXX Kal 0qcra TTJV Siaoyicrjv (F, o-Krjvrjv) JJLOV iv vp. lv is paraphrased by thetarg. Jon. pm3 np nra)HW, "I will set the Shekinah of My glory among you." In the next verse we have "the glory of My Shekinah." The word Shekinah which is used as a periphrasis for the divine name is closely associated with the conception of the divine glory (K"lp "ipk, Heb. ip) as we see from the last two passages and throughout the Targums. Cf. also Targ, Jon. on Gen. xlix. i, " the glory of the Shekinah of Yahweh": or simply "the glory of God" as in Onk. on Gen. xviii. 33. It is employed also as a rendering of " face " when used of God: cf. Deut xxxi. 18, where 3D TndK ("I will hide my face ") is rendered TU3P p? DK, "I will remove my Shekinah ": and of "name" in the same connection: cf. Targums of Onk. and Jon. on Ex. xx. 24.

In the Mishnah and Talmud the Shekinah is the mediator of God's presence and activity in the world. Wherever ten persons pray together, the Shekinah is in the midst of them (Pirke Aboth ill 9 (150-200 A. D.); Berach. 6 a): also where three are gathered together to administer justice or where two meet to study the Law (Pirke Aboth iii. 9). Where a man and his wife lead a pious life the Shekinah is present. Before Israel sinned the Shekinah dwelt in each individual (Sota, 3"): and this relation was possible afterwards: cf. Pirke Aboth iii. 9.

From the Shekinah proceeded a brilliancy or splendour (i. e. Vt). In this the blessed were to share in the next word: cf. Berach. 17, "They delighted themselves in the brightness of the Shekinah (nratfn VTD DOna). On this " brightness," which is apparently rendered by our author by Sofa, see note on xxi. 23.

As our author thought in Hebrew, this line and the next would probably have run in his mind as 3 DJJ Dnta nratf run per afrrwv KT. On a-Krjvovv used of the inhabitants of heaven, cf. xii. 12, xiii. 6: see also vii. 15. With the thought compare Lev. xxvi. u, u Oyvw rrjv SiaorjkTjv (F, o-KTjvrjv: so Mass. 33 D) fiov iv vuv. 12. fcol lorouuv vuv 0cos icat vpct? rco-0 JJLQV Aao?. Ezek. xxxvii. 27, jcat rrai 17 Karao-Kq-vaxjts AOV ev aurois ical TOMU avrots 0 o ical avrot iov cowrai Aao't: xliil 7; Zech. ii. 14 (10), viii. 3, Karaanc iakrio

Xaol autoo. If this reading is original the idea appears to be the same as that underlying John x. 16, where though there is but one flock (iroip. vrj) and one Shepherd, there are many folds (avxat). Each Aaos forms a fold in the flock, of which God is the Shepherd. Possibly, however, Xaot may simply mean as in the vernacular " people." But John does not so use AW, and Aaos seems to be the original reading. See crit. note on Greek text in loc.

cat aflros f Ocos JUT adrwv farai a, M v Oc s t

The above text appears in three forms in the MSS, and none of them is satisfactory, i. That which is preserved in KQ and many cursives and omits avrwv 0cp? can hardly be original, independently of its weak attestation; for not only is the parallelism against it (cf. also xxi. 7), but without avruiv 0cos the line becomes an otiose repetition of the idea in the first two lines. The preceding line, KCU avrot Aao! avrov ftrovrai, requires some such parallelism as 0cds aurwv.

2. Since, then, the shortened form of the text in KQ cannot be accepted, we have next to consider that attested by A, vg, s 1 s KOI afrds o 0cos ftcr avrwv orai avrwv tfcos. Although the line is rather full, the sense is not unsatisfactory- "And He God with them shall be their God," or " God Himself shall be with them their God. 9 But this unemphatic position of avrfiv before 0cos (i. e. the vernacular use of the possessive pronoun see

Abbott, Gram. p. 419 sqq.) is against our author's usage and is not what we expect here. 1 Since in the preceding line the avrov in Xaol afrov has its normal possessive force in this position, we should expect 0 o? afouv in the present line. As " they shall be His peoples," so He shall be "their God. 11 3. Instead of afow fafe, which is against our author's usage and also against the context, which here requires a real possessive, P and some cursives read 0cfo avrwv. This is the reading the context leads us to expect, but its attestation is of the poorest character. It can only, therefore, be regarded in the light of a scribal emendation.

From the above examination of the MSS it follows that the original text has not been preserved in any MS. The corrupt would be emphatic owing to its proximity to avros (see Abbott, Gram. p. 421, note i), or (b) al avros carat 0cos avrwv. In any case the sense would be: " And He will be their God." The usage of our author would certainly be in favour of (b): cf. xxi. 7.

4. Kal axcfyei KT. See note on vii. 17. al 6 Odratos ofc lernu In. The idea of this line but not the diction is suggested by Isa. xxv. 8, "He hath annihilated death for ever " (man yta mni), which section of Isaiah possibly belongs to the 2nd century B. C. Cf. I Cor. xv. 54, KatCTTofl?; 6 Odvaros cts vwcos. It will be observed that, whereas Aquila and Theodotion incorrectly render as an Aramaic phrase by e vt os and the LXX by our author gives the right sense in a paraphrastic form. For first century A. D. testimonies to the belief in the coming destruction of death, cf. 2 Enoch lxv. 10, "All corruptible things shall vanish and there shall be eternal life," and 4 Ezra viii. 53; 2 Bar. xxi. 23. See also Moed Qaton, iii. 9, where it cites Isa. xxv. 8.

Since death is destroyed (cf. xx. 14), there is no longer any need of the tree of life. All the faithful have won everlasting life. There can be no more death, there can be only " more life and fuller."

otfrf irfroo ofrc itpauyi) ofa ir6ios ofc Icrrat In. Cf. Isa. xxxv. 10, li. ii, "and sorrow and sighing (nmttt pr) shall flee though occurring very frequently in our author is never elsewhere found in this unemphatic position in our text; nor is afrog. afrifc is found once in xviii 5, but there in a source used by our author, crou is found several times in this position: see ii. 2, 19, notes. This unemphatic use of the genitive of afrtfr, though very frequent in the Fourth Gospel, does not belong to our author.

away." In our text the subject consists of three elements, and so also does the LXX of Isa. xxxv. 10 and li. n, but the words of the LXX differ from those in our text, WSpa o8vn? KOI Awny ical orrcvayfufc. See also Isa. lxv. 19; i Enoch x. 22, xxv. 6; 2 Enoch lxv. 8-9 (A), "They will live eternally, and then, too, there will be amongst them neither labour nor sickness nor humiliation nor anxiety nor need."

XXTT. 8. ica! ITK Kairfocpa ofc lanu In. This verse forms the fourth line of the stanza, the first three lines of which xxi. 4 abo we have just dealt with. That this verse belongs to that stanza, not only the subject matter, but the very diction is evidence. Thus av loroi eri, which is not found in our author outside the description of the New Jerusalem (xxi. i-4 abc, xxii. 3-5), has already occurred twice in this stanza, i. e. xxi. 4. The words themselves are based on Zech. xiv. 11 (TW nwt6 Dim) but not on the LXX. The word ara0cAa (syncopated from Karavo0cAa) means here, as the context shows, a curse, i. e. an accursed thing, and not an accursed person. In itself icaralcta could mean the latter, as va0eia (= D jn) can: cf. Gal. i. 8; i Cor. xvi. 22; Rom. ix. 3.

KCU 6 0p6pos TOU Ocou Kal TOU dp iou KT. On this conception of " the throne of God and of the Lamb," see note on xxii. i. Owing to the fact that in the next line only God the Father is spoken of, critics have inferred that KOL rov dpvtov is here an intrusion. But, as I have shown in the note on xxii. i, we find in i Enoch lxi. 8, 9 an excellent parallel; for, though the Elect One (i. e. the Messiah) is seated on God's throne as Judge in Ixi. 8, in Ixi. 9 the praises of all present are addressed to God and not to the Elect One. Moreover, in our text, xx. 6 e, the avrov refers to only one of the two Divine Beings in 6 d. Cf. iii. 21, which speaks of Christ as seated on God's throne, while in iii. 19 the O. T. words of Yahweh are used by Christ as His own. ol Souxoi afrrou Xarperfaoucrik xrx. Cf. vii. 15, note.

4. OI KKTCU T irpoatnrok aurou. Cf. Matt v. 8; Heb. xii. 14. This vision of God, which was withheld from Moses (Ex. xxxiii. 20, 23), is promised to the faithful in Messianic times in Jerusalem in T. Zeb. ix. 8, fyccrlc avrov ev Icpowoawt a promise which appears also in Ps. Ixxxiv. 7 (LXX and Vulg.) tyftprcrat 6 0coc TWV lew cv Siav. But this is not the vision face to face that is designed in our text and also in 4 Ezra vil 98. In the latter passage the vision of God constitutes the seventh and supreme bliss of the righteous.

"They shall rejoice with boldness, Be confident without confusion, Be glad without fear;

VOL. II. 14

For they are hastening to behold the face of Him whom in life they served, And from whom they are destined to receive their reward in glory."

The capacity for such vision involves likeness of character: cf. i John iii. 2. Moffatt aptly compares Plutarch (De Iside, 79), who writes that the souls of men after death " migrate to the unseen " and " hang as it were upon Him (God), and gaze without ever wearying, and yearn for that unspeakable, indescribable beauty."

KOI fd ofoyta afi-rou fat TWK petrui afirou. See notes on vii. 3, xiii. 16, ziv. i. Cf. also iii. 12.

5. ical ri ofc rrcu fa. Darkness is at an end for ever. This clause appears to be the source of the corruption in xxi 25. The expectation here expressed is not found in the O. T. but as regards heaven at all events is definitely taught in Philo, De Josepjlo) 24: et yow Jouaiflefy Stacvtrreiv ctra TIS TWK irpayiarcav, cvpiarct TOV ovpavov 17i. cpai aiawtov, VVKTOS icai ircunjs ovaas aAero;(oy, arc ircptaafuroAcvoi dcrJevrots KOL dm parot? astaorararc cyyco-tv. Cf. also 2 Bar. xlviii. 50. But the conception in our text is infinitely finer. The light of the New Jerusalem is not due as in Philo to a multitude of unextinguishable and unadulterated lights, but to the light of God's own presence always and everywhere present. The conception could be deduced from Isa. Ix. 19, "The sun shall be no more thy light by day; neither for brightness shall the moon give light unto thee; but the Lord shall be unto thee an everlasting light"

ical ox 2 ouerik XP " " ors Xrixrou ical ws Xiou. Cf. xxi. 23. The future Ifovo-iv (A vg. s lp 8, Tic.) is to be preferred to cxovcrtv. All the verbs in this description of the New Jerusalem (xxi. i-4 abc, xxii. M) are futures. As contra-distinguished from the heavenly Jerusalem, that was already in being and was to come down from heaven for the Millennial Kingdom, the New Jerusalem, which is not created till after its close, is not yet in being. As regards the former, observe the occasional present and past verbs in xxi. Q-xxii. 2. The phrase? fjxiov (AP: coro? M me s 1 2) had best be regarded as dependent on xpetav. Such an irregularity is not unfamiliar in our author. In fact we have ZX LV w i tn an acc- n n T 7 an with a genitive in xxi. 23. os 6 Ocfo OITUFCI fir afirou's. The construction here eir, A, etc.) differs from that in xxi. 23, rj (a TOV 0eov avriyv, and in xviil i, and the sense differs likewise. In xxi. 23

the meaning is clear: not the physical luminaries, the sun and moon, but " the glory of God did lighten" the Heavenly Jerusalem (cf. also xviii. i). But here the Greek omm iif avrovs differs from that in xviii. i, xxi. 23 alike in construction and meaning. First, as regards the construction, it must at once be conceded that it is peculiar. If our author had wished to express the thought "shall shine upon them," "give them light," he would have said am avrots: cf. xxi. 23. Hence later MSS omitted the ri, and herein they are followed by WH, Bousset and others. Other editors, such as Alford, Swete, and Moffatt, rightly follow KA here, but do not explain the anomaly. We can get a good sense, if we explain it as a Hebraism. When regarded from this standpoint we next recognize that Kvpios 6 Ocbs orrtcrci ITT avrovs is a rendering of Ps. cxviii. 27, J? "IKJ5 ta, where for i n our author found TK or T n, which latter he changed into TK Here the Aramaic Targum and the Syriac, Ethiopic, and Arabic Versions similarly transform the two clauses into one and presuppose the text to have been "P n and not "ikJV Here, therefore, the fcri reproduces?. 1 Having discovered the source of our author's words the discovery of their meaning ceases to be difficult In Ps. cxviii. 27 the words are a shortened form of the priest's blessing in Num. vi. 25 by the omission of V3B (see Oxford Hebrew Lexicon p. 2i b), which in its fuller form recurs several times as the footnote shows. Hence we should here render " The Lord God shall cause His face to shine upon them." Here there is personal relation indicated between God and the blessed individually. In xxi. 23, on the other hand, no such personal relation is indicated. The Holy City is lighted up as a whole by the glory of God instead of by the sun and moon. Thus the Face which the saints will see in xxii. 4 will shine upon them in eternal benediction (xxii. 5).

paaixeucrouaiv els rods alwas TOP ausfui. This everlasting reign of the saints in the New Jerusalem stands out in strong contrast with the Millennial reign in the City which came down from heaven before the Final Judgment, xx. 4.

The Epilogue.

xxi. 6 b-8, xxii. 6-7, 18 16, 13, 12, 10, 8-9, 20-21. INTRODUCTION.

i. On this epilogue, which contains the declarations of God, of Jesus, and of John, see p. 154. That they come from our author cannot be contested, though they have been transmitted 1 In Num. vi. 25 we have fy (LXX M), in Ps. zxzi. 17; Dan. ix. 17 Sy, and in Ps. cziz. 135, and-n in Ps. Izvii. 2. In all cases the LXX renders by frrl. But the LXX does not use fwrlfrtv in these passages but in the utmost disorder, and no doubt defectively. The reconstruction here given is, of course, tentative. First of all, xxi. 6 b-8, as containing a declaration of God, singles itself out for con,-sideration. It cannot possibly belong to the period after the Final Judgment; for hope is still held out to the repentant, and the doom of the second death has not yet been pronounced against the finally impenitent. It must, therefore, belong either to the period of the Millennial Kingdom or to that of our author. The thought and language are in favour of the latter hypothesis. Thus 6 FIICWV in xxil 7 brings vividly before us the experiences actual and apprehended of the faithful in the years 90-96 A. D.: he is the warrior faithful unto death, to whom promise after promise is held out, as in ii. 7, n, 17, 26, iii. 5, 12, 21, xii. ii, xv. 2. Again, xxi. 6 d, vu rp Surtovri 8axru IK ri irrjyrp rov vsaro? r s an Swpcay, clearly presupposes xxii. 17 as having preceded it; for there we have the divine gift described without the article: 6 0W Xa cra vswp fcoijs Swpcw. But for the recurrence of the Supeav here we might have explained the articles in xxi. 6 d from vii. 17. As regards the sorcerers, fornica-tors, murderers, and idolaters we are told (xxii. 15) that in the Millennial Kingdom they will be excluded from the Heavenly Jerusalem: here they are adjudged to be cast into the lake of fire (xxi. 8).

Hence xxi. 6 b-8 is to be taken as the divine authentication of the Apocalypse as a whole, which God had given to Jesus Christ to make known to His servants (as stated in i. i). This declaration of God is then followed by the declaration of Jesus that He had sent His angels to testify these things to the Churches in xxii. 6-7, i8 a, 16, 13, 12, 10, and the Book closes with the testimony of John, xxii. 8-9, 20-21 (see note on i. 1-3). In xxii. 6-21 more than anywhere else in chapters-xx.-xxii. we have the disjecta membra of the Poet-Seer. We have already assigned xxii. 14-15, 17 to the section dealing with the Heavenly Jerusalem which comes down to earth during the Millennial Kingdom. The re-arrangement of xxii. 6-22 just given is suggested by the text itself and confirmed by i. 1-2 (see note in vol. i. p. 5 sq.), and is therefore not improbably the order intended by the Seer. It is, of course, fragmentary. With a view to its arrangement, we observe first of all that Jesus is the speaker in 12-13, l6 "id likewise in 6-7; for in these last two verses the speaker is distinguished from the angel who showed the Seer the things which must shortly come to pass, and the words "behold I come quickly" in 7 are naturally spoken by Christ Moreover, as Konnecke and Moffatt have recognized, 12-13, 16 can be restored to their original order by reading them as follows: 16, 13, 12. Thus this section is to be read as follows: 6-7, 16, 13, 12. Verse 10 still the words of Christ comes next, "And He saith unto me, Seal not up the words of the prophecy of this book; for the time is at hand."

I have bracketed 11 as conflicting with xxi. 6 b-8, which apparently refer to evangelistic appeals during the Seer's lifetime. xxii 18, as coming from Christ, gives His imprimatur to the book. xxii. 8-p as describing the action of the Seer in relation to the angel at its close, and xxii. 20-21 as giving the Seer's final testimony form the natural close of the Apocalypse.

Traces of the hand of the editor are to be found in two passages: see 3 ad fin. Cf. 3 in Introduction to xx. 4-15 (p. 182).

2. Diction.

"T 6. T AX+a ital TO O. Cf. L 8, xxii. 13. 4 dpx?) ital TO: cf. xxii. 13. T fci+wm (cf. vii. 16) S Srw la TTJS Tnjyfjs TOU IWTJS Bwped: cf. xxil 17, vii 17.

7. 6 KIKWK: see under i. foopai aur 6co s: cf. xxi. 3.

8. TOIS. ofcuo-i xai irlprois xal apfakoif xal clswxo-Xdrpais: cf. xxii. 15. TJJ Mf TI "MuoUi: cf. xix. 20, xx. 10, etc.

6 Odkatos oftcurcpos: cf. ii. n.

gyrr, 6. dvrcixcr T. ftyycxo? autou: cf. i. I, dnroorctxa? a T. Ayy. avrov.

Sci ai T. Bodxois afrrou. IK rdxct: a verbal repetition from L i.

7. lod pxofiai Toxij: cf. ii. 16, Hi. n, xvi. 15, xxii. 12. fjiandpios 6 Tvjpuv T. Xcsyous T. irpo+rjtcias T. fhpxiou TOUTOU: a summary of i. 3 (and the last of the seven beatitudes in this Book), xxil io, 18.

18. paprupm: cf. L 2. T. Xlyous r. irpo+t T ios rrx.: see on 7 above.

16. yw. jfiri M ra itrx.: cf. L i. elju (a. Aaucis: repeated from v. 5. 6 donr p. 6 frpuikife: already in ii. 28.

18. y r6 AX a KCU-rd fi: cf. i. 8, xxi. 6. 6 irpfrros ical 6 Icrxaros: cf. i. 17, ii. 8. 4 PX KC " Ttfxos: cf. xxi. 6.

Id. Iftod ifpxofiai raxij. See on 7 above, diroftoufai iicdor r6 2pyoy OT! K odrou: cf. ii. 23, Scooxo. ifccurrq icara ra Ipya 10. X yci fiot: cf. v. 5, vil 13, x. 9. p?) ff payi f: cf. X. 4. T. X yous T. irpo Tcias T.? ipx. TOUTOU: see on 7 above.

6 itaipot ydp iyyus: cf. i. 3.

8. itdyii iwdkrijs: cf. i. i, 4, 9. I i ra irpocricuvtjvat 2uirpoo0CK TF irobttk: cf. xix. 10, which, however, is a doublet of this passage. Elsewhere John uses irpoo-Kwciv Ivwrwv: cf. iii. 9, xv. 4 where this phrase expresses simply homage.

cf. L i, iv. i, xvii. i, xxi. 9, 10, xxii. i, 6.

9. TWK njpojKTw T. X6yous T. 0i0X. Totfrou: cf. i. 3, iii. 8, 10, xii. 17, xiv. 12. T 0 Trpxncun rok: see note on vii. n.

90. paptupw: see 18 above, mi: see i. 7 (note). Spxop" Toxrf: see on 7 above.

Apv: see L 7 (note).

3. Idioms. The constructions are almost wholly normal. Here as elsewhere in xx. 4-xxii. the text has apparently been normalized by the editor of this section.

Johannine xxi. 6. w I: for this partitive use of ev after Sisovcu cf. iii. 9. Not elsewhere in N. T. save in i John iv. 13.

8. TOIS Seixofc. r6 pipes afirwk: a pure Hebraism: see note v.

XXII. 8. 6 dicouwk: used here as an aorist or perfect as elsewhere the participle is used in our author: cf. SCIKKVOVTOS, similarly used at the close of this verse.

Non-Johannine xxi 6. TW II WITI 8 cra. According to our author's universal usage elsewhere we should expect avroj after Sokro) in this connection: cf. ii. 7, 17, 26, iii. 21. Here apparently the editor has omitted it and so normalized the text.

XXI. 8. rfj Xipif) TJJ icaioilif) may be another such instance: cf. xix. 20.

The Epilogue of the Apocalypse consisting of () the declaration of God) xxi. 6-8: (2) the testimony of Jesus, xxii. 6-?, , 16, j, 12, 10 , P-p (3) and that of John, xxii. 8-9, 20-21.

Here more than anywhere else in chapters xx.-xxii. have we the disjecta membra of the Poet-Seer. These fragments clearly form the Epilogue of the Book, and a study of these fragments leads us to recognize them as coming from three distinct speakers God, Jesus, and John. In xxi. 6 b-8 God is clearly the speaker. In xxii. 12-13, 16, and likewise 6-7, 10, 18, Jesus is the speaker, for in 6-7 the speaker is distinguished from the angel who showed the Seer the things that must shortly come to pass, and the words "behold I come quickly 1 in 7 are most naturally spoken by Christ, and likewise 10, 18. Moreover, as Konnecke (followed by Moffatt) has recognized, 12-13, 16 should be read as follows: 16, 13, 12. Thus the original order of the testimony and declaration of Christ was most probably: 6-7, 16,13,12, io n, i8 i8 b-i9. The book then closes with the testimony of John xxii. 8-9, 20-21. xxii. n, i8 b-i9 appear to be interpolations.

This order, which is suggested by a study of xxii. 6-22, in itself harmonizes with that given in the first two verses of the Apocalypse, where we are told that (i) God has given to Christ this revelation to show unto His servants: (2) that Christ has sent and signified it by His angel to His servant John: (3) that

John has borne witness of the word of God and of the testimony of Christ.

XXT. 6 b-8. The declaration of God as to His own Bein His willingness to be gracious to the repentant His promise of being a Father to him that ovcrcomcth, and His denunciation of the craven-hearted the unbelieving and impure as destined to be cast into the lake that burneth with fire and brimstone the second death.

6 b. yrf cifu T "AX+a KU T a Here as in i. 8 (where see note) these epithets belong to the Eternal Father, whereas in xxii. 13 they are used by Christ of Himself.

4 dpx) Kal rd TOS. Cf. xxii. 13, see note on i. 8.

y TU S wm feru In TTJS in)Yi)s KT. Based on Isa. Iv. i. See note on vii. 17.

TOO tfctos Tfjs IWTJS Supcdv. Observe the articles. We have v8wp (unj 8o)cav in xxii. 17 which is explicable if xxii. 17 precedes, but not so if the MSS order of the text were correct. On the distinction between (JSwp 0179 and vxov fanjs see ii. 7, note.

7. 6 KUCW KXyiporop o-ei rauro. The victor is here contrasted with the craven-hearted in 8. The ravra here refers to the Millennial blessedness, the new heaven, the new earth, and the New Jerusalem (xxi. I-4 110, xx. 3-5). Of these " he who conquers" is "the heir" (fcxiftwouos). The collocation of K rfpovoimjr i in this line and avros 2anu xoi vios in the next but one shows, as Swete remarks, the close affinity in this respect between our author and St Paul: cf. Rom. viil 17, ct 8c rcicva, icai K r)povop. oi; Gal. iv. 7, ci 8c uio?, ical Jcaiypovoxos Sia 0cov.

KOI caofiai aurw 0c5s. This promise was made frequently in the O. T.: first to the founder of the nation, Gen. xvii. 7, 8, while that in the next line, KOL avros rrai fuu v o9, is first made in reference to Solomon as a representative of the nation, 2 Sam. vii. 14, and in Ps. Ixxxix. 26, 27 in reference to David. Nowhere in the O. T. can the individual as such claim God as Father. This claim is first found in Sir. xxiii. i: later in Wisdom ii. 16 (see note on Jub. i. 24 of my edition). But in the N. T. the normal attitude of the faithful individual to God is that of a son to his heavenly Father. Here only in our author is this conception brought forward. This sonship is realized in some true degree in the present life just as surely as the thirst for righteousness (r 0m) is in some true measure satisfied here.

We have here the list of those who have disfranchised themselves from the Kingdom of God and gone over into the Kingdom of outer darkness. Of these there are mentioned eight classes, which fall into three divisions, the first division comprising three classes, the second three, and the third two.

First division rots Sctxot? 1 KCU dhrurrois ol The S W are not "the fearful 11 as in the A. V. and R. V. but "the cowardly" or "the cravenhearted," who in the struggle with the Beast have played the coward, denied the faith, and rendered worship to Caesar. ociaia has always a bad meaning, and St. Paul declares, 2 Tim. i. 7: ov yap cwcy rjfi. lv o 0eos incvut Sctxtas. A man may fear and yet not be Sctaos. In fact the most courageous man is he who, notwithstanding his fear of the real dangers that beset his advance, goes sturdily onwards. But this fear in the N. T. is either o8os a middle term capable of a good or of a bad interpretation according to the context or cvaafao. Cf. Phil. ii. 12, ficra f6fiov KM Tp6pov rrjv lavrw (rotrrpiay carcoya ccrtfc.

TOIS. diriorois. In our author ovicrro? means primarily "faithless," "untrustworthy." This is to be inferred from the use of n-urnfe: cf. i. 5, dxro Iqo-ov Xptorov 6 uaprv? 6 irurro?; ii. 10, ytvov WIOTOS xpi Oavdrov; ii. 13, iii. 14, xvii. 14. Thus the

CMTWJTOS is closely allied to the Sctad? that precedes. As such the MTIOTOI are not coextensive with the Sctao for there are other grounds than cowardice for such disloyalty. But the avtorot owing to the ScxvyAcvot that follows immediately may suggest the idea of immorality: cf. Tit i. 15, TOIS Sc bttuaiio'ois jcal dvtbrot?. 16. ? Scavictoi OKTCS icai atrei cts. Furthermore, the irtoroi appear to embrace not only the Christian who denies his faith, but also the pagan who rejects it

TOIS. pscxiryp KOis. These are those who are defiled with the abominations referred to in xvii. 4, 5, connected with the worship of the Beast and generally with the impurities of the pagan cults, including unnatural vice. Cf. Hos. ix. 10; 2 Enoch x. 4, 5, "This place is prepared for. those who on earth practise sin against nature, which is child corruption after the Sodomitic fashion, magic-making, enchantments, and devilish witchcraft. lies. fornication, murder": Apoc. Pet 17, osrot rjouv ol fudvavres ra o-wxara avro)v arc ywatkcs avcurrpc o-ACVOI at 8c fter avraiv yvvaikis. at crvykOtfn curai aaAiya-ais as 1 In rtfa W decxott. rb lupot afrrqw we have a Hebraism where S is used in introducing a new subject: see Oxford Hebrew Lexicon, p. 514 = D7Q. a? 73?. Cf. i Chron. xxiv. i. omptoid pnn ="Andas for the sons of Aaron their courses were ": also vii. i, zxvi i, 31 (where the LXX reproduces by the dat); 2 Chron. vii. 21; Eccles. ix. 4. In Ezra x. 14 the LXX has this construction, though it is not found in the Hebrew, where possibly the 7 has been lost; wow ro? t 4r r6 rir V A roxro, Ma. unya TTH Va. The more usual construction in Hebrew would be a nominativus pendens resumed by Dpvn.

1 This meaning of Ttrr6i f t. (faithful," "loyal," is also found in 2 Bar. liv. 21 (where see my note), though elsewhere (except possibly in liv. 16) in that book it means " believing r: cf. xlii. 2, liv. 5, Ivii. 2, lix. 2, Ixxxiii. 8. On 4 Ezra in this respect see Box, pp. 67, 143.

? avrjp vp yweuka. This class must obviously comprise all the pagan world that is so defiled. We thus observe that, whereas the first three classes are closely associated in point of character, their comprehensiveness steadily widens from faithless Christians to the whole body of the impure whether Christian or pagan.

Kal tofcucri nal irlprois nai tappcutois. In xxii. 15 these words are found in the reverse order. These sins have already been referred to in ix. 21, c row ovov avrcw ovrc c rsv apiakav avrcov ovrc IK TTS iropvcias avruv (see note). See also Gal. v. 19-21, where iropvcto, xxpicucux and ovoi (in some MSS) appear amongst many other vices. In i Tim. i. 9 we have fo po ovoi;, irrfprots, and in Jas. ii. 1 1 ovos and fun cia are combined. The opLMKois are " sorcerers," as their association with the cioaa-Aarpai? in the next line shows: cf. ix. 20, 21, where they are similarly associated.

eftuxoxdrpais ital iracri TOIS + U6rik. Cf. ix. 20, xxii. 15. Idolatry is the cardinal sin against which our author warns his readers. Hence the primary reference is here to Christians. As the idols are lies so all the idolaters are liars. The insincerities of heathenism, the frauds of its priests as well as all the falsities of Christians are here referred to (cf. xiv. 5). Lying and duplicity are denounced in the O. T. but in far stronger terms in the N. T.

T plpos OUTWK. The avrwv resumes the eight classes mentioned in the preceding datives. On these datives see footnote, p. 216. TJJ Xipif) TJJ Kcuoitevfl rrx.: cf. xix.

20, xx. 10, 14, 15 and note on ix. i: 2 Enoch x. 2, "And there were all manner of tortures in this place. 4. This place, O Enoch, is prepared for those who dishonour God, etc." 6 Odratos 6 Scurepos. See note on ii. n.

The Testimony of Jesus, xxii. 6-7, 16, 13, 12, 10 n, 18

XXTT. 6-7. That these are the words of Const is to be concluded from the declaration in 7, KCU 28ov cp ofuu rayy. Moreover, there is a special fitness that He, who is designated n-toro? al dai tm in iii. 14, xix. n, should authenticate the words of the prophecy of this book as irurroi KCU 6 vjowol (6).

6. dsroi ot X6yoi vtorol ital Xi)6iyoi. Christ here authenticates the words of the prophecy of this book and as 6 irtoro? KGU txrjotvfa there is a special appropriateness in His so doing. Besides He is therein fulfilling the very task given to Him by God in i. i, where we are told that God gave Him this revelation in order that He might make it known v (. rrjv dirokaxv iv) OKCV avrp (i. e. Iqcrov Xpurrq) 6 cas Setfai rots 8ovxot avrov. Cf. 4 Ezra xv. i, a, "Ecce loquere in aures plebis meae sermones 218 THE REVELATION OF ST. JOHN XXIL 6-7,18.

prophetiae, quos immisero in os tuum, dicit Dominus. 2. Et fac ut in charta scribantur, quoniam fideles et veri sunt."

6 KUPIOS 6 Oeds TW Trvcufidrwk T K Trpo4T Tw This is certainly a strange expression. Some scholars (Bousset, Moftatt) regard the plural as an archaistic detail (cf. i. 4), according to which there are a variety of angelic spirits that inspire the prophets. If we take this in the sense that various angels were sent at various times to instruct the prophets, it is quite unobjectionable, irvcu-Lurra is used of the archangels in our author: cf. iii. i, iv. 5, etc. But though the sense is unobjectionable, the words themselves can hardly bear this meaning. The irvcvpara are best taken with Swete to be the prophets' own spirits filled by the One Spirit mentioned in ii. 7, xiv. 13, xxii. 17. When the prophet spake as a prophet, it was his spint that was active (i. 10, xvii. 3, xxi. 10). Hence it seems that the text should here be interpreted as a similar expression in i Cor. xiv. 32, wcvpa. ro, irpotfrrj-ruv irpo rais virordwcrat, where it is the prophets' own spirits that are referred to. The divine title in our text has no connection of any kind with the very frequent designation of God in i Enoch xxxvii.-lxxi.; 2 Mace. iii. 24,. " Lord of Spirits." In Num. xvi. 22, xxvii. 16 the divine title "the God of the spirits of all flesh " (" ww nnnn T K) has only a general reference to mankind as a whole and not as in our text to the special class of men. TWK irpo Twy. As in x. 7, xi. 18, xxii. 9, John associates himself here with the Christian prophets.

TOP ftyycxop aurou. Here Christ speaks of the angel of xvii. i, xxi. 9 as God's angel, and yet in i. i, xxii. 16 he is described as Christ's angel. The statements are not incompatible. 8ei ai TOIS Souxois. Iv Tdxeu This clause is repeated from i. i. In fact the words dwotciacy r. ayycxov avrov 5ci ot r. Sovaoi? avrov a 8ei ycvccrlai ev rax i combine 8ct at T. Sovaots avrov, a Set ycvccr0ai fr ra;(cc and diroorccxa? 8ta rov ayycxov avrov in i. I.

7. Kal ISoo cpxopai rax Cf. xxii. 12, where as here it is from the lips of Christ; also ii. 5, 16, iil u, and xvi. 15, which as we have already seen should be restored after iii. 3.

paitdpios 6 n)pwt rods Xlyous icrx. This is the last of the seven beatitudes of the book (see note on i. 3). It is a short summary of i. 3, and thus the Book ends as it began in declaring the blessedness of those who have kept the words of the prophecy; but, whereas it is John that pronounces the first beatitude (i. 3), it is Christ that pronounces the last 18. paprufw 4y irdm rfi ditouom, rods X6you KT. Here the speaker is, as Swete urges, still Christ, who gives His solemn imprimatur to the Book. Moreover, as in 16 tioprv rat vu? ravra the TOVS Aoyov? is to be taken as the accusative after and not after dcoiwri, as is usually done: " to every- one that heareth I bear witness to the words of the prophecy of this book." As in 7, 10, Christ uses the same phraseology, r. Xoyovs r. irpo rcta? r. 3tj8Xtov rovrov.

16. Ey "li)rous faefu ra T ftyycxli pou. These words recall i. I, jcai Jcrijfuivcv diorooretxa? 8ia rov yycxov avrov, and xxii. 6, 6 0cot. AWcrrcixi TOV 5-vyexov afoov. According to Westcott (Add. Note on John xx. 21) dhroonrexXto "conveys the accessory notions of a special commission and so far of a delegated authority in the person sent." It is strange that Abbott (Johan-nine Vocabulary, p. 227) ascribes to these verbs almost the contrary meaning: " We are perhaps justified in thinking that amxrrcxXw means 'sending away into the world at large, 1 but ITCMTU sending on a special errand." Our author, at any rate, appears to use them as synonyms.

fijuk: cf. also xxii. 6. The angel of Christ attests the contents of this book (ravra) to the members of the Asian Churches. Others think the fyuv refers to the body of prophets in the Johannine school.

fytf clju ftf I KOI T yfros Aaueift: cf. V. 5, 6 Xlwv 6 IK T S vxipiousa, fj W a Aavets: Isa. xi. i, And there shall come forth a shoot out of the stock of Jesse and a branch out of his roots shall bear fruit; xi. 10; Test. Jud. xxiv. 5.

"Then shall the sceptre of my kingdom shine forth, And from your root shall arise a stem. 1 In His own person Christ is at once the root, and the stem and branches that spring from the root, and thus combines all the Messianic claims of the Davidic family. Thus He forms the climax of Jewish Messianic expectation. Our author lays more stress on the Davidic descent than Christ did Himself: cf. Matt. xxii. 42-45.

6 dor ip 6 Xapirpl?, 6 irpuii s. Here Christ is Himself the morning star, which in ii. 28 is promised to the faithful. The idea is ultimately derived from Num. xxiv. 17, "There shall come forth a star out of Jacob," but in the Test. Lev. xviii. 3, and probably in Test. Jud. xxiv. i, this passage has been definitely associated with the hope of a Messiah from Levi an expectation that was abandoned early in the first century B. C. As Christ is the realization of all that Israel hoped for in the past (pi a icrx.), He contains in Himself the promise (cf. Luke i. 78) of all that is to come (6 forw. 6 iryxwvoc) as " the Light of the world," John viii. 12.

13. In this verse the Son claims all the attributes of the Father. In the next verse (i. e. 12) it follows naturally that He designates Himself as the Judge of all the world.

tyfc T A +a icrx.: cf. L 8 (note), xxi. 6, where it is the title used by God of Himself.

6 irpdrofi itol 6 l0x Tos. See note on i. 17, ii. 8 in both cases of Christ 4 dpx4 w T This title is used by God of Himself in XXL 6.

The phrase 17 Jx T is an abbreviated form of an ancient Orphic saying, which is first recorded in Plato, Leg. iv. 7, 6 pfr 3 0cd (oxnrcp u 6 raaotfc Afyos) (Ipxip re KCU rcxcvr v cat ufoa TWV itu r clWmw fyw. Thus Plato in the 4th century B. C.

speaks of this saying as even then an ancient one. A scholion on this passage gives the original form of it and an explanation: Otov jib TDK Styuovpyo? (TO ts, iraaaiov Se 6yov Aryct rov Op itco?, os IOTIV osros" Zcvs fyxij, vs ccrcra, AIDS 8 fc iravra TCTUKTOI, Zevc Trv6fjirjy y 04179 re neat ovpavov dorcpocvros cat lp ACV ovros cbs irotiTwcov atrtov, rexevr 8i as rcxikoy, fi rra Si d5 cf titrov ircurt irapcav. We might compare the Pauline statement, Rom. xi. 36, i avrov icai avrov ical cis avrov ra iravra, .?. God is the initial cause, the sustaining cause, and the final cause of all things.

This Orphic logion was well known in the ancient world. In the first century A. D. it was familiar to the Palestinian Jews, as we know from Josephus who quotes it in c. Af. ii. 22, 6 0cfa. avros avr tal TTCUTIV avrapki;?, a. pxq ai fiecra icat rcxos ouro? TW irarrcov. In his Ant. viii. ii. 2 it appears in almost the same abbreviated form as in our text: u rov ISiov Oebv. Ss. Apx f a t rcxo? rwv airavrw. In later times it was adopted by the Talmudists and given a Jewish turn in the third century A. D. by Simon ben Lakish, who strove to derive this ancient Greek Orphic saying from the Hebrew word J1DK (Jer. Jeb. xii. 13; Gen. R. Ixxxi.); "for. fit is the first, D the middle, and D the last letter of the alphabet this being the name of God according to Isa. xliv. 6, explained Jer. Sanh. i. 18 I am the first having had none from whom to receive the kingdom; I am the middle, there being none who shares the kingdom with me; and I am the last there being none to whom I shall hand the kingdom of the world" (quoted from Jewish Encyc. i. 439). It is hardly needful to draw attention to the forced nature of this explanation or to point out that D is not the middle letter of the Hebrew alphabet being the i3th from the beginning and the zoth from the end.

Turning now from Jewish to Christian writings, we find that the early Christian writers were well acquainted with this ancient Greek saying. This phrase lies behind the text of the Kipvyui Ilerpov: els 0efe mv, 85 opxV T KTCUV lirotio-cv KCU rcxov? ttowrfav? X- Justin Martyr (Cohort, ad Gent, xxv.) quotes the saying from Plato but ascribes it to the Law of Moses. Irenaeus (Hatr. iii. 25. 5, "Et Deus quidem, quemadmodum et vetus sermo est, initium et finem et medietates omnium quae sunt habeas"; Hippolytus, Rcfut. omn. Hacr. L 19; Clem. Alex. Protrcfb. vi. 69, Strom, ii. 22. 132; Origen,. Cels. vl 13; Eusebius, Praepar. Evang. XL 13, p rjv auros fyaif at flcwarov i)Si 12. ISod ipx 0! 01 Ta X- Cf. iii. n, xxii. 7, 20. itol 6 pou fur Ifou. Cf. xi. i8 d. 6 iurftfc p. ov is here "the reward which I give." Cf. Isa. xl. 10, isov 6 zwrflos avrov ACT avrov: Ixii. II; Wisd. v. 15, KOL iv jcvpicp 6 uo-0os avrwv.

airosoufai itdrrw 6 TO Ipyok OTTIK afrrou. Cf. ii. 23, XX. 13; Rom. ii. 6; Prov. xxiv. I2 b (LXX, Ss dtrostsaxrtv efcaar Kara ra Ipya avrov); Jer. xvii. 10; Ps. Ixl 13, OTI rv dvofitocrcis cicaary Kara ra tpya avrov. Our text seems to have been before i Clem. xxxiv. 3.

10. Here also Christ appears to speak, as Bousset recognizes. There is force in His command to issue the Book immediately; " for the time is at hand." As contrasted with Jewish Apocalypses, such as Daniel (cf. viii. 26, xii. 4, 9); i Enoch i. 2, xciil 10, civ. 12; 2 Enoch xxxiii. 9-11, xxxv. 3, etc., which were not to be divulged till distant generations, our Apocalypse is to be made known by the Seer to his contemporaries. The older Apocalypses were referred to as sealed (cf. Dan. viil 26, in order to explain the withholding of their publication till the actual time of their author.

rods X6yous T. irpo T)Teias KT. Cf. xxii. 7, 1 8. In all three cases these are the words of Christ: cf. also i. 3. 6 icaipof yap tyyifc. This clause and the preceding are combined by our author in L 3. The same idea underlies the clause pxouu ra v,

11. 1 6, iii. n, xxii. 7, 12, 20, which is only used by Christ 11. These words can refer only to the contemporaries of the Seer. But, since xxi. 6-8 refer also to his contemporaries and still proclaim the possibility of free and full forgiveness, this verse appears to be a later addition. In xxi. 6 d those who thirst after a new life are promised satisfaction, whereas here the door of hope is closed absolutely and finally against every class of sinners. Ver. 1 1 assumes that finality in character is already arrived at, and an unswerving persistence in good or evil, though there is still some interval between the vision and the Second Advent; for the circulation of the Book among the Churches (ii.-iii.) and the faithful observance of its teaching (xxi. 7, xxii. 7) postulates some such interval. And yet the interval is not expected to be long; " for the time is at hand " (i. 3, xxii. 10). In Dan. xil 10, 1 1 no such consideration for the sinner is shown. Besides in our author the whole body of the neutral nations have to be 1 Cf. the Egyptian prayer quoted by Reitzenstein (Primandres, p. 277):, dpx4 a rtfxot rip djctrjjrou frcws.

evangelized on the Second Advent when the Millennial Kingdom is established: cf. xiv. 6-7, xv. 4, xxii. 2, 17, xxl 24-26. In the face of such an expectation n is an impossibility.

d5lk1)r Tfe ical A SIKCUOS iicaiocri5inf K iroitjadrw Sn, ital 6 ftyios dytao rw Iru

We have already on the ground of their contents rejected these lines. As regards their form and diction there are further objections, though these are not unanswerable in themselves. First, as regards their form, it will be observed that, whereas universally in our author the second line is parallel with, i. e. reproduces the first not in identical but in similar terms, or more rarely the second and third lines (as in xxii. 13, 12) reproduce the first, in 77, however if is the third line that is parallel antithetically to the first and the fourth that is similarly parallel to the second. This form of parallelism is not found in our author, though there are approaches to it. It is, however, possible to regard the first and second lines, and the third and fourth as respectively instances of synonymous parallelism. But the antitheses between the 6 asufstv and the 6 dticcuo? and between the 6 ptnrapos and the 6 aytos and between dkicrarco and Sikcuoo-vnv 7rot7o-aro are in favour of our taking the stanza as we have done above. Next the diction is remarkable. Thus aicctv, which occurs twice in this stanza, means here " to act unjustly," " to sin," whereas in the nine cases where it occurs previously in our author it means "to hurt," "to damage." Next pvwapos (cf. dwro0 , ooi iracrav pwrapiav in Jas. i. 21 in like sense) occurs only here in the N. T. in the sense of internal defilement (cf. Job xiv. 4, rk yap a0apo? ftrnu airb pvwov; once of external defilement in Jas. ii. 2), pvtTavorjvai here only in N. T., and aytao-0jjicu, "to purify oneself internally " here only in our author.

18 b-19. As Porter (Messages of the Books, p. 293) remarks, these words form "an unfortunate ending of a book whose value consists in the spirit that breathes in it, the bold faith and confident hope which it inspires, rather than in the literalness and finality of its disclosures." But these clauses, to which there are abundant parallels

in other books, as we shall see presently, are not in the opinion of the present editor from the hand of John. For (i) these words presuppose that John looked forward to a long period elapsing before the Second Advent, during which the Book would be exposed not to the errors incidental to transmission but to the deliberate perversion of his message both in the way of additions and omissions.

But we know that John looked for the speedy Advent of

Christ and the Millennial Kingdom an expectation which is expressed repeatedly in the words Zpx 0 1 Ta X " JI xxii. 7, 12, 20. 2. The style is unlike that of John. Thus we have rov Xoycovtov Pt3 iov 1-175 Trpo iTcias Taifns in 19, whereas, as in xxii. 7, 10, 18, we should expect r. Xoyu? r. Trpo rcias r. ifi iov TOVTOV. Next after TOVS Xoyovs in 18 we shall expect, not kf avrdi, but Iv avtov. Again, instead of d cxc?. TO p, cpos avrov diro rov vxov rrjs oi? s we should expect (tycxei. TO tcpo? avrov v nj vxp TI S anjs: cf. xx. 6, xxi. 8, or TTJV c ovo-tav avrov ri TO (uixov Tiys G: cf. xxii. 14. 3. The nature of the penalty is not what we should expect. The extreme penalty that can befall the evildoer in this Book is not the plagues singly or collectively, but the being cast into the lake of fire. The plagues are concerned with temporal punishments, not with eternal. Exclusion from the tree of life is mentioned, it is true, in 19. 4. i8 b-i9 introduce a wrong note in these last verses.

On the above grounds I have bracketed these clauses as an interpolation.

Next, the custom of appending such warnings claims our attention. We first find them in Deut. iv. 2, ov irxxrtfqo-ccrfc Trpos TO pfjpja. o eyoj cvrcxXoKU vuv, KCU OVK d excite atT avrov: xii. 32: i Enoch civ. 10, "And now I know this mystery, that sinners will alter and pervert the words of righteousness in many ways, and will speak wicked words." As opposed to this, Enoch requires that they should " not change or minish aught from my words" (civ. n). In the Letter of Aristeas (33-41 A. D.?) 310-311, it is said that, when the Greek translation of the O. T. was completed, "they bade them pronounce a curse in accordance with their custom upon any who should make any alteration either by adding anything or changing in any way whatever any of the words which had been written or making an omission. This was a very wise precaution to ensure that the book might be preserved for all the future time unchanged." A terrible judgment is foretold (2 Enoch xlviii. 7-8) for those who tamper with the words of this book. In Josephus (c. Ap. i. 8) the writer claims a most faithful transmission of the ancient books of the O. T. 8 Xov 8 Icrrlv 2pyp, irw? jjficls TrpovtflCV TOIS iyois ypdfjLfmurt roa-ovrov yap auovos rfbrf irctpyxrjkoros ovrc irpoarotlvai TI? ov8cv ovsc d cxciv avrcoy ovrc fuTatfcivai TeroxxiKcv. It was not unusual for writers, Christian and Jewish, to attempt to secure a faithful transmission of their works by appending solemn adjurations that the scribes should in no wise change or tamper with the text. Cf. Irenaeus in EusebluS, H. E. v. 20. 2: 6oa o ere rov pjftaypa. il6p. cvov TO j8i? Xtbv TOVTO. tva m? ax? S Acrcypaiw a! Katopqway? avro Trpos TO avrtypafav TOVTO. KCU TOV opkov 6xotcos icraypa cis: and Rabbi

Meir in Sota 20 " My son, be careful; for it is a divine work: if thou writest, were it but a letter more or less, it is as if thou wert destroying a world."

it jupot odtofi dvo TOU dxou xrx. The Holy City mentioned here is that which is associated with the Millennial Kingdom. The tree of life was in this city (xxii. 2).

8-0, 80-81. John's testimony and closing words.

8-0. Of these verses we have already found a doublet in xix. 9-10 (see notes), which was probably from the hand of the disciple that edited the Book after John's death.

a KY Wifv)s 6 AKOUWK Kat px rwk Cf. 2 Cor. xii. 4, jfieovcrcv ajpitTa, Dan. xii. 5, "And I Daniel saw." At the close of his words the author gives his name as at the beginning (i. i). Observe the participles are in our author's usage equal to aorists or perfects.

ihreaa irpcxncufrjcrai Ijiirpoabck TUP irobwc TOU ayyaou. See note on xix. 10. Worship in the sense of prostration is here involved, though not divine worship: cf. irpoovcwciv amriov in iii. 9, xv. 4 of simple homage. Yet even such homage is refused by the angel. The phrase may be equivalent to irpoo-Kwfjo-cu avrov (see notes on xix. 9-10 (5), vii. 11).

TOU SeikPiwro's poi TOUTO. Cf. i. I, iv. i, xvii. i, xxi. 9, 10, xxiI i, 6. Here the participle = Sctifairo?.

0. Spa fi cruhouxos aou dpi KT. Our text appears to be the source of Asc. Isa. vil 21, "And I fell on my face to worship him, but the angel who conducted me (or rather 'showed to me i. e. fa 28 c LWW: for the Ethiopic is capable of this meaning and the Latin and Slavonic Versions = instructed me) did not permit me but said unto me: Worship neither throne nor angel: and viii. 4-5, What is this which I see, my lord? 5. And he said: C I am not thy lord but thy fellowservant." The Apocryphal Gospel of Matthew iii. 3 (Tischendorf, p. 59) seems also to show signs of the influence of our text: " Benedic me servum tuum. Et dixit ei angelus: Noli te dicere servum, sed conservum meum; unius enim domini servi sum us." Our text is a strong prohibition of angel worship (fywjowa rwv dyyew, Col. ii. 18). That this was practised by the Jews before the Christian era is to be inferred from Tob. xii. 15, "I am Raphael, one of the seven angels: 12. When thou didst pray. I brought the memorial of your prayer before the glory of the Lord:" Jub. xxx. 20: Test. Dan vi. 2, "Draw near to God and to the angel that intercedeth for you; for he is a mediator between God and man:" l Test Lev. v. 5, where Levi prays to the angel who conducts him to make known to him his name that he might l This idea of an angelic mediator is found already in Job v. I, zxxiii. 33 sq.; Zech. i la.

call upon him in the day of tribulation, and the angel replies: " I (i. c. Michael) am the angel who intercedeth for the nation of Israel 1: 1 i Enoch Ixxxix. 76. The fact that frequent admonitions against the worship of angels are to be found in Jewish writings confirms the view that this cult did prevail in Judaism. Cf. Mechilta Sect. TW, Parash. 10, where R. Ismael ben Blisha (flor. 100 A. D.) forbids the worship of any kind of angels (quoted from Lueken, p. 6): Jer. Berach. ix. 13 where men in necessity are bidden to pray to God and not to Michael or Gabriel: Aboda Zara, 42, where offerings to Michael are denounced as offerings to the dead. In Shabbath i2 b men are commanded by R. Jehuda (4th century A. D.) not to pray in Aramaic since the angels did not understand Aramaic. On the other hand, in the Jer. Qiddushim at its close (Lueken) permission is given to ask the angels for their intercession. For other proofs that, notwithstanding strong prohibitions against the cult of angels, this cult did survive in Judaism, see Lueken, Michael 6-12.

From Christian sources we know of the prevalence of angel-olatry among the Jews: cf. Preaching of Peter (Clem. Alex. Strom, vi. 5), prjfo Kara lovsaiovs rc)3cr0c, ai yap cfcctvot. owe Mvravrai Aarpcvovrcs dyyexots: Celsus in Origen, c. Cels. V. 6, wpwtOV oflv TCOV Iovsatav 0avia ctv tov, ct. rovs. dyycxovs trcSavcri.

That this superstition passed from the Jews to the Christians our text is sufficient evidence: cf. also Col. ii. 18; Asc. Isa. vii. 21, viii. 4, 5; Justin Martyr, Afol i. 6, AAV CKCIVOV TC, KCU TO vap avrov vibv ixOovra. ical rov rv aaAcuv ciroAeww KOI c ofiotovACTay yaoav dyyextov orpardv, irvevLia re TO 7rpot7jtikov o-c dze a cat n-poo-Kwovfiev: Athenagoras, Suppl. x., xxiv.: Clem. Horn. iii. 36.

TOP 1Tpo T TOK Kal TOK TtjpoUKTWK TOO? X6yoU9 KT. HCFC, 3S WC have shown in the notes on xix. 9-10, the prophets and the ordinary Christians are practically placed on the same level, whereas in xix. 9-10 the prophets are exalted far above the ordinary Christians, no mention of whom is made.

TOK rqpoditOi rods Xrfyous. Cf. i. 3, iii. 8, 10, xii. 17, xiv. 12, xxii. 7.

TOU 0l Xuu TOUTOU. Cf. XXU. 7, IO 18, 19, T Off TTpoT-

Kdmf)rok. See note on vil n.

flo. X yci 6 fciptupwk Toora. Christ is again the Speaker. The 6 Aoprvpcok goes back to xxii. 18, where Christ solemnly attests the truth of the words of the prophecy of this book.

1 Cf. Asc. Isa. ix. 23, "Iste eat magnus angel us Michael deprecans semper pro humanitate."

9 The four chief angels are spoken of as intercessors in I Enoch ix. X, 3, the Watchers in zv. 2. VOL. II. 15

Not Zpxofuit raxrf. Here for the third time in this chapter (see 7, 12) our Lord declares that He is coming speedily. On vat, see note on L 7.

Ajwfr- Ipx 0 1 "ipu li)ro. On this, the initial and primitive use of tli v, which solemnly assents to the utterance of a preceding speaker, cf. v. 14, note, vii. 12, xix. 4.?x ov ""pic is the Greek equivalent of the Aramaic NT) 3id (= "our Lord, come"). 1 See- 0v. A2- and Hastings' B D. on " Maranatha." The Aramaic is actually found transliterated in z Cor. xvi. 22, and in the Didache, x. 6:

A ris ayios IOTIV, ct TO ofc icupw v li)irou. This designation is found only here and in the next verse in our author.

21. X Pf TO " Kupiou Ivjcrog p-era irdrrwk TWK dyitti This benediction, which is unusual in Apocalypses, is an indication that the Book was intended to be read in the Church services. In the Pauline Epistles ol ayiot includes the whole body of the baptized. But in our author it appears to embrace only the faithful members of the Church. Cf. v. 8, viii. 3, 4, xi. 18, xiii. 7, 10, xiv. 12, xvi. 6, xvii. 6, xviii. 20, xix. 8, xx. 6, 9. It is not used at all in the Johannine Epistles.

1 This explanation of Dalman, Wellhauscn, etc., is preferable to that which is generally accepted in the Church Fathers, i. e. ut)ava0i=Kme po f "our Lord has come."

I. THE TEXT. THE GREEK MANUSCRIPTS OF THE APOCALYPSE.

Uncial Mbs containing the Greek Text of the Apocalypse or part of it. The enumeration is that of Gregory, except in the case of KAC.

K (iv). Petrograd. Sd. 5 2. K signifies the original text, where the original scribe or a later one has intro- duced an emendation. K K b K 0 cb etc. are various correctors of the MS. 1

A (v). London. Sd. 8 4. A signifies as K above. A corrector. 8 C (v). Paris. Sd. 5 3. Contains i 1- 19, 5 14-7 14, 7 17-8 5, 9 16-io 10, n 8-i6 13, i8-i 9 ft. 025 (ix). Petrograd. Formerly P. Sd. a 3. Contains i-i6 u, I 7 1 I 9 21 20 9-22 6.

046 (x). Rome. Formerly Q or B Sd. a 1070. 051 (ix-x). Athos, Pantokrator 44. Contains u 16-i3 1, i3 8-22 7, 22 i6-2i w j tn a commentary of Andreas in cursive. Photographed for Prof. Swete. 052 (x). Athos, Panteleemon. Formerly r 183. Contains

GREEK CURSIVES OF THE APOCALYPSE.

i (xii-xiii cent.). Maihingen. Formerly r i. Sd. 18 (1364 A. D.). Paris. Formerly r 51. Sd. 8 411. xi). Paris. Formerly r 17. Sd. 8 309. xi). Frankfurt a. O. Formerly r 13. Sd. a 107. x). Cambridge. Formerly r 10. Sd. c 1321. xvi). Dublin. Formerly r 92. Sd. 8 603. xv). Leicester. Formerly r 14. Sd. 8 505. x). Paris. Formerly r 2. Sd. O 1.

1 The photographic fa gimijg edited by Professor Lake for the Clarendon Press has been used for this edition.

91 The photographic facsimile edited by Sir Frederic G. Kenyon (1909) has been used for this edition.

Gregory's enumeration of the MSS is adopted in this edition, but for the convenience of those who use Von Soden's text I have added the latter's enumeration.

88 (xii?). Naples. Formerly r 99. Sd. a 200.

91 (xi). Paris. Formerly r 4. Sd. O 14.

93 (x). Paris. Formerly r 19. Sd. a 51.

94 (xiii). Paris. Formerly r 18. Sd. O 81. 104 (xi). London. Formerly r 7. Sd. a 103. no (xii). London. Formerly r 8. Sd. a 204.

xiii-xiv). Rome. Formerly r 40. Sd. B 408.

xv). Rome. Formerly r 25. Sd. B 503.

xiv-xv). Berlin. Formerly r 87. Sd. a 404.

x xi). Rome. Formerly r 20. Sd. B 95.

xi). Munich. Formerly r 82. Sd. a 106. (xiv). Rome. Formerly r 44. Sd. c 1498. 181 (xi). Rome. Formerly r 12. Sd. a 101. 201 (r 357 A. D.). London. Formerly r 94. Sd. 8 403. 203 (mi A. D.). London. Formerly r 181. Sd. a 203. 205 (xv). Venice. Formerly r 88. Sd. B 500. 209 (xiv?). Venice. Formerly r 46. Sd. a 1581. 218 (xiii). Vienna. Formerly r 33. Sd. B 300.

241 (xi). Dresden. Formerly r 47. Sd. 8 507.

242 (xii) Moscow. Formerly r 48. Sd. B 206. 250 (xi). Pans. Formerly r 121. Sd. O 10.

(xiv). Athens. Formerly r 122. Sd. O 42. (xi). Paris. Formerly r 102. Sd. a 216. (xvi). Paris. Formerly r 57. Sd. B 600. xi). Oxford. Formerly r 6. Sd. O 11. i).

xi). Oxford. Formerly r 9. Sd. am.

xv). Hamburg Formerly r 16. Sd. a 500.

xii). Paris. Formerly r 52. Sd. a 205 (xiu). Turin. Formerly r 83. Sd. B 303. (1331 A. D.). Florence. Formerly r 23 Sd. 400. 368 (xv). Florence. Formerly r 84. Sd. a 1501.

385 (xv). London. Formerly r 29. Sd. a 506 386 (xiv). Rome. Formerly r 70. Sd. B 401. 424 (xi). Vienna. Formerly r 34. Sd. O 12. 432 (xv). Rome. Formerly r 37. Sd. a 501. 452 (xii). Rome. Formerly r 42. Sd. a 206. 456 (x). Florence. Formerly r 75. Sd. a 52.

459 (1092 A. D.). Florence. Formerly r 45. Sd. a 104. 467 (xv). Paris. Formerly r 53. Sd. a 502.

xiii). Paris. Formerly r 55. Sd. O 80.

xiii-xiv). Paris. Formerly r 56. Sd. o 306.

xiv). London. Formerly r 97. Sd. S 402.

xi-xii). Oxford. Formerly r 26. Sd. B 101.

xi-xii). Oxford. Formerly r 27. Sd. a 214. 522 (1515 A. D.). Oxford. Formerly r 98. Sd. B 602. 582 (1334 A. D.). Ferron. Formerly r 103. Sd. B 410.

616 (1434 A. D.). Milan. Formerly r 156. Sd. a 503.

617 (xi). Venice. Formerly r 74. Sd. O 18.

620 (xii). Florence. Formerly r 180. Sd. a 207.

x-xi). Rome. Formerly r 24. Sd. a 53. xiv). Rome. Formerly r 69. Sd. a 400.

627 628 632 664 680 699 (xi). London. Formerly r 108. Sd. 8 104.

civ), civ).

xiv). Rome. Formerly r 22. Sd. a 201. xv). Zittau. Formerly r 106. Sd. 8 502.

xi). Cheltenham. Formerly r 107. Sd. 8 103.

xiv). Paris. Formerly r 123. Sd. Ai 43. xiii-xiv). Athens. Formerly r no. Sd. 8 304. xih). Athens. Formerly r in. Sd. c 585. xii). Athens. Formerly r 112. Sd. 8 203.

808,, 824 (xiv). Grottaferrata. Formerly r 113. Sd. 8 404.

866 (xiv). Rome. Formerly r 114. Sd. a 1375. 886 (1454 A. D.). Rome. Formerly r 115. bd. A 50.

919 (xi). Escurial. Formerly r 125. Sd. a 113.

920 (x). Escunal. Formerly r 126. Sd. a 55.

922 (1116 A. D.). Athos. Formerly r 116. Sd. 8 2oa 935 Athos. Sd. 8 361.

986 (xiv). Athos. Formerly r 117. Sd. 8 508.

1006 Athos. Sd. a 1174.

1064 Athos.

THE REVELATION OF ST. JOHN 1734 Athos., 1740 Athos.

1745 Athos.

1746 Athos. 1757 Lesbos. 1760 Serres. 1771 Athos.

1773 Athos.

1774 Athos.

1775 Athos.

1776 Athos. 1778 Saloniki.

1785 Kosinitza, Sd. S 405.

1795 Kosinitza. Sd. 0215.

1806 Trapezunt. Sd. a 1472.

1824 Rome. Sd. O 61.

xii). Athens. Formerly r 124. Sd. a 202.

1828 1841 1849 1852 1854 ix-x). Lesbos. Formerly r 127. Sd. a 47.

1069 A. D.). Venice. Formerly r 128. Sd. a no.

x-xi). Upsala. Formerly r 129. Sd. a 114.

xi). Athos. Formerly r 130. Sd. a 115.

xiii). Athos. Formerly r 131. Sd. a 1587. 1859 Athos. Formerly r 371. Sd. a 402.

1862 (ix). Athos. Formerly r 132. Sd. O 1.

1864 Athos. Formerly r 327.

1865 Athos. Formerly r 380.

1870 (x). Chalkis. Formerly r 133. Sd. a 54. 1872 (xii). Chalkis. Formerly r 134. Sd. a 209. 1876 (xv). Sinai. Formerly r 135. Sd. a 504. 1888 Jerusalem. Formerly r 495. Sd. a 118.

1893 Jerusalem. Formerly r 500. Sd. a 117.

1894 Jerusalem. Formerly r 501. Sd. a 1670. 1903 Athos. Formerly r 513.

1955 I9S7 xiv). Rome. Formerly r 39. Sd. a 403. xi). Paris. Formerly r. 64. Sd. O 15. xv). Rome. Formerly r 78. Sd. a 505. xi). London. Formerly r 93. Sd. a 119. xv). Rome. Formerly r 91. Sd. a 1574.

2004 (x). Escurial. Formerly r 142. Sd. a 56.

2014 (xv). Rome. Formerly r 21. Sd. A 61.

2015 (xv). Oxford. Formerly r 28. Sd. a 1580.

2016 (xv). London. Formerly r 31. Sd. a 1579.

2017 (xv). Dresden. Formerly r 32. Sd. a 1582.

2018 (xiv). Vienna. Formerly r. 35. Sd. Av 46.

2019 (xiii). Vienna. Formerly r 36. Sd.

2021 (xv). Rome. Formerly r 41. Sd. a 1572.

2022 (xiv). Rome. Formerly r 43. Sd. Ai 01.

2023 (xv) Moscow. Formerly r 49. Sd. Av 66.

2024 (xv). Moscow. Formerly r 50. Sd. a 1584.

2025 (xv-xvi). Paris. Formerly r 58. Sd. a 1592.

2026 (xv-xvi). Pans. Formerly r 59. Sd. Av 501.

2027 (xhi-xiv). Pans. Formerly r 61. Sd. a 1374.

2028 (1422 A. D.). Paris. Formerly r 62. Sd. Av 64.

2029 (xvi). Paris. Formerly r 63. Sd. Av 66.

2030 (xii). Moscow. Formerly r 65. Sd. a 1272.

2031 (1301 A. D.). Rome. Formerly r 67. Sd. Ay 41, 2032 (xi-xii). Rome. Formerly r 68. Sd. Av 11.

2033 (xv) Rome. Formerly r 72. Sd. Av 00.

2034 (xv). Rome. Formerly r 73. Sd. Av 60.

2035 (xvi). Florence. Formerly r 77. Sd Av 80.

2036 (xiv). Rome. Formerly r 79. Sd. Av 40.

2037 (xiv). Munich. Formerly r 80. Sd. Ax 46.

2038 (xvi). Munich. Formerly r 81. Sd. Av 600.

2039 (xii). Dresden. Formerly r 90. Sd. a 1271.

2040 (xi-xii). Parham (Curzon). Formerly r 95. Sd. Ap 11.

2041 (xiv). Parham (Curzon). Formerly r 96. Sd. a 1475.
2042 (xiv-xv). Naples. Formerly r 100. Sd. Av 400.
2043 (xv) Petrograd. Formerly r 101. Sd. Av 67.
2044 (1507 A. D.). Vienna. Formerly r 136. Sd. Av 601.
2045 (xv) Vienna. Formerly r 137. Sd. Av 66.
2046 (xv). Vienna. Formerly r 138. Sd. Av 68.
2047 (1543 A. D.). Pans. Formerly r 139. Sd. Av 67.
2048 (xi-xii). Paris. Formerly r 140. Sd. a 1172.
2049 (xv i)- Athens. Formerly r 141. Sd. a 1684.
2050 (1107 A. D.). Escunal. Formerly r 143. Sd. a 1273.
2051 (xvi). Madrid. Formerly r 144. Sd. Ay 08.
2052 (xvi). Florence. Formerly r 145. Sd. Av 64.
2053 (xiii). Messina. Formerly r 146. Sd. O 31.
2054 (xv-xvi). Modena. Formerly r 147. Sd. Av 600.
2055 (xv). Modena. Formerly r 148. Sd. Av 58.
2056 (xiv-xv). Rome. Formerly r 149. Sd. Av 49.
2057 (xv). Rome. Formerly r 150. Sd. a 1576.
2058 (xiv). Rome. Formerly r 151. Sd. O 40.
2059 (xi). Rome. Formerly 1152. Sd. Av 10.
2060 (1331 A. D.). Rome. Formerly r 153. Sd. Av 48.
2061 (xv-xvi). Rome. Formerly r 154. Sd. a 1588.
2062 (xiii). Rome. Formerly r 155. Sd. O 80.
2063 (xvi). Rome. Formerly r 157. Sd. Av 61.
2064 (xvi). Rome. Formerly r 158. Sd. Ax 62.
2065 (xv). Rome. Formerly r 159. Sd. Av 608.
2066 (1574 A. D.). Rome. Formerly r 160. Sd.
2067 (xv). Rome. Formerly r 161. Sd.
2068 (xvi). Venice. Formerly r 162. Sd.
2069 (xv-xvi). Venice. Formerly r 163. Sd. Av 69.
2070 (1356 A. D.). Athos. Formerly r 164. Sd. Ai 408.
2071 (1622 A. D.). Athos. Formerly r 167. Sd. Av 70.
2072 (1798 A. D.). Athos. Formerly r 168. Sd. Av 80.
2073 (xiv). Athos. Formerly r 169. Sd. Av 47.
2074 (x). Athos. Formerly r 170. Sd. Av 1.
2075 (xiv). Athos. Formerly r 171. Sd. Av 48.
2076 (xvii). Athos. Formerly r 172. Sd. a 1570.
2077 (1685 A. D.). Athos. Formerly r 174. Sd. Av 71.
2078 (xvi). Athos. Formerly r 176. Sd. a 1686.
2079 (xiii). Athos. Formerly r 177. Sd. a 1373.
2080 (xiv). Patmos. Formerly r 178.
2081 (xii). Patmos. Formerly r 179. Sd. Ay 21.
2082 (xvi). Dresden. Formerly r 182. Sd. a 1682.
2083 (1560 A, D.). Leyden. Formerly r 184. Sd. Av 602.
2084 Constantinople. Formerly r 506. Sd. a 1586. 2087 Basel.
2091 Athens. Formerly r 511. Sd. Av 602.

2116 Athens. Sd. Ao 70.

2136 Moscow. Sd. c 700.

2138 Moscow. Sd. o 116.

2186 Athos. Sd. Av 28.

2195 Athos. Sd. a 508.

2196 Athos. Sd. a 1687. 2254 Athos. Sd. Av 604. 2256 Athos. Sd. a 1577.

2258 Athos. Sd. a 1770.

2259 Athos. Sd. 2286 Athos. Sd.

There are thus 223 Cursives according to the above enumeration, which is based on Gregory's list, Griechischcn Handschriften des NT. (pp. 48-1 22). 1 1 In his list of MSS of the Apocalypse on pp. 360-361 there are six omissions and two or more wrong insertions. Von Soden (Schriften des NT. I. i. 289) reckons the number of Cursives as 222. Thus with the seven Uncials there are altogether 230 (or 229) Greek MSS of the Apocalypse.

THE MSS AND VERSIONS COLLATED FOR THIS EDITION: ABBREVIA-TIONS: SYMBOLS: ITACISMS.

UNCIALS. Of the Uncials A and N have been collated afresh from photographs of these MSS published by Kenyon and Lake respectively. For the readings of C, 025, 046 the editor is dependent on Tischendorf, and for 051 on the readings given in Swete's edition under the number 186.

CURSIVES. The following 22 Cursives have been specially photographed for this edition: 18, 35, 149, 175, 205, 325, 337, 386, 456, 468, 617, 620, 632, 866, 919, 920, 1849, 1934, 2004, 2020, 2040, 2050 Of these the following are defective: 205, 337, 468, 866, 919, 920, 2040, 2050. 205. Defective: xvill. I4a7nj 0ci airo crow. XX. 9 TTJV irapcu-Joxrjv T. aytw, i. e. one page lost through carelessness of the photographer.

337. Defective: x. 4-xi. i and xxii. 17 Xeyovo-a to end wanting. 468. Defective: xix. 18 ai o-apicas lo-xupuv. xxii. 17 chrara 2Xov wanting.

866. Defective: contains only vi. 17 i?Acpa r. fyyjJs. xiii. 12 rov Oijpcov irtiurav.

919. Ends with xix. 6 usaruy iroaAwv KCU a.

920. Ends with xxii. i KOL? Scc c.

2040. Ends with the words at roiros, xx. n. Photographs incomplete.

2050. Defective. Omits vi. i cal ciSov. xix. 21 TWK crdpicwv avraiv.

These 22 Cursives are generally quoted as 88, or 81, 80,19, accordingly as one or more are defective. See under " Abbreviations " below.

For the readings of most of the remaining Cursives cited in this edition the author is indebted to Tischendorfs NT. Graece (ed. oct. 1872) and to Hoskier s Concerning the Date of the Bohairic Version (1911) for select readings from the following 26 Cursives: 180, 181, 256, 337, 367, 368, 467, 582, 664, 680, 743 1075, 1948, 2014, 2025, 2026, 2028, 2029, 2030, 2031, 2032, 2033, 2034, 2037, 2038, 2043. Where readings from the Cursives cited by Tischendorf are not to be found in Tischendorf, they are derived from Hoskier.

CORRECTIONS ON THE MSS

A original text. A = correction and similarly in the Cursives.

K = original text The lead of Tischendorf has been followed in distinguishing the different hands engaged in correcting K. On these different correctors (as many as fifteen ranging from the iv to the xii Century) and their dates see Lake, Codex Sinaiticus, pp. xvii-xxiv. Lake differs from Tischendorf in differentiating certain of the correctors. Into this vexed question it is not necessary to enter here.

VERSIONS. For a short description of these Versions see the Introduction to vol. i. Latin.

Tyc =" Tyconius' Text of the Apocalypse, a partial restoration," published by Prof. Souter in the J. T. S., April 1913. Pr = Text of Primasius in Die lateinische Apocalypse edited by Haussleiter, 1891. fl = Palimpsestus floriacensis in Haussleiter's volume just mentioned.

gig = Codex Gigas. A fresh collation made by Dr. Karlsson in 1891 for Bp. John Wordsworth of Salisbury, and put at my service by his collaborator Professor White. vg = Vulgate (editio minor), edited by H. J. White, 1911. Syriac.

s 1 = Philoxenian Version, edited by John Gwynn, 1897. s = Harkleian or Syriac Vulgate, s sometimes is used to indicate the consensus of s 1 and s 2. Armenian.

arm i. a.8.4 = oid Armenian MSS edited by F. C

Conybeare, 1907. arm = Armenian Vulgate. Egyptian.

bo-Bohairic Version of the New Testament, vol. iv., edited by G. Horner, 1905. sa = Sahidic Version. Partial collation furnished to the editor by G. Horner. Ethiopic.

eth = Ethiopic Version, edited by J. P. Platt (new edition), 1899.

ABBREVIATIONS AND SYMBOLS

Or 1 = the Greek text, which accompanies the recently discovered Scholia of Origen on the Apocalypse, i. e. in Harnack's edition, Der Seholien-Kommentar des Origenes ur Apokalypsc Johannis, 1911. This text is not Origen's, though the Scholia probably are. It should be numbered as Cursive 2293 (x cent).

Ofmfcfew. Qrigen's text of the Apoc. in his Commentary on Matthew, vol. iv. p. 314, in Lommatzsch's edition. Similarly Or cd " " 7 means Origen's text of the Apoc. in Contra Celsum, vol. xx. p. 117, of Lommatzsch's edition. Origen's works are occasionally quoted to show that Or 1 cannot be his text.

r Words so enclosed are taken by the Editor to have greater claims to be the original than the alternative printed in the margin, t t Words so enclosed are corrupt. The Editor's restoration is occasionally given in the margin. Words so enclosed are restored by the Editor. 1 Words so enclosed are interpolated.

+ =add = omit. v, = transpose, pr = prefix.

28 (18. 35) = the 22 Cursive MSS collated for this edition less by the two MSS 18. 35. Where certain of these MSS are defective the symbol may be 21 or 20 or 19 or 18 or even 17.

Words in heavy type in the text are restorations of the original text as in 3 1 7-w.

ITACISMS. Itacisms are not recorded in the case of the Cursives nor yet of the Uncials excepting A and, and not even the itacisms of these in such common instances as t for ci (iso? for ezSof). Such itacisms as c for at or vice versa in these two MSS are recorded, since this itacism has in one case led to a corruption of the text. Thus Gwynn and Swete have rightly recognized that irccn eiri in; 16 is corrupt for irotot m, the corruption being due originally to the mis-writing of iraurrj as irccn?. In 9 AM write irccn for iraurrj a fact unrecorded by Tischendorf. In fact A writes w r-twice for mucr- out of the five times where it occurs in the N. T. and M three times. Other common unrecorded itacisms are t for 17 and o for, or vice versa.

CHAPTER L AIIOKAAYOTS IOANNOY.

I. A7rokaxvias Irjrav Xourrov rjv 2Scoicev avrg 6 0co? Sei ai rots Sovxovs avrov, Set yevcrdai ev rayei, " ccrifuivcv dirocrrcixac Sia rov ayyexov avrov r Sovxcp avrov laxixvfl, 2. os ifjULprvprfa-cv rov Xoyov rod 0cov ical T V ftaprvMOF Ii; o-ov Xuorov, ocra ciScy.

Itoawov (Icoavov) KCA 205. 2004 IOMLWOV 175. 337. 920. 2040 17 euro, rov aytov Ituawov bo euro. Icoav. rov eoxoyov (+ tjv ev IIaruui n; vtcrw c catraro 620) 325. 620: airok. rov ay. Icuav. rov dcoaoyou 1 8. 35. 386. 456. 468. 2020 Or 8 Icnay. rov 0eox. cai rjyatnjfjlcvov airo. 1934 airoic. (+ rov aytov 919) Iwav. rov cox. icat cvayycxiorov 046. 919 a? rok.; cycvcro is rov (+ aytov s 1) Icoav. rov vayy. (+ viro rov 0eov S a) CK Ilarfuu ny KIO-W et? iyv 3. rjorf vwo Nt; pdvo9 Kaco'apoc S 1 2 i) airoic. rov airtxrroxov Icuav (+ teat cvayycaurrov 025) 025 vg airoic. rov ay. atroar. Icoav. rov cox. 632 f an-oic. rov ay. IONKV. rov airoor. ic. cvayy. rov 0cox. rjv t8cv cv Trarxw nj V O-CD icvptc cvxoy. 2050.

1. avoic. n) K fiopr. I. X. airojcaxv us Iwawov rov cvayyc-Xtorov arm 4: airoic. laxiwov ca9o9 ciscv I. X. eth rjv. oo- cyiaprvpitO-ci ns ycvaiev? exc Icoawtv rov a rov KVfpvioa, 2050 iyv 84 179 arm 2 8 " avru avri; 046 ayuus K ic. tot. significans Tyc:. TCA CV eth airoorrctxa? nuntianda Pr fl: eth: +avra bo rov 88. 2015 rw oovxw avr. 1854 Or 1: rov Sovaov avr. A Icoavct K.

9. ver. 2 arm 1 oa cpoot. T. X- utoprvxav rov Xoyov arm 8 Pr Xpurrav 181 I om 2O4O: +rc i: iv arm 4 (ariva curt KOI ariva (or a: 62o) xf"? ycvcotfai ravra I. 88. 104. 181. 205. 209. 432. 468. 620. 632. 1957. 2015. 2020. 2023. 2024. 2037. 2041. 2067 al: + oi artva cto-cv 42:.

3. Makotpios 6 dvaytvakncwv

Kal ol dkouovrcs rovs Xoyovs rijs vpcxfnjttias Kal rqpovvrc? ra cv avrj ycypafi-Acva, 6 yap Kacpot cyyvs.

4. Icdowi;? rats cnra cfcicai; riai rais cv Tfl A7t

Xaptf vuv ical flprjvrj airo 6 av Kal 6 v Kal 6 cp oicvo?, (0) 5. cal diro Ii? rov Xpurroi) 6 taprv? 6 irurros, 6 irpcororokos rwv vckpcov Kal 6 dpxiv T f facrtxccoy rijs y s.

Tai dyairaivri i ftas Kal Xvvravri fia? CK rcuv aiapriuiv tyuaiv cv r3 atman avrov, (a) The MSS add here an early interpolation: ical d 4 rwv rrd vrev-Opfaov avrov. See vol. i. 11-13.

8. paitapios pr KOI eth: + ci 2050: uuucaptot arm 4 bo o avaytv. KOI arm 4: 01 avayivoxrkovrcs bo o OKOVCOV gig arm 1- 8a T. Xoy. r. irpot. K. o akovcov arm 2 r. Xoy. r. irpof.-arm 4 rovo Xoy.-HTOVTOW C: TOV Xoyov K 046. 2042 irpotjrjrias KC 93. 104. 314: +Tavny 104. 336. 468. 620 gig vg s 1 2 arm 2 bo: + TOVTOV T. 3i3X. iov eth KOi 2 + ot 2040 nypowreo- iroiowrco- arm 4: TTjpwv gig arm 1 2 3 " cv avrrj fl: cir avn?0- 2050 bo o yap K. cyy. arm 1 3 Kcup. cyy. 2OSo.

4. IwakKtjs Iwavipr K: pr a cypa rc eth: + scribens haec Tyc

Towr 2 + owato- 2050 cipiviy + multiplicetur Tyc airo re Tc avo o ov AKC O2. i. 60. 82 a deo patre Tyc avo o ov AKC 025. i. 60. 82. 88. 104. 181. 314. 336. 424.

432. 620. 628. 632. 1957. 2015. 2020. 2023. 2036. 2037. 2041. 2050. 2067: airo rov o cov 6 1. 429. 617. 1934: ab eo qui est fl gig vg s 1 2 bo: airo 0cov o wv 046. fll (-432. 620. 628. 632. 2020. 2050) al mu Or": airo icvptov o CDV 2016 o 8 205o cpxou. +omnipotens Pr Kai 4 s 2 rwv 2 AM 88. 241. 2036: a C 046. 91 (- 205. 620. 2020) al pntt Or" s 1 2 arm 8: a COTIV 025. i. 205. 620. 2020. 2023 al arm 2: a curiv 2019 arm 4 avrov 2oi8 bo: rov 0cov 88. 2015. 2036 Pr fl: Iio-ov Xptorov eth 5. xai airo I. X. et a filio hominis Tyc: eth ocr fuaprvs trtotoor COTIV 172. 2018 Pr gig vg arm 4 eth o irpon-or. "who is eldest" arm 2 8: +CK i. 1957. 2041 al ruv vckpcov "among the dead" arm 1- opxcov fuipnxr 2050: +iravrov bo)9ao-i-Xcitov K (corr. by scribe himself to faorixcwv) arm 1- 1 8 Or 1 r ( ) ayairwvrt A C 046. Al (- 205) al 1 1 Or 1 arm 4: rw aycanp-avti 025. I. 6i. m 88. 205. 1957. 2015. 2019. 2036. 2037. 2038. 2041. 2067: oo- ifyamyorcv 172. 2018 fl gig vg arm 1 2 8 bo lyiocr 1 205o: via eth Xvoxivri A C i. 88. (104). 181. 314. (620). 628 2015. 2019. 2020. 2036. 2050 Or 1 Pr fl s 1 2 arm: Xovo-ovri 025. 046. 91 (-620. 2020. 2050) al pl gig vg eth: cxovo-cv 172.

6. KOI 7rott7r v fta? fao-txciav, Upci? r 0ea ical irarpt avrov, aura) 17 Sofa cat TO Kpavo? efc TOVS aftovas TCOV auvwv isov cpxcrat ftcra rov

Kal o rcrai avrov was foaxp. bs Kal otrtvcs avrov ckcvrty0-av,

KOA KOtfovrai cv avrov wacrai al fv ai TTJS yijs. vat, (a) The MSS add here an early inteipolation. 8. 716 elu rd "AX0a al r 0, X yei Ktfptof 6 0e6f, 6 t Kal 6 Kal ipxtpcvot, 6 varnncpdrup. See vol. ii. Eng. trans., footnote, in loe.

2018 bo: Awavti K. rcov TTJOT aiapruur icixtovov Aovo avri n; CK IKTCI rov fa07TOiov aiftatOO" K. vowoo- K. TTMrjaravtt Tffuar ftao-ixciov ccparcvxa K. Xoixravri T xao- airo rav aiapruuv cv r. at tart avrov. cat CTrotiyo-f?;zao- jsacrtaetav tcpcur Krx. 104. 620. (336. 459 628) 17iacr 2 K: uw eth c Atfc i. 61. 88. 181. 2015. 2019. 2020. 2036. 2037. 2038. 2050. 2067: airo 025. 046. 81 (-620. 2020. 2050) 250 al 1 Or Pr fl gig vg bo? r. atapr. peccato Pr i;tcov VJLUOV eth: A i. 181. 336. (620). 2067 Pr cv r. OILL. avr. arm 1 8.

6. eiroit)oe Attc 025. SI (- 386. 456. 468. 866) 250. 2037. 2038. 2067 Or 1 s 1 2 bo eth: Trooro-avri 046. 42. 69. 104. 325- 33 6- 3 6 7- 385. 456. 459- 4 8. (620). 2019 lyLtacr K 025. 046 al pl Pr gig vg d (s 1 8) arm: tip. iv A 42. 325. 367. 456. 468. 517. 2016. 2020: rjjlw C: v as eth: regnum nostrum fl: nostrum regnum vg d:325 ao-t ciav up to-AK C 21 (-325. 456. 468. 2050) 250 alp m fl vg-: ao-txeiav xat icpcur c 88 Pr gig vg d: "worthy of his kingdom and priests" arm 1 4: ftatrixciav lepanicqv s 1- 8: Saartxtiay ayiav eth: jfourixciov icpcicr 046. 2050: fiacrixcicr KCLI tcpeio 025. I. 2015. 2019. 2036. 2038. 2067 a l arm 2 s ft: j8ao-ixctov uparcvia 42. 61. 69. (325). 367. 456. 468. 517. (620). 1854 Or bo icai 2 arm 14 bo avrov fl arm 1 avrw. aAiyv Pr arm 1 ic. TO Kparo?. OATV arm 4 r. accovas TOV atuva K TUV aicovuv KG 046 al pl Or" fl gig vg S L arm 2 8: A 025. 88. 325. 456. 468. 498. 2015. 2036. 2037. 2050 bo 7. ftcra ciri C sa eth rov25o. 2018. 2038 ve cxov + oLtiyv 35:-fcoefi gig arm 1 2 8 1 o croi AC 025. 046 alp- Or 1 "– 1 Pr fl gig vg eth: o rovrai K i. 181. 2038. 2067 Or s 1- 2 arm bo avrov 1 i. 205. 209 arm 1 8 woo-iravrccr s 1 2 arm: +o 172: vavrco-, irao bo ofoa pot icai arm x o Baxpoi. s 1 arm 2- 4 avrov 2 K icoirovtai o rovrai (-crai Pr) Pr fl bo arm 1- 8): o ovrot KOI jco ovrat eth

ew avrov i. 241 arm 1: r K 2050 Of Pr fl bo irao-ai. yier omnis terra Pr voi + KOI s 1
1 roc aAiyv fl arm 1: vac bo a v + Kai Xeyci arm 1.

8. TO ax o Afitc 025. 046. 81 (-620. 632. 2020) al 9. "Eyco Icoavv?, 6 dsex o?
vicov KOI O-UVKOIVCUVOS ev rfi OXufct KOI acrixctigi KOI i 7roxor ev Jiyo-
ov, eyeioiiyv ev Tjj v o-c) 17 Ka ovfjL vg IIatACf Sta TOV Xoyov TOU 0eov teal
TIV fiaprupiav I IO. eyevoiiyv ev irvcvucm ev TJJ Kvpuucfj rjfiepq., icat jjjicovcra r
icyaa-Tv 6Vio-0ev AOIT us craxirtyyos Xeyovoi II. O 0Xeve ypttyov cts t3Xiov, cal
WLU OV rats eirri gig arm 1 4 bo: TO a i. 88. 241. 385. 620. 632. 2020. 2023.
2037. 2038. 2039. 2042. 2067 al Or 8 Pr fl vg: + icai eya K re 2 I am arm 1 3 t) +
(T;) apx " (TO) Texoo- N i. 6i. m (88). 172. 205. 250. 1854. (2015). 2018. (2019.
2023. 2036. 2037).

2038. 2050 Or 111 v Or 1 gig vg bo Xeyei Kvpios o 0 o 2050 Xcyei 88 o 0 oo- S
arm 1: +Kat 620 arm 2 8a icai o rjv arm 4: " and who is " arm 2- 3: " unto aeons "
arm 1 o 4 1934 cp oA. + KCU 386: + Kvpioo- arm 1- 2 o 6 046. 2015. 2036.

9. fyw + tfu bo: icai eycu eth IOXIVTTO- K CTWKOIVWVOO- C 025. 2036
al: crvycoiv. A 046 205. 250. 468. 2020. 2037. 2038. 2050. 2067 al s 1:
KOIVCDVOO- 21 (-205. 468. 2020. 2050) al mu s 2: + vfuiv s 1 2 eth KCLI part ia
A C 046 al pl Or Pr fl gig vg arm 1 2 3: c. ev TTJ ftaa-tx (+ vxov eth) 025. i. 104.
205. 620. 2023. 2038. 2067 al eth: rrjo- foeriaeiao- arm 4: OTI TJ ? curixeia bo: S
lt2 KCU wop., ev. lrj(r. arm 1 4 cai 8 + v rrj s 1 iwrox. + TI; s 1- 2: + o ou rjarav
bo: +8ia nyv viroftovrfv vfjuov eth cv Iiyo-ov R C 025. 2020. 2050 Or 1 " lt lg gig
vg s 1 bo: ev Xpiorco A: ev Iiyo-. Xpwrr. c c Pr vg d s 2 eth: Irjo-ov Xpurrov i. 205.
1854. 2015. 2036: ev Xpiorto Irjo-ov 046. 21 (-205. 2020. 2050) al pl Or fl arm 2
" Kaxovfjitvt i: 7rikaxovp, vrj 2050: Xeyoxevr; 141: Sta 1) Kat C 6cov Kvpiov 620
icai TTV tapr. AC I. QI. 172. 242. 325. 424. 432. 1934. 2015. 2016. 2018. 2020.
2036 Pr gig vg arm 2 4 " bo: u a T. papr. K 025. 046. 21 (-325. 1934. 2020) al 1 Or
8 fl s 1- 2 arm 1 8 eth Iiyo-ov A C 025. 181. 2015. 2019. 2020. 2036. 2050 fl gig vg
arm 4: Xptorov arm 1: Irjcrov Xpurrov K c c 046. 21 (-2020. 2050) al pl Or 1 Pr s 1
2 arm 2- 8 bo.

10. yek. cv irvcufi. "and (a) there was in me the spirit (holy i)" arm 1 2 8-: pr eyw
A: pr eyo Iwiwrjo- gig: pr icai S 1 ev trvcvuuiti ev rq 2O5o cov. iey. OTTIO CV (336.
2020 on-io-co) AOV A 336. 202 o. 2067 arm 1 eth: oirio-w p, ov ov. (+ craxirtyyos
2015) ftey. C 025. 205. (2015). 2037 al Pr fl gig vg s 1 2 arm 2 bo: (ov. OTT.
xov ficyax. 046. 2040 al pl Or 1: ioVTO" OTT. Xeyovotyo mot oxr craxTrtyyocr
xcyaxiyo 2050: xuviyo" ftey. 336. (2050). 2067 OTTIO- CV tovarm 4 poxiriyyocr
pr ian; arm 1- 8- 4 eth.

11. Xcyoun s Xeyovcrav K c c Pr fl s 1- 2 arm 4: Xoxovo o- 920.

cfe "Etycerov teat cfc Sftvpvav iral cfc Ilepyaiov xal cis vat ipav Kai cfc Sapcis al
eis iaa8ca iai jcal cfc Aaoktav.

X 2. Kal cwcrrpc ra JAcvciv r v tfxavrjv ijris A Act ACT ctov.

jcai cvurrptyas cuw cwi Auxvias xpvora?, 1. Kal cv yltccrco TWV Av vicov 3iotov
v26v dv0pairov, cvcsvicvov irorjfn mu trfpicfrixritvov wpos rots uurrois 2039. 2040:
oivovcncr 2020: 104: +LMW 1854. (2050) arm 1 8 bo eth:-J-cyco ox a ic. TO a
irpamxr K. o ca xarocr (cai) (025.

104) 620: +cyi ctu ro a K. TO a (o) TTMOTOO- K. (o) ccr aroor (KOI) I. 6l. 336.
628. 2019. 2020. 2023 0C7T. K I o a 172. 424. 2018. 2020 Pr s 1 bo X r Mr
Actnyo- 2040: aicova-ci l)O T + TO K icai irei rov arm 4: et mittem fl KOLI I bo
CKicaipruucr + racer cv 1 77 curia bo: + raur (oiwatcr) arm cv cra. cv Sfivpva cra.
arm cwr 2 7 bo: ewr 2- 8 arm 1 icoi 2 6 Pr: icai 2 i49- 201. 2015. 2042. 2067 KOI
cur Stvpv. post 0varccp. pon K 2ivpvav C 025. 046. 21 (-205. 620. 2040) al s 2:
Smyrnam fl: Smirnam Pr gig: pvpvav A i. 177. 205. 620. 628. 920. 2017. 2018.
2024. 2040: ftvpav 104. 2040: Zfa, vpvav K vg s 1: Zpvpva arm Ilcpicafiov 2050:
ctr varctpav (-rtpav AC:-rrjpav 046. 2050) (AC 046) 69. no. 172. 314. 424. 1854.
1957. 2018. 2020. (2050): Tyatyram fl: Tyathiram gig: Thyatiram vg: c r (Shxit
ipcur I. 2038: cur Ovarccpa (-rrjpa 620. 632) fet 21 (-205 2020. 2050) 250. 2037.
2067 al: cv 0varctpour 025. 205. 209. 2019: Tiatirae Pr: Thyatera bo cat 5 +jcat
2040 K. cur Saps.: post Aaos. pon K c 2ap3. ap8cicr 620: iaa-Sca iav Afitc 025.
046. 104. 205. 456. 522. 620. 919. 920. 1849. I 955- 2004. 2015. 2017. 2039.
2042. 2050 bo: Aasca-f iav 21 (-205. 456. 620. 919. 920. 1849. 2004. 2050) al pl:
"Phrygia" arm 1 Aaostktav A C 110. 205. 2015. 2042. 2050 al bo: Aaosucciai 025.
046. 21 (-205. 2050) al pl: Laudatiae Pr.

12. Kai A C 025. 205. 632. 2020. 2050 Pr fl gig Cyp vg S 1 2 bo: exec 2016:
KOI CKCI 046. 21 (- 205. 632. 2020. 2050) al 1 CT-urrp. ACTT. at CWUTT. cuw
coiwersus respexi ut viderem. et vidi Pr fl: rcorpc a c? Ac a bo j8A r. l i8civ 2050
(s 1) r. u)v. CAOV TOV Aaaovvra MM 2050 caaaci KC 046 al Pr fl gig vg (s 2)
arm 2 8 4: Aaaci A arm 1: caoaiycrc 025. i. 104. 620. al s 1 ACT cuov iot arm 8
cmorpefao- 2050. (Pr fl) arm 1 Avxv. CTTT. pvr. 2050: arm 1 1.

13. luu 1 ann 1 j CIMO-CD AC 2004: yuccrov K THIV AC 025. I.

14. i) 8 iccc axty avrov fcal at rpi cs XCVKOI a Zpiov Xevkov,(a) iceu ol 6t0a jiol
avrov us Xo irvpog, 1 5. jcal ot irosc? avrov 6unoc xaxicoxifciq) Kaptyy f ircir- at
fiivi) avrov cot Dn; vsdvcoy (a) MSS add a gloss At xtcfr. See vol. i. 28.

181. 205. 459. 2015. 2020. 2037. 2038. 2042. 2050. 2067 Tyc Pr fl s arm
1- 2- 4a bo: row rra N 046. 21 (-205. 2020. 2050) al 1 Or gig vg arm 8 Xv v. +
TWV xpwwv 172. 250. 424. 2018. 2023 gig vg T arm 4 ofiotovj oxotwxa A s 1 (
= axr oAoudfia) ho sa: oMMOor 1854 rov viov rov a?0p. s 8 viov K 046. I. 35. 6
1. 69. 104. 110. 172. 175. 177. 201. 250. 325. 337. 386. 456. 617. 620. 1934.
2015. 2016. 2018. 2021. 2042. 2050 al: vio) AC 025. 1 8. 205. 468. 632. 919.
920. 1849. 1854. 2004. 2020. 2037. 2038. 2040. 2067 al p Or 8 Pr Cyp fl gig vg
arm avopwrov + ai s 1 cvcovtcvoor. ircpic ioyaCioor 1854 irorjprj KG 025. 046 min
fere omn: irosrjprjv A (2050) TTDOO- v 172. 2018. 2020: cwi Pr fl bo: inter Tyc
Aaoroio- C 025. 046. 250. 2037." 1 al 1 1: ftafour A 35. 60.432. 1957. 2015. 2023.
2036. 2037. 2038. 2041. 2067: taor0our K 104. 205. 209. 385. 498. 620. 632.
2042. 2050: + avrov s 1- bo eth j xpvow A C: xpvo-w 620: xpwip K c 025. 046 min
omn Tid.

14. T) 8c KC. Tpix- " but the hair of his head " arm 4 rp4x ca Tp l X atar 2050:-f
ttvrov s 1 arm 2 Xcwcat Pr fl arm 1- 8 sa wol A 35. 175. 386. 617. 620. 632. 920.
1934. 2020. 2040 al mu Or 8: okTit C 025. i. 1957. 2015. 2023. 2036. 2037. 2038.
2041. 2042. 2050 2067 al: ohTTrep 205. 209. 242: KCU uxr 046. 18. 250. 325.
337. 456. 468. 919. 1849. 2004 al j OKT CHOV. otfrti. aur. arm 2 cpiovj + icat no

s 1 Xcwcoi Kaoapov arm 4: no Pr fl Cyp s 1: + KCU 2019. 2050 gig vg s 1 arm 8 eth oxr x iwv arm 1- 2- 8- 4 coo- OKTCI (2019). 2020. 2042: KOJL bo: aut (corrupt for ut) Tyc. cu 3 Pr 15. Kai- 104. 620 Pr oAOiot OLUHOKT 920 avw 025. 104. 175. 620. 2017. 2042. 2050: aunchalco (auri-calco Pr) Libani Tyc Pr: aurocalco fl: auricalco gig: orichalco vg: "burnished brass w bo: +Kai gig CINT.-rrtirvp. 498. arm 1 8 4 OKT s j arm 2 8 cv c Pr fl j irtwpw vr AC Cyp Pr fl: wcirvwowa) M 205. 209. 336. 620. 628. 2050 gig vg s 1: ircirvMtfAcvoi 025. 046. 81 (-205. 620. 2050). 250. 2037. 2038. 2067 al 1 Or: ignitos velut in fornace ignis Tyc: " refined amidst a furnace fiery " arm 8- 8 c. 17 ov. vs. iroxX. arm 4 v arwv iroxXwv Tr rj0ovr Xaov 2050 (cf. Dan. io).

VOL. II.- 1 6 1 6. ical CXCDV cv rjj 8c ia X CI P avrov dorcpas eirra, al cvc rov OTOflaros avrov pofifaia Storotos o cia cwo- pcvojacvi;, ical i) oiris avrov uc 6 j Xtoc atvci cv r0 SWOACI avrov.

17. Kal ore ctsov avrov, fcrco-a irpos rovs irosac avrov ax vcxpoy icai I KCV rifv Scav avrov cv cc Xcyuv

Mi; fo3ov cyw ciu 6 irpwros ical 6 1 8. ical 6 av Kal cycvoMv vcjcpd?, al Bov (fay CIAI cis rove auovag raiv atavav 9 ical c xo Ta fcxcis rov Qavdrov Kal rov ps 16. Kai 1 1854 bo sa cx v K C C 025 046 21 (- 2050) 2037. 2038. 2067 al pl Or 8 s 1 2: ctxcv 172 250. 424 2018. 2019: habebat Pr fl gig vg arm: A 2021. 2050 v r. 8. x- WT.

arm 4 cv 2O5o Set x 1 P 1 avt- A C 025. 35. 61. 69. 172. 175. 181. 205. 209. 242. 250. 432. 617. 1934. 1957. 2016. 2017. 2018. 2019. 2023. 2036. 2037. 2038. 2041 al p: 8((ta avr. x CL P L 21 (-35. 175- 2 5- 6l 7- 9 20- T 934- 2040. 2050) al 1 Or 8: x P 60. 920. 2015. 2040. 2050 Tyc Pr fl gig vg arm 2: x L P L airr-rrj 3c ta 046 acrrcpccr A 1934. 2O2I pop t. Stor.1 irv vp, a S 1 of a205. 209. 242. 2050 arm 1 3 4 (bo) ckTropcvoi. pendentem Tyc atvct OHT o r; Xt(xr K Pr Cyp fl arm 4 bo: " like the sun flashing appeared" arm 1- 8 o205. 20 9- 2 4 X- 43 2- 49. 628. 632. 2020. 2042 aivei atva)v 2067: "was flashing" arm 4 cv n; 8w. avr. arm.

17. eircoo A C 025. 046. 35. 205. 325. 337. 456. 620. 632. 2020. 2050: CTTCO-OV 18. 175. 386. 617. 919. 920. 1849. 1934. 2004. 2037. 2040 al irpoo- cwr K 42: ri 2033 s 1 OKT OMTI K: tthTci K c arm: icai OKT Or 8 bo C KCV AC 025. 046. 21 (- 35. 205. 2050) al 1 Or: posuit Pr gig vg: CITC KCV i. 35. 61. 205. 2015. 2023. 2036. 2037. 2038. 2050. 2067: inposuit fl Cyp 8e. avr. A C 025. 046. 21 (-35. 205) al 1 Pr fl gig vg arm eth + X pa K c i. 35- 6l- 20 5- I 957- 2 i5- 20 37- 20 38- 2041. 2067 s 1- Acywv + fioi i alp arm 1 2 8 py 0)8 K: 4-Iwawe Pr 0 irpair. o wpwroroicoo- A: " beginning " arm 1- 2 o corx- o 2050.

18. it. o lw Pr gig: "I am life" arm 1 2 8 KCLI I K bo arm cycv. vckp. l: " I am (+ same 8) who died " arm 1- 2- 8 fl: 4- at nr v tot eth toov arm 8 row atovov 2O2O aiaivwv AK C 025. 2019. 2050 2067 Pr Cyp fl gig vg bo arm 1 2 ": +aii; v K 046. 21 (- 2020. 2050) 250. 2037. 2038 al Or 8 s 1- f arm 8: 2020 1 TV K ta s 1 Xcwr A C 025. 35. 205. 250. 325. 456. 468. 620. 632. 2020. 2037. 3038 al.: icxciow 046. 21 (- 35. 205. 325. 456.

AIIOKAAY S IO ANNOY 19. ypdifov ovv a Ktu a curly xai tcxXct yiyccrdac p ra ravra.

20. TO fjlwrnjpiov rav cirra aorcpuy ov9 ctscs lire-rij Sc tac u ras cirra Xv tas ra xpvcrav ot cirra acrrcpcs ayycxoi ray lirra ccriy, at at Xv vtai at cirra lirra CKK. rjruu curty.

468. 620. 632. 2020) al mu Or 1 rov flay. K. r. 08. A C 025. 046. 21 al 1 Tyc Pr fl gig vg s 1- (bo) arm eth: TOV os. K. T. OF. i. 2015. 2019. 2036. 2037. 2038 al.

10. OUK i. 498. 620. 2020. 2050 arm 1 8 8! a s 1 8 cisco- o rei bo: opacr arm 1 2 8 cat a cmrtvarm 1 8 bo icat 1 arm a a 2oso icai 2 bo a s s 1 icxXci Set 2050: 8ei icxXciv K: Set icxXci C: Set 2050 ytv roai AK 21 (- 35. 386. 468. 617. 632. 2050). 250 al pl Or 1: ycycoru N C 025. 046. 35. 61. 69. 314. 386. 468. 617. 632. 1957. 2015. 2019. 2023. 2036.

2037. 2038. 2041. 2042. 2050. 2067.

20. ouor Atfc 025. i. no. 181. 205. 209. 2037. 2038. 2050: CDV 046. 21 (- 205. 2050). 250. 2037. 2067 al 1 " Or" ctsccr opaa- arm 2 j ciri rrjtr c(. KC 025. 046. 250. 2037. 2067 min omn Or 1 s 1 arm 4 bo: r rrj Sefio A 2038 Pr fl gig vg s 1 8 arm 2 8 eth: cv rq ipi arm 1 K. TWV irra Xvxww 498 Pr fl arm 8 Too- is 385. 429. 522. 919. 920. 1849. 1955. 2004. 2039. 2040. 2042 rocr xpvcrar498 s 1: TQIV wvow Pr arm 8: + ravra corny 201: + ravra ctortv 93. 386 aorcpccr + cirra bo ayy. ciow ayy. urtv rwy cirr. ic cx. 498 Pr fl gig Vg: rwv CUT. KK Tjru v curtv 01 ayycxot arm 2 cio-iv 1 K KOI 01 at CTrra. ciriv 6 2 at Xv v. at cirra AC 025. 046 gjg V g s 1 2 eth: 01 Xv v. cirra 218. 429 2018. 2019: cirra v. K I. 6 1." 367. 2038: ai cirra Xvxv. K 35. 205. 250. 632. 1854. 1957. 2020. 2037. 2050. 2067 al Or I 01 cirta + ao-asccr 025. i. (35). (6i.). 69. (205). 1955. (1957)- 2 3 6- 20 37- 2038. 2067 bo:-I- at xpwai 2050: +at xpwrai ao- 8cr S 1:-Hot 172. 241. 250. 424. 2020 arm cirra 6 io4. 498 Pr fl (arm 4?). Only these authorities attest the original text (see vol. i. 34-35; vol. ii., Eng. trans., footnote, in he.). The a! fora belong! to

CHAPTER II.

I. T? Ayycxoi T cv E ccrip cvcicxiprtaf yxtyov

Tasc Xcyct Kparw TOUS fora dai-cpas cv T Sc c avrov, 6 jrcpiirartuv cv iccnp row Wa Xv vwiiv rovv 1. TM ayycxu T CK Extent ciotxtjatcmr Since John's usage elsewhere attests the originality of this unique grammatical construction (see Gram, in vol i.), I add here a summary of the documentary evidence for it in 2 1 and in the six other passages where it originally occurred, 2 s- lft 18 3- 7- 14. This evidence is sufficient to establish the originality of TO ayycxw rw in all seven passages: when reinforced by the evidence of John's usage elsewhere, it is irresistible. I have accordingly restored the original reading in 3 1- 7- 14 where the Greek MSS fail us.

2 1 T. ayy. TW AC (2019) s 1 arm 4 Pr (though he reads: angelo ecclesiae Ephesi). In the note Pr. refers to the peculiar constiuction in the text: Dativo hie casu ecclesiae posuit, non genetivo; ac si diceret Scribe angelo, huic ecclesiae, ut non tarn angelum et ecclesiam separatim vide-atur dixisse, quam qui sit angelus exponere voluisse, unam videlicet faciens angeli ecclesiaeque personam. 2 T. ayy. TW A (2040 r. ayy. nycr o) arm. 2 12 T. ayy. TO 2050 s 1 arm 4 sa. 2 18 T. ayy. TO A Epiph 1 " Pr s 1- arm 4 r. Orw 1 but does not replace it by nycr. 3 1 T. ayy. TW Pr s 1 8 arm 4. 3 7 T. ayy. TOI Pr arm 4. 3" T. ayy. TCO arm 4. The difficulty of the reading led to the occasional omission of uuqaruur in 2 18 (A), 3 14 (919. 920. 2040), 3 1 (s 8), 3 T (arm 4). It is interesting to observe how the evidence for the original reading grows weaker as the

text advances. The assurance of the scribes grows as they write. On the individual passages the chief variants are given below. TW ayv.1 TOUT ayycxour arm 1-: pr KOL Pr fl gig: bo sa eth begin 2 1–"18 3 1 7- M with xot (bo sa) ypa ov TO cv E era ddcxitO-ioo AC: TO) rtfar cv. cxicx. 2019: ro CF ECO-D cv rrj cic-cxTcrta arm 4: ro cv cicicxicrca E cotw s 1: npr cv E co-w ccicx. K 025. 046 min fere omn Or": Ephesi ecclesiae gig vg: ecclesiae Ephesi Pr bo: n? r E co-twv cic Xi ruur i. 2020 fl arm 1 1 8 Xryci 4- Kvpuocr 172. 250. 424. 522. 2018. 2039 xparwv + wavra Kat s 8 I Scfia x p Tyc s 1: 8c ia x pi 172. 250. 2018 arm 1 4 bo sa I avrouj + xcifw K o 8 cat arm 1 1 8 cv ftccr. cLttccrw AC: rt i cura 498. 620. 628. 2020 Tyc s 1 arm Lf: T. X. T. cirra xpwr. 2042 xp wrl)V O2 5- 4 min fere omn: XP WT UV AC: 2050 j.

2. OZSa ra 2pya crov, KO! rov xdvov ical r y wropjovyv crov, ical ore ov 81177 faoroicrai gaicovs, teal cvcipacra? rovt Acyoprac Javrovs an-oaro Aov? ical OVK ffal cvpct avrovs 3. mu viroiov v ical jsaerracra? Stet TO ovota ov ical ov iccicovriakcs.

4. aaA" fx w at ro or r n v Ay"n7v crow rijfv irpumjv 5. furtyAovcve ovv troqcv ircwcimcaf, xai Acravoiprov ical ra irpwra cpya iroiijow ci 8c Lwy, Ip oiat (rot ical icintoro) TTJV Kv yiav (rov IK rov roirov (a) MSS add gloss r M lurwvfyrw.

8ov 337 eth. T. coir. 385. 429. 522 ic. T. inro u o-ov ic. T. icoir. o-ov 632 rov KOWOV AC 025. 35. 60. 181. 205. 209. 432. 1957. 2015. 2019. 2023. 2036. 2037. 2038. 2041. 2042 Pr gig vg s: TOVO KOITOVO arm 1: rov KOTTOV crov K 046. 81 (-35. 205). 250. 2067 Oi s 1: rover Koirowr crov arm 2 8 4 bo I crov 8 Pr arm 1 8 nai 3 A bo: +ot a arm 1 ov ovvrj Socrr. J ov ptutTafcur arm 1- 3 Swicn; 2042: owci 620. 2050 Sacrra ac 025. I. 2020. 2038 KULKOV bo feat 4 over arm 1 cavrovcr 18l. 2067: +CIVCLL vg c f arm atnxrroa,. AN C 025. 94. 337. 2038 vg aim 1 2 4:-f ctvat K c c 046. 81 (- 337) al mu Or 1 Pr gig vg T s 1-; Kat cvp. avr. iff. K. cvp 0rjrav cvdairootoxoi bo.

8. KOI uvofi. ex 2 1 8. 424. 2018 VTTOI. eg. (+ K. OX. nliar iracracr K) ic. e)3aot. AKC 046. 21 (-35. 205. 620. 2020). 250 al mu Or 8 vg s 1- 8 arm 4: et habuisti patientiam et tolerasti Pr: cifeat. (tftairruraa- I. 61. 2037) K. VTTOA. e (l) 35. (6 1."). 1957. 2015. 2020. 2023. 2036. (2037). 2038. 2067 al: c aot. AC c. virouu c. 025. 104. 205. 209. 336. 459. 620: VTTOJL c. K cjsaor. avrovcr gig bo CXCMT habuisti Pr K. cj9aor. 432 oia 3i4. 2016 icat ov iccfcoiriakCor AC (s 1 2): K. OVK. cicotriacracr K 025. 046. 21 (620. 2020). 250. 2037 al 14 Or 8: et non (nee Pr) defecisti Pr gig vg: KOI KCKoirtajcaor 336. 432. 628. 2020 arm 8: Katjcoiriafcoer I: KOLI jccicoirtaoracr 620.

4. axX AC 025. i. 385. 620. 2015. 2020 2037. 2038. 2042. 2050. 2067 Or: axA. a K 046. 21 (- 205. 620. 2020. 2050). 250 al: KOI 205 cx0 Kara crov + oxiya gig njv irpwrrjv crov ayainjv A a rjkaa- AK C 025. 046 al omn T1: ac ifcccr N C.

5. jaKTjjioKtucrok 1854. 2O2O owprs 1 arm 1 2 4 eth iro cv ooev 386: ITOKT bo ircirrcufcocr (- cor K) Axc 046. 91 (- 35. 205. 620). 250 al mu Or Pr Cyp s 8: ckircirrcofcoor 025. i. 35. 104. 205. 620. 1957. 2015. 2023. 2036. 2037. 2038. 2041. 2067 gig vg s 1 ic. jwav. s 1 arm 8 K. r. wp. coy. woiijtrov bo 6. claAa rovro X ts AMTCIS ra epya TWV Nucoxatrcuv, cdyu flurak 7. "O Igaiv ovs dkowara) rt TO H-VCVACL Acyei rats eicjcai; o tai9. TJJ vtfcvrt SOHTOI avrp t ayetv evc rov v ov Tijs feo s o fort? e v rep mapaovunp rov tfeov.

8. Kai rip Ayyeaxp rp ev Sivpvj? Jmexipr jac ypctyov Tasc Xcyct 6 irpahro KOC 6 cvrxaros, fa eyevero vacDo xal ifyo'cv 9. OKa rov T V 0 fyw KOU rrjv nraxctav, jcat r K phatrfafjiiav cie r v Xcyovrwy Jov acovs c7vai lavrovt cat ovic ciortv, laAa o-wayaryrj rov Sarava.

eth I cpya + rov gig arm o-ot Atfc 025. 2050 gig vg s 1 bo sa: 181. 2041 arm 1-: + ra v 046. 21 (-2050). 250. 2037. 2038. 2067 al 1 Or Pr s arm: +rax i Kivrjri + Kara aw 325. 456 c r. row. avr. s 1 cav ci 35 leravotjcreicr (-a-ur l) 35. 104. 498. 620. 2050: ftcravorjo- 205: p Tavoijrrj Tyc.

6. CXCUT +aya ov Pr ori iccr. ori futrifa- 2040 a A arm 2: sicut Pr jcayw cyw s 1 arm 1 ' 8 eth.

7. oua cora s 1- 8: + aeovciv bo eth: aures audiendi Pr arm 1 2- 4 oucoveno 617 irvevfta + ayiov arm 1 2 4 eth raw 4- 7rra A CKKA–f raur ctrra C: +icat s 1 avrco AC 025. 046. 21 (35. 205) Or 1 Pr Cyp yg s 2 arm eth: M 35. 60. 205. 209. 1957. 2023. 2041 Tyc gig Vg S 1 ev TO) irapas. A C 046. 21 (-35. 205) al mu Tyc Pr Cyp vg s 1- 2 arm 1- 2 3 4: ev ACO-W TW irapaowaj K c- c 025: cv ico-a TOV Trapaseto-ov i. 35. 61. 205. (CACO-O) 205). 250. 1957. 2015. 2018. 2019. 2023. 2036. 2037. 2038. 2041. 2067 gig arm bo TOV 0eov A C 025. i. 6i. m 205. 2015. 2019. 2036. 2037. 2038. 2067 s 1 arm: + pov 046. 21 (-205) al mu Or Kx " Or 1 Tyc Pr gig Cyp vg s 2 arm 1 2 3- bo eth.

8. TW CK See note on 2 1. TO A arm 4: TYJO- C 025. 046. 21 min re11 Or eth: Tiycr + o 2040 ev vpvrjo- ckKAipriacr A: Smirnae ecclesiae gig (vg) bo: ecclesiae Smirnae Pr s 1: ev Zfjivpvrj KK, rfriaa- K: ev Sfivnny KK. C 025. 046. 21. 250. 2038. 2067 al mu s 2 arm (Zfi.): rqor e ca. rov Sxvpvaiov arm U8a: cjc Ai? o'tacr ftupvatcov i: Si. vpvatav dccxio-iao- 2015. 2036. 2037: 2tvp. AC 025. 046 min oinn? ld gig s 2 arm 1 2 3 bo: Zivp. K vg s 1 arm 4 TTXUTOO- irpwrorokoo- A o 2 2016. 2020. 2041 o co-g. "without end" arm 1: +o vpwroo- TDV vecpcdv 69 oor A C 025. 046. 35. 205. 468. 620. 632. 2020. 2050 Pr gig vg s 1 2 arm 1 2 4 bo: i8. 175. 325. 337. 386. 456. 468. 617. 919. 920. 1849. 1934. 2004. 2040 al mu e orcv vivit gig vg: revixit Pr.

9. OXNI AC 025. 93. 241. 2so com Pr gig vg s 1 bo sa eth:-f ra epya KCU K 046. 21. 250. 2037. 2038. 2067 Or 1 Tyc s 2 10. ft-g oJov iov icxXci JoaAciv 6 Sta0oxo9 J VLUOV efc vaamjv, Iva ir ipar0vjT cat fyifrc O ujiv fjfjLCpuv SCKO.

yivov WIOTOS a pt 0avarov, ical Saxro) croc TOV rrffavov rrjs (an?.

II. O X a)V ov aicovo-ara) rt TO TrvrdLta Aeyct rats jcjcx 7O'tats. O pucay ov ft 8tkrjfrfj cic rov Bavdrov TOV Scvrcpov.

1 2. Kai T dyycaw TO) h Ilcpyaia) fca o-ia? ypdtftov Tasc Aeyct 6 pofiffxiiav rrjv Storoxov r v arm: 4- TO, cpya ic. r yv V7rop. ovrjv arm 4 irrw tav 025. 046. 21 (-620) Or: irraxiav A C I. 498. 620: 4-orov gig vg s 1 bo eth rrjv pkaart. 4- rrgv K s 1- 2: Taor ft acrfrjijuar arm 1 2 3 a: blas-phemaris Pr gig vg: " I found not one " bo c A C 046. 21 (-35- 20 S) almu P f g V S sl a bo: 02 5- 35- 2 5- J 957- 2015. 2019. 2023. 2036. 2037. 2038. 2041. 2067 Ol QVT.

Jovs. 2015. 2036 (s 1) lovuctfv N C 2050 arm 1 cavrovo- cwu 2019 ivai 468 s 1 eavr. 336. 620. 628: avrovo- 314.

2016. 2019 K. owe eco-iv arm 1 ararava + uriv K c- Pr gig vg arm 1- 8.

10. p-Tj AC 046. 2020. 2023. 2050. 2067 bo: ftrjscv K 025. 21 (-2020. 2050) Or
1 Pr gig vg s 1 2 eth a ov 35 ficxXcur 0e tr arm irarxw A C 025. i. 35. 104. 172. 205.
468 (TTOO-XCC 620). 1957. 2015. 2018. 2019. 2023. 2036. 2041: iro civ 046. 21
(- 35. 205. 468. 620). 2067 al mu Or" tsov A C 025. i. 18. 61. 69. 104. 250. 620.
2018. 2019. 2020. 2036. 2037. 2038 al mu Pr gig vg s 1 arm bo: +817 046. 81 (-18.
205. 620. 2020. 2050). 2067 Or 1 s 2: +yap 2050 eth: +KCU 205 o Staff. ftax. 920.
2020. 2040 s 1 2 eth fia iv A C C 025. 1 8. 35. 205. 250. 919. 920. 1849. 2004.
2020 al: 8oactv 046. 175. 325. 337. 386. 456. 468. 617. 620. 632. 1934. 2037.
2040. 2050. 2067 al Or 1: Sauciv a tv K I cf vi. o 8caj3. K I. 2037. 2067 al gig c af
S4 iva Tmpao-0. J tva Trttpaqrjrt i: tva irctpao-ft? 920 K. c. Xt r. gig I C X 1 7 T A
1854. 2019. 2038 Pr (bo): CXCTC C 025. i. 181. 2050: efijrre no: e T M 046. 21
(-2050) Or 8 Tyc vg S 12 6 u . + fjl ya v)v 2050 S K. lyn. Tyc gig ificpcov A C 025.
I. 35. 104. 172. 205. 250. 620. 1957. 2015. 2037. 2038. 2050. 2067 al: dierum Pr:
rjpapao- 046. 21 (35. 205. 620. 2050) al mu Or 1 Tyc s 1- 2: die bus gig vg yivov K
ytvco-tfc. irtaro4. VJLIV s 1 a pci 2050 ficxpi 632. 2020.

11. ouoj wra s 1 2 arm 1 4: +a cov iv bo eth: +audiendi Pr arm 1 4 TO-hayiov arm
1 2 eth T. cicicx. arm j o vucwv o yap vikuv bo.

Id. TW ayy. J Toto- ayycxoio arm 1 2 8 TO) cv II. cicicx. 2050 (save that it reads
ETcpkaAw): see note on 2 1: TW c?

13. Otsa irov Karotkcif,

Sirov 6 Opovos TOV Sarava,

Kal KpatCis TO OVOML ioi, ical OVK qpvtprai rgv irurriv fuw xal Iv rats Depots f
Avr ras, t fufprvf totfc 6 VUTTOS iov, is dirckricv i; wap vjuv rov 6 Saravas Karoikcl,
14. dxX 1 (0 Kara arov oxtya, 5ri cvcis K i KpatOwras r)v Stsaxv Baxaa, 5s coacnccv
T S Baxak 0axciv crkavsaxov anriov rw via IcrpaijX, IIcfyatov s 1: TIU cv ny Ilcryaiov
CKicxiyo-ia? arm 4: TO cv T. CKK n. sa: nyr cv ITepyaflo cickAqcriao- all Greek
MSS (-2050) Oi 8: Tiycr Ilcpyafiauov (Ilcpyaicuv 1) cicjcxi? rtar arm 1- 2: Pergami
ecclesiae gig vg s 2 bo: eccles. Perg. Pr eth Xcyei + Kvptoo- 205 T. of. T. 8urr.
s'-ethj.

18. 0180 A C 025. 2020. 2050 Tyc Pr gig vg s 1 arm 1 2 4 bo sa eth: +ra pya rov
icai 046. 21 (2020. 2050 orov ra cpya KOI 325. 456) al p Or s 2 arm 8 wov KOI ori
arm a Kparcicr ckpar crao- bo: Kparowiv arm 1 8 " ftov 1 crov N pvr; cri + nomen
meum et gig TVJV irtor. TOV iriorov arm 8 Kai 8 AC 1957. 2050 gig vg s 1 bo eth:
K 025. 046. 31 (-2050) al pl Pr arm 2- a cv TOUT avraio- 325: in illis Pr i Acpatir
AC Vg s 1: +ravraur arm 1 2: +cv raur K: +OMT 046. 81 (-35. 205. 620. 2040.
2050) al Or (arm 8): +cv our K 6 025. i. 35. 104. 205. 250. 620. 1957. 2018. 2023.
2036. 2037. 2038. 2041. 2067 (s 2) (arm 4): +in quibus fuit gig: +CKUO- i. 6i. n:
+pov (cv) owr 2040. (2050) Avtiirao- K C 025. 046. fil (- 325. 337. 456. 2050) al
1 vg: Antiphas Pr: Anthipas arm 8: Antipax gig: AFTCMTOO- AK C 42. 82. 93.
325. 337. 367. 452. 456. 498. 202 1. 2024. 2050 Or: avtcwrao- s 1- 2 arm 4 bo:
eth o fuipr. KU o fiaprvo- 172. 2032 s 1: vcur taprvo- arm 2) nov 3 1 8 1. 2019 arm
1 bo: +Kai Pr o TTCOTOCT-f-ori iracr uuiorvcr (+LWU s 1) ir rror 2059 s 1: OTI
xaprvcr iov irioroo-(y)mmT o irtarcvcuv ann- "X- jjuw 4 AC 61. 69. 2050 Or 1 s 2:
K 025. 046. 21 (-2050) Pr gig vg (arm) bo xr av ckravoy 2050: o airckrav 205: ov

airckTCtvav bo eth 1 ori72. 314. 2016 imp vuv irap VMOV 920. 2040 s 1 arm 4a: c vfuav arm 2: +CKCC 632 OTTOV o 2ar.

KatOik. 2O2O S 1 14. oxX. AKC 025. 35. 205. 620. 2020. 2050 al Or": oxXo 046. 91 (- 35. 205. 620. 2020. 2050) 250. 2038. 2067 al KUTa rovk:-fxeyeiv Pr arm 8 4 oxiyaarm 1 2 8 eth on. Kpar. ovofjiara Kparovyra bo or4C Pr vg s 2 c cia e fi 15. OVTCDS l a Kparowras rip Stsaxfjv Nucoacuru 1 6. fieravorjo-ov ovv ct 8c 117, Zpxofjlai roi ra v, cu Troaciipra) ACT" avrw fr r fiojufxuy. rov orotartfe ton.

17. O x ov okovo-arai

T TO irvcvfmi Acyct rat? tkK rjriais.

T5 VLKUVTI SOMTO) avtw rov jcat ovra avrw njtov Acveijv,

KOL CTTI r v fi fov ovojia Kaivbv yeypaiLtckov o ov8cl otScv ci AIJ 6 Aa? ayciv. A Si8axv v TOU 4 2- 4 6- 2019. 2020 csao-Jccy A C 025. i. 2015. 2036. 2037. 2050. 2067 al Pr gig vg: co'ai 046. 21 (-2050) al ma Or" s 1 2 arm 1 8 8 bo: Sioao-w arm r Baa. AC 104: v rw Baa. I. 94: rov Baa. 21 (-35). 250. 2037. 2038 Or 1: tv rai Baaaax rov Baa. 025. 35. 2067 et comm. in 250. 2037. 2067: Baa. 046: K Baaaic 025. 21 (- 386. 620. 1849. 2040. 2050) Or: Balac gig vg arm: Boaocuc C 046. 620. 1849. 1854. 2040. 2050: Balaac Pr: Boaaau 386 jsaaetv 3axW c: ex axctv 2050: ao-iact A row re 2050 aycti Asc 025. I. 35. 205. 522. 632. 1957. 2015. 2019. 2020. 2023. 2036. 2050 Or Kum JLM Pr gig vg s 1 arm: TOV ay. 42. 325. 336. 367. 456. 468. 620. 628: KOI fay. 046. 18. 175. 250. 337. 386. 617. 632. 919. 920. 1849 1934 2004. 2040. 2067 al Or" (s 2) etsciiaod. vg arm 2: cisuaodutov 1854: de sacrifices Pr.

15. au Kpar. o jcparcoy 2050 KpatOwraa Kparovyra bo: arm 1 2 3 Niicoa. AC 046. 18. 175. 325. 386. 456. 468. 617. 919. 1849. 2004 al: rov Nucoa. K 025. i. 35. 104. 205. 337. 620. 632. 920. 1934. 1957. 2015. 2020. 2040. 2050 al (arm 4a bo): "of Nicolaus" arm 1 2 8 ofuuctkr AKC 046. 21 (-35. 468. 2020) Or Pr gig vg s 1- 2 (arm 4): o HWTCD i. 61.: t v uo-co 2037 arm: otoioxr o (w 468: rjv 2067) fuo-co 025. 35. 42. 181. 468. 2038. 2067: 202o arm 1 2 8 bo sa eth.

16. OUK AC 046. 21 (-35) al ma arm 1 bo eth: towr arm 8: K 025. i. 35. 61. 69. 1957. 2015. 2019. 2023. 2036. 2037. 2038. 2041 Or 1 Pr gig vg s 1 2 arm 2 ci 8c firf KOI bo OXM 6i. 69. 1 8 1. 2020. arm 1 2 8 eth: OTI K iroacicj cmroactito-ai 205 avttav crov 2050 Pr: avrov arm 2- cvtyc rov OTOA. xov arm 1: + CF rrf airctai; 17 tt av9pwirta 104. 336. 459. 620. 628 (from the Comm. of Andreas).

17. our ura s 1 2: +CUCOVCIK bo eth: aures audiendi Pr arm 1- irvcvxa + ayiov arm 1 1 eth eicicaiyo-. + ori bo r 1 8. Kcu r dyycxf rj cv 9uarctpois fcicxi? rias ypctyov Tasc Xcyei 6 ulos rov 0cov, 6 CXDV rovs d 0axAOvs ox Xoya irvpd?, ecu ot iroscs avrov op. oi. oi xaxKoxij3ava, 19. Olsa o-ov ra pya, icai rqv dytttnv ical r v iricrnv KOI TTJV Siaicovtav KOL rrjv icai ra cpya o ov ra tt ara irxctova rwv Trpomov.

vucovri 025. 046. 21 (-620. 2050) alp 1: TO vucovvri AC: avrco AC 025. 046 min fereomn Or: K 61 Tyc gig vg d T s 1: +0aye 025. I. 35. 6I. 11 104.-205. 468. 620. 632. 1957. 2015. 2023. 2036. 2037. 2038. 2041. 2067 Oif Tyc gig arm 4a: + TOU ayciv 42. 69: +"food" arm 1 2 8 TOV navva AC 21 (- 35. 205. 468. 620. 632. 2050) al Or": p. avva 69: TO uavva 046 gig vg arm 2 3: c TOW pawa K 468. 1957- 2019. (2050) Tyc Pr S 1 2 arm 4 bo: avo rov p. avva i. 35. 6I. 1 " 104. 205.

468. 620. 632. 2015. 2023. 2036. 2037. 2038. 2041. 2067: cnro TOV uxov 025: cwro TOV v ov Ttfjcr farjt arm 1: 4- ayciv 172. 250. 2018. 2050 rov KCicp. ro KCKpvix vov 2050 gig vg Saxrcu avtw 2 t 2020 arm a XCVK. K. rt r. r s j?. 2 iftov C KCUVOV KCVOV C 175. 2040 yeypaAi. cyycypa ificvov 919: Pr: + r avri r bo o ovscicr. Xai3. i o R oiscv ct cv 205. 209 bo: + avrco 2050 (.

18. TO CK euareipour CKicxvicriour See note on 2 1. rco cv 0var. A: v uar. CKicxio-iacr C: ra ayy. Trja- CKKX. rco cv 0uar. Epiph 455: ecclesiae qui est Tyatirae Pr: ro cv ckicxicrta rrj cv Ovar. s 1: TCU nfo- ckicxi ricur ri r cv var. s 2: qui in Theatrea ecclesia arm 4: TQV cv var. CICKX O-. M 025. 046 min omn vld Or 8: Tyatirae ecclesie gig: Thyatirae ecclesiae vg: ecclesiae Thyaterae bo: TUV uartpatwv arm 1 2: rrja- varetptdv KK r)cr. 2020 (arm 8) 0uarctpour K I. 18. 35. 175. 205. 250. 386. 468. 617. 919. 920. 1934. 2004. 2037. 2040. 2067: Ovartpour AC: var pour 025. 149. 201. 632. 1849. 1955. 2036. 2050: 0varctpo)v 2020: 0van? pi? 046. 620: 0ikit ipi7 69. 93. 104. no. 177. 325. 337. 456. 498. 2021: Thyatirae vg: Tyatire gig CKKX O-IOO- A arm 1 rouo-of Oa fjl A 2019. 2020 Pr gig vg (arm 3 8 4): rov o oxiov s 1: + avrov C 025.046. 21 (-2020). 250. 2037. 2038 ap 1 Or s 2 (arm 1) Xoyo Xoi K Pr: Xatiroow 1854 x 0 Xi avu 025. 104. 175. 620. 2050: auricalco Pr: eramento thurino gig: onchalco vg: " unto brass of Libanan " s 8 arm 1-:" unto brass smelted" arm 8 ": "burnished brass" (xax oxi0avo(r) bo eth.

19. TO cpy. naii8i T7yv(2O2o) iricrr. K. r. ay air. K. r. BULK. 1 8 242. 2040: TI? V aya? r. K. r. Siaic. K. r. irurr. I K. r. ayair. +0-01; S 1 bo eth riyv 2 C 2020 Trwrr. J + o-ou s 1 bo eth rrjv 8iakOVtdk ca"N r 7v 8 2O2O Scaxoviav J + o ov s 1 bo 2O. dxXa c co Kara crov

Sri ctyci? Ttv yvyaiira Ic aj8cx, 17 Xeyovcra cavr v irpoifnjTiv,

Kal 8t8atK i, ical irxavp TOUS uv? Sovxovs iropv vcrai KOI fayclv etsaxo0vra. a I. MU fowa avrfl xpovav iva fjLcravojjoy,

Kal OVK Icxicrcy fteravo crcu fc TTS iropvctac avrfj.

22. tioi) pd Xu avryv tit K LVIIV,

Kal TOUS noi vavtas LLCT avri? cfc 6 i lw p, ya T v 9 (a) (a) Interpolation follows here: Idr M? terwoijo-owii 6t rwr p w adrift. See Eng. trans, vol. li. footnote, iv. dy is not followed by the indicative in our author.

eth TTyv 4 A 2019 crov a 2023 Pr crov J + icai I irxccova X poia 175. 617 1934.

20. axXa A 046 min mult: aaA fetc 025 35. 69. 104. 175. 205. 314. 385. 617. 620. 1934. 1957. 2015. 2016. 2020. 2037. 2038. 2050. 2067 al Or 1 CXD Xcyeo arm 1 2 8 Kara rov AC 025. 046. 21 (-35. 632. 2050). 250 al mn Tyc vg s 2 bo eth: o-oi arm L2 8a:-t-iroxv K 35. 181. 632. 2019. 2022. 2038. 2050 gig s 1 arm 4a: +? roxXa 2015. 2036 Pr Cyp: +oxiya i afaicr A C 025. 046. 21 (- 2020. 2040. 2050). 2037. 2038. al mu Pr Cyp gig vg: a rjkao- N c 506. 2019. 2050. 2067 Tyc s 1 2 arm bo eth: aji-rjo- 241. 250. 424. 2018. 2040: irour 2020 ywaika KC 025. i. 104. 205. 468. 620. 2019. 2020. 2038. 2050 Tyc gig vg arm 2 8a bo eth: +rov A 046. 21 (-205. 468. 620. 2020. 2050) al mu Or 1 Pr Cyp s 1 2 arm 1 4 rip Kajsex A: lafa cx: Zezabel Pr Cyp arm 1 2 4- y Xcyovo-a A C: 17 Xey t 046. 21 (35. 205. 2O2O. 2050). al mu Or" gig vg bo eth: rrjv Xcyowav K c 025. i. 35. 205. 1854. 2019. 2020. 2038. 2050: "who declared" arm 1 4 eauriyv AC 025. 21 (620): avrrfv K 046. 104. 141. 336. 620. 628 j Trpo Tiv AK'C 21 (-620. 919. 2004. 2040. 2050) al

mu Or": prophetissam gig: irpo reiav X: irpotfrrjtrjv 025. 046. 104. 172. 620. 919. 2004. 2019. 2038 2040. 2041. 2050: propheten Tyc Pr Cyp vg: + emu fit 2050 s 1 arm 4 I K. diowicci Sturkctk Pr Cyp vg: ai Sisacncaxov? bo Trxavaj 7r avav Pr Cyp Vg i8axo0. ay. i. 2019 (Soixo. TO eio oxo vrov? arm 1 8 4: de idolothytis vg (bo): de sacrifices (- ficio gig) Pr Cyp gig: arm 2.

21. v. 21 205 icoi 1 Pr arm 1- 4 avny avrrjv 2040 DICTOF. fjl ravorj(T i 620. 2050 K. ov Oc. furav. N (arm): K et ACV Qt i Lierav. 2020: K. ou LLCTCVOIO-CV (post avnyo-) I arm 1 ' 8 exi rck A Pr Cyp eth: fcxci K C 025. 046 min om11 Or" gig vg s 1 2 Tropvetao- C 025. 046. 21: iropvtacr AK j avripr ravrrjcr K: CDV K. ov fuT vovjrav arm.

22. isou 8 ov 2020: +cyo i faxXw AC 21 (-325.

23, icai TO rcicva amft farafcrcva ical yvaxrovrai irarai at

Sri fya ccfu 6 Ipavvw v tpob KOI ical ScmTCD fyuv jcournp icari ra ipya 24. fyuv Si Xfya TOW Xotirotf rots c v Seroi 06 c ovo-iv r v 8i8ax v ravnv, omvcs ovic fyvaxrav rol paota rov Sarava, as Xcyovcrtr, 95. irx v? X rc Kpfttijowc xpi ov 456. 468. 632. 2020. 2050). i. 250. 2037. 2038. 2067 Pr Cyp vg arm: ? oxu 025. 046. 325. 456. 468. 632. 2020. 2050 Or"

i bo eth: icaaw K icxiiv vkakrv A: KOUVOV arm 1- 8 tt: gig bo eth: icaaw K icxii v fvkakrjv A: KOUVOV arm 1- 8 tt: luctum cod. ap. Pr: "pains of a couch "arm 4 fuix wravtur 61. 69 Pr Cyp ftcr avno-J avrrjv 2050 ftcyax. arm 8: maximam Pr Cyp vg arm nfravorjcrawriv AK: Acraro o-oxriv C 025. 046. 21 (2050) al pl Or: x-Tavoi7rci 2050: fji Tavorj(rrj 469 Pr Cyp bo sa eth CK. T. cpy. avr. bo sa aynyo- C 025. 046. 81 (- 35. 205. 468. 632) al mu Or 1 Pr Cyp gig vg s arm 4 eth: avrwv A i. (35). 61. 181. 205. 468. 632. 2019. 2023. 2036. 2037. 2038. 2067 vg- T s 1 arm 1- 8 tt.

88. not 1 A 620 arm 1 bo sa avrrja- avrw 205. 209 arm 84 v CUKT 468 0av. vio 2019 fpawuv AC: cpcwcov K 025. 046 min omn: scrutator Cyp Pr vc. K. icops. ap8. K. vc. arm 1- 4 bo eth: renis et cordis Pr Kapsiav s 1 (arm 2) awosoxrci) 2050 vftivarm 1 2- 8 bo icataarm 1 2- 8 ra. cpya cpya C: rrjv Kapsiav 2050 vuov AK C C 025. 21 (- 2020. 2050) Pr gg vg s 1 2 arm 4 eth: avrov 046. 2020. 2050 vg 0- d arm 1- s bo sa: avrwv arm: K.

84. Be 4 68 s 1 TOMT A. OMT. TOICT ev XCUTTOKT N rowr 1 82 94. 2041 TOUT cv TOIO- 0var. XOITTOUT 2050 TOUT ev var. TWV Ovartpattdv arm 1 8 rotir 8 205 arm 4 0varcioio- K et c- c 81 (149. 620. 632. 2050): Ovartpotcr AC: Qvar pour 025. 620. 632. 2050: va-njpioir 149: varrjpaicr 046: 0varcipaur 61. 69: varetpiy K: Thyatirae vg: Tyatirae Pr: Tyatire gig ocrot OTI 205: OOTMT gig I OVJC I K I xwo-iv c w gig: cfia ere arm 2 8 octMecr OVK ovoc Tyc ouic arm 1 yvwrav cyicorc Tyc arm 8 f3a9 a AC 046. 81 (-205. 2050). 250. 2067 al mu: (lathi K 025. I. 205. 2015. 2019. 2036. 2037. 2038. 2050: (ro) ftajooa" bo: altitudmem Tyc Pr: altitudines gig vg our Xcy. arm 4 uxr a arm 1 2 8- jaxXo AC 025. 81 (-337. 632. 2050) al mu Tyc gig arm 4: 0oxci K 046. i. 61. 69. 177. 337. 632. 1957. 2023. 2050 Oi Pr vg arm 1 8 bo eth.

86. irxtji o o ow s 1: " more than what " arm 1 8 Kpanja-art "and is with you" arm 1- 8 a pt KC 69. 177. 2087 26. Kol 6 VIKV Kal o rqpuv a u rcaovs TO cpya fiov, 8dcra avrw l owriav cvl rv lovv, 27. ical Trofftavci arrows cv pdfistp o-is pp a?

ra o-jccvty ra jccpautfa ourTptfcraf, as icdyo) ccxi a irapa rov irarpos fiov, 28. ical Soxrcii avr4 rov dorcpa TO? irpauvov.

29. O c w ovs djcowratO) T TO irpcvua Aeyci rai?

025. 046. 21 al pl: ov 205o: coxr A 241 av iy 0 Atfc 025. 35. 205. 468. 620. 632. 2020. 2050 Tyc Pr gig vg s 1 8 bo: avolfai 046. 18. 175. 325. 337.,386. 456. 617. 919. 920. 1849. 1934. 2004. 2040 al pl.

26. Kai 1 io4. 336. 522. 620. 628. 2020 arm 1 2 8 o 8 2O2O npw KPUTCDV 468 a pt rcx. s 1 ra cpya fiov a pci Tcxovo- 2050 eth c cm T. c6V. 7rik: Ta cflny Tyc.

27. K. woipj iroiuuveiv (1854) s 1: et reget gig vg:. iroixa-vovcriv arm 1 2- avrovo-avrov arm 8 crioijpaj + KCU rvvrpu i avrovo 2050:-f tcai Tyc arm 1 8 wo- O-KCVOO KcpaLtucov arm 8 a bo o-wrpt crat A C i. 104. 2020. 2037. 2038. 2050 al. Possibly a slip of the author for owtpiftovrat, or rather (rwrpiftrjo-ovtai: otfl pi o-ctat 025. 046. 21 (- 2020. 2050) ai mu Or: confrin-gentur Pr vg (s 8): comminuentur Tyc: o-wrpurcrc s 1 (an itacism for owrpt crai): confringet eas (placed before oier 1) gig (rwrpl l t (-ovo-tv arm 1- 8 s) avrovo- (avrov arm 8) arm bo eth ovroxr yap s 1 icayco cyw arm 1 8 j.

28. aurw avroio- arm 2 4 irpuwov C 025 al omn fere: A 046. 2038.

29. v. 29 Pr ovo- ora s 1 2: + axovciv bo eth: aures audicndi arm 1 4 irvevAa + aytov arm 1 8 eth.

CHAPTER III.

I. Kal TO dyyc a TW Iv Sapsccrtv ccicxio-ia? ypairor Ta3c Xcyct 6 l cuy Ta 7rra 7rv vp. ara TOV 0cov Kal rovs CTrra aorepa?, Ol6d orov Ta cpya, OTI ovoua cyei? ore f s Kat i 1. rcai 1 Pr TW ayy. TOCO- ayyeaour arm 1 1 1- TW ft S. CKK. See note on 2 1. ecclesiae qui est Sardis Pr: rw ev ny c c-K rjria Sapsccov s 1: TW cv 5aps. s 2: TOI cv (raio-) Sapsi ria cicica o-caio-arm 4: rqor CF S. CK. AK 025. 046 min omn Or 1: ecclesiae Sardis (Sard. eccl. gig) gig vg bo eth: no- 2aptstica- (Sapuwv 2. a): nyo- CK 2op S. KK Yfrtai r C cirra 181.

a. ytvov yprjyopuv, Kal orippiow ra Xoara a fytexAov airo avctv, ov yap tvprjka rov r lpya 1 vcn-Xypvpeva VWTTIOV rov 0 o5 AOV.

3 b. fjLvrjpjovtv ovv irws czX as ai 7 011011?, icat rqpci teal taxapio? o ypvjyopuv Kal-rrjpuv ra tuarta avrov, iva XT yviro ir piirarfj 9 ical jsAcirakTiv r v do- xtxrvvtv avrou.

2015 TOV 0cov386 pya + cat Pr s 1 ovona + "of the health" bo cm TCT AKC 025. 35. 205. 250. 620. 2020. 2037. 2038. 2050. 2067 al mu Or 1 Tyc Pr gig vg s 2 arm 1 2 8 4 bo: KCU (170- 046. 21 (-35. 205. 620. 632. 2020. 2050) al p: Kdl OTI 170- 632 s 1: WVTOCT arm tt icai 3 + OTI s 1.

2. yirou icai yivov s 1: yevov 1854 ypvop yp7yopav: vigilans et stabilis Pr cmypio-ov AC 025. 35. 175. 337. 468. 617. 919. 920. 1849. 1934. 2004. 2020. 2040 al Or: rrrjpi ov g 046. i. 1 8. 205. 250. 632. 2037. 2038. 2050. 2067 al Tyc Pr gig vg s 1 bo eth: cmptfcdv 620: TJiprpov 42. 141. 201. 325. 385. 386. 429. 456. 468. 522. 2015. 2019. 2036 s 2: Traifljukrov arm 1 2- ra Aotira Tyc eth: rover Aonroixr (01) s 2 a ot s 2: on arm: ci Sc XT;? bo cjicaAov AKC 025. 172. 181. 250 424. 468. 2015. 2018. 2019. 2020 2036. 2037. 2038. 2050. 2067 Oi 1 Tyc Pr gig vg s 2 arm 4: (or T?)x AA. cv i. 104. 336. 620: r (oi c)iicx c(r 046. 21 (-468. 620. 2020. 2050). 93. 201. 498 al s 1: ftcaAcicr arm bo airooavw AfccC 025. I. 620. 919. 2020. 2050,

al mu Or 1 (atroovrjo-Kfiv 468. 2015. 2019. 2036. 2037) Tyc P f g g v g s 1 8 arm 4 bo: an-o? oaA. iv 046. 21 (-35. 468. 620. 919. 2020. 2050): airo? axciv 35. 1957. 2023 cupipea cvp-rjkav 046: invenio vg: +orc ori s 1 irttrxyp. r. cpy. o-ov 141 S 1 pya AC 1.: ra pya K 025. 046. 21 al 1 Or 1 irctrxiy-pu)xcia2Ol. 386 cvajmov + icvptov 35. 205 xovl. 205. 2038. 2067 al p Pr s 1 arm 1- 8.

S 1. pnrifoveuc pr KOI eth ovvk 69 Pr gig s 1 arm 1 2 3 4 eth rjk. K. i rjta(T 2050 S 1 K. TKOIKT. K. r pci A C 025. I. 35. 104. 172. 250. 468. 620. 1957. 20.-0. 2037. 2038. 2041. 2050. 2067 gig Vg s 8 arm 2- 4 bo: K. rjnovaracr rrjpti s 1: rjkovcracr riypci arm: et audita custodi Pr: 046. 21 (-35. 468. 620. 2020. 2050) al mu KCU ri7p iarm 8 eth.

xvi. 16. isov or Pr arm 3 epxoiai cpx rac K (sed corr. prim, man.) 241. 2020 Pr s 1 arm 3: 4- cfat ii?? eth icx mcr + ra v 2019: +KCU 205 o ore K rrjpiov n v 1849 n-cpi-irarct 104. 522. 2015: vepiirarrfo-rj 2O2O: Trcpiiranorei 2019 Xcrrovo-t i. 2015. 2019. 2036. 2038: videat Pr avr. " their shame appear " arm 1 2- 3).

irotav apav ij a iir erf 4. XXa 3x 6X170 ovoiara ovic ijioxwav ra luarta avruv, iccu ircp rariproimriv ACT AOV cv Xcvicot?, ori tot cio"ir.

5. "O VIKUV ovrcus ircpiJaxeirai v tiartots XCVKOL?, ncal ov fii) jaxa a) TO ovoia avrov cic TI S pl3 ov rfjs KOI ofioxoyio-Q) TO Svofia avrov cvunrioy rov Trarpos fiov fcal cwoiriov rov dyycxav avrov.

3 C. ow 620 yprjyop. AR etc.: yMyopiyo-cto- 104. 620: fjl Tavor)njr N Pr: icravotyoto- iiysc (icai bo) ypiyopio-CMr 2050 bo I fw 1 pr. veniam et subitabo adventum meum ad te Pr 17 01 AC 025. i. 35. 181. 468. 2015. 2037. 2038. 2067 vg c d f arm bo: + tm crc M 046. 21 (-35. 468) al gig vg a T s 1 2 arm 4 eth yvwr AC 025. i. 35. 175. 205. 468 617. 1934. 2037. 2038. 2067 al: yvcocny K 046. 21 (-35. 175. 205. 468. 617. 620. 1934. 2050) Or 1: yvcixrct 104. 620 459. 2050: necies gig vg: non scies Pr irotav cop. i; " my coming " arm iroiav cupav oiav oipav (N): irota copa l8l. 367. 632. 2050.

4. axXa AKC 69. 468. 2020 Or: axX 025. 046 min pi: 35. 205 arm a CXCMT c w s 1 arm 4 bo c. ox. ovouu A C 025. i. 35. 205. 2015. 2020. 2037. 2038. 2050 al Or 8 (Pr) vg s 1 1 eth: ex- OK. ox. gig: oxiy. eg. OVOA. 046. 21 (-35. 175. 205. 2020. 2050) al: oxiy. OVOA. eg. 61. 69. 175. 314. 522. 2016: +mu i a AKC 025. 046. 21 (-35. 205. 468. 2020) al Or 8 gig: 01 35- 2 S- 209- 432. 468. 2015. 2020. 2036. 2037 2038. 2067 Pr vg: at 522 ro tuariov Pr avr. cavrcuv C: +ficra ywaiicoo' bo eth 7T pt7rat77r. J TT plirarrjtov A: Trfpurarovcrw 620. 2050 V ga. f. T s i arm: ambulaverunt Pr vg d arm 2 icr cxovarm 4: o)7rtov fjiov s 1 ore KOI s 1 ori. eio-tv eth om. here and trans, after XCVKOUT in ver. 5 ciow + icat avan-avo-iv OVK c ovo-i?. K. o cpxofieioo- (from 4 8) 35.

6. outwa A C 1 8. 35. 456. 920. 1849. 20 4 1 Or 1 Pr gig vg s 1 8 arm 4 bo: ovrio 325: ovroer N c 025. 046. 21 (-18. 35- 325- 456. 920. 1849. 2004. 2050). 250. 2037. 2038. 2067: avroo- 2050: ovroo OVTUMT 467 Trcpt ax. ircpi axXcrai C irtpipeftxrjrai 2050: irept axovo-tv avrov? bo: eth airaxa ra) 2020: cfaxct ovo-tv bo sa ro ovox. avr.

1. 2015 avrov l– avrcdV s 1 arm bo c c r. t)9X. v 2040 I r. fawyo- TCDV (nvrcov 920. 2040 ro ov. avr. 8 avrov gig cvanr. 1 fiirporv V K K. cvanr. r. ayy. avr. 32 5. 456.

6. O IXCOP ovs

TI r nrcvia Xeyct rats 7. Kal r5 dyycxu) T fr Ocxascx a tacxiprtas ywty ov T dvolyw ical ovscit icxcurct Kal jcxciw jcai ovscls ivotyct, 6. v. 6Pr ow cura s 1 2: +aicoveiv bo cth: aures audiendi arm 1 4 TirevAo + ayiov arm 1 2 eth.

7. nai 1 Pr TO) ayy. roicr ayycxoio- arm 1 roi cv ia. c X. See note on 2 1: ecclesiae qui est Filadelphiae Pr: rw v fciaa-Scx ia arm 4: TITCT cv ix. cx all Greek MSS Oi: Philadelphiae ecclesiae (gig) vg S 1 bo: nycr taascx xuv (-tcuv 3) cfdcx iao-arm 1 2 8 ixo8e io C 025. 046. 205. 325. 386. 456. 919. 920. 1849. 1934. 2004 al mu: hxa8ea iar A 620. 2050: fcixasca cia 18. 35. 175. 337. 468. 617. 632. 2020. 2040 al mu I KK rjrmitr K Xcyci + xvpiocr 172. 2018 o ayiocr o axrjo. C 025. 046. 21 (-2050). 2037. 2038. 2067 al 1 Oi 1 " 36 B 1 1 arm 4 bo eth: o ayuxr u a T 6 17 2. 2018: sanctus et verus Tyc Pr gig vg arm 1- 8: o oa. i0. o aytoo- Atf: o axiyd. 2050: o ayycxocr ax ivoo- Oi 8 o 8 337 nyvk icxeiv A C 025. 046. 21 (-35. 205. 468 617. 620. 2050). 250 al mu Or PMl46 Oi 8: icxci3a I. 35. 69. 172. 205. 468. 617. 620. 2015. 2019. 2036.

2037. 2038. 2050. 2067 Or" 1 " 3: (+omnes eth) claves Pr s 1 arm eth Add A 2020: rov AS (Aals 632) K 21 (- 620. 2020. 2050). 250. 2037. 2038. 2067 al pl: rov OIKOV (from Is. 22 s3) rov Aavcid bo eth: rov asov 104. 218. 336. 459. 620. 2050 arm 1- 8 o avoiyow teat awyw I icai 2 bo jcxcto-ct A C 025. 046. 21 (- 205. 620. 632) al pl Or pllu Or 8 arm 4 bo: cxe rq 104. 385: icxctct i. 61. 205. 314. 632. 2016. 2019. 2023. 2037.

2038. 2067 Tyc Pr gig vg s 1 8: icxcto) 2015. 2036 (arm) cx. (sine add) A C 025. (35). 205. 468. 632. 2020. 2050 al Or- 1 " 8 Tyc Pr gig vg s 1 2 arm 4 bo:-f-avnyi 046.! (-35 2 S- 468 632 2020. 2050) al mu Or 8 arm 1 8 8 rat (A: +o 2015. 2036) K HDV A 025. I. (35). 172. 205.

25O. 314. 468. (2OI5). 2OI8. 2OI9. 2O2O. 2O23. (2036). 2037.

2038. 2050. 2067 Or 1 11 46 Or 1 (s 1 8) (bo): u fcxcict C 61." 2016 al gig arm 4: et qui claudit Pr arm 8 8-: icxctci Tyc vg: ct fjiij o avotytov (+ icac ov eio avoi ci Or 8) 046. 21 (- 35. 205. 468. 620. 2O2O. 2050) al Or 1: ct XT; o ayoiywv KO. L KXctav 42. 104. 432. 459. 620 Kat 4 quod Pr avoiyei AC 025. 6 1." 205. 2019. 20 37- 2038. 2067 Or Tyc Pr gig vg s 1 8 arm 4: avoiywv 468 (arm a): ayoi ci (-vfa) 046. 21 (-205. 468. 620). 250 al 11111 Or 1 ""- 6: avoify 104. 385. 620.

8. Otsd (TOV ra? pya ibov ov8uko, Ivdrriov crov Ovpav ty ovscfc owateu icxf unu afrrqv In tucpav Ixcw Svvouv, icai CT pipra? ftou TOV Xovov, al owe pvrjcru) TO 6Vou, a iov.

9. 28ov 8t8a etc TJ S crwaycyi? TOW Sarava, TOV Xcyovrcov cavrovs lousaiovs etvat icai owe AXXa 7roiipro avrovs? va f ical irpoo-Kvinqo-oiwriv cvcomov ruiv iro8ov crov, jcal yvwotj ore yu riydirrj(ra crc.

IO. ort Ir piycras TOV Xoyov ri s VTTOAOV S tov, icayw crc rqprjro K rijs wpo? TOV irctpao-pov T S AcxXovon9 ip tuau. evi r s OIKOVXCT?;? 0X779, 7T ipdo-ai TOVS JcatOtjcoviras errl 8. oifc. r. T. cpy- Pr T. cpy. o-ov K s 2 cpya + KOI TI iriartv crov bo: +KQI S 18 eth vp. CVOTT. crou avcwyx. 920. 2040 avecoyt. AC 046. SI (- 205. 2O2O. 2050) al Or 1: qpcwyi. K 025. 172. 205. 2016. 2018. 2020. 2050 17? icai i. 6i. m f 2037. 2067 eth: bo: OTI arm s avrrjv (35) 2023. 2038 Pr gig vg arm 4 ortl + ov 2020. 2036. 2037 pikp. SV. pusillas. vires Pr CXCMT e ci I. 1957- 2037 T. Xoy. ra, pya 920. 2040: TOW Xoyovcr arm 8- 8.

0. iou icai tsov s 1 Sio AC: 8csoka K: SiscuAt 025. 046. 91 (-205. 620. 2050) al pl Or 1 gig: 8i6 o UH 205: 8i8ou 620. 2050: Scocrw Pr vg bo eth Satava + cic Pr s 1 2 TWV Xey. rover Xcyorracr bo otxXa-eth tsov 2 cat i. 181. 2023. 2037. 2038. 2067 i owiv A C 025. 69. 82. 201. 218. 314. 386. 632. 2015. 2016. 2018. 2019. 2036. 2050 arm: rjfao-iy 046. 21 (-386. 632. 2050). 250. 2037. 2038. 2067 al mu Or: lyfco I isou. rjfova-LV eth icat 2 + irottcra) airroucr iva bo irpoa-Kvvrjcrovcriv AMC 025. I. 42. 82. 149. 201. 2016. 2036. 2050 arm: irpoo-icwiyo-akrtv 046. 21 (-149. 2050). 250. 2037. 2038. 2067 al Or 1: + o-c (o-oi) MH wwowrai bo vjf. cvcmr. T. wo8. o-ow jc. Trpoo-icw. Pr icai 8 + iravr cr bo yvwa-iv AC 025. 046. 21 (-2050). 250. 2037. 2038. 2067 Pg s 2 arm s a: yvwcromu 2019. 2050. 2087 vg s lvid: yvwwtcu 2023: yvwrq M 69 Pr arm 4: yvcikjrct Or cyco AKC 025. 205. 250. 468. 620. 2020. 2037. 2038. 2050. 2067 Or gig vg s 1 2 bo eth: O46. 21 (-205. 468. 620. 2020. 2050) al m Pt lyyatricra 149. 2040 o-c ai 2020.

IO. on ftat A arm 4 TOK Xoyov AOV iccu rrjv VTTOJL bo eth 11. cp oiai ra)(v Kparct o Iva prfitls Xafy rov orc avov rov.

12. O vikwv irottpro) avrov orvxov cv r j wuj rov 0cov pov,

Koi ypd fa cv avrov TO ovopa rov 0cov iov, Kat TO vofjM rijs iroxecos rov 0cov AOV, rijs Katvijs Ic3owraa? yx, 17 Kara atvowra IK rov ovpavov diro rov 0cov fuv, Kal TO OVOMl fjLOV TO KatvOV.

13. O cvcov 085 avcowara) r ro irvfvfuL Xcyci rat?

14. Kat ra ayyexxp TW v Aaosiiciigi KK rjar as Tasc Xeyci 6 Aniv, 6 ftdprvs 6 TTKTTOS cat ax; ivo9, KTto-ccos rov 0cov, icayco icai 8ia rovro cayo eth riypiyo-a) N: ftrjprjo-a arm eth nyo 1 cupcur r. irtipao-p. TI F 2O5o: rrjcr wpao' s 1 bo ireipaotet 4-travrao- arm 1 2- 8 bo Karot owrao- bo).

11. epx- tsov cpxojtai 468. 2015. 2019. 2036 al vg 1 L T arm 1 isov p. eth Setcr Xafy 7 Xa no ra u 104. 336.

459. 620 Aiyow (ne) quis alms Pr: (ne) alms Cyp 1 8- 4) o-ov + KOC s 1 arm 1 eth.

2050 (arm 1 12. o PUCW rov VLKUVTO. arm ovrov avro) N 920 Or 8 cv arm r. vaw TO) ovoxart 920. 2040 tov 1 385. 2019 Or s 1 Kai i. nyo TTO DO- rov ov xov 2O5o eri N arm 2 or avrov C 2015: r avro 61. 2019. 2036. 2037: super illud Tyc: +ro OVOJM. pjov KOLL 2020 r. 0. p. K. ro ovofjl. O46 K. r. ov. TIJ Trox. r. cov AOV i. 181 S s: icat duo-ai avroio- rov otcoi LLOV arm 1 rov Ocov xov 9 s 1 eth: rov Trarpoo-tov bo n; cr Kaivrjcr iroxccoo- rov Trarpocr p. ov bo i; Kataftatvotvtra AN C 025. I. 141. 181. 205. 432. 459. 1854. 2015. 2050. 2087: 17 Karapfwovo-a 025: n o Kara9aivovoio K: 17 Kara aivei 046. 21 (- 205. 2050). 250. 2037. 2038. 2067 Or 1 CK. r. ovp. s 1 arm 1 sa CK A C 025. 046. i. 33. 205. 325. 337. 456. 468. 2020. 2037. 2038. 2050. 2067 al Tyc Pr gig vg bo: airo 18. 175. 386. 617. 620. 632. 919. 920. 1849. 1934. 2004. 2040 al rov 4 632 airo 386. 620 arm 2 8 4 xov 6 A C 025. 35. 205. 468. 632. 2050 al Or 0 Tyc Pr gig vg S L arm 8 4 bo: 046 21 (-35. 205. 468. 620. 632. 2050) al mu arm 2: avrov arm 8

JCOivO? + KOt S 1.

18. v. 13 Pr ow wra s 1 1: +OKOV IV bo eth: aures audiendi arm 1 2 8 4 rt TO irv. cocxi70- urarm 4 HTCVLUI arm 1- eth 14. TW ayy- roio- ayycxoar arm 1 2 ro cv Aoo CKK. See IJOte on 2 1. ro cv Aao8. cv CKK. arm 4: n? o- cv Aaos. CKK.

1 5. OTSa o ov ra ort OVTC ifrvxpo? et ovr carof. o cxov jruxpbs V 1 froros.

1 6. ovnos, ort iapos ci icat ovrc f lvxpos OVT curoy 1, AcxXo) (re cxccrat CK TOV OTOUUITOS ftov.

17. OTA Xcyets ort ITAova-to? ctxt icat ireirxovrtyka ical ov8ci xpetav fya), ical OVK olsas ori crv c7 6 Taxatirupos ical 6 cactvo? al rvXos ical yuuvos, 025. 046 min fere omn: TIO Aao (Aaoicetao- 919) 919. 920. 2040: Tfj cv Aaos. ckKXio-uur 18: Laodiciae ecclesiae gig vg: ecclesiae Laudatiae Pr: rvja- ckKXrycrtao- Aaosticciao- (-jcuur bo) s 1 arm a bo: rtja- ckKX onacr Aao3ikCbv i arm 2 8 Aaosocta AKC 104. 149. 201. 620: Aaci8iicia 2050: Aaosuccia 025. 046. 21 (- 149. 620 2050): Laudatiae Pr: Lavodike arm 4 o ativ-f KCU N icat 2 A 025. 046 21 (-620. 2050). 250. 2038. 2067 s 2 arm: o 69. 104. 459. 620. 2015. 2036. 2037. 2050: cai o C 82 bo oxi70ivoo- + icu M s 1 arm 1 2 3- eth 17 apxn airapxn 2015. 2036. 2037: am ap; ppr arm 4: + TIJO pxn r 2l rma: atr X 7 0 " e I TI 7 " lft o" Ti K: nyo KTijo-cokr 1849: TTO- TTIOTCWO- 201. 386 TOW 15. OTI s 1 I forcer. lrvxp 0(r 2O S- 2O 9 arm 1- 2- f I o cxov vxp- o V rroo A I. 241 arm 1- 2- 8 o exovj 025. 046. 205. 522:-f-i; s 1 170- CMT 046. 336. 620.

2017.

16. outuwr. uxpo7 arm 2 ovrwo- on OTI ovrwo- K bo: ort 1854. 2019: sed quia (quoniam Pr) Pr gig vg: cat s 1 ia p. ovrc feor. A 025. 205. (2050) al vg s 1: JCOTOO- owe jrvxp 00 " (N)C 046. 21 (- 205. 2050). i al mn s 2 arm 3 bo: K. OVT coroo- owrc fnxP- 6o Pr gig arm 1- 2 4 a icat ovrc. oroAaroo- fioveth owe 1 A C 025. 046. 205. 617. 632. 2020. 2050 vg arm 8: ov 21 (-205. 617. 632. 2020. 2050) al Or 8 (s 1 2) fco-rocr +ct K c irvxpoo- +ct K 2050 xcxXo) o c cxccrat CK r. OTOA. fiov n-avo-c rov oroiaroo- crov K Cfico'at cixccrat 046. 617. 919. 1934: cuv K c: atico-at 2050: "judge" arm 1 a 8:-Mot cxeyx" o 250. 2020 TOV OTOLU Tip fcapouur bo fuw rov H arm 1 2- 8.

17. on Tt 18: icat eth ort AC i. 35. 172. 175. 205. 242. 250. 314. 617. 1934. 2015. 2016. 2018. 2020. 2036. 2037. 2040. 2050 al gigvg s La bo: K 025. 046. 21 (-35. 175. 205. 617. 1934. 2020. 2040. 2050). 2038. 2067 al Or 1 Cyp cta ct s 1 K. irarxovr bo sa ovscv AC 181. 2038: ovscvoo- M 025. 046. 21. 250. 2037. 20 7 O 1 I X W 1 c X CMr 62 1 260 AHOKAAY IS IOANNOY XIL 18-10.

1 8. rv4 otAevo roi dyopwrat trap 9 Ifwv yfnxrlov

K Trvpof tva irxovnpy f, icat IJMTUL Xcvira tva ir pi axg KOI firj avcpi00 ij aurxwiy T S ywiwjnpos rov, al KoaAovpiov fyxpto-cu rovs axitous crov 19. eyw ocrovs v ia Ary w al inuoevw OVK icat o 1 K 2019. 2050 I rax. ci K 2050 o raa. caccxocr " weak and miserable bo: cxcivcxr eth o 2 A 046. 91 (18 205. 632. 920. 2004. 2040. 2050). 250 al Or 1: KC 025. i. 1 8. 61. 69. 205. 241. 632. 920. 2004. 2015. 2019. 2036. 2037. 2038. 2039. 2040. 2050 cxctvocr AC 104. 620: cacctpcxr K 025. 046. 91 (-620) al pl: oxifjoivoa- 1854 ic. yvpvocr K. rv Aoo- 104. 1 10. 336. 620. 632. 2050 gig arm 4- a eth jr. rwf. s 1 1.

18. cnifip. rvui)3ovacvo-ci 2015 arm 2 8: consuletyc rot H-ow 2020 arm bo eth: +Xa3c arm 1 2 8- ayopoo-oi ayo-paaov 2020 (Tyc) arm 1 2 8: Xajsctv eth irap iov I72.

250. 424. 498. 2016. 2018. 2038 Trap CA. XP V(r- AKC 025. I. 35. 205. 2015. 2019. 2023. 2036. 2037. 2050. 2067 al Or 1 Tyc Qyp g g y g sl f arm: XP 1- f - 46. 91 (- 35- 205. 2050) al bo sa: +cfuF eth c c myocrj cv TTvpt bo eth: CK wpacr 046 I Trxovnyo-ewr 620. 2050 iiartov XCVKOV Pr Cyp Xevica Xamirpa bo: Ttita arm 1 cva ircpc)3ax. ircptj9axc(rdai s 1 2 iva 2 Pr gig vg bo eth ircpi axXi; 046. 61. 69. 172. 205. 617. 1934. 2015. 2036. 2037: TTCpt axct 104. 2050 fawtpuorj favr) 69 Or: + cv CTCH Pr ato-xvn ao wxrwiy 025. 35. 104. 205. 620. 2019 KoxXovpicw A 025. 35. 6 1. 205. 522. 632. 920. 1849. 1957. 2004. 2019. 2023. 2038. 2040. 2050 al Or 1: icovx-Aovpior I. 1 8. 919. 2037: Jcovxovptov 385. 2015. 2036: KoxXvpiov C 175. 250. 325. 337. 386. 456. 468. 617. 620. 1934. 2020. 2067 al: Koxvpiov 046: collide Pr gig: collyrio Tyc Cyp vg ijxpurai (cv X. 2050: e x. 620) A C 94. (104). 336. 459. 468. 620. (2015). 2019. 2037. 2050: fyxpurat 104. 2015. s 1 2: cyxp"-ov 025. I. 35. 6I. 1854. 1957. 2023. 2036. 2038. 2041. 2067 eth: munge Tyc gig vg: ungue Pr Cyp: "give to " bo: " lay " arm 2: cyxporiy 2020: iva cyxpurct 046: iva cyxpun 91 (- 35. 205. 468. 620. 2020. 2050) Or 1: ra cyxp ur W 2 5 + CTTI 60. 432. 1957. 2041 arm r. w 0. crov s x P cmur 104. 2050: jsXc rcur 620 arm 4.

10. eye ori ryw arm 1 8 bo sa cav ay K 2019. 2050 foxcve AC 046. 91 (-35- 205. 468. 617. 620. 2020). 250 m: fr ov 314. 617. 2016: ftxokrov K 025. i. 35. 205. 468. 620. 2020. 2037. 2038. 2067 al: vrnpov 1957: rede Pr ow io4. 181. 336. 620. 2015 arm 1 2 8 icat 2 arm 2. eth.

20. ISov lemKa krl TTJV Ovpav ical fcpovar lav TIS ojcovctty w? AOV eu dvot 0 rrjv Ovpav, KOI curcxcvvrouu wpdf avrdv irai ficumtcrcu ICT" avrov feat avrof ACT iov.

31. 6 yucca? 6(Mra avrcp jcaftcrai rr JAOV fr Tjj 0povp AOV, cos dya ivtkrjcra KCU fcctfura fura rov varpo? fum Jv rf Bpovip avrov.

22. O? x (OV coikrarco Ti TO irvcvia Xcyet rats flo. isou-f rxwor 0: ore iw bo: icat c ov eth nri antepr aicovcn avoi ct 2050 aicovoi;. AOV KU Or Joll I and elsewhere avotfo) K: avotfei 18. 2050 s l: +JLOI Or 10 11 Pr bo eth icai 8 M 046. 21 (- 205. 468. 620. 632. 2020. 2050) al mu Or Pr s 1 arm 4: A 025. i. 104. 205. 468 620. 632. 2015. 2019. 2020. 2036. 2037. 2038. 2050. 2067 Or jo u gig vg s 2 arm 1- 8- oo et h W p thr avrov s x owfipru "will dwell" arm 1: "will rest" eth ciov-fin trono meo Pr: +"in my kingdom w arm 1 2 8.

81. o Pikttp pr jccu S 1 2 eth fcayco cyco S 1 bo eth.

88. v. 22 gig ovo- wra Pr s 1-: +0x01 1? bo eth: aures audiendi arm 1 4 uvevxa +ayuk arm 1 eth.

CHAPTER IV.

I. Mera ravra etSov, icai tsov vpa vc yicin; v r ovpava), Kal 17 KDV irptotrj fjv ffkOwra as craa.7rtyyos Xaxovo s ACT CAOV, Xcywv Avajsa a8c Kol 8ct c0 o-oi 8ci ycvco cu icra ravra.

1. ficra pr icai arm 1- (bo) eth icai 1 Pr bo sa eth eth I 0vpav 620. 2050 eth itvewyxcvr; AK 025. I. 2016. 2O2O. 2038. 2067: TKeaiyACVTjv 2050: avcoiyicvi; 046. 81 (-2020. 2050). 250. 2037 al Or 1: rfvoixorj arm 1 Tyc: arm 4 KOI +i8ov K Pr I i; 1 49 1957. 2020 wn + rj Xoxovo-a fur CAOV bo 17 irpwmj s! 17? 170- 205: eth OKT + 011 7 bo eth o-axirtyya Pr gig s 1 Xaxovnr Xaxovo-av K Pr gig: Xaxovaa 522: Xeyownro- 141. 218. 1849. 1955: cxaxipjrcv s 1 arm 8 XFWV AK

046. 81 (-35. 205. 468. 620. 632. 2020). 250 al mu Oi: Xcyoinra K 025. I. 35. 6I." 205. 468. 632. 1854. 957- 2020. 2023. 2036. 2037. 2038. 2067: at Xcyovoa pot 2019: KCU Xcyowno- 104. 336. 620: KOI Xcyovo av gig: KOI cxcycv s 8 eth avaSa avaftifoi A am o-c 205. 386 a ocra A 8ci 817 2050.

3. cv0caf ycpoAipr iv urcvuum

KCU i ov Opovos IKCITO iv Tp gal irl rov Opovov KajACv 3. icai 6 KOL0Tqfi vos oioios opcurct Atfly bunri8c KCLI icai Zpis fcvjcad0cv rov Opovov OMHO? opcura 4. ical cvfcxo0cv rov Opovov Opovov CIKOCTI rcwapc?,

KOI cirt rove r 0povovs cucoo-t rewapas" 1 irpco-? vrcpovc 2. cuocw AM 046. 91 (- 35. 205. 620. 632. 2020) al Or" Pr gig vg s 2: CUCIKT 8e M: icai cv ccocr 025. i. 35. 104. 205. 620. 632. 1854. 2020 al s 1 armf 1 2 4) eth: KCU arm 8 bo toov ioov arm 1- 8: ct3ov tsov bo: i8ov etsov Pr CKCITO 2050 bo: positum Pr (arm 1 2 8) v T. ovp. CKCITO 468 eth cv T. oup. 632 rov Opovov AK 046. 21 (-35. 205. 632) al mu Or 8: TOV Opovov 025. i. 35. 205. 632. 1957. 2015. 2019. 2036. 2037. 2038. 2041. 2067.

3. K. o Koofipciw AM 025. 046. 42. 61. 93. 104. 337. 452. 468. 506. 2019. 202 1. 2050 Or 8 Tyc gig vg s 1 2: et his qui sedebat Pr: 21 (-337. 468. 2050) al mu arm 1 2 8 4 bo eth opacri 205: opacrtor 2050 At0o i6uv 2020 arm 8-: ioov Tyc vg s 1 2: arm 1 bo tocnr. K. o-op8. Xi co Pr iaotri8i acririsi 920: i aairiot 2050: + o-xapayso 337: + icai a-papa-you 046. 42. 1 80. 452. 468. 506. 1854. 2021 cat 2 i854 arm 1 1 crap3ia AK 046. 21 (-325. 337. 456. 468). 250. 2037. 2067 al mu Or 1: sardi Tyc: sardo Pr: crapotm 025. i. 632. 2019. 2038 al gig bo sa eth: sardinis vg d: sardmi vg: sardion s 2 arm 2 8 4-: sardon s 1: i854 tpto- 025. 21 al pl Or 8 Pr gig vg bo eth: tpcicr K c 046: icpeur A 2015. 2036 arm 1 2 8-! Kvuxaotv KVK O 920: icvicxcu cv 1 8. 104. 20 1. 205. 336. 620. 632. 2017. 2024. 2036. 2037. 2038. 2039. 20 5: KVfcxo) 241. 2019. 2020 Opovov +OLVTOV 2O2O: + et ipsa sedes gig otoioo2 A 025. i. 35. 104. 181. 314. 429. 632. 2019. 2036. 2037. 2038 Pr vg s 1 2: oxotoi 2015 arm 1 2 8: o otov 205: opoia 35. 241. 468. 620. 632. 1957. 2016. 2023. 2037. 2041. 2050. 2067 oiomixr K 046. 21 (-35. 205. 468. 620. 632. 2050) al Or 1 oi. op. O-A. K. KVK. T. Op. K opao-ci o-ftapaysivo) AN 0 025. 35. 205. 250. 468. 620. 2037. 2067 al Pr gig Vg: opao-ct uaydivu 2050: opao-et o-xapays(ov (riapay8ou arm) S 1- 2 arm 1- 2-: opoo-cto- (rxapaysiv 69: opao-to- o-fiapaysivuv 046. 21 (-35. 205. 468. 620. 632. 2020. 2050) al Or: wo-(632) opcuricr rmapay8ov 241. 632. 2020: opaorccixr orAopcucsov (arm 4) bo.

4. Kiu 1 AM 0 025. i. 35. 205. 468. 620. 632. 2020. 2050 al Or Pr gig vg s 1 arm 1 2 4- bo eth: O46. 21 (-35. 205.

TT pl3 fix.1Jfji VOVS lUlttw A. CVCO19,

Kal CTTI rag Kcfa as avrfixv orc ovovs pwrovs.

5. KOL IK TOV Opovov ewopcvovrai dotpairat icai juval Kal ftpovrai Kal brra AaAirase? rrvoos Kai6fl vai evwtriov TOV Opovov t (a) 6. KOL ewirtov TOV Opovov us 0aacuro-a vaxiinrj opaia jcpvaraaAfp, Kal (b) Kvicacp TOV Opovov Tco-o-apa a ycAOKra 6f0a fjuiv cAirpocrfcv ai oiricrocv (a) A gloss is added here: ft lore? r eirra i-rcvtara TOV Oeov. See vol. i. 117.

( ) A gloss added here: frilcrff rov Opbvov Kal. See vol. i. 1 1 8.

468. 620. 632. 2020. 2050) s 2 arm 8 fcv Xo0c 920: jcvicaw 2015. 2019. 2036.
2037. 2067: KVfca. u0 v 1 8. 104. 205. 336. 620. 2017. 2039. 2050 0povov
+ ct8ov Tyc arm 4 flpovovol AK 250. 424. 2018 Tyc: Opovoi 025. 046. 21 al pl
Or s 1- 2 bo cwoo-i 1-I-KUI 104 al Tco-crapco- A 025 mm pi: rco-o-apur 2020. 20
qo ica4 8 2oi7 arm 1 c ri T. K. T. ov K 2017 Tyc arm 1 rt T. Opov. IK. T cro: 025.
35. 632 s 1 arm 2- bo eth: iri T. Bpov. row cue. TCO-O-. 046 mm pi Or": super
thronos viginti quattuor vg (gig): in quibus seniores sedentes erant xxiiii. Pr: ri T.
cue. TCO-O-. Opov. (92O. 2040) A 93. 94. 920. 2040. 2050: cue. Tco-cr 2 2020
arm 1 rco-o-apoo- Tco-o-apio- 2050 Qpovova 920. 2040: + t8ov 1957. 2023 2041 al
vld KO. irpco-. 2020: Ka xevot 7rp 72vt 3oi Pr (arm 2- 4- a) TTfpifafixrj vout 1934:
irtpi3 3 rjp. cvoi Pr ir(pi3 3- A 025. 35. 2015. 2036. 2037 Pr v g g g: + 046. 531
(-35). 250. 2038. 2067 (s 1 2) Or ifjuitiw ACVKO) Pr gig: ifianour-K 2050 arm 4
avroiv c orrco-gig: + IXOF arm 1- 2 pvo-covo- M.

6. TOU Opok. TOV Opovw s 1 cmropcuovrai c ciropcvovro 104. 620 vg d arm
bo eth (?) ocrrp. K. DV. K. (Zpovr. AM 025. 046. 21 (-2020). 250. 2037. 2038.
2067 al 1 1 Or 8 Pr gig vg s 2 arm 2 4 bo: oorp. ic. fipovr. K. fx v. i. 385. 2020:
fipovr. K. acrrp. K. jw. s 1 iccuoi. n-vpoo 920. 2040 irvpoo- vg s 1 arm 4 Katoicvai
bo Opovov AK 025. I. 632. 2019. 2020. 2038. 2050. 2067 Pr gig vg arm bo eth:
+aurov 046. 21 (-456. 632. 2020. 2050) al mu Or s a o eoriv. TOV Opovov N 456 a
corn icai 6l. 69 Or 1 a AN 0 025. I. 2OI. 386. 2019. 2038. 2050 vg s 2: at 046. 21
(-386. 456. 2050). 250. 2037. 2067 al Pr gig vg s 1 rriv A: curtv K c 025. 046 a lfere
omn 0 02. I. 6l. 69. 468. 632. 1957. 2015.

2019. 2020. 2036. 2037. 2038. 2050. 2067 arm 8- bo: 046. 21 (-456. 468. 632.
2020. 2050). 250 al ma (s 1 8) arm 1 2 4 ra cirra TTFCviata ro ayiov vvcvfjm eth
irvcvnataj " powers (parts 4) of the spirit holy (3) " arm 1- 4.

6. 0poKOu +avrov 104. 141. 205. 209. 620 oxr AK 025. 046. 21 (-386. 632).
250. 2038 al 11 Or b bo: i. 201. 386.

7. Kai TO fwov TO irptotov oftotov Afovri, Kal TO Sevrcpov JKV oAoiov fuxrxy,
Kal TO Tptvov (ov IXCDV TO irpocrcraw us avdpuirov,
Kai TO TCTOptOV fffoV OfjLQloV acTtp ircTOAcvlp.

8. cal TO. Tcvo-cpa pa, v Ka0 cv avraiv? x a)V v wrcpvyas,( ) Kal avavavaw
OUK c ovo-iv i pas Kal WKTOS Acyovtfs "Avios ayio? ayios Kvptos, 6 0cds 6 ira
TOKpatcip, 6 i)y Kal 6 v Kal 6 cp dicvos.

(a) The following clause is interpolated here: KVK 66ev K 632 Tyc Prarm S 1
0axao-(rav 620. 2050: +OKT eth va unrj A 025. 046. 21 (- 205. 325. 456. 468. 632.
2020. 2040. 2050) vaaivqv 2050: vaxrjvtfj 2040: v tvrj 60. 205. 241. 325. 456.
468. 498. 632. 2018. 2O20. 2022. 2023 I oua 205 I oJLOiav 2050 Kpv oraxXo)
Kpvoraxa) 632. 2020 i ysrypvaAa) arm 4: "the whiteness of crystal 1 arm 1- 2 3 a
ic(ra) A 1854: "at the side of" (?) eth

OpoVQ P +AOV 2020 K. KUKA. T. poV. 385. 429. 22. 2OI5.

2050 Tyc arm 1 8 8 bo sa eth KVKXw KVKXco cv no Tco-o-apa K 025. 046. 81:
Tcotrcpa A oj0a fwvr 336. 620. 2015. 2019 cfiirpoo- cv A min fereomn: cftirpoo- c
920: cvirpoo-0cv M 025. 046: ante se Pr oirur0c 920.

7. itai 1 2050 Pr S 1 TO irpeorov TO i)ov 386 wov 2 arm 1 KOI S Pr v. av0p.
oxotov avbptmna gig arm 4:

OAOIOV TTpoO-WTTO) (o)5 TTpoftiintOV Cth) VtoV OvopwITOV bo 6th Cl)V
T. irpoo-. TCT. Icuo? 325. 456 I CXCDV A 046. 104. 620. 919. 920. 1849.
2015. 2019 Or": ov K 025. 21 (325. 456. 620. 919. 920. 1849. 2050) al: x v arm
2 4: t v arm 3: 205o arm 1 To 5 AM 025. i. 35. 61. 205. 2015. 2019. 2020. 2023.
2036. 2037. 2038. 2050 al Or: 046. 21 (-35. 205. 2020. 2050) al im dxr avbpwirov
A 42. 2019 vg s 1: quasi humanam Pr: OKT av ptutroo- 025. i. 35. 61. 104. 205.
620. 1957. 2015. 2020. 2023. 2036. 2037 2038. 2041. 2050 S 8: avoptairov 046.
21 (-35. 205. 325. 456. 620. 2020. 2050). 250. 2067 Or 8 arm 1 2 8-: OAOIOV av
pcon-ov 2018: coo- oiotov av pcotra) M Kai 4 Pr TO 205 aiov 4 AK 025. 35. 468.
620. 632. 1849. 2020. 2037. 2038. 2050. 2067 al Or 8 Pr gig vg s 1 8: 046. 21 (-35.
468. 620. 632. 1849. 2020. 2050). 250 al eth (which om. ((DO? thrice before).

ra rcov. l a bo TO AM 025. 18. 35. 205. 620. 632. 919. 920. 1849. 2004.
2040. 2050 al Or 1: 046. 175. 325. 337. 386. 456. 468. 617. 1934. 2020. 2037.
2038. 2067 al w Ka6 ev avroiv A 025. 35. 104. 172. 181. 205. 250. 620. 2015.
2018. 2036. 2038. 2067 al: singula eorum Tyc gig vg: cv cxaorov avtwv K 2O2O
s 1 bo eth: O Ka.0 cavtO J. 6 J: Kao cavrcav 2050: cv Kao cv 046. 21 (- 35. 205.
620. 2020. 2050) al Or: singula 9. Kai ovav Sttmrovow TO. a So'fav icai TIXTJV
KOL ru aptcrrtav rj Kaorjfjavw crrl r3 Opovp, rep akri cts rove aiawa? raw azcovcov,
IO. irccrovvrai ot ctieoa-t rcwapc? irp r3vrcpoi frtinrtov rov KOq- fjLCVOV rl TOV
00OVOV, icat irpoakwrjcrovo-iv TO awi cfc rovs atavas rav aiavay, icat 3a ovrw rovs
orc avov? avrav cvwirtov rov 0povov, Xeyovrcs

Pr: + OTOKT 250. 424. 2018 s 1 xov A i. 42. 61. 82. 104. 172. 336. 429. 522.
620. 919. 1849. 1918. 1955. 2017. 2019: ov 046. 21 (-205. 620. 919. 1849. 2020.
2050). 250. 2037. 2038. 2067 al Or 8: exovra 025. 2020. 2024. 2050: ct 2015: x v
205: i ov K 61." Tyc Pr gig vg arm 4 ova Trrcp. o aajaw KVJcaodev airo rcuv OKV
CDV etraj cv, yciovr bo: 4-a7ro TWV ovv aji icat ciravcu, Trrcp. e Kvicxo ev KOI
y fiovrlV of8axfjm)v s 1 Trrcpvycov 046 icvicaodcv + icai 046 al p: +cfo v 61. 69
K. o-o i cao cv teat c u cv Or 8: 218. 522. 2015. 2018. 2020 arm cora0ci cfcu cv
1957. 2050: ante se et retro Pr yexovra i. 2020: cxoira 2037 o Oaxfjiovcr 620. 2036.
2037 icai 8 quae Pr OVK e ovo-tv ovx (orav K: non habebant Tyc Pr gig vg-d arm 4
iyx. ic. VVKT. aaAa iravrorc 2050 rjfjltpula–f re 632 Aeyovrea 1 A 025. 046. 21 al
pl Or: dicentes Pr gig: Acyovra no. 385. 1955. 2023. 2041: dicentia vg: +ro 2050
ayioo- ter A c 025. 205. 386. 617. 620. 632. 920 2004. 2037. 2038. 2040. 2050.
2067 al Pr gig vg s 1- 2 arm 1 2 4 bo eth: semel Or 8: bis 18. 181: sexies 141. 2020:
octies: novies 046. 35. 175. 250. 325. 337. 456. 468. 919. 1849. 1934 al mu arm 8
a KUMOO- + o-afiauq 205 o 1 K o eoo-2050 Or 8 arm 1 1 o eoo- o Travr. rafiaa6 o
TTOVTO. 35. 104. 620. 1918. 2015. 2019. 2036. 2037 o waiT. raw 0 ov eth o 2 K
2019 o coi ic o rjv 35. 201. 205. 250. 386. 2016. 2019. 2O2O. 2023. 2067 (arm) bo
sa c. o tav 620 cut o epx- eth.

9. Saxroucrik A 025. i. 632. 2015. 2019. 2020. 2036. 2037. 2050. 2067 al:
8curo0-t(v) K 046. 61. 69. 104. 181. 205. 620. 1854. 1918. 2017. 2038 Or 8:
owi(v) 31 (-205. 456. 468. 620. 632. 2020. 2050) 250 al: 6Wet 42. 141. 517: oo
325. 456: dederunt gig s 1 arm: dederant Pr ow. r. fwa aa Swo-owtv 2050 8ofavk
arm 2 a cat 2 2O5o arm 2- cvxa-piorciao- A arm 1 8: cvxopiorciav 2015. 2017. 2040:
2O5O ra povco A 2050: (in) trono Pr: rov Opovov 025. 046. 21 (-2050) al Or 8: +xai

irpoo-Kvvrjo-ovtriv (-orcixrii 2040). 920. 2040: + ai s 1 TO fcokrt. ctTt rov tfpovov
919. 1849. 2004 TW fwvri. aigWCDV vg rwi ai(i)vav 1854 aim 1: +aAiv (-f Kat)
2017. 2040 Or 8 s 1 arm 2: +cv0 uo- Pr.

10. ircffourrai. T. aiway 175 arm 3 a ircaovirai. KOI npoo-Kvvrjcrovo-tv KCU
irpocrkwqaouaiv wwiriov r. a0. o II. A tof cl, 0 Wplo? KCLl 6 0COS
    Xaj8Lv TTJV 5o av KCU r v TIA V KOU r v 8vvauv, art (rv cmcra? ra traira,
    KOI 8ia TO 0 X. r)p, d crov 5 crav jcat cue. T. wperJ. eth irccrouvrai iritrrovaiv vg
(procedunt corrupt forprotid.): cirwrrov Pr vg d T (procedebant corrupt for procid.):
circcrov arm 1 CUC + KU min p s 1 (arm 1) rcao-amr rcarcrapicr 2O2O. 2050:
rc(rraMir 620 cvuwriov. Opovuv bo ruv icafl. C7rtpr gig arm irpwrkwijcrwo-LV 18.
2004: irwo woven 6I. 11: trpoercicwow vg- ft d- f v: adorabunt (corrupt for adorabant)
Pr cur r. atoiv. TCJV. auux. TOJ cuvrt s 1 ru rtarm 4 ctcr rover awtfvacrarm 1 aicovcuv
+ awjv K 205. 2017 s 1 arm 2 cai 3axov-riv A c (?) 025. 21 (-620). 250. 2067 al Or
8 gig vg a c f s 1 2 arm 4: it. JoaAovo-iv K 046. i. 6i. m 172. 181. 429. 620. 1854.
2015. 2017. 2019. 2023. 2036. 2037. 2038 bo: K. 3aaAov vg dr: mittentes Tyc Pr
arm a awov 205 cvawr. T. 6pov. 92o. 2040.

11. ci ccrrtv arm 2: +Kvptc K o Kvpuxr AK 046. 21 (-35. 205. 620. 2020). 250.
2067 al m11 Or 8 s 1 2 arm 2 8 4 ho: icvpic 025. i. 35. 69. 104. 205. 241. 336. 620.
1854. 1918. 2015. 2019. 2020. 2036. 2037. 2038 Pr gig vg arm 1-: +i iv s 1 ic. o
6W i?ii cu 1 o25. 35. 69. 104. 205. 241 336. 620. 1854. 1918. 2015. 2019. 2020.
2036. 2037. 2038. 2067 Pr gig vg arm 1 2 a bosaeth o 2 N 468. 2050 Or 8 (i wy AN
025. 104. 205. 620. 2020. 2037, 2 3 20 S 1 P f gig v g s 1 arm bo eth: +o ovpavtocr
172: +o ayiocr 046. 21 (-205. 620. 2020. 2050). 250. 2067 al mu Or s 2 Swolfjuv.
av. ny v 620 np 2 N riyv 3 A 8wauv + Ktu 69 ra AK 025. I. 35. 205. 2015. 2019.
2020. 2023. 2036. 2037. 2038 2050 al: 046. 21 (-35. 205. 2020. 2050). 250. 2067
al Or iravra + jcat Sta crov curt? s 2 Sta bo Sia tfea art crov A: 8ta rov OtxyimToo-
o-ov 617 (s 1): ex voluntate tua (tua potestate Pr) Tyc Pr i crav K. c ct r6 haec sunt
constituta Pr vpav KU 2019 iycrav AK 21 (-18. 35. 468. 620. 2020. 2050) Or Tyc
gig vg s 1 2- arm 4: ov icrav 046. 18. 69. 2020: citri 025. i. 35. 104. 172. 250.
468. 620. 1854. 1957. 2018. 2023. 2036. 2037. 2038. 2050. (2067): rycvcro bo:
+iravra eth ckrio-0. K. curi 2067 K. ckTiaftycrava: "and stand sure" arm 1 2 3-: a

CHAPTER V, I. Kot ctsov lire TJJV Sc iai rov KafcjfjLtvov evl rov yeypavtevov
ew0ev KOL rrurpw 1, Katcvtftpayurpivov cr payicrty If 0er eirra. 2. ical effiov
iyycxov urxupov K pvoxrovra ev 0)17 fieyaa0 Tic ios vot ai TO)i? Aiov KOI Xvcrai
ras 0- payisas avrov; 3. KOI ovoyw waro cv rep oupavy r o 8c r TT S yi s ouse 1
WTOKCITW rfc odrc 6H yi s dvoi ae TO 3ift iov od8c 9Xevciv avrd. 4. ai evAatov
iroxv 1. KOI +ficra TOVTO Cth T. Se. + u ev jlt o-D Or 1: +TOV Pr Cyp ty8A.
yeypaAi. K. co"o vl A 025. 046 min omn Tyc Pr gig vg Cyp Or 1 " 5 xl XMr PM
XXT Or 8 bo eth: ciirooo-
    K Or 0 m sa omrtw A i. 69 al Or E " L- Ite-
    Fhil nr.36,
    Or s 1 arm bo eth: a foris gig: foris Tyc Pr vg: + KU oiricr ev KOI ciirpoo' 35: +
u oirto- 2038: +K C 42. 337. 468 arm 1 2 8 Karco pay. J co r payia A Fov 337: Kat
ox iy, cfO 920, 2040.

9. tisokj i icowra gig: +aaAof 172. 250. 2018. 2050 s 1 1 Krjpva-a. urxypov K wjpwnrovra + u Xcyorra eth ev AK 046. 81 (-35- 2020). 250. 2067 al mtt Or": 025. i. 35. 172. 1854. 1957. 2015. 2019. 2020. 2023. 2036. 2037. 2038. 2041 Or p, xt 37. mil. T. 36 I lgs4. + KU Xeyovra (Pr) arm 1- a

Tier +e0Tiv i vg a uxr AK 025. 35. 205. 2020. 2038. 2050. alp (Vs 1: +emv 046. 81 (-35. 205. 2020. 2050). 250. 2037. 2067 al Tyc Pr gig Cyp s 8 1.

8. eoukato K 81 (-205. 2040. 2050). 250. 2037. 2038 al: rfiwa. ro A 025. 046. 1. 6l. 69. 104. 2023. 2036. 2040. 2050. 2067 al Or: Swatat 205: + ovrc 2050 Tyc Pr Cyp (arm) ovpavu AK 025. i. 35. 172. 205. 241. 632. 1957. 2015. 2019. 2023. 2037. 2038. 2067 al Or 1 " T- Tyc Pr Cyp gig vg s 1 arm bo eth: +avw 046. 21 (-35- 205. 632. 2050). 250 al Or s 2 1 ovse 1 A 025. i. 35. 104. 205. 620. 1957. 2015. 2020. 2023. 2036. 2037. 2038 al: ovrc K 046. 91 (-35. 205. 620. 2020). 250. 2067 al mu Or 1 ewi T. yip ev Ty yij s 1: +Katw 386 ovse WOK. r. yiyo-K 181. 201. 386. 1854. 2023 arm 1 eth: post ovro pon i. 2037 ouse 8 A 025. i. 35. 104. 314. 620. 1957. 2015. 2023. 2036. 2037. 2038: owe 046. 21 (-35. 386.

620). 250. 2067 al mu Or 0t? Aiov +icai Xwoi TCWT avrov S 1 owfie 8 025. I. 35- 104. 314. 1957. 2015. 2023. 2036. 2037. 2038: ovre AK 046. 91 (-35. 205). 250. 2067 al Or 1: KM 205 s 1 arm 1-: ou yap arm 8: sed neque Pr Cyp jffaeireiv e)8Aeiroi arm 8.

4. v. 4 A 522. 2050 KOI K 025. i. 181. 2015. 2019.

5. at els K rwv Trpfo-ftvrtpwv Xeycc pot Mi) xxcuc iw (VIKTJO-W 6 Xew 6 rijs vxif lovsa, rj pi a Aavct8, dvotu TO fit, P ov Kat ras cirra o pavisas avrov. 6. Kat etsov ci ie(7a rov Opovov Kol rstv rcoyrapw uw ai CP ftevy raw irp crfivrfpj)V apviov to canicos 1 UK io-0ayicrov, c wv xepara rra Kat 5 0aaju, ois curd, a- ot euriv ra cnra uvcvLiara rov 0cov, TreoraxAfw 1 cis Travav TTK 2038 gig s 1 2 arm 2 4: +ryo 046. 21 (-2050). 250.

2037. (2067) Or 15 xlt 176(p " xl Or" Tyc Pr Cyp vg arm 1 8 cxaoav K: cicxcov K L iroxu Troxwi 046: iroxXot I arm eth: iroxAa 205: iravrco- bo: 0r phl1 xxv cvpc cvpcoyv 2020: upe0i; cr Tai K ayoi ai + cai avayvojvcu I. 35. 205. 1957. 2019. 2023 2037.

2038. 2067 arm TO JiJX.-rrfv crfpayia arm 1: KO. I Xuo-ai arm 2- " Xttrciv airro Xwrat rao- o- paytsacr ovrov Pr S 1.

6. Koi 1 +cwrwcpt0i7 2050: +i8ov Tyc: +iyx fiot bo Xryei eiircv Cyp Vg S 1 bo xoi 205 gig arm isou +yop 2050 o 2 K 69. 2015 s 1 bo sa: +ov i. 2067 77 wfa f piiiyo- arm bo eth: +TOV 35. 205. 2023 avoitai A 025. i. 35. 104. 205. 468. 620. 1957. 2015. 2019. 2020. 2023. 2036. 2037. 2038. 2050. 2067 Or p8 x! mi xxv Pr gig Cyp vg arm bo eth: avoifei s 1 2: o a otfcur 18. 2039: o a otyajv 046. 21 (18. 35. 205. 468. 620. 2020. 2050). 250 al lnu Or Kcu 2 +Xuo-at K 2067 arm 2 8 eirra s 1 arm 1 2 " bo eth o payiow + St 2040.

6. CIOK isov KGU A: ctfiov Kat tsov 172. 2018 Tyc vg ev i O"a). u Qy (-f-fat 620) 62O s 3 cv xco-u) rov Opovov Qpovoi Tyc ciiecro) 1 A 2050 icai 2 + i ctrw Pr arm TWV rto-cr. ioxdv (TO) reoxrapa oa Tyc cy o-w 2 Pr S 1 arm 4: eAjteo-w A irp (r8. +OKT arm 1- a COT KOO- A 025. 046. 21 (-149. 620. 2004. 2050) al mu Or": eor KOKr K i. 104. 149. 172. 2004. 2015. 2017. 2019: COTIKOKT 620. 2050: 2038 arm 1 2 a)o-i8. 632. 920. 2016. 2024. 2040. 2050 arm bo sa co- ayu,. ccr

payta-pevov 104. (920). 2016. 2017. 2020. 2038. 2067 arm" " e wi AK 046. 104.
429. 620. 919. 2015. 2017. 2019. 2050 Oi s. c ov 025. 21 (-620. 919. 2020) al rau
K. o0ax. 7rni2O5O 01 AK i. 172. 205. 2020. 2038. 2067: a 046. 21 (-205. 2020).
250. 2037 al pl: arwa 241. 498 ra 250. 2037 2067 rra 8 M 046. 21 (-205. 2050) al mu
Tyc Pr gig Cyp V ga. c. s i 2 arm DO. i. 181. 205. 2038. 2050 vg 4 h eth wcvfjlara
irvcvia eth: powers arm 2: powers of the spirit arm 1 8: (parts of the seven) graces of
the spirit arm 4 rov Otov Trv vfiara I: rov 0 ov arm 1 0cov +ra i. 42. 104. no. 205.
336. 620. 2036. 2037. 2038 (s 1-2) arm 1- 2- bo an-coroxicvoi A: airecr-raxicva K
I. 205. 2020. 2023. 2036. 2037. 2038. 2050 (s 2): "sent down" bo: airoorrcxXoiei
a 046. 21 (-205. 2020. 2050). 250. 2067 al mu Or 8 s 1 arm 1 8: arm 4.

yfjv. 7. KOI ri.0 V Kal ctxi cv IK rf); 8 tas rov KasrjfjL Vov fal rov Opovov.
8. Kal ore caa? cp TO ? t? Aioi, ra rcwcpa wa KCU oi cucocri Tccnrapcs wpeo-
jsvtepot ctrccrav cvcuirtov TOT) apviov, c ovres Kifldpav Kat taxa? xwras ycutovcras
tfvitaiavwv (a) 9. Kal poverty ux v Katnp Aeyovtes
"Aftos et Aa? iy TO ? t? Atoy
KOU vol(at Tas 0-0payt3as avrov,
Kal yopacras TO) 0ea) cv TO) aiiart orov ua. ry5 Kal yxaicrcny? Kal Xaov) MSS
add gloss: a? elrtp 7. KOi 2 bo ctxiy ev +TO 3ifi LOv I. 104. 205. 620. 2019. 2050
Pr gig Cyp vg- b c d fi s 1 bo sa: +avro eth CK +n r eipoo- 620 arm 1 2 3 Scfiao- x
L P 0(T gl: +TOU cov Pr Cyp TOV Ka. TTO- Ka0rip. wov (sic) Opovov-f TO ? i?
Aiov 250. 2020. 2037. 2067 Tyc vg.

8. cxapckJ aperuisset vg yst Atoi +KCU arm 8 Tco-o-cpa AK 2 020: T (7(rapa
025. 046 al pl: 01 CIK. reo-cr. Trpecr?. Kat T. TCO-CT. coa eth Tco-orapcwr 620:
Tecro-apio- 2050 evanr. T. apv. crrcoroi 205 7T o-av A I. 104. 325. 337. 452. 456.
506. 517. 620. 2023. 2050 Or 8: OTCO-OV 046. 21 (-325. 337. 456. 620. 2050).
250. 2037. 2038. 2067 al mu ckaoroo-;(O T O fet e ovreo 1 Kat ci ov arm 1 2s a
ckaoroo- +avrov S 1 2 Ki apav Kttfapao- I. 104. 205. 385. 468. 617. 620. 1957.
2019. 2023. 2037. 2038. 2041. 2067 Tyc Pr gig Cyp vg 0iaxao- vaxao- 2050: faoarjv
s 1 arm 1 2 3 a Xpwraa xp v ao r N XP va "n v sl arml 3 a I yeftowao- xeorao- 620 bo
sa: ycxovo-av s 1 arm 1 2 3 a Ovptapjatw-f- supphcationum Pr Cyp f at A 025. 21
(-2050). 250. 2037. 2038. 2067 al 1 s i. 2 Or 8: a K 046. 2019. 2050 curt rjcrav arm
1: eortv arm 8- at Trpocrcixat A K 025. 046. I. 35. 205. 241. 250. 468. 620. 632.
1957. 2015. 2019. 2020. 2023. 2036. 2037. 2038. 2041. 2050. 2067 Or 1 " xlv 3 s
1 2 arm bo eth: n-poo-c xat N 18. 61. 69. 172. 201. 218. 386. 424. 632. 920. 1849.
2040 al mu Or 8: 7rpoo- vxiv 82. 93. 104. no. 175. 177. 242. 325. 337. 385. 452.
456. 517 617. 919. 1934. 1955. 2004. 2021. 2024 I TCOV aytwv optbjy aytcov Or.

9. icai 1 S 1 asovo-Lv aowrtv A: asovrco- Pr s 1: cantabant Tyc arm (bo):
cantaverunt Cyp: + OMT Tyc Katvi wsiyv Pr Cyp vg Kauvrjv + Kat s 1 arm ct +
Kvptc gig vg v: + Kvptc o ccxr lyxwv arm 8 avotfat Avo-at s 1: resignare gig co- ay
a co- aycur 620. 2050: ijyop). TO) B (O A (eth see below): 4-iftao- K 025. 046. 21
(- 205. 620. 2040. 2050). 2037. 2067 al pl Or 8 S L (arm) bo sa: iyop. i uur rcu u
172. 250. 336. 424. 620. 1918.

10. icai evottaas avrov? Tp ep AWV ftaa-ixtiav icat tepcts, icai r ao-tacvovaw" 1
fcrl Tifc yijs.

11. icai clow icat rfttovera tjntivjjv dyyeaaii iroaAuiv jcutcaip rov 0povov,(a) Kal f 6 dnfyxos avrir ivpta cs jivptaow icai;(tata8cs Xtataow, 1 2. Aeyovres KOV xevaaj; faov 1 ortf TO dpvtov ro rfayfjl9vov Aafr?? TJJV Svvafuv icai wxovrov Kal crwfriav icat ur vv icat Tti-jyv ical Sdfav icat cvaoytav.

13. icat irav KTio-fia 8 CK TW ovpavv KOI iirl TJJS yfjs Kal vtrokavw (a) M SS add a gloss here: cai rwv ftta jcal rwr vpcffpvrtpw, 2OI6. 2OI8. 2038. 2050 Pr gig Cyp Vg: ifop. ra 0ca i uioiv 1 80. 205. 2040 sa: iyop. 17100- (-eth) cv r. CUA. crov r. co s 1- 2 eth: cv rco aifuLTt crov 632 atftari OFOiari 2040 irakrcov ua. ai jc. yxoxrcrcok ic. Xawv. c voiv arni 3 4 KCH, yaoxro o- s 1 arm 1 j. 10. ouroucr rjfuur Pr gig vg 4 arm 1 2 8: ex iis eth TW 6W rjfji v A ftaa-t tav AK 2050 Pr gig Cyp vg (s 1) arm 4 bo: in regnum dei eth: fao-tacur 046. 21 (-2050). 250. 2037. 2038. 2067 al pl Or 8 s s i p ur icpatciov K:-f cat ysao-tacur s 1 eth icat 8 eth paorixcvovcrtv A 046. 18. 325. 386. 456. 617 919. 920. 1849. 2004. 2020. 2037. 2040- al s 2: ? ao-iaewoixrii K 025. I. 35.82. 91. no. 172. 175. 177. 205. 250. 314. 337-429. 468. 620. 632. 1934. 2038. 2050. 2067 Or 8 al gig Cyp vg s 1 arm 4 bo: eth: fao-iacwoAci Pr vg arm 1- 2 s.

11. KCU cisok sa eth tovrfv A 025. 046. i. 69. 205. 2023. 2036. 2038 al p Or Tyc Pr gig vg arm 2- 3- tt bo eth: OHT vrjv M 046. 21 (-205. 337). 250. 2037. 2067 al mu s 1 2 arm 4 sa: tixr fwrj 337 TroaA. o)! ayycxoiv 920. 2040 Pr TroaAwv 62O arm 2) KVJcxul KVK oqcv i: KVKXwotv 468 icat 8-Hcvcxu) Pr arm 1)- 8- Kai TUV irpco-p. i arm 1 icat t v o apibp. avr. arm 8 uptasccr ivptas. icat Pr gig vg pvpias. uyuas. fivpuur arm: ftuptao- pvpiasw s 1- 2 icat cxtad. txta ciif xiatasco- x tacr s 1- s x " 8wv arm 2- s: +icat s 1.

12. XcyokTta Xcyoi-cov 498. 920. 2020. 2040. 2050 Pr vg Kpa ovtco- arm 1 oftov K 046. 21 min omn nd Or 1: ojtocr A (s 1) COTIK ct s 1 co- ayA.1 co- 0payarxcvov 2020 rqv 2019 arm 1 Swauv. cvxoytavj "praise and riches and honour and glory" arm 1 W. jcat arm 2- icai 1 920. 2020. 2040 Traovrov AK 025. i. 35. 205. 2020. 2037. 2050. 2067 al arm eth: rov irxovtov 046. 21 (-35. 205. 920. 2020. 2040. 2050). 250. 2038 al mu Or 1: rrjv fao-taciav bo: divinitatem vg: xryaaoirpcirciav arm 4: 920. 2040 icat 8 + TIV 386 bo icai arxw bo arm 1- 8:-f icat y8acrtactav eth icat 4- 6- 6 + TTJV bo icat cvaoyiav arm 1- 8.

13. o A 046. 21 (- 35. 205. 468 620) al Or gig s 1 bo eth: TO K: 620:-Mortv 025. i. 35. 172. 205. 250. 241. 468. 2015.

rip yip KOI fat n? s faxdwip forty, ai ra ev avroi? iravra, Xfyorra hi ro 0pova KOI r j dpny 17 cvxoyta KOI ij Tti al Sofa KOI TO xparoc efe row aiaivas rwv atuvayv. 14. ical ra rcwcpa 5a ZXcyov Auv, al ot rpco'frsrcpoc cwra?

2018. 2019. 2023. 2036. 2037. 2038. 2041. 2050. 2067 al Fr vg s 2 (arm) eiri n; r yipr cv ny yiy i. 2037 Pr s 1: eiri yi; r 336. 2015. 2036 ic. wo, r. 7770- A 025. 046. 21 (-920. 2040. 2050). 250. 2037. 2038. 2067 al Pr gig vg 0 "- s 1 2 arm eth: K 69. 181. 218. 241. 920. 2040. 2050 ve d f " arm 1 2 8- bo ai 4 +ra K (bo) eth:-l-quae sunt vg f ri T O- 0axor-OT T (nyv Qaxavvav 2020) 241. 2015. (2020). 2036. 2037 (ev HI Oaxao-oy K Pr gig vg (s 1- 2) arm bo eth): + cm(v) A 21 (35- 205. 2020. 2050) al: +ci COTIV 025. 046. I. 35. 205. 429. 1957. 2023. 2038. 2041. 2050. 2067 al: +ooracrnv 172. 250. 424. 2018 Or 8: +o rrw s 1 KOI ra 2oi9: et quae-cumque sunt Pr cv 2 r 2020 avroio- ea vg- f " v: eo vg 0- ": + sunt gig: +icai 42. 61. 69. 241. 632. 2015. 2037 iravra ifcowa Xcyovrao- 025. 1 8. 314. 2017. 2039. 2050 al p Or 8: irovro r K. Xeyokra A I. 69. 181. 2038: Travra xat TK. Xcyovrao- K 424. 429. 2019 gig S 1 (bo): vavra K. I K. Xryovrwi 250. 2018: iravra K. IJK. Xeyoira s 8: Trairao- ipr. Xeyorrao- 21 (- 18. 35. 2050). 2037 al mu Tyc Pr vg: Travrao- KCLI T K. Xeyovrao- (-TWF 172). (172). 522: vavra K. iravratr IJK. Xcyoyrao- 046: iravra ic. ipc. iraxiv Xcyovra 35: iravra Xeyovra eth ro Kaoyp. rov fca icvov S 2: o KaoripiikHr arm rco 0povu A 046. 18. 175. 250. 325. 337. 456. 617. 620. 919. 1849. 1934. 2004. 2050 al: (in) throno Tyc Pr vg: 0povo 141: rov tipovov K 025. I. 35. 205. 241. 386. 468. 632. 920. 1957. 2015. 2019. 2020. 2023. 2036. 2037. 2038. 2040. 2067 al mu Or 1: (supra) sedem gig ai 6 AK c s 2 arm 1 2 oi rw opvui) bo TO) apviu ro apvtov arm 1- a: + rj 919 i; cuxoy. icparoo- u blessed exalted (2) and glorified (+ and almighty 3) " arm 1 2 8 if O25 iy s 9i9 ai TO Kparoo-l iravroicparopoo- K (cf arm 8): arm 1 14 rwv aiwvwv arm 2 Tyc owivcov AK 025. 104. 172. 201. 205. 250. 2018. 2050 al p Or" Pr gig vg s 1 1 arm i.4. 4-a Tyv 046. 21 (- 205. 2050). 2037. 2038. 2067 al mu arm 8 eth.

14. K. r. Tfov. t a cxcy. O T)K Q20. 2040 ra 2O5- 620 rarcrcpa A 2020: rco-crapa K 025. 046 min" 1 Or cxcyov AK 025. i. 35. 104. 205. 620. 632. 919. 2015. 2018. 2019. 2020. 2023. 2036. 2037. 2038. 2050. 2067 al Or Pr gig vg s 2 arm: cxcycy 172. 250: Xcyovra 046. 18. 35. 175. 325. 337. 386. 456.

CHAPTER VI.

1. Kal ctsov ore j? voi cv TO apviov fitav c c rwv iirra teal ijjfcoucra evos fc ruiv rcoxrapcov (paw Acyovros cls 2. cat ezSov cat isov iirrros ACVJCOS, ical 6 KaovffjL vo lif avrov fyiov rofov, Kal 60rj aura) orc avot, cat c J A0cv vtkaiv icat tva 468. 617. 1849. 934- 2004 s 1 (bo) ajwv AN 025. i. 35. 69. 314. 2015. 2019. 2020. 2036. 2037. 2038. 2050. 2067 Oi 8 bo sa: TO aiipf 046. 21 (35. 920. 2020. 2040. 2050). 250 al nm ai 2 arm 01 + eucoo t T oro-apeo Pr vg v cireo-av AN 025. i. 104. no. 172. 250. 337. 429. 468. 620. 2018. 2019. 2023. 2050. 2067 al Or 8: rcow 046. 21 (-337. 468. 620. 2050). 2037. 2038 al mu: 4- cvonrtov avrov arm 1 2 3 cwwav KCU eth Trpoo'e-Kwiyo-av + viventem in saecula saeculorum Pr vg d:-f avroi arm 1 1.

1. nai fura ravra bo i5ov Pr eth ore ANC 025. I. 104. 205. 314. 620. 1957. 2020. 2023. 2036. 2037 al Pr gig s arm 4 bo: on 046. 2O (- 205. 620. 2020). 250. 2067 al pm Or" vg arm: 2038 vjvotf ev rjvvfcv N fiiav I ic ruv ctrra A C 046. 20 (-205. 325. 456). 250. 2037. 2067 alp Or" Pr gig vg s arm 8 8 4 eth: cirrao25. i. 205. 314. 325. 456 2015. 2016. 2023. 2038 al arm 1 bo sa o- payiow N (suppl. N c) f ai 620 bo sa cvoo- CKI957: voo- 920 2040: c woo- arm: eic N 468 Aeyovrocr Acyovrcov N: arm o tuvri 3povrriarpr eth fuvrj AC 046. 20 (468. 919. 920. 1849). 250. 2037 al pm Or 8 bo: wnyv N 506. 919. 1957 gig vg arm: oi o- 025. i. 314. 2016. 2038. 2067: fuvjj 104. 172. 468. 920. 1849. 1955 Ppovrrir ftpovrw s 1:-J-Acyovrocr A: + Xcyova-av arm epxov AC 025. I. 35. 60. 82. 94. 241. 432. 1957. 2015. 2019. 2020. 2023. 2037. 2038. 2041 Or 8 vg 4- " bo sa: cp ov ante CDCT ov. ftpovr. 2036: p op, ai arm 1: p ov KCLI tse N 046. 20 (-35. 2020). 61. 104. no. 172. 201. 250. 314. 385. 498. 522. 1955. 2016. 2018. 2067 Pr gig vgd- " v s eth.

2. KCU 8oi046. 20 (-35. 205. 468. 620). 250 al mu Or 1 Tyc Pr vg d- f- ": pr ai 7icowra s 1 not 1 bo CTT avrov eir avra i. 61 (?). 2037 exwv habebat vg arm:

tenebat Pr rofov sagittam Pr (vj 0cv errrjxOcv Or: arm 8 vtcwv KCLI tva VIKVJOTJ ut vinceret et victor exiit Pr vwcwv pr o A arm 2- 4 KOI tva vikTrjot) KOI cvuc crcv K bo sa: K. tva vim rct I. 2023. 2038: ic. tva vik7 T7j (-o-ci 2019) Kat CVIKICTCV 2017. 2019:. cvifnorcv K. iva vucqatj s 1: vwccov ateth icat fl 5o6 vg gig s 2 arm I.

3. Kal ore yvoitw rrjv r payi8a TTJV Scvrcpa?, fjkOixra rov Scvrepov Jwov Xcyonro? Ep;(ov.

4. Kal e i X0 v axXos ITTTTOS irvppos,

Kal r5 cat ifvp cir f avrov f r c8o'0ij avrcji 1 Aajsciv TTV ctpqnp p. aipa 5. Kai ore vot ci riv o payi a r v rplrrjv, jjjicouo-a rov rptrov pov Xcyovros "Ep ov.

ical ctSov, icai isov iinros icxas,

CTT autov c (iv (vyov cv r ctpc avrov.

3. i)poi p wfev K T7p o- payt8a riv cvrepav Axc 025. I. 172. 205 250. 314. 424. 2018. 2023. 2038 Tyc Pr gig vg arm: nyv owepai (7paytsa 046. SO (205). 2037. 2067 al pl Or 8 cpx olj AC 025. 046. 20 (-205. 386. 468). I. 6l. 69. 82. 104. no. 314. 336. 385. 498. 522. 1955. 1957. 2015. 2016. 2019. 2023. 2037. 2038. 2041 al mu Or vg s bo sa: cp oiat arm: cpxov teat t8c K 141. 172. 201. 205. 250. 386. 424. 468. 1918. 2018 2022. 2067 Tyc Pr gig vg d- v eth.

4. itai c T)X0cf at (c)isov cat isov (K. isovbo sa) t(rj 6. K 250. 424. 2018. 2067 bo sa axXoo-Tyc s 1 arm 2 bo sa Trvppoo- C 35. 175 201. 241. 242. 325. 429. 456. 468. 498. 617. 1849. 1934. 1955. 1957. 2023. 2024. 2037. 2041. 2067 al mtt Tyc Pr gig vg s arm 2: irvpoo- A 025. 046. i. 18. 61. 69. 104. 1 10. 172. 201. 205. 250. 314. 337. 385. 386. 620. 632. 919. 920. 2004. 2020. 2038. 2040 Or 1 TQ Ka077ju. vo pr tv A v avrov A C 025. 046. 20 (- 18). 250. 2037. 2038 al 1 " 11 Or 8: r avrto i. 18. 172. 2015. 2037. 2067 al p: super eum Tyc Pr: super ilium gig vg avrw K C 025. 046. 21 Or 8 vg s arm bo sa eth. The avrco should stand in the text: cf. 2 7 17 26 3 12 21. It should be restored (?) in 21: AK C 2016 Tyc Pr gig Xaj8e arm 2- c nyo- 7170- C 025. 046. 20 (-205. 620). 250. 2037. 2067 al 111 Or Tyc Pr gig vg s eth: N C: cica 104. 205. 209. 336. 620. 1918. 2038: airo nyo- yip I. 2019 al p icai iva, A C 025. I. 35. 172. 205. 250. 2018. 2019. 2020. 2038 al Or 8 Tyc Pr gig vg s 2: cat 046. 3 (- 35- 205. 2020). 2037. 2067 alp" 1 S 1 bo crtfrafawriv AC 1849. 2019: o- o ix7t(v) K 025. 046. 20 (- 1849). i. 250. 2037. 2038. 2067 al pl Or 8 ta atpa icyaxiy- A bo sa eth.

6. tjkOifek rgwfa K: yvoiyq s 1 rqv cr paytsa nyv rptnv njv rpir. crtfrpay. i. 2019. 2020 al: TJ rfpayio- 1 rpins 1 iicovon cisov bo cpxov AC 025. I. 35. 60. 91. 104. 241. 336. 432. 620. 1918. 1957. 2020. 2023. 2036. 2037. 2038 Or 8 gtg vg-K s 1 bo: + ai i c K 046. 20 (-35. (620). 2020). 61. 69. no. 172. 181. 201. 250. 314. 385. 498. 522. 1955. 2016. 2018. 2067 Pr VOL. IL 18 6. oca! rjKoixra fc favyv cv ficvnp TWV rco'crapoii yuv Xcyowrav Xolvi flrirov Srjvapiov,, icat rpeis xptvucts Kptoutv Srjvaplov, icai TO cxatov icai rov olvov prj do Kijo s 7. Kat ovf vot cv rv (r paytsa r v rcraprov, cowra QN V rov rcraprov aov Xeyovros TEpxov.

8. KOI ctsov icai 3ov nro; at 6 KaorjfjLtvos lirdvu) avrov ovopa, avnj) 6 0avaroc.(a) al o60rj avrg 1 owrla. Im TO rcraprov r (a) Here follows an interpolation: Kal 6 gftip i o otf0ei per airoo. ( ) Here follows an interpolation: dtorretrcu y fiopfalq, Kal fr ipf fr Oavdrtf Kal vrt rw Bypiw rrjt y y.

vgc. d. g-. w s s. + et fc Kai l 3o v o 4 6. 20 (- 35. 205. 468. 620). 61. 69. no.
172. 181. 201. 314. 498. 506. 517. 522. 1955. 2016 al Or 8 gig vg c- " s l eth KOI
i8ovpr ann l eth: KOI bo ITTTTOO- pr oxXocr arm 1: pr icai c i? A0cr eth xcxaaj
ieyao- 919. 2020 CTT avrov CTT avra) I. 2037. 2067 al p c wv habebat Tyc Pr vg
arm.

6. wr wmrjir Axc 025. 35. 181. 314. 2038 Or l gig vg: oxro46. 20 (-35). 250.
2037. 2067 al l Pr s arm bo sa eth I cv ULCO-W cxxetro) AC: c c ULCO-OV s 1:
xecrov 35. 205 rco-o-apcuv 8 35: s x arm l I oxov + uo onp acrov bo eth Xeyowav
Xcyovroiv gig vg arm x 04 " r w 920 Sivaptov + evocr Pr gig vg d Kpiowv A C 025.
i. 181. 205. 20 6. 2038. 2067 s 2: icpiftyo- 046. 21 (-205). 250. 2037. al r Or l s l
ovaptov 2 pr row A: +CIOCT Pr vg: 69. 181 KOL TO bo sa KOI TO cxacov KOLI
TOV otyov 2019 Tyc Pr Vg S l eth aikTfivrjor asucrjo-ur 025: abtkrforjrovtai arm 1.

7. Ti F o payisa T? K Tetaprt vj rqv rerapnyv cr payisa 2020. 2038: nv o- pay. r.
35 iKowa pr ai 325. 456 avijr AN i. 35. 1957. 2015. 2019. 2023. 2036. 2037. 2038
alp Or vg s l eth: pr nv 205: tfwvyjcr 2067: C 025. 046. 20 - 35- 2 S)- 2 5 alpm Pr
gig s a arm bo sa row rcraprov fwovj ro reraprov fwov C: rcraptov s l ip ov AC 025.
I. 104. 620. 632. 1957. 2015. 2019. 2020. 2023. 2036. 2037. 2038 al p Or 8 vg– s
l bo sa arm 4: + u ise 046. 20 (-620. 632. 2020). 250. 2067 al pm Pr gig vg c d T s
2: + tse eth: cp ofuu arm.

a KM 8ok046. 20 (-35. 205. 386. 468. 620. 632). 69. 250. 314 al mn Or l gig
vg c T arm l eth I icai i8ovpr s l eth: HOI bo: isov arm 2 wnroer pr KOI c qx0cv eth
wnroo-xxwpcxr MTTPOV xxwpov Pr s l x pov Xcvicoo- 920. 2040: pallidus Tyc
gig vg (Pr): " reddish w arm l l o Kaftyievoo- oc ravw avrovj avrov-C 025. I. 181.
205 avrw + rjy Tyc Pr: avrov S l o flavarocr 025. 046. 20 (-35. 920. 2040). 250.
2037. 2038.

9. Kcu ore ijjvot cv Tiyv 7T fj. Tmjv ar payisa, etsov VTTOAcarci) rov OwtHHrn-
jplov rots rvxas TGV c0- ayu. evav a TO? Xoyov rov flcov ical 8ta Ti)v fiaprvpiav fjv
el ov.

10. teal cicpa av fu)irfi xeyaafl Acyovrcs
V QK wore, 6 ScotToyifs 6 yiof ical ov jcptvct? ical eftstkcts ro alxa M c TWV
jcatoikovvtcov rl r s yijs; 2067 al pl Or Mt 1!1 I8? Or": o C 35. 336. 432. 920.
2023. 2040. 2041: o aoavarotr A oarjo- infernus Tyc Pr vg d f?: inferus V g. c. g. a
n Anienti" bo iKoaov i C 025. 046. 2O (-35). 250. 2067 al pl " Or" Tyc Pr gig vg
arm 1-: cucoaov ci i. 35. 1957. 2015. 2023. 2036. 2037. 2038. 2041 S utcr avrou
AC 025. I. 35. 104. 498. 620. 1957. 2015. 2023. 2036. 2037. 2038: ACT avrov
s 2: avrw M 046. SO (- 35. 620) al pm Or 8 Tyc Pr gig vg s 1: avroio- (also ruriv)
Or Mt " 80 17 avrw 046. SO (- 35. 468). 250 al pm Or 8 Pr gig vg S L 2 arm bo sa
eth: csofliy avroio-AKC 025. i. 35. 468. 2015. 2023. 2036. 2037. 2038. 2067 al p
TO TCTaorov + p. pot 452. 2015. 20x9. 2036. 2O37 i quattuor partes vg tv6avarat
ev325: cv nj 6 i ff i bo VTTOTIOV ipicov
TO T TO. ptOV TO)V OrjpkDV A.

9. TTJK irc imf)K ff payisa AC 025. 046 al: rrjv (rfpay. rrjv c. K Tyc Vg c: rrjv c.
r pay. K c 35: rrjv cr pay. T. v p. vnrfy 6 1. 69 s 1 2 arm 14 a TOV wioanyptovj-l-Toi;
0cov Tyc Pr Cyp TCOV cor ayieiov AC 046. 20 (-35. 205. 920). 250. 2037 al pl
Tyc Pr gig Cyp vg s 2 eth: pr TOV avopwrwv K 025. i. 35. 60. 181. 205. 209.

432. 1957. 2019. 2023. 2038. 2041. 2067 bo sa: TOO- ecr ayxcvacr s 1: TOIV car
paytaxckcov 104. 2 1 8. 336. 920 Or 8 Sta TOV Xoyor pr a TOV cov icai arm 1 8io 2
A Pr gig Cyp bo sa paptvpiav AKC 025. i. 241. 632. 2015. 20x9. 2036. 2037. 2038
Pr gig Cyp vg bo: ejcjcaiyo-iav 2020: +TOU apvtov 046. 20 (-632. 2020). 2067 al
pm Or 8 s 2: H-Iiyo-ov s 1:-f Iio-ou Xptcrrou 172. 250. 424. 2018: + awov Pr Cyp
arm 1 2 8 eth t v i ov K c i v rxpv K.

IO. CKpa a A C 046. 20 (- 35. 205. 632. 2020). 250 n pm p r Qyp D0. K paj ov
02. i. 35. 205. 632. 2016. 2019. 2020. 2036. 2037. 2038. 2067 Or 8 gig vg s: airov
arm 1- Qwrj p. ya rj A C 025. I. 35. 104. 205. 385. 620. 632. 2O2O. 2037. 2038.
2067 al mu Or 8 Pr gig vg Cyp s (arm) bo: fwtrjv u. cya i)v 046. 20 (-35. 205. 620.
632. 2020). 250 al m11 I ax tvoo- pr o i. 172. 429. 468. 620. (2018). 2037. 2067 c
3tjccur Cfcicqcrcur ftt e TOV AKC 046. 20 (- 35. 205. 468. 620. 2020). 250 al 1 "
11 Or 8: an-o TO V 025. i. 35. 104. 205. 468. 620. 2015. 2018. 2023. 2077. 2038.
2067 al p: cat rov 2020 ciri TT J yiorj in terris Pr Cyp.

II. KCLL eo o0i? avrots CKOOT OToar;

Kat Ippcorj avrols Iva avaurawrovrat ert povov LUicpdv, frii KUI ot oiwsovaot
aura)? Kat ot dsea ol avrcov airokrcvvco'lfat a KCU aurot.

12. Kat l8ov ore TJ oifcv T V rtpayl a rip cat crctcrios . eyas eycvcro,

Kat 6 ipatos eyevcro fieaa? a

Kat 17 o-eaiyi oaiy eyacro a alia 11. cboor). OTO T Xcuki) eso T o-av. aroaai
Acvicai Pr vg (Gyp) arm 1 avroio- cicaotO) AKC 025. 35. 61. 69. 104. 205. 250.
468. 620. 632. 1957. 2018. 2019. 2020. 2023. 2036. 2067 al p arm 4 bo: eis
singulis Pr gig Cyp: illis singulae vg: aurowr 82. 91. 93. 181: cicaotci046. SO (-35.
205. 468. 620. 632 2020) al mu Or 8 arm 1 2 8-: cicaano avrwv (2037) 2015. 2037
s eth eppeqrj fp rj M 35. 241. 522. 620. 632: cppyorj 172. 242. 250. 1957. 2018.
2024. 2039: oqrj 2038 avrours 1 avairav-o-ovrai A 025. 046. i. 104. no. 522. 620.
2015. 2019. 2036. 2038 al p: avairava-vvrai C 20 (-620). 250. 2037. 2067 al pl:
avairv V(TWT(U 69: avairavraa-0ai Or 8 TI (CTTI K) pov. XIK. C 025. i. 18. 205
632. 2015. 2036. 2037. 2038. 2067 vg s 2 bo sa: XP OIOV CTl " fw A: crixpopov
046. 20 (- 18 205. 325. 456. 632. 2020). 250 al pm: in nva xpov. xtc. 2020: n
UK. Xpov. 241. 2019 eth: eowr Kaipov xpov. UK. s 1: xpovov 325. 456: UKpo?
Or 8: ert fuKpov gig: UK. cri xp v- Cyp: XP W- f 11- arm eaxrj-hov i. 18. 35. 205.
1957. 2015. 2019. 2023. 2036. 2037. 2038. 2041. 2067 al p Traiypw oxriv AC 385
gig vg s arm bo eth: 7ra?7paxrukri(v) K 025. 046. 2O (620. 632. 2040). I. 250.
2037. 2038. 2067 al pl Or": irkqpukrovo-i 620. 632. 2015. 2016. 2019 2036. 2040:
impleatur numerus Cyp KCLI 01 (rwsouaoi 2019: Kai 046 Cyp vg bo KU 01 asea ot
Kat 386 ot LicaAovt or A C 025. 35 205. 620 Or 8 vg s 1 2 bo: pr Kat 046. 2O (-35
205. 620). 2037 al mu (Cyp) ot icaA. avokTtw. qui occidentur gig airokT vieo-0at
AKC 35. 82. 93. 94. 175. 205. 241. 250. 325. 337 456. 617. 919. 920. 1955.
2004. 2018. 2024: +UTT avniv K (del. K c): atTOKrcvcor at 1 8. 42. 91. 104. 1
10. 172. 242. 385. 386. 468. 506. 620. 632. 1849. 1934. 2015. 2016. 2017. 2019.
2023. 2024. 2036. 2039. 2040. 2041: airokT iv crocu 025. 046. I. 6 1. 69. 336.
429. 498 Or 8 (vel rcvco-ftu): avooavctv arm OKT at avrot Kat 3 85. 2020: exemplo
ipsorum Cyp.

12. i8oki8. 94. 141. 385. 429. 522. 1849. 1 9SS- 2039- 2040 Tyc eth ore TVOIV ore ewfev (rjwfa K c): pr Kat 025. i. 35. 42. 61. 69. 181. 205. 209. 432. 468. 1957. 2019. 2023 2041 Pr rrfv o-fpayi8a rrfv Krrjv nyv CKT. o-0pay. Pr Tyc pr tsov A Vg r: a)(r s 1 iryacr cycycro KC 025. 046.

13. KOI ol dorepes rov ovpavov rerav cis T V yijv, OK OTJKIJ jsoxXci TOW oxviflovs wro dvciov xcyaxov crcioievi

Kai irav opos KOI vfjros CK Tov TOUW avrw 5. Kai ol frurtxcis r yi Kai 01 icyioravcs Kai 01 txiap ot teat ol irxouoioi Kai ol ur vpot Kai ras fiovxos Kai cxcvpos Kpwfav caurovs cis ra OTTTJXata Kai cis ra? irerpas TQI 6pcav.

30. 250. 2037. 2038. 2067 alp 1 Or 8 Pr arm 8:- A 2016 Tyc gig vg arm 4 cyevcro ficxocr AC 025. I. 35. 205. 2015. 2019. 2020. 2036. 2037. 2038. 2067 Tyc Pr gig vg arm 4: 046. SO (-35. 205. 2020). 61. 69. 104. no. 172. 201. 250, 314. 498. 5 22- 1 955- I 957- 2016. 2018. 2023. 2041 al p Or 8 oxr. Tpi ivocr eth o-akcocr ao-KOO- S 1 f) vtxrjvri o rj Afctc 046. 80 (35- 20 5)- 2o6 7 alpm Or 8 Tyc (gig) vg s 1- 2 bo eth: "the moon wholly" arm 1 2 3 a: 0X17 025. i. 35. 172. 205. 250. 1957. 2018. 2023. 2037. 2038. 2041. 2067 Pr sa oxr atia cicr aita 1934: wo- Pr gig arm.

13. TOU oupavou TOU Ocov A: Tyc Pr vg d f: de coelo (post 7T (rav pon gig bo eth) gig arm bo eth en-co-ay A C 025. i. 104. 337. 429. 2015 al p Or: CTTCO-OV 046. 80 (-337). 250. 2037. 2038. 2067 al mu arm 4: " wen shaken down " arm 1 2 3 cio-rrfv yyv 7ri TT? V yyv 241. 468. 2038 s 1: super terrain vg arm 4 (bo): gig OTVKTJ + o-cioicny (Tyc) jsoxXci AC 025. 046. 35. 61. 69. 2019. 2023. 2037. 2038. 2067 T)C Pr gig vg arm 4: airo? axXci 2015. 2036: ? axei i: j axXovcra K 1 8. 172. 205. 250. 336. 429. 468. 498. 620. 1918. 2039 Or"s:)8axowa 20 (-18. 35. 205. 468. 620. 2020) 42. 93. 94. 141. 201. 209. 218. 241. 242. 385. 424. 452. 506. 517. 522. 1955. 2016. 2017. 2O2 1 al p: atTofoxowa 2020 wro airo K 69. 2016 arciov ficyaxov A C 046. 20 (-35. 205). 250 al lnu Or 8 Pr gig vg: 025- i. 35. 2015. 2037. 2038. 2067: A yaxovtyc. wro icy. (TCioiev) aiciov 205 (rcioici (TaxruoAcn; A 181: r o-ACVOU 456.

14. o i aire wpwr arm T 2 a bo: CTOKT s 1 arm 4: i- 0r eth oxr jstjsXiov xat oxr ? i? Xia s 1 cxio-o-oicvov AC 046. 35. 69. 82. 104. 250. 337. 468. 2023. 2040 al mu Or 8 Tyc Pr gig vg s 2 bo eth: ix ro-ouirov 025. i. 2019. 2023. 2036. 2037. 2038: exurroxcvor K 20 (-35. 337. 468. 632. 2040). 1 10. 314. 1957. 2016. 2067 al p: cixunroicyoor 632: cxurcroirai s 1: cixi arm bo npocr njo-crocr C 046: jsowocr K: insulae Tyc Pr vg: pr iracra s 1 bo sa avro)i CKtn?0iprav N C 025. 046 mm p: : airtkCivrjaav A:-ccraxcv orar 920. 2040.

15. Kai 8 A x L ia PX 1 irxovcrioi i. 2019, 2020. 2038 16. KOLI Xcyovortv rots opeo tv icat rats irerpats nco-arc e lywis icat icpityarc 1740 dvo irpoo-coirov rov icaflip- ftevov eirt rov Opovov Kal diro ri opy s rov dpvtov, 17. ori X0cv ij i7tepa ij xcyaxi; r 9 opyijs avrov, icat rts Svyarat ora vac; al p icat ot terxvpoti. 181. 2019. 2038: ott 2024. 2O 4 I icat cxevdepoo' AC 046. 90 (-35. 205. 2020). 250 alp m Or 8 Pr gig vg S: icat TOO- excvtfepoo- K 025. I. 35. 205. 1957. 2015. 2020. 2023. 2037. 2038. 2041. 2067: K arm 4: at irarreo- ot cxcv cpot arm bo Trcrpcur otrao- arm bo.

16. KOU Xeyouo-ik dicentes Pr: icat tirov arm 1 roto-opcatv cot rato- Trerpato- bo arm 4: Tyc: icat rato- wcrpato- arm 1- irco-are A 025. 104. 2015. 2036 Or 8:

flwrre C 046. 20 I. 250. 2037. 2038. 2067 al pl: 7TC(T Tou K jcpwrarc Kpv erat S:
Kpv f T 385 I awo irpoorwirov. rov apvtovarm a rov ica i;-fifvov. rrjar opyrjrs l eirt
rov Opovov AC 025. I. 35. 69. 104. 205. 241. 468. 632. 1957. 2015. 2019. 2020.
2023. 2036. 2037. 2038. 2067 al mu Or 8: eirt ro Opovu K 046. 20 (- 35. 205. 468.
632. 2020). 250 al mu: supra sedem gig: super thronum (Pr) vg a7To K c l rt K.

17. OTior. tj t) cpa r ficyax 71)0- opyrja aurou r; ficyaxr; TTyo" opyntr avrov ificpa
18 T7 1 2OO4. 2020 17 ficyaxi 69. 325. 456. 517 avrov A 025. 046. 20 (- 2020).
250. 2037. 2038. 2067 alpi Or 8 Pr arm 1- bo: avrwi C 2020 gig vg s 1 2 arm 4 sa
rra0r vai rw r)vcu 141. 242. 617. 1934: rrrjv(u, 250. 429. 2018. 2019:-f ante ilium
Pr arm 1-8 bo.

CHAPTER VII.

I. r Mcra 1 rovvo elow rco-rrapas ayycxovs oroxra? iirl ra? rco-crapa? yovta r s
yijs, Kparofwas rovs rcwapag ai eiovsr TIS 7 5, Tya x irvcj; avcAO? eirt r s y s iiyre
eirt r s axao-OTys II; T e? rt 1. fcra AC Or 8 Pr gig vg sa: pr cat K 025. 046 21. 250.
2037. 2038. 2067 al pl s arm 8 (bo) eth rovro AKC 046. 21 (-205. 468. 920. 2040).
250 al pm Or 8 s arm eth: ravra 025. i. 61. 205. 241. 468. 920. 2015. 2019. 2036.
2037. 2038. 2040. 2067 Pr gig vg bo Tttrarapatr 1 C 025. 046. 21 (-35. 866) Or 1:
T nraper A: K 35. 866 eirt per Pr Teoxrapatr 8 A C 046. 21 (- 35) Or 8: Tccrcrctpco-
025: o 35 icparovkrao- pr icat 337 s arm 1- icparowroo-. avciow r. yiyo- eth

KG 025. 046. 21 (- 35) Or 8: recrrropco- A: 835 npr yipr 2020. 2037 s 1 bo sa I
wcrj irvevcny K 172. 205. 250: irvcet 2019.

r t n" 1 ScvSpov f. 2. Kal etsov dxXov ayycxov avaftalvovra dhro T favaroxijs 1 i
Xtov, c ovta o payisa 0cou wvros, KOI Kpav 1 iwh avjj cyaxfl rots rcwapo'iv dyycxot?
ols c8o'6 avrois dstjciprat riv "W 0 yi v ical rijv 0axaoro-av, 3. Xcycov M f 081 17017
rvpr yi v ire 1 TTV d 0axacrrav prc ra 8cvSpa, a pt rpayirw v rovs Sovxovs rov 0cov
wv cvl rwv icTaliriov avruv.

4. Kal jjffcovcra rov apiopjov TOW co payurACFayy cxarov rco'ora-rcwapcs x 1
5 payurfifvoi IK Trcwn5 (Or): ir (n7 920. 2040: flarent Pr vg ft bo aveLior pr o C
61. 69. 506. 522. 632. 919. 920. 1955. 2040: Pr vg f v arm 2: 01 cwexot bo em
TT T yrj(r A: in terris Pr ri n r oxao-o-jyo- TTO- A: +fjirjt cm TOF vorap v bo eiri TI
Scvspov C 046. 21 (-35- 205)- 2 5 alpm Or" (Pr gg v g): wuwso iw K 025. i. 35.
205. 1957. 2015. 2019. 2023. 2036. 2037. 2038. 2041 s 1: CTTI Sevspov A: cirt
(ra) 8cv8pa s 2 r arm bo eth.

3. oxXof ayyexof 42. 325. 456. 468. 620. 866. 1934. 1957.

2036: axXov Pr axXov. avaflauvovta KOL avcftij axXoo-ayycxoo eth ava aiyovra
avaftavra i bo avarox o NC 025. 046. 21 (-18). 250. 2037. 2038. 2067 al pl Or 8 s
2: avaroxwv A 18. 2039 (s 1) o- payi8a et N c o-ayisa N ov pr TOV 325. 456. 468.
620. 866 iitoor pr rov 468 cxpa cv KC 046. 21. 250. 2037. 2038 al pi Or Tyc Pr
gig vg s arm bo: ccpoy A 025. 2067 t wr) fi ya rf t(ivyv pfyaxy 866 reo-crapcriv et tf
5 rco-o-apco- N: 5 35 ayycxoio- fwoio arm 4 oio- cso i eo quod datum esset Pr avro
r35. 336. 337. 2015. 2023. 2036.

2037 gig vg I astkTcrai axroxccrat arm 1.

3. Xcyu J +zvroio- Pr bo eth akTytnrc asim rcrai K: +lurjtt Or 10! 6 iiyrc nyv
axao-crav C 025. 046. 21 (-866. 2020). 250. 2037. 2067 al 1 O 0 16: Aif nyv 0.
K 866 2038: KO. I TI V 0. A 432. 452. 2020. 2021 Or bo sa jbnrc 2 prjbc K 866

axpc (-r) A C 025. I. 35. 181. 2038 Or j016: axpio- ou 046. 21 (35). 250. 2067
al pl Or: axpto- av 94. 2015. 2036. 2037: iva arm 8 o- payuro)i r o- payuroicv 337.
2016. 2020.: " I shall have sealed " arm 1: o- paytotyrc bo: afpayurqwri eth TIWV
24i. 2015. 2039. 2040 Tyc s 1 bo sa eth.

4. Kai t)KOVra. eo payurjicw A rov apibpw p2O. 2040 cor payuricvctfv + art rov
ftcranrov avrwv bo cicarov. cor payicrtcKOf i8. 141. 385. 429. 919. 920. 1849.
2OO 4- 20 39 2040. 2067 cicarov retro, rcotrapco 025. 205. 386. 620. 866. 1934:
cxarov KOJL rcotr. rcororapco- C 82. 104. 172. 175. 250.314. 325. 337. 456. 468.
617. 632. 1957. 2018. 2041: (ocarov) acarov xai rcoro-. KOI rcflraapca- 498 (2020):
cxarov rco-o-. KO. I rcoxrapeo- 69: p fi S 046. I. 35 al mu: cicarov rco-crcpakOvra
(rco-o-apakovra A) A: CK. rco-cr. 8 A ccrpay rie oi AKC 025. I. 35.

IK tv y Pov3rjv Scoow xixiascs, (a) 7. c c cwxijs 2v4 a cvc jkvx? s Aevl e 1 fv fjs
Icrcra ap Scieica txc 8. cv vxijs Zafiovxuv ftoscica

CK vx7s Bci'taAciv Swseica x-w es eo-payto-ievoi, 5 C eic fv rj; Fas 3o3c ca xi
6. cic vx?7s Acrip 8(oscjca cic (a) On the restoration of the original order of the text,
see vol. i. 207 sqq.

205. 632. 2020. 2037. 2038 al mu Or 10 3q BM11C) Tyc Pr gig vg s 8 bo: (r
paytorA vwv 046. 21 (35. 205. 632. 2020). 69. 82. 104. 201. 250. 314. 498.
2016. 2017. 2018. 2036 al p Or 8: s! sa: + em r. JICTWTTWI avrwv bo vtoiv Icrpa
X vuuv- arm 2- 4 eth: lo-pa Xttto s 2.

5 h. ca payiap. cioi A C 025. 35. 468. 632. 2020 Or 8 Pr gig vg s 2:-p. vai 046.
21 (-35. 468. 632. 2020). 82. 201. 314. 385. 498. 1955. 2016. 2017 al p:-fteiwv
69. 104. 522: s l arm 3 4 bo eth Povfiyv A C 025. 046. 175 Or 8: POV LV 61. 69.
104. 201. 337. 498. 617. 919. 1955. 2004. 2015: Povftip, i. 18 35. 93. 386. 456.
468. 620. 632. 920. 1849. 2017. 2019. 2020 2036. 2037. 2038. 2040. 2067: Pov?
ct 60. 91. 172. 205. 385 1934. 2018. 2023. 2041: Povpcw 250. 2016: Pov3rjfjl 314
325. 506. 517. 620. 866. 2024: Ruben Pr gig vg: Rouben bo.

7. CK 4ux. IUJJL. 8w8. x X. K 172 Acvi Acvci K: Aevi et lo-a ap s 1 Icro-axap
A 025. 6l. 104. 385. 522. 919. 1955. 2017 al p Or 8 vg arm 1 2 3: lo-a ap C 046.
21 (-919) s 1 arm 4 bo: Isachar Pr: Ysacar gig.

8. CK 4ux. Zap. 8wo. X tx- 1849 Zafiovxw. IOKTI; 1934 I(oo-i7. BcvtaAciv K
2015 Beviaictv A 025. 920. 2038: Bewauv C 046. 21 (-456. 620. 866. 920) al pl Or
8 Pr gig vg s bo: Bciiafup 242. 456. 620. 866. 2017 ccr payicr-fitvot A C 025. 35.
205. 468. 632. 2020 Or 8 gig vg s 1 bo:-ACVCU 046. 21 - 35. 205. 468. 632. 920.
2020. 2040) al lim: 92O. 2040 Pr s 8.

5 C. CK 4ux. Tos. 8w8. X ix. K Tos Aav 42. 325 (pr man. scripsit in marg) 336.
456. 620. 866: Aas i: Oath Pr.

6. CK 4ov An)p 8w8. X ix. Or 8 Ne oxin A 046. 6 1. 69. 175. 314. 325.
429. 456. 617. 620. 866. 919. 920. 1849. 1955. 2004 al vg: Nephtalim arm 1- a:
Neptalim Pr gig: Nc oxi M s: Nc oxiv C: Nc ox 69. 201. 386. 517. 522: Eph thalim
bo: Ne 0axcix 025. i. 18. 35. 61. 104. 172. 205. 241.

9. MCTOL ravra
KOI Mow oxxo? iroxus, Sv pt0fi7 ru avrov ovsei? vvaro 9 IK irairos e0vovs icat v
wr KGLI Xaak KCLL yxaxrcroiv, corarrc? CVCOTTIOV rov Opovov KOL ivwriov
rov dpviov, t ircpifcJXiyjlcvovs f oroxas Xcvicas, Kat (xnvucc? fr rats

Xcpcrlv avrcov I o. icat Kpdfcavcrtv xovfl xcyaxT; Xeyovrcs
CTTI T 242. 250. 337. 385. 468. 498. 632. 1934. 1957. 2015. 2016. 2017.
2O18. 2019. 2O20. 2O23. 2O24. 2037. 2038. 2039. 2040. 2041.
2067 al mu Or" I cic va. Mav. 8a8. X- 620. 866 Mavao-(ny K 025. 21 (- 175.
205. 620. 866). i. 250. 2067 al pl Or Pr gig vg arm: Mavao-crryv C: Mawaao A:
Mavaoty 046. 175. 205.
  2037. 2038 s: Dan bo.
  9. jura pr KCLI s 1 arm 1 bo eth KU i8ov K 025. 046. 21. 250. 2037. 2038. 2067
al 1 Or" Tyc gig s 2: A Pr Cyp vg s 1 bo sa: isou C oxxoo- iroxw C 025. 046. 21.
250. 2037.
  2038. 2067 al pl Tyc gig s 2: iroxvo- Or": oxxov woxw A Pr Cyp vg s 1 bo ov et
K ocr K: icoi A avrov A C 025. i. 61. 69. 205. 2019 al p Or" s bo: 046. 21 (-205).
104. 172. 201. 241. 242. 250. 314. 385. 429. 498. 522. 1955. 1957. 2015. 2016.
2017. 2018. 2023. 2024. 2037. 2038. 2039. 2041. 2067 al p Tyc P r gig Cyp vg
csvvaro A C 046. 21 (-205. 2040) al pl: i vvaro P25. I. 61. 69. 172. 205. 241. 250.
2015. 2023. 2037. 2040. 2067 al mu Or": Swaroi 2038 arm 4 c iravrocr tovoo- CK
irairuy 0vov Tyc gig vg arm 8- 4 vxwv fv rjr s 1 Pr Cyp KOI Xacov feat yxoxrrov eth
corcorco- AK 025. I. 35. 205. 1957. 2004. 2019. 2023. 2024. 2037. 2038. 2067
al p s: corwrao- 046. 21 (-35. 205. 2004. 2020). 250 al mu Or": coromov C 2020:
ecrrwra 93. 1955: stantes Pr gig Cyp vg cvowriov 1 nri A ir ptp px. Tip. vovcr AK
C 046. 21 (-35. 205. 2040). 250 al pm gig: 7rcpi3e? XT Acvar 242. 2040: ircp j
Xi7xcvoi K c 025. I. 35. 205. 1957. 2015. 2019. 2023. 2037. 2038. 2067 al p Or"
Tyc vg: Kat ircpi? cj3Xwicioi s 1: et erant amicti Pr Cyp otvtxeo- A C 025. i. 35.
104. 172. 205. 250. 2018. 2019. 2020. 2037. 2038. 2067 al p gig vg arm: palmae
fuerunt Pr Cyp: foivikao- N 046. 21 (-35. 205. 2020). 61. 69. 201. 241. 242. 314.
385. 429. 498. 522. 1957. 2015. 2016. 2017. 2023. 2024. 2039. 2041 al mu Or":
Kioapau bo cv raio- x f ltLV P r i? ow Pr gig Cyp.
  10. icai 1 i. 2067 bo. Kpalotkriy Kpafovr a- i. 2067 bo s 1: tkpa ov Pr gig Cyp
vg arm j Xcyoirco- pr icat 2067 s 1: cxcyov arm 1: KOI cxc ay arm 2 (T co rov 6tov
A (in marg.) bo: 0 0 I. 2037 (poSt TO) a CITi TO) BpoV.) TO) KO CVO) K II. Kai
irawcs ol ayyexot IOTI KCIOW Kvvcxtp rot; Opovov Kal rwv Trp r3vt piv Kal rgv
Tcoxrapaw UMIV, Kal lirccrav vanriov TOV Opovov farl ra fl-poo-coira avtaii Kal
irpocrekvvrfa-av TS 0ep, 1 2. Xeyovres
  Aiiji v evxoyia Kal 8d a Kal 17 cro ta
  Kal 17 cvxapioTia Kal 17 TIAI) Kal 17 Svvau?
  Kai 17 icr vs TO) 0 j MOP cfc TOVS aiuwas row aiowa)? diiyv 13. Kal a7T
Kpi(h els CK rov irpco-jsvrcpctfi Xcycov lot Ovroi ot Trcpt eysX icvoi ras oroxas ras
XCVKOIS rtvc9 curiv Kal TTO CV 14. ical Lprjka avra) Kvpte iov, o-v otsa?. Kal
ctn-cv tot
  Oirroi cio-tv ot cpxopwoi IK rj?9 0Xi cu s T
  Kal Zirxvyap ra? oroxas avrtov,
  Kal IXcvkavav avras cv ra aifuxrt rov apviov.
  (suppl. K c): pr Kai s 1 CTTC TOJ 0povw A C 025. 81 (- 205. 468. 632. 2020).
250. 2067 al lnu: eiri TOV Oporov K c 046. i. 104. 205. 468. 632. 2019. 2020.

2036. 2037. 2038 al mu Or's 1: super thronum Pr Cyp vg: supra sedem gig TOI awoo rov apviov K:-f icr TOW aioivao- TO V atcuvwv aii K (del. K c).

11. 01 K (suppl. K c) loriyiccmrav AK (- Kto-a K) 025: tvrrjkicrav C: eionKiyo-av 046. 104. 919. 2017. 2018. 2036: cim? Kcio-av 21 (-205. 919). 250. 2037. 2067 al pl Or 8: Lorrrj Kco-av i. 205: stabant Tyc Pr gig vg arm bo KUKXw eiowrtov bo 7T rav A C 025. 42. 181. 325. 337. 468. 517. 620. 866 al p Or 8: CTTCCTOV 046. 21 (- 325. 337. 468. 620. 866). 250. 2037. 2038. 2067 al pl evwtrtov. Trpocrajtrov airrwv CTTI r. irpoo; avrcov cvowriov T. Qpov. bo sa eth TOV Opovov A C 025. 35. 205. 920. 2020. 2037. 2038. 2040. 2067 al Or 8 Pr gig vg s 1 arm- 3- a bo: + aurov 046. 21 (- 35. 205. 920. 2020. 2040). 250 al S 2 eiri Ta irpooxinra CTTI irpoo a7roy I. 2038. 2067 bo: arm 1 Kai Trpoo-ckw o-av TW 0 (o s j Kai CTrco-av. Xeyoirecr CTTI T. Trpoo-coira avrcov cvonriov T. Opovov TOV O QV 12. apj pr ayuxr ayuxr ayioo 205 cvxoyia. 8o a- s 1 eth Kai 17 ro ia A arm 4: ante 17 8o a pon 506: post K. 17 cvx a P toTta pon 2067 17 cu apicrria i; K (suppl. K c) rj np. fi eth Kai rj KTYWT bo: Kai 17 x a P tcr arm L 2: i) c ovo-ia arm 8 TU coi TOV 0cov bo: TD Kvpico arm 1 TO) co) arm a aiqv C 2015. 2019 Pr.

18. oirckpior + fjiot Tyc gig: Xeyci AOI arm 1- eth CK K 1957 Xeywv pot gig arm 1 2 8- eth: xoi Tyc arm 4 TOO- oroxao TOO- Xcvkao-J TOO Xcvkao 1 crroxao-2015. 2036 I Toor 2 C I TIVCO- urtv Kai eth: euriv i. 181. 2038 17X60? veniunt vg f- arm 1-.

14. xai bo sa ftprjua AKC 025. i. 205. 2015. 2019. 2036. 2037. 2038. 2067 al p Or": rov 046. 21 (- 205). 250. al pm: dixi Pr gig Cyp vg: Xcyw arm 1 Kvpie uv C 025. 046.

1 5. Scot TOVTO curiv cvbnriov TOV Bpovov TOV 0cov,

KCU Xatp vowiv avra ACpas ical yvjcro? cv TW pcup avrou, teal 6 Jca0i7j, cvo? cvt frov 0povovf crmvowci cv avrovs.

1 6. ov irctvcwrovcrtv CTI ov8c Sufrjcrovo-iv cri, ov8c M) iraurg? TI avrovs 6 17X10 ovsc wav jcavfia, 1 7. on TO dpviov TO dva MOW rov Opovav Troimavct avrovs, ical otyijo'ci avtovs cirt an s myyas vsutcov gal c axctyci 6 0eos irav Sakpvov CK rav of0axfj. i)V avrcov.

21 (-205). 250. 2037. 2038. 2067 al pm Or" vg s arm 8 4 bo: tov A i. 205 Pr gig Cyp arm 1 w v Xcyct gig arm 1 ot pxopcvoi qui venerunt Tyc Pr Cyp eth: qui veniunt gig vg arm bo c TTO 0Aurcar ncr utcyaxicr a? ro tfaiirccixr xcyaxicr A CTrxwav AK 046. 18. 35. 175. 205. 468. 617. 620. 632. 1934. 2020 Or Tyc gig vg Cyp s arm bo: CTrxarwav 42. 82. 201. 325. 337. 385. 386. 429. 452. 456. 468. 498. 522. 632. 919. 920. 1849. 1955. 2004. 2021. 2024. 2040: cirxareivav I: VKCLVOLV 2015: Pr f KCH exewcapav avrowr Tyc: "made them glorious" bo Kat 4 62o. 866 avrao- As 025. i. 35. 60. 93. 181. 205. 209. 432. 468. 1957. 2015. 2023. 2036. 2038. 2041. 2067 gig vg Cyp s arm 4 bo: avrao 2037: 046. 21 (-35. 205. 468). 250 al mu Or" Pr arm.

15. oia TOUTO pr cat 046. 2015. 2036. 2037. 2067 riv rj Qov eth Xarpcvovcriv So a ovo-tv eth o Kabrjfjl vocr his q ii sedet Pr Cyp cm TOV Opovov AK i. 61. 172. 205. 250. 385. 2015. 2018. 2019. 2020. 2023. 2037. 2038. 2067 al mu Or" s 1: CTI TO) Opovw 025. 046. 21 (- 205. 2020) al mu: supra sedem gig: in throno Tyc Pr vg Cyp O-K IXOO-CI r avrovo- N 0- c: yivcikTfcci avrovo K: ytvwo-KCt ir

avrovo- K c: habitavit supra illos gig: inhabitavit super eos Cyp: habitat super eos Tyc: inhabitavit in eis Pr: " dwelleth in them " arm 1 2 3- I.

16. eri 1 A 025. 046. 21. 250. 2037. 2038. 2067 al 1 " Or 8 gig: K 2019 Pr vg Cyp s arm 3 4 bo sa ovsY + 117 A 61. 69 Or 8 Sti iyo-ovo-iv Sn ao-ovo-tv tc 385: Swf o'wariv 025. 69. 2038 crt 2 A 046. 21 (205. 2020). 2067 al pl Or 8 vg s 2 arm 2 bo: umquam Prcp: 025. i. 141. 172. 205. 250. 424. 2018. 2019. 2020. 2037. 2038 gig s 1 arm 1 8 4 a: + " neither shall they toil " bo pi) waicn; m an emendation of Gwynn and Swete of fwy way an A 025. i. 35. 69. 2015. 2019. 2036 al p: ov p. v) ir (TTfj cirt 046. 21 (35. 2020). 250. 2037. 2038. 2067 al pm Or 8: ov fit) ir crqrai CTTI 2020 o 17X0)0- o 2020 2037: "cold" arm 1 2 3: "shadow" bo irov Tyc arm: TO 314. 2016 icavxa-f patientur Pr Cyp.

17. aya IICOTOK cvumov bo eth Trotxavct AK 025. 046. I. 35. (n. 69. 104. 205. 314. 429. 468 620. 866. 2015. 2019. 2020. 2023. 2036. 2037. 2038. 2041. 2067. s arm sa: reget gig vg Cyp: irotAcuvci 21 (- 35. 205. 468. 620. 866, 2020). 42. 82.

CHAPTER VIIL I. Koi ow jjvot cv TTJV o- pavtoa rrjv cffioup, Jycwto o-iyiy fr Ttjj ovpawji uwpov.(a) 3. Kai f aaAos f ( ) iyycaos j Xtfcv KCU- cvrra0ty hri r ro tfwukmjpun 1 exw Xiftavwbv xpvtrow, ical 4 o0i? ryrfov gfl j fofuapara roaAa, 2Va ow Tat irpoo-cu;(a? s TOW dyiw TTOLVTW m TO Qwruurrripwv TO xpwow TO evumoy TOV Opovov, 4. cat aiety (a) Verse 2 is restored in what appears to have been its original form after 8. See vol. i. 218-222, 224. (J) Read eli.

91. 141. 172. 201. 218. 241. 242. 250. 385. 424. 432. 498. 522. 1955. 1957. 2016. 2017. 2018. 2021. 2023. 2024. 2039. 2041 Or 8: regit Pr: ircpttraret ACT ainw bo oosyiprct Atf 025. 046. i. 35. 61. 69. 20. 2015. 2019. 2020. 2036. 2037. 2038. 2067 al p Or 1 Tyc gig Cyp vg s arm bo: oo ya 21 (-35. 205. 2020). 42. 82. 91. 104. 250. 385. 429. 2016. 2017 al mu Pr coi7rj (oxroo- I. 2020. 2036. 2037. 2038. 2067: CDTV KOI CTTI s 1 inryoo 1 fontem Pr arm bo KO. I. c axci ci. o Sax v avrcov 2020 cfaxei i efcxct 35 o Otocr s 1 arm 2 4 iraf Sakpvoi irolv Spakvov K 17ravta Ta ovifcpva 69 arm: Sa pvov eth CK TDF o Boxffmv AC 025. 046. 21 (- 325. 456. 468. 620. 866. 920. 2040). 250. 2038 al 1 " 11 Pr gig Cyp vg s: euro TWV o 0ax-fuDv K 61. 104. 241. 325. 456. 468. 620. 866. 920. 2015. 2023. 2024. 2036. 2037. 2040. 2067 al p Or 8 vg d T.

1. Koityc orav AC: ore N 025. 046. 21. 250. 2037. 2038. 2067 al Or 8 1 cnyiy twvrj bo yiio)pov AC 337. 498. 1957: rifuMpiov (i- K) K 025. 046. 21 (-337. 866). 250. 2037. 2038. 2067 al 1 Or 8 s: semihora Pr gig: media hora Tyc vg: wpav bo.

8. ayycxoirs 1 7X ev c Adcv 69: before axXoo- arm 1 2 ri TO Bvffuumjpiov A 025. I. 35. 205. 2019. 2023 al mu: tm TOV foo-iooritymov K 046. 21 (-35. 205). 69. 104. 250. 314. 385. 2015. 2016. 2018. 2037. 2067 al! nu Or 8: em TOV flimaernypiov C: ante altare Tyc gig vg arm 1 eth: super altanum Dei Pr: "at the altar" arm 2 8 4 cxw KU ix v arm 1 2 eth: xei arm 8 I ifio. vorrw Xifavov TO C VAIOUITO supplicamenta Pr iva 6Wcis 1 owct AKC i. 35. no. 172. 201. 250. 337. 386. 632, 2015. 2037. 2038. 2040 al p: owiy 025. 046. 21 (- 35. 3 2 5- 337- 3 86- 456- 632. 2040). 250. 2067 al mu Or 8: u 69. 314. 325. 456. 2019 TOUT irpoo'cvyoto- Tao-cvxao 2 5: orationes gig arm 1: de orationibus vg T: " along with the prayers n bo Ovo-uurrriptqv + TOV 0eov Pr TO wimnw TO K arm 1 2 s tt.

4. awpt) o Kairw K c: amftrj Kaarvoa K: o 506: av 3rj arm 8 1 wv 6vp, uifuLnjv supplicationum Pr TOUT 6 KCL7TVOS TO)V OvfluLfjUOftoV Tttts irpoTCVXCUS TWV dyi(l)V dyyexov cvunrioi TOV 0cov. 5. KOI cta. i ci 6 ayycxos TOP XiJaveotov, KCU yciircj avrov cic TOV irvpoc TOV Ownaumjplav, KOI Iftaxtv cts T F yiyv, ai iycvavtO f ftpovral KOI dorpairai ical ara t " (rciorias.

2. Kal flow f TOV? CTrra f (a) iyyovs (3) KO! r crav 1 afrofc W V f C7rra f (a) craxiriyycs. 6. xal ol t a f (a) dyyeaoi ot ras f fora t (a) craxmyyas qrofficurav avrovs tva ra 7ricruxri.

(a) Read rpccs in the first two cases after the noun but without change of order in the next two. See vol. i. 218-223.

( ) The interpolator of viii. 7-12, to whom the changes in the text are due, added here of cinoy rov Beov trr icaa'tr. This termination ao-tx of the perfect does not occur elsewhere in our author, who uses-av.

orationum Pr s 2 arm 4 bo: de orationibus gig vg: ow r. TTfkKrcv aur eth ipor tipuv arm 1 2 TOV ayyeaov TOV 498. 2020: rov ayycxuv 69. 205 arm 2: rov apxayytxov arm 1 v(jyjri. ov arm 1: pr TOU bo TOV 0eov arm 1 4.

5. cixtj ck cycmurcv arm 1 a rov Xij3avorov ro iftavwrav 104. 141. 205. 218. 424. 2019. 2024 KOL cycjuu avroveth avrov avro 104. 205. 218. 424 rov wrtacrrrptov-f rov cov Pr: pr rov ewi s 1: "of Gehenna" arm 2 cfeacv K 046. 21 Or 1 Pr gig vg s. arm bo eth: cfaxAcv 025: cxa3oy A jspovrai x. aorpaircu K. uivat A 336. 2020 s 2 dlp): ftpovrai K. iuvai x. acrrpairai K 046. 21 (35. 2020). 69. no. 172. 250. 314. 385. 2016. 2018 al p Or Pr gig vg s 1 bo eth: ovcu K. ftpovrai K. curroatrcu 025. i. 35. 2037. 2067 al mu Tyc arm 4: wvoi K. aorpairot K. fipovrai 104. 2038: The order of all the MSS is corrupt. We should expect aorpainu first, since not only in point of fact the lightning is seen before the thunder is heard, but also because this order is preserved always elsewhere in our author: cf. 4 n 19 i6 18. St. John is an observer of nature, and was not guilty of this blunder. It is due to the interpolator of 37-12 T ne original order was aorp. KCU uvcu KOI jspovrat as in 4 6 11 19 i6 18. The hopeless order of A ftpovr. K. oorp. K. wv. is most probably due to the interpolator. The readings of K 046 Pr vg s 1, of 025 Tyc, are obvious attempts at correction. KCU o-etoyioo- 242. 617. 1934: O-CIOAOI 209 Or 1 arm 2 8:-f tyucr vg v arm 1-a: + cyevcro icyacr vg.

8. roua cirrai. 506: TOW 205 TOV covarm 1: TOV Bpovov 620. 866 arm 4 corrKGum AKC 025. 046. 81 (-35. 325. 456. 468. 2020) Or 1: cicmKcicrav 35. 468. 2020 s: cor xco-ay 42. 314. 325. 456. 517: stabant gig: stant Tyc eth: stantes Pr vg bo tsofaicrav KG 025. 046. 91 (-18. 919. 920. 1849. 2004. 2040) Or 1 Pr gig vg s bo: c8o0i; A 18. 172. 919. 920. 1849. I 955- 20 4- 201- 2 4- 20 4 I arm: Q i acceperunt Tyc o-axiriyyeo— iva traxirurithri 920. 2040: tubas Tyc I.

6. 04 cxoitCff A 025. 046. 21 (- 468. 620. 866). 250. 2037.

13. Kai ctsov Kal jjjKOwa evos derov ircrobiciov v lecroupav xatt AeyoitOS covfl ficyaafl Ovat ovat ovai rots Katotkovow ri ri?? CK TOW Aowrwv ctfvun TJfc raairiyyo rcuv rpcwv ayycaiw rail AOKTUI oraairt civ.

7. Kal 6 wparos coraxirurcv jcal cyevcro axa a Kal irvp icuyucpa cv acfum,

KOt ifi r)0r) cfc-nyy yijv.

Kal TO rpirov TIS yis icarecaiy,

Kal TO TplTOV TtoV Scvfyxok KatCKttl,
Kal iras opros x- 0 5 KatCKaiy. 8. Kal 6 SCVTCWS ayycaos ccrdxirto-cv 2067 al 111 s arm 1 2 8- bo eth: 01 K 468. 620. 866. 2019. 2038 Or 1 arm 4 TOO arm a avrouor A: cavrovo- c 025. 046. 81. 250 2037. 2038. 2067 al 1 1 Or S L 2 bo: CTT avrovo- 69 raairurixrt 4- rovr craa.7nyyar arm 1- 8: + TOW irra craaTriyyao-arm 2.

18. KU Soi's 1 eth Tfjkowra + favrjv Tyc vg arm 1 2 a evoo- N 025 arm bo sa a-ov AK 046. 21 (- 205. 468. 620. 632. 866). 250 al mu Or 8 Tyc gig fl s arm 1- 2- a bo eth: ut aquilam Pr: ayyexov 025. i. 104. 205. 241. 468. 620. 632. 866. 2015. 2019. 2036. 2037. 2038. 2067 arm a iretotcvov bo ev jifcrovpavrjfjlatt cv fjlccrovpavlo-fjlOLTL i: in medio caeli et terrae eth Acyovroo-J et dicentem Tyc eth fwvrj tyax-rj + TMO-104. 432. 2015. 2023. 2036. 2037. 2041: uv77 Tpio-35. 2019: fxiv. icy. before Aeyovroo- gig fl: Tyc s 1 owuj twice only i. 2038 eth TOCO- KarolKOvcrtv A 025. I. 35. 104. 205. 2037. 2038. 2067 al mu: TOW KatotkOWTao- M 046. SI (- 35. 205). 61. 69. no. 172. 242. 250. 314. 385. 2016. 2018 al mu Or CK TWV AOMTIDV (OVCDV-nyo" o-aaTTiyyoo- K rrja- fuvrjr rtov craxiriyyutv S 1: cic T. ffxavrjcr r. AOITTWV craa.7Tiyyciv s 2: jbciva)i TTJCT o-aairiyyoo Pr.

7. o irpwroa A 025. 046. 21 (- 2020) al 1 "" 1 Or s arm 4: + oyycaoo- I. 250. 522. 2015. 2019. 2020. 2036. 2037. 2038. 2067 Tyc Pr gig vg arm 1 2 3-" bo eth I Kai 8 Tyc Acutiyxcva A 046. 21 (-205. 2020). 250. 2037 al pl Or Pr gig vg s: ftcuy-025. 181. 205. 209. 432. 2020. 2038. 2067 Tyc cv evi. 2038 alp: vsan 205 s 1 2: e r otxa Pr gig J3 rjor Tav 172. 250. 424. 2018 s 1-2 KOI TO TKTOV rqo-yiyo-KatCKai7i. 2018 arm 1 4 TpitOv 1 Sevrepov arm 2 8 KOTC-Kai; L 8 KatCKavouv fl: Karccaixrcv arm 2- 8 a cat TO rpirov rw Scvspcuv icat Kai7o46. 175. 456 al p gig arm 8-: KOI Karckajj irav Scvspov eth TPITOF 2 J Scvrcpov arm 2 KOTCKOI; 2 Tyc arm 2- 8 bo Kac irao- x P Toar k pocr Kar Karj arm x P TOr XAcopoo o opr. o xawpoo- 104. 201. 386: iravra voprov hupov arm i. 8. 8 D0 Awpoo-1 rqor yiyor s 1 Ka. T Karj eth.

8. ayycxoa K s 1 coo- pr cycvrro 920. 2040 s 1 irvpi AK

Kat os opos Lteya irvpt Kaidicvov i3 rj0rj cb rijfv 0axao-o-av, Kat cycvcro TO rpirov riys tfaacurcrijs atxa, 9. Kat dirc0avcv TO rpirov rwv Kricrfuircov rov cv r 0X00-07; ra gal TO rpirov rv irxotw i f6dp-rjtav. IO. Kat 6 rptroc ayycxos ccraxirto'Cv

KOI crrco-cv CK rov ovpavov asrnjp icya? KCUOACVOS as Xatiras, Kat CTTCO-CV CTTI TO rpirov rav irorajjuav Kat t eirt TCLS Triyas t rov v attov, 1 1. cat TO OVOJLOL rov acrrlpos Xcycrae 6 "Ai'tv os cal fycvcto TO rpirov rssv voartov as aufwoos, Kal TroxXol TQK dv cutrojv dirc0avov CK TXUV vsarcov ori 025. i. 35. 205. 250. 2020. 2037. 2038. 2067 al mu Or 8 Tyc Pr gig fl vg s 2 arm 2 4: irvpotr bo: O46. 21 (-35. 205. 2020) al pm S 1 arm 1- a 8X 17 crrccrcv s 1 arm OMT opoo-p, ya irupt irvp xrya ucr opocr eth cycvcro eywqorj K Tpttov Seurcpov arm 2 atia in sanguinem Pr.

0. TO rpitOK 1 + ftepoo- (C 172. 250. 424. 2018. 2019 Pr gig fl vg bo sa eth: TO Scvtcpov arm 2 s rwv KTUTIATCDV piscium Pr: animalium fl arm 4: creaturae vg: pr iravrw s 1 2 bo TOW v Tiy axoo-o A 025. 205. 250. 2020. 2037 al mu Or" fl s bo eth: i. 181 Pr vg: r vq 6. 21 (-205. 2020). 2038. 2067 al mu: eorum quae in mari creata sunt gig ra e orra ivxao- ra ovra iftvxrjv (+ OT; O- bo sa eth) K bo sa eth:

Ta e ovra Tao- jvxw 42. 242. 468: rotv ovrt v Tao" u ao- 35: TO c ov tyvxn v s 1: habentium atiimas Tyc: Pr fl Btc Oaprja-av AN 025. (i). 35. 42. 60. 181. 432. 1957. 2015. 2023. 2036. 2037. 2041 s 2 arm 1 2: 8i (f6apr) 046. 21 (-35. 205). 250. 2038. 2067 al pl Or 8 s 1 arm 3: tf0apjj 205: corruperunt Tyc: penit Pr: interiit gig fl vg.

10. ayyexoa S J Xafwroxr irvp eth: H-Trvpoo- bo Kat 7rca-ev 2 Pr fl Tptto + pcpocr 2019 Pr fl vg bo sa eth KOI eirt TOO-mryao- TWV vsattuv A: vsatOO bo Sa.

11. TOU oorcpoa-i- TOVTOV Tyc Xryetot exeyero 104 arm 4 o Airt ocr A 025. 046. 21 (-2020). 250 au m Or 8 s: o N rtc i. 69. 104. 2019. 2020. 2037. 2038. 2067 al p a lfiv6otr K c: aiav0tov N (+ Kat Xcycrat H del c) bo: a tv oicr 2067: absintium Tyc: absintus Pr: absinthius gig vg- d- v: absentius vg f: absin-thus vg: habsintus vg c: absentium fl: " bitterness " arm 1- 2-: " wormwood " arm 4 rptrov + ncpoo- Or 8 Pr fl gig vg bo eth cycvcro ytvcrat I. 2019. 2038 al p wcr a livo(xr (-ov Or 8) 2038 Or 8: sicut absintium (alloe bo) Pr gig vg s 1 bo sa: quasi absentium fl: cur a ivoov A 025. 046. 21 (-620. 866. 1934). 250. 2067 al pl s 2: cur atyivqiov 104. no. 336. 620. 866. 1934. 2015. 2023. 2036. 2037 gig vg: "bitter" arm 8; "into blocxj 12. Koc Tcvapros ayycxos raxir rcr Kai cirxijyi; TO Tpnw TOV 17X101;

KOI TO TplTOV Tlj (Tcxl Kal TO TpltOV TW OOTCpw, IVa (TKOTW0fl TO Tpitov avrcov i f ij iwpa ity av0 TO THTOV avn KOI 17 vv f j into wormwood" arm 4 ex TWV vsatuv ore efrupav Vrav (ab) amaritudine aquarum (Pr) fl arm 1 1 eth: ort crupov o-av ra vwa s 1 CK TWV wi TOV A.

18. ayyc oo S 1 cirxiryiy tvxyfc arm 1: +KCU ccrkOTiotfj; Cth I TO Tpitov TOW lyxiov KOI 1 934 TpitOv + fji pot (thrice in this verse) Pr fl gig vg bo sa eth KM TO TPITOV nyo- o- X i r fl iva

O KOTMT) TO TpitOV avTUlv + Kat JK. OTUrblf)TLV S 8! KCU UTKOTUrorj (- 07o-av s 1) TO TPITOV ovrwv 1 7 2. 2 50. 2 o 1 8 s 1 arm 1- 8- 4: KCU CCTKO-Tio iy arm: iva o- otwr oxrt bo: ut minus lucerent Pr: iva O-KOT. T. rpitov avtcov xai eth 1 17 cpa. w text corrupt: bo alone (KOI TO Tp. avrwv fjnj favt rjfjltpaa- KOI oiowixr WKTOV) either preserves or recovers original sense. Pr fl and eth attempt to recover it. See below. Evidence as follows, y qicpa fav7j TO rpnov (Toprov A) avriytr A 025. 35. 2037. 2038. 2067 al mu Or 8: eu TO TPITOV avnp w owy rj(O46. 522) ijjjupa 046. 175. 325. 337. 456. 468. 617. 620. 866. 1934 al pm j (avttdv for avncr 18. 69. 141. 385. 429. 522. 632. 919. 1849. 1955. 2004. 2015. 2024: avrow for aur cr 386: avrrjo- 920. 2040: TO rpirov aur o 202o): et dies eandem partem amitteret Pr fl: et dies non luceat terciam partem gig: et diei non luceret pars tertia vg: KCU 17 i? pa OVK c aivc TO Tpvrov avnja- s 1: Kai 17 xcpa OVK c any KOI TO Tpitov arm 1: "and the third part of them had not light and day " arm 8: IT; exuvwo-iv Kai TO rpnov cpour xai WKTOO- eth y w(nocte vg f T: noctis vg d bo eth.

CHAPTER IX.

wpq- I Kai o f ircfunros f ayyexos co'axirurcv ot Kai clsov aorcpa CK TOV ovpavov reirtUKora 119 rip yiv, aurw 77 KXcis TOV fptatos 1 9 d vwov 1. KM. cffaxmffcK i849 KOI cisov eth aorcpa. irarndKora M: aorcpao-. irctrrukoraar K aorepa CK TOV ovpavov Tcnrcukora aorepa Trcirrcoic. CK TOV ovp. 920. 2040 arm 4:

CK TOV OVp. OOT. 1TC1TT. gig CICT TTJV ftJv ffl Tip yyfr 498. 2020 S 1
bo sa: vpocr TTJV yipr 385 o6rj eswkav bo 17 KXeur TOO- x DO eth TOV pcatoo-
TOV tp a. Tav s 1 I TITO- ajsvo-o'OV gig.

2. Kal yvoifa TO tptap rjJs aftwrcrau, Kal v 3i) Kairio? fc TOV pcaros
OK Kan-foC KCLfjLLVOV flCyax f,
Kal ltKOTvorj 17X105 KOI 6 dr)p IK TOV icairvov TOV
Kal IK rov fcairvov jjTXtfov aicpiiscs cts r v y v, ical So0i? avtots c ovo-ta UK i
cnxrw c ovo tav ol o- copirtot 4. icat ippcfcj avrats tva jii; asik crovo-iv rov 6prov-rijs
yijs oisc Trav xxcopoi ovsc irai 8ev8pov, ct KT; TOVS dvtfpcinrovc otrtvcs OVK c
oixrtv TT)V o- paytsa rov cov CTTI 9. Kai i)KOi c TO 4p ap nrja apuaaou A 025. I.
35. 104. 172. 241. 250. 620. 632. 866. 1957. 2015. 2019. 2020. 2023. 2036.
2037. 2041. 2067 alp Or 8 Tyc Pr gig fl vg s 2 arm 1 4: O46. 81 (-35. 620.
632. 866. 2020). 2038 al mu vg a d s 1 arm 2 3 bo eth KOI arcfy de quo ascend it
Pr KCLTTVOCT CK row pcaroo- awr I. 172. 325. 456. 2018. 2021 K c: 7rt TOV
peatOo- rwv 0pcarov S 1 OKT icatrioo- wo- A: axr CK Pr fl icainoorj K c: Kafuvocr
K icyax o- A 025. I. 35. 205. 2015. 2036. 2037.
2038. 2067 al mu Tyc Pr vg fl arm 1- 2- 8 bo eth: gatoiciipr 046. 21 (-35. 205.
2020). 250 al mu Or 8 s 2: fieyaxiyo- Katoxei o' 141. 432. 452. 2019. 2020
(ftcyaxoi;). 2O2I gig s 1 arm 4 icai 8 oo- Pr fl cvkOTioorj A 6l. 69. 181. 2038:
covcoriordi? K 025. 046. 21. 250. 2037. 2067 al pl Or": tenebris obscuravit Pr fl o
p ao-riyp 205 CK row KOLITVOV TOV ptatCKT icat K (but not K c) Pr fl arm 1 2
TOV peatOo- TWV pcarcuv s 1: rrja- icaxevov arm 8.

3. Kairrau + TOV peatoo- Tyc vg f- T: 0pcatoo arm 1- cur iri arm bo avraur A 025
21. 250. 2037. 2038. 2067 a pl Or 8: avrour M 046. 104 ovo ia + cat Ta fccvrpa
avrtuv arm 1 wo- txovo-iv efovo-tav similis earn quae habent fl: rjv e ovo-tv s 1: ixr
Ktvrpa o Kop7riov arm 1 2-: iva yciaitai oxr eth Tiyo yiyo- pr wi s 2 arm 8 bo eth:
arm 1- 2-.

4. cppcoij A 025.21 (-35). 2037. 2038. 2067 alp 1 Or 8: cppi01? 046. 172. 250.
2018. 2024: cpcd?; 35 avraur A 025. 21 (-18. 919. 2004). 250. 2037. 2038. 2067
al pl Or 8: avrotor K 046. 18. 6l. 69. 172. 919. 2004. 2039 asikijo-ovo-iv A 2019:
astkio-axttv K 025. 046. 21. 250. 2037. 2038. 2067 al pl Or 8 Tyc Pr gig fl vg ovsc
irav x w P ov (c wrote x w above Sc pov) Tyc arm: LnSc irav vpov 2020: rat TTO. V
P V s 1 x upov. Sevspov bo iravsevspov Scvspa s 1: Trav arm 1: iravra 8ev8pa arm
2 8 4- ct ya rovo avdpoitrovcr + xovovcr 1957. 2023. 2041 al: nisi tantum homines
vg arm rpayt8a cr paytsav 82. 866 rov eov i. 35. 181. 241. 2015. 2036. 2037. 2067:
rov Xptcrrov arm 1 Acronroiv AM 025. I. 181. 2015. 2036. 2037. 2038 gig vg 0- 1:
H-avrtdv 046. 21. 250. 2067 al 1 Pr vg. fl s arm 1- 2- eth.

VOL. ii. 19 5. KOU cooori avrots era py faofcrtivaxrw avrov?, oaA iva 3curavtr
77rorau uva? ireitf.(fl) 6. cal cv rats icoats fcctyais finjtroww 01 avopwroi rov

Kal ov fiijf r upokriv 1 avrov, Kal ciriovfjLrjffowriv airooav lv Kal tvy i 6 Odvaros
air avrvxv. 5ioim 7. xal ra oioiwtara TWV avyuow Aoia 1 Tinrois

KOL ctrl Tas jec axas avruw as crrtfavoi oioiot xpwtp, Kal ra irpoffwra avrv us
irpovawra avopwirwv.

(a) Text adds gloss: col 6 jscwcww aiTw ws ftwwur (TKOprlov trw 5. xai cso6r)
et dictum est Pr eth: dictum est fl avraco-025. 046. 21 (-2004). 250. 2037. 2038.

2067 al pl Or 8: avroto-AM I. 104. 181. 2004 airokrciioxrir (181 770-0)(7 920. 2040 tva 2 S T jsao-awo- o-ovrat AK 025. I. 35. 181. 2019. 2O20. 2038: paoravhrqwri 046. 21 (-35- 2020). 250. 2037. 2067 al pl Or": cruciarentur Pr (gig) vg fl: cruciarent Tyc arm ho eth avrw wo- patravio-flOtr 149 Trawny 21 (- 149. 468. 620. 866 920. 2020) Or 8 Tyc gig fl vg s s arm: TTCOT AK 025. 046. 104. 149. 172. 620 866. 920. 2020. 2038 al mn: irecny r. s 1: irxiyfiy 60. 432. 452. 506. 2021. 2022. 2023. 2041: 80107 367. 468 bo sa eth.

6. CP Tcua Tjfupaia cxcivaur Tyc: tv rrj rjfjitpa ccan; arm 1 1 fiyi o-oucriv JTOWTIV 60. 82. 93. no. 175. 325. 452. 456. 468. 517. 1957. 2024. 2041 01 avopwroi Pr cupokrtp A 025. 35. 172. 181. 205. 209 250. 424. 2015. 2018. 2023, 2036. 2037: cvpiforowriv 1 046. 21 (-35. 205. 325. 337. 456. 468. 620. 866. 1849). 104. no. 201. 241. 242. 314. 385. 429. 498. 522. 1957. 2017. 2019. 2024. 2041. 2067 al mu Or 8 gig fl vg: cvpyvwrw I. 61. 69. 82. 325. 337. 456. 468. 517. 620. 866. 1849: cvpovviv 2038: inveniunt Pr airooavcw rov Oavarov 104 ftvyei A 025. I. 35. 181. 2019. 2020. 2067: fayy K: cu crai 046. 21 (- 35. 2020). 250. 2037. 2067 al 1 Or 8 Pr gig fl vg s arm bo eth o Oavaroa air aviw A 025. I. 35. 205. 2015 (av). 2019. 2O2- 2O 3 2037. 2067 al mn Pr gig fl vg s arm 4: air avnav o Oavarov 046. 21 (-35. 205. 2020). 250. 2038 al mu Or 8 arm 1 2 8-: o Qavarwr 104.

7. TO o wi fjiata TO oMuaAa gig s arm 1- 8- bo oioia 025. 046. 21. 250. 2037. 2038. 2067 al pl Pr vg: oxotoi N (s): OAOIW-fiota A: oxokoia Or 8 arm 1 2-: opotov arm 8: similes erant fl arm 4 avrwvj-foxotwfta Or 8 oiotot xpwci AK 025. i. 35. 172. 205. 250. 429. 2015. 2018. 2019. 20 36. 2037. 2038. 2067 al p 8. feat Jt av Tpi as us rpt as ywaucan, icai oi 6Sowcs avroy cos Xcovrcov 9. icat ical 17 uvT7 rcuv irrepvycdV avrcov a on? pfidrtav 9 tirirctfv TroaAaiv rptxpimov eis iraaetoy.

IO. ical I OV(TW ovpas 6ioias oricoptriois ical jccprpa, icai cv rats oupais avrujy fj e ovcria a ruy asuacrat TOW? avopiairov? fjifjvas ircrrc.

1 1. l owtv if avrujv 3ao-taca rov ayycaoy-nys ? ucro ov, ovofjlO. avrw K patott A a88ov.(a) (a) Text adds gloss: ai v r EXXivtictJ foojia fyei AToxXisw. Observe below how Pr fl vg add et Latine habet nomen Exterminans a fact which shows how glosses arise.

Or 8 Tyc Pr gig fl vg s (arm): " of colour of gold " bo: xwcroi 046. 21 (35. 205) al pm KCLI TO. irpoo-omra. av0pawrav arm 2.

8. eixoi AK: ci ov 025 046. 21. 250. 2037. 2067 al pl Or: c ovt cr 2038 Pr fl: arm 1 28 a rpt ao1 icai at rpt co avrcuv (arm 3) arm 1- 3- rptxao2 2020 fl: rpixccr arm 1- 2- 3- yvvaikw yvvo-LKoar arm 1- 2- 8- a: ut mulieres fl wcr 2 + osoirccr fl vg d XCOVTCDK Xcovroo- arm 1- 2- a iorav fl s 1 arm.

9. itai cixak. (Titjpoua- 920. 2O4O Oti)pakar 1 2020: pectora Pr oxr Oupakao- 18. 919. 1849. 2004 gig on Pr fl arm 2 wnrwv pr icai 337. 468: 325. 456. 620. 866 7roaA. av bo Tpcyoi rwv iro acrficvcov bo.

10. icat CXOIKUH icai et ov 2020. 2067 Tyc Pr vg arm 1 8 8 4: fl ovpacr oAoiao-J ovpat oxotai fl: oAotuia arm 4 j ofjiouur 025. 046. 21 (-35. 617). 250. 2037. 2038. 2067 al pl Or 8 Tyc Pr gig vg s arm 1 2 s bo: ouuatcr 617: OAOIOUT AM 69: oiouixr 35 I o-Kopiruucr o-jcoptrtcu s 1 arm 1- 2 3 a: o-Koprritov vg: cncopiruuv icrav fl icevrpa icai CF A C 025. 046. 21 (- 18. 205. 2020) al pm Or 8 s 2 arm 3- 4 bo: jccrrpotcr KOI cv Pr fl: jccvrpa i; v cv vg f- T: iccrrpa (Sc) ev s 1: ecu i. 1 8. 61. 104.

141. 172. 205. 209. 241. 250. 424. 2015. 2018. 2019. 2020. 2036. 2037. 2038. 2039. 2067 Tyc gig vg eth: KOI ev arm 1: ncrrpov (ai arm 2) v arm 2- a i efovcrta avrcov A 025. 35. 172. 205. 209. 250. 424. 2018 al p gig vg bo: pr KOI i. 2019. 2038. 2067 Or 8 (Pr fl) vg l s 1: c ovcriav cxovcriv 046. 21 (- 18. 35. 205). 69. no. 201. 242. 314. 385. 429. 498. 522. 1955. I 9S7-2015. 2016. 2017. 2023. 2024. 2037 al ma s 2 (pr icat 241. 2036): (KCU) cfoixrtav i ov arm 1-: c ovcrtav ovcrai 18. 61. 2039: 104 eth asikTo-cu A 025. i. 35. 172. 175. 205. 242. 250. 314. 617. 1934. 2015. 2017. 2018. 2019. 2036. 2037. 2038. 2067 al p Or: pr TOW 046. 21 (- 35. 175. 205. 617. 1934) al mu ircvre sex Pr.

11. exoucriv AK 205. 314: pr KCU 025. I. 250. 2037. 2038 al Or gig s: KCU ci o? 2067 Pr fl vg arm 4-: CXOVG-OI 046. 21 (- 205) 12. "H oval 17 xta airijAflev 28ov ip TOLi 3u Svo oval xcra ravra.

al mu Tyc avrcov facrtaca A 025. (025 adds in mg. but writes avrov). i. 35. 61. 69. 205. 2015. 2036. 2037. 2038. 2067. Tyc Pr gig vg s 1: r avrcov Wiactcr 2019: cavriov rov jsacnaca K arm 4: Soo-iaca r avrcov 046. 21 (- 35. 205). 250 al ma Or s 2 arm: fturtaca cir avrov 18. 172. 452 (or avrovo- 104: VJT avrcov 336): I facrtaca + rov apxovra A: fl rov ayycaov nycr a)9vrcrov riycr ajsvotrov rov ayycaov A rov ayycaov Afct 025. I. 35. 69. 104. 205. 632. 2015. 2019. 2020. 2036. 2037. 2038. 2067 al mu Oi arm bo: rov 046. 21 (- 35. 205. 632. 2020). 250 al nm ovoxa avrcol pr co K: co ovoxa 94 Tyc Pr fl (+ est) vg: ovoxa avrov 2067 aSasSwv A 025 al p Tyc vg s 1: ajsjffoasow 046. 325. 429. 456. 468. 517. 620. 632. 919. 1849.! 955- 20 4: atyfoascov 172. 250. 920. 20l8. 2040: a aasStov 42. 82. 93. HO. 337. 452. 506. 2020. 2021. 2024 al p: a3j8a8tov i. 18. 35. 60. 91. 175. 181. 201. 314. 386. 617. 1934. 2015. 2016. 2023. 2036. 2037. 2038. 2067 Or gig arm 8: a?? a8ov 2019. 2041: a? Aa ow 61. 69: arm aged don Pr: ababdon fl: albagos arm 1: nabathdon arm 4: magedon bo KOI cv rq AK 025. i. 35. 205. 314. 2019. 2038 al p gig s 1: cv 8c rr) 046. 1 (-35. 205. 325. 456. 468. 620. 866. 920). 250. 2037. 2067 al pm Or 8 s 2: v rrj caA vik?; 8c 325. 456. 468. 620. 866: cv nj Sc TT; 920: graece autem Tyc vg: graeca autem lingua Pr: graeca lingua fl: " who is called in " arm 1 8 caAi vtc cxXi visi K 205: +p crci 2020. 2067: crvpiaici; s 1: "Armenian" arm 1 8 ovoxa ct 2019 gig: ovoxa e cov 522: " is called " arm 1- 2- 8: Pr vg arm 4- a eth airoxXvcov pr o 2038 bo: airoxvcov 522. 2023: apohon Tyc: apollion Pr: perdens gig: apollyon fl arm 8: "destruction" arm 1 2: "destroyer" arm 4: + latine perdens Tyc: + et latina lingua nomen habens exter-minans Pr fl (vg): + " who is called destruction in Armenian " arm 1- 2- 8.

12. i) ouai TJ fiia ovai xia K: ovai y xta K c: pr ifiov arm amjxOcv 7rapr) 0cv 2015. 2036. 2037 arm 1 2 3 isov pr KOI Tyc Pr fl vg- v: arm 1- 8- eth epxcrat A 21 (- 632. 2020). 69. 104. no. 385. 429. 2016. 2023 al mu Or s 2 arm 1 bo: cpxovroi K c 025. 046. i. 172. 250. 632. 2015. 2017. 2018. 2019. 2020. 2036. 2037. 2038. 2067 vg s 1: secuntur Pr: venient Tyc crt ai 432. 2019. 2037. 2038: en KCLL at 241: alii Pr: alia gig: i. 104. 498. 2023. 2067 Tyc fl bo eth Svo ficvrcpa 104: secun-dum fl arm 1 4 bo xcra ravra. KCLI A 025. i. 35. 172. 205. 250. 632. 2015. 2020. 2023. 2037. 2038. 2067 al mu Or gig vg s f: also Pr eth but xcra ravra: icai xcra ravra 046. 69 Tyc: xcra ravra icat (u 469 s l bo sa) are joined to ver. 13 by K 21 (-35. 205. 632. 2020). no. 241. 242. 385. 469. 2016. 2024. 2039 ai mu s l bo sa.

13. Kcu 6 f SKTOS f iyycxos fraxTrurcv poi ai jjfjcowa tfxavrjv fiiav IK rwv fccpatw rov Ovvuumfplov TOV

Xpwov rov franriov rov fcov, 14. Xfyovra r g f CTOI f dyyexai, 6 ZXWF " ffaxiriyya 9evr

Avow rovs revcrapas ayycxovs rovs Sfscicpovf ITTI r iroratq) W 15. Kd! cxvtft-prav ot rcowipcs ayycxot ol firoifiao-fjifvoi eis r v opa? iral iffiipav KCU A va al cviavrov, tva airofcrcivaxrtv TO rpirov TWK avopunrwv. 1 6. icai 6 apiofjio rov arparcviaraiv rov unrucov 8 13. KU K (see above) nyy itav 69 Or":

K c 2067: av K 2020 arm 1- a8- bo: iwviyv icyoxiyv 172. 250. 424. 2018: vocem, unum vg: unum Tyc Pr gig Cyp uav c c raw Kcparwv K (uao- CK raw Kcparaiv K c) iccparaiv AK 2015. 2036 gig vg s bo sa eth: pr rco-o-apuv 025. 046. 21. 250. 2037. 2038. 2067 al 1 Or Tyc Pr (Cyp) s 1 arm: OHDV arm 8 c flwwurnfpiov + del Pr: arcae Cyp cvonriov +rov povov bo eth.

14. Xeyoira AN Tyc Pr gig vg Cyp: Xeyorroo- 046. 21 (- 35. 205. 468. 2020) al mu Or: Xryovo-af 025. I. 35. 104. 172. 205. 468 1957- 2015. 2018. 2019. 2020. 2023. 2036 al p: Xcyownjo- K 2067: Xcyoiv 141 cirro) A 2038 o t w rat c ovri 172. 250. 424. 2018 rco-0-apcur T rcrap cr K 172 TOIKT Sc8cievoixr. ayycxot (ver. 15) bo, but not sa eth rt cv 93. 104. 432 TD 1849 I T0) ficyoxo) + iroraAO) 025: arm 1 2 a cv pan; 046: pr TO) 468: eufraten Tyc Pr gig Cyp: Al Frat sa.

15. cxuor)(rak cxvirrjorprav A ot rjtOt aa cvoi 01 K 1 8. 522.

2O21. 2O39: Oi TrpoJJTOLfia(TflCVOL 2Ol. 2O 6 Kttl rjfjLtptlV A O2.

35. 205. 2037. 2038. 2067 al mn Tyc Pr gig vg Cyp: u ctcr n v rjii pav 046. 21 (-35. 205. 2020). 250 al mu Or" s eth: KOI TTJV rjp. cpav 1957. 2015. 2020. 2023. 2036. 2041 bo sa: K i I iw + Aiyk I Tptrov + xepoo- 432. 2015. 2036. 2037 Pr Cyp gig vg bo sa eth.

16. TOU tinrtkou AM 025. 046. I. 35. 61. 69. 104. 205. 2015. 2019. 2019. 2020. 2023. 2036. 2037. 2038. 2067. al p Or 1: rov wnrov 21 (-35. 205. 386. 2020). 42. 82. no. 336. 38. 1957. 2Ol8. 2023 al mu: rcuv imrw 386 ovo- ivputsco-. aptopov arm 1 Sur fivpcasccr uvpcasov A 025. i. 205, 2016. 2019. 20 3 Or 1 (Cyp): Svo ivpiasaiv nvptascur K: fivpcasco- tvpraw 046. 21 (- 205). 250. 2037. 2067 alp m: myriadis myriadum Tyc: octo-ginta milia Pr: vicies milies dena milia gig vg avroiv +ut 17. r KOvou TOV fyiopbv avrwv. xal OVTOK dsoy TOVS imrovs

TQ Opdvtt (fl) jcat TOVS jca07i6ovs iw f avrv t fyovtas 0apa ac irvpivoi KCU ai KC aaai roiv fmvw a Kc aaai Acovrcui,

Kai TWV 0TOAatUv avyW ekiropcvcrat irvp KOI Kairvos KOI 0CIOF 1 8. airo raw rpiif wxijyv TOVTWV air Krav9vj(rav TO rpfaov TWV

K TOV irvpdf cat TOV Kairvov KOI TOV tfctov TOV raw OTotatwv avroy. 19. 17 yap ovcria rov ttnrwv v rp oroam avraiv COTIF ( ) al: ai)rozf 4v f avrats f as (a) The text is corrupt and defective: faowra r. djt dv a W may be an intrusion. After opret we should restore Kal TOVS Kaorn vovi tr airois, which has been lost through hint. Next, for ecu r. Kaff vovs AT tairo f 1 orraj above read tal ol KafyfjMKH tr avroi)s txovrts.

(6) Text adds an interpolation here: ai rats oipcu f airwv, at 70 oipai amv Ajuouu 0060-1 fypwai 0a dj. See vol. i. p. 253 sq.

occiderent tertiam partem hominum Pr rjkowa. eth. After fivuaow two lines appear to have been lost.

17. KCU ourua. opooci s! ovrwtr 2O2O Tyc Pr arm 1 2- unrowr unrikOwr 046. 69 Or 1 I irl CTravw K c oirao Tr pi r)fjl vovr bo vajavyoihT KGU 0 tooctcr Kap Sova ctov s vokiv ivovcr oiakivowovo- 325. 456: uuctvoivowr 620. 866: hyacmthmas Tyc: hyacintinas vg: iacintinas Cyp gig: spineas Pr KCLI Oaubeto- eth (cec cur 0vo6W K: Oiufcur M r: "god-like" arm 4 TWV VTOIMLTW rov oroiaroo- 35 Tyc Pr gig vg Cyp s 1 arm 1 2 8- ciwropcvctai rop U To 2020. 2067 wp 18. airo pr KCU S L 2 arm bo: wo I row rpuov irx cov rovroii TWV C: Tptwr K Or 1 arm L: irxi o v i. 2038: TW rpiwi Tovrwk Trx wv 205 I awkravoijiray airckTavoy 468. 498. 2019. 2020 gig vg Cyp rpitov +icpor gig vg bo sa eth TOW irvpoo- A C 03 S- I- 35- 20 S- I 957- 20I 5- 20I 9- 202- 202 3- 20 3- 20 37- 20 3 Or" Vg Cyp: airo TOV irvpoo- 046. 81 (- 35. 205. 2020). 69. 104. 250 2067 al 1 " 11: pr u s 1 arm 4 TOV jcairvov AK 046. 81 (- 35. 866). 69. 104. no. 250. 385. 2004. 2036. 2067 alp Or vg Cyp bo sa eth: pr ex C 025. i. 35. 314. 2016. 2037. 2038 al gig s: pr airo 866: arm 1 1 TOV 0 ov A C 046. 81 (-35). 250. 2067 al " 11 Or vg bo sa eth: pr 025. i. 35. 314. 2016. 2036. 2037. 2038 al p gig s TOV KTrop VOfjL vov Cfciropcvoicvov 104: ruv cciropcvo-ftevwv 2015. 2019. 2020. 2036. 2037. 2067 bo CK row oroiatCDv ut TOV oroLuitxr 205. 92O. 1957. 2040 gig vg Cyp s 1 arm 1-!, 10. unr)? TOITIDV A cv ro trrofuiti avw cori? KOI w TOUT 20. Kttl 01 XOUTOI Ttov dv MOITtdV, Oi OVK V KTavor)Tav V Tttls irxiyyat? ravrais, fovsc fkTworjorav CK TWV cpycuv rov L P V avrcw, a ii) irpoctKVKiprovoii ra oatiowa Kai ra. cisoxa ra xpwa Kai ra dpyvpa Kai ra XO KQ. KOI ra iowa, KCU ra va. iva, ovre 3A. c7mv Svvairai ovrc okovctv ovrc Trcpiirarciv, 21. Kai ov i T votyrav K rwv ovuv avrwv ovrc CK ruv appja. Kuav aurwv ovrc CK r s iropvcias avrujv ovrc etc ruv cacixctttov avrov.

ovpaur avrav cv rater ovoaio- Kai cy ra arrobuirt avrwv T; V 2O2O. 2037: in ore et caudis eorum erat Pr KOI cv roio- ovpaicr avriav i.

2019. 2038 avruh rciv i7nro)v 385: +COTIV S 2 at yap ovpai. a8ucovo-tv b 1 oiotat C: oiotot 2023: erant similes Pr arm 1 2 8 4 o eo-ii A C 025. i. 35. 61. 69. 1957. 2015. 2019.

2020. 2023. 2036. 2037. 2038. 2041. 2067 al p Or Tyc Pr gig vg Cyp s 2 arm 1 2 4 bo: o ct arm 8: o cwv 046. 21 (-35. 2020).

25O al m11: OfloLOLL TWV Ofaw 20. C OVOTOl CYOVO-OXT K: c ovo-aur K r 025. 2019: c owi? C 2038. 2067 KC0axao- + draconum Pr asixovo-tv Siicovo-av 2020: qfeow Pr arm 8- s- 4- bo eth: astk o-ovo-iv arm 1: + avopunrow-rrtvrt fjujvaur bo eth.

20. oi 2 g g arm 8 4 bo irxiyyaio- + avruv K ov8c. XCioaw avrcuv QI9 ov8c K 046. 61. 69. 2020: ovrc A 025. I. 35. 205. 429. 632. 2019. 2037. 2038 al p Pr gig vg Cyp bo: ovc21(-35. 205. 632. 919). 104. no. 172. 241. 242. 250. 314. 385. 429. 1955. 1957. 2015. 2016. 2017. 2018. 2023. 2024. 2036. 2067 al Or TWV cpywv rov cpyov S 1 irpwrkwrprowriv A C 104. 452. 2019: irpoorkinnprwo-u 025. 046. 21. 250. 2037. 2038. 2067 al 1 Or 8: adorarent Pr vg 0 4 v-: adorent gic vg-Cyp ra Saiiovta icai ro Saiiovt rj 2020: arm 1 ciooixa + id est simulacra Cyp: + aimay arm 1- 8 XP VOU XP vrcua: XP wrug Or B KOI ra x a K(l (xaxKca K) AKC 025. 046. 35. 468. 2020. Or Pr gig vg Cyp. s arm bo eth: 21 (- 35. 205. 468. 2020). 42.

82. 104. no. 201. 218. 241. 242. 314. 336. 385. 429. 498. 522. 1955. 2016. 2019. 2024. 2039 a l p I ""i vaW tt 743- I0 75 sl bo eth owavrai A C 025. 046. 18. 35 104. 149. 205. 241. 250. 468. 632. 2004. 2015. 2018. 2019. 2020. 2023. 2024. 2036. 2037. 2067 Or 8: owanu 046. 21 (-18. 35. 149. 205. 468. 632. 2004. 2020). 2038 al pl: s 1 afcovctk. ircpiirarciy arm 1 ovrc aicovci? Cyp.

21. pcrcroijow + CK TOVTWV ovrc 2020 ovtov avav gig: (f vrjcr arm 3 oirrc CK TOJV ooxakuuv avrwv Cyp arm 8 apfiakiuiv A 025. 046. 104. 2038 al p Or: apiakuv sc 21 (-35. 205. 468. 632. 2020). 250 al nm: ajtttk i(i)v i 35. 205. 468. 632. 2020. 2037. 2038. 2067 al: " sorcery" arm 1 8-:

CHAPTER X.

I. Kol ciSov daXov dyycxov Mr vpov jcarajftuvovra cic rov ovpavov, ircptj3c)9Xi7Li vov vc cxiv, Kat rj Iptc M rrjv KCtftaxrjv avrov, Kai TO irpoo-coirov avrov toy o iXtos Kat ot irdsc? avrov a5 orvxot wvpds, 2. Kat l w " X L P l a wov j8t? Xapt-stov vcwyAcvoy. Kat 201KCv rov wosa avrov rov 5c tov evl ri s flaxaoxns, rov 8c evcowiov cwi rijs yifc, 3. feat icpafcv ov xeyaa. UXTTTCD Xccuv ical 3rc ikpa cv, Xaxi o-av at CTTTO ftpovral ra? javruv

"divination" arm 4 iropvciao- ironyiiao- AK: iropvuur c 025. 866 ovrc c c rwv icxcitarcdV avruv Pr s 1 sa factorum Cyp.

1. KCU cibov. Karapaikorra Kat icra ravra aaAoo- ayy.

eth axXov ayycxov Attc 172. 205. 250. 2018. 2019. 2020. 2038. 2067 Or Tyc gig vg s arm 1 24 ft: 104. 336. (620. 866 axov) Pr: axXov 025. 046. 81 (-205. 620. 866. 2020). i. 2037 alp m co vpov S 1 arm 1- cic airo 337 icat 17 tpto eirt riyv KC axiv avrou arm 8: Kat i tpto- arm 4 rj (c) tpur A (-etcr) K c C 046. 1 (- 205. 2020). 250 al pm Or arm 1- 2- bo: i; Opi N: tj 025. i. 104. 205. 522. 2017. 2019. 2020. 2037. 2067 al p: tpiv 2036. 2037: iprjv 2038: cptv 2015 cirt TTJV KC oxiyv AC 181: cirt rrja- Kc oxio- K 025. 046. 21. 250. 2037. 2038. 2067 al pl Or 8 TO irpooxoirov avrov + iv vg o 17X100 o 2020 orvxot orvxoo-205. 2020 Tyc vg (-vg c) s 1 arm.

2. Kai 2020 I c wv ANC 025. 046. 21 (35. 205. 468. 632. 2020). 250 al mu Or": Karcxwi 2020: et cv I. 104 205. 241. 468. 632. 1957. 2015. 2018. 2019. 2023. 2036. 2037. 2038. 2041. 2067 al p Pr gig vg arm: cxct 35)3t3Xapt8tov AK C 025. i. 2067 al p Or s: 0t3Xt8aptov K C C 35. 60. 61. 69. 104. 205. 241. 432. 468. 632. 1957. 2015. 2019. 2020. 2023. 2036. 2037. 2038. 2041: t3Xtov 046. 21 (-35. 205. 468. 632. 2020). 250 al mu Pr gig: libellum vg qvcwyxcvov KC 025. 104. 172. 205. 218. 250. 424. 2016. 2018. 2038. 2067: 7yv (uy-ACVWV i: avewyAevov 046. 21 (-205). 2037 al pl Or: A bo rov 8c tov C j rqr Oaxaararjcr rvfv 0oxacro-av I. 2037. 2038 al p rov 8c cvoivviov cirt nyor yrja- 866 no yiycr nv yiyv I. 201. 386.

8. xnrcp pr Kat Tyc arm 1 8-: UKT ore vg fivxarat rugiens Pr bo CKpafcv 2 +UKT K (del K c):-hicyaxiy (fruvrj arm at cirra)9povrat c: cirra fwai K: at i. 91. 94. 104. 866. 2067 arm racr eavriov wvacr ratar cavrcov cavato ((104 gig s arm-: Pr TOO-cavrcov avao-. (ver. 4) ypa ctv 4. ai ore caiprav al cwa fipovrai, jjtcaXov ypa av xai ovau favrjv IK rov ovpavov Acyowav S payuroy Xiprav al ra Ppwralj xal j aura ypcw s.

5. leal 6 dyycxos ov ctSov ccnwa ciri rip 0axacrn? f al cvi T S pcv r v xcipa avrov T K Sc iav eis rov ovpavov, 6. Kol uuxrcv ev Tcs (urn cfc TOVS aiwvas TOV atwvuv,

9 CKTMTCV rov ovpavov al ra cv avrui, KCU TTJV y v cat ra Iv cat r v daxacro-af xal ra b avr, ort pdvos ovkcn 7. ixX v rats i xu T S ov 9 rov f 8Wftou f dyyexou, orav, xat crcxccr TO iixm piov TOV tov, ws arm 1 8 I TOO cavruv covao. (ver. 4) jspovrai 1 386. 620. 866.

4. or ocra K 432. 2036. 2037 Pr gig ftpovrai 1 +voces suas vg ijieaXov AC 046. 61. 69. 82. 181. 201. 218. 386. 452. 498. 920. 2020. 2024. 2038 Or 1: cuxXov K 025. 80 (-386. 920. 2020). i. 104. no. 250. 314. 385. 2015. 2037. 2067 alpl I icai ore. ypa civ " And I heard the things which the seven thunders said: I was about to write them also." bo e TOV ovpavov + TOV c08oiov s 1 o- payurov nota tibi Pr a ocra K 94: o s 1 rra C gig arm 8 icai 8 Tyc vg bo py avra Atfc 025. 046. 20 (- 35). 250 al 111 Or 1 Tyc Pr gig vg s 8 arm 1-8: ovra arm: py avro s 1: ura raura i. 35. 60. 181. 432. 1957. 2023. 2036. 2037. 2038. 2041. 2067 ypa o- ypa a- 205 Or: ypa eicr I. 35. 60. 432. 1957. 2019. 2023. 2036. 2037. 2038. 2041: ypa rcur 104. 522. 2015 ypa w 2067.

5. o ayycxoa TOV ayycxov Pr vg 0– corura 42Q. 498. 522. 2016. 2020 gig f iypcv pr oo s 1 I TJJV Scftav A i. 35. 2019. 2038 vg s 1 cur TOV ovpavov in caelo gig.

6. KM tpooci +o ayycxoo Tyc cv ro fwvrt. cv avnf Tyc ev TW (ovrt AK 025. I. 35. 104. 175. 205. 314. 617. 1957. 2015. 2016. 2017. 2019. 2023. 2036. 2037. 2038. 2067 al p: per viventem Pr gig vg: ev K 046. 80 (-35. 175. 205. 617). 250 vw Or TWV auovwvl i. 181. 241. 632. 2038. 2067: + apjv 336. 620. 866. 2019 KOI ra cv avri arm 1 bo KCLI rt v yrjv Ktu ra cv ovny A i. 181 jcoi Ta cv avn 1 2f6 arm 1 bo f cv avrf cv avroto- 2015. 2036. 2037 KCU rrjv Baxacrvav KU ra. cv avny K C 025. 046. 80 (- 205. 2020). 250. 2037. 2038. 2067 alp Or 1 vgs'arm 2 8: AK 141. 205. 429. 522. 2016. 2017. 2020. 2023 Tyc Pr gig vg s 1 arm 4- cv avnf ev ovrour arm 1 OVKCTC corrai ovkcri cart K 141: ov carat crt i. 2036. 2037: crt ovic COTOt S 1.

7. axK gig bo: owe s 1 i or Hunyo- Tyc s 1 arm 8 rov

TOVS cavrov Sovxovs rovs irpo ras. 8. cat rj tfxtivrj rjv rfkovcra CK TOV ovpavov iraxiv f Xaxowrav ACT ciov ical Xcyovaui f Y? ray Xajsc

TO filfixLov TO Jjv qyfjL VOV TO CV X 1 P TO yy Xov TOV COTOTOS C1TI Tij? faxawis ical rt-rijs yi s. 9. icat diri X0a irpos TOI ayycxov Xcycov avnp Sovvat xut TO ? t3XaDt8tov. icai Xcyct mot Aci? c icat jcarac aye avrd, icat irticpavct crov T V icotxtai, axX cv TW ordxart o ov lorai yxvicv u c3So ov ayycxov TOV ayycxov TOV cjsSofuw K: TOV C ficxXct 1 8. 104. 172. 429. 522. 1849. 1957. 2015. 2016. 2018. 2019. 2036 at A C 025. 046. 20 (- 35. 386. 468). i. 250. 2037. 2038 al 1 Or" vg- s 1 2 eth:35. 60. 201. 386. 432. 468. 1957. 2023. 2041. 2067 Pr gig vg c f v bo arm: tune vg 4 ercaco-01 A C 025. SO (-35. 205. 468). 250. 2038 alp m s: +yap bo: Tcxeor i. 35. 205. 468. 1957. 2015. 2019. 2023. 2036. 2037. 2041. 2067 Or": Texccrlct 046. 104: Tcxccr vat 35: finietur Pr (gig vg arm) wtr o 60. 432. 1957. 2015. 2023. 2036. 2037. 2038. 2041. 2067 s 1 arm 1 2 4-: ocr 35 ewry-yextorcv cvityyexto-atO 35. 60. 93. 181. 432. 506. 1957. 2015. 2023. 2036. 2037. 2041 Or 1 TOVO- cavrov 3ovxov0- A C 025. 35. 205. 2020. 2038: TOVO- Sovxovo-cavrov Or 8: rover ovxovo- avrov 046. SO (-35. 205. 2020). 250 al mu s 1: Tovo-avrov Sovxovo- 69. 2019: TOUT cavrov Sovxoto I. 2037. 2067 al p: TOUT avrov

Sovxotcr 2015. 2036: Toto- Sovxoto- avrov 498 gig arm 1 2 4: per profetas servos suos Pr: per servos suos vg arm 8- bo TOVO- irpo ip-acr pr teat K eth: roto- irpo rjtalO- i. 498. 2015. 2036. 2037. 2067.

8. Kai i) wit) t)K Tjkouaa KOI ixovo-a tfrwrjv 104 Pr (gig) vg 1 S 1 arm 4 Xoxovcrav. Xcyovo-av AKC 025. 046. 61. 69. 104. 1957. 2019 (+ fiot). 2038 (Pr) gig vg s 1 arm 4: Xoxovo-a. Xcyovcra 20. I. 250. 2037. 2067 al pm Or 8 icat Xcyovo-av Pr: + AOI arm 2 I wayc +icat 91. 175. 242. 314. 617. 1934. 2016. 2017 Pr vg arm 2 8 0tJXtov AC 69. 314 Pr gig vg: c? Xopt-Stov X 025. i. 2038. 2067 ap Or 8 s: Xtsoptov 046. 20. 250. 2037 al pm i vcwytcvov A C 025. i. 61. 172. 250. 2018. 2019. 2038. 2067 al: aycctfyAcvo? 046. 20. 2037 al mu Or 1: s x CVX M C arm 8: cv 3i4- 2016: cic x pwr 2019 Pr gig vg 0oxoo–oiyo-. yiyor- s 1.

9. Kai ain)XOa. Xafje s 1 aimj 0a A 336. 498. 517. 620. 866. 2024 Or 8: a. mi 6ov C 025. 046. 2O (-620. 866). 250. 2037. 2038. 2067 al pl Xeyoiv avro Tyc: avtto Pr Sowat AKC 046. 20 (- 35. 205. 468. 2020). 250 alp"" Or 8 Tyc Pr gig vg s 8 arm 4: 800- 025. i. 35. 205. 468. 1957. 2015. 2019. 2020. 2023. 2036. 2037. 2038. 2041. 2067 bo fitflxapiiov A C 025. i. 2038. 2067 al p Or 8: fitpxapiov A: jfysXtov K al p (Pr gig vg): fiip t apior 046. 20. 250. 2037 al pm Xa c icat jcata ayc avro avro icat xara ayc M: Xa3c avro icat Kara ayc avro K c eth IO. Kat txaflov TO itixoptstov IK-rijs cipbs rov dyycxov KOL Kartyayov avrd, icac rjv iv r orduian w yxvicv ws icxt icat ore fyayov avrd, iirikpdvoy rj icotxta AOV. II. ical Xeyouo-tv un Act re iraxiv irpo rcwrat M, Xaofc cat cftcaw jcal yxucnrats icat tfaortxcvow roxXots.

arm 11: accipe librum et devora ilium vg: Xojsc avro o-oi bo o-ov o-ot s 1 np icotxtav Tyy icapstav A Or 8: + CTOV s 1: cv rrf icotxta arm 1- I coroi yxvicv Pr: yxvicv s 1.

10. Kuj–OT Pr icai exaysov. icatC ayov avro gig pifixjopaw AC 025. i. 2038. 2067 alp Or 8 s: fybXioi K 046 2O (- 35- 2 S)- 2 5 almu (v g): Xisapiov 35. 60. 69. no. 205. 432. 1957. 2015. 2017. 2019. 2023. 2036. 2037. 2041: libellum Pr KCU ijv. c ayov avro Pr arm 1 yxwcv oxr xcxi A 046. 2019 arm: coo- Acxt yxvxv KG 025. 2O. 250. 2037. 2038. 2067 al 1 Or 1 gig vg s arm 4: yxwcv arm 2a: tocr text eth ore c ayov avro 25o. 424. 2018 arm 2 tirikpavorj eycito- K Pr gig arm 1 2 4 icoixui jcapsia Or 1 (but writes icotxta above) fiov + irikpiav gig arm 1- 8 4.

11. Xcyouaiiaftc 046. 20 (-35. 205. 468. 632. 2020). 250 al mu Or vg- sa: Xcyci 0215. i. 35. 104. 205. 241. 468. 632. 1957. 2015. 2016. 2020. 2023. 2036. 2037. 2038. 2041. 2067 al p Tyc Pr gig vg- d f T s arm bo w eth mx. iv irpo i?-Tcvoratl-202o: 7raa. iv- arm 2 Xaour. c vco-ij s CTTI Xaowrj cm Xaou 617. 920. 2040 s 2: an Xaovo 172: in populos Pr: populis gig vg c vccriv AK 025. i. 35. 205. 241. 468. 2016. 2019. 2020. 2037. 2038. 2067 al p Or" gig vg bo: pr cirt 046. 3O (- 35 205. 468. 2020). 250 al mu S JCGLI yxwo-crawr. iroxXour arm 1 yxoxromcr pr ciri arm 1-.

CHAPTER XI.

I. Kal C O T; ftoi xaxaios 01010? pa88a Xtywv v Eyccpc xal fjL Tprj(TOV TOV VttoV TOV COV Kal TO UOTloOT ploK Kttl TOV9 TTXMT- 1. nat csoov foi dedit mihi Pr: c8okai AOI bo fcaxauxr ioo- paftw Aaron virgae similis Tyc: harundinem auream similem virgae Pr bo (m s pl) eth oxoiocr pa?8o coo- pafibocr 2020 Xcywv A c 025. 20. i. 2038 alp m Tyc Pr gig vg: +LUH 743. 1075. 2067 arm 1 8 bo eth:

Xcyct N: icat CDVT; Xcyovo-a 2015. 2036. 2037: pr icat ctonicct (ccmicct K c c: umicci 046) o ayycxoo-K c- 046. 60. 61. 69. 104. 172. 250. 424. 432. 1957. 2018. 2023. 2041 Or 1 s 1 2 arm: pr KCU o ayycxoo- cumpfcet 2019 cyctpc AK 025. 046. 175. 325. 456. 620. (866). 920. 1849. 2004. 2037 al

CV avTf. 2. ICOl T F Ovx? Tljfv l toqfv TOV? OOV ifaqtv Kal firj amjv fiaTprfaip, Sri I860rj TOW c vccriv, cat T r v ayiav iran roinrtv Aijvus rco-o-cpcucoira al Svo.

3. ical SUKTO TOIS owtv paptvo-tv JJLOV, Kal irpot7jt i(rowrt. v tcpac Xixias SiakOo-ias ef iKOVra f ircpiJcJXiyAeiovs f OTCLKKOV?. 4. Ovroc cio-iv at Svo ixatai icai at Svo Xvxvtat at evanriov TOV fcvptov TJ S yifc

Or: cyccpoy 60. 94. 205. 2038: cyccpat 9O (- 175. 325. 456. 620 866. 920. 1849. 2004). i. 250. 2067 al oi 2 104 Tyc bo flerpiprov xcrpiprai 104. 920. 2040 rov ov arm 1 2 TO 0wuurn? ptoi-f TOV 0cov Tyc Pr: + avrov eth ev avrw illud gig arm 4 f.

8. KU TIJK aoxrjk. trpi tn ff gig Tqv avkrjv njv K c: TTJO- avx o- TTO- K: atrium autem (Tyc) vg: ara autem Pr c o-tfcv 1 A 025. 046. SI. 2067 alp 1 Or 8 Tyc Pr vg s arm 1- bo: CO-010CV M I. 172. 181. 250. 2018. 2037. 2038 s 1 voov K c: Xoov K cic9axc c ev icat Pr arm 4 c aac K c: pr KOI M: CK)8dxXc 2037 cfcoflcv A i. 35. 61. 69. 172. 181. 250. 424 432. 506. 1957. 2015. 2018. 2019. 2023. 2036. 2037. 2038. 2041 Or s: co-ulcv 025: ecro) N arm 1: cu 046. 21 (-35). 2067 al pl arm 1 8 bo: foras Tyc vg: arm 2- eth xcrpiyotcr Ltcrpi rior X: ftcTpito-cior 104. 2036 TOUT clvccrtv K: pr icai N rrjv iro w rip aytav 17 iro ur rj ayto arm 1 bo rrjv ayiav Pr vatiprawriv p, Tp-rjtov(riv A: + cv avn; bo: " that they shall trample under foot" arm 1 Tco-o-epcucovra AK: Tco-o-apacokra 025. 81 (-35) al pl Or 1: fi 046. i. 35 KOI Svo A 046 (f?). 21 (- 35. 205. 617. 919. 2020). 429. 2067 al p s arm: ai K 025. 69. 205. 250. 617. 919. 2018. 2020. 2023. 2037 Or Tyc Pr gig vg bo: ft i. 35 8. KCU irpo ntCUooupii ut profetent Pr eth: irpo rcvo-at 8 l: icat bo I Stcucoo-iao-69 if lyicokra + ircvrc K c- c 69 arm 1 2 8 wepijsejsXiyievovo' AK 025. 046. 35. 91. 104. 242. 920. 1934. 2015. 2036. 2041:-u otk c C 21 (-35. 920. 1934)- I-250. 2037. 2038. 2067 al pl Or Tyc Pr vg: amictis gig O-OLKKOWT saccis Tyc Pr gig vg T.

4. 01 Suo cxauu rcat i. 2038 at 1 K c: 01 K: 2OS s 1 2 cxaiat avxcuai A: axatat C at Svo 2 AK C C 025. 046. 81 (- 205. 620. 866). 250. 2037. 2067 alp Or arm: c Svo 620: Svo K 205. 866 al p s 1- otevowrtov AC 025. 046. 81 (- 35. 175. 205. 386. 1934. 2040). i. 250. 2037. 2067 al pl bo: ot cvowriov 201. 386: cu 35. 6z. 69. 104. 172. 175. 205. 241. 242. 314. 424. 1934. 2016. 2017. 2018. 2038. 2040 Or: in conspectu Tyc vg: sub conspectu Pr: coram gig TOV icvpiov C 025. 81 (- 35. 265). 250. 2067 al 1 " 11 Or Tyc Pr gig vg s arm 8- 4 bo: TOV A 046: TOV 0eov i. 35- 205. 2015. 2019. 2036. 2037. 2038 al p arm: "the lord God " arm 1- TITO- yiyo- pr munpr s 1 arm 1- f: super terrain gig: f foroirc? f. 5. ai A rw avrov? 6i i dstfcjo-ac. irvp faropcvcrat IK rov oroAaros avrwv icai icarcorfici rovs fyopovs avroiv.(a) 6.

DUTCH govern TiOv i(owtiav jcacio-ai rov ovpavov, Iva JJLT) vcro? ra rjptpas rijs irpotfrrjrtias avrwv, cat e owiav cxowtv lirl rcov v ariv orpci eiv avra eis alia KCU Trarafai riyv yijv cv ircuny oo-cuu? lav

Text adds a gloss here: icol ef rtf 0e ifa-0 aiirodt dffiic rcu, ofcrwi ef bo COTWTCO-AK C 046. 91 (-35. 205. 337. 468. 617. 632 866. 920. 2020. 2040). 250 al inu

Or s: eorwrawr 866: ccrraxrat tf cc 025. I. 35. 104. 205. 241. 337. 385. 468. 617. (620). 632. 920. 1957. 2015. 2019. 2O2O. 2023. 2036. 2037. 2038.

2040. 2067 al p: stantes Tyc vg: consistentia Pr.

6. KCU ci TUT aurouff Ocxci asikijaat xac ct re tfcxowri avro Trotto-ovo-t bo?: "and they (he arm 8 4) shall desire (desire arm 4) to hurt them" arm avrovo- 0cact AC 025. 046. 21 (-468). 2037. 2067 al mu Or 1 Tyc Pr vg s a: K 172. 250. 468. 2018 gig: 0ca. ei (asocto-ai) avrovo 69 s 1 O L 0 rj 104. 2038: faxrjwi Pr arm 1 2 8-: voluerit gig vg ostinprai + sive OCCidere Tyc irvp cfciropcvcrac. asuctjo-ai 205 CKiropcvcrcu ckTropcinrrrat 6 1. 69 Or 1 arm 1 2 8: exeat Pr: exiet gig vg icat bo Kareo ici devorabit gig vg arm 1 2 3-: comburens Pr i no- K c: Tff rur K C I: OOTMT 2020 s 1 arm Icxipn? A: cx crcc 2020 Or arm 1 2 8-: c i C 025. 046. 21 (- 2020). 250. 2037. 2038. 2067 al 1 Pr s arm 4: voluerit gig vg Otxjja i avrowr AC 025. 046. 21 (-468). 250. 2037 al p Or 1 gig vg: i. 468. 2019. 2023. 2038. 2067 al mu Pr s 2: flcaiot (osim rac) avrovo- fit (s 1) asimo-ail airoicretvcu 432. 2015. 2019. 2O22. 2036. 2037. 2067 ovrcikrj A: ovra 1 8. 205. 617. 632. 919. 920. 1849. 1934. 2004. 2040 avrov pr KOI Pr: avrovo- 620. 866 s 1 arm 4 airofcravtfipat asikijorjvai arm 4.

6. OUTOI pr coi s 1: on bo eth rqv cfovo-tav AC 025 Or 1: rip K 046. 21. 250. 2037. 2038. 2067 al pl C OVO-UIK icacto-ai rov ovpavov AKC 025. I. 35. 205. 2015. 2019. 2023. 2036. 2037. 2038. 2067 al mu Tyc Pr gig (vg) s: + KOI after c ovo-tav Or: rov ovpavov c ovo-iav fcacurat 046. 21 (35. 205. 2020). 250 al mn: rov ovpavov icxciorat 69. 498. 2O2O icxcurai arm 4 vcrocr ftp xn l- 2O 37- 2067 al p: vcroixr ftpfxl 49: wovcr fipf r) 2020: vcroo- yspc ci 429. 522. 2015. 2017. 2019. 2021: Katafiaivrj veroor s 1 arm 4: pluat Tyc vg: imbrem pluat Pr: pluat pluvia gig: " they rain w arm 1: + eiri nyv yiyv bo eth rocr yntpcur iv rowr cpour i. 2037 Tyc Pr (vg) s 1 arm 4: pr irootur bo npr Trpo iyrctoo- avrwv 025. 21 (- 617. 920. 2040). 250. 2038. 2067 al mu Or Tyc Pr gig vg s 1 2 arm: nyo- Trpo rioo- avroiv 046: avrcov rrja- irpo retao- I. 617. 920. 2037. 2040 al pl 7. Kal orav Tcxco-axrik rrjv papruptav avrcov, TO Orjpiov TO ava)ftuvov CK Tijs dJwro-ou ironact ACT avraw 7roxcj, ov Kae vttaqcrci avrov? Kal ewrokTCicr avrous. 8. KCU TO irrwfia avrv errl-njs irxatCtas rijs iroxcas TJJs fjltyaxrp, ijris jeaxcitai trv yiatikU7 2d8oAa ical Afywrros, orrov ical 6 Kuptos avruv coraupcoft;. 9. ical 3 iravrw IK TWV Xawv Kat vxwv ical yxwo-owv Kat c0i av TO irrwAa avtuv

CITi TOIK VWaiv (TTp f W auTtt OTpc Clv Ttt Vlta S 1 I C7TI TCDV vsatOv omnium aquarum Pr cur atia in sanguine gig KOI K c: K cv TTOOT; ir rjyrj ocraktcr cav cxio'oioriv AKC 025. I. 35. 205. 2015.

2019. 2020. 2023. 2036. 2037. 2038. 2067 al p Or Pr gig vg S arm 1- 8- eth: cv irao-i; irxiryiy after Ocxvjcrwrw 046. 81 (- 35. 205. 617. 920. 20 20. 2040). 250 al mu cv Traot; irxiy? Axc 025. 81 (-617. 920. 2040). i. 2015. 2019. 2023. 2036. 2037. 2038. 2067 alp Or 8 Pr s (arm 8- a): cv 046 al p vg (arm 1- 4): cv gig: 6i7- 920. 2040 cav av C 2020 cxiyo-cuon ortv C: cxaxriv 69. 498. 2019. 2038: dcxowiv 181.

7. icai orak Tcxcaucriv 6i7 (but not 617). 920. 2040 Or (through homoeotel.) arm 2- 8 Tcxco-wo-iv Tcxco-oixrt i. 2037. 2067 avtoiv TTCT (avrcuv KCLI TTjv eth) wpo rTetacr (-av eth) avraiv bo eth I TO fajpiov-H TO Tcraprov A TO avaftawov K c: TOTC avafialvov R: TO ava? atvav A: quae descendit Tyc a uo-crov axao-otyo-

s 1 ficr avtfov woxc tov Atfc 025. 046. 81 (- 205). 250 al mn Or Tyc Pr (gig Vg) S: iroxciov ACT avroiv I. 205. 2019. 2037. 2038. 2067 al p voojo-ci VCUCTOT; C: vwoyoty 104: vicit Tyc icai airokTCvct avrovo- i. 172. 181. 498. 2019. 2021. 2038 feat DO airokTcvct occidit Tyc.

8. TO TTTwia AC 046. 31 (- 35. 205. 2020) al mu Or" Tyc arm 8- bo: Ta Trrayiata K 025. I. 35. 172. 205. 250 1957. 2018. 2019.

2020. 2023. 2036. 2037. 2038. 2067 al p Pr gig vg s arm 1 2 4 CTTI Tiyo-Trxatciao- CTTI TWV Trxiatctwv s 1: in plateis Tyc vg arm 4: in platea gig: in medio Pr: " in the midst of their street " arm 1- 2- 8- a: pr corai- c bo sa: pr eao-ci 432. 2015. 2022. 2036. 2037: pr proicitur Tyc: pr ponet Pr: pr jacebunt gig vg d T arm 4: pr posuit eth-nyo- Trxarctacr eth froxcwo–nyo- ficyax o- rqr Acyaxio- woxcaxr 205: cv rrj Troxei rq p yaxrj arm 1- 8: + pufti 94: + arata 2015. 2036. 2037: + jacebunt vg- c Sosofta-f Kat cyyvo- o irorauwr K c: Segor arm 1 4: +Kai Ba uxwv arm 4 cai Aiywrroo- Pr: Kat Topoppa 2019: + icat Ba)9vxov arm 1 8: "of Khemi" bo OTTOV Kat Kat M I. 61. 69. 104. 172. 181. 250. 424. 910. 2018. 2019. 2038. 2067. s 1 bo eth avtoivj c: K: tyiwv i (.

9. pxriroucrikj ? Xc owtv Pr gig vg arm 1- bo eth Xocwr. vxcov- K s 1 bo vxwv pr TWV 046 KQI c6Vov I Tyc arm 1:-f "they shall look upon " bo TO Trrwta. ifutrv Pr A C 046. 81 (- 35. 205. 2020. 2040). 250 al pm Or

Tpcts Kat fluru, KOI ra Trrwxara avrwv OVK d tovcrtv JAa. IO. Kat ol fcaroiicoi-wcs cwi TJ yi s xaipowtv cir avrotf Kat cv xuvoirat icai 5u0a irci ovo-tv aaA Aots, on ovrot ol Svo 1 1. Kal tcra ras rpcts fjfltpas KOI r)p. urv n-icoia ui s CK TOV 0cov urfj 0 v cv avrots, Kal cona-ay liri TOVS irc8as avtcov, ical

Tyc arm 1- 8- a: ra Trrwiara 025. i. 35. 205. 1957. 2015. 2019. 2020. 2023. 2036. 2037. 2038. 2040. 2041. 2067 gig vg s arm 4 bo Kat ijucru Attc 025. 35. 429. 432. 2015. 2023. 2036. 2040 al p Or 8 Tyc gig vg s arm 4: Kat 046. 21 (- 35. 2040). 250. 2037. 2038. 2067 al pm ra m-cowita" ra owxara 2037 arm 8: TO o-cuxa 69: "their bones" arm 1 2- afaovo-iv ANC 025. i. 181. 2015.

2019. 2036. 2037. 2038 Tyc vg: a o-ovo-tv 046. 21 (- 2040). 250. 2067 al pl gig s arm bo: a tao-t 2040: a nycrtv Or 8 xv a (A) K 025. 046. 21 (-205). i. 250. 2037. 2038. 2067 al pm Or" Tyc gig arm 1 2- bo: iviymov C 2019: zvtjxara K c 205. 522 al p Pr vg s arm 3- 4.

10. 01 KatoucoukTCff pr iravt r bo 7rt Tiyo" yiyo? rt nyv yrjv 172. 314: eiri 2OI5 2036 x al P vcrlV olprjo-ovrai 2020. 2067 Pr gg v g s arm 4 bo CTT avrour ev avrour 2015. 2020. 2036 wfpaivovral AKC 025. I. 35. 181. 205. 2015. 2019. 2036. 2037. 2038. 2040 Or 8 arm 1- 2 s tt: epulantur Tyc: tv pavor rovrtu 046. 81 (-35- 20 S-2040)- 69. 104. no. 250. 314. 2067 Pr gig vg s bo Kat V(fpaw. eth ircA ovo-tv A C C I. 35. 205. 2037. 2040 al mu Or 8 Pr gig vg s bo eth: Trcxtrowrtv K 025. 2015. 2019. 2036. 2037. 2038 Tyc arm 2- 8- 4 (sa?): SUKTOVO-IV 046. 21 (- 35. 205. 2040). 250. 2067 al mu a r)Xoir axX ova-C 517 ovrot s a ot Svo TTpofrjtcu ot irpojr Tai ot Svo K: Trpo rot Pr TOVO- Karoi-Kovrracr cirt rrja- 7170- eos per plagas Tyc.

11. Tcwr rpciv AC 046. 21 (- 35. 468 1849. 2020). 2037. 2067 al pl Or 8 s 2: racr K 025. I. 35. 69. 141. 250. 432. 468. 1849. 1957. 2015. 2018. 2019. 2020. 2023. 2038. 2041 s 1 arm 1 3 4- bo: arm 2 I CMUT Kat lyxto-u rj pacr after lyiton; 69. 2015.

2020. 2036. 2037. 2067: Kat 69. 2020: Kat rjfuo-u arm 1 2 rjfjlurv rjpio-ov AN: TO-TJMCTV C oi; cr f wv s 1 arm 8: bo CK TOV cov 468. 617. 632: CK arm 1 2 4 bo CK TOV 0cov CMTiX cv ctori? A0ci CK TOV Ocov C I cto"i? A0cv cto'cxcvo-crat bo eth cv avroto- À 94. 2015. 2019. 2036. 2037. 2040 Or 8: cv C 025. I. 35. 104. 181. 2020. 2038: cto- avtoixr 046. 21 (-35. 2020. 2040). 250. 2067 al mu Tyc Pr gig vg arm bo sa eth: cir avrovo- 1957. 2023. 2041: s L2 = cv avroto-or cur avrowr cor o-av anyorovrat 2020 bo eth ain-Dv + Kat nrcvia urjr drco cv CTT avrowr s 1 cwcirco-cv AC 025. 35. 325. 337. 456. 468. 620. 632. 866. 920. 2037. 2038 al p Or 8: cirttrco-ctrat 2020 arm 1 2 8 bo: circcrcv K 046. 21 (- 35. 325. 337. 456. 468. 620. 632. 866. 920). 250.

; rrc0rcv brl rovs faupovvras avrovc. 12. ical fyovouv tinn v iv") IK rov ovpavov r Xcyowrav 1 avrotc Ava9atc ov Kal aw- etc rov ovpavov 4v r vt cxp, ical ffwp crav avrovc o P avvJiv.

13. Kal iv fc v 7 r upa iycvcro crctcrAos icya, Kal TO Sarov r 5 iroxcax tfirccrcv, ical aircicravtfitOav v Tp o-cur cp 6vofiara dv0pa-irav txtasc? euro, Kal ol Xotrrol oy8ot ycvovro ical csaucav Sofav rji c9cf rov ovpavov.

14. H oval 17 Scvr pa dir Xtfcv isov 17 oval 17 rpmy cp erai 2067 al p eth: cycvcro S 1 rovo- ccopot rocr rcw tfccupovvroyv C 025.

Id. Pr t Kouoak A C 025. 429 al p vg s: rjkova-a 046.

21 (-2020). 250. 2037. 2038. 2067 al pm Or Tyc gig arm bo sa: okowrorrcu 2020 tfhwijv ficyoxiv CK rov ovpavov de caelo vocem magnam Tyc wrjv icyoxi; v. Xcyovo-av (Xcyovou 046) A 046. 21 (-35. 205. 2040). 250 al pm Or 8: uvipr fjl ya rjfr. Xcyovo o- C 025. I. 35. 60. 181. 205. 432. 1957. 2015. 2019. 2023. 2036. 2037. 2038. 2040. 2041. 2067 avrour A 2015 Tyc gig: avrovo 2016 ava? arc A C 025. 325. 452. 456. 506. 2019 Or: avaftrjre 046. 21 (-325. 456. 620. 866). 250. 2037. 2038. 2067 al pl: ovaJ ir 620. 866: ascende Tyc: " rise ye up and come up " arm 1 a c ccupio-av c0capow 498. 2020 s 1: "shall see" bo avrovo- "their going up" arm 1- 01 cxfywt pr iravt o- arm 1- 8.

13. KOI CK A C 025. i. 35. 205. 250. 2037. 2038. 2040. 2067 al mtt Or Pr gig vg s arm 1 a bo eth: KU 046. 21 (- 35. 205. 2040) al mu Tyc arm 8 4 opa A C 025. i. 205. 2019. 2037. 2040 al p Or Tyc Pr vg s arm 1- 2t 8 bo eth: ipucpa 046. 21 (- 205. 2040). 250. 2038. 2067 a l pm gig arrfl4 I Y I TO orrai arm 8 bo

KOI TO (ixrrc TO C Scicarov y 046 bo: oa8ckarov 175. 2017: + ucpoo- bo eth r o- v eweo-av s 1: " was swallowed up w arm 1- tt I ovofjuaau avopwrw xtxtosco-cirral numero LXX milia hominum Pr: pr fcoc s 1 ovotara av panrqivj arm 1: ovofiara avopwirot s 1: avopunrot, arm 01 XOHTOI-I- av poiiroiv arm 4: " after that " arm 1-f fjito3oi, cycvovro cv oSoc cycv. C: cv fo3D iycv. M 69 Or Pr (sunt missi) s 1: in timorem sunt missi vg: "fear (+ great arm 1-) was (shall be arm 2) in all " arm 1–:" were astounded " arm 4 1 cycvovro icot ycvoAevoi 2015. 2036. 2037 TOV ovpavov Tyc s 8: + et terrae Pr: rw ev rw ovpavo s 1: " heavenly " arm 1- 2-.

14. i) oiiai i) Scurcpa rj 1 M c i. 172: pr KOI 386: pr cfiov arm 1-: tsov at ovai at fivo s 1 awq 0cv naprjxOcv K 2015. 2036. 2037: amyxtfov s 1 isov pr Kat vg s 1 arm 4 bo: 104. 205. 209. 218. 314. 2018 arm 8 eth: KOI arm 1 2-" eth isov rj ovot 17 rpcn; cpxcrot AC 025. i. 35. 2019. 2020. 2038 al p Or" Pr (vg) s (bo): tsov

17 Tpiny ovot cp erot 2015. 2036. 2037: ov ovat ij rptrrj cp crat 15. Kai o tl)88p t fyycxos Aroxirtw xal fycvoiro KOVCU rp ro

"Eylrcro ij flavixua rov xooytov row icvptov wr ical nov

Xpurrov afrov,

Kal jfturtxcvvci cis rove alawac rwv aiupw. 1 6. ical ot ctfcocrt rcwapcs irpeo-jftvycpot ot fruirior rov 0cov feaftf-M eiri rove flpoyous avrur lirco-av cvl ra ffpaninra avrov xai irpocrckvv ow rip 0c Xeyovres 2040: 17 ovai 17 rpvnj (ra v) cpxcrat 205: tsov cp crat 17 ovai 17 rpirrj K 2019 gig: 17 ovat 17 rpin; t5ov cpxenu 046. 81 (- 3J. 205. 2020. 2040). 250. 2067 al mu epxerai veniet vg (arm 1 2-"-): cai? Xv0c s 1: tr. after ra v 205.

15. Ku + ore arm 1 2 3 a o cj38oiocr ayycxoer ecraxirurcv oc eirra ayycxoi co-axiricrav arm 1 o A icai 8 arm 1 4- cycv-roto K: eycvero K arm 1 " 8- tfxavai xcyoxat wny icyaxiy arm 1 8 eth: jivti arm v TW ovpavu K TOU ovpavov arm 1 8 bo eth Xeyor-Tcr A 046. 18.61. 69 82. 93. 1 10. 314. 325. 336. 429. 432. 452. 456. 506. 517. 522. 617. 620. 866. 919. 920. 1849. T 955- 20 4 2021-2039 Or 8: Xryowat NC 025. 21 (- 18. 325. 456. 617. 620. 866. 919. 920. 1849. 200 4)- 2 5- 2037. 2038. 2067 al pl cycvcro rj facrixcta rycfOvro at ftturixfiat, I. 104. 205. 2038 17 frurixcia pr waaa arm 1 2 TOV KOO-IOV huius mundi gig vg: 2015. 2037 Pr arm 1 rov icvpcov JH. W pr KOI 1934: rov Otov rjpw 2015. 2020. Pr: KCU rov foov rjfjuw s 1: rov xvpiov rov Q OV I KDV bo KM rov Xpiorov avrov Irjaov Xpurrov 205. 1934. 2015 (pr rov). 2036. 2037 arm 1 2: ccuarm 4 fao-txcwci oonxcvct 69. 172. 325. 336. 456. 517. 620. 866. 2015. 2018. 2036. 2037: regnavit gig s 1 rover aiuwgur + rat eicr rovo- atwvcur arm 4: rov ouora bo ro)F eu(uki)i + aup M 94. 141. 181. 2020 vg c arm 2 bo 91 1.

16. OI T N A bo ctioxrt rco-o-apcor A C 025. 1 8. 175. 205. 250. 386. 617. 920. 1849. J 934- 202- 20 37 20 38. 2 o67 al mu Or 8: K 046. 91 (-18. 175. 205. 386. 617. 920. 1849. 1934. 2020). I. 104 al p: ctkOTi Kai rcoxropco- 429 al p ot vwrrtov K 025. 91 (-35. 205. 2040). 250. 2037. 2067 al pl Or" s arm 1 2 4-" bo: qui in conspectu del sedent Pr (gig) vg: ot A 046. i. 35. 6 1. 69. 104. 181. 205. 209. 2038. 2040 Gyp arm 8 rov Ocav A C 025. i. 35. 205. 1957. 2015. 2023. 2036. 2037. 2038. 2040. 2041. 2067 al p Pr gig fl vg s 1 arm 1- 4 a: pr rov povov 046. 21 (- 35. 205. 2040). 250 al pm Or s 8 arm 8 ra tcwi A 025. i. 35. 104. 632. 1957. 2019. 2020. 2037. 2038. 2067 al p Pr gig vg Gyp (s) arm bo eth: pr ot 61. 69. 205 Or 1: Kaorprtu K C C 82. 2040: ot KO VTOI 046. 21 (-35. 205. 632. 2020. 2040). 250 al 1 1 1 cirt rover Ipovov cirt 0povov arm 1 circoxw. rco cw arm 1 crccrav. OVTWK arm 4 ovrwv bo circtrov A(K)C 025. i. 104. no. 337. 429. 620. 866. 2016. 2023. 2067 al p Or: drco-ov

VOL. II. 20 17. Ev apirtovfjL V o-ot, Kvpcc 6 0cos 6 6 ftv KOI o 7Jv 9

Sri etx as ryv 8vvauv rov Mat fao-txcvow. 18a. irat ra?0? i7 cftpytcrftprai,. KCU Afcy 17 opyi o-ov, A. al 6 Kcupos Sia 0 tpa TOVS Sta 0ctpoiras T yijv, f. iral 6 ffaipo? TWV V Kpwv Kpiorjvai g. TOVS fufcpol? KOL TOVS Acyciaovf, f. gal Sowat TOV p. i(roov TOIS Sovaotf rov, e. rots irpo ifrais fcal rots ayiots 1 Kal rots o 3ovui Vois TO ovoia arov.

046. 21 (-337. 620. 866). 250. 2037. 2038. (2040) al mn: pr KOI M 2040 TCI nyxxrunra TO Trpoo-anrov fl bo xai 2 bo sa TU eo gig: " the Lord God " arm 1- Acyovrco- cxeyov arm 1: KOI cxcyov arm 2-).

17. oroi o-c 046 Kvpic Kvpuxr M 2038 o 0ecxr + rjimv 2015.

2036. 2037 gig vg arm 2 o 2 K c: K cov. i" gig eth oijv + KCii o pxop voo- o i. 35. 1957. 2OI5. 2oig. 2023. 2036.

2037. 2040. 2041 al p (bo) OTI pr K U K C: icai arm: oo-arm 1- 2 cta ao cixi co- C o-ov rrjv fieyaaiyv arm 1 bo.

18. pyi(T0Tjra K c: upyurorj K: opyurorja-av 149. 201. 2015. 2017 al p icai 2 ort bo o ov + r avrow 2020 (icai ca apat ai

A arm 2: quique exterminandi sunt Pr: et conrumpantur fl: Sia epctcr bo 8ta ipovtar AN 046. 21 (- 35 468). 2037 al" 1 Or 8 arm bo eth: 8ia 0 arrcur C 35. 60. 104. 172. 241. 242. 250. 468. 1957. 2018. 2023. 2041 Pr gig fl vg Cyp s: 0-porrao- 025. I. 2038. 2067 Kaipocr K ijpot C: 4-7170- cpio-caxr bo I TCOV VCfcpdv TtdV 10)1 617. 920. 2O2O: TOVO" V KpoVT bo icpt Tvat Pr: jcptvcur arm 8: icpticu bo TOVCT xtfcpovo KOU rover Acyoxoikr AW C Or: TOIO (pr icat 2020 gig) ufcpour Kat TOIO-utcyaxoto- K 0- 5 025. 046. 21. 250. 2037. 2038. 2067 al pl Pr gig fl vg Cyp s 2 arm: TOUT ftucpour meta TCOV tcyaacov s 1. It is possible to explain the variation of tenses as due to the dislocation of lines h and g. Thus A C preserve the ace. (TOW icxpovor in apposition to the subject of Kpioyvat) even after the transposition of the line after u TOMT fofl. o-ov. Next comes the corrector's stage: the ace. is changed into a dat to agree with TOIO- fof. Possibly the original order was a, b h y g, c, d, e, . The TOOT jjlLKpowr m-A. would then qualify TOIKT Sea dccpoirtur KT. In any case the order in the MSS is wrong. Sowat + avrour bo jrai TOto ayio r Pr gig TOCOT ayioio icai TOIO- (K) o? ovu, cvoto- TOW aytovo- KO. I rowr fofiovpcvowr A (a correction?): Toto- ayio o Kato i: icat35. 205. 2015. 2019. 2036. 2037. 2038 al p arm 1 2- aytoto–f-o-ov 617. 920, 2020 j.

19. KOI rjvotyrj 6 vaos rov 0eov o v rj ovpavcj), ical jciiarros rijs 8ia0i? Ki? s avrov ei TW vcus avrov, ical fyciwro dorpairai KOI DVCU al fipovral KOI (rcurios xal 19. tjvoiytj AK (nvvyrj) C 025. I. 35. 61. 69. 104. 172. 205. 250. 1957. 2015. 2018. 2019. 2023. 2036. 2037. 2038. 2040. 2067 al p Or eth: i? votx 7 046. 81 (- 35. 205. 2040) al mu o cv rw AC 61. 69. 172. 250. 2018. 2020. 2040 Or 1 gig fl arm bo eth: OK 025. 046. 81 (-2020. 2040). 2037. 2038. 2067 al pl Tyc vg s j ovoavco + aya K (del. M c) ux fliy csoftp C rrjo- tabrjmfcr avrovj rov ov arm avrov 1 AC 025. i. 35. 172. 205. 250. 2015. 2018.

2019. 2036. 2037. 2038. 2040 al p gig vg s arm 1 2 8 4: rov KVUOV 81 (-18. 35. 205. 386. 2040). 2067 al pl Or: KVBIOV 046. 18. 104. 1957. 2039: rov 0eov K 201.386 fl eth: Tyc bo cv ro vow arm 2: pr" which is " arm 1-8 eth avrov 2 s 1 bo cyevovro: cycvcro K KOI avai KOLL ftpovrai Afcc 025 046. 81 (- 2020) Or Pr arm 1 2)8- sa eth: tuvoi. ?MVTCU 69. 172. 25a 498. 2015. 2019. 2020. 2036. 2037 gig fl s (arm 4) bo: xat wvac 314. 2016 Tyc: u ?OOJTCU vg cai O-CKTIOCT A C 025. I. 35. 205. 2015. 2019. 2020. 2023. 2036. 2040. 2067 al p Or Tyc Pr gig fl vg s arm 2 4- eth: at o creiaiocr 181: cai crcuriot 172. 250. 424. 2018. 2037. 2038 arm 1 bo sa: 046. 81 (-35. 205.

2020. 2040) al mu arm 8 ai xpxafa fityaxrj Tyc.

CHAPTER XII.

I. Kat a-t fji LOV ieya wfqrj iv rip ovpavw, yv ircNj? cj8Ai;ien7 rov JAtoy, fcal (rexijny vtrojcarcu ruv irow aur s, icat fart r s ccax s avr s arc avos aotcpcov 8a Scka. 2. icat v yaorpl r 2xovo a, 1. xai Pr: + tsov bo ircpifitpxrjfjxtnrj irepiJXcroio A 1 17 o-ea. i17 N c: r o-eaTiip N: 17 I. 175. 498: +1 2020 aarepaii a. Kav6w s 1 Oejca AKC 025. 046. 81 (-35. 337) Or: Scca Svo i. 181. 2037. 2067: iff 35. 337. 2015. 2017 al p: xxii 8. CK yofrrpi cxouoo erat praegnans ventre Pr: in utero habebat fl: "she was with child" arm 1 2 8- KOL Kpafa K 2040 vg c-: Kat A 025. i. 35. 2015. 2019. 2036. 2037. 2O 3: Kai cupakcv C Pr fl vg t?: dcpafav 81 (-35. 1849. 2040). I. 104. no. 172. 250. 2016. 2067 al mu Or vg 11 s 2: Kpa(cv 046. 1849 al p arm 4: vcpamv 35?: KOI eirwiv gig arm 1–: who cried out" arm 8: et clamans vg" s 1: po(owa bo uvovcra pr KOI A s eth KOI fiacravtfrntvt KOI bo: et cruciabatur Pr fl: " and in many pains she was nigh " arm 1 rcxciv pr rov 468. 2040.

Kap po ci wivowra KCU faowtfouifrn TCKCIV. 3. KOI atyft? 5 AAo OTflCiov cv TJ ovpavqs KOI isov Spavotfv ftryas mjppo CXDV Kc axas cirra cal Ktpara Scvra, al cvl rav KC axas avrov cirra Stao iara. 4. Kal 17 ovpa avrov orvpct TO rptrov raw acrrcpwv rov ovpavov, al Zftaxw avrov? cis r v yj v. icac 6 8pakov ewijkcv fronriov ri s ywaucof rijs ftfxXowns rcjceiy, iva 5rav TCO; TO TCKVOV avrfp 5. ical CKCV vtov, Jwrcv, 6s ficaAct irotLuuvctv Travra ra pdpp ri r)pa KCLL fipirdoftrj TO rlfcvov avr s irpos roi COK ical irpo rov Opavov UVTOV.

3. fcyoa irup(p)oa A 025. 051. I. 35. 172. 205. 1957. 2015. 2019. 2023. 2036. 2037. 2038. 2040. 2041 al p Tyc vg s 1 sa eth: KC 046. 81 (- 35. 205. 2040). 250. 2067 al mu Or Pr gig fl s 2 arm 1 2 8- (bo) icyao- +" exceedingly" arm 1: "it is very great" bo iruppoo- A 025. 051. SI (-18. 205. 337. 386. 617. 919. 920. 1849. 2004. 2040). 2037. 2038. 2067 a! mu Or 8: rufus Tyc Pr gig fl vg eth: irvpoo- C 046. r. 18. 205. 250. 337. 386. 617. 919. 920. 1849. 2040 s: "fiery" arm 1 2 8-: "of colour of fire " bo: arm4: + OLUHOOT irvpt eth cirt TOO- c oaocr circ TIJO-Kc oxi o- 205 (arm 1 2): cirt rcur cirra icc axao 1 arm 4 avrov avrw A 172 cirra 2 I. 181. 2038.

4. ij oupa aurou gig: avrov i o-upct trahebat Tyc Pr fl vg TOW aorcpctfv K c:-f-ro rptrov K rov ovpavov i. 2067: rwv v ro ovpavoi S 1 avrovor H- K rov ovpavov arm 2 4 eio- nyv yip arm 4 conykcv COT KCI C s: cony 61. 69 nyo- tcxXovo o-reicciv bo eth: " who wished to bear " arm 1- 8 sa rccctv TIKT IV 051. 35.432. 1957. 2023. 2041 T KIJ–i; yyki; arm L2- ro TCKVOV avncr arm 4 TCKVOV Trotsiov 2020: filium gig vg bo: natum Pr fl avn r bo icara ayi;-f avro(v) arm 3:-f avro(v) o 8ocucav arm 1 2 a tva. tcara ayi; iva cav rcm; ro TCKVOV o Spaicctfv Karaifxiyr avro bo: iva orav TCKT; jeara ayi; ro TCKVOV avnyo-eth.

6. rriktv 4- 1 ywiy Tyc arm 1- 8- viov Tyc Pr arm oporcv AC: opo-cvn 025. 2038. 2040: appcva K 81 (- 2040). I. 250. 2037. 2067 al pl Or: apcva 046 xcaAct Trotiatvciv "shall shepherd " arm 1- 2- 8: recturus est Pr gig fl vg wavro ra 0vri ra c ny 205. bo: " his people " arm 1- 2 cv pafibw A C 046. 91 (-35. 205. 2040). 250. al 1 Or 1 Pr gig fl vg s (bo): 025. 051. i. 35. 181. 205. 498. 2015. 2037. 2038. 2040. 2067 icai 2 Pr ifptraa AC 025. 91 (- 386. 2040). i. 69. 104. 250. 2037. 2038. 2067 al 1 Or: wvaxfa 046: rjpwayij K 60. 241. 385. 386. 432 1957. 2016. 2023. 2040. 2041 TCKKOV irotow 2020 I avrrjcr bo irpoo 2 i. 205. 2019. 2037. 2038 al p J.

6. KOI y ywy l nrycv cfe r v Iprjiwv, ovov fy foe? roirov TOiieurifvok diro TOV 0cov, tvo i Vpc owu l avr v i upas xtaia? owoaias if KOvreu 7. Kai lybm irrfacioc b rj ovpafty

Mt a X Mai o2 ayycxoi avrov TOV Toxci o-at icra TOV ical 6 Spokco? Tox i crcv o(ol ayycxcu avrov, 8. ical OVK furxwrw omi TOTOS cvptfty f avrwv f 3ri ev T ovpawp.

6. i) l 2O5 OTTOV e ct. airo rov flcov "where was her place (a place for her arm 2-) prepared of God" arm!: "which hath there a place prepared of God" arm 4: cat (bo) cur rov roirov OF ip-oifuurcv avn? o coo bo sa etb c ci ci c 2020 fl vg s ckci 1 AK 025. 046. 21 (- 2020). 250. 2067. al pm Or s l arm 8 4: tr after TOITOV 205. 241. 632 gig: C 051. i. 69. 2019. 2020. 2037. 2038 al p Pr fl vg s l arm l f ip-otfaaoyicvovj pr awry arm 8:-f-ovny arm 8 airo TOV 6W AKC 025. I. 35. 1957. 2023. 2037. 2038. 2040. 2041: OTTO 205: wro TOV 0covo46. 21 (-35. 205. 468. 620. 866. 2040). 250. 2037. 2067 al m!l Or B: wo 0eov 468 620. 866 eicci 2 tr after avn 468 Pr fl: 5i s l Tpc axriv A 025. i. 1 8. 205. 250. 617. 2020. 2037. 2040. 2067 al mu Or 8: cfcrp axriv 046. 31 (-18. 205. 617 2020 2040) al mtt: TM owivkC 051. 2010. 2038: cfcroc ovo-tv 429. 522: "she may be fed " arm l avnvj N: avrov K: 69 arm l t uur Sioicoo-Mio- C KOVTO A 025. 91 Or 8 (arm 8-): +ITCVTC K (arm 1- 8 8): cxuur SIOKOO-IOO- (046: oo-f 2015: ocuf 69:;(ix. KOI BICLK. KOI (frrjk. s: mille ducentis quadraginta gig: " a thousand two hundred and ninety " bo.

7. voxcfioo l + xeyao- gig bo o o re A s 2 TOV Troxei crcu AC 02 S- 35- 432- 1957- 2019. 2023. 2040. 2041 al p: Or 1: rou K 046. 21 (-35. 2040). i. 69. 104. no. 250. 314. 385. 429. 2015. 2016. 2017. 2037. 2038. 2067 al"" l s 2: ut pugnarent Pr fl: pugnabant Tyc (gig vg) arm 1 8 8: iroxciowrco- s l arm irraj Kara I. 201. 386 al p KOI o Spamov. avrov KOI o Spcucwv KOI ot ayycaxu avrov ciroxci o-av 205 8 KOI o Spaicwv rov Scvrcpov s l l.

B. nai sed fl arm 1: arm 4 wxwrev A fll (- 35. 205. 337. 1849 (2020). 2040). 250 al mu (bo) eth: urxwav (+ poo- avrov K) C 025. I. 35. 205. 337. 1849. 2015. 2019. (2020). 2036. 2037. 2038. 2040. 2067 al mtt Or l Tyc Pr gig fl vg s (arm): Mr vov 046. 69: + iroacpw per avruiv bo ovoc A C 046. 81 (- 35. 205). 250. 2067 al ma: OVTC 025. i. 35. 205. 2019. 2037. 2038 al p Or rovoo vp 0r) avrvni Tore cvpc i: K: TOTTOO- 69 cvpcfivj ovrwv AC 025. 046. i. 69. 2020. (2040) al mu Or gig vg: 2015. 2036. 2037. 2067 Tyc (Pr) fl s 2: evpcft; ovrow K 0 35. 1849.

9. KOI tp ij0r) 6 Spow 6 ficya 6 etyis 6 6 icaxovAcios Ata Soxo? ai 6 Saravas, 6 irxavwi T V ouovpavyv okqv cjsX fty cis i v yi v ecu ol ayycxoi avrov ACT avrov l3 rjoi orav. XO. cai ijicovcra fyavrp ficyclXiv cv r j ovpawp Xcyowrav Apri cycvcro ij o am; pta cat iy Suvait? ical faarixcta rov 0cov LUOV at ij c ov0ra rov Xpiorou avrov, ore iftkr Ori 6 canfycop rail a8 X v WLV, 6 Kanryopgtv avrovs onrtov rov 0cov AWV rjp, pas KOI WJCTOS.

1 1. icat avrol cvaci rav avrov Sta ro atia rov apvtbv, cat 8ta TDK Xoyov r s taprvpta? avruii, ical owe rryamfouv rrjv ia; v avro)i a pt 9o. va. rov.

2019 s l arm: cvpcft; avrco 21 (-35. 1849. 2020. 2040). 104. IIO. 250. 314. (385) al mu TOTTOO- avrov eri ev rw ovpavw cvptqrj Pr eri K ct 104. 2015. 2036 s arm.

9. o ficyaa o O KF o teyacr cx tcr K I. 2067: o ofuT o ficyacr 617. 920. 2040 Pr
bo: ficyoxr o io- 2038 o o wr pr KOLI. arm 2 o AiaJ. cat eth xac o Sarakcur AC 025.
I. 35. 2038. 2040. 2067 al p Or 8 s: KOI M bo: o 046. 21 (- 35. 2040). 250. 2037
alp o irxavwv. yi Tyc I o iraavwiJ qui seducebat Pr (bo) eth: qui seducet fl cfavflri pr
cai gig fl s 1 2): u CTTCO-CV arm: " the lion fell " arm 1- 2 f ACT avrov c Xiydi
rav 506. 2015. 2036. 2037: tcr avrov 051. i. 35. 2038: ejxiy-Orjcrav Tyc arm 1 c
Xiosyo-av en-cow arm 3: CTTCO-CV arm 2.

10. Tjicouaa rjkovcrav 2037. 2040 ffxavrjv ficyaxiv. Xcyov-crav wvtcr fjuryaxvjcr.
Xcyovoi r 2067 fi ya rjv arm CK TO ovpatco cic rov ovpavov 205. 2040 Tyc Pr gig s 1
arm 1- 4: after Xcyovo-av I. 2037 al p: 452. 2021 aprt Pr: i3ov s 1 icai 17 frurixcta Ifl
I cat i; cfovo'ta rov Xpurrov avrov Tyc S 1 Xpiorov icvptovc fi rjrj Ka. T 3 rjorj I. 35.
2023. 2038. 2067 al?: exclusus est Tyc: u hath fallen " arm jcanrcop A: Karrjyopoa-
C 025. 046. SI. 250. 2037. 2038. 2067 al 1 Or": "the betrayer" arm 4 row ofcx cov
rjfjuav s 1 o Karrjyopuv qui accusabat Pr vg s 8: "who was betraying " arm 4 avrovo-
A 025. i. 205. 2015. 2019. 2036. 2037. 2038. 2067: aimo? XC 046. 21 (- 205).
250. alp 1 Or: bo 0cov + KOI rov icvptov (Ii o-ov Xpurrov) arm 1- W i ficuv 8 i. 61.
69. 522. 2015. 2036. 2037. 2039. 2o6 7 arm 1 2- bo eth.

11. Kat 1 ort bo: arm 2 avrot ovroi: Pr vikr)arav superatus est Pr avrov ab ipsis Pr:
s 1 8ia ro aiia Sta rov aiiarocr 69. 2019 arm 1- 2- a: cv TOI atiart s 1: Sta TO ovopja.
2015. 2036. 2037 rov apvtov + rov 0cov arm 1- 2 rovxoyov C arm 4: 12. a TOVTO
cv paivcr0c ot ovpavol rat ol cv avrots oval TTJV yrjv KOI rrjv daaaoxrav, art Kat 3r)
6 8ia3o os irpos vias, c;(iv OVJJLQV cyav, ct af or o iyov Katpov cgcc.

13. Kal ore ctscv 6 SOCLKUV ore ifixirjor c rrv yijv, csuo cv r v vwauca iyris
Irciccv rov axrcva. 14. icat 66rj(rav TQ ywauu at ovo wrcpvycs rov acrov rov
ftcyaxov, tva wcyifrai cis r v Zprjfjlov

CIS roV roTTOV avTty?, O1TOV Tp f Tai K 1 KaipoV KOI KOilpoVS Ktu rov
Xoyov arm 1 2- 8: TO aiuta bo nyo- Aaprvoiao r v C: rciiv fiaptvpictfv arm 4 avrcov
avrov 172. 205. 241. 632. 2022 arm i u 8 ort bo ovc ov A rqv X Tacr fax 0- I 7 2- 2
SO-424. 2018 vg d f v arm 4 avrwv cavrwv K c a pt ficxpi 468. 620. 632. 866.

18. ia pr Kat 205 eth 01 ovpavoi A 051. i. 35. 241. 429. 632 1957- 2015. 2019.
2023. 2036. 2037. 2038. 2040. 2067 al Or arm 1-" 1 bo eth: 01 KC 025. 046.
21 (-35. 632. 2040). 250 al mu S: o ovpavov arm 2- 3: ovpavoo- arm 4 ev avrotcr
a-Krjvowrttr A 025. 046. 21 (920) Or s: cv avrour Kartwicrjvowtta C: Karotkowrta-
cv avrour K (Pr fl vg bo sa eth): "all (arm 8: ye arm 1) who are dwelling ('the
dwellers' arm 8) in them (it arm 8 4-)" arm: v avrour jcarotkowrco- 385. 429. 506.
522. 920. 2016. 2037 (gig) TTJV yyv KO. I rrjv Baxao-aav C 025. 35. 2015. 2036.
2038. 2040: pr cio- fit: pr rotor fcaroucovo-i i. 2037: TT V ayairrjv KCLI rrjv
Qaxavvav A: rq yq KM. rrj Oaxaurm) 046. 21 (35. 2040). 250. 2067 al pm Or": vae
terrae et mari gig fl vg s arm bo eth: vae vobis (tibi Tyc) terra et mare Tyc Pr jcarcfy
KoraSatvci s 1-): "is fallen" arm 1- 8- Sto oxocr "dragon" arm 1 2 3 4: "adversary"
arm 8-! vfuur avrovo- s 1 ex v pr o i. 2037 arm 8 c wv Bvpav icyavj Atyavk arm 1:
icyov jov 2067: c wv Ovfjlov utcya 2020: cum ira ingenti Pr I.

13. o Spaicw on cl v)6r: ort t Or) o Spaxatv K c
"fell" arm 1 2 8- eth but both = cSXiyfty cstu cv CDICCV K c csuo cv c: csuofccv
gig oxrcva KC 025. 35. 61. 69. 2040 Or 1: apo-evav A: appcva 21 (-35. 2040). 250.

2037. 2038. 2067 ap 1 apcva 046. 2015: viov s 2: "child" arm 1: "male" arm 4: "male child " arm 2 8-: rov veov (rov) app va 506. 680 bo sa eth.

14. cboofio-af csotfi K c 205 S 1 arm rrj ywa Kt avrrj bo at, 8vo 7TT 3iry o-irrcpvyco- Svo 468 at Svo AC 025. 35. 104. 18i. 517. 2015. 2019. 2036. 2038. 2040. 2067 (s 2): arm 1 2 8: ot K 046. 21 (35. 2040). 2037 al pl Or 1 s 1 arm 4- bo eth arcopyco- + (at) Acyaxai bo rov acroyj rov K arm bo: pr OHT Pr bo rov ticyoaov arm 1 bo irmraij irrrarai 046. I. 919. 2015. 2020. 2036: ircotrat 386: +17 ywiy bo cur rqv cpifiov 1. 181. 2037 cwr 2 Tyc arm 1 2- 8 avriyo- bo eth cwrov rpc crai A C 025. i. 35. 201. 314. 386. 2015. 2019. 2036. 2037. 2038. 2040 al p

Koipov VQ irpoo-uirov TOV fycws. 15. icat J oacv o ctytf c TOV oroAaros avrov owcru rijf ywatkOf vswp u irorafiov, tva avrqv vorafio 6prjtOV iroufarg. 1 6. KOI ipvfflrprcv rj yy TJJ ywatkt, cal jjfvotfcv y yy TO orofia avrrp icat Karcrtfv TOV vmaiav ov ciaxcv 6 opokcav K rov OToAatos avrov. 17. icat cpytcrtfi; 6 Spaicaiv cirt T j ywatkt Kat di7n A,0 V nth rai iroxcbtox ftcra TUI Xotiruk TOV (nrtpfjlatos avr, TWV njpovvriav ras Ivroxas TOV 0cov icat;(6VTiv r v fjLaprvpiav Irjrov.

1 8. ical lovdfrrj lirl rrjv aiiov T S

Tyc Pr gig fl vg s 2: pr tva Or": owov Tp rat 506. 517. 2017: otruxr Tpc iyrat 046. 81 (-35. 386. 2040). 250. 2067 al mu S 1 ckct Tyc Pr fl vg bo eth: before oirov gig Katpov Kat icatpovo- jcatpovcr Kat Katpov arm 1: Katpov-Kot Katpov arm 8: icotpov arm 2 v K: Kat Katpov K c Kat Kotpovo Kat 456 S 1 Kat i Katpov C IHUTV K c: ifuo-ov K.

16. cpaxcy cxa3cv A: vircpc? axcv 104 CK TOV OToiarocr avrov tr. after TTO-ywatkOO I OTTICTO) T. yvvatkoa after iroraiov bo sa v p 38s- 429. 522: "venom" arm 2 OKT iroraAov to fl-oraAOv 18: arm a tva. irotiytny bo avn; v worafio-faprjtov irotrja rf iroirjcrr) avrrjv TTOTap. ofoprjrov C aimv Atfc 046. 81 (- 35. 205). 250. 2037 al Or 1 Pr gig vg s: TOVTT; V 025. I. 35. 104. 205. 2038. 2067 al p iroraAO opiTOv 71-01770-77 Troraxo-fopifrov irotio-ct 104. 2019. 2038: perderet Pr: faceret trahi a flumine vg: faceret ictu fluminis trahi ad se gig.

16. Kat cpot)Or)acv. yuvaikt bo Kat 1 sed Pr rrj ywatkt y ri 3371 V r? HI-250.424.452.2018.2019.2021

Pr gig arm 1-4 TO oroia TOV oroxatoo- 18 Kat Karcirtcv. OTOAOTOO- avrov S 2 C 004 Kat 8 bo TOV n-oraAOv ov TO vup o A arm 1-: TOV n-oraiov o 456: TOV Troratov vsatoa bo c)8axcv cvc3axcv 046 Or 1: avcxa)3cv 61. 69 (69 after ywatkt ver. 17 repeats Kat tjvotf cv. avcaaicv): " poured out" arm 1-2-a CK TOW orofuft TOO- avrov " upon the woman " arm 4: OTUTCD TTTO ywaixoa bo: arm.

17. Kat upyuroi). yuvatkt arm 1-4 copyta'tfi; opyuroi) 046. 104. 2019. 2038: iratus Pr o Spakwv Pr irt C Pr j TTOLrjaai TroacAov K ftcra pr Kat 2040 TCUV Xotmiv TOIV cirt-Xotircuv K: nyo- ywatkoo- Kat arm 1: arm 2 8 TOV o-Trcpxaroo-de semine Tyc Pr vg avnpr TITO- ywawcoo- bo TOO- cvroaao-J riyv fvroaitv Pr arm 1 Irprov AK C 025. 046. 81. 250. 2037. 2038. 2067 alp Or gig vg s arm 8 4 bo: pr TOV 046. i. 104. 110: TOV flcov K: 0eov 522: Jesu Christi Pr vg c arm 1 2 eth (.

18. ver. 18 Pr arm 2 ecrrafty A C 61.172. (205) al Or Tyc. gig vgft. a. r. T s s arm i. s et h. OTa 02. o 4 5 B ai (-205). 250. 2037. 2038. 2067 al pl vg s 1 arm 4- bo.

CHAPTER XIII.

I. Kal ctsov CK rip faxaoxris Oijplov avajftuvov, cj(ov Kcpara Scvca cat KC axas euro, (a) KOL cvl ras Kc axas avrov fovonara 1 2. Kal TO OTJDLOV o etSov yv oiotor flrapixct, jcai ot Trofe avrov as apicov,

KOI TO OTOMI avrov d? orota Xcovros.

Kal cswkcv avrs 6 Spakuv riv 8vvauv avrov ical TO? Opovov avrov Kal Ifovcriav p ydxijv.

3. Kat uav e c rov icc axuiv avrov rov avarov avrov l (Oavfjlacrorj 0X17 y t OTrtvo) rov Brjplov f, (a) MSS add a gloss to prepare the way for xvii. 12: al Art rflr Kepdrur avrov Stica dia Mira. See vol. li. English transl., footnote m f.

1. Kai cisok CK Trjcr Oaxaoffi)r 205 CK TT; O-
Jcuyov CK no- axao-o-iyo" after avaftawov (Tyc) Pr s 2 arm eth Qrjpiov afaj8atvov Tyc:-f fieya arm 1 c ov cxw I. 104. no. 429. 522. 2016. 2017 K para Seca KOI Kc axao- cnra Kcpara 8cka KOI I: Kcpara Scka. xc axaa cnra vg arm 1- 2: Kcpara Scka 468 roar KC axaor rr v K ax. tfv arm avrovj avrwf (025) ovojxara A 046. 21 (- 2040) al 1 "" Or" vg s 2: ovo a C 025. i. 2015. 2036. 2037. 2038. 2067 Prgig s 1 arm bo eth ft a(T(jr)fjiia(r ycyjaiievok bo.

2. TO 6i piokj bestiam Pr gig: bestia vg TJV OMUOV- 172. 2015. 2018 Tyc Pr vg yv i. 181. 209. 2038. 2o67 cora gig arm 1- avrov 1 Tyc wol similes gig apkov A C 025. 046. 21 (-35. 632. 2040). i. 250. 2037. 2038 al mtt Or": O KTOV 35. 61. 172. 201. 241. 385. 429. 522. 632. 1957. 2037. 2039. 2040. 2041. 2067 al p oroia 2 2O2O s 1 arm 1 2 Xcorroo-AC 025. 046. 250. 2037. 20 3 8- 20 7 al pl Tyc Pr gig vg arm bo sa eth: Xcovrwy K 61. 69 Or 1 s avrco avrov 866 o K rqv Bwafjuv avrov Kac rov Opovov avrov ai arm 1 KOI rov Opovov ovrov2037 KOI cf ovcriav fteyoxiyv 385. 429. 522. 919. 1849. 1955. 2004. 2024: KOI 104. 2038: + COOKC? avrw A.

8. icat 1 + 3ov 2040. 2067 Tyc vg 4 f xtav fua arm 1-: unum caput Pr: irxiyjyv (?) bo CK O46. i. 205. 2019. 2037. 2038. 2067: CTTt bo avrov cirra Pr axr A C 025. I. 35. 205. 385. 2015. 2019. 202- 20 3- 2037. 2038 al p Or 1: oxrct 046. 21 (- 35. 205. 2020). 250. 2067 al niu: t v arm 1: arm 2 8 I 4. teal wyxxrckWitorav T(j) opokom

KOi wpoo-CKWito-av r ro Oijpiov 1 Xcyom?

T OLLOIO? TW 0i? pup, gal TIS Swatai Toxeut rai ACT avrov; 5. Kal cso? avrw oroia Xaxovv tcyaxa al JXcur rjuas, (a) (a) On the restoration of 5 b to its original place before 7, see vol. ii., English transl., footnote in loc.

ccr payicrieviyv 386. 1957. 2037. 2067: co ayieny (?) arm 1: o- ayio- bo: occisum fuerit Pr avrov 2 046. 205: row tfavatov K (corr. first hand) ctfaviacrfliy A 051. i. 181. 2015. 2019. 2036. 2037. 2067 gig (s): ctiaviacnwfy C: c avwwrcv K 025. 046. 21. 250 al pl Or 8 bo: admiratae sunt Pr 0X17 17 yq cv 0X17 Tiy yq 051. i. i8i. 2015. 2019. 2036. 2067: in terra gig: gentes inhabitantes terram Pr: + KOI iKoxovflijo-ei eth OTTUTCU TOU fajpiov O7rir0 TOU Orfpiov 2020: post bcstiam illam gig: ad bestiam Pr oirto-o) TOU flihwov irnn nnso, corrupt for rrnn nnxia. See vol. i. 337, 351.

4. TW 8pa om. Trpocrdtukijaak 2 i. 385. arm 2 bo Spakovri Byptw arm 1 ort cswfcc. tfqptu) 1 bo on esukcp A C 025. 172. 181. 205. 209. 250. 424. 2015 (ore). 2018. 2019. 2036. 2037. 2038. 2040. 2067 Or Tyc Pr vg s arm 4: +o Spokcji arm 1: TW Seswkori 046. 21 (- 205. 2040) al pm: TW 8om 61. 69: qui dedit gig arm 8- rqv cfowiav rqv Or 1: + avrov arm L 4: omnem potestatem suam Pr TO puo 1 TO)

6ypio 920: aimi) arm 1 Xcyovrccr,. 0i? piu S 2 KOI irpowkwya-av TO Brjpiov 051.
181. 205. 2038. 2067 arm 2 4- ft TO ftypiov A 2036. 2037 al p: TW (hipua tec 025.
046. 21 (- 920). 250 al 1 Or 1: TW frrjplW 920 Twr 1 ovscio arm 1 TW Orjpni) +
TOVTW s 1 2 bo eth: ilhe bestiae Pr KQI S A C 025. 046. i. 35. 60. 61. 69. 172.
181. 205. 241. 250. 432. 452. 632. 1957. 2015. 2018. 2019. 2020. 2023. 2036.
2037. 2038. 2040. 2041. 2067 Or" Pr gig vg s bo eth: if Tyc arm: 21 (-35. 205. 632.
2020. 2040). 104. no. 314. 385. 2016 al p Swatai A C 025. i. 35. 172. 205. 250.
498. 920. 2015. 2018. 2019. 2020. 2023. 2036. 2037. 2038. 2040. 2067: Swaroo-
046. 21 (- 35. 205. 920. 2020 2040) all" 11 Or 8 1.

6. KOI csofc). pxaa Tjfucur i. 2016. 2017. 2038 Pr oroia arm 1 Xoxow Aoxowrocr
205: Xaaciv arm 1 2 3 bo eth: loquendi gig jsXaa uoo- KG 201. 386. 2020. 2040 al
p vg(ft) d s 2 bo arm 1- 2: jsXacr iyuat 620. 866 vg c- f- v: j8Xao-Tfia A 172, 181.
241. 250. 424. 632. 2015. 2 18- 20 3 6- 20 37 2o6 7 flhitrfaijuav 025. 046. 21 (-386.
620. 632. 866 (920). 2020. 2040) al lliu Or s 1 arm 8: blasphemare gig: +ycvco-6lai
arm.

6. Kal ijvot cv TO OTOKZ avrov cis jsXao uas irpos TOV Mov, JXaa fnprai TO
ofOia avrov gal TIV O-ICI F avrov, r ical rovs 1 cv TW ovpav crnvowra?. roh 5
b. ai csofli; avrf (awria irotrjoui fifjvas rcovcpaicovra al ivo, 7. gal 0ty avry ironam
irdxcjuiov icra TWV ciytuv ical vucfyrai gat iioftj avrw efowia fcrl jrao-av vxrv Kal
Xaov ical yxwro-av fcal c6Vos.

8. Kot irpoo' Kvno' ovo' cv avrov iravres ol Katoutovvrts CTT! TI S y55 Tot;" 1 ov
yeypairrai TO ovoxa r avrov 1 v T(p tjsXta) T?? anjs TOV dpnov TOT) cv ayievov
ATTO ax, Ko- ourwr 6. itai 1 deinde Tyc To 1 175. 337. 617. 1849 twr jsW quao-
AK i. 94. 172. 250. 424. 2018. 2019. 2040 vg: cur j9Xao- Atav 025. 046. 21
(-2040). 2037. 2038. 2067 al 1 Or Tyc gig s 2: in blasphemia Pr arm 1-: Xao- ctv
s 1 arm 8 bo eth 0Xao 0i7Liio-ai pr KOI bo eth: KCU effxao- wyo-ev arm 1 2: ivo
)8Xao-0i;iiyot7 S 1 avrov 2 N c: avrof K KOI rqv (ncrjvrjv avrov C KOI TOWT ev
T. ovp. o-Kivowrao K c 025. 046. I. 205. 632. 2020. 2037. 2038. 2067 al m vg
bo arm: TOVO cv T. ovp. o-Kiyv. A C 046. 21 (- 205. 632. 2020). 250 al m Or 1
Tyc s 2: TOV ev T. ovp. crmpowtoo' (eth) Pr gig eth: TWV ev T. ovp. o-Krjvawrwv
s 1: rip cv T. ovp. arm 1 2 o-Kiyrovkratr o-myvowreor X: oucovkrao 386. 2019:
Karoikouvrao- 149. 201: vkVfvriv arm 8-: cjcxcjcrovor arm 8: arm L2.

5 b. xai cbo6r). iroit)ffai arm 4 a c ovrta M voujaai, AC 025. I. 94. 181. 632.
2015. 2019. 2036. 2037. 2038. 2040. 2067 Tyc Pr gig vg s eth: +o dexct K: pr
mxcuov 046 31 (- 632. 2040). 250 al pl: +Ta Tcpata a e cxiyo-c eth: fl-oxcitdat 6 1.
69 Or bo sa: ironjmu iroxc o-oi (roxciov arm 2) KOTa TWV ayiw KOI vikT (ra. i
avrovo KUI c8o (+ avrwv arm 1: + cfowia arm 2) : Tco-o-apakOFTa 025. 21 (-35).
250. 2037. 2067 al pl Or 1 1 TCO-O-. neat Svo A 336. 620. 866 2040 Tyc gig s:
icai ttc 025. 21 (" 35)- 2 5- 2 37- 2o6 7 alpl 0 Pr v g: ffl 4 6- 35- 2015. 2019. 2036.
2038 alp: (KCH) Svo arm 2.

7. aim 1 + efovcria 386. 920. 202O iroirjaai. avrw 2 AC 025. i. 61. 69. 181.
2038. 2067 arm sa tr 7 after 7 b s 2: after 5 arm 1- 2 8 arm 1- 2- 8 Tron rai iroxcuov K
046. 21. 2037 al m Pr gig s 1 2: 1. 172. 250. 2018 al p Or Tyc vg pera TWV ayiwv
Tyc vnoo-at vicitpr c ovo-ta K c: c ovo-iavm irao-av Qvxrjv irao-aar TOO- tfrvxacr

bo eth xai Xaov icat Xaowr C arm 4: 051. i. 35. 1957. 2019. 2023. 2038. 2067 Tyc arm 1- 2 bo.

8. irpoincui7)oxinriv irpoo-tkwrprav Pr vg T arm 2 8 eth avrov AC 046. 21 (-35. 205. 468. 2020. 2040). 250. 2037 al Or: 9. El! TIS fyct ofc ducovo-aroi. 10.

cz TIS I tovTOvf O8c low lj VTOAOV KOI i) 1TIOT15 TOIV Oytw.

OVTCD H025. 051. 1.35. 104. 172. 205. 468. 1957. 2020. 2023. 2038. 2040. 2067 al p: Tyc iravrco-. yi r ircwra 17 yi arm 1 cirt 920. 2040 T. yipr Tiyv yiyv 920 ov ou C Pr: own A: u ov s 1: ov ov K (but K om. ov) 025. 35. 175. 205. 250. 386. 617. 632. 919.1934. 2020. 2037.2038. 2040. 2067 al pl Or 8 Tyc gig vg s 8 arm bo eth: ov OVTC 046. 21 (- 35. 175. 205. 386. 617. 632. 919. 1934. 2020. 2040). 385 al p: A) OVTC no ycypanrat ycypaimevoi s 1 TO ovoia AC 046. 21 (- 35. 2040). 250. 2038. 2067 0 " Tyc Pr S 2 bo: ra ovoiara M 025. I. 35. 2015. 2036. 2037. 2040 gig vg arm eth: s 1 avrov AC: avrctfv K 2040 s 2 arm: K C 025. 046. 21 (- 2040). 250. 2037. 2038. 2067 altf Or 1 Tyc Pr gig vg s 1 cv ri 046 bo TW 3i3Awo

S 1 co- ayicvov eo- payicrtcvov I. 242. 336. 2020 Tyc airo vpo s 1: prtovprethl.

9. ct TUT CXCL oorur c ct arm 2: o c uv arm 8 4: 01 c ovrco-arm 1 ow wa s Pr arm: + audiendi arm bo eth.

10. cur aixpixwonak 1 Atic 025. 046. 3;. 205. 2015. 2020.

2036, 2038. 2040 vg-c l arm: +airayct 250 Or 1 gig vg- T s: + flrayci 2018: +vrayet bo: at xaxumrtav atrayci 424: ai fiax-wnav i. 61. 69. 241. 632. 2017. 2037: c ct ai Liaaxixriav 051. 21 (-35. 205. 632. 2020. 2040). 110. 201. 314. 385. 498. 522. 1955. 1957. 2016. 2041. 2067 al: aixioatfti ct (. Tiprci 2019). 104. 2019: captivum duxerit Pr cur atxioacixnav 2 A 218. 2oi80r 8 gigvgs: C025.046.21.1.61.69. IO 4 IIa 201- 2 4 X-314.385.498. 522. 1955. 1957. 2015. 2016. 2017. 2019. 2036. 2037. 2038. 2041. 2067 arm bo wrayci (rvvayti i. 2037: vadet vg: et ipse capietur Pr ia aiw 12 AC Or 8: ia aipo K 025. 046. 21. 250. 2037. 2038. 2067 alp 1 airokTav vai 1 A: On this Hebrew idiom see vol. i. 355 sq.: an-okrctvct K 632. 2015. 2036 (gig S 1-): airouratvci 051: OWXWCTCWCI 250. 2018. 2040 Or 8: affoKTcpci C 025. 046. i. 35. 104. 172. 205. 506. 620. 866. 1957. 2019. 2020. 2023. 2037. 2041. 2067 al p arm 4 bo eth: Occident Pr vg: 21 (-35. 205. 620. 632. 866. 2020. 2040). 69. 82. no. 314. 385. 429. 2016. 2017. 2038 al p arm 8 avrov pr oci KC 025. 046 al mn Pr vg s 1 cv fuxxatfnr AC 025. 046 Or 1: cv iaxupa K 35. 205. 620. 866. 2040 s arm 4 bo:21 (-35. 205. 620.

2016. 2017 al p: OITOKTCVOVOTV avtov 866. 2040). 69. 82. no. 241. 314. 385. 429. airoftravovat ammcrav6 rcnu gig s 1 sa eth: en II. Kal cffiov axXo Orjpiov dvafaivov CK rijs yfo jcoi ct cv Kcpara Svo ouia Spvp, ical f iaaa. i f 12. ical r v cjovo-iav rov irpwrov Orjpiov iraarav iroict avrotij Kai iroiei TI V yijv Kal rovs ev avrfl icaroikOvvra? iva yxxr-

Kwiyo-ovo-iv TO Orjpiov TO irpwrov, ov Mfpaircvorj jj Tr rjyrj rov Oavdrov avrov.

13. Kal TTOUI (rrjfji La uiryaaa, iva Kal TTVO troij) CK rov ovpavov bo sa v7roAoit7. irwrrco s 1 vtToxoviy sapientia gig 7rto-Tto J 0 i lir 498. 2020 I ay KDV-f fuikopios cart bo: +iakaKcr-HO9 Kat ov Oavfjiacrtl arav eth.

11. cisop t8ou 617 OyplOv Tyc avajurovl ava aivvovc: avapawatv 104 8vo tr after aovtco 2020: Ka duo 181: 21 (-18. 35. 468. 620. 866. 2020. 2040). 42. 82. no.

314. 385. 2016. 2017 al p arm 8 oiota ovoia C: outotov bo: Kat ofioiov rjv s 1 apiiw pr TU 620. 866 arm 8- 4-: opvtov Pr vg s 8 cxoxci On the corru)tion of the Hebrew source here, see vol. i. 358 sq.: Xoxct gig: a ow bo Spaicwv pr o arm.

12. TOO irpurou 0Y)piou rov Brjpiov rov irporrov 69 Troxrav Pr arm 4 wotct 1 ciroui 2020 Or Pr vg s 2 arm bo: iroii rei 172. 250. 424. 2018: iva TTOttcrci s: Trotctrat 051. 35 CICUTTIOF avrov Kaipr arm 1 iroiei 2 A C 025. I 205 620. 632. 2015. 2019. 2036. 2037. 2038. 2040 al mu Tyc gig: wonrjwi 172. 250. 424. 2018 s 1: 7Tout 046. SO (-205. 620. 632. 2040). 69. 104. no. 314. 385. 2016. 2023. 2067 al Or 8 s 2: fecit vg arm bo: ri Pr arm 8 nyv yiy Kai cvonriov 025 Kai 8 Pr rovo- cv avny Karoi-Kovrrao tr cv avrrj after Karoikovirao C 61. 69 gig vg eth: inhabitantes terram Pr: eos qui in ea sunt Tyc iva irpoo-Kwr)-o-ovo-iv AC 69. 104. 429. 522. 2019. 2038: Kat irpocncvrq-o-oiwriv S 1: iva vpoo Kvvi? o-ocriv 025. 046. 20. 250. 2037. 2067 al pl Or 8: ut adorent Tyc gig arm: ut adorarent Pr: irpoo-Kvitv K: adorare vg ro Orjpiov TO irpwrov rcu Orjpua rco irxorw 172. 314. 452. 468. 2018. 2021. 2040: bestiam priorem Tyc (Pr) rov ftmitov A avrov 2 O25 6 1. 69. 632 Pr vg.

la iroici 7rotr?(7 t 172. 250. 2018 Tyc s 1 arm 4 bo: cirotci 2016: fecit Pr gig vg arm L2 8 a o icta ficyaxa 172. 250. 2018 ivakai irvp AKC 025. I. 172. 250. 632. 2018. 2020. 2038. 2040. 2067 al p gig vg s 9: ita ut ignem Pr: u 205 Tyc s 1 arm 4 bo eth: iva ev iraavi? irony (iroici 2015) irvp 2015. 2036. 2037: Kai irvp iva 046. 2O (- 205. 632. 2020. 2040) al mu Or 1: wp iva 61. 69 irolij (ntuci 2015: 70117017 250. 2018 Pr gig vg) c rov ovpavov Karaftuvciv (Kara aivviv C: KaraZqvai 172. 250.

cis rip yfjv cvwrtov iw aydpunrcov. 14. ecu irxapp rovs s cvi rijs yjjs a ra o ieia esofl?; avra TTOITJO-CU cvuirioi TOV Oypiov, Xeycw rois Karoucovow crl rijs yijs irouprai ciicdva r 0i? pfp fc X CI w yv " ax a W s " w- I 5-xat 60i) favr f Sovvai Trvevta r cucon rov Oypiov, iva teal Xaxicrp WHIN TOV Oijpfcv, at 701170 iva 3croi av pi) vpoo-tcvv-rpww rrjv cucova rov Grjpiav avokTavbwriv.

2018: discendentem Pr) AC 172. 250. 424. 2015. 2018. 2020. 2036. 2037. 2067 Tyc Pr vg arm 1 2 8-: de celo faceret descendere gig: iron; (TTOICI 025. 2040) Karafttuvtiv CK TOV ovpavov K 025. i. 2038. 2040 al p s arm 4 bo eth: CK rov ovpavov KaraSaivr) (-v i 104. 314. 429. 522. 2019) 046. 80 (-205. 2020. 2040). 104. 314. 429. 522. 2019 al rau Or 1: Kara aivrj CK rov ovpavov 205 CMT rip yrp AKC 025. i. 205. 250. 2037. 2038 al mu Or 1 gig vg: ri TTK yip 046. 30 (-35. 205. 2040). 6z. 82. 104. no. 314. 385. 1957. 2016. 2067 s arm 1- 8- bo: ri nycr yi r 69: 3. 2040 Pr arm.

14. irxara, irxain rci s bo: seduxit Pr: irxavav arm 1 rover Karoucovrroo- A C 025. 046. 205. 468. 620. 632. 920. 2020. 2040 Or 1 Pr gig vg s arm bo eth: pr row ctovo- 051. 20 (- 205. 468. 620. 632. 920. (1849). 2 o 20 2040). 82. no. 314. 385. 429. 2016. 2017. 2023 al CTTI n r yip terram Pr vg: nyo- yiyo-arm 1- 8ia ra o tcia. ciri riyor yrjo 046 s 2 ra o icia TO rrjfji tov arm 4 Xcyw Xcyov 046. i. 61. 69. 201. 386. 620. 2040: Xcyovroo- 046.: et dicit Pr irot o-oi pr KOI K cuco a tikovav A 2038 oo- AC 025. 046. 61. 172. 218. 250. 424. 2015. 2018. 2019. 2036. 2038 Pr gig: o K 20. i. 2037. 2067 al pl vg s 1: xr Or 1 e ei A C 025. i. 250. 2020. 2038 al mu Pr gig vg s 1 arm 4 bo: x 046. 20 (-2020), 2037. 2067 al mu Or 1 s 2 np trx.-qyrjv AC 025. 35. 205. 250. 620. 632. 2020. 2037. 2038. 2040. 2067 al 1 Or": irxi o- K: nyv O46. 20 (-35. 205. 620. 632. 2020. 2040). 42. 61. 69. 82. no. 141. 201. 314.

385. 429. 452. 498. 506. 517. 522. 1955. 2016. 2017. 20 2 1 bo rqcr pt atno- (pr airo 6 1. 69 Pr) cat cfipcv (l o-crat arm 1 2 8) AKC 025. 35. 61. 69. 250. 632. 2020. 2037. 2038. 2040. 2067 al mn Pr gig Tg s arm bo: at c o-cv airo (+ npr vkiflip 336. 620. 1918) Tip iaxatpao- 046. 20 (-35. 205. 632. 2020. 2040) al mu Or 1: np ta. K. tjo-fv airo r. ir Tiy. r. la. 205 yayupqcr AKC Or: la aiwur 025. 046. 20 al.

16. aotT AC 025. (The feminine may be due to the gender of the Hebrew word rpn; but the late emendation in M 025. 046 must be adopted): avm K 025. 046. 20. 250. 2037. 2038. 2067 al pl oowai C arm 8 Bowu nrcvuui AK 025. i. (35). 205. 2037. 2038. 2040. 2067 al mu Pr gig vg s: 046. 20 (- (35).

1 6. KOI iroict 9ravra9, rovs uirpovs rat TOVS tcyaxous, at rov? irxovo-iov? al TOVS irrco oi, Kal rovs Acv cpovs ical TONS Sovxovs, tva Sa ny avrocs apapa irl rr CC avrov rs 8c ta? cirl rd 205. 2040). 250 al mn Or 1 wa KOI a rjrr rj CCKOIV rov Orjptov C 69. 336. 468. 617. 620. 2015. 2036 s 1- arm 4 bo (but not sa eth) tva ai Pr arm 2-: KOI 104. 205. 2020. 2037. 2040 gig arm 1: on arm 8 Xaxrjovj Xox o-et 104. 522. 620. 2040: cxaxci arm 8 I ai 11-0117017. pptou 2015 ai 70117017. airojcrak-wj teat airofcTeivai ocrot eav AT; irpoo-Kvvrjcrovo-LV r. Brjptov KCU r. eucova avrov bo 0117017 (on this Hebraism (= irot o-ai) see vol. i. Introd.; raw. 10. i. ( )) A 025. 046. 20 (-468. 617. 620. 2004. 2040). i. 2037. 2067 al pl Or Pr gig vg: TTOIIO-CI K 61. 69. 250. 468. 522. 617. 620. 2004. 2019. 2036. 2038. 2040 s: cirocct arm 8 eth iva A 025. 104. 506. 2019. 2037. 2040 Pr gig vg s arm: K 046.80 (-2040). 61. 69. 172. 201. 250. 314. 385. 498. 522. 1955. 2015. 2016. 2018. 2036. 2038. 2067 al p Or vg- cay av K I. 205. 2037. 2038 al mu: 2Oi6. 2040 Trpoo-Kvvrj-o-oxrtv A 025. 046. 2O. 250. 2037. 2067 al pl Or": irpoa-Kinnrjcrowriv K 051.69. 104. 452. 2016. 2019. 2038 arm 1-: adoraverunt Tyc: adoraret Pr: adoraverit gig vg: adorabant arm 8 ryv tkOva A I. 2037 2067 alp: TTJ CIKOVI K 025. 046. 20. 250. 2038 al pm Or Tt v ikova rov Orjpiov TO (hjpiov icai Tq r cifcova avrov Tyc bo TOV Orfptov-f iva 051. i. 35. 632. 1957. 2023 al p: fneque acceperunt inscriptionem in fronte aut in manu sua Tyc airokTavbuta-iv avokravbrjvai 6 1. 69 Or 8: airoicrctvai bo: occidatur vg c- d- t T.

16. irotci iroirjo-fi K c vg s arm 1- bo: fecit Pr itxpovo oaovo- Pr arm 4 rovor 2 K icai s s 1 Trxownowr. K 2036 icat rovo irrv ow KOI rovo- cacvpowrj Pr:. excv pouo- ar m a caevfopoixr. 8ovxoihrj- 62O. 1918. 2019 eth cai TOVO- cxevtfepovo- 205. 2038: icai TOW 8c7irorao- S 1 tvabo Soxriv (own K c) A C 025. 046. 35. 42. 60. 61. 69. 172. 181. 250. 314. 432. 468. 1957. 2018. 2019. 2020. 2023. 2037. 2038. 2041 al Or 8: Soxrct i bo: 80x117 051 arm: Saxroxriv 82. 104. 175. 205. 336. 429. 498. 522. 617. 620.919. 920. 1849. 1955. 2004. 2015. 2017. 2036 al pl: Scootwonv 18. 91.

94- 141. 201. 209. 325 337. 385. 386. 456. 632. 1934. 2016.

2067 al: 8o0i7 s: Xafaxrt 506. 2040: habere Pr vg avrour K aimo K: axXTXoio- gig: 5o6. 2040 Pr vg apay pa. AKC 025. i. 172. 205. 241. 250. 498. 522. 632. 2015. 2018. 2019. 2020. 2036. 2037. 2038. 2067 al p Tyc Pr gig vg s arm 2- 8 4-: opaytara 046. 20 (- 205. 632. 2020. 2040) al 1 "" Or: TO xtyayja avrov jo6. 2040 arm 1 rye- tipocr. TTTO- 8c too- TOW x-P v. TWV oc uovs Tio1 20(-35. 205. 2040). 42. 82. no. 201. 314.385. 429. 498. 517. 522. 1955. 2015. 2016. 2017 al 17 Kai 181. 2020.

arvv, 17. Kal Iva iij rts Swirai dyopcurat fj irwxfprat tl 6 fytov TO dpayfioj TO ovofia TOV Qtjpiov i) rov pioJibv TOV iatot avrov. 18. r OSc 17 cro ui mv 6 jfx wv " w rfy rov Apiofjubv TOV Orjptov, dprffios yap Avopunrov larrtv Kal 6 avrov aiccxrtoi KOVTCL 3.

2038 arm 2 8 4 bo TO ACTWITOV Atf 025. 90 (-35. 205. 468. 920. 2020). 250 al mn Or Tyc arm (bo) eth: pr ovro 2020: TOW ACTWITOV C: TWV irrowrwv 046. 051. I. 35. 205. 468. 920. 2015. 2037. 2038. 2067 Pr gig vg arm 1 8 4 avrov 2 2015 Pr.

17. icai 1 Atf c 025. 046. 20. 250. 2038. 2067 al pl Or" gig vg arm 1- k: K C 314. 2015. 2017. 2036. 2037. 2041. Pr s arm 4 bo: sic ergo facient Tyc fu? rur uqow 172. 250. 2018 SWTJTOI A C 18. 35. no. 141. 172. 205. 241. 250. 385. 429. 432. 468. 632. 1849. 1955. 195?- 2004. 2018. 2019. 2020. 2023. 2040 al mu Or" Tyc Pr gig vg s 2: Swarm 025. 046. 051. SO (- 18. 35. 205. 468. 632. 1849. 2004. 2020. 2040). i. 61. 69. 104. 201. 314.

2015. 2016. 2017. 2024. 2036. 2037. 2038. 2067 al p arm 1 2: owio-crou arm 8-4 a bo: S ayopao-ai. ircoxiyorai 172. 250. 2018 17 wa Xiyo'iu Tyc: KO. I irioxijtrat arm 8-: +CTI 172. 250. 2018 s 1 p, ij fjajr C o e wv oc: y c cov i: c iy arm 1 2-: 04 CXOVTCO- Tyc TO ovo a rou Qrjpiov A 025. 046.80 (2020). I. 61. 69. 104. 172. 201. 250. 314. 385. 498. 522. 1955. 1957. 2015.

2016. 2018. 2023. 2036. 2041. 2067 al Or" vg: TOV oioiaroo- TOV Qrjpiov C 2037. 2038 Pr vg 0-d-f-v s 1-2 arm 8 eth: TOV Orjpiov y (icai 2019) TO ovofia avrov K 2019. 2020 bo: pr 17 Tyc gig arm 4:-f jj TOV apiofiov TOV (hjpiov 046 17 Kat Pr arm 1-2 TOV uptopov TOV opi0iov eth.

18. tj ox ia sapientiae Tyc com c ct Or": tr before 17 ia gig: +Kat s 1 vow pr rov i. 172: over N 325. 620: ow 69: vovo- 1918: o-o iap arm 1-8 rov apto ov TO ovopa, 61. 69. 2019 avbpunrov cortv- 205 cat o apiofioa 1 avrov S 1 cat AC 025. 046. I. 35. 60. 94. 205. 432. 632. 1957. 2015. 2020. 2023. 2036. 2037. 2038. 2040. 2041. 2067 al mu Pr gig vg s 2 arm 1 2 4- bo eth: 20 (-35. 205. 632. 2020. 2040). 61. 69. 104. no. 172. 250. 314. 385. 498. 522. 2016. 2018 a! Or" Tyc avrov + cartv C 025. I. 35. 60. 94. 205. 432. 1957. 2015. 2020. 2036. 2037. 2038. 2040. 2041. 2067 Tyc gig vgc s 2 arm 1 2- bo cucoo-tot (-ai:-a 025. 104. 336. 385. 620. 1934. 2037. 2038. 2040. 2067). (rjkovra (+ KCU 2037 8) e A 025. 104. 149. 336. 385. 620. 1934. 2037. 2038 2040. 2067 Pr gig vg s bo: xfr 046. 2O (- 149. 620. 1934. 2040). i. 69. 250. 314. 429. 498. 1957. 2017. 2018. 2019. 2023. 2036. 2041 al mu: xifr 2015: efaicoo-ia CKO e C: arm 4 Iren. v. 30. i: DCXC Tyc.

XIV. I 2. Q C rj VTTOfjLOVTJ TWV dyiw TTIV, Oi TTpoWTCS Ttts rov fcov ica! TIV wurriv liprov. 13. u ijjicovo-a unp Ac rov ovpavov Xcyown Fpdirov Ma aptoi oc vcicpol ol cv Kvpup diro nf-oricovtCV av apri. vai, Xcyci TO irvcvua, iva avairaio'ovtat fc TV jcoirw avrov, ra yap pya avrav aveoxovi ACT avrcov.

xiv. 12-13. On the restoration of these verses to their original context, see vol. i. 368-369.

xiv. 12. 8e tj tnrojaoin) o Sc virotevuv Jicra bo: r8c 8c 17 wofjioVTj eth o8c69 I 1 7 I 934 cfrivj + Sc i. 35. 69. 104. 205. 620. 1957. 2023. 2036. 2037. 2038. 2067 al: tr beiore 77 UTTOIOK; Pr gig oi r povrrco- rov ri7powro)v K 2004. 2019. 2020. 2040 rov ? COV I. 2067 WWTTAV + TOV 35. 432. 1957- 2O23- 2O4I

IlO-Qv -hxpto-rov 582. 1948. 2014. 2015. 2034. 2036. 2037. 2042 arm 1- bo: +xapi7erovrat 35.

13. +urr v. Xcyoucrqa jurrjv. Xcyoinrav 386 C COVTO- + O TIT p. fya rj(T bo K TOV ovpavov Acyovo-iyo-l Acyovonyo- (+ utoi 2020) K TOV ovpavov K 2020. 2037 AryovotTO-J + MH 051. I. 35. 205 468. 632. 1957. 2015. 2019. (2020). 2023. 2036. 2037. 2038. 2041. 2067 Pr gig vg d arm 1 2 8- ypairov bo oi vcicpot eth cv Kvpta) AK 046. 2O. al pl Pr gig vg arm bo: +IJIJLW s 1: C 025: (TW) ecu s awo viyo-Kovtecr "should they rise bo aw apri joined with what precedes P 35. 205. (337). 468. 498. (632). 1957. 2004. 2040. 2041 al s arm bo: joined with what follows 046. SO (- 35. 175. 205. (337). 468. (632). 2004. 2040) al mu Pr gig vg: without punctuation A C 051. 175 vat, Xcyei AK C 025. 632. 2004. 2020. 2040 al Pr gig vg s arm 1 8 4: icai Xeyei 205. 2018. 2019. 2041 arm 2: 046. SO (-632. 2004. 2020. 2040). 69. 104. 1 10. 314. 2023 al mu: voi 620 bo irvcvLwi + To ayiov 2004. 2040 arm 1 2 8 eth, Afetc avairava-ovrai 04 046. I. 620. 2038 al p arm 3 8 4: avairavo-cdvrat 025. 2O (- 620). 250. 2037. 2067 al pm: avairavcov-rat 05 1: avairavovrac arm 1: requiescant Pr gig vg: + air apri bo cic a7ro6l. 69 icoircov cpycuv 6 1. 69 TOV KOTTCOV avrcov Ta yap cpya avro)v okoxov cc TWV icoirctfv Tcav cpycov avrcov Ca- a. KO ov0r)Tti bo Ta yap epya. ficr avrcovs 1 Ta yap A C 025. 336. 506. 2004. 2020. 2040 Pr gig vg s 2 arm 4: ra 8c 046. 80 (- 2004. 2020. 2040). 250. 2037. 2038. 2067 al pl arm 1 2 8- eth j avrwv + KOI otyi o'ct avrovo-cur anyo irrjytfjv vfiatoiv DO (nd).

VOL. II. 31

CHAPTER XIV.

1. Kal ciSov KOI csov TO apviov lords iirl TO Spot oi itrr avrov cwarov Tttro-cpcucovra Tcoxrapcf c ovo-cu TO ovoxa avrov KCU TO OVOACL rov iratpo? avrov ycypat-ACVOV cirl TWV Acranrctfv avrwv.

2. ical ijjfcowra f)vrjv CK roo ovpavov arc Koviyv vsarcuv rroxXcov jcat a9 KCU 17 ctfvq jyv rjkOwra aw i0apa8a)V Ki0api(ovtCiv cv rats ictdapai? avruv, 3. jcal Sovo-tv o 01107?

rov Opovov cat VWTTIOV rcov rcovapoiv OXDF neat ro 1. icai cisok KCU isou et ecce vidi Pr: KOI yxcra ravra eth I Koi 1 gig ai i8ov gig Cyp bo (cf. eth) TO apviov. Stcuv supra montem Syon agnum stantem gig TO apviov Attc 046. SO (- 35. 205. 468) s arm 8 a bo eth: TO 025. i. 35. 205. 250. 468. 1957. 2015. 2018. 2019. 2023. 2037. 2038. 2041. 2067 al p arm 1 2 ecrroo- A C 025. 2036: CO-TWO- 046. i. 205. 250. 2020. 2037. 2038. 2040 al p: tortjkoo- 2O (- 205. 2004. 2020. 2040) 2067 al mu: comykuio- 104. 172. 2004: stans Tyc: stantem Pr gig Cyp: stabat vg eirt TO opoo- Stwv m opotr C ACT avrov A C 025. 35. 205. 2020. 2037. 2038. 2040. 2067 al Tyc Pr gig vg Cyp s 1 arm bo eth: + apiopoo- 046. 20 (- 35. 205. 2020. 2040). 250 al inu S 2 CKCM-OV TCo-o-cpakoira Tco-o-apco- A C: Karov rcrcrapa-Kovra Tcoxrapcor 025. 250. 386. (620). 1934. 2O2O. 2037. 2040. 2067 al pm: ckatov T ora-apa. Kovt o-oup ar 149: pis 046. 20 (149. 386. (620). 1934. 2020. 2040). i. 2038 al pm CXOVOYU pr at 69: C OVTCO- gig vg: habebant Pr Cyp avrov KO. I TO OVOJJM 025. i TO ovopo I04. 336. 522. 620 avrov 3 385 yeypaxicvov pr TO A b 3: eyycypaAcyov 385: KCLIO VOV i.

2. WKijk 1 2 8 XOVTO- 2067 wioyv 1 92O I CK TOV ovpavov OKT fwrjv 620 I (fxwrjv vsaraw troxXwv KO. L as favyv bo wviv 2 Tyc Kat OKT vrjv povnyo-Ltcvaaiyo- 2015. 2036 KT 2 aut Pr: arm 2- a nyv 3 Tyc Pr ftpovrrjo' tcyaxicr J N c: fjLcya ij(T 8: Pr: Ppovrqv JLeyax-rjv Tyc bo j cat 77 twr TJV jjkOwra AficC 046. 80. 250 al pl Pr s 2 bo: KOI s 1: icat fwyv (-rjr 2067) rKowra 025. i. 1957. 2015. 2036. 2037. 2038. 2067 arm 8: et vocem quam audivi Tyc gig vg: u rjkovo-a wo-aw)v arm 1 J oxr 8 1. 1957. 2038. 2067: + tovrjv arm 4 K loapwotov Ki6api ovtav Kioaptasov Ktoapifcovra s 1: Kioapwo'ova- bo cv raicr Kioapata avrcuvj avtcov C: cv T. K. avrov s 1: Pr bo.

3. Kai aftouffiv cai (bo) asovrco- 743. 1075 sli2 O eth: et 3- KOL Ovsctc ISVVOLTO ML0CIV T V el j f at cxarov rccra-cpokovra 4 ovroi ol dicoxov ovvrcs Tj apvup OTTOU av virayct. 4 d ovroi Topdo-Qrjo-av dwrd (a) Text adds following interpolation: 3 d. oi yoxwx ot drd rif 4 b. o5rof etoi ot aerd ywatkv OVK ttioxfodrpav xarflpot ydp eliri. (6) Text adds gloss: jcal TV cantabant Pr gig vg arm oxr wosp AC i. 35. 2015. 2019. 2036.

2037. 2038. 2040 al p vg s 1 sa: oxr fet 025. 046. 20 (- 35. 2040). 250. 2067 al pu Pr gig s 2 arm bo eth: cv wfy (icam?) bo wsiyi Kaivrfv 1934 icatviyv +Kai iyv K (vjv above the line): pr jcai arm 8 CKOTTIOV rov povov 42. 498. 1918. 2020: + rov Otov gig arm 1 3 icat 2 42. 498. 1918. 2020 rco-o-apoiv 2O5 Kttl TCOV 7Tp CT)8ut po)V C arm 1 8 Kttt 8-h ClonrioV

K gig s 1 arm 2- 4 a ouscto- ovse tcr 046. 20 (- 35. 205. 620.

1934. 2O2O. 2O4O). 110. 20T. 385. 429. 1955. 2Ol6. 2Ol7. OVK arm 4 eswaro Atfc SO (-386. 617. 2040) al: i waro 025. 046. 250. 386. 617. 2037. 2040. 2067 al pl: ov 8warat 2038 (arm 8): iSviaiiyv arm 4 fta civ dicere Pr gig vg (-): to know " arm bo eth ci prj cats 1 at K c 104. 620. 1849. 1955. 2004. 2015. 2017 cfcarov rco-o-cpaicovta rcao-apco AK C (C): cicarov rco'o-cpafcovra itav K: r ororap (T C: eicarov rcaaapakOvra TCO-orapco- 025. 386. (620). 1934. 2040: cicaroy to" I: pp 046. 2O (-386. 620. 1934. 2040) al mu x wi o" Pr airo nyor yiyo- quae empta erant de terris Pr).

4. OUTOI. av uirayci oirroi curtv ot akoxovtfowrecr. oi tcra ywaikuv. yap curty 205 ovroi curiv A (205) cioxw o-av cioxwav ra itaria avrov bo ewrtv 2 permanserunt Pr Cyp ovrot 2 Attc 025. i. 2015. 2020. 2037. 2038. 2040 gig vg g s 1 (arm 1 2- 3 a):-t-cto-tv 046. 20 (-(205). 2020. 2040). 250. 2067 Or" Tyc Pr vg d f Cyp s 1 arm 4 bo oi 2 K oicoaov owrcor cucoxov io-avrccr 920 S OTTOV av A C 025. I. 35. 172. 205. 250. 314. 1957. 2015. 2018. 2019. 2020. 2023. 2036. 2037.

2038. 2040. 2067 al mu: av 1849: OTTOV eav 046. 20 (- 35. 205. 1849. 2020. 2040). 61. 69. 104. no. 201. 241. 242. 385. 429. 1955. 2016. 2017. 2024 al m Or wrayct AC 104. 172. 336. 620. 2015. 2019. 2038 s 2: vadit Pr: virayi? K 025. 046. 21 (-620). 250. 2037. 2067 al pl Or s 1: ierit Tyc (gig vg): "shall go" arm rjyopacrfa rav A C 025. I. 172. 250. 2015. 2018. 2019. 2036. 2037. 2038. 2040. 2067 al p Pr gig vg s 1 (arm 4) bo eth: pr vn-o 1170x 046. 051. 2O (- 2040). 69. 104. no. 314. 385. 2016 al mu Or" S 2 airo raw avtfpunrov C airapxn AC 025. 046. 2O (-620). 250. 2037. 2038. 2067 al pl Or gig vg s arm 4 bo: av apxnr K 336. 620. 1918: ab exordio Pr (placed after rm apviu): eth ro apvtu pr cv K: rov apviov arm j.

6. Kai elsov axXov 5yyexok UTTOUFO? fr fyorra cvayyioF aiuftoy evayycxtw lirl TOW Art Tij yi s at CTTI iray 30FW KOI fvkrp ical Aaov, 7. tojffiffrp TOF 0eov xat Sore a r w, at rMXTJCvfipratC TW von rairt TOF OUXIF K cat TTK y K icai axcurray cat myyas vsatwk.

5. KM ori S 1: Pr ev TCO crroiart avrwv ov cvpca; Atc 025. I. 35. 205. 1957. 2015. 2019. 2023. 2036. 2037. 2038, 2040. 2041. 2067 al Or 8 Tyc gig vg s: in quorum ore non est Pr:

OVX CVK01? V TW OTOAOTl ttvTCUV 046. 80 (-35. 205- 2040). 69.
82. 104. no. 250. 314. 385. 429. 2016. 2017. 2018 al (bo) eth
Of Ttt) OTOtoTt V TOIO- OTOfuUTl arm bo Cvfioflr XMT I. 2037 al p arm 8 OLMOHOI yap f rtv N 046. 80 (-35). 250. 2037. 2038. 2067 al pl Or vg ft- c d s arm L 2 s 4 bo sa eth: on aicoiot CIO-IF 5 T- 35: TV A C 025. 181 Tyc gig vg f-h T: et inventi sunt sine reprehensione Pr aAwtoi aiwttrot 104 c riv + ourw curtv oc akoxov0owrcr ro apvia) 2 1 8. 242. 250. 617. 1934: + "before God" arm 8 1.

6. oxXok ayy w A c c 025. 35. 1957. 2023. 2036. 2037. 2040 al mu Pr gig vg Cyp s arm bo eth:- 218. 250 2018: oaXof K 046. SO (-35. 2040). 2038. 2067 alp m sa: oyyfxo Tyc vtrofuvov AC 051. 20 (-617. 919). 69. 250. 385. 1957. 2016. 2018. 2036. 2037. 2038. 2067 al: irctcoicvov 025. 046. i. 617. 9 1 9 al: veraptvov K ev 35 ico-ovpanfiart N c: iccroi ovpavrjfjuttt, K: ftco-ovpafMTian I: ovpavcu attan s 2 c OKra + ex avrw s 1 1 cvayycxurat AC 025. 046. 20. 2038. 2067 al pl: cvayycxunur at (K) 60. 218. 250 2015. 2018. 2019. 2023. 2036. 2037. 2041: pr cpx f L vov 2015. 2036. 2037: cuayycxi(oira bo cirt 1 Asc 025. 218. 250. 2018 s 1: 046. 20. 498. 2037. 2038. 2067 al 1 TOW itatotkowroor A 051. 35. 61. 69. 2015. 2036. 2037 al p s Tyc: TOW Kafhiiwawr C 025. 046. 20 (- 35. 2020). 250. 2067 al 1 1 S 1 Pr gig Vg: TOW ca i vow (+ u 2019) TOW xatOCDcowrao- I. 205. 2019. 2038: TOUT fta icvour 498. 2020: Cyp arm L 2 8 rt rip yiycr arm 1 KOI iri vav. Xaw Tyc wi I. 2015. 2019. 2036. 2037. 2038 4v tjv KOI yx Kraaf KM aoy Aaow. vxao- K. yxawcray s 1: traaav fv. K. wavra Xaov ic. murav yxaxrcrak bo.

7. CY K K: tr after xcyoxiy 104. 620: Xcyovra 051. i. 35 Pr Cyp cv CKUVT icyaxiy CF A: magna voce vg: Tyc 8. Kai XXoc Scvrcpof fyycxos ipcoxovprcv Xcywv "Erco-cv ftrcarcf Ba? vxuf rj tcyaxi?, 4 cv rov oivov TOV 0viov irp Tropvctas avrifc rcirrfruecr iravra ra fcvy.

9, Kai XXos fyycxos rpcros qkoxovaprc? avroit Xcyov cv wty

E? Tt? TTpoO-fcWCl TO fojploV Kai T1)V Clkow avTOV, xal Xoi avci r ro xapayMi 1 cvl f rov ucrcoirov f avrov ij rip x P metuite potius Pr Cyp rov Otov AKC 025. i. 35. 205. 250. 1957. 2015. 2023. 2036. 2037. 2038. 2040. 2041. 2067 alp Pr vg Cyp s arm 1- 2 4 bo: TOK mptoi 046. 20 (- 35. 205. 2040) a lpm jy C gig arm s aurtf gofdv 2015. 2020 avrou I. 104 ra iroiyfo-avrt AKC 025. I. 35. 205. 250. 1957. 2018. 2019. 2023.

2036. 2038 2040. 2041. 2067: pr avrai 94. 104. 336. 620. 1918. 2020: avrov irotrptavra 046: avrov rov irwrpavra. 046. 80 (35 20 5- 4 2O 2O2a 2040). 2037 al ma: avro rov iroirpravra 468: deum qui fecit gig arm 8 KOI 6a turrav AC 025. 314. 2040: KOI Oaxturvaa- I: KOI TTV Baxaartrav K 046. 051. 21 (- 2040). 250.

2037. 2038. 2067 al 1 " 1 bo: KCU 2oi9 Pr vg 4 Cyp arm L8 Tnjyaxr vsaroiv racr mjycucr TWV vsanov 61. 69: ra v8ara bo: omnia quae in eis sunt Cyp arm 1-.

8. oxXoa Scurcpoff ayycxcxr A 046. 30 (- 18. 35. 205. 2040). i. 250. 2037 al mu Pr arm 1- s 8 4 bo: SCVTCKXT 69 Tyc vg eth: ayycxocr K 4 2040 s 1: axXor ayexor5cvrcpov C: axXocr ayycxocr SevrcpckT K c 025. 18. 35. 60. 94. 104. 141. 205. 209. 314. 432. 1957. 2015. 2023. 2036. (2038). 2041. 2067 s 2 aim: oxXcxr 2019 gig rjkO ovoi)(T v i) 8v 205: qicoxovlec s 1: +avrotcr 468. 620: + OVTW Pr s arm L a- bo eth Xeywv. i; Koxoi rcv (ver. 9) K (suppl. K) 325. 456 Xcywv + ev Ki)i jucyaxq 205. 620 circo-cv cireo-ey A 025. I. 35. 241. 432. 632. 1957. 2015. 2019. 2023. 2036. 2037. 2040. 2067 al p Tyc Pr gig vg s arm 2-: " is fallen, is lost w arm 4: r rcv K C 046. 90 (- 35. 325. 456 632. 2040). 250. 2038 al mu arm 8 bo eth: circo-cv mercy CTTCO-CV arm 1 1 ij CK rov AC 218. 250. 424. 506. 2018. 2020. 2039. 2040 Tyc vg s: if K 025. 046. 20 (-325. 456. 2020. 2040) al mn Pr gig arm 4 bo: ore CK rov i. 2019. 2037. 2067 rov tfvpov rrjcr iropvcuur nyr jropvcuur rov Ovfwv 920 rov Qvpov i. 2037. 2041 1170-npr iropvuur K C C 046: arm 4 avnyo-Tavrrp 046. 82.

104. 175. 337. 385. 617. 620. 919. 920. 1849 J 934 a l p I

A 025. 046 min 5 00111 Tyc vg eth: reirrwicav K 181 (-KCV). Pr arm 4 bo sa: rorocqiccv 919: biberunt gig.

0. KOI 386 oxXoo- ayycxoo- rpcroo- AC 025. 046. 20 (325. 456. 1849). 250. 2037. 2038. 2067 alpm gig v g s arm 8-: oyy ixr 10. KOL avro? vierai TOV olvov TOV OVJJLQV TOV 0cov

TOV jccjccpoo'Acvov dvcparov cv rcs Trorrjpiy rfjs opyfp avrov, Kal paauvuror-jcrercu cv irvpl KOI tfciy cvctnrtov ruw dyyea. an ai cvairtov TOV dpiiov.

11. Kai 6 icairvdf rov facravcoyiov avraw ck auova? auoiwv jcat OVK c ovo-tv arairawrtv JyAcpa? at VVKTOS, ot Irpoo-Kwovircs TO Orjpiov KOL TJJV cticova avrov, ical ci TIS AaA? avct TO xapayAa rov ovoiaros avrov. (a) fa) Vers. 12-13 have been restored to their original context after xiii. 1 8.

oaAoo" rplToa- 1849: oaAoo- ayycxoo i coxov o'ev rptrocr K: aaAocr rpiroo-ayyexoo- arm 1- 2- 4 bo: tertius angelus Pr eth: rpiroo- i. 6 1. 69: ayycaoo- 181 avrowr avrw A Pr arm 1 2 8 v tuvrj ifyoaiy 617: voce magna Pr gig vg: bo irpotncwci irpo(TKvvr (T i. 2020 arm 8 bo: adoraverit vg: "hath worshipped 1 arm 8 a TO ryptov ro OrjpuD C 468. 2040: TO vo-taorrpiov A: ro iromjpiov 69: tr ro frrjpiov before irporicvv i i TTJV CIKOWL TI; cucovt 104. 468. 620. 1918. 2040 avrov avrcov C cat 8 C 69 XaA? avct Xi crat arm 2 bo: " hath received " arm 1- 8 a TO Xapayxa 250. 432. 2015. 2018. 2019. 2036. 2040 arm 1 28t "S 1 2: Xopayia AK 025. 046 min pl. TO is here necessary. Its absence is due either to a slip of the author or to a primitive corruption. Xflpayfut nomen Pr: + avrov s 1 2 arm (i 2 s. fl) TOV CTOMTOV roi fictciwrco K rj cm Tiyv x cc a awov s arm 1 avrov 3 6i. 69.

10. itai 1 bo eth otvov" Tronyptov arm 1 2- s TOV 0cov TOV icvptov S 1: avrov 61. 69: arm x aicparov Pr Cyp TO ironyptw CK TOV ironrjpiov A 104. 336. 620. 1918 rrjo- opyio- TT; V opyqv A (avrov Pr arm 1 2 a)8ao-av r i70etat 3a. o-avur6rj rovtat A 6 1. 69. IIO. 2004. 2019. 2040 bo TWV ayycxcoi A 506 bo: T. ayy. avrov eth: ayycacoif aytwv K 025. 35. 6 1. 2004. 2020. 2040 gig Vg S sa: ayycxoiv icat aytwv 2038: aytaw ayycxcui 69 (+ ayi(uv 2019): raw aywuv ayyc oy 046. 20 (35. 2004. 2020. 2040). 250. 2037. 2067 ap 1 Pr Cyp arm 1- 2- 8- 4: " God " arm a apviov povov s 2.

11. TOO paaravuffou tor men tor urn vg arm 8- 4: de tormentis Pr Cyp: arm 12 a avrtov avrov 104. 205. 336. 452. 1918. 2021. 2023 arm 2 cur oicovao-. avaflaim 620 cur aicovao (+ TCUV K) atcdVwv AN 046. 20 (- 205 468. 920. 1934. 2004). 250. 2038 al pl Pr gig vg Cyp S arm: cur atwa audvoo C 205. 2015. 2036: cur auova auuvctfv 025. 051. I. 6 1. 69. 104. 468. 920. 1849. 1934. 2037. 2067: cio- audvcuv 2004: "for ever" bo avaftuvci ascendet gig vg c d- T Cyp arm bo: tr before o-oicovao- roiv OUDVOIV Pr arm bo sa (eth) cxovo-iv habebunt Pr Cypl tr after PVKTOCT 35. 2020 TO Orjpiov KOI njv ccicovaj 14. Kai ctsov, KOI ifiov v f rj VKrj,

Kal fal rrjv vc cxqv f Kajicvov ojxotov f vlov dvfyanrov, CXCD? cvt riyv K fa T v aurov rrctavov xpixrovv Kal cv rjj X CI P avrov Spciravov 5 u. (a) (a) Text adds here a doublet of xiv. 18-20 from another hand. See vol. ii. 3, 18 (ad fin.), 21 sq.: 15 Kai AXXor Ayyexor fjkBev tic TOV vaov, Kpdfar tv 0WFJ iwytixp rf Ka.6-rii. Uvy dirl TTJI vcfexrji Iltji fov rb dptiravbv row icai Otpurov, ftri Xtfev r ftpa Oepurai, 6n Qtipdvoii o Oepifffaot rijt yijt.

roi Oripuv KOI rrj tixovi 468. 2019. 2040: n; eikovrj 104 TO I. 205. 2037.

14. xai cisok K s 1 eth KCU t8ov bo eth vc caiy Xcvoy nubem albam Tyc Pr: nubem candidam vg bo cm rrjv vtfaxriv Kaorjfjltyov supersedentem Tyc riyv vc cxi rrf vc cxiy 2004 Kaorjjjl vov ofjLOiov ica icvoo- oiotocr I. 104. 205. 620. 632. 1957. 2023. 2037. 2067 al oioiov Tyc eth viov AK 046. 42. 61. 69. 82. no. 201. 218. 325. 337. 386. 429. 452. 456. 517. 522. 919. 920. 2016. 2017. 2021. 2024. 2036 Tyc: vtcov 2015: woo- i: viov 025. 506: viu C 051. 80 (-325. 337. 386. 456. 919. 920). 104. 250. 314. 2037. 2038. 2067 al mu Pr gig vg S 1: TOD wo s 2 avopwtTov pr rov S 2: av6pu7ra 620. 2020 CXCDV A 025. 046. 20 (325. 456. 468. 2004. 2020. 2040). I. 314. 2037. 2038. 2067 Tyc: pr o 2041: ov K C C: c ovra K 42. 325. 385. 45 2- 45 6-.468. 506. 517. 2004. 2015. 2036. 2040 Pr vg: c otti 2020 gig CTTI rrjv Kufxixrjv A 18. no. 141. 201. 385. 386. 429. 522. 632. 919. 1849. 1955. 2015. 2020. 2036: cirt TTO- KC axicr KC 025. 046. 20 (- 18. 386. 632. 919. 1849. 2020). 250. 2037. 2038. 2067 al mu: in capite Tyc gig vg: super caput Pr cv rrj tipi CTTI rrjv cipa s 1 avrov 2-f habens Tyc:-f " he had " arm 1- s- ofv Xevicov s 1 1.

15. oxXoa ayycxoa 2016. 2020 CK rov vaov tr. after Kpafav A: Pr vaov + avrov K: ovpavov 051. I. 35. 104. 181. 205. 336. 632. 2015. 2023. 2036. 2037. 2038. 2067 al p arm 2- 4 a ev wny icyaxiy + Xcyaiv bo eth: (arm 1-): CF fji yaxrj TTJ tovr i: Pr ircn ov. nyo- 7170- S 2) icai cp rovarm 2 lyxflei + rov 051. I. 35. 181. 2019. 2037. 2038 i + oxw 104. 620 alp 6 punu AC 025. 046. 20 (-18. 468.

632. 919. 1849. 2OO4. 2O2O. 2040). 250. 2037. 2038. 2067 al mu: pr TOV 18. 385. 468. 632. 919. 1849. 1955. 1957-2004. 2023. 2040. 2041 al p: TOV 0cpur4, ov K 2020: "of (the) reaping of the earth" bo ort cftyoavft?. yiycr s 1-W bo efiypai Orf " is arrived " arm 1- 2- s-.

16. ver. 1 6 arm o Kaorjfjlcvocr. vc fxrjo- s 8 rt npr. avrov I 7170- vc cxio- AM 241. 336. 498. 2019.

1 8. Kat 3XXos dyycxos e JAdcv IK row Bwruumjpwv (a), ical v Acycov crov TO Spciravov TO o v cal rpvyiycrov rovs ftorpvas ri s dfwrexov rijs yi ori jjjKAaarav at ara vxai avris.

19. at?faxcv ( ) TO Spcvavov avrov cis r v y v, icat cypvyqo-cv rrjv atfrcxov rijs yis, icai f2axcv cfc rgv Xivov rov 6vp. ov rov Bcov rbv ftcyav.

jcal Mcplffov 4j yy. 17. Kai AXXot 776X01 ttfxOev IK rod raod rod oitparf, fyuv ical avrdy dpbravov 6 6.

(a) Text adds a gloss: 6 CWF ttowriav M rov irvptt.

(6) b dyycxos is here added by the interpolator of 15-17.

2020. 2037. 2038. 2067: i v vc cxT C 025. 35. 175. 205. 250. 468. 617. 620. 1934. 2004. 2040 al pm: Tif v ea. i? 046 2O (- 35. 175. 205. 468. 617. 620. 1934. 2004. 2020. 2040). 42. 61. 69. 104. IIO. 201. 1955 KOI e0 pir077 77 yi; KOI c cpio-cy TT; V yi; y vg f- v: demessus est terram fl: bo.

17. ver. 17 6g. 2039 cfrX cv X cv 046 vaov. ovpavo) ovpavov bo TOV cv ro ovpavoi rov IO4. 141. 620. 1849: rot C: pr rov 0cov arm 4: avrov cv ro OVMIVOI 205 ai avroa! bo sa Spciravov ojv pofjlfxuav o ctav bo (also in ver. 18).

18. c(T XOck A 2038 Pr: tr after 0vatamipiov 35 e c TOV tfvoriacmpiov Pr: de ara del fl o ex v AC s gig vg (arm) eth: o K 025. 046. 20 ai omn fl bo tqwrivtv-f cv SO (-35. 205. 325. 337. 456. 468. 2004. 2020. 2040). 69. 104. no. 250. 314 al p c cuvtycrcv c cpa cv s wny A 046. 337. 920. 2004. 2016. 2020. 2040 fl gig vg s 1 arm 1- 2- 3- a eth: pavyi? C 025. SO (-337. 920. 2004. 2020. 2040). 250. 2037. 2038. 2067 alp 1 s 8 bo: "tongue" arm 4 Xcywi K C: Xcyw K: s j ircfurov. ofv cat arm L 2-: " come thou " arm 8 wcwrov + rv s 1 o-ov ro 8pc? ravov + o ov 385: TO Spciravov o ov K jsorpvao- fioravaa- 201. 386: ftorpva- 2015. 2036. 2038 TTO-aAircxov vine-arum fl: I arm 1 ort rjkfjulO-av. aimo- bo rjkfjlarav (rj-A: rjy- 620) at ara vxat A C 025. I. 35. 104. 205. 468. 620. 632. 2004. 2015. 2020. 2023. 2036. 2037. 2038. 2040. 2067 al gig vg (fl) s a: Kfuurcv 17 oro vxiy 046. 20 (- 35. 205. 468. 620. 632. 2004. 2020. 2040). 250 al mu arm 1 2 4 avno- ANC 025. I. 35. 205. 468. 632. 2004. 2015. 2020. 2023. 2036. 2037. 2038. 2040 al mu gig vg fl s 1 arm 1- 4 eth: cv ovriy arm: npr yryo- 046. 2O (- 35. 205. 468. 632. 2004. 2020. 2040). 104. 250 al mu s.

10. cpaxcr A C 025. 046. 35. 205. 620. 632. 2004. 2020. 2040: misit gig vg fl: c c3axcv SO (- 35. 205. 620. 632. 2004. 2020. 2040). 82. 104. no. 172. 250. 385 al ci5 rrjv yijv AC 2O. ical liranqoy y Aipw?? u0ev rrjs jroacco?, c i? A.0cy alfia IK-rijs Xijvov L pi rwv orastw xixiw c a oriiy.

025. 046. 80 (-2020). 250. 2037. 2038. 2067 al pl gig vg fl s f bo: cwi rqr yiycr K 498. 2020 s 1 arm 1- 8- car nyv Aivov. rov ficyav A(C) 025. 046. 20 (- 205. 386. 620. 632. 2004. 2040). 61. 69. no. 141. 242. 314. 385. 452. 2016. 2017. 2021. 2022. 2023. 2024. 2039. 2041 al p s 2: rov flcyav i8i. 424: cur rov yvov. TDK icyav i. 201. 386. 498. 522. 1957. 2038 al: ctr Tt v rjvov. rrfv fjicyaxrjv 104. 205. 250. 620. 632. 2004. 2015. 2018. 2036. 2037. 2040. 2067 s 1: in torculari (-ar fl). magnum Tyc Pr fl: in lacum. magnum (-am gig) gig vg rjvov axwvav C: + TOV owov 2020 TOV 0viovj rov Bvfjmv 386: 337. 620. 2004 arm 1 2-.

80. fwatfjoij CTranyerci (-av eth) arm 1 2 bo eth: eruhj i if yvoo o Xiyvocr 205. 336. 498. 522. 1957. 2004. 20191 2020: rrjv X-qvov bo: in torcolari Pr fl arm 1 2 8 cfo cv AC 02 rrjv X-qvov bo: in torcolari Pr fl arm 1 2 8 cfo cv AC 025. 046. 20 (-35. 205. 2020). 250 al 11111: c o X i. 35. 205. 2015. 2020. 2036. 2037. 2038. 2067: extra Tyc Pr vg fl: a foris extra gig no2 TOV 452. 522 arro orastwv ri oraotwv s 1: per stadia Tyc vg: per stadios Pr (fl) ixiw ctaxoo-wv AK C C 025. 35. 386. (620). 632. 1934. 2004. 2040 Pr fl gig vg bo sa: xiatwk Siakortwv 506. 680: ax 80 (-35.

386. 620. 632. 1934. 2004. 2040). 61. 69. no. 314. 498. 2015 al: x e-2037: 2036: OCKCL Kat ef eth: mille quingentis gig.

CHAPTER XV.

2. (a) Kat czSov a5 Odxatrav vaxivrjv AcuyAcvty? TTVJI, icai vuctovras CK TOV Orjpiov KOL IK-nys cifcdvos avrov ical K TOV pi6funt TOV ovoiaros avrov rrwras TTI T V axao-o-av T V va Lvrjv t (a) xv. I. is an interpolation: Kal cldor AXXo v lov r rf otpavf (dya, Kal 0avfiaort6v, dyyaovj irrd x o " ra f Xifyai eirrd? if draf, 6n fr oivatf ttextabr) 6 0ivt6s TOV 0eoo. The subject of xv. I. is not touched upon till xv. 5, where the phiase Kal Aerd raora cttov shows that a new section and a turn subject begin. See vol. i. 106 and footnote; vol. ii. 30.

L 0aufi, aotOK Bavfuuriov 61. 69 ayycxov angelos stantes fl ir rjyat cirraj 920. 2015. 2016. 2O2O. 2036. 2037. 2067: irro 2OI9 cv avraicr cv Tavrais 35. 205. 2015. 2036. 2037. 2038: in his Tyc.

8. uaxitfjk vitreum perlucidum Tyc at TOVO- VIK. coramur CTTI riyf axao-arav et super mare stantes uidi eos qui. uictoriam fcrent fl: et superstantes uidi eos qui. uictoriam ferent Pr i0da TOV flcov, 3. KOI 8ovcriv(a) Tip TOV dpviov

Mryoxa KOI 0avuurra ra ipya crov, fcvnc, 6 0cos 6 iravtOKpatoip oucatai KOI (Ur imi at osoi rov, 4. rfe ov nj oty0fl, Kypic, ical 8of acrfi TO OKOIA orov, ocrtos; ovi iravra TO. c 0ny f) ovnv

KOI irpoarkWTJvawrw Ivwiriov o-ov, ort ra SucaiuJiata o ov tyaycputfqow.

(a) Text adds a gloss: i ysV Mww wt TOU 5o 5Xou roo 0roo xaf.

mowtCwr C CK rov Oyp. KOLL cic r o- cucoroar avrov AC 025. 18. 35. 205. 250. 2037. 2038. 2067 al s arm 1 2: CK T. ft KOI rrjv cue. avrov M 104. 336. 620. 1918. 2020 Pr fl: CK

Tl S CMC. KOI CK (22) TOV Ol)p. ttvTOV (2O4O) 046. 20 (- 1 8.

35. 205. 620. 632. 2020). 61. 69. 522 al: CK TOV ftyp. avrov 632: bestiam et imaginem illius gig vg bo sa eth: bestiae Tyc xai CK TOV apt0uv A C 025. 046. SO (- 35. 205. 468. 620) al s arm 1-: et numerum gig vg bo: KOI CK TOV apayfiatoa-avrov KCU (2Oi8. 2019. 2036) CK TOV apispov 051. I 35- 205. 250. 468. 2018. 2019. 2036. 2037. 2067 Kat CK T. apiti. avrov 620 Tyc Pr fl corwraer Tyc arm 1 T. va t, vyv fl Pr eth I Kiqapao- A C 025. 35. 632. 920. 2037. 2038. 2040. 2067 al pl bo sa: roor Kiftipocr 046. 20 (- 35. 632. 920. 2040). 82. 104. no. 172. 201. 250. 385. 498. 2018. 2022 alarm 8 4-! TOV 0cov pr jcvfuov K: fl I.

3. Kai as,. TOU 0couc Kajbo aowriv asovrao- K 743 107;. 2067 Tyc Pr fl vg s 1 8 bo nyv 1 92o Mwvo-coxr A 046. i al 1 ": Moxrccixr 025 al m TOV Sovxov AM 025. i. 35. 205. 250. 632. 1957. 2015. 2020. 2037. 2038. 2041. 2067 al: Sovaov 046. 20 (- 35. 205. 632. 2020). al pl icyo a KOI 0avbuwrra Ta cpya orov magna et mirabilia operati sunt Tyc o 0cocr o 620 I KOUU. at o8ot crov Sikaia KCU axijdiva ra cpya crov s 1 arm 1- 4 o ftoffixtvar jsao-cxcvor N 429. 632: ? acnacv N 1 8. 94. 241. 385. 522. 919. 1849, 2004. 2039: pr tu es fl TCOV c0iw A c 025. 046. 051. 20 (-2040). i. 69. 104. no. 250. 314. 2037. 2038. 2067 al gig Cyp arm 4 bo: omnium gentium Pr fl arm 1 eth tt C 94. 2040 Tyc vg s: "of aeons and king oi all Gentiles" arm 2-.

4. TMT pr Kai 2019 arm ov pi) crc ov K 2040 fafirftr) Afttc 025. 046. l. 61. 69. 181. 205. 241. 632. 2019. 2022. 2040, 5. Kat ftcra ravra ctsov, at yvoiyrj 6 vaos

uaprvplov (a) tv r ovpavy, 6. cat l XBov f ot cwa ayycaot f (t) pi cxovtCf T 5 ctTa iraiyas K rov vaov, cv8cvj, cvot f Aiov f (tf) OLfjarpov Kal 7rc0ic axrAcvoi ircpl ri mq6rj

So) For the probable origin of this corrupt phrase, see vol. ii. 37 sq. b) Here the hand that inserted xv. I changed Ayyexoi rrd into at Irrd dyy. and added ol Jfxorret raj frra rxiffds. M See vol. ii. 38.

2036. 2037. 2038. 2067 Pr fl gig arm bo: + o c 051. 30 (- 205. 632. 2040). 104. no. 250. 314. 385 al pl vg s eth cvptc6i. 69 Pr gig arm eth ao-ct AC 025. 046. 18. 175. 325. 456. 617. 632. 920. 1934 al: ris ov o ao-ct 2040: So cun? M i. 35. 104. no. 5- 337- 3 8 5- 3 86- 468. 919. 1849. 20 4- 2020. 2037. 2038. 2067 al pl: 8o ao-oi 205. 620 ftovoo- pr o 35: pr (rv cc 468 s 1: tu solus Pr gig arm ocrioo- A C 025. i. 205. 2015. 2036. 2037. 2038 al s 1: pius Pr. vg Ctg: ci ocrtoo- 632. 2020: oo-uxr ct 2019 al: pius es vg- 1 T: ayioo- 046.20 (205. 632. 2020. 2040). 104. no. 250. 314 al p: ayuw ci 2040. 2067 al: sanctus es gig arm 4: sanctus et pius es (es et dignus arm 1) fl arm 1- 2: oo-too- ct u Stkatoo- s 2 iravra ra c0n? AKC 025. I. 35. 205 386. 2020. 2037. 2038. 2067 al Pr fl gig vg s arm bo: iravra 2040: iravrco- 046. 80 (-35. 205. 386. 2020. 2040). 69. 104. 250. 314. 385. 2022 al pl cvonriov o-ou + JCVMC A 205. 2040 arm: ro ofoia o-ov bo ra Sue. crov e avcpcu io-avj Siic. cvanriov orov fav. K: (Sticaioo-) ci s 1 c avcpo io-av magnificata sunt vg 0 i.

6. wu 1 Pr fl icra Tavraj ACT aura C iccu J 4- isov Tyc Pr vg arm: tsov bo rgvoiyrj arm 4 o FOOO- + TOV cov 620: Tyc I Tiys o-ici iyo- +1 0- aytotr gig: 17 o-icin; Tyc cv TO ovp." pr o s 8 arm eth.

6. e t X6ok A M 025. 046 al omn: c X av C: e i; A0ci A oi cirra ayycxot 01 ayycxoi 01 cirra 325. 456. 468 CH c ovrco 1 AC SO. 250. 2037 al s (arm) bo: ot K 025. 046. i. 242. 2036. 2038. 2067 al: habentes gig fl vg: cum (vii plagis) Pr c TOV voov A C 025. i. 35. 104. 205. 241. 385. 620. 632. 2015. 2019. 2022. 2036. 2037. 2038. 2040. 2067 al gig fl vg s: tr before oi 8 201. 386 s l (bo): c TOV ovpavov 60. 1957. 2023. 2041: 046. 2O (-35- 205. 386. 620. 632. 2040). 250 al Pr arm 1 2 cydcsvAcvot AKC 025. i. 35. 2040 al Tyc Pr gig fl vg s l arm 4 bo: pr oi rjo-av 046. 80 (- 35. 2040). 250 al 1 (s) arm 1- Ae0oy Ko-Sapov AC 242. 2O2O m. 2039: lapide mundo vg 1): Aivov Kaoapov 025. 051. 8O (-2020 11). 104. 250. 2037. 2038. 2067 al 1 s arm: Atvow naoapw 046. 61. 69. 94. 498. 2019: linteamine mundo vg 4: lintheamen mundum gig: lino mundo Tyc: linea munda Pr: linteamina Candida fl: iradapov? Xmn M: "with garments of linen" bo apirpw Aaiirpovo- K (bo): 7. cat tv cic iw Tccrcrapcov jw 2owcv row cirra ayycxot? cirra Xa? xpvoras ycuurixras rov 0VAOV rov 0cov rov uvros cis rove avac TWV abavtov. 8. KOI cycuor0i? 6 vao? fcan-yov cic r s 86 rp rov flcov al cv ri s Swofuois avtov, gal ovcl? csvvaro curcx0ctv cis rov rao? axpt rcxco-0okTiv al cirra irxiryal raw cirra dyycxcw.

irpov 2017 Tyc gig s 1 arm 1 8-: et Candida Pr (arm 4): candido vg: 386 fl coi a i. 205 bo wepi i. 181. 2016. 2037. 2067: ciri 2015. 2036 Tyc s 1 bo sa eth.

7. CK K i. 104. 181. 336. 620. 2036. 2037. 2038. 2039. 2067 arm: unus gig fl vg CK 205 cwra 8 K xpvo-ao- Pr S 1 arm 2- ycfuwcrcur 325. 456 rover acoiveur rov auowov rov O4dva rov OUDVOO- 367. 468: + aup fet 181. 205. 209. 2015 S 1 bo.

8. o WMMT o!934: +rov tfeov gig arm 4 Kcanrav AC 025. i. 35. 205. 620. 632. 2020. 2037. 2038. 2040. 2067 al: pr rov 386: fumo Pr fl gig vg arm: pr CK rov 046.

2O (- 35. 205. 386. 620. 632. 2020. 2040) 250 al s bo K I 468 s 1 arm 2 8- bo eic Pr arm 8– tow. AC flo (-2040) al 1: y w. K i. 250. 2037. 2040. 2067 al mu curcx civ tr after vaov K: cx civ 620 a XP l axpur ov C at cirra irxi at septem (bo) plagae illae Pr bo: septae illae plagae fl rra 2 025. 051. i. 35. 60. 94. 181. 1957. 2015. 2023. 2036. 2037. 2038. 2041. 2067 gigl-

CHAPTER XVI.

I. Kal Kovo'a ftryaai Kov 9 cic rov vctov Xcyovcns rot? cwa dyycxots "Yiraycrc jcat cicxccrc ras cwa 0iaxas rov Ovfiov rov Otov ct?

1. M Y axi ar +orr)r AC 046. 42. 61. 69. no. 175. 325. 337. 386. 456. 468. 920. 1934. 2016. 2022. 2040 al bo sa: K 025. i. 18. 35. 205. 250. 617. 620. 632. 919. 1849. 2004. 2020. 2037. 2038. 2067 al l Pr gig vg 011070- 4-eic r. ovpavoveth c rovvaov A C 025. i. 35. 205. 250 632. 2020. 2040. 2067 al s arm: tr after Xcyownpr 2037. 2038: cic rov ovoavov 42. 367. 468 arm 4 bo sa eth: 046. 90 (- 35. 205. 468. 632. 2020. 2040) al pl arm 8 icoi 2 i. 104. 181. 205. 337. 620. 2015. 2019. 2023. 2036. 2037 al gig arm 1 bo dc ccre A C 025. i. 181: ccx arc 046. 051. 90. 250. 2037. 2038. 2067 al 1: CKICCXCTC (cf- 61) 61 69 cmra 02S- I. 35. 1957. 2015. 2023. 2036. 2037. 2038. 2041 fl bo eth taxiurj + quas accepistis Pr CK rrjv yrjv ciri n yip s 1: arw bo: cur r. ircwrav yip eth: fl arm 4 I.

rip yqv. 2. Kal irfj.0cv o irpwros KCU c cev T F fnd rjv afcov cfc rijv yrjv KO! cycvcro cxtcos KOXOV ol irovtfpov cm TOWS dy0pairov.(a) 3. Kal o Scvrcpos l(e ttv rrjv faaxrjv avrov cis r v laxacnrav jau cycvcro atia us vc poi5, at iracra iw r) oi awxicv, ra cv Tfl 0axaw0. 4. Kal 6 rptros e cck r v (Jia rjv avrov cfc TOWS iroraAOV? neat ra? myas TWV vsarcov feat ycvovro (a) Text adds the gloss: rods xorrat r6 x YAa rov jpfou xcu rodt vpofficwowrat r cticdvi avroo. See vol. ii. 43.

(3) Text adds an interpolation 5: xai JKowra rov dyyaou rwv Worwr X WTOJ, in order to introduce 5 b-7. These clauses 5 b-7 originally followed after xix. 4, to which context they are restored in this edition. See vol. ii. I22sq. f Ii6sq.

9. KU ainjx6. cur nji yi)Ktt irpwroar +ayyc ocr 172. 181. 218. 250. 2015. 2018. 2019. 2036. 2037 arm 1 2- bo eth cio- cm i. 35. 205. 1957. 2015. 2023. 2036. 2037. 2038. 2041. 2067 S 1 rrjv ytffv Ttjcr 7770 2038 I KXT KOLKOV feat vovrjpov

C KOV (-KOCT K C) iroVTfpoV KO. I KOLKOV N. KCLKOV A 1849! KOLKW KOI 2o67 bo eth: vulnus pessimum magnum Pr: ulcus saevum et malum fl: vulnus magnum (saevum vg) et pessimum gig vg cm cur i. 35. 205. 1957. 2015. 2023. 2036. 2037. 2038. 2041. 2067 al: in gig vg bo TO apayAa tr after 0i uov 620:-h nominis Pr icoi 6 fl rover 8 IO4. 385. 620. 1918. 2015. 2036. 2037 (wpoarkW. tr after cucora I. 2037 rrj cucow rrjv ccicova K I. 35.

2036. 2037. 2067: arm 2 8. icai oscur. C CXCCK K Scvrcpoo- A C C 025.94. 2040 Pr fl gig vg arm 4 eth: +ayycaoo- 046. 2O (-2040). 250. 2037. 2038. 2067 al pl s arm 1 2 8- bo cycvrro + iy oxoorcra fl gig s 1 eth aifjLa UHT vcicpov mo- aita vcicpov 104. 181. 205. 620. 1918. 2038: velut mortuis sanguis fl oxr vcicpov Pr oxr oxri M: i. 209. 468 nfxn hxnr A ionyo- AC 2040 eth: foxra K 025. 046. 051. i. 35. 104. 205. 620. 1957. 2015. 2020. 2037. 2038. 2041. 2067 Tyc gig vg s 1- 2 arm a bo sa: quae erant viventes fl: 2O (35. 205. 620. 2020. 2040). 69. 1 10. 250. 314 al Pr arm 1- 8 TO. AC 2038 s 2: TCDV 2040: K 025. 046. SO (- 2040). 250.

2037. 2067 al Tyc Pr fl gig vg s 1 bo cwrctfavci tr after 0X00x717 1948. 2014. 2015. 2034. 2042 arm 1- 8- CK ny 0ax. rc rip vqAcuriflr K L 4. Tpitoor + ayycxocr 051. I. 35. 172. 205. 250. 1957. 2018. 2019. 2020. 2023. 2036. 2037. 2038. 2041. 2067 s arm 1 2- bo cwr cirt It 051. 94. 2016 Pr vgbo sa TOO- A C 025. 35. 60. 1957. 2022. 2023. 2036. 2038 2040. 2041 Pr fl gig arm bo: pr cis 046. 80 (-35. 2040). i. 250. 2037. 2067 al s: pr cm 94. 2016 vg cycvovro A 2019. 2040 Pr fl gig s arm 2 bo sa eth: cycvcro KC 025. 046. 80 (-2040). i. 250. 2037. 2038. 2067 ap 1 vg 8. Kat 6 rcrapros c cx cv "7 fufap avrov cvt rov ijfxiov at 09 avrj feavuaruroi rovs dv0po7rovs cv ITVM 9. cat cjcavumcr-Biprav ot avflponrot icavua ftcva, at c Xaox fiiprav TO ovofta rov 0cov rov cxovroc T V V l(owiav ciri ras irxirya? ravras, cat ov flcrcvoqow Sovvat avrp oof av.

IO. Kai WA7TT05 c cxccv r fv faaxjjv avrov ri rov Opovov rov fojptov Kal cycvcro 17 frurixcta avrov crooraiftcvi; (a). at fta-flranro rag yxdxnras avrfix rov irovov. u. cat cSXao fiitO-ay rov 0co rov ovpavov ic TWV irovcdy avrwv icai CK rtuv IAxak avrtuv, KOI ov ftcrcvoiouv rwv? pywv avrcov. 12. Kat o licrof

(a) Several clauses lost here: see vol. ii. 45 sq.

5. row oyyexou angelos Pr TWV voarwf pr rov art 2040: tr after Acyovroo- 205: quartum gig.

8. rctaproa AC 025. 046. 175. 325. 337. 468. 617. 620. 632. 920. 1849. J 934- 2004. 2040 al gig vg s 2 arm 8 4: +ayyexoo- K 051. i. 18. 35. 205. 250. 314. 386. 456. 632. 919. 1957. 2015. 2018. 2019. 2020. 2023, 2036. 2037. 2038. 2041. 2067 al m Tyc Pr vg s 1 arm L bo sa eth ri in gig vg Kavfiarta-ou, row avbp. v (K 2038) irvpt AM 025. 35. 205. 2020. 2038. 2040 gig s 2: aestu afficere horn, et igni vg: iravp. cv irvpi r. avop. 046. 90 (- 35. 205. 2020. 2040). 250 al pl: ignem et aestum inicere hominibus Pr cv TTVM xavpart xeyaxw bo.

9. icaujia facya icavfiari ficyaxo) 94. 2015. 2036. 2037: bo fftxaa- fjaiauv Afetc 025. I. 205. 2019. 2020. 2036. 2037. 2038. 2040. 2067 al Tyc Pr gig vg s 1 arm 1- 2- 4 bo: + ot avopwiroi 046. 80 (- 205. 2020. 2040). 250 al pl s 8 arm 3 TO ovota cvcuiriov A: icara rov ovoiaroar 2040: cur ro ovopa, 2015: arm a nv AK 025- 35- 60. 181. 205. 432. 1957. 2019. 2023. 2038. 2041. 2067: C 046. SO (- 35. 205). i. 250. 2037 al pl arm bo ov 10. Trcjiirroa A C 025. 046. 20 (- 35. 205) gig vg) s 2 arm 8- 4 sa eth al: + ayycxoo- 051. 35. 172. 205. 250. 1957. 2018. 2019. 2023. 2036. 2037. 2038. 2041. 2067 al Tyc Pr vg s 1 arm 1- bo: ayycxoo- i rov Opovov rov Opovov 2020 covcoroyicvi A C 025. 90 (-456): co-KOTMrAcviy K 8 0 046. 456. 385. 2015. 2037. 2067 cuurwvro AKC 025 al mu: CLUXO-CT. 046 al mu c c airo K 031. 35 Tyc bo sa rov vovov doloribus suis Tyc.

11. ver. 1 1 Pr rov Otov r. ovx ro ovofw. rov faov (+ rov avp. S 1) 1957 s 1 icat tk rwv cxicoiv avr. K 172. 2022. 2031 arm 4: ot cic. r. tpywv avrwv bo ex 8 O25 205. 2020. 2038. 2067 cxicwv cxicowwv 2020 flcrcvoqo-cv tr after avrcov 8 468 CK row. cpy. avruv

W. CKTOV + oyycxoo- 051. 35. 172. 205. 250. 620. 632. 1957. 2015. 2018. 2019. 2023. 2036. 2037. 2038. 2041. 2067 Tyc Pr rip JHaxrjv avrov hrl TOV iroraiov TOV icyw rov r Efypaiv KCU Itypavor) TO vswp avrov, iva froifuurlp ij 68ds TWK fiurtxw rsxv ion rowroxtyf 1 rj tav. 13. at c! iw c rov orofurrt rovdraroxw opojcovroc cal fc rov oroxaros rov 0t; puv KCU rov oro'iaw rov cvowpo tytOV DTcviara Tpta ik

0apm(tf) 14. f faropcv-crat f ( ) rl Tov jscunxcts ri s oucovAcnp 0X75, truvayayctv avrovs ck rov 0cov rov (a) Text adds gloss: wi Jdrpaxot 14. Tip rotoorra (nyuetia.

(3) K 051 change A cropcverot into tkropevcffdai. Corrupt for tkropeva-pera the change being made by the interpolator of the preceding words. See vol. ii. 48. Pr (see below), recognising the need of this participle, inserti it after rpla, and some Gk. MSS. insert tkrofxvqtrra. after Sdrpa oi.

(c) MSS insert here as xvi. 15 a verse which originally stood after iii. 3 and where it is restored in this edition.

gigvg d s 1 arm L2 4- bo avrov placed after taxi v A C 046 al mtt: tr before r. iax. 20 (- 18. 35. 205. 632. 919. 920. 1849. 2004. 2040). 42. 61. 69. 104. 201. 314. 452. 498. 517. 2017: 920 ciri in gig vg: per Tyc r. TTOT. r. try. rov tcyav iroraiov 051 rov 8 AC i. 69. 172. 250. 2015. 2018. 2036. 2037. 2040. 2067 bo sa: 025. 046. 20 (- 2040). 42. 82. 104. 201. 314. 385. 429. 432. 498. 522. 1955. I 957 20I 6- 2017. 2019. 2022. 2023. 2038. 2041 al pl ewfp. cfp. 046 r)pcu(h siccavit gig vg avrov 2 i. 181. 205. 2019. 2038 bo row Jao-iaecuv venienti regi Pr: regi venienti gig: regis arm: Tyc rwv 2 s 1 avaroxwv A 051. i. 35. 314. 468. 1957. 2015. 2020. 2023, 2036. 2037. 2041 S 1 bo: avaroxipr KC 046. 20 (- 35. 205. 468. 2020). 250. 2038. 2067 al s.

13. cior c6 K c rov crroi. r. S. T. Orjp. K. K CK
T. OTTO4. T. plK. K. C 325. 337. 517. I9I8 CK TOV OTOA. T. 0tyx
Kai20!9 arm 1 rpia akdoap. AKC I. 35. 104. 205. 620. 1957. 2015. 2019. 2020. 2036. 2037. 2038. 2040. 2041. 2067 al mn Tycvg s 1 arm 1-: 046. 20 (- 35. 205. 620. 2020. 2040). 250 al 1 arm 8: akao. 92o: Tptagig: tres exeuntes inmundos Pr oxr flar-pa oi oio- (okrct K) Sarpa ow K 94. 498. 2019. 2020. 2023: K e 2067: + cmropcv cvra 241. 2015. 2036. 2037 14. Q ai oyu)v + aka0aftiv 2040: Satiovwv oji. I. 35. 205. 2015. 2019. 2020. 2023. 2036. 2037. 2038. 2067 al I a(+ KCU 2015) CKiropcvctai A 20 (-205. 620. 2040). 69. no. 250. 314. 385. 429. 498. 1957. 2015. 2016. 2017. 2018. 2023. 2039 al pl Tyc: a cjciropcvokrat 046. 104. 336. 620. 1918. 2019: onropcvco ai K 051. I. 2022. 2036. 2037. 2038. 2040: a ciaropcvco-lai I: CKiropcvovrat K: cinropcvcrai 205: et exeunt (procedunt gig vg) Pr gg vg arm 4 eth: bo ri ur K TIJO- owe. T. yi r KCU (2037) T. out, i. 2037: T. yrp bo oaip i s 1 arm 8 bio rw o5i. I.

16. iwu (rvnyaycv avrovs els rov row toy ffaxovpcvov Ejspaum Ap Mayciv.

17. Kal 6 ov tfexeev TTV uftitv avrov evi rov tpa ai J)X0cv wq tcyai; rov vaov Airo rov Ipovov Xcyowa Feyovev 18. ai cycvovro aorpamu KOI uvai ieat ftparrai, ical 0 00710 cycvcro ficyac, olo ov cycvcro ty f ot r av0panros cycvcro 1 evi rip yfr 205. 2019. 2022. 2038. 2067 al rip iffl T. icy. K 6l. 69. 2020: ad diem magnum vg: diei magni Tyc gig: n r cy. A 2040 bo: npr i fu ekctno- r. uy. 046. 051. 90 (- 205. 2020. 2040). I. 250, 2037. 2038. 2067 al Pr s: n r qi. cicctyipr 205 rov 0eov domini Tyc arm 1 1.

16. vwiflayw rvnyyayov K 5 s: crwaf ct vg s 1 arm 1 8 avrovo-s 1 rov 1 K 6l. 69 arm bo roirov ITOTOAOV A rov 6i. 69 bo rov icoa. c3 pa. Tyc op iaycuv AN 051. I. 35. 104. 172. 205. 241. 250. 468. 620. 632. 1957. 2018. 2019. 2020. 2023.

2036. 2037. 20 38 3 4- 2 (7 s arm 4-: hermagedon vg: ermagedo gig: ermagedon Tyc: armageddon Pr: ermakedon bo: piycow 90 (- 35. 205. 468. 620. 632. 2020. 2040) al S 1 arm 8: mycsow 046: ioxesooiv 61. 69.

17. KOI o 08. KM ore K (cai o f K c): +ayyc or c- e 051. i. 35. 172. 205. 250. 468. 1957. 2015. 2018. 2019. 202 3- 2036.

2037. 2038. 2041. 2067 al Pr gig vg s 1 arm 1- bo nri r. ocpa eta- r. acpa 051. I. 35 61. 69. 205. 1957. 2015. 2016. 2023. 2036. 2037. 2038. 2041. 2067 al s 1: in acre (-a gig:-em v g) Pr gg v g I W 8 1? A i. 181. 205. 209. 2038 K A i. 94. 181. 205. 209. 617. 2019. 2020. 2037. 2038. 2040. 2067: cwro 046. 90 (-205. 617. 2020. 2040). 250 al pl vaov AK 60. 61. 69. 2040 Pr vg s arm 8 bo sa: +rov ovpovov 046. 90 (- 468. 2040). 250. 2067 al pl: ovpavov I. 94. 181. 241. 2015. 2019.

2036. 2037. 2038 gig arm 8 4-: (+ ovp. rov 468) vaov KOI 468 eth aro rov Qpovav rov Otov K: mu (2Oi) airo r. Opov. rov tfcov20i. 386: o5i gig.

la Kai + cv9c(i)(r 386 aorpdir. K. fw. K. ftpovr. A 42. 82. 141. 2015. 2019. 2036. 2040 al Pr gig vg arm 1 bo sa eth: ftpovr. K. oorp. K. dv. K. ftpovr. K: ootp. ic. ov. 046: ftpovr. K. oorp. K. 40v. K 6 920: oorp. K. Ppovr. 205. 181. 2038. 2067 Tyc s 1 arm 4: w. K. ft. icac oorp. I. 2037 al: oorp. K. ftpovr. K. KDV. 051. 90 (-205. 920. 2040). 61. 69. 104. no. 141. 172. 201. 250. 314. 385. 432. 1918. 1955. 1957. 2016. 2018. 2022. 2023 al s s (cycvcro 1 AM i. 35. 61. 69. 205. 1957. 2015. 2019. 2023. 2036.

2037. 2038. 2040. 2041 al Tyc gig vg s arm 8 4- W bo: 046. 90 (- 35. 205. 2040). 250. 2067 al 111 Pr sa otoo- ov cycv. ovrw ficyao- et signa magna Pr ouxr OVK cycvcro our ov cycvovro K: ouxr ov ycyovcv 920 a ov ex qua die gig avqpwrwr cycvcro A bo: 2020 arm 8: avlpuirot cycvovro K 046.

n? Xtkovrof rturAo ovrcu ftcyas. 19. fcai(a) at iroxcts rwv? icrav KOI Bajsvxoiv ij tcyaxi; ipvyrgrj cvwtrtov rov 0cov Sowat avtjj ro ironjptov rov otvov rov Ovjiov TJ; S ojyfs vrov" 2O. at ircura njo-os fyvycv, neat opiy ov ivptqrjvav. 21. icyd Xi; ax raxavrtata garafruvct cw rov ovpavov irt rov? irovc cal i3 jaur4TJjliio'av ol Avopwroi rov eov ovt xcycia.? iorlv (a) MSS insert before a the words: a2 tf yero r Xif iryaxi; cb rp(a See vol. ii. 52.

35. 61. 69. 181. 2019. 2036. 2038. 2040: oiavtipwrot, (ovpavoi 506) cycvovro (1957: ycyovao-iv 337: cycvovro ot av p. 205) 051. 20 (35. 2020. 2040). i. 104. no. 250. 2037. 2067 al pl Tyc gig vg s arm 2 4 sa em no" yi r 69. 104 r Xncovroo O-CMTIOO- ovroi ficyaor bo: tr after cyevcro 8 arm 2 OVTCD ovm) i. 498. 2015. 2018. 2020. 2037. 2033. 2040 al.

10. at iroxcur rj vo ur K s 2 at 20 1 5. 2036. 2038 circerav AK C 046. 051. 35. 104. no. 337. 452. 468. 498. 620. 2015. 2020. 2023. 2038. 2041: circo-ov 2O (-35. 337. 468. 620. 919. 2020). I. 69. 250. 314. 2037. 2067 al pl: circo-cv K s 2 Souvat pr rov K 632. 2015. 2036 2037 ro tror. CK Pr TO K 2040 rov 2 K bo r. Ovfi tr before r. oivov 468 eth: tr after ojyiyo- Pr: + ccu s 1: Tyc r. opy. 6i. 69 gig arm avrov K bo: rov ov 2019 eth.

20. Kai 1 i irao-a viyorocr c vycv omnes insulae fugierunt Pr arm bo eth 0017 pr omnes Pr:-f cat 2015. 2036. 2037 cvptqrprav + rorc ot afro avaroxoiv cv orrcu cirt Swrfuur teat, ot airo ovoyutfv cur avaroxao- carat yap 0Xt rur xcyaxi; ota ov ycyovcv atro KCLTa3o rj(r KOPV ovs ov ft? yevtrat 468.

21. fj yaxi))8tata 920 j OHT raxavr. tr after Karaftaiv i 920 I coo- 202 2 Pr Karafatvcij tcar rj s 1 arm bo rov Btov 386 c c cirt 205 7r. rjyrfa-. oxo i r 92O ccrrtv cycvcro Pr vg rj irx. avr. vg avn r O46 arm 2-: tr before ij wxiyi; 205: a mj 1 8. 69. 104. 175. 250. 325. 386. 456. 617. 620. 920. 2015. 2016. 2020. 2037 1: vrov 181. 385: a grandine Pr).

VOL. II. 29

CHAPTER XVII. I. Kol Jjxfcv etc fc TW l iyyw, rir ttfmn rk jirri

TO Kpifm Tifc iropwjs Tifc ftcyaxip Tijs Ko i;wts CTI vsarwv roxXv, 2. ftc s ftropvcwrav 01 fturixcfc ri?? yfo ical iicOvr0iprav oi Karoucovm? T V yijK c rov otvov 1 Topvcta? avrijs.

3. Kal dwnjkcykcv pc cis nfuf fr irycvLtari. xal ctsov ywcuxa t ov Kaorj fvrjv hrl Orjpiov KOKKIVW yetovra 1. ijxOcv cf cv A cur TUT 104 arm 3 4 CK K 2015. 2040 ayycx. laxeur Tyc r. CXOVTWV qui habebat gig (fxoxiyo-ev dixit Tyc ACT cfu Xcy. Tyc Xcywv-f fioi i. 205. 2015. 2036. 2037. 2038. 2067 T. icy. s 1 ijSat. iroxX. AK 025. I. 172. 181. 205. 218. 250. 2015. 2018. 2019 2036. 2037. 2038. 2040. 2067 bo: iw vsat. TCOV iroxX. 046. 80 (- 205. 2040) al pl arm.

8. juo ijcr +" sinned and" bo I cirowcww ro jrcv vopvw bo sa KOI. avnp Tyc Pr cicdw rav cwducrav 205 01 Kar. T. y. tr after avripr I etc airo 920 owav oucov K? iropvcieur iropvtjv 205.

3. airt)vcyKCirl av vcyfccv 920: duxit Pr: tulit Tyc gig (me MH 386 cpiyywv +TOTTOV 2040 w A 025. 046. 35. 175. 205. 325. 468. 617. 620. 632. 1934. 2020. 2040 Tyc Pr gig Cyp vg bo (arm): i8, 82. 93. 141. 201. 218. 325. 337. 385. 386. 429. 456. 498. 506. 522. 632. 919. 920. 1849.!955- oo4-2024. 2039 al ctsovj isa A cm +TO 920 Brjpiov Att 35. 175. 205. 617. 620. 632. 1934. 2020. 2040: +TO 18. 325. 337. 386. 456. 468. 632. 919. 920. 1849. 20 4 I " " K 1 K y 4 6 I yct. (ver. 4) u 8 468 yctokra A 025 (s 2): ycfioi K 046. 051. 20 (-468). 1.61.69". no. 172.201. 241, 250. 314. 385. 498. 522. 1955. 1957. 2015. 2016. 2018. 2019. 2022. 2023. 2024. 2036. 2037. 2038. 2039. 2041. 2067 (s 1): ycicdv 104. 429. 2017 avofmTa A 025. 046. 30 (-35. 175. 205, 617. 1934). 61. 69. 104. no. 201. 241. 385. 429. 498. 522. 1955. 1957.

2017. 2O22. 2024. 2039: OFOUMW I. 35. 61. 172. 175. 205.

250. 314. 617. 1934. 2015. 2016. 2018. 2019. 2023. 2036.

2037. 2038. 2041. 2067 I CXCDV A 104. 201. 429. 919. 2017: CXOVTO. K 025: c ov 046. 051. 80 (-468. 919). I. 250. 2037.

2038. 2067 alp 1 I KC. CTTT. K04 I ficktt KOLL If ywlf. Tl T yrjr (ver. 18) 025. 2020. (On this addition see Tischendorf, crit note in he.) j, ai fccpara 8c a.

1TOptvpoVV JCflu KOKKIVOV, KOI KCXPWCDICITJ r pvOl1f JCOi Alg TlUW ai flapyaurat?, Igowa iron; piov xpwrovv fr rg x pl avr s yciov JSeavyiarcov al ra fadoapra rrp jropraas afcnys. 5. icat Iwi TO icranrov avri s ovoia ycypajflcyov,

BABYAON H MEFAAH, H MHTHP TON KAI TON BAEAYFMATON THS PHS.

6. KGU ctsa r v yvwuica ic vowai ic rov atwitos TWV dyeiuv cai rov arxaros rctv faaprvpuv (a) Tyc Pr vg a. rm =ropnw, which the parallelism in the next line requires. See vol. ii. 65.

4. qr y I irop vpow vop+vpav 051. I. 35. 175. 181. 205. 250. 314. 617. 1934. 1957. 2015. 2019. 2023. 2036. 2037. 2038. 2041. 2067 al p: 7roptvpa s 1 icai 2 I957 cai 8 A I. 104. 250. 424. (620). 2018. 2019. 2020. 2022. 2037 al Tyc Pr gig vg s arm 8 4 bo: 025. 046. 80 (- 620. 2020). 2038. 2067 al mtt s 1 arm 2 Kf pwrwp. VTj Tcpticc;(poToyacn7 250. 424. 2018: KexpikraiAcya s 1: "gildings embroidered" arm 2 xpvo-ta A 046.80 (-35. 205. 2020. 2040). 250. 2067 al mu: xpwci) 025. i. 35. 205. 1957. 2015. 2019. 2020. 2023. 2036. 2037. 2038. 2040. 2041 At0. rtfu. fiopy- arm- Ai0. TIA. Ai0ovcr rtuovo s 1: i0our rtuoto- s 2 arm pipy. Aapyoptrcur s 1: " pearl n arm c owa. T. n-opk. avnp 025 CXOVCTO pr ai Tyc s 1: et habebat Pr WOT. xpw. i. 205. 1957. 2015. 2019. 2023. 2036. 2037. 2038. 2041. 2067 al: tr xpwr. after avnpr 1 920 ev ri s 1 yctov AK 046. SO. 250. 2037. 2038. 2067 al pl: ycio)y K 104. 201. 429. 2017: pr KOI s 1 arm 8 4 ?8ex. ra oica. s 1 8ca.1 cavviatoo- s 1 arm 4 (bo): abominatione vg 1 (-nem) Kat bo I ra ako. J T. (uca apiara 2039: inmunditia vg 8 c t g. h. v.-tiae Pr vg (s 1):-tiarum Tyc vg (bo) T. wopy. gig avr o 2 A i. 35. 104. 172. 205. 241. 250. 468. 632. 1957. 2015. 2016. 2018. 2019. 2020. 2023. 2036. 2037. 2038. 2040. 2041. 2067 al Tyc vg s 1 arm 2 eth: nyo- yio-046. 80 (- 35. 205. 468. 632. 2020. 2040) al m11 gig arm 8: totius terrae Pr Cyp: avrrja-KCLI TTJO" ytyo K s 2: avrrjir fura npr yip oai r bo: arm 4-.

5. orafaa ovofmra 18. 919. 2004: s arm 2 eth vanpcov sacrament! Pr: cv iwrnyptcd arm 8- r. ropv. gig iropvwv fomicationum Tyc Pr vg (arm 2) T. yi r totius terrae Pr (.

6. cisa (isa A) AK: cisoy (i ov) 025. 046. 051 mm 1 ex 1 A i. 35- 104- 172. 205. 241. 429. 468. 632 2015. 20I 6 2017. 2019. 2023. 2036. 2037. 2038. 2040. 2067 al mu Pr gig vg s: K 025. 046. 90 (-35. 205. 468. 632. 2020. 2040). 69. 82. HO. 250. 314. 385 al mu T. atA. ra aiAari K 2O2O;

Ecu efovfwura isov avr v 0ava icya. 7. KCLI cfow AOI 6 716 (rot yyexot Ata rt clavfuuras; r eya cxi) croi 1 TO tvonpiop TIJS pfl KOI TOV fttykov TOV foota oitos avriyi, row fywos ras ewa

KOI TO Sera Kcpata. 8. TO fov ct c f v KOLI OVK forty, nrdyeir AcxXci vaflatv tv IK rift ajsvwov, KOI cfe atruxctai r wruya 1 KOI lavfuurftprovrai 01 KatOUcowrc? Ivi rfp yjjs, wv ov yeypamrai TO ovofui rl TO fiifixiav Trp fu cwro Karajsox s KWTAOV, jsXcirdvrw TO TI v cal OVK IOTIF KCU irupcorai.

sanguine Tyc arm xai 2 AK 025. 35. 205. 468. 632. 2020. 2040 al mu Tyc Pr gig vg s arm bo: 046, 80 (- 35. 205. 468.

632. 2020. 2040). 82. 1 10. 250. 385 al CK T. ttlji, CK 3H.

2016. 2041 al: sanguine Tyc arm upr. atjtvptw A: pr ayiw 325. 468. 620 Iiyo-ov pr TOV 2040: +Christi Pr: i. 2019. 2067 arm a ts. aur. 0avi. uy. bo tr iswv avr. after xcya K 2020 s 1 avnyv 6i. 69.

7. cpw aroi A 046. 80 (-35. 205). 250 al mu gig s eth: K 025. i. 35. 61. 69. 1957. 2019. 2022. 2023. 2036. 20 7. 2038. 2041. 2067 al p vg: tibi ostendam Pr bo TO arm T. yvv. huius mulieris Pr Tov 8 KU 2020: pr KU i. 2036. 2037 Tao- 205 arm 1 4 CUT. K. Pr vg SCK. iccp. Pr vg.

a TO 0i piok pr u Tyc arm eth o 8ecr Tyc ijv if A: pr o arm KOI sed Pr: s 1 bo airwxciav + irae Tyc vrayci A 181. 468. 2037: vadit Pr s 1 (eth): wayw K 025. 046. 90 (-468). 250. 2037. 2038 ap 1 s a arm (bo): ibit Tyc gigvg) 0avuur 77owrai A 025

s: 6avparovta. i K 046. 80. 250. 2037. 2038. 2067 min onm: mirabantur vg- f- " arm
a ot KOTOIX. pr irarrco- Pr arm 8 4 bo TI rye yipr AK 025. i. 35. 175. 205. 250.
617. 1934- 2037- 2038. 2040. 2067 al gig s arm 8 4- bo: rqv yvp 046. 80 (-35. 175.
205. 617. 1934. 2040) al " 1 Pr vg: rip yip arm 8 ov ycypairr. J OVK cycypavrat A
TO wopa A 046. 80 (35. 175. 205. 468. 617. 1934). 69. no. 385 al mu s j arm 4
bo: Ta ovoiata K 025. i. 35. 175. 205. 250. 468. 617. 1934. 2037. 2038. 2067 al Pr
gig vg s 1 arm 8 eth: +avno? arm ri 8 cv 2036.

2040 Pr gig vg s 1 arm TO ty8W A 025. 051. i. 35. 175. 205. 250. 314. 617.
1934. 1957. 2016. 2019. 2023. 2037. 2038 al: TOV ftijsXunt 046. 80 (-35. 175.
205. 337. 617. 1934. 2040). 69. 82. 104 al mtt: T ftipxtu 337. 2040 Pr gig vg s 1:
fapxa 2036 (arm) j8X rovrwv jsXcirokrco- i. 35. 1957. 2019. 2O22- 2 2 3 2041 Pr
gig vg T. (on) i? v AK 025. i. 35. 205. 2020. 2037. 2038. 2040. 2067 alp Pr gig s
arm bo: OTI rp T. 046. 80 (- 35 2 05 2020. 2040). 250 al o TI so apparently Pr vg d-
Y arm 2: on 046 mm 0 11 gig vg fcc f h bo arm 8 4-: AK 025. s would support either
reading cortv corai 386. 920 KOI + waxiv K irapeonu AK 025. 046. 051. 80 (-632).
69. 104. 250. 314. 2067 al 1 " 11 Pr arm 4: wapcemv K i. 181.

9. QSc o vovs o IXWF rofiav at cirra KC axat cwa(a) IO. jsao-txcts ( ) cto-iv
ol ircvrc cvcow, 6 els forty, 6 XXo? ovro jXfcp, ical orav 2X00 oxiyov avrov Set
ACtvat. 1 1. at TO Orjfxav, S v teat ovic farcy, cat auras oysoo? cwty, ical CK
TOW cwa cvrrty, KCU els dircoxctay virayct. 12. Kal ra Scvca jccpara ctscs Scvca
Bao-txctt ctcrtv, otrtw frurtxctay OVITCD fxafoy, AAXa cfoutrtav of facnxci? uay
apay afjifldvowtiv fjara rov Qrjpiov. 13. ouroi xtav

Here follows a gloss giving a second explanation: 6n? drf?, Arov 4 ffipnu T avrutf.
Kal. The same gloss adds errd.

241. 336. 632. 2019. 2036. 2037. 2038 gig s arm: cireow bo: vg.

9. ufo o muff o ex cro. joined with what precedes 046. 18. 69. 201. 337. 385.
386. 456. 498. 522. 919. 920. 1849. J 9S5 d: "he who hath heart with (and eth)
wisdom let him understand " bo eth 8 cosc pr et Pr: 046 o c wv TCO ovri s at KOI
2040: osi CTTTO 6i. 69: tr after eio-iv I r crravo) 6 1. 69 OTTTOU. CTT avrcov ubi.
supra illos gig S: super quos Pr vg bo eth.

10. icai 1 620 atr. CTTT. cicrtv A 025. I. 35. 205. 241. 632. 1957. 2019. 2020.
2036. 2037. 2038. 2040. 2041. 2067 al Pr gig vg s (arm 8- 4-): rr. far. curiv K bo
sa eth: ftatr. fwrtv cur. 046. 20 (-35. 205. 632. 2020. 2040). 250 al mu (arm 2)
circcrav crrccrov SO (-35. 337. 468. 920). 42. 69 82. 104. 250. 2067 al o 1 pr KOI
i s 1 arm bo: + 8e 2041 Pr eth 8 cmv pr owe bo: superest Pr o 8 pr KOI vg arm bo eth
avr. Set uctvat A 025. I. 35. 69. 2037. 2038. 2040. 2067 al: avr. uve fei (8 K): Set
avr. ftctwu 046.80 (-35. 2040). 250 al mu (Pr) gig (vg).

11. icai 8 468. 2040 I icai 8 K avroo- A 025. I. 35. 175. 205. 250. 617.
632. 1934. 2037. 2038. 2067 al Pr gig vg (s 1) bo: ovnxrko46. 20 (-35. 175.
205.617.632. 1934) al (s 2) oyxxrl pr o K 452. 2017. 202 1: octavo loco Pr c. CK. r.
CUT. COTIVJ cum sit ex vii Pr j wroyei vadet vg: ibit Pr (arm 8- 8).

1 oirikca hii Pr f Jao-ixeiai bo oviru OVK A: ovrco K axXa AN 69. 2040: axX
025. 046 min pl: bo arm 4 oxr Scwrtxcto- regni Pr piav wpav una hora Pr gig vg a. ft.
0i? ptov "having followed the wild beast" bo Xa 3avovonv pr ov 620: accipient gig
vg 0 41 7: tr after (hjptov 920 ftcra rov Orjplov post bestiam vg.

18. OUTOI + omnes Pr yvwx v cxoucriv AK 025. I. 35. 205. 2037. 2038. 2040 alp Tyc (Pr) gig vg (arm): 046. 80 (- 35. 205. 2040). 250 al mu sa CXOVCTIV habebunt Pr rrjv 61. 69. 2038 arm 8- cfowtav A 046. flo (- 35. 205. 386. 468. 920). 250 al mu arm 8-: pr nyv K 025. i. 35. 172. 201. 205. 385. 386. 468. 498. 920. 1957. 2018. 2019. 2023. 2036. 2037. 2038. 2041. 2067 l I vovcru, KLI TTJV Svyauy Ktu Ifowtav avrtw Tj (a). 17. yap 0cos CDJCCV cfc TOS Kapoyus avrcw iroujcrai avrov,(; ecu Sovcai T V fcuriaciay avrw rj Iqpup, i pi rcxcffproirat o2 Xoyoi rov 0eov.

16, Kal TO 8c a cpara ctscs fcai rft 0i; ptov, OVTOI xunproiknv r v iropvip, xai vjprjfjlWfianrjv irwrpowtLV amjv Kal yvAwfr, jcai TO? o-apjca? avr ayovnu, jcai avr v Katcwcavvovo-tv cy irupi 1.

14. ovrot ftrra rov dpviov iroxeii rovni, KCU TO Apvtov vuao-ei avrov's, ori irvpcos cvpiw oriv icat curixev? ftcurixiw, Kal ol ACT avrov xxi ol cal cicxckrol cat irtorot. ( ) (a) Text of xvii. 14-17 dislocated and glossed. On the restoration of the original order, see vol. ii. 61, 71 sq.

(b) A. doublet here follows ml rottJMu dx "ivkpip: see crit. notes below, and cf. xvii. 13.

(f) What was originally a marginal gloss on xvii. I text adds here: 15. ml ebr MU T Mara A ctfter, off i) rfpnj ca rcu, Xaai ica2 c y ca2 cavruv i (s): arm 2- St TW 0iyp. diabolo Tyc owovffiv 94. 2036. 2037 Tyc bo: aowowi 218: tradent Pr vg 17. Ocoff Kvptoo- 6 1. 69 csuiccv Tyc airrwv 1 avrov K r. yv. avr. K. iroiijvai 94. 620. 1918 arm 8 8 eth avrov avrwv K c ic. mwicrai Atav ykwti A 2036. 2037 Tyc gig vg: et esse illos in (+ uno arm 18 4 bo sa eth) consensu (-fet metu Pr) Pr arm 2- 8. Q gth Kflu mutiaaj. K c uoy yvwt v K 025. I. 35. 2019. 2022. 2037. (2040). 2067 al: 046. 20 (- 35. 2040). 250 al mu: fuor 172. 2018: +avro)K 2040 s 1 KOLI gig vg bo oowai dabunt Tyc: ut dent gig vg njf 2 bo sa avrwv 2 avrw A: avrov 046. 61. 69: 2036 Pr arm 2- bo sa Tca. eo-0 oirai AK 025. 051. i. 35. 181. 205. 209. 432. 1957. 2023. 2036. 2037. 2038. 2041. 2067: rcxcr0axrtt 046. 80 (-35. 205). 69. 104. no. 250. 385. 20i6alp!.

18. a ctsccr tr after ptov 205 eth K. TO Oypiov TO arm 2: TOV ptov arm 3: + o ciov (Pr): Tyc arm 4 i odio habent Tyc TTMrpawnv (irotovo-iv Tyc) avr v K.

025. i. 205. 632. 2020. 2036. 2037. 2040 al Tyc gig vg s 8 arm 2 sa: Tron roimTiv avnjv KU (bo) yvwiyv Troirpowrw (- rwrw 617) avnp 046 in C-). 80 (- 205. 632. 919. 920. 2020. 2040). 250 al bo eth: xat yvm v vovrja-ovtriy avnjv 424. Pr s 1 arm 4:. yvivniv 046. i. 82. 141. 218. 498. 919. 920. 2016. 2019 avr. ay. 1 632 ayovrai ayuvrai 1 8. 632: edunt Tyc xarokavcrovarivj fcavo-oixriv 1. 181. 205. 2019. 2020 cv A 80 (-920). 2037. 203. 2067 al 1 bo sa: K 025. 046. 172. 250. 920. 2018 Pr gig vg. 14. woxcp)rourii iroactowiv Tyc arm 2 ot ACT avrov 1 8. ical y ywij rp czSc? ccrrtv ij roais ij ptydxr 1 c owa quicumque cum eo erunt Pr 1 11X177. aca. trtcrr.1 cxx.

. VKFT. Icalp-. Pr K rjtOi Ktu gig Kttl 4 Vg"c 'tll. T t ori I. 2037 cgackTot KOI no. 2020 1 wca. vurr.1 172. 2018. 2036. 2037: 01 cftacicroi. 01 mcrrot bo cai 205. 2067.

16. curcr A Tyc Pr ve s arm 4 bo sa: Acyw K 025. 046 mm gig arm 2- ft: eth toij+angelus Tyc ra voaro rovra: ravra ra vsara K c ctwj oiow 104: vides Tyc: +icai

rj ywrj 175. 617. 1934 ov super quas Pr Cyp s 1 1 17 K vopvr mulier Tyc bo Aaot pr icat M cat o Aot vg o Aoc. yxaxro-at 920 o A. CMTIV K. cftoy K. yaoxro-. turbae (+ et gentes Cyp) ethnicorum et Inguae sunt (sunt et linguae Cyp) Pr Cyp: " multitudes of nations " bo (, 18. eorik Pr s 1 if icy. TOV B OV 920 if K 18. 201. 386. 2039. 2040 T. pturtxcwv r. junaciwv M arm 2- bo eth: arm 4: +TWV 336. 620. 1918 npr 7170- AK 025. 18. 35. 175. 205. 468. 617. 632. 1934. 2020. 2040 Tyc gig vg s arm bo eth: terrarum Pr: pr ri(o46). 325. (336). 337. 386. 456. (620). 632. 919. 920. 1849. (1918). 2004 al mu.

CHAPTER XVIII.

1. Mcra ravra ctSok aaAov ayycaov Karaftalvovra IK TOV ovpavov, ovo-uxy ieyaa.7, KO. L 17 yvj tywurfrri IK rrp Sofo avrov.

2. ai Kpa cv iv urx pf 1 favij Arycu?

Er (r v, TT (r V Baflvxtav rj ucyaaty, KOL cyefcro Katoucrjrijpiov SCUAOVWUK, cat tv akT ITOITOS opvcov okaodprov Kol (a) Text of these last two lines is uncertain Possibly we should read Byplov for rrerfparoi (cf. Jer. 1. 39), cf. A 250. 424 Pr gig s below: or else, with 250. 424 Pr gig s 1, read an additional line: U fv a, K vdrrot 6ijpiov dxaddprov.

L irro Taura pr KOI 051. I. 35. 104. 205. 250. 468. 2020. 2037. 2038 al gig vg eth: et Pr oaA. ayy 35. 175. 242. 250. 617. 920. 1934. (1957). 2016. 2017. 2023 aaAov crcpw 1957: i. 6 1. 69 arm 4 CXOKTO pricoi 205 eth fiey. gig arm ex 2 airo 386: +TOV Trxxrurtrov avrov cat bo eth.

2. Cfcpa ek ccecoafcy A c v A 025. 35, 432. 452. 1957.

3. ore IK rov olvov rov 0vtov rrp ropwiaf uvrijs varra TO. vvy t icat ot fariacit TVJS yjjp per avrijs cwpvcwav, at ot fynropot ri)s y s IK rip iwaflcoc rov orpipov? aurip lirxovnprav.

2019. 2023. 2036. 2038. 2040. 2041 Tyc vg (bo): K 046. 90 (-35. 2040). i. 141. 181. 241. 250. 336. 385. 429. 522. 1918. 1955. 2037. 2067 Pr gig lo-xvpa wny (+ icyaai7 i. 181. 2067: + ai tcyaxi? 205. 2019) AM 025. 046 20 (- 18. 620. 632. 919. 1849. 2004). I. 181. 250. 432. 452. 1957. 2019. 2023. 2036. 2037. 2038. 2041. 2067 vg s 2 (arm 4 eth): urxypav farrjv 18. 141. 241. 336. 385. 429. 522. 620. 632. 919. 1849. 1918. 1955. 2004: KDVT Acyaarj (+ MU targvpa Pr) Pr gig s 1 arm 8- (bo): fortitudine Tyc Aryuw 025 bo tireo-ev 2 A I. 35. 104. 172. 205. 468. 632. 1957. 2019. 2023. 2036. 2037. 2040. 2041. 2067 Tyc Pr gig vg s arm 8 4: K 046. 20 (- 35. 205. 468. 632. 2040). 250. 2038 al mu arm 8- bo sa eth: + r cr 025 J BoJ. pr rj 046. 61. 69. 2067: +17 0X10- bosa eth KOTOOC. habitatio etrefugium Pr ovuftovudK AK 046. 2040 Tyc Pr gig vg: Sotuow? 025. 20 (-2040). 250. 2037. 2038. 2067 al uxakiy 1 3 Pr vavroa 1. Aeito Aevov 2 omms immunditiae et iniquitatis Tyc iravroo1. vaatt? 2 18. 205 wcvpatOo + oatioviov 620 axob. 1. opvcov 025. I. 61. 69. 104. 181. 242. 617.919. 1934. 2016. 2019. 2020. 2036. 2037. 2038. 2067 s 1 arm 1 1 K. icuotfACFov 1 A 336. 620 gig arm 4: K 025. 046 min fere omu (Pr) vg s 8 bo sa eth: + et omnis bestiae imraundae Pr ran-. 8 456. 632 opvtov uov A afcatf. 8 Q20 ic. on icvov 8 ic. ftcucwruvov 18: 6i. 69. vg (- vg 6): pr Kat ravrocr Brjpiov axa aprov 250. 424: + et career omnis bestiae immundae et odibilis gig s 8 1.

3. T. OIK r. 9u i. K 046. 20 (- 35. 205). 250 al pl Tyc s 8: r. 0vfu r. otv. 025. 051. i. 35. 172. 205. 241. 432. 1957. 2018. 2019. 2023. 2036. 2037. 2038. 2041.

2067 gig arm 8 4- W eth: T. wv. AC vg: T. 6vfjl. Pr s 1 T. Bvp. T. iropv. T. n-opv. T. tfv. C T. iropv. 2i8 S 8 ir r. vavr. r. Pr JTCITOTIKCV 94. 432. 2019. 2036 (s 1): TTCTTOKCV (ITCTTW- 35. 2037). 025. I. 35. 2023. 2037. 2038. 2041: jrarukcurt (irciro- 242. 498. 617. 2020). 051. no. 175. (241). 250. 337. 468. 522-617.

632. (1918). 1934. 1957. 2016. 2017. 2020. 2024. 2039. 2067 al p Tyc gig vg s 8 arm 8 8-: rorromcay AC: wfirtumcaori(v) K 046. 90 (-35. 175. 337. 468. 617. 632. 2020). 61. 69. 104 al p arm 4 bo eth JUT avr. ciropv. ot ACT avr. iropvcwravrer 256. 336. (620). 628 Tyc arm 8-: ACT ouriycr Pr T. yip 3 aunyo-I. 920 r. Bw. bo crrpiKovcr arprjvov C 149. 201. 241. 2037. 2067 (.

4. Kcu jjjtfovora ftxXTjv wqy IK rov

E A0at r afaijs 6 Xnos ioi; 6 Xafc 0c tva iiy (rvwcoivwifcnpc rat? aiamai? avnjs, gal IK iw Trxi wv OVTTJS iva py Xafyrf 5. 5ri oxXi707rav avnjs at aiopruu fypi rov ovpavov, KOI cuqioicvcrci 6 0co9 ra d uc iara avrijs.

6. airosorc avrjj us cat ical Siirxwarate Stirxa Kara TO, Ipya. avn)?

ev TO TTonptw c fccpturei KCpooratC avr Suraovy 4. axXijk n)K axXiyo- wnpr C 2067: 2020: axX. arm 8 4- bo Xeyouo-oy-n r 2067 c cx arc AK 2036. 2038: e ex0CTC 025. 051. I. 35. 205. 1957. 2017. 2023. 2037- 2041. 2067 Tyc gig vg s arm bo: c cx0c C 046. 80 (- 35. 205. 2040). 250 al pl Pr c avripr tr after fiov KC 025. 2020. (2067) eth: i. 110. 181. 2038 j cf air 2067 o 2O5. 2038. 2067 iva386 crwcoiv. AKC: ovyicoiv. 025.046 min omn ai 2 s a K. K T. irx. avr. O25. 051. 35. 2038 I T. trxrjyw nj(r irxijyrp gig s 1 Xafcp-c Xaflqrc 386: jsXafyre 051. 2036. 2037 (Tyc Pr). 6. aim) 1 awn; s 1 (bo): auraiv arm 2: 92O a pi c a 025: uxpi 2037 cjtnyiov. + avnpr 18. 35. 82. no. 172. 337. 385. 456. 632. 919. 920. 1849. 1955. 2004. 2018. 2022. 2023 al p: + avrour 386 eth Btoo dominus vg: dominus deus Pr avnja 3 avrw Tyc arm 2.

6. airosotc. auttjcr et (Cyp) ideo reddidit ei duplicia (dupla Cyp) Pr Cyp au-osorc arosisaxnv arm 2- aai 1 vg (-vg) o 8o)KCF +vfuv 051. i. 35. 175. 205. 468. 617. 632. 1934.1957. 2016. 2037. 2038. 2041 gig vg T arm 2 4: +i? fui 2067 arm 8- u 2 K eth rxoxrarc(9rxiurarc 18. 2004) AKC 046. 80 (-35- I 75- 205. 617. 620. 632. 1934. 2020). 61.69.82.93. 110. 385. 2022. 2024. 2039 al mu Tyc gig vg: + avnj 025. 051. i. 35. 104. 175. 250. 617. 620. 632. 1934. 1957. 2016. 2037. 2038. 2067 al s arm 4 bo: + avnyv 205: + avra 2020 (Siiraa A 025. 046. 051. I. 35. 104. 175. 205. 250. 617. 620. 632. 1934. 2016 2020. 2037. 2038. 2040. 2067: pr TO KC 18. 61. 69.110. 325. 337. 385. 386. 456. 468. (632). 919. 920.1849. 2004. 2022 (ra) Surxa AKC 025. 35. 175. 617. 620. 632. 1934. 2p20. 2040 Tyc Pr gig vg s arm bo eth: +axr K ai avn? (avrw 69) KOI (6i. 69) 046. 80 (-35. 175. 617. 620. 632. 1934. 2020. 2040). 61. 69. 82. 110 sd mn ra 149 ev T D TTonflnw in calicem gig iror puo AC 025. i. 35. 175. 250. 325. 617. 1934. 2037. 2038. 2040. 2067 Tyc Pr (gig) vg s arm eth: 62o: +aun7rko46. 80 (-35. 175. 325. 617. 1934. 2040). 69. 104. no. 385 bo w wo- 172. 2020 bo cxcpao-cv + VUK

AIIOKAAYMS IOANNOY XVm. 7-8.

7. ova fiofflurcv avnfv col Icrrpiyvwuw, wovrov Sore afrij jsocravuriov 8n fr T J Kapow a s Xy T4 Kaftfluuu jsaatxarcra 8. a TOVTO iv ua l f flavaros al ir os ical Xinos, t(a) al b mpl fcarakav o-crat, art wrxvpos o 0 K P tl as a T Vt 9- Kal r wi l jrf

owlu ff ra I fl fwr awjs iropycwravtCS Kal otprvia(ravt, Srap 0 ir w TOK (a) On this line see vol. ii. ioa 632 Kepacrare remixtum est Gyp Pr: " shall be mingled arm 2 avrf avrrjv 046. 620.

7." KTO pr Kat Pr arm 2 OVTTV Afcc C 025. 046. 0 (-35. 175. 205. 632. 1934. 2020. 2040) al: avn c I. 35. 69. no. 175- 205. 250. 632. 2020. 2037. 2038. 2040. 2067 al pl roo-ovr. 3orc xcpoo-arc i Sore owc 025: datur Pr

Gyp (arm 2) Sore aw. s x avny gig K. wo. 05I. I. 35. 60. 181. 432. 1957. 2023. 2041. 2067: +populo suo Tyc on 1 ecu i: SIOTI 2036. 2037: +KOI 205: O5I. 2038 Xeyei + Babylonia Tyc ori 2 + iyw 172. 250. 2018: i. 620. 2067 Kobryim A C 025. 35. 175. 617. 620. 632. 1934. 2020. 2040 gig vg s arm 8-: jca6 u 046. 61. 69 arm 2 bo: KO WO- 18. 82.

no. 325. 337. 3 8 5- 429- 45 6- 5 22- (6 3 2)- 9i9- 9 20- 18 49- SS-2004. 2022. 2024. 2039 al p: + Kobwr 468: + oxr 205: ciu fca bxr 201. 386: sum Pr Gyp jsao-txio-cra jfturtxcvovra G OVK cifu non possum esse (esse non possum Gyp) Pr Gyp.

8. imtpa opa 6 1. 69 Pr eth avr o- pr r s 1 (arm 2 3-) avaroo-J Bavarav 046 arm 2 got 1 AM 025. 35. 205. 620. 920. 2040 Tyc Pr gig vg W 2 arm 8 4- bo: 046. SO (-35. 205. 620. 920. 2040). 82. 1 10. 172. 201. 250. 314. 385. 429 498. 522. 1955. 2018 al arm 2 rat 8 i8 cv irupt tr after fcarajcaud. (arm 2) bo eth icaroicavdicrcrat icaraicav erokrai Tyc: fcavftprfrat 337 o 0COO- A 2040 vg eth: o Qiocr o Kvpwr K: mpuxr o Ototr N 1 C 025. 046. 80 (-175- 617. 920. 1934. 2020. 2040). 250. 2037. 2067 al Tyc Gyp gig s 2 arm 3 4- bo: Kvpuxr 141. 175. 242. 314. 617. 1934- 2016. 2020. 2041 Pr s 1 arm 2: Kvp. o 0coa o wavtQKparwp 2036: Kvpuxr o vavrokparup 2037 Kpwur Kpivw K i. 175. 250. 314. 617. 1934. 2016. 2036. 2037: (qui) iudicabit Tyc vg.- 0. KXauomrai A i. 18. 205. 2019. 2004. 2038. 2067 al p:

Kcnrvov 1-175 irvpomrcco? avnjs, 10. OTTO uafcpolcv COTTKOTCS Sea ror f6pov TOV SacravtoTov aftrifc, Xcyovrcs Ovac, ovat 17 irdxt? 17, Bafoxwv iroxi9 17 OTI AI upp X0cv 17 fcptcri? O-ov. 11. ical oi cfiiroMH rijs yi s KXatowtv ical irwqoixnv cv avriyv, 23. ptt oi 3jurooot f o-ov t i o-av ot Acyiorravcs T yijs (fl) I I b. OTI TOV yopjov avtcav ovsels ayopa ct OUKCTI, (a) This line is provisionally restored here: see vol. ii. 102, 112. But it is best to take it as a gloss on II.

icxavo-ovo-tv C 025. 046. SO (18. 205. 2004). 250. 2037 al 1 KXawovrai (-crowrtv) +avnrv 025. I. 35. 2O J. 2036. 2037. 2067 S 1:-f-Tavrtyv 2019 2038 cat co. 92O icai 8 bo r awi7 6i. 69 Pr avny A I. 205. 498. 2019. 2020. 2036. 2037. 2038. 2040: avrrjv C 025. 046. 20 (205. 2020. 2040). 250 al: avntO- 2067: avrcov 620 ot 1 i8 K otp v. N 456:-H KCLI orrcva cikTiv fcc c " c SXciramTtv tsakriv X: XctTOvcriv 051. 522. 2017. 2038 irvpoxrcoxr irrtikrccoo- K.

1O. airo pr icai Pr arm 8 COTIJCOTCO COTWTCO- 2040: OT KOVTCO 2036. 2037: otTTo ovrat arm 8- bo T. fo(3. 1849 1 Tov)8ao-av-ia-iov TOV jsao-avmTxov 1849 (arm): tormentorum gig: arm 8- Xfyovrcor icat Xcfowiv s 1 arm 8 8 tt: arm 4 ouai 8 +OIMU 172. 250. 2018 s 1: I4I. 2019. 2038 17 1 1934 17 icy. Pr I 3a3uxa)v pri7 172. 250. 2018. 2023 io- vpa o upa 2036. 2037 fjua copal xtav upav A 2040: pr cv I. 2020. 2037. 2067 i? X0 v A o-ovj eius gig.

11.-njcr Ytja OTOU 456: 4- o-ov K: terrarum Pr fcxaiovcrtv ic. irci owrtv A C 025. I. 35. 205. 1957. 2023. 2037. 2038. 2040. 2067 (Pr) gig: fxawowi (-o-ovrai

2036) c. Trevfl o-ovo'i (-Oowriv 314) 046. 20 (- 35. 205. 2040). 250. (314). (336). (1918). (2036) vg s 1- 2 arm 8 (bo): X. KOI s 2: KOI ravfl. 336. 620. 1918. 2036: rat 8 bo: flent plangentes Pr cir avr. tr after jcxaiovo-iv 2020 CTT cv A I. 2036: c 051. 181. 2019. 2037. 2038. 2067: pr c eavrovcr 468: Pr avn; v C 025. 94. 336. 620. 1918. 2017 gig vg (Pr): avri7 A 2O (620). 104. 250. 314. 1957. 2022. 2023 al mu: avtito 61. 172. 2018: avrow 046: cavrovar 051. 181. 2038: cavrour I. 2019. 2036. 2037. 2067.

88. on AMC 025. 046. i. 35. 175. 250. 617. 620. 1934.

2037. 2038. 2040. 2067 Tyc Pr gig vg s arm 2 4 eth: 10 (35. 175. 617. 620. 632. 1934. 2040). 82. 201. 385. 429. 498. 522. 1955 bo oi 1 A 2040 o-oii 325. 2019. 2036 ow 386.

ll b. aunav avrt)r 172. 2016. 2020 OVKCTI (KCU OVKCTI 620. 1918: OVK corev 456: iam Pr: arm bo eth) joined with what 12. yotw xpwrov KOL dpyvpov Kal Xioov TIUOV u iapyapitoiv, KOI jsvcrowov Kal troptjuvpas Kal criptkov ical KOKKCVOV, Kal irav (v ov Ovivov ical trav CTKCVO? iketfxivtivov Kal irav (TKcvos IK r (vxov riuorarov, 13. KOI KivvafjUDfjLOV Kal aittfloy xal fouatara, Kal tvpov Kal Xipavov Kal otvov, precedes 035. 1957. 2023. 2036. 2037 Pr gig vg s 1: joined with what follows AC 046. 19 al pl s 8: without punctuation K.

12. xpwrou xpvcrow C 025. 620. 1918: XPOTIW 94. 2019 opvvpovjopyvpow C 025: apyvpiov 94. 181. 201. 386 Ai0. TI. Aipow rtuowr C 025 (bo): Atftoi nuw Pr s arm 2 uopyaptiw K 172. 2018. 2040 Pr gig s arm 8- 8- ft: lapyopitoir (-TOUT A) AC 025 bo: polpyapitov 046. flo. 250. 2037. 2038. 2067 al pl vg I 0wnr. KOKKIVOV sirici et purporae et coccineae vestis Pr ftwrtrwov AC 025. 046. 80 (- 35. 205) al pl gig: ftwrtrivwv K: j8wnrov 051. i. 35. 205. 1957. 2019. 2023. 2036. 2037. 2038. 2041 Vg K. iropt. A iroptvpar KC 025. 104. 205. 620. 632. 2018. 2037. 2040: iropjvpov 046. 051. 20 (- 205. 620, 632. 2040). i. 69. no. 314. 385. 2037. 2067 K. o-ipuc. i. 920 o-cptkou Afctc 025. 046. 051. 104. 620. 1849. 2017 al: orypikOV 20 (-386. 620. 1849) al pl: OTHKOU 172. 386. 2016. 2018. 2019 TOV (v w. TifjuwtOLTov omne lignum mcensi et omne vas ligneum et omne vas eburneum preciosum gig K. TTO. V fva, Ovw. et omnis ligni citrei Pr: tr after rip. bo (vxov O-KCVOO- A: (vxww 025 exc. K. TT. O-KCVOO- arm 2 K. TTQ. V O-K. CK fvx. gig Tav o-Keikxr 2 Pr CK C 94 (v ov C 025. 046. 20 (-2040) al fere onm Pr s (arm) (bo): Xioov A 2040 vg eth rifuomiroi Ttfuov S 1 oxKOv. vifypov. fmLpfjuipov xafaov. ri rjpov. iopiopoy S 1 bo a Kov KO. KOV C K. 0-18. arm 8 K. fwpi. i.

18. Ktwap,- A C 025. 046. 19 (-35. 205. 620. 919. 1934. 2020). 104. 250. 2038 al p (Pr) vg: uvap- 046. i. 35. 69. 172. 205. 314. 620. 1934. 2020. 2022. 2023. 2036. 2037. 2067 al mu gig bo KUvafjlufjlOv (KLvafuDfiov) AC 025. i. 250. 2037. 2038. 2040. 2067 al mu vg gig s arm (bo): KivvaLuoiov (Ktvaiaiov) K 046. 19 (-35. 2040) al mu: cinnamum Pr K. aiaAo? A C 025. 35. 93. 172. 181. 218. 250. 314. 2016. 2018. 2019. gg v g s 8: K 046. 20 (-35). i. 2037. 2038. 2067 al pl Pr s 1 arm bo Bvfuaimra 0viiaxa i. 2037. 2040. 2067 Pr gig arm 8 bo:-fuitoar 046. 6l. 69:-Aarciy 201. 386. 620 vg K. pvpov C jjojpov pupw 386 (arm 8): pvpav vg s 8: (rtvpvav 2036. 2037 Aifevov ipavw vg owov. caaioy 175. 218. 242. 250. 314. 617. 1934. 2016. 2017 K. oivov A C 025. 35. (175). 205.

Kal Jfaaiov Kal crcusaatv Kal crirov, ical KTyvy KO! irpofto. ro, (a) cat v a? avopurrrotv. (b) 1 5. ot Zfjoropoi Toimui, ol iraovr?; cravtCS dv avri?, Airo fmKpofav 8ia rov t63ov rov SacravcaAov aur s icxatbrrcs al 1 6. Acyovres oval i; iroat? ij Acyaai;, ij ircptfaftxvjfmfvri pwro-ivov KOI irop vpovv ical icac Kcxpvo-ufjlcvi xpvcria) KOI At g Tifup KOI Sri Aia atpa riprjfjluorj 6 TOO-OVTOS Traovros.

(a) Here follows an interpolation: Kal frrrwv ctf fcdw? jca2 crwidrwy. See vol. ii. 1 02.

(3) Verse 14 is restored after 21: see vol. ii. 105. 108.

(617). 632. (1934). 2020. 2040 al Pr gig s arm bo sa eth: O46. 20 ("35- I 75- 632. 205. 617. 1934. 2020. 2040) al mu:. otvow Vg atov caatov vg K. rcuu Pr rcu8. vx ar rcu8aacakr. orrov. KTTJVWV. irpofiarw. iru wv vg jc. (TIT. ic. icr. s 1 icai 9 bo erirov orirov 620 bo j KTTJVTJ K. irpofiata A C 025. 35. 205. 2037. 2038. 2040. 2067 al Pr gig (vg) s 2 arm 8- 4- bo sa: 046. 2O (- 35. 205. 2040). 250 al mu arm 2:. irpojff. 42. 1957 ttnro) anrovcr 2040 s arm 2: equi Pr pcs v A C 025. 046. i. 1 8. 205. 632. 919. 1849. 2004. 2037. 2038. 2067 al mu: HUW 051. 2O (18. 205. 632. 919. 1849. 2004). 82. 104. 250. 314. 2016 al mu: pcw 61. 69. 2022: xow Pr s arm 3 4- pcw icai arm 2 bo o-wi. KO. I 337- 386 arm 2 (cniLLariv crctffiara s: craiia bo: fru w 61. 69: mancipia (-orum vg) Pr vg: porcorum Tyc: mulorum et camelorum sa K. fax avop. et diversi generis animalia Pr: K. iru v avqponrov bo eth: Tyc.

15. TOOTW avrrjcr Pr: crov bo avrrjcr 1 crov bo arrjcrovrai stabant Tyc 8. T. oj8. T. j8. avr. Tyc icaaiokrcflr (icaavo-ovo-if s arm 2 bo eth) A C 025. i. 18. 35. 175. 250. 617. 632. 1849. 1934. 2004. 2037. 2038. 2040 Tyc Pr gig vg s 1 arm 8 4- (bo) sa: pr at 046. 325. 337. 386. 456. 468. 620. 632. 919. 920 al s 2 arm 2 eth KCU bo ircvtfowrco-J TTCV GTOVO-CK s 2 arm 2 bo eth.

16. Xcyorrca- (Aeyowiv 046. 522: cpowriv arm 8 eth) A C (046). 1 75. 325. 337. 386. 456. (522). 617 al mn Tyc gig s 2 (arm) bo sa (eth): pr 1025. 051. 19 (- 175. 325. 337. 456. 617. 620). 250. 2037. 2067 Prvgs 1 arm 4 (eth) own 1 + 0-01 bo I ovoi 2 AKCo25. 35- T 75- 2 S- 6l 7- J 934- 2 20- 2 O37- 2038. 2040 al Tycprgigvgs arm (bo) sa eth: +01 11172.2018:-fo-otbo: 046. 10(35. 175. 617. 1934. 2020. 2040) al mu i TToa. TI icy 17 p yaxvj iraxur 2020 bo iy icy. 17 ircpfapl. K iy 8 A 17 Trcpi A. quae vastata est gig I pwor. K xpvrwp, vri 325 PWTO-. KOKK. A 1 ftvaa;. TTOJ.- Pr PWTO-IVOV (flwivov 025. jsvorcrwov i) 17. KOI iros Kvfapvrjnfi teal ires 6 brl rovov vxcw, KOL vavrat Sow rrjv Odxcwav Ipyaforrat, avo fjLOKpoocv corqaav 1 8. Kal JXcjron-es rov Kairrov TIJS irvpacrecit avn, Acyorrcc T 6iota T iroxei rg (jltyaay; 19. KOI r cj8axov"l ow rl aviw, xal cpa(av cxaioms Kal ircvlowrc?, Adorns Ovat, oval f) Troxi? ij icyaxiy, . 35. 175- 2 5- 6l 7- 6zo- 2 37- 2 3 8 1 Tyc (Pr) gig

V ga. c. f. g. h. jsvoro-ov 046. 18. 337. 386. 456. 468. 632. 919. 920. 1849. 2004. 2067 al Vg 4T vopqvpaw A C 046. 19 (-325. 386). 2037. 2038 al pl: 7ropfvpav 025. 94. 141. 172. 201. 241. 250. 2018. 2019. 2067 rat 025- 175. 242. 617. 1934 KOKKLVOV KOKKtva s 1 I Kai 8 051. i. 2036. 2038 arm 4: 17 eth Ke pvcr. Kc pixrcoxcfoy K: icc pvo-uAcva s 1 (bo): arm 4 XW D AC 025. 046. 19 (-35). 250 alp 1: xwo-o) K 051. i. 35. 61. 69. 1957. 2019. 2023. 2036. 2037. 2038. 2067 al: auro Pr gig vg: pr cv KC i. 35. 1957. 2019. 2023. 2036. 2037. 2038. 2067 AiO. rii. Xioour riuowr s 2 arm 2 8- Ttftwu 046 sa lopyaptny ANC 025. 2040 Pr arm 4 bo (sa): lapyapiraur (-rao- s) 046. 19 (- 2040). 250. 2037. 2038. 2067 1 fere omn Tyc gig vg s arm 2- 8 fua in hacgig iflwyuwtfr pvj 0rj 051. I. 2036. 2038 o 025- 2040.

17. o 025. i. 314. 1957. 2016. 2017. 2036. 2037. 2038 al CTTI TOU-OV irxco)v pr rt TOW Trxotwv s 1: iri TWV Trxoiuk (+ o I) ouxocr i. 2037: Trxcw iri TCOV iraoto)v 2016: super mare navigans Pr (bo sa): (qui) manibus navigat Tyc TOTTOV (pr rov K 046. 468: pr ilium gig) A C 046. 19 (-35. 175. 617. 1934) al mu gig vg s 2 arm: TOIV irxoiwk 025. 35. 181. 250. 314. 617. 1934. 1957. 2017. 2019. 2023. 2036. 2038. 2067 rrxcwv navigabat (-avit Vg) gig vg c K. vavr. epyafovrai bo ocroi T. Oa. epyajovrai quotquot mare operatur Tyc T. 0ax. cv TIJ axacroty Pr gig vg v arm 8: mana (mari vg dtf) vg 0- 1– epyafon-ai morantur Pr conyo-av stabunt Pr arm.

18. Kai eicpaja 2020 Pr icai 2067 arm 4 tkpafav AC 025. 172. 2018. 2038. 2040 Tyc gig vg s 2: c Da ov K 046. 051. 19 (-325. 468. 920. 2040). I. 250. 2037. 2067: CKXaioy 920: Ctfxawav avrqv s 1: CKpavyaj ov 42. 325. 468. 517: Kpa ovcrw arm SXeiroirccr opwvrecr i Kairvov C 025. 046. 19 al fwe omjl Pr Tyc gig s arm bo sa: rmrov A 60 vg rur C iroxct + ravnj C gig vg arm bo.

19. tpaxok (-av C) C 046. 19 (-325. 617. 2040) al " " vg s (bo): cjdoxXof 025. 051. 325. 385. 617 gig: rc8oxov (erc axXok 2040) A 2040: mittentes Pr ovv 2o r. KC. ripr Kc oxi o- K 2026 bo avrcov cavrwv C Kat 2 arm 2 4 bo Kpa av (+ twvr) icyox arm 4) AC 2018 vg s arm 4: tkpa ov K 025. 046. 19. 250. 2037. 2067 a gig: clamabunt Pr: ircvqavvrco-arm 8-: arm 2 KXatovreo- K. ircv6awt r A I: pr KOI 325.

Iv j Trxoim rav iravrcs ot c ovrcs ra irxotia TQ tfaxavo;, f lc T S riiidn ros avr s on it i pa pi a. f ( ) 21. Kal pcv cts ayycxot icrxvpot Xiflov as Avxtvov Acyav, ical f? axcv cts riv tfaxacrcrav Xeytov

Ovrws oppyfutn 3 rj(hjartt(U Bafoxwy 17 fjlfyaxrj iroxic, Kal ov i vp 0jj In.

14. Kal 17 otrojpa crov r s ciritfvfuas ri dinAtfc? avo crov,

Kat Travra ra Xiirapa ical ra XaA? rpa atrcoxcro airo orov. ( ) (a) Text corrupt. We should read: 6rt u w t aijr j: cf. vers. 10, 1 6, and see vol. ii. 106 sq. Ver. 20 is restored to its original context after 23- b. See vol. ii. 92 sq.

( ) On the restoration of the order of the text, see vol. ii. 92, 105, 108.

(V) Here follows a gloss: ical OVK TI ov w aura evfrfo-oixriv. On a possible explanation of it in connexion with the loss of 22 b which I have restored, see vol. ii. 92, 109, and footnote in loc. of English transl.

468 arm 3-: 325. 468: tr after Xcyoireo- 325. 468. 517 Aeyoireo- (+ voce magna Pr) Atfc i. 172. 2018. 2040 Pr vg (arm 2 8a) bo: pr Kai 025. 046. 19 (-325. 468. 2040). 250. 2038. 2067 al pl gig vg 0 s arm 4: 468 vg 1 ouat 2 AC 025. 046. 19 (- 337. 468. 2040) Tyc Pr gig vg s arm sa eth: +ovoi 172. 250. 2019: K 141. 337. 432. 452. 468. 506. 2019. 2021. 2040 bo 17 wox. 17 ftey. j rj icyaxq iroxur 1849 TO i. 35. 172. 175. 617. 1934. 2018. 2036. 2037. 2038. 2067 al cv T. 0ax. avnjcr de mari et de pretiis eius gig c r. nx. avr. Tyc rjprjfjuuorj cpyptoor) I. 2036. 2038.

21. xai 1 pr teat cxpa cv av7v bo K. pcv tr after ur vpoar bo ctcr ayyexocr irxypor i6. ir a. Xtft A. The letters between a and X are not visible, but the space is only enough for five or six. MT + C aurwv 337 ayy. to– TCDV ayycxoiv raiv s 1 urxypoa-lo-vupov (tr after ibov N) K 141. 149:

Tyc s 2 Xi0ov OKT bo: Xi ov 2oi9: wo- arm 2 oxr coo-el 2036. 2037: ad magnitudinem Pr x, vxtvov (ivxucov C) AC: molarem vg (bo): uvxov 025. 046. 19.

205. 2037. 2038. (2067): molam (-ae Pr) Tyc Pr gig so2 arm: Xi0ov K (2019) iteyav ieya 2019. 2O2O: tr before coo- 2067 ovroxr pr ort M 620: hoc Pr vg arm 2 J3a3v t i pr ilia Tyc ficyax vo iar LccyoxotToxio- 2067 iroxicr-Pr crt + cv avn K 046. 61. 69.

14. TJ otrwpa pomorum (-a vg) Pr vg: hora gig (arm 4): arm 2- 8 17 C o-ov 1 placed after oircupa A C 025. 2040 (Pr) V gac f. g h. r. tr a er vxycr 046. 19. 250. 2037. 2038. 2067 gig vg d s 2 arm: in both places 172. 2018 s 1: bo rrja cirt0vuor AnoKAAY l2 IQANNOY XVIH. 82.

22 ". KCU CJHDVTJ jcttfoptpsojv KOI f LLOOTIKCOV f ov fjaf clKOwrqjj cv o-ol err (0 jcal un? (a) avxip-wv) cv crol 3ri.

ov f; aicovo-00 cv crol cri" 22. jcai was TC VITT TTOOTS Te nys ov LM) cvpcofl cv rol CTI.

ICOl OVJ7 ov IT; akOwrq cv crol Iri a) Necessarily restored, yet found in eth: see below.

17 ciritfviua Pr s 1 amyx cv discendent vg 11 arm 2 ra 1 6i. 69 I Xiirapa piirapa N: 4-crov 2040 ra 2 A 025. 046. 10 al fer omn: C 2036. 2067 cwnoxero AC 025. 046. 19 (-35. 620). 250 al arm 4 eth: airoixovro K 35. 104. no. 172. 336. 432. 620. 1918. 1957. 2018. 2023. 2041 gig vg bo sa: perient Pr: cariox 2067: am? X0cv 051. I. 2036. 2037 S 1 arm 8- OVKCTI-h avra jsXc rcto' gat s 1 ov fiiy avra Att 2018. 2020. 2040: avra ov IT; C 025. 046. 19 (- 35. 175. 617. 1934. 2020. 2040) al gig vg: tr avra after evp. i. 35. 175. 250. 617. 1934. 2037. 2038 (arm) evpij-crovo-tv A C 025. 1 8. 172. 250. 424. 2018. 2019. 2039 v s (arm 2) bo: cvp cr (-cur 104. 620). 046. 19 (- 18. 35). 2037. 2067: cvptjcretcr (- r 051). 051. I. 35. 432. 1957. 2023. 2038. 2041 Pr gig arm 8 4: + ovrc irv ao- avqptdirw rov XOITTOV tfjitropeufrrj 241. 314. 2016 K. oviccrt. cvprjorowriv joined with ver. 15 by 172. 2018. 2019 s bo eth.

2. Kai uinr). aoxiricrruk KCU ov prj akowfhj cv avn; faavri iovo-ucov KCU Kioapaa- KOI avxov KCU xoviy craxTrtyyoo- ov p. rj akcnxrorj cv avr?; eth. Here observe that the Ethiopia has already restored the missing words in 22 b x icat 1 i Tyc: ov8c bo eth Ku? apa)ow Kioapacr s 1 arm 2 bo eth) AOVO-UC. o-axirj s 1 avxirrwv avxurrcav 620: sinfoniacorum Pr avx. cai bo o-axirurrcov AC 025. 046. 19 al fere omn gig: o-oxwiyyov (-00- s 1 arm 2) K 172. 2018 s arm 2 4: o-oxirty vg bo: fistularum Tyc: tibicinum Pr: + KCU 2020 crot avnj gig vg c- f eth.

8 C- d. 4 nei ftivrjv K bo I Wfi rftr pr ony C 920 s 1 eth.

22 " b. K. mo-Tcx?- cti 6i. 69 s 1 arm: tr. after cv o-oi cri 2 104. 620 TOO- TcxyitTTo- i9i8 iroxnyo- Tcxnyo- C 025. 046. 19. 250. 2038. 2067 Pr gig vg s 2: AK bo: + rtvoia 1918 o-oi 1 avri7 vg T eth K. wviy fivxov. cri 2 AC 025. 046. 19 (18. 919. 920. 1849. 2004. 2020). 250. 2037. 2038. 2067 Pr gigvg arm 2 bo: 18. 141. 172. 385. 522. 919. 920. 1849. Z 955- 2004. 2020 s arm 8 eth ivxov pvqov C oxovo- ov fif) (ftfivy iv rol fri.

2O, E6 paivov fcr 46177, ovpavc, ical ot otyioi feat oil dwcrroxot ical ol OTl llcpivCV 6 0COS TO KptfjM VflmV 23 f. ore fr Tj) apuaiciip t orov f(0) cirxavijatyrav irdvra ra 24. feat cv avrj alia irptxfrrjrv cat dytw tv ical irdvrwv rav icrtayfjl vwv CTTI r s yi s.

(a) Read cvpc i; 046: ai7; 91. 175. 250. 314. 617. 1934. 2016 (rot aim; 23- b. icai 4Koa. Ti C 025. 046. 19 al fere onm Pr gig vg s arm 8 4- bo: A 506 arm 2 ai 046 vxymi–Kai av arm 8 any okovo-Orj 620 i C Pr gig vg S 1 cri 2O. eu pairou exultate

Pr s arm 3-: cv paivcrcu (-craxrav arm 2) arm 2 eth r ovriy ovpavc Tyc bo? r cv A 522 avn; A C 046. 19 (-18. 35. 617. 2004). 250. 522 gig: ovnyv 025. 051. I. 18. 35. 617. 2004. 2018. 2019. 2036. 2037. 2038. 2067 al Tyc Pr vg u ot 8 A 025. 046. 19 (- 35). 250. 2037. 2067 al pl Tyc Pr vg 1 "- 11- T s arm 8 bo: C 051. i. 35. 2038 al p gig

V gc. d arm 2 4. a (eth) cwrcxrroaoi. irpo irat eth.

28 f. apfiaxia A C 025. 104. 172. 2019. 2038. 2067: apxaiccta 046. 19 al pl: (rater) apiakUucr Tyc gig vg S 1 bo: maleficiis Pr crov avrvjcr arm 2: avrtuv eth CTrxavi icrav CTrxav-170-00- 172 s 1 eth.

24. CK OOTTJ Tyc: in te Pr eth aiia A C 025. i. 2020. 2036. 2037 al p: aifjua. ro. 046. 051. 19 (-2020). 250. 2038. 2067 al p evp 0rj cupc0i? o av 69. 104. 620. 1918 c. irarr. s j Kat 8 Tyc I ca ayicvwv co- payto-ficvcdv 2020 (arm 2 8-): pr a te Tyc: + oywuv 468.

CHAPTER XIX.

I. Mcra ravra rjkovau s fmvr)v fjlcyaxrjv o ov iroxXov iv rf ovpavy Xcyovrctfv 17 crtdT pta xal rj oof a ical Suvamis rov Qcov 1. pcra raura. (ver. 6) xai t)Kouora KT 632 utera

A C 025. 046. 19 (-35. 468. 2020). 250 al pl Pr gig vg s 2 bo: pr icai 051. i. 35. 468. 1957. 2019. 2020. 2023. 2036. 2037.

2038. 2041. 2067 s 1 arm eth wr Afetc 025. 046. 19 (-620.

VOL. n. 23 2. Sri ahrjoival KOI Siicaiat at icptcrcic avrov ovi ftcptvcv Tyy iropvrjv rqv fltyaxrjv, rv yv T0 7ropicia ical ifcoyinprcy TO aljpa raiv Sovacw avrov ic 3. ical Scvrepor

AXXiXovia-ical 6 Katrvos avrit? avaftuvei cfc TOVS aiawas rcov 4. Kal ttrco-av ol cikOcrt Tewapco- irpcovsvrcpot ical ra rcotrcpa

TW 0cp Tp Ka0rjp. fvp brl rp 0povp Xcyovrc?

632. 2020). 250. 2037 al vg bo: tr after fjlcya rjv 2019 eth: i. 104. 181 241. 336. 620. 632. 2020. 2038. 2067 Tyc Pr gig s arm neyox v xcyoxov 337. 632: tr after iroxXov 1957. 2023. 2041 al: i. 141. 2036. 2038. 2067 Pr arm 4 o Xov woxXov oxxwv iroxXcoi Pr vg f s 1: tubarum multarum vg fl- v arm 2: aquarum multarum vg d woxXov arm 3-: H-clamantium voce magna Pr Xcyovrcw dicentis gig: Xcyovo-ap no: +ro i. 2037 O-WT. Sofa eth o-wnpiaj laus vg g v 17 Sofa (+ at rfrifitf 632 arm 2- bo sa) K. 17 Sw. AN C 025. 35. (632). 2019. 2020. 2036. 2037. 2038. 2040 Tyc vg s 1 arm aa bo sa eth: 17 Svi. ic. 17 Sofa (+ K. 17 Ttfti7 S 2) 046. 19 (- 35. 632. 2020. 2040). 250 al pl gig s a arm 8: ic. 17 Sw. K Pr arm 4 T. 0cov i7uwov 2067 TOV 0 ov A C 025. 046. 19 (-632). 250. 2038 al pl gig bo sa: ro 0ea 241. 632. 2019 Tyc Pr vg s arm: jcvpuo TCD Otto I. 2037 rjfjiqtv +est Vg.

8. a T)Oikai cicpivcv axrjorj 468 ori 2 qui vg: + sic Pr iropinrjv iroxiv 69. 94. 209. 241. 632. 2023 17x10-. iropvcia avnrjo- bo 17x10-. yjjv 2O26. 2031. 2037 arm 8- I c0dcipcv KG 025. I. 172. 632. 2019. 2036. 2037. 2040 al: oie00ccpei 046. 19 (- 632. 2040). 250. 2067 al: cjcptycv A I iroppcia C 025. 046. 19 al pl: iropvta Attf Kai + KO- 2040 avrov 2 avr o- K eic x por A C 025. 046. 19 (- 35. 620. 632. 920). 250 al:

K rycr xcipoo- i. 35. 620. 632. 920. 2018. 2019. 2036. 2037. 2038. 2067 al: de manu Tyc gig s 2 sa eth: c (row) upvv Pr vg s 1 arm 8: x V 00 " arm 2 bo.

8. itai 1 s 1 cipqicav AK 025. i. 35. 172. 2018. 2036. 2037 2038: ipr)Kao-w 61. 69. 201. 250. 386. 2040 2067 al: rav (-ov 2020) C 2020: dixerunt (= eiprjkav or CITTOV) Tyc Pr gig vg s arm 2-) 4 sa eth: cip ccv 046.19 (35. 386. 2020. 2040) al bo j o 386 avnjff avrcov Tyc: de ilia Pr: i. 241. 632. 2067 avaJoivci av 3atv v 172. 2018. 2020 s 2: wcfty 2036. 2037 S 1 arm: avafyo-crai bo.

4. circaa A C 025. 046. i. 325. 337. 498 620. 2023. 2036.

0o ios on ravra CKMITOS 6. OTI atfm ayuav KOL feat alia avrots ewicas 1 ire O UM curt?.

7. Kal jjjcovcra rov Owuumjpiov Acyovro?

Nat, icvpic, 6 0eo 6 iravtOKpdrup, axrjoival KCU oyxatat at cpurets crov.

(a) On the restoration of xvi. 5 b-y to their original context, see vol. ii. 1 1 6, 120-124.

2038. 2041: CTOTOV 046. 19 (-325. 337. 620). 250. 2037. 2067: tr after irpco-0. 620 ot (69) cucoo-t TCO-GT. irptofi. A 046. 18. 61. 69. 201, 337. 386. 920. 1957. 2004. 2019. 2036. 2037.

2039. 2067 Pr gig (s 1) arm: ot irpccr?. ot etxoort rco-or. MC 025. 10 (-18. 337. 386. 620. 920. 2004). i- 250. 2038 al 1 vgs 1 ewe. TCO-O-. xs 046. i. 35. 337. 468. 919. 920. 1849. 2004. 2038. 2040 al Teo-o-eoa Atfc: reo-crapa (ft 35. 456. 2040 al mu) 025. 046. min pl wa TW (9i9) Opovu ANC 046. 19 (-35. 386. 468. 620. 632. 920. 2020). 250 al pl: TWV 6povw 025: rov (2O37) pwov I. 35. 386. 468. 498. 620. 632. 920. 1957. 2019. 2020. 2023.

2036. (2037). 2038. 2041. 2067 al afirfv axXyx. 35: arm 4 7 I ouijx. Pr 1. fcuca xvi. 6 1. fcucaiocr +domine vg d eth ct 104 arm 1 2 8- o A C 025. SO (-337. 617. 632. 919. 920. 1849. 1934) al: ocr 046. 61. 69. 82. no. 141. 337. 385. 429. 452. 522. 617.919. 920. 1849. 1934 al pl: arm 8- J "is" arm 2 8– ocrtoo- AC 046. 175. 250. 325. 337. 456. 468. 617. 620. 919. 1849.!934 2004. 2020 al mu arm 2: o xr xr M 025. 051. 35. 94. 181. 201. 205. 314. 386. 517. 632. 920. 1957. 2015. 2016. 2018. 2023. 2036. 2038. 2041. 2067 al (arm 4): sanctus vg: u 00100- 2040 s: et sanctus gig arm 1 8 a sa eth: KU o oo-too- i. 18. 424. 2019. 2037: et qui es pius Pr: bo.

6. oipi 1 aeiara M 620. 1918. 2019 ayutix. irpo-tijrwv 2o6. 2017 s 1 arm 8 1 aytcov fjmprvpw bo teat 8 ideoque Pr arm 1 8-: bo aiuui avrour Scdwkcwr (csamcaa-) AC 025. 046. 20 al fere wam vg s 2: otxa csaixao- avrour M gig s 1: cowacr avroco- aiia 6 1. 69 Pr (arm 4) sa (eth?): cowcur aiia avroio- bo: arrow arm x Sesowcao- AC arm 2 4: eswicoo- K 025. 046. 0 al oml1 miv (irlv C) A(C): irieiv K 025. 046. 80 al 8 omm ofiot pr ovtp K: pr ort 336. 620. 628. 1918 Pr (gig) s bo (sa) eth: pr ut 7. TOO 8ua. XCYOKTOV A C 025. 20. 250. 2038 al 1 vg f-i s arm 4 bo: pr ex 046. i. 2037. 2067 vg d W arm 1 2 8: favrp ex xix. 5. Kat fxavrj ITO rov Opovov i rj 6cv 4yowra

Alvcirc TJ) 0 p yfmMV, TTCLKTCS Ol Soiixot avroV ical ol tofiovfji vot avrov, 01 fjukpol KOI ol ficyaxoi. 6. ical ijffcowra os ak)v o;(Xov iroaAov cat us tavrjv vsarcnv xoxXuv ical OK tfwvrjv ftpovriav urxvpuv, Xcydvrcv ori cfao-txcwcv icupios, 0cos 6 Xuxoicv ical dyaxXutftcv, at Swo-oficv riyv So dv avr ori X0 v 6 yaio? rov dpvfov, icai 17 yw avrov rotxaorcv (arm) r. 6W. Xcyovorav 2019 arm: alterum (aliam vocem Pr) dicentem (-ens vg) Pr gig vg: ab altari dicens vg v axi?0tku.

cuat arm 1- (bo) eth ow u o Sicaioo- bo xat 8 bo. TJT. 6. 4 Kij. e tjx0 K. Xcyouaa AK 025. 046: vtu. ctyxBov. Xcyovcrai N: arm 2- 4 OTTO AC 046. 19 (-35. 175- 617. 632. 1934). 250 al mu: K M 025. I. 35. 175. 241. 242. 617.632. 1934- iqSS- J 957 2016. 2017. 2019. 2023. 2036. 2037. 2038. 2041. 2067 al mn tyorov AKC 025. 10 gig vg s arm 8- bo: ovpavov 046 61. 69 Pr c i? X0cv tr before airo r. Opov. K: S 1 TCD co AKC 025. 046. 325 al p: rov 0cov 10 (-325). 250. 2037. 2038. 2067 al 1 rjfjlwv vuov Pr: +otfcirc 2040: 1 8 arm 4 icoi 2 A 046. 10 al onm Pr gig vg s arm 8- bo eth: C 025 avrov dominum Pr: ro OVOJLCL avrov s 1 uicpoi. pcyaxoi Pr oc fttcpot pr icai i. 2023. 2037 al arm 4: pr iravrco- S 1 oi 8 175 ic. ot y. J icra rwv icyaxcuv s 1 bo ot 4 6. wa 1 AK 025. 046. 10 vg s bo: tr after WTJV 2019 s 1 arm 4 eth: i. no. 172. 181. 2016. 2018. 2037. 2038. 2067 Tyc Pr gig arm 8- o X. iroxX. ovxcov TroxXcoy s 1: tubarum (-ae vg) magnarum (-ae vg) Pr vg"- d- T cwr 2 025. 046. 10 (- 386) Pr gig vg s arm 8 4- bo eth: A 181. 201. 314. 386 Tyc vfiar. fl-oxX. ftpovr. icrxo r I Pp mrr + ToxXwv icai 468 CO VMDV magnorum vg 1 Xeyovrwv (-ovo-wv N:-OVOT 2067) A( ) 025. 172. 314. 2018. 2019. 2020. 2036. 2037. 2040. (2067) al Pr gig vg: Xcyovrccr (-TOO- 620). 046. 18 (- 35. 2020. 2040) al ma: Xcyovracr 051. i. 35 al: dicentes Tyc KVDUXT o 0eoo- AK 025. 046. 18 Tyc gig vg s 8 arm bo sa: o 0coo- o KVMOO-: o fcoo- o 0coo- 2038: o 0C00- 051. i. no. 181. 2019. 2067: nipioo- Pr s 1 o 0 or A i. 2023. 2040 Cyp s 1 arm 2 4 bo sa eth: +r)nw K 025. 046. 18 (-2040). 250. 2037. 2038 2067 al 1 " 1 Tyc Pr gig vg s f arm 3- o mvrokp. gig.

7. x ai P w F kcK X ai P Av (Kal X a P ACV Arm 4) 1 Arm ayaxXicuficv AM 025. i. 94. 172. 181. 2018. 2019. 2036. 2037. 2038. 2040. 2067:- AcOa 046. 18 (2040). 250 al 91 u 8 s 1 W. r.

8. fccu isoft; avrfi Iva ircpt? aai; rai

PVO-O-IVOV afjlirpov caOopdv. (a) 9. Kal X yci fuu Tpoafov Mafcapiot 01 cfc TO Scurvo? rov rov apvlov (a) An incorrect gloss follows in the text: rb-yip pfoffivo ra rwv A-yiwr rfrr. See vol. ii. 127 sq.

(3) Text adds a doublet of xxii. 6. 8-9: ol X y AW Offroi ol Xtfyot at dxiyitrol roo Btw thiv. lo. ical rera tfjnrpoffocv rwr xo wv airrou irpoffkVvfyrtu avr. Kal X y uuu "Opa j J ffirfotafc ffotf ciu ical TWI dcx i roi; raw i-)(kvtW T IV imprvplav Ivpov rtf 0ej Trpwrktrtpov if ybp fiaprvpia Irpov arir Tpoifirjrcut. See vol. ii. 128-129.

avr. glorificemus nomen eius Tyc arm 8 owoicv AM 0 Pr gig vg arm 4: cwcoicv (owoytcv 2019) 025. 2019. 2036: atcv K 046. 051. 18. i. 61. 69. 104. 241. 242. 250. 314. 1957. 2018. 2023. 2024. 2037. 2039 al mu: " we give " arm 1- 8-: o acwp. 2067 cf. Tyc arm s T. oof. avr. AK C 025. 046 min pl gig s eth: aurcor. 8of. Pr Cyp Vg avra avrtav K: avrov I. 175. 18 1. 250. 617. 1934. 2017. 2038 I ywiyj wfjufrr K c-: sponsa gig: +1; WI T; arm 8- 4 I avrov airrw arm 8 bo: I. 104. 181. 336. 620. 1918 eavnyvj avrrjv 18. 2037.

8. KOI 4-KOi 1934 ircpc aaiTcu vtpiflaxrfr A: 7rcpt)aaAipm 69. no. 172. 522. 2023. 2037: ircpt? c Aip-at 175 AaLwr. KO. Aftc 025. 104. 620. 1957. 2040 Tyc Pr gig vg a cf g h v arm 8 bo eth: 051. 35. 2036. 2038: Aawr. icai KO. 046. 18 (- 35. 620. 2040). 250 al pl vg d s 8: Kao. icai Xafjar. I. 2019. 2037. 2067 s 1: XCVKOV Xax7r. (ayatiov sa) icatf. (ica. Kat Xafiir. arm 8) arm 8 4 sa Svo-trivov 2 + mundum Pr: + Aevjcov arm 8 r. aytcov tr after tarty i al gig vg s 1 1.

9. Xcyci xoi arm 8 Aeyci ctircr s 8 bo: ctirov S 1: +CICT (CK) TIDV Trpco-vrcpcuv arm 8 ypoiw Troatv s 1: i. 2037. 2038 eur i49 TO AK 025. 18 (-386. 468. 620. 2020) al pl: TOV 046. 172. 336. 386. 468. 498. 522. 620. 2020 rovyaiov AK C 046. 18 (- 620). 250. 2067 al pl Pr vg sw 8 arm 8 8 sa eth: K 025. i. 336. 620. 1918. 2019. 2036. 2037. 2038 gig arm 4 bo apvtov-Heart s 1 K K rjfji voi + icat Siyc KGU airioi rco oxr 8ci (from the comm. of Aretas) 314. 2016. Aeyei 2. ciow arm 8 ic. Acy. iot 2 Ars c 025. 046. 18 (- 2020). 250. 2037. 2038. 2067 al pl (Pr) gig vg (s) arm 8 4 (bo) sa: K 314. 522. 2019. 2020 eth cai 8 + iterum Pr Aeyei 8 CITTCV s bo Aoyoi + fww K s 8 ot 8 A 91. 242. 1934 (b 1): K 025. 046. 18 (- 1934). 250. 2037. 2038. 2067 al pl arm 4 sa a ijotvoi vera et iusta Pr arm 8 oaiyfl. rov cov ctcrtv A 025. 046. 18 (- 35. 2020. 2040). 250 al 1 gig V g. c. d. th. T s. ax ft clrif Te OV 05!. j. 1957. 2020.

2023. 2036. 2037. 2038. 2067 (Pr) arm(8 4: rov 0cov a rjo. cio-iv K c 522. 2040 vg.

10. circva AK 025. 35. 325. 337. 386. 456. 620 al mu: rcrov 1 1. Kcu ctSov rov teal Bov iinros jcat 6 Kalqicm bf avrov jcaxovflCPOf irtcrrdf ml axiftm, jcul iv JC0100W0 gptvct xai? roxcAc 12. 01 8e fyfcafiol avrov a9 Xo irvpos, cat lirl r v K ax v avrov Stao uiara iroxXa (at) (a) Here follows an interpolation: d ctfrfc.

046. 1 8. 175. 468. 617. 632. 920. 1849. 934- 20 4- 2040 al mu Cfmrpoffv CKonrcov 046 r. iro8. 620 avrov rov ayyexov 620. 1918. 2040 irpoo-Kvyiyo-ai avrco (avrov 046) AK 046. 18 Pr gig vg S 2 arm 1: KOI (bo sa) nyxkTCfevnpra avrw 025. 2036. 2037. 2038 s 1 arm 8- 4- bo sa eth Xey rcv s bo fun arm 4 opa f y + TOHyotyo- 2017. 2040: vide ne feceris Pr gig vg: pr fitj irpoo-icwct 468" eth: " obey (see thou art evil, and he said to me arm 2). Fall thou (arm 2) not down before me " arm 2- 8- opa bo trwbovxocr pr on Pr bo eth: + yap gig arm 2 8 I crov 2 K 314: + KOI i. 181. 2038 Ii crov 1 pr rov 241. 429: +XPMTTOV Pr arm: (ro) icvpia arm 2 9rpoo Kvn; o-oiJ+AaaAoy s 1 if yap fuipr. irfarov sanctificatio enim testificationis Pr j TO w. nrp irpo. spiritus est et prophetiae gig: "the spirit holy which is in the prophets" arm 2 Iiycrov 2 A 025. 046. i. 35. 61. 69. 181. 336. 2019. 2023. 2036. 2037. 2038. 2040. 2067: pr rov 18 (-35. 1934. 2040). 250. 314. 2018 al pl: rov viov 242. 1934 wpo iy-reiao- aai ctacr 2037 bo.

11. icai 1 KCLI (bo) Jtcra ravra bo eth: Pr 7jvcayp, cvov A 025. 432. 2067: avcwypcvov 046. 18. 250. 2037. 2038 al pl c. tsov tinr. Xev. 632 icax. vurr. K. axrjq. 046. 18 (175. 617. 1934). 250 al pl s bo sa eth: vocatur (vocabatur Pr Gyp vg arm 9) fidelis et verus (verax gig: + vocatur vg- c- f- h) Tyc Pr Cyp gig vg armw 4: irurr. Kax. jc. 0X17. K: JcaxovLwoo- A 025. 051. I. (35?)- 9 1- r 75- 181. 242. 314. 617. 1934. 2016. 2017. 20 3 6 2037. 2038. 2067 arm 8- ft ic. K 8t c. icpcrcc Tyc: aequuni iustumque iudicat Pr K. irox. Tyc bo.

Id. 01 Se + oi K: KU 01 Tyc bo wo- A 172. 250. 1957.

2018. 2019. 2040 al Tyc Pr gig vg s arm 2- 4 bo sa eth: 025. 046. 18 (- 2040). i. 2037. 2038. 2067 al arm 8 ciri. r. c. tv rrj K fa rf 61. 69: in capite gig vg c ov et habebat (habens Pr: portabat Cyp) Pr Cyp arm a ovopa (+icya Pr) ycypaixeiov A 025. i. 35. 104. 175. 241. 242. 617. 632. 1934. 2016.

2019. 2036. 2037. 2038 al Tyc (Pr) Cyp gig vg s 1 arm bo sa: ovoxara (+ iroxXa arm 2) yrypatxLtoa 42. 325. 336. 468. 517. 620. 1918 arm 4: ovofuau ycypaAtcya (920) KOI ovoia (ra ovofutra yrypaiicva arm 8) 046. 18 (- 35. 175.

13. xal ircpi cj3Xi?Acvo? iidvwv r ft ftafjLjuvov cutarc, xal Kcvcxirrai TO 6Voyu avrov 0 Aoyos rov 0cov.

14. Jcai ra orrparcviata ra cv ixji ovpawp Koaovtfci avrf finrois Xcvfcoi?, cvScoviwoi rivwifov Xcvkov 1 Kaoapov.

15. ai eic rov crrouaros avrov cvnropcvcrai potato. ofcta, fva cv avrfl iraraffl ra 20r 7, ai avro? Trotiam avrov? IK pa? p VLrjpfr KOL avro? Trarci r v XTVOI rov otvov rov VAOV rijs 5py5s rov 0cov rov Travrokparooos; 325. 468. 617. 632. 1934). 250. 2067 al mu s 2 arm 8 1 ycyp. o ovo N o arm 8 avroor qui accipit gig:+fiovoo- 2026 bo eth.

13. irepipepxy)ji ior circumdatus est Tyc arm 8 8: vestitus erat vg: erat coopertus Pr frfafticvov A 046. 051. 18 (- 2040). i. 2037. 2038. 2067 (s 1) arm sa: ircpipcpafiiciov K: Trcpipcpavrur-icvov K cc: pfoavti(ri vof 025. 2019: cppakraricvov 172. 250. 2017. 2018. 2040. Similarly Tyc Pr gig Cyp vg s 2 arm 8 bo eth aiLum pr v 175. 218. 242. 250. 314. 617. 1934. 2016. 2017 K KX. ijrai AK C 025. 046. 18 (-35. 175. 617. 620. 1934) al 1 vg 1 T arm 2 8 a (sa): KC C I; (TO ovoia) N: xaxcirai i. 35. 175. 242. 250. 617. 620. 1934. 1957. 2016. 2019. 2023. 2036. 2037. 2038. 2067 al Tyc Pr gig vg i h s 1 arm 4: Koaovucvoo- (s 2) bo TO ov. avr. avr. TO ov. 69: bo.

14. itoi 1 Tyc Ta otpat. TO orpatCvta gig bo Ta 1 6l. 69. 2038 Ta 2 025. 051. 18 (-325. 468. 617. 620. 920. 2020). 241. 242. 250. 429. 1957. 2023. 202 4 1 Tyc Pr vg s 2 sa: avrov 2017: Atf 046. i. 61. 69. 94. 104. 172. 181. 314. 325. 336. 468. 498. 517. 617. 620. 920. 2016. 2018. 2020. 2036. 2037. 2 038 gig sl (arm) bo eth cv r. ovp, TOV ovpavov (rwv ovpavtav 468 s 1) 468. 920 s 1 (arm) eth: TW 204o: bo: tr after avrw gig ipcoaov0ci rjkoxovtiow 051. i. 2020. 2037. 2038. 2039 I 0 ttTTTOto- (ev ttTTTOto- 620) XcvlcOUT AK 025. I. 1 04. 62O. 2OIQ. 2020.

2037. 2040. 2067 al p: cirt ttnrotcr XCVKOUT 046. 18 (-35. 620. 2020. 2040). 250 al pl: i7nroi7roxAoio5i. 35. 181. 2036. 2038 cvscsvicvoi cvscsviwour K: vs Svieva 632: cvscsvxciw 920: pr feat S 1 ftwa-Lvov XCVKOV (Aaiirpov 94. 2037 bo) K 025. 046. 18 (-2040). (i). (94). 250. (2037). 2038 alp 1 Pr Tyc (gig) (s 1) arm 4 (bo) (sa): XCVKOV ftwrnvov (Xcvkojsvotrivov 2040) A 2040: + KOI K i. 456. gig s 1 sa: Xcvfcoy arm 2- 8 XCVK. Kab 104 s 2: ao. Kat XCVK. arm: CDTOO-XCVKOV (corrupt) eth Kaqapov purpureum gig: bo.

15. aurooj avttav s 1 arm 2 bo cxiropcverat exiebat Pr arm I u ciu AM 025. i. 35. 2019. 2020. 2036. 2037. 2038 al gig vg s

BACIAEYC BACIAEHN KAI KYPIOC KYPinim.

17. Kal fffiov eva ayyexov COTUTOL fr T J rj i(p, KOI cpa cv vjj icyaxj; Xcywv TTCWTI TOIS opvcois TOIS ircroficvois ev i o ov-panjutan Acvrc crwav0iyr ci? TO Sctirvov TO fteya TOV 0cov, 18. tva ayiyrc o'apxas frurtacwv KCU o-apjcas xiaiapxwv a orapjcas urxvpwv jcal o-apicas nrirctfv al TOV Ka(h p. Viv cir avruiv, fcal o apjcas iravrcuv (a) Text adds: 6rl r6 Iid eu. See vol. ii. 137.

arm bo sa eth: pr owoioo- 046. 18 (- 35. 2020). 250. 206 alp 1 Tyc Pr s 2 ev avny cv avrw 2020 s 1: ex eo Pr irata ij irata ci K 104. 385. 620: irataoo-iv s 1: iraparafri 325. 517 Ta c0viy pr irokra 498. 2020 gig sa icai 8 Tyc irat vary Pr

T. 01V. T. OvfjL. S 1 T. VXOV (+ JCOl I. 2OI9- 2036. 2O37- 2038.

2067 al p arm 8) placed after oivov A 025. 046. 18 (- 2040) al pl Tyc vg s 2 arm eth: tr after opyipr K sa: tr before TOV OIPOV 2040: Pr gig bo rrjcr opyi r pr Kai 2040: s 2 arm 4-: + avrov 620 tfcovj + magni Pr.

16. KOi 1 avroo- Tyc exei A: + ri (Tyc) TO tpjanov (ra iAatia atrrov S 1: TO tcranrov 2040: +avrov 920 bo sa eth) icai (s) K 025. 046. 18 al onm Tyc Pr gig vg s l 2 arm (bo sa eth) ciri K bo sa TOV f"pov TOVO- fji7jpovcr s 1 arm 4 I avrov 920 OKOia ycypait.-arm 4 ovo ia pr TO i. 2037: gig vg.

17. CKO A 025. i. 35. 104. 241. 632. 1957. 2020. 2023. 2038. 2040. 2041. 2067 al Pr gig vg eth: oaXov fet 2019 s 1 arm 4 bo sa: + oaAov 172. 250. 2018: 046. 18 (-35. 632. 2020. 2040). 2037 al pl Tyc s 2 arm 2 expose? A 025. 18 (- 18. 2040) al pl Tyc Pr gig vg s arm: CKpa cv 046. 18. 181. 2040: icpa iy bo wny A 025. 35. 175. 250. 468. 617. 620. 632. 1934.

2020. 2037. 2038. 2040. 2067 al 1 Pr gig vg: pr o K 046. 18. 61. 82. 104. 325. 336. 337. 386. 456. 468. 632. 920. 1849. 2004 al Tyc arm 4- 1 bo sa Acycw 35. 617 irouri TOUT opv. J vavra ra opvea arm 2 bo Trocrt 2040 S 1 T. ITCT. cv ftco. caell Pr ITCTOA. AM 046. 18 (-456) al pl: TTCTWI. 025. 456 al (rwax(h)T 051. i. 2037. 2038 Pr TO (TOV 91. no. 385. 452.

2021. 2041) owvov TO fjifya (tr after 0cov 920) AK 025. 046. 35. (91. no). 325. 337. (452). 456. 632. (920). 1849. 2004. (2021). 2040. (2041). 2067 al: TOV fctirv. TOV ftcyav 18. 172. 175. 201. 242. 250. 314. 336. 386. 468. 617. 620. 1918. 1934. 2016. 2017. 2Ol8. 2O2O I TO ficya TOV 0. TOV ftryaxov 0eov 051. I. 2019. 2023. 2036. 2037. 2038 arm 2-a eth TO i ya gig.

18. icat aapk. x 1 2023 arm o-apicao 4 Tyc K. r. Kab. travrwv 6i7 avrtov 025. 046. 17 (-617). 250. 2037. 2038. 2067 al pl: avroto K: avrovo- A 61. 69 o-apkao6 pr raor 18. 632. 1849 iravroiv airavrwvo46: +TWV 1934: i. 2067 s 1 bo I TCI. 314. 2067 icai 7 AK 025. 17 (-632. 1849. 2020) al p re cot Sovxw mu fuKpw jcai ftcyoxtdK.

19. cat etsov TO rove Jatrtxfts rij yijs at ra arparcviara avrwv crvnry-leva ironprai rov voxciov icra rov KO ICVOV cirt rov ttnrov ai ucra rov orparcvAaro? avrov. 20. xal mao-tfty TO Oijptov, teal 6 cvsoirp

ACT avrov 1 6 cvsoirpo qn 6 mnipras ra rqpcui CVUTTIOV avror, 6 per fr ofe lirxan ow rods Xafowas TO xapayta rov Iqptov KCU Tois 5 Trpoo-Kwovrras ITI ctcoval avrov aivres cj9Xi auv ot Suo cfe r v T j e 6w Atikiv rov irvpoc 1 9 Katoicviys 0cup. 21. fcal ot Xocirol dircfcrdi-Ajaav ev r poi a i rov KO ICFOV M rov tinrov, rjj i Qo xrq IK rov ordiatos avrov, ai raira ra Spvca l opracrbifrav IK rwv o'apicttk avrwv.

Tyc Pr gigvg s bo: 046. 61. 69. 241. 429. 522. 632. 1849. 2020 UKOOIV AK025. i. 172. 175. 242. 250. 617. 1934. 2018. 2019. 2036. 2037. 2038. 2040. 2067 al mn: + 046. 17 (-175. 617. 1934. 2040) al mo icyoaidv pr iw K 2040.

19. npior + KCLI ra orparcviara avrov s 1 K. r. frur. tr after yi r 920 I yi r oucov cno- 620 K. ra orrpar. Kara ra rpar. (sic) avrwf M 025. 046. 17 (-456?. 620?. 920?. 2040?). 250. 2037. 2038. 2067 al pl Tyc Pr gig vg s arm 1- bo: avrow A 314. 2016 arm 8 sa o-wryyuva tr after n-oaciov 2040 rov AK 046. 1 7(35- X 75- 386. 617. 2020. 2040) al 1: 025. i. 35. 175. 250. 314. 386. 617. 2020. 2037. 2038. 2067 al p Mnrovj + (rov) ACVKOV Pr arm bo sa eth icra 2 bo sa eth rov orpor. row orparcvfuiruv s arm.

80. xai Pr icr avrov (icra rovrov I. 2023. 2037. 2038) o K (i). 35. 69. 432. 1957. 2020. 2023. 2036. (2037. 2038). 2041. 2067 (Pr) vg s 1 arm 1 4: ot (o 025 arm 2) fwr avrov (+ mu bo) o A (025). 2021 (arm bo): ot ACT avrov ot (424) 424 arm 1: o wr avrov 046. 17 (-35. 2020). 250 al pl gig s 2 cvs. cvsoirpo TOi 424 arm 1 cv oco- orxav. r. CIK. avr. quibus signis seducti erant adorare imaginem bestiae et qui acceperant caragma illius Pr XajsovrcurjirxavqXTacr 177. 180. 337 TO xapayxa ra xapaypara 456 TOW trpocricw. ot irpcxricwowrco- gig: rwv irpoo-KWOWTUV s 1 TTJV cucoya K 920. 1918 2020: rrj cticovi AK C 025. 17 (- 920. 2020). 250. 2037. 2038. 2067 al 1: TO x Wf" 046 fwitfo-J irai Karifirpov KOI s 1: pr KOI s 2: rov Wrar arm 1 4: ohrao- bo: Pr e Xi o-av ft rjbr rovrat i. 2019. 2020. 2038. 2067: fjbaxov arm bo sa ot Svo tr after Btiw 920: avrovo-arm L. a. TOixr Svo bo sa eth: 45 gig arm 4 r. mp. r. icatoA. rqv leaiofi. irvpt cat bo rrp jcaioftcnpr AK 025 Pr vg: rrjv fcacoACi F 046. 17 al 01 " 11 gig bo cv tfciw ev r 0cuu i. 172. 175. 617. 2018. 2019. 2023. 2036. 2037. 2038 al: et in sulphur gig: trat 0 iov s 1: igne et sulphore Pr (cf bo). 81. pouaaia + avrov 2040 I nnrov + (rov) XCVKOV Pr eth I oc 1!

airo 920 opvcaj cptrera 617 j.

RESTORED ORDER OF THE TEXT. CHAPTERS XX. 1-3, XXI. 9-XXII. 2, XXII. 14. 15. 17.

XX. I. Kai ttov ayycxov jcarafatvovra IK rov oupavov, fyovra Tf v icxeiv riys Ajsuwov avrov.

jou hpatrjo-w rov opafcovro, 6 oi? o os cortv 8iij8oxos KCU 6 Saravas, ical lo o-cy avrov Xta? n, 3. fcai 2j3axcv avrw efc rip aWow, icat cxcurcv KCU fofodyurw ravu avrov, tva i irxav cn; rt ra ravra Sc! Xv vai aurov uicpov XP VOV s. 1. ayycxok pr axXoy c 2017. 2050 Tyc s 1 arm 1 + OX OV 336. 620. I918 6K T. OVp. K I K tv KX sa eth: 620). i. 104. 620. 2037. 2067 al oxvow ficy. J oxvcrcow ftry. iry. Pr rt T. x pa A 046.

18 (- 2020). 250. 2037. 2038. 2067 al pl: cv rq X H K 2020 Tyc Pr gig vg s arm bo sa eth.

2. o o M7 o opxaiotr A (s?): rov o iv rov ap aiov K 046. 18 al omn: serpentem (pr ilium Pr: anguem Tyc) antiquum Tyc Pr gig vg: rov opxuov 2036 oo- A 046. 18 al omn: o K 2050 eoriv cognominatus est Pr 8ia? oxoo- A 046.18 (- 2020. 2050). 250. 2037. 2038. 2067 arm: pr o N 69. 498. 2020. 2036. 2050 arm 11 bo sa K. o crar. 2050 ai 2 bo sa eth o 8 A 046. 35. 175- 250. 325. 337. 456. 617, 1934. 2020 al mu: o5i. i. 18. 386. 620. 632. 920. 1849. 2004. 2037. 2038. 2040. 2067 al (o) o-aravoo- AK I. 175. 617. 632. 2016. 2036. 2037. 2038. 2040. (2050) Tyc Pr gig vg s 1 arm bo: + o irxavwv n v oncovicn o rjv (6i. 385) 046. 051. 18 (-175. 617. 632. 2040. 2050). 250. 2067 al 1 1 s 2 i. en; K. efax. avrov K- 8. Kai. apuatrok arm 4 eth ocxcto-cv tfyrtv (+avrov i) I. 181. 2036. 2037. 2038: cs otv KU K L(r v arm: +ro orow, avnp bo sa co oayicrcv 4- ff payii eth erava) avrov ifuvaxr avrov A Trxwijtrt) (-tret K) AK I. 2036. 2037. 2038. 2040 al: irxova (-17 2050) 046. 18 (- 2040). 250. 2067 al pl m tr after vif s 1: i. 69. 141 Tyc bo eth ra 1 35: pr Travra s 1 a pi. en; S 1 a pi a pio av 2050 rcxco- J rcxco- ttxri 141. 241. 386. 2067 ra 2 051. T. 181. 2036. 2067 iera AK 046.

xxi. 9. Kal X0cv cts c TWV CTrra iyyexuv TWV fyorrwv ras rra taxas, f TWK yciovrwv t TWV cirra iraiyaw TWV lazaret)?, cat caax crcv ACT CAOV

Xcyaiv Acvpo, 8ci a crot riv VUK TV r v ywauca rot) dpviov. IO. cat atnyvrvc AC cy irvcvLum CTTI opos ftcya cat vt Xov, KOI 2Sci cv tot Tiv Troxtv T V dytav Icpovcraxi t jcara-fiatvowrav IK TOV ovpavov airo TOV 0cov, 11. otxrav r v av TOV 0cov 6 axrrqp avrij OLUHOS Xtiftp rifiudrar, 019 18 (- 35- X 7S- 6l 7- 1934- 205) almu T Y C Pr gig vgw s 1: pr KOI i. 35- 175- 617. 1934- 2050 al vg r arm bo eth: +8c 385. 429 s 2 Set Xv0. avr. Xvtfio-ctot s 2: Xvo-ci (cxvo-av arm 2) OVT. arm 1- 2 Xv0. OVT. A 046. 18 (-35. 175. 617. 2020) al mu: K i. 35. 175.

250. 617. 1957. 2016. 2020. 2023. 2036. 2037. 2038 2041. 2067
Pr gg v g Xvorjvai Xwat Tyc s 1 ujcpop xpov. 2050: pr CTI bo sa.

xxi. 9. cur o irpoiroo 172. 2018. 2020 c i. 172. 205. 2018. 2020. 2036. 2037. 2038. 2067 rro 2 gig vg TWV ycAOVTQv AK 025. 181. 2036. 2038. 2050: rtav yczovo-wv K p: rao-ycftovcrao- I. 104. 2037 (s): ycxovo-ao- 046. 18 (-2050). 6l. no. 385. 1957. 2016. 2023. 2037. 2067 al mu: plenas Pr gig vg: c ovcrao- 2018 Twv 4 AK 025. I. 35. 104. 172. 205. 632. 2018. 2023. 2037. 2050. 2067 al s arm 4 bo: 046. 18 (- 35. 205. 632. 2050). 250. 2038 al mu at 2 bo sa Scvpo + oi vg arm 2-4: + iva bo sa TIV ywatka (pr at arm 1-: + ou 42. 2017) placed after wi iv AK 025. 35. 172. 218. 250. 2018. 2020 Tyc Pr gig vg s (arm 1- a) bo sa eth: tr after apvtov 051. i. 205. 2036. 2037. 2038. 2067 al: tr before T V vtyi. 046. 18 (35. 205. 2020). (42). 104. no. 385. 2016. (2017). 2023 al pl arm 4.

10. amjkcyke rjveymv 2050: duxit Pr: tulit gig: sustulit vg ev Trvevft. Pr CTTC AM 172. 2018. 2050: CTT 025. 046. 18 al pl opotr opovo- 2020 KOI 205 bo cat 8 arm 2 bo sa AOI ic 149. 325. 620. 1934 iroxii AK 025. 046. 18 (-35. 175. 205. 617) al pt Tyc Pr gig vgs arm 1- 2 4 bo eth: + rrfv pcya ijv 051. i. 35. 175. 205. 250. 617. 1957. 2016. 2023. 2036. 2037. 2038. 2041. 2067 alarm ryv 2 KOI 051. i. 35. 175. 205. 250. 617. 2016. 2036. 2037. 2038 arm a cic T. ovp. A 025. 046. 18 (- 18. 175. 617. 2004) Tyc Pr gig vg s arm bo eth: OTTO T. ovp. 18. 175. 2x8. 250. 617. 2004. 2016. 2017. 2018. 2039 OTTO T. 6. AK 025. i. 35. 104. 205. 241. 632. 1957. 2020. 2023. 2036. 2037. 2038. 2050. 2067 al Tyc Pr gig vg s 1 arm bo eth: c T. 0. 046. 18 (-35. 205. 386. 632. 2020. 2050). 250 al 1: 6i. 201. 386.

11. CXOUCTOK. 6cou A 522: rrjv ft)Ti ovo-av avrqv 2050: TJ ccrriv oyio 17 yci 80 770- bo T. Sofav + airo K gig: lumen claritatis Pr T. dcov-f-icoi i. 104. 205 Pr s 1 arm 1- (bo): +cv rj vj ywrj TOV apvtov 17 ava Icpoiwax i wo 6cov Koa-fjajorjar rcu KOI So dcr0i7crctai 743. 1075. 2067: arm 4 o f xrn)p OVT. oxr 12. fx ovo " a tl os M y 1 irvxcovac Scoscjca, ical TTI rots irvxuxrtv dyycxovs Swscka, icai ovdxara foiyeypaAACva, COTIV ra ovotara TWF owcica 0vxuv vuiv Ioyxu; X 13. diro dvaroxTTS irvxww rpctc, xal dwo floppa irvxawes rpcif, cal no- avyvfcr s 8: cv avny (170- ro arm 4: + I? P arm 1) arm oiouxr + ccmv Pr: bo arm 1 Xi6 riui. Xiflov (-aw arm 1) rtuov (-cov arm 1) arm 1 bo: Xt0our rifuour arm 8: arm 4 rtuirarci rifuco gig vg s 1 DCT Xi6 tr after tocnrist arm 4: o5i. i. 35. 94. 104. 181. 205. 241. 632. 2020. 2038. 2050. 2067 arm 2: oxr oxr bo icpvoroxXiiovrt AK 18 (-18. 337. 617.

632. I934 2O20. 2O5O): KpvTTabj. ovTl O2. 046. I. 1 8. HO. 172. 337. 385. 498. 522. 617. 632. 1934. 2018. 2020. 2036. 2037.

2038. 2050: sicut crystallum (cristallo gig) gig vg: refulgent! in modum cristalli Pr: "crystal-seeming (-gleaming arm 1: arm 4) and (arm 4) luminous (living arm 2-) " arm.

Id. cxouaa 1 OVTI K: txpwrav 172. 2018 Tyc: +rc I. 2037. 2067: et habebat (-et Pr) Pr vg wlrj ov latum Pr x owra cgovo-av 104. 172. 2018. 2050 al Tyc: e oirowr K: pr cai 2036. 2037: KCU 2067 bo: o c ct Pr: at ct c arm 1- eth Soscxa 1 if? 046. 35. 205. 337 ic. ri T. irux. ayy. 8co8c caa 2050 Vg f arm 4 ri TOW truxomTiv 025. 046. 18 al fepe omn: cwi TOIKT Trvxcovcur K 94: in portas (4- habens gig) Pr gig ayy. angulous Pr vg- c- T: pr TOW bo 8a)S Ko s 175. 617. 1934. 2020 i Seicasvo 18 (-35. 175.

205. 617. 1934. 2020). 104. HO. 172. 201. 498. 522. 20l8. 2023.

2024: iff K 046. 35. 2O I ovoiara 1-I- avrw K S 1 ciriycypaiyutcva ycypafiACva gig Vg c 4 T S 1: eyyeypaiicva (evy- 2050) 94. 2050. cf. inscripta vg- fa eariv. IcrpaiX arm a a eoriv Pr arm 3 ra ovoiara A s: tr after IcrpaiX 2050: ovoiara (o oxa bo) 046. 18 (-35- 205- 2 5) almu gg V 8 arm bo: N 025. i. 35. 205. 241. 432. 1918. 1957. 2023. 2036. 2037. 2038. 2041. 2067 Pr arm 2 Swscka 8 ifi K 046. 35. 205 viwv AK 046. 18 (- 35. 205. 386. 920. 2050). 250. 2038 al mu: pr TWV 025. 051. i. 35. 104. 1957. 2023. 2041. 2050 al arm 4: i8i. 201. 241. 386. 517. 920. 2017. 2036. 2037. 2067 s 1 arm 1 2- loyxnjx pr TOV 201. 205. 386. 2017. 4036. 2067.

18. omtoxtja A 025. i. 205. 2017. 2020. 2037. 2038. 2050. 2067 S: avaro wv 046. 18 (- 205. 2O2O. 2050). 250 al icai 1 2- s 051. i. 205 arm 1 4- Tyc Pr ai 2 8 2037. 2038. 2067 ftoppa (-pacr 2050: ftopa 920). vorov. SVCTACDV K c 025. 046. 18 (-386). 250. (2037). 2038. (2067) al tore onm Tyc Pr gig vg s arm 4: fioppa. ftoppa. vorov K: ftoppa. SVO-ACIIV. vorov (iecnyftjspmwr i) A I: SIMTLUDF. poppa. vorov 386. 1957 arm 1 1: vorov. floppa. Svoyuiv 522: vorov. owMOP. poppa (bo): + ot airo fjL rrjfjippuw irvxo-veer rpcwr 2037. 2067 rpfiol 8 8 y 046. 35. 337.

diro Fdvov irvawkcs rpcis, Kal dvo 6Wiay irvaajycs Tpcis. 14 u ri TCI OS rfjs wdacais 2;(av Octexibus idcKo, Kal cv auraiy Sasoca Mfuau rwv a CKa airooroaw TOV fyviav. 15. Kal 6 Xaxwv ACT fywv cfycv ifvpov Kaxaioy xpixrovv, tva Acrpiprj; rrp iroxtv tcai TOVS irvauvas avns Kal TO Tcfyos avrjf. 1 6. KOI 17 Troxis TCTpayawos Kcirai, KOL TO II KOS avr oow Kal TO iradvos. Kal iroxiv TO) Koaatu cvl r otOtous 1 Swscka ixtaswv TO al TO v ros avr s ura COTIK. 17. Kal muri Pr arm 1 CXDV A 025. 046. i. 104. 498. 522. 1849. 2017. 2038: t ov M c 051. 18 (1849. 2020. 2050). 250. 2037. 2067 al pl: habens gig vg: ci c 2020 arm 8: habent Pr: K 2050 arm 1- 2 4 ctcx 8o Sckaj 149. 1948 bo eth: THI C-Xtow Tpcur 2050 Swseka 1 i K 046. 35. 205. 337 K. eir. avr i. 104 cir avrcdv in ipso gig: pr ycypaiicva (-ov bo) bo eth i)8 Ka ovofi. apviov 2O o o o8eca 2 t)? (pr TWV 35) 046. 35. 205. 337: Sekasvo 93. 94: i. 104 Pr bo ovoftara ovofm bo DOW 8 tS K 046. 35. 325. 337: Tyc s 1 arm 1 1 TOV apviov pr KOI Tyc Pr: TOV viov s 1.

15. xai 1 2050 arm 4 ficrpov oaaAOv AK 025. 046. 18 (- 2050). 250. 2067 al pl Tyc gig s 2 arm 4: harundinem (aUream) ad mensurarn Pr: icrpov Kaxapov M c 517. 2016. 2O5ocfmen-suram harundineam vg: terpov Koaa ov s 1: tctpov i. 2036. 2037. 2038 arm 2- bo etb: Koaaiov arm! icrpitGny uttprjw 046. 104. (2050). 2067 K. T. TTV. avna s 1 arm 2 K. TO Tft oir (rarctxn Pr ar" 1 bo eth) avnycr (vg) AN 025. 175. 205. 617. 632. 1934. 2020. 2050 Pr gig vg s arm bo eth: O46. 051. 18. 35- 3 2 5- 337- 3 6. 456. 620. 920. 1849. 2004 al 1 1.

16. aimjff tr before Tcrpaywocr K: arm 1 Kot 8 A 2050 Pr vg s 2 arm 2- 4- bo eth: K 025. 046. 18 (-2050). 250. 2037. 2067 al 1 1 gig s 1 arm 1 irxatoor + avnpr s 1

arm TCD Koxaiu AK 046. 18 (-35. 175. 205. 617): pr tv 025. i. 35 175. 181. 205. 250. 617. 2016. 2017. 2036. 2037. 2038. 2067: harundine (pr de vg) Pr gig vg sa: bo arm art per gig vg: ab Pr oraouo- (-ov K) A (c) 046. 18 (- 205). 250 al pl: oraow K 025. i. 205. 2018. 2036. 2037. 2038. 2067 0Scka AM 025. 2050: iff 046. i. 35. 205. 632. 2018. 2038: Sekosvo 18 (- 35. 205. 632. 2050). no. 201. 385. 498. 522. 2016 al mn xuw AK 025. 35. 632. 2020. 2050 Pr gig vg s 1 bo: pr KOI 046: +icka (046. 35). 046. 18 (-35. 632. 2020. 2050). 250 al mu (s 2): arm 1 TO fiipcoo 1 pipcovcr bo sa: pr KOI 2020 s 2: + avnpr s 1 arm I iraatocr–avnyr 2050 s 1 arm 2 4- bo saeth K. T. woo- arm 2 avnto ao5. 2050 Pr gig arm.

17. C)ACTPT OIK (-rpicrcy 620. 2050) AK 025. 35. 620. 2037.

2038. 2050. 2067 al p Pr vg 0- 4 T s arm: cucrp gig vg- f bo: 046. 18 (-35. 620. 2050). 250 al mu I T ixpr xo M: muros avrrjs (KOLTOV rccnrcpaftoira rcr(rapw m ow, perpov ay6ptnrov t o 1 8 KOI Jl Cv8dA7(ris TOV TCC OVS dvTljs MOTTO, tat 17 TToais xpucriw Kadapov OJJUMJW vaxy Kaoapy 19. 01 0cj, exiot rov Tcfyow rijs woacws tram Xtvai repp 6 0eficaio9 6 irpwros Zooms, 6 Scvrcpos owr cipoc, 6 Tfm

Ygc. d. r KatOK rcotrcpax. T (T(r. 8 cat cfcaroy Tfotrcpacovra A: Kaiw ftf K: ppx 046. I. 18. 35. 104. 325. 337. 456. 632. 920. 2004. 2020: nonaginto octo gig rco-o-cxuc. Tco-o-apaxovra 025. 175. 205. 386. 617. 620. 1934: (TtpakOvra (crapakovra 2050) 1849. 2050 Teo-crapwy rccrraDtr x ta o" 2050 TTI XWV mxttw K: rrasiay arm a: Pr bo ftcrpov LLCTKU s 1: fitrpa (placed before injxuv S 8) S 9 bo I a pootTOv ovpavov 2050.

18. K. i) K8w ju TOU T ix- in structura murus gig i; 1 AK C 025 Tyc s arm L 2-: i v K: yv y 046. 18. 250. 2037. 2038. 2067 al pl Pr vg bo cvsoii? crtcr AN C 498. 2020: cv SOJACUTI N cf gig: cvscuo-io- 2050: evsoAio-icr 025. 046. 051. 18 (-2020. 2050) al pl aunor 175. 2050 Tyc arm 4 1 laotrio- ex lapide iaspidi Pr vg (arm 2 4): pr wo- bo: Tyc pw. ca0. xpwto) Ka apw 2014. 2034. 2036. 2042 vg: xpwnov (p r CK Pr) ica apou Pr s arm 1 4 ofioiov ofmia 051. i. 35. 205. 2036. 2038 Pr: pr KGLI gig voxo) Att 025. 046. 18. 175. 337. 456. 617. 920. 1934: vcxco (vcaAo) 385. 498) 35. 205. 325. 386. 620. 632. 1849. 2004. 2020. 2050 al pl Kaoapw 025 rj who- xpwiov. a0aoo) civitas aurum mundum (purum gig) simile (+ et gig) vitro mundo (puro gig) Tyc gig: ipsa vero civitas ex (vg) auro mundo similis vitreo (simile vitro vg) mundo Pr vg: i iro r (+ oaiy arm 4) XDWIOV Kabapov oiotov (or ofwia) vaaoi Kaoapw s arm 1 2 4-: "the city was wrought of gold pure like glass pure " bo: otoia 17 voxur wr rjar i Trotrcrtcr ecrrt cv xpvcrito Kaoapu) eth.

19. 01 06jic ioi A c 025. 046. 18 (- 35). 250 al mu Tyc vg sa: pr KOI K i. 35. 104. 2018. 2023. 2036. 2037. 2038. 2067 s arm bo eth: pr ubi gig: + autem Pr n? cr iroxcwo- + OAOIW 2050: Pr vavti t0. ni omnia ex (ex omm Pr) lapide pretioso Tyc Pr: ioour TIUOKT s 1: iravrcov XI CDV rifuuw arm rtuw Kektxri?- fjLfvOi 205 K KOTfjir)fj. CVOl-ACKO) 1849. 2O0 4 I. 2050 Tyc

Pr gig arm o 0c. lacnno- arm 4 o cuxuxr pr KOI s 1 arm 2 eth: +TOV re ow arm 1- 2: gig TTXUTOO- ctcr K o 8 pr KOI M Tyc s 1 arm 8 eth oratr ctpocr rax.7r i)oa 2017:-17900- 051. 2020. 2050:-ipoo- 025. 046. 2004 Pr vg gig bo: saffyrus Tyc o 4 pr KU K s 1 arm 2 eth. (Also before o 6 and ver. 20 o 1 9 K arm 2 eth add KOI: s 1 except ver. 20 o 8- 9) TMTOO- (also X.

20. 6 Tcvapros criapaysos, 6 Wiwros crap8ovu, 6 CKTOS rap8iov, 6 fftofjlO? Xpiwroaitfos, 6 oysoo? JipuaAos, 6 cwros roira toy, 6 Socaros;(pwwrpao os, 6 cvscvcaros a av0o? j 6 Sa8ckaros a bic v wonros 21.   icai ot SajScxa irvawvcs Saiscica xapyapirai,

Ava els CKOOTOS TQJV irvawvcav j v cc cvos fuapyapirov

KOI rj iraarcid TT S irdacws pva-Lov Kabapov fc vaaos Scavyis.

22. icac vaov owe cz8ov cv avrjj, 6 vap icvptos, 6 cos 6 iravrojcparup, 6 vaos avr s icai TO dpviov (a) Lacuna restored by means of xi. 19. See vol. li. 170 sq.

2020) 046 min mu vg c: tapx- 2018. 2050 vg f 8 v s l bo: Koaiow s 2: sardonius (-icus vg 1) Tyc vg d.

20. orpapapsoo l acr ap- 2050 o-apsovvf o apowv 149. 1934 al p: o-oaoovuf 2024: crap8iow (-w 2050) A 2050 o-apstov trapsiotr i. 35. 104. 205. 2020. 2037. 2038. 2067 al p Pr vg v: sardinus (-onium Tyc:-inon bo) Tyc vg v bo: o-aptsov (o-ap ov s 1) s fypuaAoor K min pl vg s: fypiaAoo- A 385 (Tyc) Pr gig: fypva-Aioo- (-iov 025: JipuaA- 046: fypiaA-1) 025. 046. 051. i 61. 104. 175. 617. 2016. 2036. 2037. 2038: fypvaAiyo- 2050: fivprj Xocr (? vptaA- 2023 bo) 149. 2023 bo cvaroo- A 046 mm pl: CWOTOO-025. 051. 35. 205. 241. 242. 385. 522. 632. 2016. 2023. 2037. 2038. 2050. 2067 al mn: ff K TOTraftov TOTraow K (s 2): TOTTOV- iov (ron-avow s 1) 025 s 1: irafiov 456: topaxmos Pr dopation bo xpwoirpao oo"-ov A:-iocr K c:-o-o-oo- 104 Pr vg g:-woo- 42. 325. 517. 620. 1918 Tyc:-TTOO-OCT (-irao-a-oo- 498: TTOOTOCT 61. 141. 2024). 61. 82. 141. 337. 385. 429 456. 498. 522. 1849. 2024: chrysoliprassus vg fv vakivoor wtkivbivov Tyc (bo): iacinctus gig aAC0vcrroo- A 025. 046. no. 175. 325. 456. 617. 620. 2004. 2038 al mu:-ivoo- N: aic0woo- K c 051. 18 (- 175. 325. 456. 617. 2004). i. 104 al pl: aii co-oo- s 1.

21. 01 Swscica wuxw ctr duodecim portas Pr: ideo Tyc D fiopy. Pr Scuscica 2 N 2030 bo fuipyapirai-f-cio-iv vg ava iva A 2018: pr cai 456: pr e r s l cwr + KO. L 025 Tyc vg s 1: 205 TCDVirva. fjULpyaptrov bo T. irva. rjv 5Pr Trvacovwv irvaidv 498. 2020: +cov K cf pr OKT 025. 046. 61. 2036 iraar. T. iroa. plateas eius Pr xpva-. Ka0. ex auro limpido (puro s 1 arm 1 2-) Pr s 1 arm 1 2- oxr ai 051 Tyc vaaoo- (-ov 205) A 025. 046. 175. 205. 456. 617: vcaocr (vcaA- 385. 498. 2020) min pl 8iavyi r Siavycer 205 L 22. KOOF OUK cisov OVK ci8ov vaov bo sa eth cv avnf cv avro) 149: eth o yap ort o K: o yap o K c nvptocr o (K) 0coo AK 025. 046 min pl Tyc Pr gig vg s 2 arm 2 4 bo sa: 0coo- 337. 1934 eth: Kvptoo- 920 s 2 arm 1 o 4 A s 2: aurocr s 1: M 025. 046 23. KCLI ij iroxif ov xpciav fgci rov y iov ovsi TT S acvctfcriv avrjj, 17 vap 5d a rov 0cov tyururtv avriv, icai 6 Xvx? os avnj? TO apvtbv.

24 wcpiiratijo'owtv ra lovrj Sea rov

KOI ol frurixcic-nys yij cpovoriv riv 5o av avrwv cis avrijv, 25. Kal ol irvxwvcf avns ov fty fcxcigT0imriv icpas f vv yap

OVK corai foci f. (a) 26. Kal oftrowiv r v So av cal r v rifirjv rstv iqvuv cfc avriv, (a) Read ml wvtcrk. See vol. ii. 173.

min omn o vooo- ovr. COTIV tr after opvtov Pr rriv 104 TO 2050 apviov + "the only begotten son (2) of God (+ is 2) altar of holiness " arm 1 2 K. TO apviov joined with what follows 046 s 1 1.

28. iroxur +avrrj 498. 2020 cx civc arm bo ovsc ovrc 2050: KOI arm 1 2-" iva et Tyc aivaxrikJ aivovo ivo5i. 2050: faivrj Pr avny As 025. 046. 18 (35) al pl Pr gig s

eth: pr cv K c 051. 35. 1957. 2023. 2037. 2041 al p vg bo sa: avrrjv 2018. 2036. 2067 al p (arm 1-2-a) avif- 17 yap AM 025. 35. 175. 205. 617. 2020. 2050 al Pr gig vg s arm 1- bo eth: avriy yap y 046.18 (- 35. 175. 205. 617. 2020. 2050) al mu arm 4 0cou icvpiov Pr C WTMTCV OTI CI Pr eth: oirto- i. Tyc vg d T arm 4 ovnyo- O. VTOV KOI 2037: + coi 2036: +COTIV 2021 Tyc gig vg s 1: +rjv arm 1 2.

24. comrj + TCOV o-wfoxevwv i out T. WTOO cv TQ on 2050 Tyc vg T Kat ot 2050 f f poverty (afferent gig vg bo: con-fere nt Pr) AK 025. 35. 2020. 2050 Tyc Pr gig vg s arm 4 bo:-f OVTW (avn; 205) 046. 18 (- 35. 2020. 2030) al pl rip A 025. 3J. 632. 2020. 2050:046. 18 (-35. 632. 2020. 2050) al p 6o av AK 025. i. 35. 60. 94. 241. 632. 2020. 2036. 2037. 2038. 2050. 2067 Pr gig (vg) s 1 arm 4 bo sa: + KCLI (+ TIV 250) Tixiyv 046. 18 (-35. 632. 2020. 2050). 42. no. 201. 209. 242. 250. 385. 429. 498. 522. 2016. 2017. 2024. 2039 al mu avrwv AK 025. 35. 632. 2020. 2050 al mu Pr gig (vg s 2) arm 4 sa: TOV cOvwv (205) 046. 18 (-35. 632. 2020. 2050). 250 al pl (bo): + K at r v nfurfv (+ TWV C0VUV s 2) vg s 2 bo verses 25, 26 337.

26. 01 2O5 oiirvx. avr. l tr after icxcurtfomriv sa eth; p, epour rjfi pa K: + KOI wicroor arm vv(yap KU w arm l bo OVK OVJCCTI 205 arm 1 2- coroi cortv 617 Tyc arm 2 4: yv arm 1- cicci tr before OVK mv Tyc.

26. OUTOWTIK ponet Pr: i? ovo-tv bo 00 1 1 (ourovcrtv bo a) nyv 2 2050 Sofdv + avrwv bo eth Tinyv– avrcov bo eth rwv cowvjra 0vrj bo eth ceo- avrrjv (in ilia gig: in ea Pr AK 025. 35. 205. 632. 2050 Pr gig vg s arm 4 bo: +iva curcxlukriv 046. 18 (- 35. 205. 632 2050) al 1 J.

37. rat ov IT) curcxlty efc avrr)v f irav KWVOV f (a) KOC frocwr jsScxvyia xai cvsot, I pi? ol ycypaifickoi fr rf 0i0Xfy rip (urp rov dpvv.

ixil I. Kai i8c(cv MM iroraAov vfiaroc anjt Xafwrpov f ftpw raxXov, im- ropcvoAcvov i rov Opovov rov 0cov KOI rov dpvtov 2. fo MOW rijs irxarc las avr s,

KOI roV TTOTOlol) frratfcy KO. I IKlwtv vxov tys, r woiovvl jcaoirovs fiuscjca, rotfr

Kara i va CKOOTOV dirostsovv l rov fcapirov avrov icat ra vx a rov (vaov cis Ofpa-muiv rwv e voiv.

(a) Primitive corruption for rat Kotv6t. As the rest of the verse (cf. xxii. 15) shows, only persons are contemplated: cf. vol. li. 173 sq. arm 4 (definitely restore the text. s u 8 are susceptible of either text.

87. itai 1 vg bo curcadi? cttrcx wo-iv K: curc 0oi 2050: eoroi s 1 cur aim?? cir avn 2050: in ea Pr gig vg: cicct s 1 arm L way KOIVOV " anyone corrupt (of evil will arm 1-)" arm iroudV AK C 61. 94. 2021. 2032. 2050: rrotow 025. 046. 051. I. 35. 175, 250. 617. 1934. 2037. 2038. 2067: faciens Tyc Pr vg: o iroiwv K 18 (-35. 175. 617. 1934. 2050). 42. 82. 93. 104. no. 141. 201. 241 336 al pl s (arm 4): quod facit gig: ot TTOIOWTCCT bo jmeavyia pr OKTCI K KU cvfiocr vitae Pr 01 ycypafificfOi 01 cyycypauu 2016. 2050: ra ycyoafiicva s 1: quorum nomina illorum (sua arm 2) scnpta sunt arm 1-8 v fm bo TCD j3tj3X tf TT; ftifixw 2050 rtftr fon r Pr s 1 rov opviov rov avpavov K: rov fttft tov 2050: illius agni Pr.

Hdli. 1. irotojioi AK 025. 046. 17 (-35. 175. 205. 617. 1934. 2020) al mu Tyc Pr gig vg s arm 1 4 bo sa eth:-f- Kaj0apov 35. 104. 175. 205. 209. 218. 242.

250. 506. 617. 1934. 1957. 2016. 2017. 2020. 2023. 2036. 2037. 2038. 2041. 2067: pr Ka. Qa. pov i arm vsaroo- wqo vo op wv arm 4: wvra vsaroa- arm a: aquae vivae gig vg-c-f (onyo Tyc Xofurpov Xaiirpoo- 2050: Xafurpov gig: candidum Pr eth: pr Ka.0a. pov nai s 1: i4i. 2020. 2038 Tyc OKT wrtt 175. 617 (cpvoroxXov-oo-2050:-rra ov 632: + KOI s 1 rov 1 K 0povov oroAaroo- 61.

    8. CK jicaw CAICO-CU A 2050: pr ai 2050 gig s 1: per mediam (plateam) Pr npr Trxarcumr rwv iraatCiaiv s 1 arm 1-: n r iroxcoxr 1934 Kat 1 ri s 1: +nri s 2 rov iror. tr after uuiqcv Tyc Pr vg s 1 cmvfcvj eitfcv K cket. (vx, wiycr K: O CF c cjccttfcv A 046.17 (- 35. 205. 632. 2050). 250 al pl gig s 8 arm 1- bo sa: OTCV0CV05I. i. 35. 205. 632. 1957. 2018. 2023. 2036. 2037. 2038. 2050. 2067 s 1 Jvxov "trees" arm irotow K 046. 051.

    17 ajfewomn. rowy l Ka ft 35. 205. 337. 617: decies gig arm 1: + KU S 1 Kara w a (jjLrjvav A) CKaorov VOL. II. 24 14. Maxoptoi ol Trxwovrcs ras crroxas avrwv, tva Ibrai rj f ovtrta avrok rl TO vxov r s KCU TOIS Trvxakriv curcxlaicrti cts riyp iroxiy.

    15. e a ol mpcf icat ol icat ol iropvot ical ol ovcis ical ol cloxoxatpai, ical iras ixu)v ical TTOUOV i 1 7. ical TO nrcvfia ical ij VUA I; Xeyowiv ical 6 dicoiw ctiratQ) "Ep ou ical 6 St aiv 6 Icxcd? Xa?

    (-Sov 175) A 175. 250. 617. 2037. 2038. 2067 al s 1?: icata p, rjva CICOOTOV (cicaotOo- 2020) QTrosisovo- K 35. 2020. 2050 al: K. prjva (arm 1) eva cicaorov airostsow (-Stsorra i:-Stsow 051. 2038) 05 1. I. 205. 2038. 2067 (arm 1): K. JA. atrostsoro- CKaoroo 325. 337. 456. 620 al S 8?: K. fu airoistsovo- (-Stsow 386. 632) dcaorof 18. 386. 632. 1849. 1934. 2004 al: K. x. airo t8ovcr cicacrtQ) 046. (141. 1918): persmgulos menses et (Pr gig) reddens (reddentes Pr) Tyc Pr gig: per menses singulos reddens vg d v: per menses singulos (singula vg- f-) reddentia vg c-f- atroses. T. icaptr. avr. bo eth T. icaptrov TOW Kapwova- K s 1: TOV I. 18. 61. 141. 385. 429. 632. 1849. 2004 aimw avrtdv 2050 arm: 205 T. fvx. TWV fvxwi M arm: avrov s 1: + icatayycxXcrai 175. 218. 617. 2016. 2017 TWV K: "the eyes of the" bo.

    14. irxuforrco (-arrca 104. 2050) TOXT aroxcwr auruk (+ in sanguine agni vg 1) AK 104. 2020. 2050 (Pr) vg sa eth: inuowrco-TOO CKroxoo" avrov (ciov 2067) 046. 17 (2020. 2050). 250. 2037. 2038. 2067 al pl gig Gyp s armw4– bo: (qui) servant mandate haec Tyc iva s 1 arm 1 orat tr after avroiv 2 bo sa avrcdv 8 + OKT 8e 17 cfovo-ia N TOIO- irvx. TW irvxxovt s 1 bo: + ov fty 2050 urcx0axriv ctcrcxcvo-ovrat s 1 arm 4 bo cur rfjv a-oxtv-f rrjv ayiav Pr: TT; O- iroxcomr (+ TOW flcov arm 1) arm 1-.

    15. c. apfjiaxot tr after ctoxoxarpat s 1 c fw + c (icat s 1) s 1 bo sa: foris autem remanebunt Pr arm 1: " and there shall go forth " arm 4 eth icweo- KOIVOI s 1 01 fappakoi malefici Pr icoi 2 Tyc ot 6 175. 1934 8 Xoxatpai + venefici Pr: + "adulterers" arm 1 woo- AK 046. 17 (-175. 205. 617. 632. 1934. 2020. 2050) al mu: +o i. 104. 175. 205. 250. 429. 617. 632. 1934. 2016. 2017. 2020. 2032. 2036. 2037. 2038. 2050. 2067 al mu: Travreo- ot 94 arm bo eth txcov cat irouov A 046. 17 (- 175. 617. 1934). 2037. 2038. 2067 al pl Tyc Pr vg sw2: irouav cat (l-o 2018. 2032) ixwv K 91. 175. 218. 242. 250. 424. 617. 664. 1934. 2016. 2017. 2018 gig: TTotowrco-arm 4 bo: txowrco- arm: txowtccr Trotctv eth.

17. icai 1 Tyc TO N bo vvevia + aytov arm 1 eth iy

CHAPTER XX. 4-15.

4 Keu ci8oi ras rv ac TWV ircircxcfcc(r6n0y 8i r v rvpiav Iicrov ( ) d KCU 8ta rov Aoyov roo 0cov, e KCU OITIV ov irpoo-cicvnyo-ay TO Orjptor ov r v cifcova avrov, KCU owe Z a3ov TO xdpayfia Ivl

Kal ekok Ipovovs KOI iiaiourav iff avrovg, (a) I have restored 4 b to their original place after 4. See vol. it 182 sq.

g Xcyovo-iv cxcyov 051. 35 cpx 01 1 artn I Kcu. cpx v arml e h o 1 18 o OKOVCOV qui vidit gig: pr his Pr cp ov icoi Pr icai 4 arm 1 o 2 456 exer0c0 + et bibat Pr o Icao? pr icat 209. 218. 2050 s 2 arm sa: gig s 1 Aa? cto Xaj ctv Tyc s 8 arm: pr KOI s 2 Cuqcr pr rye-2030 1.

zz. 4 c h. xai cisok (2050) Cyp: KCU AN 046. 18 (- 2050) al omn Tyc Pr gig vg s arm: v pi bo eth T. ircirexekKrxevcoy-KI CVWF 175:-Krjp. wuv 201. 386: T. irciroxcii7Ac ov A: occisorum Pr gig Cyp: decollatorum vg: TOO- Trctrexfktcrxcvacr s 1 K. omvca ct Ttvccr ow K cf et si qui Pr gig: "they are those who" arm 1 2- 7rpot Kwrf(rav irpocrtkVvovv 386 TO (TO 920) Orjpiov AK 046. 18 (- 18. 35. 175. 337. 617. 620. 2040) al pl: T (TO 620) (hjpiw i. 18. 35. 175- 2 5- 337- 6l 7- 620. 1957. 2017. 2023. 2037. 2038. 2039. 2040. 2067 al ovsc ovrc 051. i. 35. 175. 250. 617. 2037.

2O38. 2O67 al pm TTfv LKOVa AM 046. 18 (- 62O. 2O4O. 2O5O). I. 250. 2037. 2038 al 1 1: rrf CIKOVI 104. 620. 1957. 2023. 2037. 2067 al cxojsov cxoj3c 1 8 xapayp + TW Qypwv 2040: +eius vg TO ICTWTTOV AK 046. 18 (-386. 620. 2050) Pr gig arm bo: TWV trrortrwi 104. 181. 201. 336. 386. 620. 1918. 2036. 2037. 2050. 2067 vg: +avrctfx i. 35. 1957. 2023. 2036. 2037. 2038 s 1 arm bo sa eth cm 2 2040 T. x t P a Tatr X cc P ar 3 V 8 s:! Sef IOF x pa a 1!

4 b. cicaoiaai sedentes Pr arm 1 K. Ka0uray (TOUT) Koouratrt bo nrl ciravw 1934 avrow avrour 2050 icai arm L 2 bo Kuia cso.- 386.

AHOKAAYWS TOANNOY XX. 4-6.

4 1. icat tfrrjo-av KOI tpcurt wrav ftrra rov xpurrov l ia inf. (a) 5 b. avrrj rj dvaarao'iff irptarrj.

6. Maicaptoc KOI aytos o Ivcov ficpos fr rjj Avaoraurct r0 vpwrff, tin. Tovnav 6 Stvrepos 0avaros OVK fy i ovriav t aaA. 1 (fowrai tepcts rov 0cov al rov Ypwrrov, fcal Jao-iaevvowiv ficr avrov ra tata CTT;.

(a) Text adds 5: ol Xotrol rwr veicpv OVK tfoav AXK rexerffp ra gfxia fr unobjectionable as far as diction is concerned but rejected as a gloss on the following grounds advanced by Mr. Marsh, (i) It is prosaic and made up of words borrowed from 4 3 or 7. (2) If it were original we should expect it to be introduced either by ical used adversatively or W as in 2i 8. The asyndetic construction in 19 is not parallel, for there the thought of the preceding sentences is simply developed further. (3) It spoils the metre. (4) 5 b follows more naturally a positive than a negative statement.

4 l. K. cltjaak K. tpaaix. over i V(rav (sic) 2050 K. irav K. Pr Kat 1 hi omnes Tyc: ot s 1: ovroi (+ ctariv ot arm 1-) arm 1- eth: bo sa e(fyo av clinpray 920:)o-ovrw arm 1- 4 eth: + ficr avrov bo cj8arixcvo av j8aertxcv(roikriv (-oixrtv arm 4) arm 1 4 eth rov i. 2017. 2038. 2067 r. xpwrov lesu Pr x 1! AK i. 35- 175- 181. 250. 424.

617. 1957. 2017. 2023. 2036. 2037. 2038. 2041. 2050. 2067 s 1 arm 2 4 bo: pr TO
046. 18 (-35- J 75- 6l 7- 20 S) all1 s 2: arm j.

5. 01 XOITTOI. x X. en) A 046. 35. 175. 250. (617). 632. 1934. 2020. 2037.
2038. 2040. 2050. 2067 al p Pr gig vg (arm) bo sa: Kl8(-35.175. 617.632. 2020.
2040. 2050). 61. 69.104. no. 385 al mu s oi Aowrot A Pr gig vg: pr KCU 046. i. 35.
175. 181. 250. 336. 617. 632. 1934. 20x6. 2020. 2023. 2037. 2038. 2040. 2050.
2067 arm 4 bo (sa) eth: KOI p ra ravra arm 1 TWV vcjcpctfv pr CK arm 1: avrutv Pr
vcicpcor A 35. 1934. 2020. 2040. 2050 al gig vg arm 4 bo sa eth: avqpunrw 046.
175. 250. 424. 617. 2017 efi rov av cm; o-av i. 250: iprcrai (-ovrat arm 4) arm
rexccrfty rexeo i cu 2020: rcaccr okri 2036. 2037 avny pr ore 104. 336. 620. 1918:
pr KOI s 1 eth: haec est itaque Tyc.

6. iakapioa pr KOI 18. 632. 1849. 2004. aycoor ic. o ayiocr 2050: 61. 69 v rq
ayaarao-cij+ravn; Pr: + avrov 920 art pr on 2050 arm 4: pr KOI s 1 arm 8 rovrcov
rovrov (-TW 69) 61. 69. 385. 2036 Tyc o ovvr. Bay. o Oav. o Scvr. i. 2023.
2036. 2037. 2038 axX aaXa K rov 0cov K. rov purrov pr icat K: TO) Oca K. TO
xptora) 2020 s 1: rov Irjrav xpurrov (0 ov K. rov itvp. w r. xp"""- arm 1) arm)8oria.
cvo-owiv K 046. 18 al om11 Tyc Pr gig vg s arm bo sa: fcwriatvowiv A ACT avrov
AK 046. 35- J 7S- 617. 632. 920. 2020. 2040. 2050 Tyc Pr gig vg s arm bo eth:
ftcro ravra 18 (-35. 175. 617. 632. 920. 2020. 2040. 2050). 82. no. 141. 201. 242.
336.498. 1918 r. x A. my ann 1 ra K 046. 61. 69. 94. 241. 386. (632). 920. 2020:
A 051. 18 (386. 632. 920. 2020). 250. 2037. 2038. 2067 al 1 arm-4-.

7. Koi orav rcxco-00 ra txca frry, Xvftprcrai 6 Saravfc c rfv icjp avrov, 8. KOI
c(cxcvvcrai irxaviprai ra Zovi; TO Iv rais ywvuus r f yi s, rov Faiy Kal Maydiy,
owayayctv avrovc cfe rov iroxciov, 6 api0iof avraw arc 7 apfu rijs tfaxduro s. 9. teat
av dtyow firl TO irxarof rijs yis, ACCU ikwcxcvo-av r v irapcu,-fto rjv rwv dytw al
riyv iroxiv r v fiyamjfjlCvrjv. al fcarcjft? irvp T di4 TOM IK rov oupavov rai Karc
aycv avrovc. io. feat 6 Sia oxos 6 Trxavuiv avrovs iftkyqrj cfc r v Xifunp rov irvpog
ical eiov, ovov KCU 7. otttk Tcxc90v (ore crcxco crav i: ore crexco- i; s 1) AK 35.
175. 250. 617. 2020. 2037. 2038. 2040. 2050. 2067 al Tyc Pr gig vg s arm 4 bo sa
eth: fura 046. 18 (- 35. 1 75. 617. 2020. 2040. 2050). 61. 69. 104. 385 al pl arm 1
2- avrov arm 12- bo eth.

8. cjexeuo-ftai bo irxan o-ai KOI frxanprei (+ TOW Sovxow KCK bo) vg arm 1
bo ra cftny A 046. 18 (- 386) Tyc Pr gig vg s 2 arm 8- 4 (bo) eth: pr mm 2036 s 1
(arm 1-): ra 386 ra 2 A 046. 18 (- 149). 250. 2037. 2038. 2067 al 1 1 Tyc Pr gig vg
s 2 arm 4: K 61. 69. 149. 172. 2018 s 1 bo sa TOMT i. 69. 432 Tcoxrooo-t rerpao-i
K: rco-o-apa 617 r. yrftr K rov 1 AK 046. 18 al: K bo sa r. Twy K. M. o-way. avr.
" Gog and Magog shall be gathered" bo eth Maywy AK i. 1934. 2036. 2037. 2050
bo sa: pr rov tt 046. 18 (- 1934. 2050). 250. 2067 al 1 " j owayayciv A 046. 18 (-35.
175. 617). 250. 2067 al pl s 2 arm i. 2. sa: pr icoi K 051. 35. 175. 617. 2016. 2017.
2036 s 1 arm 4: at crwayci 181: et congregabit (-avit gig: trahet Pr) Pr gig vg rov 8
AK 046. 18 (-175. 617) alp 1: O5i. i. 175. 250. 617. 2023. 2036. 2037. 2038.
2067 cov 2050 avrcov AK 046. W (-3S- 75- 6l 7- 1934- 2020) al pl (s) arm 1 2–: i.
35. 175. 242. 250. 617. 1934. 2020. 2023. 2036. 2037. 2038. 2067 Prgig vg arm 4
wr ij wrei 42. 82. 104. 201. 325. 385. 386. 456. 498. 620. 632. 920. 1918. 1934.

9. KCH arcpi oav 6i. 69:-fdiabolus et populus eius Tyc irxaroo- altitudinem Tyc gig ckvicxcixrav A 046. 18 (- 35. 175. 337. 617. 620. 1934. 2020. 2050) 82. no. 385. 2023 al mu: Kwxoxrav M 051. I. 35. 104. 175. 250. 337. 617. 620. 1934. 2016. 2020. 2037. 2038. 2050. 2067 r. mptfift. r. ay. + KCU Tip iroxiv TCDV ayiov 046. 498: njv iroxiv n r irapeifoxipr rov ayiav S 1 r. rjyamjfiivrfv dilectorum Tyc: rrjv KOUVTJV bo: rrjv aycav eth KOTC I; ascendit gig irvp. cr r. Xtin; v R eic airo 051. I. 35. 93. 205. 620. 2038 c r. ovp. A 94. 181. 2036. 2037 Pr: pr airo (eic 051. i. 35. 93. 205. 2038) rov (35- 2038) B OV K 025. 051. i. 35. 93. 104. 205. 2037. 2040. 2050 al vg s 2 arm 4: 4- airo rov 0cov 046. 19 (- 35. 205. 2040. 2050). 250, 2067. al 1 Tyc gig s arm 1- 1 bo sa eth.

10. KOI Oeuxi A 025. 046. 19 (- 325. 620. 632. 2040. 2050). i al sa: KCU (62o) rov 0uov K 42. 94. 104. 172. 218. 241. 250.

TO Orjpiov Kal 6 rrevowpo i? ii? s, ecu Saouvuroyo-ovrai Tipapas ical WKTOS ck rovs alcavas TCUV aluwv.

II. Kal ctsov tfpovov utcyav ACVKOV ical rov icad cvov lir taflrov, t(a) of ATO rov ( ) irpootuwov tyvycv y ical 6 ovpavot, ical TOTTOS ovx cvpiij 12. ical ctsoy rov j vcicpov? rovs xcyaaovs Kal rovs fucpovc eotorras cvanriov rov 0povov, jcal)3i Xia oixftprav, ical jcal ikpiorfo-av ol vcicpol lie rair ycypatytciwv v TOIS irara ra cpya avrcuv.

(a) Wrong construction due to editor.
( ) An interpolation by the editor (?); cf. vi. 16, xii. 14.
325. 336. 632. 1918. 2017. 20i8. 2023. 2036. 2037. 2040. 2067 al: TTJV Kaiop, inrjv mpi (ta bo) 2050 bo: 2O38 cat 8 A 025. 046. 10 (- 205. 2050). 250. 2037 al pl Tyc Pr gig vg s: K i. 205. 1957. 2050 s 1 arm 1 2 4 bo sa eth icoi 4 +OTTOV K: 620 o rcvooirpo. + ijorja-av 2050: ot l v otrpofr rcu Tyc arm 1 ftacravurorjo-ovtai + CKCI 2050 cio-. r. atcuv. r. aicov. I. 181. 2038 arm j rov audvcav 24i. 336. 2067.

11. 6poKOF ftcyav bo sa xeyav iry a 2050 icyav (-fcai 2050 Pr arm 1 4 eth) XCVKOV A 025. 046. 10 (- 18. 175. 205. 337. 617. 2020) al Pr gig vg s arm 1 4 bo sa eth: i. 175. 205. 230. 617. 2020. 2037. 2038. 2067 arm: jacyavi8. 337 cir draw K 2020 S bo sa avrov AM I. 2020. 2040: avrov 025. 046. 19 (2020. 2040). 250. 2037 al pl: aura) 218. 2018. 2038. 2067 rov Afet 025. 2040. 2050: O46. 10 (- 2040. 2050) al pl irpoo'cmrov + avrov 2040 S arm 1 8 rj yrj jcat o (2O5o) ovp. AK 025. 046. 10 (- 35) al pl gig vg s bo sa: o ovp. K. rf fl 35. 60. 432. 1957. 2023. 2041 Pr arm eth avrour eorum Pr bo: ab eis vg: in illis gig.

18. ficyox. pucpouv 046. 91. 175. 242. 250. 506. 617. 1934. 2016. 2017 bo r. (KOI K) icy. K. r. LUKD. (r. pikp. K. r. ftcy.) placed before COTWTOO- AK 025. 046. 35. 205. 632. 2020. 2037. 2038. 2050. 2067 al mn Tyc gig vg s arm 4- bo sa eth: placed after corwrao- 91. 175. 242. 250. 506. 617. 1934. 2016. 2017: placed before rovo- vccpow 104. 620: i. 18. 82. 93. no. 201.

325 337- 3 S- 3 6. 42Q. 45. 456. 498. ST- 522- 632. 920. 1849. 2004. 2024. 2039 I COTCDTCUT cpcinr. r. Op. Pr arm 2 coromur 6l. 69. 82. 429 CVWTTIOV cirt K: cycmrtov CTTI M c Opovav Otov I. 2037. 2067 al 0i0Xia fliflhoi 2050: fiiflxLOv 386 votx io-av ri t)V Btj K: rjvtivxrj KOI axAo 3i3Xiov rjv 0rj K c j 5. 046. 1.61.69.172. 175.218.242. 250. 1934.2016.

13. Kal ffioikcv f 4 Odxacra-a f (a) rovs VCKBOVS rovs cv f avrjfrt (a) jcat 6 0avaros Kal 6 17 tfowav rovs vckpovs rovs cv Kat CKHfo-av f KQOTOS Kara ra cpya avrw.

14. Kal 6 tfavaro? Kal 6; cJAijftyo-av cfc riyv Cfjlvrjv rov (a) The text has been tampered with here. The abode of righteous souls should occur instead of "the sea." Probably oi (hpavpol or a! poval (John xiv. 2) or 6 rapddeurof (Luke xxiii. 43) stood originally in the text. See vol. ii. 194-198.

(6) + offrot 6 6A. va. Toi 6 Scfrrepfo fort., Xfath) rov vvpfa a marginal gloss drawn from xxi. 8f., where it is full of meaning, but nonsensical here.

2017. 2018: ivcwxjo-av (avcw crav 35. 432. 1957. 2020. 2023). 35. 104. 205. 432. 617. 632. 1957. 2020. 2023. 2 37 2038. 2050: avotyqo-av 2067: aperti sunt Tyc Pr gig vg s arm bo: ivoi av (-cv 42. 325- 33 6- 5 7- 620. 1918) 18 (-35- 175- 20 S- 6l 7- 632.

1934. 2O20. 2050). 82. IIO. 141. 201. 385. 429. 452. 498. 522.

2021. 2024 sa eth K. oxXo)9i)8X. rjvoixn i arm rjvoixrj A 025. 35. 141. 172. 385. 2018. 2036. 2037: yvoiyri 2067 432. 498. 2020. 2023. 2041) M 046. 19 (-35); 250. 432. 498. 2016. 2023. 2038 0)170- Kpurcaxr s 1: +unius cuiusque Tyc Pr cv rowr 3i3Xoicr cv TOMT ? i? Aotcr K: librorum Pr: ciri TOV Pip iav bo eth: arm.

13. arm 1 row cv aim). vckpovo 2O2O r. VCKDOVO- r. cv avn? AM 025. 046. 18 (35. 205. 2020). 250 al 1 Pr gig vg s bo sa eth: row cv avnj (avrotcr i) VCKOOVO- 051. I. 35. 205. 2023. 2037. 2038. 2041. 2069: mortuos suos Tyc arm" K. o Oav. avrw 141. 1957 arm 2- 4 Kat o 1 2OS o 1 325. 620 ctfkav K 025. 046. 18 (-1934. 2020) al fere omn Tyc Pr gig vg s bo sa eth: COKCV A 82. 242. 1934: arm a r. vckpovcr rovo- (TOUT 046) cv avro(or A 025. 046. 18 (-35. 205). 250. 2037 al pl vg s: roucr cv avroto- vckpovo 051. I. 35. 205. 2023. 2038. 2067 eth: mortuos suos Tyc arm a: mortuos quos in se habebant Pr: mortuos suos qui in ipsis erant gig Kpior rav Karckpiorjo-av K: Kpiqrj s 1 CKOOTOCT +avro)v s 1: bo avrov A 35. 205. 325. 386. 620. 1934. 2020. 2050 vg s arm bo: avrov 046. 18. 61. 69. 104. 175. 250- 337- 456. 632. 920. 1849. 2004. 2067 sa.

14. o 1 149 Oav. 08170- gig vg eth rov vvpoa Tyc: + rrjv KOIOACVITV cv tfctco bo: + rrjv ycLtowav 0ctov eth ovroo- pr KOI K OVTOCT o Oav. (ver. 15) mtpoo- 2O5o arm 8 ovroo-. 17 Xiiviy r. irvpoar i. 94. 149. 201. 205. 452. 2016. 2021. 2038 Pr arm 1- bo ovroo-. cmv 498 o 0av. o Scvr o Scvrcpoo- tfavaroo- K 2020: o 0av. Scvrcxxr 2036. 2037 COTIV placed after Scvrcpoo- A (K) 025. 046. 18 (- 149. 205. 2050). 61. 69. no. 172. 250. 2018. 2036. 2037 vg s 8: after ovroo- 60. 432.

15. icol cf r a x cvpcfc; fv rjj ftj8Xp rip anj ycypauficvo? els rip lfivrjv rov mipos. 1957. 2023. 2041 gig s 1 arm 4: after favarocr 2067: IO4 17 XiAvi? T. irvpocr s 1 arm 4 (.

10. xai 325 cupcfty cvpc0i7rcrat K arm 1 n? t Xo A 025. 35. 104. 205. 2020. 2023. 2036. 2038. 2067 al: T 3t? Xtu 046. 18 (- 35. 205. 2020. 2050). i. 250 al pl j.

RESTORED ORDER OF THE TEXT.

CHAPTERS XXI. 5- 4 d. s b 6 a. 1-4, XXII. 3-5, XXI. 5 C, 6 b-8, XXII. 6. 7. 18 i8 b-i9. 16. 13. 12. 10 n. 8. 9. 20. 21. See vol. ii. 144-154.

XXI. 5 ft. Kai clirtv 6 Kaofavos brl f TW Bpovy f( ) 4 d. Ta irpwra dirj X0av 5 b. 8ov icaiva TTOUO Travra (3).

(a) Wrong construction due to editor.

( ) The text contains the following intrusion: 6. ical ctrlr fwt Ttyorar. See vol. ii. 203 sq. xxi. 5 should be read immediately before xxi. 6 b. Hence correct note in Commentary.

6 tt. KOI l8. 82. 201. 325. 337. 385. 386. 456. 498. 632. 920. 1849. 2004. 2021. 2024. 2039 cwrev ait gig: + AOI s 1 arm 2 4-" bo o xao. ciri r. Qpov. 2O5o ctrij cv 172. 2018. 2036. 2037 ru) 0povu rov Opovov I. 205. 920. 2023. 2038 al.

4 d. TO A 025. 051. 2038 arm 4: pr OTI ( ) 046. 18 al fere omil Pr gig vg S 2 arm 1- bo sa eth: + yap 2036 ra irpotra ra irpoftara K: ravro 2050: eiri ra vpoarwira avri r icai s 1: arm l! 2 a nX 2050: eiri ra vpoarwira avri r i A: awri 0ov 025. i. 18. 35. 104. 205. 920. 2037. 2038. 2067 al: dtrrjxOcv K 046. 18 (- 18. 35. 205. 920). 250 al mn arm 1-: + KIU (bo) isov iravra Troirjorjo-ovrai. naiva (K. tirotijorjo-av tr. eth) bo eth. 5 b. ibou pr KCU A: +t8ov 2O2I KOIVCL (iccva K) TTOIQI iravra AK 025. 172. 205. 432. 1957. 2018. 2020. 2023. 2041. 2050 Pr gig vg s 1: KaivotToiu) vavra 051. 35. 2036. 2038: iravra jcatva TTOUV 046. 18 (-205. 2020. 2050). 250 al 111 S 2: Katva iravra irouu I.

2037. 2067: iroiipra) (iroico eth) iravra icaiva bo sa eth.

5 C. For text of this line see p. 379, line 5. K. Xryci arm Xryci (CMTCV Tyc vg f s bo) A 046. 18. 325. 337. 386. 456. 620. 632. 1849. 2004 Tyc Pr gig vg 0- 11 arm 2 4-:-hnot K 025. 05 J i- 35- T 7S- 20 5- 2 S a 6l 7- 632. 920. 1934. 2020. 2037. 2038. 2050. 2067 al pl vg d f v s 1 bo eth arm 1 ypa jov ort 205: Pr ort o i. 386. 1849 s 1 arm 2 4- irurroi jc. ox ivot I. Kal ctSov ovpavov jcaivov u yijv KCUMV yap jrpairos ovpavos Kal ij Tpwn; yjj dbri A0av f Kai 17 tfaaao-o-a OVK Icrnv In.

2. KOI TTV iroxtv T K aytap Icpavcrax A Kainjv etSov

Kataftaivowrav CK rov ovpavov airo rov 0cov, Tjroifiao-fji vrjv a xvKnjv KCKOOT Ltcnv rp dvpi 3. ica ikowa WTS ieytys CK TOV Iw ij o-Kijvrj rov 0cov iera TWV

Kal o-Kipwo'Ci ACT avraiv, icat avrot Aaos (0) avrov jfcroirat, ao(feat avro? f 6 co9 icr avrwv lorai avraik co? f. ( ) (a) In the New Jerusalem God has only one Xatfo. Before the final judgment our author might have said that God had many aoi. Hence aol (AM and a few cursives) is a corruption. Otherwise if aol is the older reading, then it arose through a misunderstanding of the editor, and Xofo (025. 046 and Versions) is a nght emendation of the text.

(3) Read: afc-wr 0e6s Amu or Amu 0eds airwr. See vol. ii. 207 sq. 6 Debt per avrwv (= taijDy) seems to have originated in an excellent marginal gloss on 3 b, but in 3 it is wholly irrelevant and against the parallelism.

AK 046. 18 (-35. 175. 205. 617) al mu Tyc (Pr vg) gig s arm 1 2 4 bo sa eth: 025. i. 35. 175. 205. 250. 617. 2037. 2038. 2067 arm mor. oai0. (oa. K. TTIOT.) 4- TOV 0cou 046. 18 (-35. 205. 2020. 2050) al mu s 2 curtv tr before icoi oxi tvoi Pr vg: + TOV tfcovi7S. 250.617.

6 a. nnv Acyct K arm ycyovak (-acrtv 2020) A 2O2O S 1: ycyova 025. 046. 051. 18 (-386 2020) al few oam s arm: ycyove 386: factum est Pr gig vg: N C Tyc bo.

1. Kaiiw. Kant)? Ktvov. KWTJV M arm 4 irpoirocr KCVOO- arm 4 vpwrrj 42. 385 Pr bo arm amjxOav AK: airqxBov 046. 18 (-35- 205. 620). 42. 61. no. 201. 250. 385. 429. 498.

2017 al Tyc Pr s bo: am) 6cv 025. 82. 91. 172. 241. 522. 2016.

2018 gig vg: vopiyxF 051. i. 35. 205. 620. 2023. 2036. 2037. 2038. 2067 al 17 0oa. OVK COTI rrjv a aarrav OVK isov A T 2 1 8. 2050 OVK cortv crt OVK carat my 2050: OVKCTI coroi 205.

d. icoi 1 + ego lohannes vg T I aviav icyaaiv Pr KCUVOV iccvov K Kawqv ctfiov-2050 arm 4 f ow) tr before rip vo tv gig vg Y CK rov air 920 (arm a) CK r. ovp. airo r. 0cov AK 046. 18 (- 35- 2 S- 9 20)- 2 S- 2o6 7 Ty c Pr gig vg s arml 4 bo sa eth: airo r. 0. CK r. ovp 025. I. 35. 205. 1957. 2023. 2O 3 6- 2O 37-2038. 2041 al: owo TOV tfcor 2O2i KVA V-f-Kot Tyc.

8. not v)icoura a ieyaxtjr. Xcyounir KCLI. Xfyovcra K teyaaiyar gig arm L2 CK T. 0p povov AK 94 vg: ovpavov 025. 046. 18 (- 2050) al to OBm Tyc Pr gig s arm bo sa eth tsov tic 205 o- nvwo- twipwrw K 2050

Air 4 1 ". rat tfaxcfyci r o flcos trav 1 Sdvcpvov K 1 rov avruv,

Kat o 0avaro? OVK carat 3rf ovrc Trcvflos OVTC Kpavyy ovrc irovos OVK carat cri, zxii. 3. at Trav Kara0cAa OVK carat crt.

Kat 6 0DOV09 rov Ocov Kat rov dpvfov IV avrjj carat, jcal ol Sovaot avrov Aatpeixrowtv avnp, 4. KOI 0 IOVTCU TO irpda-UMTOl ttuTOV,

Kat TO ovoxa avrov CTTI ruiv xrrawrwv avrwv.

Tyc gig eth Xcuxr avr. tr after cowrat Pr Tyc gig Xcuxr 025. 046. 18 (- 2050). 250. 2067 al pl Tyc Pr gig vg s arm bo sa eth: Xaoi Alt I. 6l. 2036. 2037. 2038. 2050 al KCU avrocr o 0COO- fjt. tr avroiv (+ cat 2050 S 1) carat avrcov (auroto- s) 0eoo- A 2050 Tyc Vg s: xat avroar o 0 xr carat tcr avrcav 0coo- avraiv 02 c. 05 1: at (K) avroo-o flcoo- carat fitr avrcuv (ACT avruv carat 046 gig) M 046 Pr gig bo sa: at avroo carat 0coa avrcuv Kat carat OKXT ACT avrcov eth: min. thus; ACT aurwv carat 18 (-35. 175. 205. 617. 632. 2050): carat ACT avraiv I. 35. 175. 205. 241. 250. 617. 632. 2016. 2017. 2023. 2036. 2037. 2038. 2041. 2067 0COO- (+ ov 181) avtitfv 35. 175. 181. 205. 617. 2036. 2037. 2038 al: 18 (- 35. 175. 205. 617. 2050). i. 61. 104. no. 250. 385. 2067 al.

4 b c. itot 1 +avroo- s 1 o flcoo- A i. 2067 vg: air (c 522) avrwv 18. 325. 337. 386. 456. 522. 632. 920. 1849. 2004 al: 025. 046. 35. 175. 205. 250. 617. 620. 632. 1034. 2020.

2037. 2038. 2050 Tyc Pr gig s arm bo sa eth owpvovj Spaxv K CK T. o Q. avr. air avran 141. 2021 CK Atc 2017: OTTO 025. 046. 18al omn o 2 A 025. 046. 18 (-632. 2020. 2050). 250. 2037.

2038. 2067 al pl: N 241. 632. 2020. 2050 bo sa owe corot crt OVKCTt OV pi COTOt 2050 OVK COTttt. ITOVOO 172. 522. 2Ol8.

2067 ovrc. ovrc. ovrc ovse. ovoc. ovdc 2050 irevti. Kpavyrj K ovrc Kpavyrj ovrc irovoo- Tyc ovrc iroiw K: ov iroyoo- 205. 620: sed nee luctus ullus Pr OVK carat crt ovkcrt carat 2050: Pr arm 1 crt 2 crt K: ort corr first hand: i.

zzii. 8. Karaocpi fcaraytta K: avalctta 2050 (s 1?) crtj N: CKCI 051. I. 35. 104. 175. 205. 250. 617. 632. 1934. 2020. 2037. 2038. 2067 al s 1 cai J sed Pr: ort arm 1 o Qpov. corat sedes. erunt vg cv aim; carat carat cv avrrj 2050 bo sa cv cir 205 K. ot oova. avr. Xarp. avrw Pr K. ot oovxot avrov xat vfuxr OVK carat ot dc Sovxot rov 0cov bo: KOI OVK carat 0vAoa-Kara rwv Sovxaik rov 0cov ot eth Aarpcvaovo'tv Xarpcvova'tv 1 8. 82. no. 175. T8l. 205. 337. 456. 522. 617. 1849. 2004. 2020.

4. ciri pr Kat K: pr scriptum Pr arm.

5. JCCLI vv(owe? orai fri, gal ovx owtv 1 xpciav curos Xv ov icai fa yxhnt, on xvpiof 6 0eos orurci JIT avrovs, jcal facrixcwrouow cfc TOVS auovas TOV auww.

xxi. 5 C. Kat Xcyci Tpfyov ort ovroi ol Xdyot TUTTOC at clow.

6 b. Eyw ctfu To AX a ical ro Q, rj apxfj icai. TO rcxos.

Cyu) T St tom SakTO) K Tl

Scopedv.

5. coral rrw 051. 35. 175. 617 s 1: ip arm 1- m A 025. 82. 93. 2018. 2032. 2050 Tyc Pr gig vg s arm 1 4 bosaeth: CKCA 051. i. 35.104. 175. 205.617. 620. 632. 1934 als 1 arm: 046. 18. 325. 337. 386. 632. 1849. 200 4- 2020 al mu ovxcfowif Xpciav A 2050 Tyc gig vg s bo: ow cxowtv xpciav K: P tta v VK exowtv025. I. 35. 175. 205. 241. 242. 250. 617.632. 1934. 1957. 2016. 2017. 2018. 2023. 2036. 2037. 2038. 2041. 2067 al mu arm 4 sa: ou xp a 046. 18. 104. no. 325. 337. 386. 620. 632. 1849. 2O 4- 202 a l mu P r arm 1- or. Xv v. K. 2oi8 (it00- (oxr 2036. 2050: + Kai s 1) Xvxvov (2O2O: v ovny bo: sa) AN 94. 241. 632. 2020. 2036. 2037. 2050 Tyc Pr gig vg s arm 1 4 (bo sa): Xv vov (-ov i) 025. 046. 051. 17 (-632. 2020. 2050). 250. 2038. 2067 al pl arm KU S 1849 OKT yxiov A 025. 175. 181. 242. 617. 1934. 2017. 2036. 2038. 2050: lucem (lumen Pr) solis Pr gig: uroo-17X101; K i. 35. 205. 250. 632. 1957. 2016. 2018. 2020. 2023. 2038. 2041. 2067 Tyc vg s arm bo sa: KOTOO- 046. 18. 61. 82. 104. no. 201. 325. 336. 337. 386. 429. 498. 522. 620. 632. 1849. 1918. 2004 DT T A 025. 181. 452. 2038. 2050: wriei K 046. 051. 17 (-175. 617. 1934. 2050). i. 2037. 2067 al pl: inluminabit Tyc Pr vg arm 4 bo sa: ttari fa 175. 242. 250. 617.1934. 2016.2017. 2036 gig vg c htt s: inluminavit vg f arm 1 ir AK 2018. 2050 Tyc Pr gig eth: 025. 046. 17 (-2050) al fewomn vg arm 4 bo sa ocrixcvcrovo-tv regnabit super eos Tyc: jeWixcvtr avrcnv s 1 1.

xxi. 5 C. See p. 376 (adfin.) sq. for notes on this line.

6 b. eyw ciju TO A 1918. 2020 Tyc Pr gig vg bo eth: ryw ro K 025. 046. 35. 42. 104. 172. 175. 181. 205. 218. 241. 242. 250. 506. 617. 632. 1934. 1957. 2016. 2017. 2018. 2036. 2037. 2038. 2050 s sa: TO 18. 61. 82. 91. 93, 94. no. 141. 201. 325.

33- 337- 3 8 S- 3 86 4 2 9- 43 2- 45 2- 45. 49- S J 7- 5 22- 02- 632. 920. 1849. 2004. 2023. 2024. 2039. 2041. 2067 ox a A i. 205. 456. 2020. 2023. 2037. 2067 al wu Pr vg icai 1 +tyws 1 eth w +KOI 18. 82. 104. 337. 385. 386. 456. 632. 920. 2004. 2016. 2041 al if opxif K. TO Tfx. A 025. 046. 18 (- 35. 175. 205. 617. f 934) Jopx 1? fc " w 3S- IIO J 7S- 20 S- 3 8 S- 43 2- 617. 2017.

7. 6 VIKOW fcxipovoi crct ravro, KOL io-oioi avnji 0cos, ai avro? lorai ftoi v! o.

8. rots oc Scixoic cai dirtorot? icai iiocxvyAcvotf, at ovcwi icai iropvois icai apxokois,

KCU Ctscaxoxdvpai? Kttl ITOCTl Tot TCvsccTlv-

TO tcpo? avrov cv 17? Xfiv0 177 Kaiofitvy irupl teal 0cup, o cori? 6 pavaros 6 Scvycpos.

xxii. 6. Kai ctircv H Ovrot 01 Xoyoi iriorot KOL AXyqwoi, ai 6 fcvptot, 6 0co Toiv wvcvxatwv Tov irpo Tcov, dircotCixcy TOV ayyexov 2038 al p arm 4- cyo 2-f icai 205 arm 1 TCO 8wr. sitientibus Tyc (arm 1 2) TW 025 Soxrw AK 025. 35. 205. 620. 632 2020. 2037. 2038. 2050. 2067 al Tyc Pr gig vg s arm 4- bo sa: favrw (aimwcr arm 1) 046. 18 (-35. 205. 620. 632. 2020. 2050). 6r. 82. no. 172. 201. 242. 250. 385. 498. 2016. 2018 al arm L 2 7170- myiyo- A rrja- (0170- 386. 620: vivae Tyc gig Vg- c f- h- T 1 8wp av aipcao- 205.

7. o KIKUK KH o VIKQIV (+ avrocr s 1) S 1 arm eth fcxipovofiio-ci (-criy 104) AK 025. I. 35. 104. 205. 241. 432. 632 1957. 2020. 2023. 2036. 2037. 2038. 2050. 2067 al Tyc Pr gig vg s arm bo sa eth: SCIKTCI) avrw 046. 18 (- 35. 205. 632. 2020. 2050). 250 al 1 ravra irovra I. 2037: iravra ravra arm 1 2 avrto avruiv (avrour arm 1 4-) A i. 2036. 2037. 2038 arm 1 4-: avrov Tyc avroo-eorrat avrot ccroirai 051. I. 2036. 2037. 2038 arm 1 avtoriA Tyc s 1 ftoi A 025. 046. 051. 18 (-175. 325. 386. 456 620) al 1 Pr gig vg s 1 arm 1- bo: nov M 175. 325. 386. 456. 620. 2038 al Tyc s 2 arm 4 viocr o woo- 1957: moi 051. i. 2036. 2037. 2038 arm: Xcwxr arm 1.

8. TOUT Sc Bcixoicr Seixowr i 8c-j-oxr K: O25 icai 1 Cth atrtotOio- (irurrour eth) Afcc 025. I. 2023. 2036. 2037. 2038. 2050 Tyc Pr gig vg arm bo sa eth: + KU aAaproxoir 046. 18 (-2050). 250. 2067 al pl s Koi 2 i. 181. 205. 2023. 2036. 2037. 2038 al I K. iropv. Tyc gig arm 2 ic. IT. T. evfoo-ik arm 2 cvsco-iv cvarawr A (bo) avrwi carat Tyc Pr:-I- co-rat (COTIV arm 2) vg bo arm 2 cv TT; COTIV 2050 ev 62O T. MUOA irvpi ic. 0cto TOV irvpocr 2050: ardente (bo eth) ignis et sulphuns Tyc bo eth o 1 17 s o (6i7. 1934 al p) Oav. o. 8evr. AN 046.

18 (-35- 20 S)- 2 S alpl arm: vr- O ay 5 I- l- 35- 20 5- 202 3- 2037. 2038. 2067 al: Oavaroa- 025.

xxii. 6. eiiwr A 025. I. 175. 205. 250. 617. 1934. 2037.

2038. 2050. 2067 al mtt Pr vg sarm 4 bo: Xcyci 046. 17 (- 175. 205. 617. 1934. 2050) al pm gigarm L irioroi fidelissima (+ sunt vg) (Pr) vg: + curt? KOU, aytot cwrtv bo irwrr. axi?0. 2050 al: + CMTIV Pr gig vg- t T bo icai 2 bo o 1 A 61. 2018 s 1 bo avrov Sci at rots Sovaois avrov a Set ycvccru Iv ra ci. 7 Ka i8ov Ipxotai ra v. pucapios 6-nptov rovs Aoyovs T S irpotnjttia rov ? i? Atov rovrov. 1 8. taprvpa ya iravrl rf djcovovri rovs Aoyovf rij irpofr T Las rov ftiftxiov rovrov. (a)) The following interpolation is inserted here: i8 b.

6 Oet r aird? rij rxij df rdf ytypafiptvat tv rf pipxtv rovrtp. 19.

Wof curroc dird rod uxou r t f ft f cai c r t rrfxeut r t d foj, ycypapjjLtvw tv rtf ptp lp roiry. See vol. ii. 222-224.

sa: 025. 046. 17 al fereonm 0coo- + omnipotens vg Trvcviaruiv A 025. 046. 17 (- 175. 205) Pr vg- T s 1 arm 4 bo sa: rtu TrvcvLiari (rov m cvLiaroo- s 2 arm 4: ro irvcvAci eth) gig vg d s 2 arm 4 eth: r ov aytwv 175. 205 (arm): omnipotens vg: i. 2036. 2037. 2038 Twy irpotrjtav irpo Tfrw 205: T. ayttov i 250. 2018. 2036. 2037. 2038. 2067: r. ayu v irfxxf. s 1 atrcorcixcv + AC M 452. 467. 506. 680. 2021 s 8: GHTooteaAci s 1 avrov 1 + But fjltcrov rov rrjv oirrcuriav ccupaicoroo 1 Icoavvov 35 8ci ai r. S. avrov Sisafai 1849: 18- 3 2 5- 337- 36. 45. 632. 2004.

7. Koi 1 AN 046. 17 (-35. 175. 205. 617. 1934)- 2037 al 1 gig vg s: i. 35. 175. 205. 250. 617. 1934. 1957. 2018. 2020. 2036. 2038. 2067 Pr arm bo sa cpx "" tp ovrai K: cpxcrou 181 arm 1 ra v cv ra ct 181 s 1 arm 4: +Xcyct ncvptoo- 2050 r. 7rpo0.-f- ravnto- bo sa: tr after ftift iov gig: arm 1 r. fiifik. TOVTOV arm.

IB. ver 1 8, 19 181 iaprvpo (pr i) AK 046. 17 (- 175. 617. 1934). 2037. 2038. 2067 al pl: Liaprvpofuu 175. 242. 250. 424. 617. 1934. 2016. 2018 cyoi ergo Tyc: + Iwakvipr 2050 Pr TO) 1 35. no. 468. 1957. 2023. 2036. 2038. 2041. 2067 iravri TCD axovorri omnes qui audiunt Pr TOW Xoyovcr rov Aoyof Tyc s 1 arm 1- r. irpo. + ravnyo- bo sa: arm 4 eth cav rto- pr ore bo sa cjriorj CTri o-ci K 2036. 2037 arm cir aura cjriqrjo-ti N I cir avra ir avrw 522. 2037: ad earn Tyc (arm) eth ciri o-ci (-CTCU 1957. 2018. 2020) AK 046. 175. 205. 250. 1957. 2018. 2020. 2037. 2038. 2050 al pl Pr vg s arm bo sa eth: artorjo-at 051. 17 (175. 205. 1934. 2020. 2050). 42. no. 336. 498. 522. 2023. 2041 a! Tyc gig r avrov A: eir (2037) avrcd A 6 1. 2036. 2037. 2050: cv avra (avrovor arm 4) arm 4 bo sa o 0coo- or avrov (avru) A (late cursive hand) 046. 17 (- 35. 175. 205. 617. 1934) al pl Pr gig vg s 2 (bo sa) eth: or avrov (avrcu) o 0eor K 35. 61. 175. 205. 218. 242. 250. 432. 617. 1934. 1957. 2017. 2023. 2036. 2038. 2041. 2050. 2067 Tyc s 1 wairyao- Atf ("SS- X 75 205.617. 1934) al pl Tyc Pr gig vg s arm 4 bo sa eth: pr cirra 046. 051. 35. 175. 205. 218. 242. 250. 432. 617. 1934. 1957. 2016. 2017. 2023. 2037. 2038. 2041. 2067 arm.

19. icoi 1 205 cav av N af rj a cactrat 046: 1 6. cy i Irjcrov circi ra rov yycxov iov laprvp crcu vuv ravra ""cv 1 TCL ckicxitO-iats, cyw ifu fj pi a ical TO ycvo? Aaucis, 6 0rj)p 5 XaAirpos ical 6 irpuro? jcal 6 a ro 2050: contempserit Tyc cnro T. Xoy. Tavnyo- Pr arm cwro T. Xoy. TOP Xoyov 2050: +TOVTCDV M TOV pift. + Tovrov bo:

Tyc arm 1 T. irpo. placed after tyffxiov A 046. 17 (- 386. 456) al pl vg s arm 4 bo: tr before T. ? t3Xiov 201. 368. 456. 582.

I 1948. 2014. 2025. 2028. 2029. 2033. 2034. 2036. 2037. 2042: gig eth ravrrjv rovrov 201. 368. 386. 456. 582. 1948. 2014. 2025. 2028. 2029. 2033. 2034. 2036. 2037. 2042 a cxcc AK 046. 175. 205. 250. 617. 1934. 2037. 2038. 2050 al mu Tyc Pr gig vg s arm bo eth: a cxot (a cxat 325. 620) 17 (-205. 175. 617. 1934. 2050). 42. 82. no. 241. 1957. 2018. 2023. 2041. 2067 al p o foocr dominus Pr Tov 2 456 airo T. fvxov cwro T. 3i? Xiov 2067 Pr vg 1 Y bo: pr de libro vitae et vg d e A 60. 2020 bo T. iroxeoxrl TWV iroxcoiv S 1 1 70 ayuur TOIV ayiwv s 1 arm 1-: + icat CK gig Vg T(iv ycypat. TCDV cyycyoafu 20 1 8: TTCT ycypaxftcvr r Tyc Pr cv CTTI bo: 2050.

16. ojiik pr CK s 1: gig arm 1 ravra 2O5o Pr cv A 94. 250. 469. 582. 699. 2014. 2020. 2034. 2036. 2037 Tyc gig vg arm 1- 4 bo sa: rt K 046. 17 (- 175. 205. 617. 632. 1934. 2020) al pl s eth: osi. i. 91. 175. 181. 205. 241. 242. 617. 632. 1934. 2016. 2038. 2067 Pr (arm) T. ckfcx o-iaur ecclesia Tyc: septem ecclesiis Pr: pr iraa-aur bo K. ro ycvoo-J tr after Aavcts 386 TO yckoo- origo Pr Aavcts pr TOV i. 104 al: + cac o Xoyoo 2050: + KOI o Xaoor avrov s 1: "of Adam" arm 1 o 1 pr KOI 051. 35. 104. 205. 250. 2018. 2023. 2036. 2037. 2038. 2050 s 1 arm bo sa: pr uxr s 2 o Xaurpoo- KU 2oi8 bo arm 1 o 2 18 icat 8 A 205 gig vg: K 046. 17 (-205) al omn Tyc Pr s arm eth I o 8 205 Tiyxdivoo- irpoivoa- A 1957. 2038: irpuroor arm 4 i XaiirMxr. irpwtvoar AM 046. 17 (-175. 617. 1934- 2050) al p Tyc Pr gig vg s 8 arm 4- a eth: 91. 141. 175. 218. 242. 250. 617. 1934. 2017. 2050 s 1 1.

18. cy + fu gig vg arm TO ox a AK 17 (-35. 205. 2020). 250 al pl gig bo arm 4-: TO A 046. 35. 205. 2020. 2037. 2038. 2067 Tyc Pr vg jcai + cyw s 1 o irpuroo- ic. o (2041) co-xatocr 1C 046. 17 (- 2050) al fereoimi: irpomxr c. co-xatoo- A 104. no. 2014 arm 4-: tr after rexoo- i. 35. 175. 205. 242. 617. 1934. 1957. 2016. 2017.

2023. 2036. 2037. 2038. 2067 al arm 4: 205o arm 1 bo 17 op i; K. TO Tcxoo- AK 046. 17 (-35. 175.

cat 6 uo-00? AOV MT CAOV, dvoovvai ciccurnp as TO Ipyov f eorti avrov f. (a) 10. al Xcyet JMH Mif anfrpayurgs rovs Xoyovs rijs irpo irctaf TOV 3i? Xiov TOVTOV, 6 tcaipos yap eyy vs COTIV. ( ) (a) This order is against our author's use and is probably due to the editor. See Gram, in Introd. to vol. i. Read adrou tmv.

(J) The following verse is removed from the text as an interpolation; see vol. ii. 221-222: II. 6 LKW dduafffdrw fri,

KO. I 6 Hnrapfo vwavofru In, ical d IKOIOS dikOHHTunjv irotifffdrw T, cat 6 yto dywurtf rw in, 205. 617. 1934)- 250 al pl: ap iy ic. Tcaocr i. 35. 175. 205. 617. 1934. 2037. 2038. 2067 alarm rcxoo- + Xcyct o Kvptocr o Icoo-o TraitOKparcop arm 1.

12. isou pr KOI i. 2038. 2067 Tyc eth nypwv rowr Xoyovo TOV ? t? A. iov TOVTOV 104 icat bo awosooijvai t: KOI (bo) airoo io co s 1 bo I wcr. avrov Kara ra epya (ro cpyov s 1 sa eth) avrov (avrcov gig) 2036 Pr Tyc gig vg s 1 arm bo sa eth TO 325 eoriv AK 205. 2014. 2020. 2038 s 2: corai 046. 17 (- 205. 2020). i. 42. 61. 201. 250. 429. 498. 522. 1957. 2018. 2023. 2037. 2038. 2041. 2050. 2067 al pl COTIV (eoroi) avrov (avra 2050) AK 046. 17 (- 35. 175. 205. 617. 1934. 2020). 2014 al 1: i. 35. 175. 205. 250. 617. 1934. 2020. 2037. 2038. 2067 l p I- 10. K. Xcyci. TOUTOU gig Xcy. mot eth Xcyct CITTCV Tyc Cyp s bo fut + angelus Tyc o- paywntO- o- payurcur 205 Xoyovo- + Tovrovor (del first hand) irpo. + ravri7o- bo r. 9X. Tyc arm 1 rovrov eius Tyc: ravnyo- arm 1 o Katpwr yap ort o fcaipoo- I. 35. 205. 1957. 2023. 2038 Pr yap placed after Koipoo- AK 046. 17 (-35. 205. 620. 1934. 2050). 250 al 1 Tyc gig vg s arm bo sa: tr before fcaipoo- 82. 94. 141, 2036.

2037. 2050: 9i. 242. 336. 517. 620. 1918. 1934. 2032.

11. o abucw pr cat 424. 2018. 2032 Pr s 1 eth o ast c. aswno-aro) ert hii qui perseverant nocere noceant Pr: qui perseveraverit nocere noceat adhuc Tyc b (qui iniustus est iniusta faciat adhuc Tyc) m 1- arm 1 KO. L (bo) o pwr. pw. CTI (arm bo) K 046. 17 (- 2050). 2037. 2038. 2067 al pl Tyc Pr gig vg s arm bo sa: A i. 218. 250. 498. 2014. 2018. 2032. 2050 I o pviropoo- qui in sordibus est Tyc b Pr Cyp gig vg pviray0i? Ta K 94. 2017: pvirapcv roi 046. 17 (- 205. 2050). 2037.

2038. 2067 al 1: pwapw0ip-a 205: sordescat Tyc Pr Cyp vg cri 1- a 4 arm 4 bo eth Stfcatoo vi v irocijo-arcd en A 046. 17 (- 2020) al 1 gig vg s: iustiora faciat (iusta faciat adhuc Tyc) 8. Kayo IwawitS 6 ducovaiv cal ? Xcirav ravra. KOI ore covcra icai r t(3 rov circora jrxxncvncreu Ifurpocr cv raw irosw rov dyycxov rov Scikyvovros pot ravra. 9. ical Xcyct pot "Opa pij owoovxos o o ov ctii ical TOP dscx uw crov rwv vpo rjrtov KOI TOP npovyrwp TOVS Xoyove rov j9t Xfov rovrov Tp 0ej irpoo-fcvnorov.

20. Acyct 6 flaprvpwv ravra No Ipxpfuu Ta v. Aiiv cp; pn ftvptc "Iiprov.

Tyc b Pr Cyp: Sucawuftp-w crt (arm bo eth) 2020. 2036 arm 1 (bo) eth c. o ay. ay. crt similiter et sanctus sanctiora Tyc Pr Cyp: 6i. 2036. 2037.

8. itayw at eyco i. 35. 175. 205. 250. 617. 1934. 2037. 2038 al: ort cyo arm 1: cyo s 1 bo sa lomUfipr pr o 205 o 2020.

2O24 CLKOWDV K. jsXcit. TttvTa jsXcit. TttltTa K. ttkOVtoV I al ttlcOlhUV ic.)8Xeirav A 046. 17 (-35- 175- 2O S- 6l 7- I934- 2O 7 al pl gg vg s 2 arm: K 35. 175. 205. 218. 242. 250. 617. 1934.2016. 2017. 2036. 2037. 2038 Pr s 1 bo sa eth

SXctruv o ? Xcir. bo sa eth ravra avra 1 8. 2004: +xaprvpo 2050 cat 8 1934 rjkowra
K. cjsXcirov c)3Xc ra K. ijkowra s 1 arm 1 3 irov A. cJXc ra K I. 35. 175. 242. 250.
617. 1934. 1957. 2Ol6. 2017. 2023. 2036. 2037. 2038. 2041. 2050. 2067 al:
cisov 201. 336. 386. 456. 522. 2018. 2020: ore cisov (tow 046: isov 61. 104. no).
046. 1 8. 205. 325. 337. 620. 632. 1849. 20 4 a l pl: +ravra bo eth circora Att i.
336. 429. 2018. 2020. 2032. 2038. 2050: en-cow 046. 17 (- 2020. 2050). 250.
2037. 2067: eth Kwrjo-ai KOI (eth) irpoo-cicwio-a arm eth: bo sa tfjarp TWP Trpo
A Sctjcwon-oo- (Siyv- A) A 046. 17 (- 35. 325. 620. 1934. 2020). 250. 2037. 2038.
2067 al 1: Sctkiwroo- (Sucr- K) K 35. 60. 82. 91. 104. 325. 456. 498. 506. 517.
620. 1934. 2020. 2023. 2024. 2041 al.

9. Xcyti ciircv vg 1 S bo AOI 205. 325. 2050 I opa fiiyj-J-iro 70T r 2017 Pr gig
vg rvvsouxor pr ori Pr ciuj + cyo 175. 617. 1934 bo sa eth icai 8 AK 046. 17 (- 35.
175. 205. 386. 617. 1934). 250. 2037 al pl gig vg s arm 4 bo sa: i. 35. 60. 91. 175.
181. 201. 205. 241. 242. 386. 432. 617. 1934. 1957. 2016. 2017. 2023. 2038.
2041. 2067 Pr r. Xoyovo- + n r irpo rcuur 2020 Pr arm: pr rovrovo- s 1 rov ? i? X.
rovrov j rovrovo- 2050 r. 0co irpoo-Kvrqarav magis Deum adora Pr: gig.

20. Xcycij + o 0 xr 2050 o s a ravro + civai K arm 4 vai Pr gig arm aiiyv K 2050
Tyc Pr gig s 1 arm 4 p ov AK 046. 175- 205. 250. 617. 1934. 2038 al gig vg s arm
4 bo sa eth: pr vat (icai 104). 051. 17 (- 175. 205. 617. 1934). 1957. 2018. 2023.
2036.

2037. 2067 al 111 Pr Kvptc + iyfuiip bo yo-ov AK 046. 18. 35. 250. 325. 620.
632. 1849. 2004 al pl vgssa: + ptorc K c 17 (- 18. 35. 325. 620. 632. 1849. 2004).
42. 91. 201. 242. 2016. 2017. 2036. 2037. 2038. 2067 Pr arm 4 W bo: gig.

81. ver. 21 Pr i ap. T "yo-ov bo T. ic. Iiorov TOW Xpurrov 175. 181. 617. 1934.
2016. 2017. 2023 Kvptov AK 046 17 (-149. 175. 205. 468. 617. 1934). 250. 2037.
2038 al 1 arm sa: + i? fuov 149. 205. 468. 2067 al gig vg s arm 4 eth tiprov AK
506 sa: + xptorov 046. 17 al pl gig vg s arm eth ficra (ri arm bo) mm TCUV (arm)
ayuov (+ avrov s 1) 046. 051. 17 (- 2050). 250. 2037. 2038. 2067 al s arm 4- (bo)
sa: xero ITOKTOIK A vg- c- d h: ftera iravrav vwov (i?icov 2050) 2050 vg f- v eth:
i ra (circ gig) raw ayicov K gig: + ctcr TOV auava TOV cuava)V bo ax; v

K 046. 17. 250. 2067 al p vg s arm bo sa eth: A 2014. 2025. 2026. 2031. 2034.
2036. 2037. 2038 gig.

Subscription. airofcoxv rur (-cur K) laxwov AM 1854: avrofca-Xwfrur rov aytov
loxiwav 2004: a,7roka v lur rov ayiov uoawoi; TOV coxoyov (+ Kat cvayycxicrrov
1849) 3 2 5- x 49: Tcxoar ri or airoica Xv fcokT rov ayiov tuxivvov rov cvayycxtorov
82: rcxoa rrjo- rov aytov tioavvov rov Btoxoyov iao- atTOKoxv coxr 522: rcaxxr rov
airofcaxv coxr rov aytov airooroxov KOLL cvayycxtorov iwavvov 468: 046. 18. 35.
104. 149. 175. 205. 429. 456. 617. 620. 632. 1934. 2017. 2020. 2023. 2050 al.

VOL. ii. 25 IV. ENGLISH TRANSLATION.

CHAPTER I.

1-8. THE REVELATION WHICH GOD GAVE TO JESUS CHRIST TO BE
MADE KNOWN TO HIS SERVANT JOHN, AND THE BEATITUDE PRONOUNCED
ON THOSE WHO KEEP THE THINGS WRITTEN

The book 1. The revelation of Jesus Christ, which God gave unto him, its to show
unto his servants even the things which must shortly " come to pass; and (which) he

sent and signified by his angel unto his servant John; 2. Who bare witness of the word of God, and of the testimony of Jesus Christ (even) of all things which he saw.

3. Blessed 1 (is) he that readeth,

And they that hear the words of the prophecy, And keep the things that are written therein: For the time (is) at hand.

4-7. JOHNS GBEEUNG AND BENEDICTION TO THE SEVEN CHURCHES.

4. John to the Seven Churches that are in Asia

Grace unto you and peace, from him which is, and which was, and which is to come, 2 5. And from Jesus Christ, the faithful witness,

The firstborn of the dead, and the ruler of the kings of the earth. 8

Unto him that loveth us and loosed us from our sins by his blood, 1 On the seven beatitudes in this book, see vol. ii. 49.

Here John's editor interpolates the following words: "And from the seven spirits which are before his throne "; see vol. i. 9, 11-12.

1 The last two phrases=the Sovereign of the dead, the Ruler of the living. The primary meaning of rpwr ro of,. " firstborn," is wholly superseded by its secondary one of "chief," "foremost," "sovereign." See note oni. 5 (vol i. 14).

The first beatitude for those who keep the things written therein

John's greeting to the Seven Churches

Grace and peace from God and from Jesus Christ of the dead and Ruler of the living 6. And hath made 1 us to be a kingdom, priests unto his.

God and Father of t

Unto him be the glory and the dominion for ever and? ever. Amen. Redeemer 7. Behold he cometh with the clouds;

And every eye shall see him, and they that pierced him. 2 And all the tribes of the earth shall wail because of him. 8 Even so. Amen. 4 9-80. JOHNS CALL AND COMMISSION.

(His vision of the Son of Man, who is described in terms that recur in the Letters to the first six of the Seven Churches.) 1 Not "and he hath made us"; for we have here a Hebrew idiom which often recurs in our text; see vol. i. 14-15.

In this translation I generally use "tkat" to "introduce a statement that is essential to the complete meaning of the antecedent," and "who" to " introduce a non-essential statement," as Abbott, Gr. 218, footnote, recommends, this being the usage generally adopted by Shakespeare and Addison.

8 Here 6r vtrrfo requires this rendering. In Zech xii. 10, on the other hand, the same words mean, "they shall wail for him." We could also render " wail in regard to him ": cf, John xiii. 28.

4 Here all the authorities add: 8. " I am the Alpha and the Omega, saith the Lord God, which is, and which was, and which is to come, the Almighty." This verse is unquestionably interpolated, though I did not recognize this fact when writing my Commentary. This is proved by the evidence of (a) the context (or thought), and (b) that of the text (or grammar), (a) Contextual grounds. These words imply that John heard them in a vision; for otherwise he could not have heard them. But this would necessitate a foregoing statement, that John had fallen into a visionary condition or trance, such a statement as we find in i. 10 (" I was in the spirit") before his vision

of the Son of Man, or his very frequent " I saw " or " I saw, and behold "; see vol. i. 106 sq. John does not fall into a trance till i. 10. If, then, i. 8 is original, the text is fragmentary. But the words cannot come from John's hand at all, as we see from (b. (6) Textual or grammatical grounds. John never disconnects 6 0e6s (" God") and 6 irairoicpdtwp (" Almighty "), for the verv good reason that 6 raproicpdrwp represents a genitive in the Hebrew dependent on Bc6. That is, 6 0efa 6 Tavrorpdrwp is a stock rendering of mitaan vrvn (="God of hosts"); see vol. i. 20. Only an ignorant scribe could have separated the words. For John's use of this phrase, see iv. 8, xi. 17, xv. 3, xvi. 7,14, xix. 6, 15, xxi. 22. The recognition of this fact is very important, seeing that not only has no scholar recognized the misuse of this pnrase in i. 8, but none has recognized that the text in xix. 6,6 0e6r i wr vrrokpdrup (M 025. 046 Pr gig vgf s 1), is equally impossible with that in i. 8. Here such great authorities as A 2040 s 1 arm 9-4 vgs bo eth Cyp should at all events have led scholars with WH to bracket V"" s an intrusion, if not as impossible. In the LXX and in all works written by Jews in Hebrew or in Greek, nothing can intervene between 6 0efe (or xtfup) and 6 rarrojcxtrwp in this phrase.

Hence i. 8 must be rejected. By its removal the right order of thought is restored. First in i. 4-7 comes John's greeting to the churches, and next in 9-20 his account of his call and commission by Christ, i. 8 is thus impossible in itself linguistically in our author, unintelligible in its present position, and intolerable as creating a breach between i. 4-7 and 9-20.

John bid- 0. I John, your brother and companion in the tribulation den to and kingdom and endurance (which is) in Jesus, was in the isle down his w cn P atmos because of the word of God and the visions and testimony of Jesus. 10. I was in the Spirit on the Lord's day, send them and I heard a great voice behind me, as of a trumpet, saying: to the

Seven 11. What thou seest, write in a book,

Churches, 4 j t to fo t xven churches; 9-11 Unto Ephesus, and unto Smyrna, and unto Pergamum,

And unto Thyatira, and unto Sardis, and unto Philadelphia, and unto Laodicea.

19. And I turned to see the voice that spake with me.

Vision of And having turned, I saw seven golden candlesticks; man amid 13 And m the midst f the candlesticks One like unto a son the seven of man candle- Clothed with a garment down to the foot, sticks, And girt about the breasts with a golden girdle.

14. And his head and his hair were white as white wool, 1

And his eyes were as a flame of fire, 16. And his feet like unto burnished brass, as when refined in a furnace,

And his voice as the voice of many waters.

16. And he had in his right hand seven stars:

And out of his mouth went a sharp two-edged sword: And his countenance was as the sun shining in his strength.

17. And when I saw him, I fell at his feet as dead. And he laid his right hand upon me, saying,

Fear not; I am the first and the last: 18. And he that liveth, 8 and was dead:

And, behold, I am alive for evermore; And have the keys of death and Hades.

19. Write therefore the things which thou hast seen, And the things which are, And the things which shall be hereafter.

1 The text adds what was originally a marginal gloss, "as snow M; see vol i. 28.

Not "shineth," which is neither good English nor a rendering of the text. The text here contains a Hebrew idiom; see vol L p. 31.

This clause belongs to this line, not to the preceding; see vol. i. IS. 3-

L ao-XL. LETTER TO THE CHURCH IN EPHESUS 389 80. As for the mystery of the seven stars which thou sawest The seven in my right hand and the seven golden candlesticks the seven candle-stars are the angels of the seven churches; and the candlesticks 2j cl 2L are are the seven l churches. Churches, and the stars are the ideals

CHAPTERS II.-III.

LETTERS TO TEE SEVEN GHUBGHEB.

(To the angels of the Churches, i. e. to the Churches in their potential and ideal character, John addresses the seven following letters, which come from Jesus Himself, through whom alone their ideals can be realized; for He holds them in His right hand. These Churches, which are very imperfect witnesses of God on earth, are menaced with world-wide tribulation. These Letters were written by John, probably in the time of Vespasian, and edited afresh for incorporation in the Apocalypse. See vol. i. 43-47-)

CHAPTER II.

XL 1-7. (Letter to the Church in Ephesus, which is praised for rejecting false teaching, but blamed for forsaking its first love.)

L To the angel of the Church in Ephesus write:

These things saith he that holdeth the seven stars in his right hand,

That walketh in the midst of the seven golden candlesticks: 8. I know thy works, even thy toil and endurance, And that thou canst not bear evil men;

But hast tried them which say they are apostles and are not, 1 fete

And hast found them false. teachers 1 Nearly all the authorities read cu Aigrfai at Ivr frra Arrxipfei tbtw. endurance, The position of the numeral without the article in the predicate here is 2-3 parallel to that of iwri and 86ra in ivii. 9, 12, xxi. 21. But here we require the article in the predicate, since the predicate is co-extensive with the subject, and since "ike seven churches" (rtfr 6rra Ittxipncfr) have just been mentioned. Two cursives Pr fl and arm 4 rightly omit the second ford.

1 Not " and they are not"; for we have a Hebraism here; see note on 5-6, vol. i. 14.

8. And thou hast endurance,

And didst bear for my name's sake, And hast not grown weary.

But 4. But I have (this) against thee, that thou hast left thy first blamed love.

for forsak- ing its first 5. Remember therefore from whence thou hast fallen, love And repent and do the first works;

Or else I will come unto thee, And remove thy candlestick out of its place. 1 6. But this thou hast, that thou hatest the works of the Nicolaitans, which I also hate.

7. He that hath an ear, let him hear What the Spirit saith unto the Churches:

The victor TO him that overcometh will I give to eat of the tree of life, which is in the Paradise of God llfe 8-11. (Letter to the Church in Smyrna, which is praised for its loyalty under tribulation and impoverishment, and forewarned against a still worse though shortlived persecution.)

Church in 8. And to the angel of the Church in Smyrna write:

Smyrna praised for These things saith the first and the last its loyalty Which was dead, and is alive (again): uon Ul and 9 know th? tri! ulalion poverty, f ore! But thou art rich; warned And the blasphemy of certain of those 8 which say they

of coming j e J ews an(J t 8 lived But are a s y na g g ue of Satan- 10 Fear not the things which thou art about to suffer: Behold, the devil is about to cast some of you into prison, That ye may be tempted, and have tribulation for ten days.

Be thou faithful unto death,

And I will give thee the crown of life.

1 A gloss adds, "except thou repent"; see vol. i. p. 51.

1 tic ruf cy6rrw is partitive. Our author does not charge with blasphemy all who claim to be Jews. The limitation u defined further in "and are not, but are a synagogue of Satan." But the Ac here may be only a sign of the genitive; see my Grammar in the Introd. to vol. i. under IK.

Not " and they are not "; see note on ver. 2.

n. 11-17. LETTER TO THE CHURCH IN PERGAMUM 391 11. He that bath an ear, let him hear The victor

What the Spirit saith unto the Churches: J J

He that overcometh shall not be hurt by the second he reach death. of death 18-17. (Letter to the Church in Pergamum.) 18. And to the angel of the Church in Pergamum write: Church in

Pergamum

These things saith he that hath the two-edged the sharp praised for sword: its stead-13. I know where thou dwellest, and loyalty (Even) where Satan's throne is: in the days And thou boldest fast my name,. f peraecu-And didst not deny (thy) faith in me, Uon 12 " 13

Even in the days of Antipas, my faithful witness, 1 Who was slain among you, Where Satan dwelleth.

14. But I have a few things against thee, But Because thou hast there some who hold the teaching of blamed for

Balaam,

Who taught Balak to cast a stumbling-block before the i m children of Israel, doctrine

To eat things sacrificed to idols, and to commit fornica- "d life to f- exist in tl0n-their 15. Thus 2 thou too in like manner hast some who hold the mids teaching of the Nicolaitans. I4 16 16. Repent, therefore,

Or else I will come unto thee quickly,

And I will make war against them with the sword of my The victor mouth. will 1 endowed 17. He that hath an ear, let him hear with

What the Spirit saith unto the Churches. enriched powers

To him that overcometh I will give of the hidden manna, and And I will give him a white stone, personality

And upon the stone a new name 8 written, Which none knoweth but he that receiveth it.

1 AC read "my witness, my faithful one"; but i. 5, iii. 14 support the text adopted above.

8 The " thus " is justified by the statement in 14, while the words " thou too in like manner " involve a comparison with the Church in Ephesus, ii. 3.

1 Though difficulties may attach to the various explanations of the " white stone," that of the new name is clear. The name stands for the man and all therein implied his personality. For him that overcometh this personality is so transformed, developed and enriched that it is in effect a new personality, which none knoweth save God and the man himself.

THE REVELATION OF ST. JOHN H, 18-83.

Church of Thyatira praised for its growth in things spiritual, 18-19 blamed for suffering a false prophetess m its midst, 20-25 18-39. (Letter to the Church in Thyatira.) 18. And to the angel of the Church in Thyatira write:

These things saith the Son of God,

Whose eyes 1 are like a flame of fire,

And whose feet 1 are like unto burnished brass: 19. I know thy works (Even) thy love, and faith, and ministry, and endurance; And thy last works are more than the first.

90. But I have (this) against thee,

That thou sufferest the woman Jezebel, who calleth herself a prophetess,

And teacheth 8 and seduceth my servants, To commit fornication, and to eat things sacrificed to idols.

81. And I have given her time that she should repent: But she hath refused to repent of her fornication.

98. Behold, I will cast her upon a bed of suffering, 4

And those who commit adultery with her into great tribulation; 6 83. But her children I will slay with pestilence:

And so 6 all the churches shall know

That I am he that searcheth the reins and hearts.

And giveth 7 to each one of you according to your works.

x Lit "who has his eyes."

1 Lit. " and his feet"; but the possessive pronoun is really a part of the relative in Hebrew. Thus the stanza would run in Hebrew:

VM anva vry TTK Vp nrroa vnsjidi 1 Not " and she teacheth "; for we have here a Hebrew idiom; see vol. i. 14 sq.

4 See vol. i. p. 71. Here as in Hi. 9, ttotf with the present indie, is to be rendered by the future.

1 Text adds a gloss, "unless they repent of their works." These words are unnecessary. Moreover,? with ind. (furiuhripovffiv, Aft: jtrraioi-ffwriv C 025. 046), is against John's usage. The punishments in 22- b leave an opportunity for repentance but not the punishment in 23. The omission of 22 restores the parallelism and makes this stanza a tristich as the two that follow.

1 Here K L has this meaning still more strongly than in Matt. v. 15, xxiii. 32; I John lii. 19, etc.

7 i tpawuw. Ktu ffv. We have here another instance of the same idiom as in i. 5 t M= nm. jnan. Cp. Amos ix. 6 for a construction like that implied in the text. The judgments about to be executed in 22-23 wilj

H. 34-39, LETTER TO THE CHURCH IN THYATIRA 393 31 But to you I say, to the rest that are in Thyatira, As many as have not this doctrine, That know not the deep things of Satan, as they call (them) 35. I cast upon you none other burden: Only hold fast what ye have till I come.

36. And he that overcometh, even he that keepeth my The victor works unto the end shall share

To him will I give authority over the nations: 37. As I also have received from my Father, 8 87. And he shall break 4 them with a rod of iron;

As the potter's vessels shall they be dashed to pieces: 6 ceivetiie 38. And I will give him the morning star. morning star, 26-28 39. He that hath an ear, let him hear What the Spirit saith unto the Churches.

cause all the Churches to know that it is Christ that is the Judge, and that He judgeth now. In fact it is from such experience that they connect the judgments in 22 with the conclusion in 23. The judgments are in accordance with the works. Both the sins and their punishments have become actually known to them. Hence there is no eschatological reference here to the final judgment, and accordingly xai fov must not be translated "and I will jive," but according to the Hebrew idiom as rendered above. Here is mother fact tending to prove that the Seven Letters were written at a much iariier date than the Book as a whole. The Letters insist more upon the present judgments of Providence, the Book as a whole on the final judgment. 1 fyvww. Timeless aorist to be translated as a perfect = " have recog-iised"=" know." See Introd. vol. i, Gram. 4. iii. 2 Or "and."

1 This line follows 26 b immediately, as the exactly parallel construction io ii. 21 shows.

4 Or " shatter w or " destroy "; see note in vol. i. p. 75 sq. B ffwTptpcmu, is to be taken as a Hebraism and rendered by the future; ee vol. i. 77. Tyc (ut vas figuli comminuentur) Pr vg (sicut (tanquam vg) as figuli confringentur) (s") presuppose ffvrrfhfijpomu and the above ranslation. 2050 gig (s 1 emended by Gwynn)=iral ffvrrplfa afrofc wf rd itetfty KT. In any case the verb affects the fin), not the weftf.

fvrrpipovrtu (or awrpi ovrai) would have seemed more natural in our xt, since tfnj is thrice preceded and twice followed bv the plural verb in iir author (xi. 18, xv. 4). But the sing, verb occasionally? w; the neuter lural of various nouns in our author; see vol. i. Gram. 8. ii. (b). If this ems unsatisfactory here, seeing that tory is referred to in the preceding ause by ofrofr, then we must regard ffwrpiftrtu as a slip of toe writer a primitive corruption for ffvrrplpwnu or wrMtywroi.

THE REVELATION OF ST. JOHN m. 1-5.

Church in Sardis blamed for its spiritual declension, and ad-monished to be watchful and repent, 1-3, xvi. 15

Second

Beatitude for those who keep their garments clean

Yet a few in Sardis are worthy

The victor shall obtain a spiritual body, and have his name in the Book of life

CHAPTER III.

XXL 1-6. (Letter to the Church in Sardis.) L To the angel of the Church in Sardis write:

These things saith he that hath the seven Spirits of God, And the seven stars: I know thy works

That thou hast a name to live, but art dead.

8. Be watchful, and strengthen the things that remain, (but) which are ready to die: l

For I have found no works of thine fulfilled before my God. 2

Remember therefore how thou hast received and didst hear, And keep (them), and repent

XVI 15. Behold, I come as a thief:

Blessed is he that watcheth, and keepeth his garments,

So that he may not walk naked, And his shame be seen. 8 m. 8 C. If therefore thou dost not watch, I will come as a thief, And thou shalt not know At what hour I shall come to thee.

4. But thou hast a few names in Sardis Which have not defiled their garments, And they shall walk with me in white; For they are worthy.

5. He that overcometh shall thus be arrayed in white garments;

And I will in no wise blot his name out of the book of life, But I will confess his name before my Father, And before his angels.

He that hath an ear let him hear What the Spirit saith unto the Churches.

1 The epistolary imperfect here rendered as a present

"Works of thine" (AC). This judgment is more sweeping than the reading of 025.046 " thy works." Sardis has failed as a centre of spiritual power.

Lit "they see his shame."

. 7-10. LETTER TO CHURCH IN PHILADELPHIA 39

HI. 7-13. (Letter to the Church in Philadelphia in which it is given unqualified approval for its fidelity and steadfastness, and promised the honour and privileges of die true Israel (9), and deliverance from the final demonic woes in the approaching worldwide tribulation (10-11). He that overcometh shall have an everlasting place in the spiritual Kingdom of God even God's city, the New Jerusalem and bear on his forehead God's name and Christ's own new name, 12.) 7. And to the angel of the Church in Philadelphia write:

These things saith he that is holy, he that is true,

He that hath the key of David,

That openeth and none closeth, 1

And closeth and none openeth: 8 b. Behold I have set before thee an open door, 8. Which none can shut 1 8. I know thy works,

That thou hast a little power, And yet thou hast kept my word And hast not denied my name.

9. Behold, I will cause 8 them of the synagogue of Satan Who say that they are Jews and are not,

But do lie:

Behold, I will make them to come And worship before thy feet, And know that I have loved thee.

10. Because thou hast kept the word of my endurance, I also will keep thee from the hour of tribulation, Which is about to come upon the whole world, To tempt them that dwell upon the earth. 4 1 See vol. i. 86.

8 8 b- form a parenthesis, if the MSS order is followed. But the MSS order of the text cannot be right. Hence 8 are restored before 8. Thus in 7-10 there are four stanzas: the first and third of six lines each, and the second and fourth of four lines each.

1 Here ISou hu= ru un, and indubitably refers to the future, and should be so translated (so rightly in AV.). This common Hebraism (see Gesenius, Heb. Gram., transl. by Cowley, I io, where the participle=a future, is called futurum tntfans. Our author sometimes puts the present (indicative) (cf. i. 22) after tfotf, where it is to be rendered as a future: also xvi. 15, mi. 7, 12. In the last three cases the fyx 0 " may be rendered as present wing to the idea of futurity associated with the technical use of the verb, rhe same variation in the renderings of this idiom appears in the LXX.

4 The demonic temptations here referred to can only affect the unbekevea f. "those that dwell upon the earth "; see note on xi 10 in vol. i. 289)1

Church in Philadelphia praised for its steadfastness despite its weakness,

Promised the powers and privileges of the true Israel

And deliverance from the woes that are to try the faithless

THE REVELATION OF ST. JOHN HL 11-19.

The victor shall dwell (or ever in God's city and bear His name and

Christ's new name

Church in Laodicea denounced fonts self-complacency and for its spiritual destitution despite its material wealth and intellectual cukure 14-17

Bidden to seek the true riches and to repent, i-19 11. I come quickly: hold fast what them hast; Let none take thy crown.

18. He that overcometh I will make him a pillar in the temple of my God, And he shall go out no more: And I will write upon him the name of my God, And the name of the city of my God, The new Jerusalem which cometh down out of heaven from my God, And mine own new name.

18. He that hath an ear, let him hear What the Spirit saith unto the Churches.

m. 14-23. (Letter to the Church in Laodicea.) 14. And to the angel of the Church in Laodicea write:

These things saith the Amen, The faithful and true witness, The beginning of the creation of God: 15. I know thy works

That thou art neither cold nor hot: I would thou wert cold or hot.

16. So because thou art lukewarm, And neither cold nor hot, I will spew thee out of my mouth.

17. Because thou sayest, I am rich,

And have gotten riches, and have need of nothing; And knowest not that thou art (of all creatures) the (most) wretched and miserable And poor and blind and naked: la I counsel thee to buy of me gold refined by fire, that thou mayest be rich;

And white garments, that thou mayest clothe thyself, And that the shame of thy nakedness be not made manifest; And eyesalve to anoint thine eyes, that thou mayest see.

19. As many as I love, I reprove and chasten: be zealous therefore, and repent 20. Behold, I stand at the door and knock: Appeal to If any man hear my voice and open the door, I will come in to him, and will sup with him, And he with me.

81. To him that overcometh, I will grant to sit with me on The victor my throne, shall share

As I also have overcome, and sat down with my Father "j on his throne. f J; g 88. He that hath an ear, let him hear Fath

What the Spirit saith unto the Churches.

CHAPTER IV.

THE VISION OF GOD THE OBEATOB, FROM WHOM ABE ALL THINGS.

(With iv. comes an entire change of scene. The dramatic contrast could not be greater. In ii.-iii. we had a vivid description of the Churches, with the ideals they cherished, their faulty achievements, their not infrequent disloyalties, and their outlook darkened with the fear of universal martyrdom. But the moment we leave behind the restlessness and turmoil of earth, the moral shortcomings and apprehensions of the Churches in il-iii., we enter in iv. into an atmosphere of perfect assurance and peace, where neither the threatenings of the powers of evil nor the alarms of the faithful on earth can awake even a momentary misgiving in the heavenly hosts that serve and worship. And yet that the manifold needs and claims of the faithful on earth were the object of God's gracious purposes becomes clear and ever clearer as we advance.) 1. After these things I saw, and behold, a door was opened 1 in heaven, and the former voice, 1 which I had heard as of a trumpet speaking with me, said, Come up hither, and I will show thee the things which must come to pass hereafter. 8. Straightway Vision of I was in the spirit: 8 a throne

And behold a throne was set in heaven, Him that

And on the throne (was) one seated; sat there- 1 1 have taken these participles as finite verbs, a construction occasionally occurring in our author and in Hebrew, and very frequently in Aramaic. If rendered as participles the sense is not so good: " Behold, a door opened in heaven, and the former voice, as of a trumpet speaking with me, saying."

1 i. e. that in i. 10.

1 On the high probability that part of this chapter was written at an earlier date by our author and subsequently incorporated by him when he edited the complete work, see vol. t. 104 sq. f 3.

THE REVELATION OF ST. JOHN IV. 8-.

The four and twenty Elders

The four Cherubim

Cherubim praise God as Holy, Almighty, and Everlasting 8. And he that sat was to look upon like a jasper stone and a sardius,

And there (was) a rainbow round about the throne, like an emerald to look upon.

4. And round about the throne (were) four and twenty thrones:

And on the thrones four and twenty elders sitting! Clothed in white garments; And on their heads (were) crowns of gold.

6. And out of the throne proceeded lightnings and voices and thunders,

And seven lamps of fire were burning before the throne, 1 0. And before the throne there was as it were a sea of glass like unto crystal; And round about the throne (were) four living creatures, 8 full of eyes before and behind.

7. And the first creature (was) like a lion, And the second creature like a calf,

And the third creature had a face as of a man, And the fourth creature (was) like a flying eagle.

8. And the four living creatures had each of them six wings, 4

And they rest 5 not day and night, saying: Holy, holy, holy (is) the Lord God Almighty, 8 Which was, and which is, and which is to come.

1 A gloss is added here: " which are the seven spirits of God." On the whole line see vol. i. 117.

1 A disturbing gloss is added here: " in the midst of the throne and "; see vol. i. 118.

i. e. Cherubim; see vol. i. 119-123.

4 The following clause is here interpolated: " Around and within they are full of eyes"; see vol. i. 125.

1 Pr gig and vg-d give " rested." See next note.

1 The rendering "Almighty" is probably right, but by no means certain. The Hebrew behind rarroicpdtwp is in our author mua; see Isa. vi. 3. See footnote on i. 7 above. The specific word in Greek for' Almighty " is Tarrostvafjiot, which is found in Wisd. vii. 23, ri. 17, xviil 15. It is significant that, although jcparew has in some instances approximately the meaning of " to be powerful in the LXX (see Esth. L I; I Esdr. iv. 38, etc.), it never has this meaning in our author nor in the NT. The two words rayroirpdrwp, rarofffrauof are found side by side in the Liturgy of St. James; see Lightfoot, Apostolic Fathers, II. i. 7. In the Apostles' Creed and generally in latei the equivalent of royrwrpdrup. be sate in any case.

in later times omnipotens is The rendering " Lord God of Hosts " would 9. And when the living creatures give 1 glory and honour and thanks

To him that sitteth on the throne, Who liveth for ever and ever, 10. The four and twenty elders fall 1 down before him that The Elders sitteth on the throne, P God

And worship 1 him that liveth for ever and ever, Creator of

And cast their crowns before the throne, saying, all things, 1L Worthy art thou our Lord and God, IMI

To receive the honour and the glory and the power: For thou didst create all things, And because of thy will they were, and were created. 1

CHAPTER V.

THE VISION OF OHEIST THE REDEEMER, THROUGH WHOM ARE ALL THINGS.

(As in iv. we have the vision of God from whom are all things, in v. we have the vision of the Lamb, into whose hands the destinies of the world are committed, inasmuch as through His redeeming death He had won the right to carry God's purposes into effect. As in iv. the Elders and Cherubim worship God as the Creator, in v. the Cherubim, Elders, and angels worship Christ as the Redeemer, while the chapter closes in the adoration of God and Christ by all.)

L And I saw upon the right hand of him that sat on the Vision of throne a book written within and on the back, sealed the sealed book 1 These verbs are futures and not pasts in the Greek. But the context which cannot admit of futures. We have here no prediction of what shau be wider none could certain circumstances but (a) either an account of what the Seer saw in a P en 4 vision in the past in such a case we should have pasts, and so Pr vg d T arm 1 render (b) or a statement of the regular order of divine worship in heaven. Since the praise of the Elders follows immediately on that of the Cherubim, the context seems to favour (b. Hence the futures are to be tendered as presents. The Greek futures represent Hebrew imperfects in the mind of our author used in a frequentative sense a common usage in Hebrew; see vol. i. Gram. 10. ii. (h) But (a) may be right, and the context refer simply to what the Seer saw in his vision. Then the futures would have to be rendered as pasts, as in the Latin and Armenian Versions mentioned above. The Hebrew imperfects in the mind of our author would explain this anomaly also. In careful translations like the LXX the uncertainty of the translators as to whether the Hebrew imperfect should be rendered by the Greek present, future, or past imperfect is constantly manifest, each of these renderings being possible.

8 Lit. " were " (frar so A omitting rest of line). Other MSS and Versions: " were and were created,"

THE REVELATION OF ST. JOHN V. 8-18.

save the Lamb, whom the Seer now beholds

Adoration of the Lamb by the

Cherubim, Elders, and countless hosts of angels, 8-12 9. with seven seals. And I saw a strong angel with a loud voice, Who is worthy to open the" book, and 8. to loose the seals thereof? And no one in heaven, or on earth, or under the earth was able to open the book, or to 4. look thereon. And I wept much, because no one was 6. found worthy to open the book, or to look thereon. And one of the Elders saith unto me, Weep not: Behold the Lion that is of the tribe of Judah, the Root of David, hath 6. prevailed to open the book and its seven seals. And I saw between the throne and the four living creatures and the elders 1 a Lamb standing as though it had been slain, having seven horns and seven eyes, which are the seven 7. spirits of God sent out into all the earth. And he came and took 8 (it) out of the right hand of him that sat on 8. the throne. And when he had taken the book, the four living creatures and the four and twenty elders fell 9. down before the Lamb, having each of them a harp and golden bowls full of incense. 8 And they sang 4 a new song, saying,

Worthy art thou to take the book, And to open the seals thereof; For thou wast slain,
And hast redeemed unto God with thy blood

Men of every tribe, and tongue, and people, and nation, 10. And hast made them unto our God a kingdom and priests, And they reign 6 upon the earth.

11. And I saw, and heard the voice of many angels round about the throne; 6 and the number of them was ten thousand times ten thousand and thousands of thousands, Id. saying, with a loud voice:

Worthy is the Lamb that hath been slain

To receive the power, and riches, and wisdom,

And might, and honour, and glory, and blessing.

1 Here the Lamb stands between the inner circle of the Cherubim and the outer circle of the Elders. This implies a Hebraism in the text See vol. i. 140. Otherwise render: "in the midst of the throne and the four living creatures and in the midst of the elders. 1

The perfect is here an aorist perfect: the RV. renders "taketh"; cf. viii. 5. See Introd. vol. i Gram. 4. v.

1 The MSS add a gloss here: " which are the prayers of the saints." The prayers and the incense were not identical; see vol. L 145.

4 The text has " sing "; but this can represent the Hebrew imperfect in our author's mind.

1 In the vision the Seer sees the saints already reigning in the Millennial Kingdom. Otherwise the verb is to be given a future sense as a Hebraism.

The MSS add a gloss here: " And the living creatures and the elders." See vol. i. 148.

18-14. (These two verses form the proper close to iv.-v., for they give the grand finale pronounced by all creation in praise of both God and the Lamb the themes of iv. and v. i-ia.) 18. And every created thing which is in heaven, and on the All area-earth, and under the earth, and on the sea, and all things that tion unites are therein, heard I, saying, Godtnd" 8

Unto him that sitteth upon the throne, and unto the Lamb, Be the blessing, and the honour, and the glory, And the power, for ever and ever. 14. And the four living creatures said

Amen. And the elders fell down and worshipped.

CHAPTER VI.

THE JUDGMENT OF THE WORLD BEGINS WITH THE OPENING OF THE SEALS BY OHKIST.

(Christ opens seal after seal of the Seven-sealed Book, and as they are successively opened a series of destructive agencies are let loose war, international strife, famine, pestilence, the prayers of the martyrs which have become instruments of divine wrath (see footnote 2, p. 403), a mighty earthquake, cataclysms affecting heaven and earth. Through these God's judgments on evil are brought to pass. But the cosmic troubles are still future, and even when fulfilled are partial and not the immediate heralds of the end, as the dwellers on the earth apprehended (see vol. i. 183, 153 sqq.).

1. And I saw when the Lamb opened one of the seven seals, and I heard one of the four living creatures saying as with a voice of thunder, Come.

9. And I saw, and behold a white horse, Vision of

And he that sat thereon had a bow; War

And there was given unto him a crown: And he went forth conquering and to conquer.

a And when he opened the second seal, I heard the second living creature saying, Come. VOL. H. 26

Vision of 4. And another horse, a red one, went forth: mlcr. And to him that sat thereon was given to take away the strife And that they should slay one another,

And there was given to him a great sword. 1 6. And when he opened the third seal, I heard the third living creature saying, Come.

Vinpn of And I saw, and behold, a black horse; fe 0 " 06 And he that sat thereon had a balance in his hand.

6. And I heard as it were a voice in the midst of the four living creatures saying,
A measure of wheat for a penny,
And three measures of barley for a penny;
But to the oil and the wine do no hurt 7. And when he opened the fourth seal, I heard the voice of the fourth living creature saying, Come.

Vision of 8. And I saw, and behold, a pale horse: 4 pestilence And he that sat thereon was named Pestilence, 0 1 So A, which omits Ac. But even if we retain At, with the great majonty of the authorities, the sense could be the same; cf. ij. 9, "the blasphemy of (fr) them." This peace is the wrong peace. Christ came to destioy it to make room for the true peace. The text recalls a saying of Christ in Matt. z. 34: "Think not that I came to send peace on the earth: I come not to send peace bat a sword." Otherwise with N, etc., render: " to take peace from the earth."

1 The sword bears here the eschatological meaning of civil and international strife. It is given by God to the faithless nations that they may destroy each other with it. See vol i. 165.

1 Ramsay (Cities of St. Paul, 430 sq.) traces these commands to ancient custom. 'The annual crops may be destroyed, but that means only scarcity and high prices; a new year will bring new crops. On the other hand, the vines and the olive must not be destroyed, because that means lasting ruin. New olive trees take about seventeen years to mature. Vines also need a number of years. This old principle of West Asiatic international religious law was taken up into the Mosaic Law." This is no doubt true, but our author is first of all and mainly dependent on the Little Apocalypse (Mark ziii. and parallels) and Zech. i. 8, vi. 2-7. See vol. i. 158 sqq.

4 The MSS add a gloss: " And Hades followed with him See vol. i. 169 sq.

8 So ftbwof most be rendered. It bears this meaning in il 23, xviii. 8, and frequently in the LXX. It=m See vol. i. 170. In Aquila and Sym-machus 131 is rendered by up6t ("pestilence"), which is unmistakable in meaning, bat in the LXX by 0drarot and not Xot f. (Hence correct footnote in vol. i. 170.) Aquila so renders it in Deut. xxviii 21; Amos iv. 10; Hab. iii. 5: Syra. in Ps. Izxvii. (Ixxviii) 48, xc. (xci.) 6; Jer. xlv. (xxxviii.) 2, and both translators in Ex. v. 3, ix. 3, 15; Ezk vi. 12, HI. 16. In Ps. Ixxvii. (Ixxviii.) 50 the LXX renders both mo and iai by ffdraror.

And authority was given onto him over the fourth part of the earth. 1 9. And when he had opened the fifth seal, I saw underneath Vision of the altar the souls of them that had been slain for the the word of God, and for the testimony which they held: JJJJJF fol 10. And they cried 2 with a loud voice, saying, on"heir n
How long, 0 Master, holy and true,
Dost thou not judge and avenge our blood 9-10
On them that dwell on the earth?
11. And there was given to each one of them a white robe; The
And they were bidden to rest yet for a little season, martyrs
Until their fellow-servants also and their brethren should S 1.".

be fulfilled,? That should be killed even as they.

19. And I saw when he opened the sixth seal:

And there was a great earthquake; Vision of

And the sun became black as sackcloth of hair, M rth

And the whole moon became as blood; 2d t a h other 18. And the stars of heaven fell to the earth,

As a fig tree casteth her unripe figs, 12-14

When shaken by a mighty wind.

1 MSS add a gloss: "to kill with sword and with famine and with pestilence (or death), and with the wild beasts of the earth. 1 See vol. i. 171.

2 Though the subject of the seal is described as "persecutions" (see vol. i. 158, 171 sqq.), in keeping with the original eschatological tradition in Mark xin. 7-9, 24-25 (and paiallels), the reader should observe that its character has been changed by our author. Here the first thought is not of the persecutors or of their victims, but of the prayers of the latter. The prayers of the martyrs, vi. 9-10, are conceived as an instrument of divine wrath. The prayers of the martyrs offered on the altar, vi. 9-10, as those of all the saints, viii. 3-4, become spiritual forces. Hence a voice from this altar, ix. 13, orders the four angels of punishment to be let loose for the second Woe, and in xiv. 18 an angel from this altar delivers to the Son of Man the divine command to undertake the judgment of the earth, while in xvi. 7 (which rightly belongs to xix., see vol. ii. 122) the altar declares, as the angels, Elders and Cherubim have already done, that God's righteousness and truth have at last been vindicated in the destruction of Rome. Thus the prayers of the martyrs and saints are conceived as bringing about divine judgment, like the other seals.

8 breffav should perhaps be rendered " were cast," seeing that vlvreir ii here used as the passive of 0dxX r=" casteth," in the next line. In In. xxxiv. 4 the same verb is presupposed in both clauses of the LXX and Sym.:. wf Turret. See vol. i. 180.

14. And the heaven was parted, Being rolled up as a scroll; l And every mountain and island were moved out of their

Men's P laces itatfo l w-And the kings of the ea? h and the princes and the f ear chief captains, and the rich, and the strong, and every 15-17 bondman and freeman, hid themselves in the caves and 16. in the rocks of the mountains; and said to the mountains and to the rocks,

Fall on us, and hide us from the presence of him that sitteth on the throne, And from the wrath of the Lamb: 17. For the great day of his wrath is come; And who is able to stand?

CHAPTER VII.

VISION 07 ifc SEAIiiNG 0? MK flpiittyijaXi TRP. ATCT.; AND OF THBIB BLESSEDNESS IN HEAVEN AFTER MABTTBDOM.

(In the preceding five chapters there is a progressive drama, advancing in a series of visions dealing first with its chief agents: (a) with the Christian Church on earth, ii.-iii.; (6) with God from whom are all things, iv.; (c) with Christ, who takes upon Himself the fulfilment of God's purposes, v.; and then with the opening of the first six Seals, which are to be followed by a series of social and cosmic judgments, vi. But with vii. 1-3 a pause is made in order that the spiritual Israel may be sealed, to secure them against the coming three Woes of a demonic character, 4-8. Thus in vii. 1-8 a pause is made in the movement of the divine drama, but in vii. 9-17 there is more: there is a breach in the unity of time, a unity which has been observed in ii.-vii. 8. But this breach is full of purpose. The sealing in vii. 1-4, though it secures the faithful from demonic powers, does not secure them from suffering martyrdom. Hence to encourage them to face these impending evils the Seer recounts the vision in vii. 9-17, in which, looking to the close of the great tribula- 1 So N ftifffflium and some Cursives. So also Isa. xxriv. 4: pip Lov 6 ofyxtrfe. But the best attested reading, Atttriaieiw, is perhaps at once original and a primitive slip for the emended form in N. If i urff6fuww be taken as the original and correct text, then it is to be rendered: "as a scroll being rolled up."

1 Less weighty authorities read " their. 1

VIZ. 1-0. SEALING OF THE SPIRITUAL ISRAEL 405 tion, he beholds those who had been sealed and died as martyrs, already triumphant in heaven before the establishment of the Millennial Kingdom. This vision is proleptic. It constitutes a breach in the unity of time. At its close the chronological order of events is resumed. Such proleptic visions recur with the same purpose later on.) 1. After this I saw four angels standing at the four corners Destrac-of the earth, holding the four winds of the earth, that no tiv c. wind should blow on the earth, or on the sea, or upon any f s e t ed 9. tree. And I saw another angel ascend from the sun- God's rising, having a seal 1 of the living God: and he cried servants with a loud voice to the four angels, to whom it was aled, 8. given to hurt the earth and the sea, saying, Hurt not x 3 the earth, neither the sea, nor the trees, till we have sealed 4. the servants of our God in their foreheads. And I heard The the number of them that were sealed: a hundred and P iritual forty and four thousand were sealed out of every tribe of S the children of Israel 5. Of the tribe of Judah were sealed f twelve thousand: Of the tribe of Reuben twelve thousand: 7. Of the tribe of Simeon twelve thousand: Of the tribe of Levi twelve thousand: Of the tribe of Issachar twelve thousand: 8. Of the tribe of Zebulun twelve thousand: Of the tribe of Joseph twelve thousand:

Of the tribe of Benjamin were sealed 8 twelve thousand: 5. e Of the tribe of Gad twelve thousand: 6. Of the tribe of Asher twelve thousand: Of the tribe of Naphtali twelve thousand: Of the tribe of Manasseh twelve thousand. 1 9. After these things I saw, Vision of And behold, a great multitude, which no man could the future number, blessedness

Out of every nation, and (all) tribes and peoples and tongues, been

Standing before the throne and before the Lamb, sealed and

Clothed in white robes, and with palms in their hands; 1 The text here is without the article. In iz. 4, where it recurs, it has the an.

1 The participle here is to be rendered as a finite verb. See Introd. Gram.

1 5-6 have been restored to their original order, in which the sons of Leah are followed by those of Rachel, and these in turn first by the sons of Leah's handmaid and then by Rachel's. See vol. i. p. 207.

Their 10. And they were crying 1 with a loud voice, saying, pnisc Salvation to our God before the TJ s i ttet jj on tne throne, lhronc And to the Lamb.

In which 11. And all the angels stood round about the throne and the angels the elders and the four living creatures; and they fell join, ii-xi before the throne on their faces, and worshipped God, saying, 19. Amen:

Blessing, and glory, and wisdom,

And thanksgiving, and honour, and power,

And might, be unto our God for ever and ever. 1 18. And one of the elders answered, saying unto me, These who are clothed in the white robes, who are they, and 14. whence came they? And I said unto him, My Lord, thou knowest. And he said unto me,

These are they that have come out of the great tribulation,

And have washed 8 their robes,

And made them white in the blood of the Lamb.

The 15. Therefore they are before the throne of God; blessedness And they serve him day and night in his temple: martyrs And he that sitteth on the tnrone sna1 1 ablde u P on tnem- 15-17 18. They shall hunger no more, neither thirst any more;

Neither shall the sun unite 5 them any more, nor any heat: 17. For the Lamb that is in the midst of the throne shall be their shepherd, And shall guide them unto the fountains of the waters of life: And God shall wipe away all tears from their eyes.

1 Here xpdfowc represents the imperfect in Hebrew in the Seer's mind, and should be rendered by a past imperfect 8 Nearly all authorities but C Pr add " Amen "; but it seems to be here a liturgical addition, as Swcte remarks: it is bracketed by WH. See note in vol. i. pp. 19,151 sq. The MSS read: " The blessing and the glory," etc.

1 We have here a Hebraism frequent in our author; see note in vol. i. 14 sqq. The RV. here, as always in the case of this idiom, is wrong "Come. and they washed."

4 Or: "shall cause his Shekinah to dwell upon them. 11 See vol. i. p. 215. The construction favour AT aftrofr is not found in any OT. version (so far as I know) except in Aquila's (Ex. xxiv. 16). In xxi. 3 of our text we have enjvovv furafrw. Now, since ffn)Hh= and Sy frequently follows pr, ffkyrow tori seems here modelled on the Hebrew, as rapou? wrd on oy jar. Cf. the presupposed interchange of V? and oy in the LXX and Theod of Dan. vii. 13, while Matt. xxiv. 30, xxvi. 64 (tptfiuw M r. rep uv) and the LXX of Dan. vii. 13, presuppose Sy, and Mark xiii. 26, Luke xxl to), and Mark xiv. 62 (Ipgtfiteror pcrd), presuppose oy.

1 An emendation of Gwynn and Swete. See vol. L 216.

CHAPTER VIII.

HEAVENS PRAISES STILLED THAT THE PRAYERS OF ALL THE FAITHFUL MAY BE PRESENTED TO GOD AGAINST THE IMPENDING THREE WOES.

(i, 3-5, 2 (restored), 6 (restored), 13. Amid the silence of heaven for the space of half an hour, when all praises and thanksgivings were hushed, the prayers of all the saints are presented before God, i, 3-5, to shield them in the coming tribulation. Then three Trumpets are given to three angels, wherewith they prepared to sound, 6, whereupon the Seer beheld another vision, even an angel flying in mid heaven and proclaiming, "Woe, woe, woe to the inhabiters of the earth," i. e. the non-Christians and faithless, because of the three Woes that were about to come upon them, 13. On the interpolated passage, viii. 7-12, and the changes introduced by the interpolator in viii. i, 2, 6, 13, see notes below, and vol i. 2i 9 sqq.)

L And when he opened the seventh seal, there followed a Silence 8. silence in heaven for about the space of half an hour. 1 And adc n another angel came and stood by the altar, having a golden t c censer; and there was given to him much incense, that he pra yers of should offer it upon 9 the prayers of all the saints upon the all the 4. golden altar which was before the throne. And the smoke of the incense went up from the angel's hand before God JJ, 5. on behalf of the prayers of the saints. And the angel took before the censer and filled it with the fire of the altar, and cast God, 3-5 it upon the earth. And there followed lightnings, and voices, and thunders, 8 and an earthquake.

8. And I saw three angels; and unto them were given three Three trumpets. "fjh r bidden to 1 viii. 2 is an intrusion in its present context and not original in its present? und tne form. It is restored in what appears to have been its original form after viii. 5. These changes are due to the interpolation of viii. 7-12. See vol. i. trum P els 218-222,224. announc-

Or "on behalf of."! "8 the 1 This is the original order as in iv. 5, xi. 19, zvi. 18. See Introd. Chap. IV. where it deals with this phrase. Corrupt order in MSS, due to inter-polator of viii. 7-12.

4 The text reads: " And I saw the seven angels which stand (Andrew. This termination-off not found elsewhere in our author, who uses-ay. Cf. xix. 3, ftfflkav; xxi. 6, ytyovav. See vol. i. Inuod. Gram. I. hi. ( )) before Goil, and there were given unto them seven trumpets. 1 6. And the three l angels who had the three l trumpets prepared to sound. 2 18. And I saw, and I heard an eagle flying in the midst of heaven, saying with a loud voice, Woe, woe, woe, to them that dwell on the earth, because of the voices 8 of the trumpets of the three angels, which are about to sound.

INTERPOLATED PASSAGE.

7. And the first (angel) sounded,

And there followed hail and fire, mingled with blood, and they were cast upon the earth: And the third part of the earth was burnt up, And the third part of the trees was burnt up, And all 4 green grass was burnt up.

8. And the second angel sounded:

And as it were a great mountain burning with fire was cast into the sea: And the third part of the sea became blood; 9. And there died the third part of the creatures which were in the sea that had life; And the third part of the ships were destroyed.

10. And the third angel sounded:

And there fell from heaven a great star, burning as a torch, And it fell on a third part of the waters, and on the fountains of waters, 6 ll. b And the third part of the waters became like 8 wormwood; And t many men t 7 died of the waters, because they had become bitter.

1 Text has "seven."

1 Here the editor of John's Apocalypse interpolated a small Apocalypse, viii. 7-12; see vol. i. 218-222. This consisted of four stanzas of four lines each. These four plagues are modelled on the first four Bowls.

8 Text reads: "the remaining voices." The addition comes from the hand of the interpolator of viii. 7-12.

4 Instead of "all green grass" the rest of viii. 7-12 suggests that in the original document there stood originally: " the third of all green grass." But why the change was made is not apparent; for as it stands it is in direct conflict with ix. 4.

Thecontext requires "of the fountains," etc. See vol. i. 234. The MSS add: " and the name of the star is called Wormwood." But this clause breaks the development of thought and makes the stanza consist of five lines instead of four.

f So 2038 Or Pr fl gig vg s 1 bo sa eth. Other authorities = " became wormwood." But the waters did not " become wormwood," but bitter in taste like wormwood.

7 We should expect: " the third part of mankind." See vol. i. 236.

12. And the fourth angel sounded:

And the third part of the sun was smitten,

And the third part of the moon, and the third part of the stars;

So that the third part of them was darkened, And f the day did not shine for the third part of it, nor likewise the night, f

CHAPTERS IX.-XIII. THE THREE WOES.

(The three Woes, i. e. (i) the demonic locusts, (2) the demonic horsemen, (3) Satan and the two Beasts. These affect only those that dwell on the earth, i. e. the non-Christians, viii. 13, who had not the seal of God on their foreheads, ix. 4. The third Woe, it is true, results in the universal martyrdom of the faithful, xiii. 15; but its power to deceive and destroy spiritually is limited to the non-faithful, xiii. 14. Thus these Woes affect in the deepest sense only those who had not the seal of God on their foreheads. Yet evil at this stage appears to have triumphed, and the cause of God on earth to be brought to an end for evermore.)

THE FIBST AND SECOND WOES.

IX. (The first Woe consists of a plague of demonic locusts, which had no power to hurt those who had God's seal on their foreheads, but only those who had not, i-i i. The second Woe consists of a plague of demonic horsemen, which were let loose from the Euphrates and destroyed one-third of the heathen world, 13-21.)

CHAPTER IX.

1. And the first angel sounded:

And I saw a star fallen from heaven to the earth, And there was given unto him the key of the pit of the abyss.

1 The text is hopelessly corrupt. There is no connection between the destruction of one-third part of the sun and the reduction of the length of the day by one-third. The corruption may have arisen in the Hebrew The Bohairic gives what was apparently the original sense: " the third part of them did not shine by day, nor likewise by night." Cf. eth. I here withdraw the note in vol. i. 237 unless so far as it traces the error to the Semitic original.

1 " Fifth," owing to the interpolation of the four plagues in viii. 7-12.

THE REVELATION OF ST. JOHN DL ofd locusts,2-3

No power to injure any save such as had not God's seal on their foreheads, 4-5

First Woe And he opened the pit of the abyss;

And there went up a smoke from the pit, As the smoke of a great furnace; And the sun and the air were darkened by the smoke of the pit.

8. And out of the smoke came forth locusts upon the earth; And power was given them, as the scorpions of the earth have power.

4. And it was said unto them that they should not hurt the grass of the earth,

Nor any green thing, nor any tree, but only the men That had not the seal of God on their foreheads.

5. And it was given them that they should not kill them, But that they should be tormented five months:

And their torment was as the torment of a scorpion, when it striketh a man. 1 6. And in those days men shall seek death, And shall not find it;

And they shall desire to die, But death shall flee 8 from them.

7. And the forms of the locusts were like unto horses pre- pared for war;

And on their heads as it were crowns like gold, And their faces were as the faces of men.

And they had hair as the hair of women, And their teeth were as those of lions; 9. And they had breastplates, as it were breastplates of iron. And the sound of their wings was as the sound of chariots, (Yea) of many horses rushing to war.

10. And they have tails like unto scorpions, and stings; And in their tails is their power To hurt men five months.

Their king 11. They have over them as king the angel of the abyss: His name in Hebrew is Abaddon. 8 1 In my Commentary (vol. i. 222, 243) and Text I have treated this line as a gloss for the reason given in vol. i. 222; but it may be original

The text reads " fleeth," which seems to be a Hebraism: i. e. = Hebrew imperfect in the mind of the writer. See vol. i. Introd. Gram. 4. i. (a).

1 Text adds a gloss: " And in the Greek (tongue) he hath the name Apollyon." See vol i. 245 sq.

appearance of the locusts, 7-10 12. The first Woe is past: behold, there come yet two Woes hereafter.

18. And the acond l angel sounded:

And I heard a voice from the horns of the golden altar which is before God, 14. Saying to the second 1 angel who had the trumpet, The

Loose the four angels who are bound at the great river 5J5 nd,

Fiinhratwi Woe the

Euphrates. dcmonic 16. And the four angels were loosed, f r 0

Which had been prepared for the hour and day and Euphrates month and year, In order to kill the third part of mankind.

16. And the numbers of the armies of the horsemen were twice ten thousand times ten thousand: 17. I heard the number of them: and so I saw the horses in the vision, And them that sat on them.

And they that sat on them 8 had breastplates of fire and brimstone:

And the heads of the horses were as the heads of lions;

And from their mouths issued fire and smoke and brimstone.

18. By these three plagues was the third part of mankind The third killed,

By the fire and the smoke and the brimstone, which issued from their mouths; 19. For the power of the horses is in their mouths; 4 and with them they do hurt.

1 Text reads " sixth," owing to the interpolation of the four plagues in viii. 7-12.

1 Text seems corrupt, but I cannot emend it satisfactorily. The fact that we have here the construction r. Kaoimtvow IT f aflrwr t a construction against our author's usage may point to the evil activities of John's editor. Cf. xiv. 15, 16, where in an interpolation the same wrong construction occurs twice. I have supposed a loss of Ar avrofo Kttl ol Kabjiuvu through hint, and corrected fyovrat into fyprrej. ojfrwj, according to our author's usage, refers to what precedes, cf. ii. 15, iii. 5, 16, xvi. 18; but it cannot do so here, for the description of the horses comes later.

1 i. t. " on the horses." The text reads: farrow? r f afrw t (=" sat on them "). This incorrect phrase seems due to the interpolator who tampered with the text. I here withdraw the suggestions in vol. i. 252 sq.

4 The text adds a gloss here: "and in their tails; for their tails are like unto serpents, having heads." But the destructive powers of the horses lie in the fire, smoke, and brimstone which issue from their mouths, and not in their tails. The gloss is due to ix. 10. See vol. i. 253 sq.

THE REVELATION OF ST. JOHN IX. SO-X. 6.

The rest 90. And the rest of mankind, which had not been killed by repented these plagues, not, ao-ai Dkl not even repent of the works of their hands,

So as not to worship demons, and the idols Of gold, and of silver, and of brass, and of stone, and of wood; Which can neither see, nor hear, nor walk: 8L And they repented not of their murders, nor of their sorceries, Nor of their fornication, nor of their thefts.

CHAPTER X.

The angel with the Little Book

The seven thunders! but their message not to be written down, 3-4

God's purposes to be fulfilled without delay, 6-7

THE BEERS NEW COMMISSION.

(This chapter serves several purposes. It was written mainly as an introduction to xi. 1-13 (the Little Book), but partly also to prepare the way for xii. sqq. (see x. n) and partly to declare that the time prayed for by the martyrs, vi. 9 sqq., when God's purposes, x. 7, should be accomplished, would no longer be delayed. Thus x. links together the earlier chapters with the later. A strong angel presents the seer with the Little Book (Le. xi. 1-13 a transmitted source), and swears that God's purpose with regard to the world would be forthwith fulfilled, 1-7. The Seer is then bidden to eat this Book and to issue other prophecies, 8-11.) 1. And I saw another strong angel coming down from 1 heaven clothed with a cloud, and the rainbow was upon his head, and his face was as the sun, and his legs were 2. as pillars of fire. And he had in his hand a little book open: and he set his right foot upon the sea, and his 8. left foot upon the earth; And he cried with a loud voice, as a lion roareth: and when he cried, the seven thunders 4. uttered their voices. And when the seven thunders uttered (their voices), I was about to write: and I heard a voice from heaven saying, Seal up the things which the 5. seven thunders have uttered, and write them not. And the angel that I saw standing upon the sea and upon the 6. earth lifted up his right hand to heaven, And sware by him that liveth for ever and ever, who created the heaven and the things that are therein, and the earth and the 1 The word is here Ar.

1 That ol rttes aftroc has this meaning here is shown in vol. L 259.

things that are therein, and the sea and the things that are therein, that there shall be time no longer.

7. But in the days of the voice of the third 1 angel, when he shall sound, 8 then is the mystery of God finished, according to the good tidings which he declared to his 8. servants the prophets. And the voice which I heard from heaven spake unto me again and said, 8 Go, take the book which is open in the hand of the angel that standeth upon 0. the sea and upon the earth. And I went unto the angel and bade 4 him give me the little book. And he saith unto me, Take it and eat it up, and it shall make thy belly 10. bitter, but in thy mouth it shall be sweet as honey. And Th See I took the little book out of the hand of the angel and ate jjj he it up; and it was in my mouth sweet as honey, and when I 11. had eaten it my belly was made bitter. And they said T 1 S unto me, Thou must prophesy again concerning mm y dsi u e peoples and nations and tongues and kings. other prophecies

CHAPTER XI. THE ANTICHRIST IN Tfgp. TTftaT. Tem 1- (XL 1-13 is a proleptic digression on the Antichrist in Jerusalem. It is a digression, because the Seer turns aside from his main theme of the Antichrist as identical with Rome and its empire: it is proleptic, because in point of time it belongs to the third Woe, when Satan has been cast down from heaven, and the kingdom of the Antichrist established, xii.-xiii. This task once fulfilled in xi. 1-13, he returns to his main theme in xi. i4-xviii. The seer here uses a source which originally had in several respects a different meaning. Its present meaning is given in the short summary in vol. i. 269.)

L And he gave 6 me a reed like unto a rod, saying, Rise The and measure the temple of God, and the altar, and them 5 nn8 9. that worship therein. But the court that is without the faithful to secure 1 Text reads " seventh." For this and other changes introduced by an them early editor, see vol. i. 219 sqq. against f See vol. i. 264 sq. demonic 1 The Greek is solecistic, and the solecism appears to go back to the Seer, rowers " And bade " is here a rendering of Xfy, followed by an inf., as in 2 xiii. 14.

1 The Greek is tftfi) MM Xlyw, which must be rendered as if it were

Mowce pm. X4yw. For like abnormal constructions, see note, vol.

i. 274.

THE REVELATION OF ST. JOHN XI. 3-14.

preaching of the two witnesses, 3-6

The Beast from the abyss puts them to death in Jerusalem! and the people of the land rejoice, 7-10

Resurrection and ascension of the two witnesses

XI-I2

Judpent on Jerusalem and conversion of the rest of the Jews temple leave out, and measure it not; for it hath been given unto the nations: and the holy city they shall tread under foot forty and two months. 1 And I will appoint my two witnesses, and they shall prophesy a thousand two hundred and threescore days, clothed in 4. sackcloth. These are the two olive trees and the two candlesticks, which stand before the Lord of the earth.

5. And if any man will hurt them, fire proceedeth out of 6. their mouth, and devoureth their enemies. 8 These have the power to shut the heaven, that it rain not during the days of their prophecy: and they have power over the waters to turn them

into blood, and to smite 7. the earth with every plague, as often as they will. And when they have finished their testimony, the beast that cometh up out of the abyss shall make war with them, and 8. shall overcome them, and kill them. And their dead bodies (shall lie) in the street of the great city, that spiritually is called Sodom and Egypt, where also their 9. Lord was crucified. And some of the peoples and tribes and tongues and nations look upon their dead bodies three days and a half, and suffer not their dead bodies to be laid in a tomb.

10. And they that dwell in the land rejoice over them, and make merry; and they shall send gifts one to another; because these two prophets had tormented them that 11. dwell in the land. 8 And after the three days and a half the breath of life from God entered into them, and they stood upon their feet, and great fear fell upon them that Id. beheld them. And they heard a great voice from heaven saying unto them, Come up hither. And they went up into heaven in the cloud; and their enemies beheld them.

18. And in that hour there was a great earthquake, and the tenth pan of the city fell; and there were killed in the earthquake seven thousand persons: and the rest were affrighted, and gave glory to the God of heaven.

14. The second Woe is past: behold the third Woe cometh quickly.

1 Vers. 3-13 are a prophecy rather than a vision. The presents in 4-6, 9-10, are equivalent to futures. The past verbs in 11-13 represent Hebrew perfects (or in some cases probably the imperfects with vav conversive); but these perfects vividly represent the prophetic future.

1 The text adds a gloss here which is based on 5 and xiii 10: "and if any will hurt them, in this manner must he be killed"; see vol. i. 284.

IVTBODTTOTIOH TO THE THIED WOB.

XL 16-19. The proleptic digression in xi. 1-13, to which x. is an introduction, has come to an end, and our author here returns to the progressive development of the divine drama in the third Woe, xu.-xiii. Though x. in certain respects links up the chapters that precede with those that follow it, yet in the order of action xi. 14 follows immediately on ix. and the main theme is resumed in the third Woe, which is heralded by the third Trumpet. This Woe apparently results in the absolute triumph of Satan and his agents on earth and the annihilation of the Church; but the two songs in heaven, which introduce it in xi. 15-18, disclose in advance the actual issues of events: their burden is that the Kingdom of the world has in the reality of things become the Kingdom of God and of His Christ, that the time has come for the judgment of the nations and of Satan and the Beast, for the judgment of the dead and the due recompense of God's servants.

16. And the third 1 angel sounded; and there followed great voices in heaven, saying,

The kingdom of the world has become (the king- Song (of dom) of our Lord and of his Christ, And he shall reign for ever and ever.

pending 16. And the four and twenty elders, which sit before God advent of on their thrones, fell on their faces and worshipped tne Lord God, saying, 17. We give thee thanks, 0 Lord God Almighty,

Which art and which wast; Because thou hast taken thy great power,

And hast become King. advent of 18. a. And the nations have waxed wroth, lennial b. And thy wrath hath come, Kingdom, h. And the time to destroy them that destroy the? h last earth, jj c. And the time for the dead to be judged final re- compense 1 Text reads " seventh"; see vol. i. 218 sqq. Each Woe is heralded by of God's a trumpet blast, Before the interpolation of viii. 7-12 there were only three servants, trumpets. 16-18 1 In the text this clause is certainly out of place. By its restoration after i8 b we recover the development of events in their true order; see vol. i.

295 sqq. "The destroyers" are the first Beast, the False Prophet, and Satan as well as their adherents.

g. The small and the great 1 d. And for giving their reward to thy servants, The prophets and the saints, And them that fear thy name.

Ark of if. And there was opened the temple of God that is in heaven; and there was seen in his temple the ark of manifested his covenant; and there followed lightnings, and voices, a pledge and thunders, and an earthquake, and great hail of the fulfilment of the songs just song CHAPTER XII.

A BETB08FEOT.

(Xn. This chapter is retrospective. Its object is to give the Rtder insight into the past in order to prepare him for the crowning evil the climax of Satan's power upon earth. But this crowning evil is not really a sign of his growing power, but the dosing stage of a war in heaven, which had already terminated in the vindication of God's sovereignty, and the hurling down of Satan to earth. Hence, however, Satan and his minions, the Roman and heathen powers, may rage, but it is but the last struggle of a beaten foe, whose malignity is all the greater, since he knows that his time is short. The vision goes back before the birth of Christ, and tells with mythological colouring how Satan sought to destroy Christ, and, after His ascension, the Church itself. In setting forth his theme the Seer has borrowed the main part of this chapter from Jewish sources, which had in turn been derived from international sources, and has adapted them though not wholly to their new and Christian setting. The closing verses, 14-16, were written before 70 A. D., and cannot be interpreted in detail of the crises of 95 A. D., when our author wrote See vol. i. 299, 331 sq. For a summary of the chapter, see vol L 298 sq.)

Ajkj n 1. And a great sign was seen in heaven; a woman Hke in ap- clothed with the sun, and the moon under her feet, and pearance 2. upon her head a crown of twelve stars. And she was the with child, and cried out in her travail and pain to be delivered. And there was seen another sign in heaven; d behold, a great red dragon, having seven heads and child 1 1 have restored this line immediately after 18; cf. xx, 12. Otherwise read line g immediately after line h (And the time) to destroy them that destroy the earth, The small and the great. "The great" would be Satan and the two Beasts: " the small " would be their adherents.

4. ten horns, and upon his heads seven 1 diadems. And Saian on his tail drew the third part of the stars of heaven, and his fail did cast them to the earth: and the dragon stood 8 before " rom the woman that was about to be delivered, that he might W ich 6. devour her child when she was delivered. And she involved was delivered of a son, a man child, who shall break 4 one-third all the nations with a rod of iron: and her child was oftne 6. caught up to God and to his throne. And the woman c n s t fled into

the wilderness, where she hath a place prepared destroy of God, that there they should nourish her a thousand this child, two hundred and threescore days. i-S 7. And war burst forth 6 in heaven: child 6 Michael and his angels had to war 6 with the dragon; rapt to And the dragon warred and his angels; and he prevailed heaven not, " d his a Neither was their place found any more in heaven. Saoed 0. And the great dragon was cast down, the old serpent, for three

He that is called the Devil and Satan, and a half

That deceiveth the whole world years into

He was cast down to the earth,

And his angels were cast down with him.

10. And I heard a great voice in heaven, saying, his angels

Now is come the salvation and the power storm after

And the kingdom of our God, and the authority of toheaicn his Christ: but are

For the accuser of our brethren is cast down, over-

Which accuseth them before our God day and night, tt""

11. And they overcame him because of the blood of the down to

Lamb, earth, 7-9

And because of the word of their testimony, Triumph

Seeing that they loved not their lives even unto death. 7 song of the 1 The position of the numeral before the noun is against our author's martyrs in usage. But this seems due to the source. heaven in c- Jpei. Here=Hebrew imperfect. honour of 1 Here ttrniite, from (mjitw, as WH. In vii. n our author uses elrn 6(in their the same sense. brethren 4 See note on chap, ii, 27 (translation), and vol. i. 75. st jll on 1 The Greek is vero. earth 6 Mtxe X Kal ol dyyexoi aflrou rou roxeaifrai. These words cannot be. explained as Greek on any hypothesis save on that of their being a slavishly " no ln r literal rendering of a vigorous Hebrew idiom. See vol. i. 321 sq. the reality 7 A pregnant expression, meaning that they esteemed life as nothing in gs comparison with loyalty to their faith, even unto martyrdom. I have rendered the ol before ofoc rr w by "seeing that" (cf. xviii. 3, xix. 3), as = in Hebrew: cf. Gen. viii. 18, xxvi. 27. This line introduces a statement of the condition under which the action denoted by the principal verb, Irtapar, took place. See Oxford Hebrew Lexicon, p, 253; Gesenius. ffeo. Gr. p. 456 (Oxford ed.).

VOL. II. 27 have al- 13. Therefore rejoice, ye heavens, and ye that dwell in them: ready ovei- Woe unto the earth and the sea; come p or the devil is gone down to you with great wrath, batan by Knowing that he hath but a short time.

coning martyrdom 13. And when the dragon saw that he was cast down to the

S tan eu e P? reecu kd e woman that had brought forth secutes Se e man And there were given to the woman the

Christian two wings of the great eagle that she might fly into the

Church, wilderness to her place, where she is nourished for a but the t j mej t j mesj an(j j, a jf a tj m e, because of 1 the serpent.

Christian 16 And e serpent cast out of his mouth after the woman

Church water as a river, that he might cause her to be swept away escapes, 16. by the flood. But the earth helped the woman, and the 3 l6 earth opened her mouth, and swallowed up the river which

Persecu- 17. the dragon cast out of his mouth. 2 And the dragon waxed
Gentile Wrot 1 e woman went awa y to ma e war
Christian the rest f her seed, which keep the commandments of
Church God, and hold the testimony of Jesus.
SATAN APPARENTLY TRIUMPHANT: THE OHUBGH ON EARTH DESTROYED.
XH 18-XIH, XIV. ld-18. (The climax of Satan's power on earth achieved in the
personal reign of the Antichrist the
Satan Roman Empire incarnated in the demonic Nero for three and stands by a half
years: the universal martyrdom of the faithful, and the e sea ", beatitude pronounced
upon them from heaven. For a summary summons of s sect on (to which xiv- I2 " J
3 belongs see vol. i. 368) see to his aid vol. i. 332 sq. The third Woe, which began
in xi. 15-19, is resumed here, though in xii. the way is prepared for this Woe by the
casting down of Satan from heaven.)
XIL 18. And he stood upon the sand of the Sea.
J Sw note in roll 330 aflf a, 1 xii. 14-16, which was written originauy of the Church
before 70 A. D,, do not admit of any intelligible interpretation in their present context,
which relates to 95 A. D. This passage, like many others, would have undergone
revision hid John had his opportunity; see vol L 299, i ad Jin. 1 332.
xm. 1-7,
THE FIRST BEAST
CHAPTER XIII.
1. And from the sea I saw a beast coming up With ten horns and seven heads, 1
And on his heads names of blasphemy.
8. And the beast which I saw was like unto a leopard, And his feet were as the feet
of a bear, And his mouth as the mouth of a lion:
And the dragon gave him his power, And his throne, and great authority. 8. And (I
saw) one of his heads slain as it were unto death; And his deadly wound was healed:
And the whole earth wondered t after the beast t; 4. And they worshipped the
dragon,
Because he had given his power to the beast;
And they worshipped the beast, saying, Who is like unto the beast? And who can
war with him?
the first Beast with seven heads and ten horns-the Roman empire incarnated in the
Neronic Antichrist, ii. 18-xiii. 2
The Beast's wound healed
Those that dwell i the worship Satan and the first 5. And there was given unto
him a mouth speaking great Beast things and blasphemies; 8 Bias- 6. And he opened
his mouth for blasphemies against God, phonies To blaspheme his name, and his
tabernacle, 4 and those that dwell in the heaven.
He rales 6 b. And there was given unto him authority to act with effect?. forty and
two months. n Sd 7. And there was given unto him to make war with the overcomes
saints, and to overcome them; the saints,
And there was given unto him authority over every tribe 5 b 7 and people and
language and nation.

1 MSS add a gloss: " And on his horns ten diadems." The position of the numeral is against our author's usage. Further, the gloss con6icts with xii. 3". Again, though the use of "diadems" is befitting in relation to the Emperors of Rome cf. xiz. 12 where Christ has " many diadems ", it is quite inapt in regard to the ten vassal kings of Parthia (xvii. 12).

Read: " when it saw the beast The Greek 6riaw row fyptov implies t corruption in the Hebrew source, nrmo (= 6rlw) is corrupt for anna = ISown or j9X6roura. See vol. i. 337. xiii. 3, 8 are a doublet of xvii. 8.

1 The three verses relating to the blasphemies of the Beast, i. e. 5 6, clearly form a tristich; and the three lines in b, 7, each beginning with xol 50ij crfry, just as clearly form another tristich. Hence I have restored 5 b to its original place.

Possibly" his shekinah." See vol. i. 352, ii. 205 sqq.

THE REVELATION OF ST. JOHN XIII. 8-18.

a And all that dwelt on the earth worshipped l him, Whose names were not written in the book of life Of the Lamb that hath been slain from the foundation of the world.

0. If any man hath an ear, let him hear.

10. If any man is for captivity, Into captivity he goeth: If any man is to be slain with the sword, With the sword must he be slain.

Here is the patience And the faith of the saints.

11. And I saw another beast coming up out of the earth: And he had two horns like a lamb, But t he spake as a dragon f. 8 18. And he exerciseth all the authority of the first beast in his sight And he maketh the earth and them that dwell in it to worship the first beast, Whose deadly wound had been healed.

18. And he doeth great signs, so that he maketh even fire to come down from heaven on the earth in the sight of 14. men. And he deceiveth them that dwell on the earth by reason of the signs that it was given him to do in the sight of the beast; saying to them that dwell on the earth, that they should set up an image 4 to the beast, 15. who had the wound of the sword, and yet lived. And it was given unto him to give breath to the image of the beast, that the image of the beast should also speak, and to cause 6 that as many as should not worship 18. the image of the beast should be killed. And he causeth martyrdom Tcxt reads of the imperfect in the source.

faithful, u See vol 353-. A alone preserves the true text here. The faith- Read: " he was a destroyer like the dragon. less receive wftg here corrupt; see vol. i. 358 sq. the mark 4 Lj t ma t image."

of the i The Greek = "And it was given unto him to give breath to the image

Beast on of beast, that the image of the beast should both speak and cause that i A "! af wy skndd ww Mp th " te. This does not represent the hand and historical fects. It is also hopelessly clumsy. I have assumed, therefore, that forehead, t) iere a Hebraism in the text akin to another we have found frequently.

10-17 j second beast was empowered to do two things: the first to give life to the image of the first beast, and the second to cause all that did not worship the image to be put to death. Thus xal roc would naturally be ai

Those whose names were not in the Book of Life worship him

Seer's admonition to be faithful in the coming persecution, 9-10

Second Beast or False Prophet from the land-the imperial priesthood, officials, and cultured classes

He makes the dwellers on the earth to worship the first Beast

His signs and deceits, 13-14

But this is a rendering of the Hebrew Cf. 4, where the past " worshipped " is rightly given.

See vol. i. 355 sq.

The Hebrew of the source all, the small and the great, and the rich and the poor, Seer's and the free and the bond, to receive 1 a mark on their admoni- 17. right hand or upon their forehead: and that no man should be able to buy or sell, save he that hath the mark, W h 0 are the name of the beast or the number of his name, to be 18. Here is wisdom. Let him that hath understanding martyred count the number of the beast; for it is the number of Third a man: and his number is Six hundred and sixty-six. 8 Beatitude

XIV. 13. Here is the patience of the saints, who keep the ad commandments of God, and the faith of Jesus. voice from 18. And I heard a voice from heaven saying, Write, Blessed ov r the are the dead which die in the Lord from henceforth: martyred yea, saith the Spirit, that they may rest from their Church, labours; 8 for their works go with them. 4 v- I2 X 3

CHAPTER XIV.

PROLEPTIG VISIONS OF THE GLORIFIED MABTYB8 IX THE MILLEN-NIAL KINGDOM, OF THE DOOM OF ROME AND OF THE HEATHEN NA-TIONS.

(This entire chapter is proleptic: that is, the orderly development of future events, as set forth in the successive visions, is here abandoned (as in vii. 9-17, xi. 1-13), and the visions of coming judgments in xvi. ly-xix., xx. 7-10, are summarised in xiv. 8-11, 14, 18-20. To this summary is prefixed a description of the blessed (i. e. the 144,000 in vii. 4-8) on Mount Zion during the Millennial reign. This is a later stage in their blessedness than that in vii. 9-17. The object of the entire chapter is to encourage the faithful to endurance in the face of the universal martyrdom just foreseen by the Seer in xiii. 15.

rocijffat, and be parallel to Sovvai that precedes. But here by a common Hebrew idiom the infinitive passes into a finite verb. Thus xal tdmhi avrj ftovrcu. ml iroiifafl is a literal rendering of vym. nns r6 jnri. In this case the imperial priesthood produce a speaking image, and cause all that do not worship it to be put to death. If we do not accept the Hebraism, then it is the image that causes the death of the faithful. But the context seems to be against this interpretation, and certainly the verse that follows is. It is the second beast in xiii. 16 thai causes all to receive the mark of the beast, and historically, as we know from Pliny, etc., it was the priesthood or official classes that did so not the images.

1 Lit. " that they should give them."

1 It is possible that ver. 18 is a later addition.

1 i e. the hardships, laborious toils incident to the life of faith.

4 i. e. not " follow after them "; see vol. i. 370. The works are the Christhke character they have achieved; see vol. i. 372 j.

THE REVELATION OF ST. JOHN XIV. 1-7.

Prolcptic vision of Christ's Kingdom with the glorified martyrs (= 144,000 that were sealed in vii. 4-7) on ML Zion in the Millennial period (= vision which comes in its due order in xx. 4-6)

The new song sang in heaven and learnt by the 144,000, a-5

Prolcptic vision of the

Evangel-isation of the world during the Millennial period, 6-7

This is done by the vision of the blessedness of the martyrs in the Millennial Kingdom, 1-5, and the vision of the doom of Rome and the heathen nations Thus Christ's Kingdom which seemed overthrown is seen in the vision to be established on earth, and Satan's Kingdom, which appeared triumphant, to be destroyed.)

L And I saw, and behold the Lamb standing on Mount Zion,

And with him a hundred and forty and four thousand, Having his name and the name of his Father written on their foreheads.

2. And I heard a voice from heaven, As the voice of many waters, And as the voice of a great thunder.

And the voice which I heard (was) as (the voice) of harpers 8. Harping with their harps, and singing as it were a new song Before the throne, and before the four living creatures and the elders.

And no one could learn the song Save the hundred and forty and four thousand: 4 C. These are they which follow the Lamb whithersoever he goeth.

4 d. These have been redeemed 1 from among men (to be) a sacrifice to God, 8 5. And in their mouth hath no falsehood been found; For they are blameless.

6. And I saw another angel flying in mid heaven, having an eternal gospel to proclaim unto them that dwell on the 7. earth, and unto every nation and tribe and tongue and people, saying with a great voice,

Fear God, and give him glory; For the hour of his judgment is come: And worship him that made the heaven And the earth and sea and fountains of waters.

1 Here it was most probably John's editor who, wrongly taking dropx to mean "first fruits 1 added the following gloss: "3. who were redeemed from the earth. 4 b. These are they who were not defiled with women; for they are virgins. 1 These clauses exclude from the 144,000 all women; for the clause " who were not defiled with women " cannot be interpreted of women even metaphorically. See vol ii. 8 sqq.

1 The redeemed are a sacrifice (dropx4) to God, but not to the Lamb. dropx4 does not mean " first fruits" here. The same interpolator who added the clauses given in note (J) has added here "and to the Lamb."

XIV. 8-14. J PUOLEPTIC VISIONS OP JUDGMENT 423

And another, a second angel, followed, saying, Proleptic

Fallen, fallen is Babylon the great, on

Which had made all the nations to drink the wine j J 1 of the wrath of her fornication. tn j of them that 9. And another angel, a third, followed them, saying with a worship great voice, the Beast If any man worshippeth the beast and his image, j JSt And receweth the 1 mark on his forehead, or upon (= vision his hand, coming in 10. He 8 shall drink of the wine of the wrath of God, order, xvi. Which is mingled sheer 8 in the cup of his anger, i7- viii), And he shall be tormented with fire and brimstone"

In the presence of the angels and of the Lamb.

1L And the smoke of their torment goeth up for everj and ever; executed

And they have no rest day nor night,

That worship the beast and his image,

And whoso receiveth the mark of his name. 4 14. And I saw, and behold, a white cloud;

And on the cloud one seated like unto a son of man, Having on his head a golden crown, And in his hand a sharp sickle. 6 1 This article is necessary; see vol. ii. 15, and text in loc, for the cursives j."" 2 and versions which support it. Jo f 5 We have here nl afrfa. Three explanations are possible, (a) The Kai is a Hebraism introducing the apodosis, and so is not to be translated; see vol. ii. p. 16. (6) It may be taken with the xal that follows in the third line as ol. d, "both. and." But this usage is not found elsewhere in our author, though it is in J. (c) It may be rendered " too." raj avvto would then ="he too." But the context is against this rendering; for it presupposes that some one else just mentioned shall drink of the wine of God's wrath But there is no such statement in xiv. 8. Besides, the phrase Ktd avrfo (in the meaning of " he too ") does not occur in our author, save in an interpolation xiv. 17, and in a Greek source xvii. n.

1 aicpdrov. Can our author have taken this word to be a rendering of-on, as the LXX in Ps. lxxiv. 9? See vol. ii. 17.

4 Ver 12-13, which pronounces the great beatitude on the martyred Church, has been restored to its original context after xiii. 18.

1 Here apparently John's editor has added 15-17, which is really a doublet of xiv. 18-20, This doublet represents the judgment as a reaping of the harvest of the wrath of God. But this figure does not belong to our author, who speaks of it as a vintage; cf. xix. 15. Besides, several constructions are against his use, and the interpolator has failed to recognise the " one like a son of man " as Christ; see vol. ii. 3, 18 (ad fin.), 21 sq. John could never have divided the Judgment between Christ and an angel or have put any angel on an equality with Chnst. It is a very stupid interpolation; for it assigns to an angel the very judgment that is to be exercised by the Word 424 THE REVELATION OF ST. JOHN XIV. 18-XV. fi.

18. And another angel 1 went forth from the altar, 1 and cried with a great voice to him that had the sharp sickle saying,

Thrust in thy sharp sickle,

And gather the clusters of the vine of the earth:

For her grapes are fully ripe.

19. And he 3 thrust his sickle into the earth, And gathered the vintage of the earth, The Son And cast it into the great winepress of the wrath of God.

treads the 80. And the winepress was trodden without the city, winepress And blood came out of the winepress even unto the wrath horses'bridles-

To a distance of one thousand six hundred furlongs.

CHAPTER XV.

XV. 2-8. (The chronological order of events in the Seer's visions of the future is here resumed. In other words, xv. 2-8 follows immediately on xiii., for xiv. broke away from this order and was wholly proleptic. xv. 2 opens with a vision of the entire martyr host, that had fallen in xiii. and are now in heaven (as in vii. 9-17) praising God for His righteousness and proclaiming the coming conversion of the nations (that had not been deceived by Rome), who would become His servants because of His righteous acts, 2-4. Thereupon follows a vision of the dooms inflicted on Rome and the nations seduced by her in the judgments of the Bowls, 5-8.) ofgodinxix. n-21. The interpolated verses (15-17) are: 15. "And another angel went forth from the temple, crying with a great voice to him that sat on the cloud,

Thrust in thy sickle and reap:

For the hour to reap hath come;

For the harvest of the earth f is dried up.

16. And he that sat on the cloud thrust in his sickle on the earth; and the earth was reaped. 17. And another angel went forth from the temple which is in heaven, he also having a sharp sickle."

1 Another, as distinct from the angels in vers. 6, 8, 9; otherwise render: "another, an angel."

1 The MSS add: " who had power over fire."

9 i. e. the Son of Man. The text reads "an angel" an interpolation due to the hand that inserted 15-17. The Son of Man is never described as an angel. It is He, and not an angel, that thrusts in the sickle and gathers the vintage of the earth. Therein xiv. 14, 18-20 is a proleptic vision of the event described in the vision in xix. 11-21 where the Word of God treads the winepress of the wrath of God.

XV. a-8. ANTHEM OF THE GLORIFIED MARTYRS 425

S. x And I saw as it were a sea of glass mingled with fire; The and them that had been victorious over the beast, and glorified over his image, and over the number of his name, m? rt y rs standing by the sea of glass, having the harps of God, fc and singing f the song of the Lamb, saying, complete,

Great and marvellous are thy works, ""5.

Lord God Almighty: gfg

Righteous and true are thy ways, His power

Thou King of the nations. and righteou- 4. Who shall not fear, 0 Lord, ness and

And glorify thy name? k; n f hl P

For thou alone art holy;

For all the nations shall come 2 3

And worship before thee; Wh sha

For thy righteous acts shall have been made manifest 6. And after these things I saw, and t the temple of the (6. tabernacle of the testimony in heaven t 8 was opened: and (during the seven angels 4 came forth from the temple clothed in fine Millennial linen, 5 pure, bright, and girt about the breasts with golden Kingdom) 7. girdles. And one of the four living creatures gave unto Vision of the seven angels seven golden bowls full of the wrath of God who liveth for ever and ever. """" c

And the temple was filled with smoke from the glory of

God, and from his power; and none could enter the temple bowk of till the seven plagues of the seven angels were finished, wrath, 5-8 receive seven 1 xv. I is an interpolation; see vol. ii. 30 sq.: "And I saw another sign in the heaven, great and marvellous, seven angels having seven plagues, (which are) the last; for in them is finished the wrath of God." This subject is not touched upon till xv. 5, as the phrase Kal perd racra ettor proves. This phrase is not used unless at the beginning of a new and important section. See vol i. 106 and footnote.

1 The text reads ml tfowtr, "and they sing" as in xiv. 3. This is the Hebrew idiom, which has already occurred frequently; see vol. i. 14 so. That this was so understood very early we see from the Versions, which render as I do in the text: i. e. Pr fl arm. We should observe the correction in K, which reads Kal Sorrat. The text here adds: "the song of Moses the servant of God and "; see, however, vol. ii. 34 sqq.

1 A meaningless expression. Either we mast excise the words: " of the tabernacle of the testimony," or, for this introduction to the Bowls go back to a Hebrew source and assume a slight corruption in the original. See vol. ii. 37 so., where it is shown that if this introduction is from a Hebrew source we should probably read: "the temple of God which is in heaven," as in xl 19. The corruption could quite easily arise.

4 Text reads: "the seven angels that had the seven plagues" a change due to the interpolator of xv. I.

See vol. ii. 38. The best MSS read Xtfor. This impossible reading appears to presuppose a murendering of the Hebrew.

CHAPTER XVI. THE SEVEN BOWU.

(These plagues are not in any sense a repetition of the seven Seals or the three Woes. Under the Seals (save in the fifth, where the prayers of the martyrs as spiritual judgments affect only the heathen), Christian and heathen alike suffer physically. The three Woes do spiritual hurt only to those who had not the Seal of God; the first two doing physical hurt as well: to those who had the Seal of God the three Woes could do no spiritual hurt, though the third could do them physical hurt Since those who had been sealed have already been martyred in xiii., the Bowls affect only the heathen world.)

First Bowl If And I heard a great voice from the temple saying poured to the seven angels, Go and pour out the seven bowls of upon the 9. the wrath of God upon l the earth. And the first went earth, i-a D0urec j ou t his bowl upon l the earth; and it became

The 8. a noisome and grievous sore upon men. 8 And the second in second poured out his bowl upon l the sea; and it became the sea, 3 blood as of a dead man; and every living soul died, (even)

Th thid " e n at were n e sea- And tne M P oure d on j he out his bowl upon the rivers and the fountains of waters, rivers and and they became blood. 8 And the fourth poured out fountains his bowl upon the sun; and it was given unto him to

The fourth 0. scorch men with fire. And men were scorched with on the sun, great heat, and they blasphemed the name of God which

"hath the power over these plagues, and they repented not

The fifth 10. to give him glory. And the fifth poured his bowl upon on the the throne of the beast; and his kingdom was darkened; tht L U. and they gnawed their tongues for pain, And they

KM i blasphemed the God of heaven because of their pains and of their sores; and they repented not of their works.

1 b, but vl in 8, 10, 12, 17 without any real difference in meaning.

8 The MSS add the following gloss: "that had the mark of the beast and that worshipped his image"; see vol. ii. 43.

1 Here follows an interpolation: "and I heard the angel of the waters saying," which is used to introduce "-7. These clauses originally followed after rbc. 4, to which context they are restored in this edition; see vol. ii. 122,8)10 Il6sq.

4 After " darkened " several clauses have been lost, in which the cause 9 of the darkness and the sufferings of mankind were given. The plague of darkness could not explain the agony of the worshippers of the Beast This plague is closely connected with the first Woe; see vol. ii, 45 sq. The phrase " because of the sores " proves that the sufferings of the subjects of the Beast cannot be explained from the text as it stands.

U. And the sixth poured out his bowl upon the great river, The sixth the Euphrates, and its waters were dried up, that the way on the might be prepared for the kings that (come) from the sun- 5 J tcs 18, rising. And I saw from the mouth of the dragon, and p art hul from the mouth of the beast, and from the mouth of the might 11 false prophet, three unclean spirits 1 going forth 8 unto march the kings of the whole world to gather them together p inst 18. unto the war of the great day of God Almighty. 8 And Sfti"

i i j i i i i i i 11 ucscrnicu they gathered them together to the place which is called more fully 17. in Hebrew Har-Magedon. And the seventh poured out inzvii. 12-his bowl upon the air; and there came forth a great! 3 7i l6) voice out of the temple, from the throne, saying, It Evil spirits 18. is done. And there followed lightnings, and voices and Jjj k thunders, and there followed a great earthquake, such as Bcastg c there has not been since men were upon the earth, so mastering 19. mighty an earthquake, so great 4 And the cities of the the nations nations fell, and Babylon the great was remembered"" before God, to give her the cup of the wine of the 90. fierceness of his wrath. And every island fled away, and 21, the mountains were not found. And great hail, (every stone) about the weight of a talent, came 5 down from follows, heaven upon men: and men blasphemed God because overthrow-of the plague of hail; for the plague thereof was 6 J? PJ f exceeding great. thc nations. 1 While our text represents God as putting it into the heart of the Parthian Babylon the two Beasts which muster the nations against Christ in xvi. 13-16; cf. for special xix. 17,19, xx. 8. judgment,

MSS add a gloss: "As it were frogs; for they are spirits of demons 18-20. working signs"; see vol. ii. 47 sq.

1 The text here reads corruptly A farotttfrrat instead of impcvfyum, which our author's usage and the context require; see vol. ii. 48 1 Here the MSS insert as xvi. 15 a verse which originally stood after iii, 3, and where it is restored in this edition. It forms the second of the seven beatitudes in our author.

4 The MSS add here: " And the great city was divided into three parts " the contents of which are against the context, while the order of the numeral is against our author's usage; see vol. ii. 52.

"cometh" Hebrew imperfect Lit "is,"

CHAPTER XVII. THE VISION AND DOOM OF HOME, xvn. 1-6, xvm.; THE INTEBPBETATION OF

THE BEAST AND OF HIS SEVEN HEADS AND TEN HOBN8, XTO. 8-17.

(These two chapters are to be taken closely together, xvii. begins with a promise on the part of the angel to show the Seer the judgment of the Great Harlot; but instead he turns aside to deal with the Beast, and the promised judgment is not witnessed till xviii. Our author is here using two sources: one embraces xvii. i-2, 3 b-6, 7, 18, and part of 8-10, xviii. (see vol ii. 55, 59 s qq 94)t wmcn was originally written when Vespasian, the sixth king, was still reigning (xvii. 10). The second is fragmentary, xvii. 11-13, 17, 1 6, and dealt with the Neronic Antichrist, the ten kings, and the destruction of Rome.)

Vision of XVIL 1. And there came one of the seven angels which had the woman the seven bowls, and he spake with me, saying, Come hither l wiu 8h W

Scarlet Th e judgment of the great harlot

Beast That sitteth upon many waters: 8. With whom the kings of the earth have committed fornication,

And with the wine of whose fornication they that dwell upon the earth have become drunken.

And he carried me away in the spirit into a wilderness: and I saw a woman sitting upon a scarlet-coloured beast, full of names of blasphemy, having seven heads and ten 4. horns. And the woman was clothed in purple and scarlet, and adorned l with gold and precious stones and pearls, having in her hand a golden cup full of abomina- 6. tionsand the unclean things 8 of her fornication. And upon her forehead (was) a name written, a mystery-

Babylon the great,

The mother of harlotries

And of the abominations of the earth.

1 Or " covered "; see note on meaning of Kexpvrwfthnj here, vol ii. 64.

1 To be taken as an ace. after ytpor, cl 3, and not as in RV.; nor as dependent on fyowo, as suggested in my note, vol. ii. 65.

1 So Tyc Pr vg arm 9. This forms a perfect parallel to " abominations." This reading of Tyc Pr vg arm may be the result of conjecture. If so, the corruption could have arisen in the Hebrew source; see vol. ii. 65.

6. And I saw the woman drunken with the blood of the saints and with the blood of the martyrs 1 of Jesus. And 7. when I saw her I wondered with a great wonder. And the angel said unto me, Wherefore didst thou wonder?

I will tell thee the mystery of the woman, and of the The beast that carrieth her, which hath the seven heads and "jeaning of the ten horns. thebeast 7 8. The beast that thou sawest was, and is not, and is about j g to come up out of the abyss, and he goeth his way into "I Jrjei perdition. And they that dwell on the earth will wonder at the (all) whose names have not been written in the book of Beast's life since the foundation of the world, when they behold tu d ra te o the beast, that 8 was, and is not, and yet is to come. 4 lb ea 9. Here (is needed) the mind which hath wisdom. The J j 867611 10. seven heads 6 are seven kings: five of them have fallen, acve are the one is, the other is not yet come, and when he kings: the 11. cometh, he must continue a short time. And the beast, sixth that was, and is not, is himself also an eighth, and is of reigns: the the seven; and he goeth his way into perdition. JSfreign 18. And the ten horns, which thou sawest, are ten kings, that but a short have received no kingdom as yet; but they will receive 6 space and authority as kings for one hour along with the beast. =- 18. These have one purpose, and they give their power and 17. authority unto the beast. 7 For God hath put it into their wno is one hearts to do his purpose, 8 and to give their kingdom unto of the 16. the beast, until the words of God should be fulfilled And ven, 11 the ten horns which thou sawest, and the beast, The ten

These shall hate the harlot, JjjJu

And make her desolate and naked, who will 1 So rightly AV. and RV. and not " witnesses "; see vol. i. 62. ind 1 It is better to follow A fordyei, "he goeth his way," here than 025. Destroy the 046 vrdy tv t "to go his way." All the time, despite his apparent recovery Q reat and triumphs, he is on the way to perdition; cf, on xvii. n. Harw T 1 Better so rendered than by " how that" (ri). I here read 6 n, not ri; Jl J J cf. drum in xvii. 11 exactly in the same sense. We have here a parody of the ' divine name: " Which is, and which was, and which is to come (i. 4, iv. 8).

4 Tdpcarcu is here=Aetf rcu (a form our author does not use, though he uses other tenses of fyx 0 aq d eaeifrrereu (xx. 8)).

8 A gloss here follows: "arc seven mountains on which the woman sitteth and they." This is a second explanation thrust in from the margin.

Text="receive."

7 The text is dislocated and glossed. 17 is to be read immediately after 13 and next 16. 14 follows on 16, because 14 records the destruction of the forces which according to 17, 16 are to destroy Rome. 15 is a gloss on xvii. i. "And he said unto me, The waters which thou sawest, where the harlot sitteth, are peoples, and multitudes, and nations, and tongues "; see vol. ii. 61, 71 sq, 74- 8 Text adds here an early gloss or doublet: " and to do one purpose "; see TO!, ii. 73.

THE REVELATION OF ST. JOHN XVIIt

And be themselves destroyed by the Lamb and the Saints, judgment implied in xix. 13) woman

Rome

And they shall eat her flesh And burn her with fire.

Rome has Men, for she hath corrupted all the earth, 1-3 14. These shall war against the Lamb, And the Lamb shall overcome them, For he is Lord of lords, and King of kings; And they that are with him, called and elect and faithful, (shall overcome). 1 18. And the woman, whom thou sawest, is the great city, which reigneth over the kings of the earth.

CHAPTER XVIIL THE DOOM 07 BOMB.

(This chapter deals with the doom of Rome, a vision of which had been promised by the angel to the Seer in xvii. i. With the exception of a few clauses, it comes from a source which our author has already laid under contribution in xvii. i-io, 18; see vol. il 94. It was written in the time of Vespasian, and several clauses survive attesting that period; see vol. ii. 93.) 1. After these things I saw another angel coming down from heaven, having great authority; and the earth was 2. lighted up by his glory. And he cried with a mighty voice, saying,

Fallen, fallen is Babylon the great, And has become a habitation for demons, And a hold of every unclean and hateful spirit, And a hold of every unclean and hateful bird 8

For of the wine 4 of her fornication hath she caused all the nations to drink; 5 1 Understand runfffoupw, rather than what I have proposed in vol. ii. 75. After 14 the text inserts what was originally a gloss on xvii. I, i. e. 15. See note 7, p. 429.

8 Text of this and the next line doubtful. I have followed A minp" 0 gig arm 4.

1 This line conflicts with the statement in xix. 3, according to which the smoke of Rome's burning is to go up for ever and ever. But this is due to the fact that xviii. is an early source used by our author, whereas xix. comes from his own hand.

K 046 Tyc s read: "wine of the wrath of her fornication." I have followed 325 (?)Pr and s l.

So a few cursives and s 1 (Ttrructv). This reading explains the impossible readings of the Uncials. This clause expresses the very same idea that is expressed passively in xvii 2 b: lwltfrfproi. fr roc ofrou rfr cf. xiv. 8.

For 1 the kings of the earth committed fornication with her, And the merchants of the earth waxed rich through the wealth of her wantonness.

4. And I heard another voice from heaven, saying, bwwch

Come forth from her, my people, theithful

That ye may have no fellowship with her sins,

And that ye receive not of her plagues. 0; nlo 5. For her sins have reached unto heaven, brance And God hath remembered her iniquities.

6. Render unto her even as she hath rendered, 1 And double (unto her) double according to her works: J-In the cup which she hath mingled, mingle unto me ntand" her double. her destruc- 7. In the measure in which she hath glorified herself don by and played the wanton, In that measure give her torment and t mourning f. 8

Because she saith in her heart, I sit as a queen,

And am no widow,

And I shall not see t mourning f. 4 8. Therefore in one day shall her plagues come, t Pestilence and mourning and famine t 6 1 See note in loc. 3 U are circumstantial clauses introduced by ml (= Hebrew)), which state the conditions under which the action described in 3 takes place. See notes on xn. n c, xix. 3, and see Oxford Heb. Lexicon, p. 253. Hence U=" seeing that," "for." The Greek aonsts are rendered by English aonsts (frbpneixrw. frxoisnproi), as Babylon is regarded as a thing of the past in these verses. In 3 the perfect is rightly used, since the results of "the wine of fornication" are enduring in the present. But in 4 sqq. the standpoint of the Seer changes. Babylon is still conceived as in being. The Greek aonsts that follow have therefore frequently to be construed by the English perfect.

This statement points to a source. The faithful have all suffered martyrdom. See vol. ii. 96 ad fin.

1 TMot ("mourning") is an idea foreign to the context here and in 8 b. It is not " mourning, " but destruction that awaits Rome. Since rlrfof = V? M, the latter may be corrupt for rn or iwK=dir(ixeto = " destruction." The same corruption is implied by the LXX in Jer. xii. n. Hence for " mourning" read "destruction." This explanation is better than that suggested in vol. ii. 100.

4 Read "destruction," as in 7.

1 First of all the order seems wrong. Almost invariably in the OT. we have "famine and pestilence." Here again "mourning" cannot be right As in 7 kf we should read "destruction." Thus we should have "famine, and pestilence, and destruction."

And she shall be burnt with fire;

For strong is the God who hath judged her.

9. And the kings of the earth who committed fornication an(ve wanton ty w tn ner s wee P d! vcr her, when they look upon the smoke of her burning, 9-10 10. Standing afar off for the fear of her torment, saying,

Woe, woe to the great city,

Babylon the strong city,

For in one hour is thy judgment come.

Dirge of n. And the merchants of the earth shall weep and mourn merchants Over her ' n. ri For no man buyeth their merchandise any more 12. Merchandise of gold and silver, and precious stone and pearls,

And fine linen and purple, and silk and scarlet, And all thyine wood, and every vessel of ivory, and every vessel of most precious wood, 8 And brass, and iron, and marble, 13. And cinnamon, and spice, and incense, And ointment, and frankincense, and wine, And oil, and fine flour, and wheat,

And beasts, and sheep, 8 and souls of men. 4 16. The merchants of these things, who were made rich by her, shall stand afar off for the fear of her torment, 16. weeping and mourning, Saying, Woe, woe to the great city, That was clothed in fine linen and purple and scarlet, And adorned with gold, and precious stone, and pearl;

For in one hour are so great riches laid waste.

Dirge of 17. And every ship master, and every one that saileth any nit 6 1 " whither, 5 and mariners, and as many as gain their 17-19 18i liv " 1 8 bv the sea stocxi afar off And cried as th? v to 0 upon the smoke of her burning, saying, What (city) is like 1 23, which is quite impossible in 23 and cannot be satisfactorily restored elsewhere in this chapter, is best explained as a gloss on 1I. It runs: "For the princes of the earth were thy merchants." In my text and commentary I have inserted it after 11.

1 A 2040 vg eth read " stone."

1 The MSS add here: " and horses and chariots and slaves. 0 See vol. it 102 for the grounds for the excision of these words.

4 Ver. 14 is transposed after 21 in this edition. See vol. ii. 105, 108.

1 The text seems corrupt here. Pr bo sa presuppose tvl 6vt instead of iwl rbrov. Hence render " that saileth on the sea, see vol. ii. 105 sq.

19. the great city? And they cast dust on their heads, and they cried, weeping and mourning, saying,

Woe, woe to the great city,

Wherein were made rich all that had their ships at sea; For in one hour are her precious things laid waste. 1 81. And a strong angel took up a stone, as it were a great Sadden millstone, and cast it into the sea, saying, tionot

Thus with violence shall be cast down Babylon, the great city, And shall no more be found. 8 14. And the fruits which thy soul lusted after of

Are gone from thee: c er Seer

And all the dainties and the splendours Rome, 14,

Are perished from thee. 4 22, 23 1 88-b- d. And the voice of the harpers and singers Shall be heard no more in thee; 6 And the voice 6 of the flute players and trumpeters

Shall be heard no more in thee.

83. And the voice of the bridegroom and the bride

Shall be heard no more in thee; 88 f. And no craftsmen of whatever craft

Shall be found any more in thee. 88 h. And the voice of the millstone

Shall be heard no more in thee: 88 b. And the light of the lamp

Shall shine no more in thee.

1 On the restoration of this verse see vol. ii. 106. Ver. 20 is restored tt the close of 23-b. On the restored order see vol. ii. 92 sq.

1 Or " with indignation." But the meaning is doubtful.

1 The beginning of the next dirge appears to be lost. On the reconstructed order of this dirge, see vol. ii. 92 sq., 108 sqq.

4 The text adds: "And they shall no more find them " (=-np OIN? nvl); but this is possibly a corrupt form of the line, which is lacking in 22 and which I have restored (i. e.-ny p VHT). But probably it is an interpolation; for elsewhere in this source i8 a w ov is always followed by the subjunctive, whereas here it is the indicative; cf. xviii. 21, 22 (ter), 23 (bis).

lowrtcfli'ssoTtf (see LXX Ezek. xxvi. 13, Sir. xxxv. 3, 5), corrupt for nnrfss" singers."

Restored as the context requires. See vol. ii. 109. It is noteworthy that the Ethiopia Version has made the same restoration, see vol ii 352. VOL. II. 28

Seer's ftp- 90. Rejoice over her, thou heaven, peal to the And ye saints, and ye apostles, and ye prophets; inhabitants p or Q gj ven j u dg men t in your cause against her.

to rejoice D8 f. For with tor 1 sorcery were all the nations deceived.

over the 94. And in her was found the blood of the prophets and doom of 23 S 4 And of a11 that had been slain u P n the earth-

CHAPTER XIX.

(Response of the heavenly host to the appeal of the Seer just made first of a mighty multitude praising God for His judgment of the Harlot City, and His avenging His servants' blood at her hands, 1-3; next of the Elders and Cherubim and of the Altar, which in like manner praise Him for that, having poured out the blood of the saints, they were made to drink each other's blood, 4, xvl 5 b-7; and, finally, of the martyrs themselves, who offer their thanksgivings, for that now the Lord God Almighty has become King and that the Bride is now ready, xix. 5-7. The Bride will appear clothed in keeping with her character, 8. Thereupon the fourth Beatitude is pronounced, 9. At this stage a vision of the destruction of the Parthian kings is to be expected (see vol ii. 114 adinit., 117 admit., and note i on ii. 436). Now that Rome and the Parthians have been destroyed, there remains only the judgment of the kings of the earth who had shared in the abominations of Rome. These are slain by Christ, and the Beast and False Prophet are cast into the lake of fire, 11-20.)

Response 1. After these things I heard as it were a great voice of a of heaven mighty multitude in heaven, saying,

Seer's Hallelujah;

Salvation, and glory, and power, belong to our God: 9. For true and righteous are his judgments; on God's For he hath judged the great harlot,

Jlsr 611 That corru P te t 16 earth with her fornication, of Rome, And he hath aven g e(j foe blood of his servants at her hand 8. And again they said:

Hallelujah; For 4 her smoke goeth up for ever and ever.

1 Text reads corruptly " thy." It. roxXto.

1 A perfect with an aorist meaning.

4 ml to be taken as a Hebraism; see vol, fa. 120,

Xtt. 4-0. SONGS OF ELDERS, CHERUBIM, MARTYRS 435 4. And the four and twenty elders and the four living Song of creatures fell down and worshipped God that sitteth on the Elders the throne, saying,

Amen, Hallelujah; praising

XVL 6 b-. Righteous art thou, which art and which wast. 1

Holy, in that thou hast thus judged: hath made 6. Because they poured out the blood of saints and prophets, saints, to

Thou hast given them blood also to drink: slay each

They are worthy."

7. And I heard the altar saying, xvit " 6 Yea, 0 Lord God Almighty, The True and righteous are thy judgments. j 7 vindicated 5. And a voice came forth from the throne, saying, by God, Praise our God, all ye his servants, and bidden

And ye who fear him, small and great.? fier 6. And I heard as it were the voice of a great multitude, Uuv.

as the voice of many waters, and as the voice of mighty mi 5 thunders, saying, Response

Hallelujah: of the

For the Lord God Almighty hath become King. martyr 7. Let us be glad and rejoice, h. ost. And give unto him the glory: SSelujah For the marriage of the Lamb hath come, in that And his bride 8 hath made herself ready. God has become

Yea, it hath been given unto her to clothe herself kin the In fine linen bright, pure. 4 rfuhe 8"

9. And he saith unto me, Blessed are they which are called comc and to the marriage supper of the Lamb. 6 the Bride made herself ready, 6-8 1 On the restoration of xvi. 5 b-7 to its original context, see vol. ii. 116, Fourth 120-124. Beatitude

On the technical meaning of this phrase, see vol. ii. 123. on those il yw i avrov; see vol. ii. 127. invited to 4 Text adds an incorrect gloss: "for the fine linen is the righteous acts of the the saints "; see vol. ii. 127 sq. Rather " the fine linen " is the result of such Marriage righteous acts, that is, the spiritual bodies in which the saints are clothed. Supper of

Text adds here a doublet of xxii. 6, 8-9. 9 b. " And he saith to me, these the Lamb are true words of God. 10. And I fell down before his feet to worship him. T f And he saith to me, See thou do it not. I am a fellow-servant with thee and with thy brethren that have the testimony of Christ: worship God: for the Jut testimony of Jesus is the spirit of prophecy." See vol. ii. 128 sqq."

THE REVELATION OF ST. JOHN XIX. 11-lfi.

destruction of the Parthian referred to in xvii. 14)

A Divine

Warrior followed armies of heaven, 11-14(1 judgment prolepti- cally described inxiv. 14, 18-20)

Smites with a sharp sword the nations and treads the winepress of the wrath of God-bearing the name of King of kings and Lord of lords, 15-16

Birds of prcy, summoned to feast on the slain

Beast and False Prophet overthrown and cast into the lake of fire, 17-18 Ifl.

And I saw the heaven opened; And behold, a white horse,

And he that sat thereon Faithful and True; J And in righteousness he doth judge and make war.

And his eyes are as a flame of fire, And on his head are many diadems; 8

And he is clothed in a garment dipped in blood: And his name is called The Word of God.

And the armies which are in heaven follow him on white horses, Being clothed in fine linen, white, pure.

And from his mouth proceedeth a sharp sword, That with it he should smite the nations:

And he shall break them with an iron rod: And he treadeth the winepress of the fierce wrath of God Almighty.

And he hath on his thigh a name written,

KING OF KINGS AND LORD OF LORDS.

And I saw an angel standing in the sun; and he cried with a great voice, saying to all the birds that fly in mid heaven, Come, gather yourselves together to the 18. great supper of God; That ye may eat the flesh of kings, and the flesh of captains, and the flesh of mighty men, and the flesh of horses and of them that sit thereon, and the flesh of all men, both free and bond, and small and great.

19. And I saw the beast, and the kings of the earth, and their armies, gathered together to make war against him 1 1 have indicated a lacuna here. Where xix. 9 b-io stands we should expect a vision relating to the destruction of the Parthian kings a destruction prophesied in xvii. 14 (see vol. li. 116 ad fin.) and implied by the epithet prtawttw in xix. 13 (see vol. ii. 133). This vision appears to have been displaced by the interpolation, o, b-io. The subjects of all other proleptic visions are rehandled in other visions in their due order. Hence we expect a vision on the destruction of the Parthian kings here in its chronological order.

046 alp and many versions read " called Faithful and True."

1 Here the MSS add an interpolation: " Having a name written which no man knoweth save he himself." It is an anacolouthon: it forms a break in the thought and is contradicted by what follows; see vol. ii. 132.

4 See note on xii. 5 (translation); also vol. i. 75 sq.

1 Text adds: " his raiment and on," see vol. ii. 137.

90. that sat upon the horse, and against his army. And the Their allies beast was taken, and with him the false prophet that diip and wrought the signs before him, wherewith he deceived jj them that had received the mark of the beast, and them ltn by that worshipped his image: they twain were cast alive birds of 21. into the lake of

fire that burneth with brimstone. And P r y. the rest were slain with the sword of him that sat upon the horse, (even the sword) which came forth out of his mouth: and all the birds were filled with their flesh.

CHAPTERS XX.-XXIL (The traditional order of the text in these three chapters is intolerably disordered and hopelessly unintelligible. The present editor has restored. so far as he can, the order of the text as it left the hand of the Seer. See vol. ii. 144-154. The restored order is given on pp. 153-154. On line 12 (p. 154) delete 6 a, and on line 17 insert 5 before 6 b-8.)

CHAPTER XX. 1-3, 1-3. (Satan chained for a thousand years, and the nations set free from his deceivings.) 1. And I saw an angel coming down from heaven, Chaining

Having the key of the abyss? f Satan

And a great chain in his hand.

8. And he laid hold on the dragon, the old serpent, Which is the Devil and Satan, And bound him for a thousand years: 3. And he cast him into the abyss, And shut and sealed (it) over him, That he should no more deceive the nations Till the thousand years should be fulfilled.

After this he must be loosed for a little time.

THE REVELATION OF ST. JOHN XXT 0-17.

Vision of the Heavenly Jerusalem the seat of Christ's Kingdom on earth for 1000 yean ments

CHAPTER XXI. 9-27.

ft,14-16,17. (Vision of the Heavenly Jerusalem, which descends from heaven and settles on the ruined site of the earthly Jerusalem. This Heavenly City is at once the scat of the Messianic Kingdom, the abode of the glorified martyrs, and the centre of the evangelising agencies of the surviving nations on the earth, during the millennial period. Though it is not stated, we must conclude that alike the glorified martyrs and the Heavenly Jerusalem are withdrawn from the earth before the final judgment.

The tree of life (xxii. 2, 14) appears to be for the new converts (xxii. 2; cf. xi. 15, xiv. 6, 7, xv. 3, 4) and not for the martyrs, since the martyrs are already clothed with their heavenly bodies and are not subject to the second death. They had already eaten of it in the Paradise of God (u. 7).

As one of the seven angels of the Bowls showed Rome the capital of the kingdom of the Antichrist to the Seer (xvii. i), so lie now shows him the heavenly Jerusalem.) 9. And there came one of the seven angels who had the seven bowls, which were full of the seven last plagues; and he spake with me, saying, Come hither, I will show thee the bride, the wife of the Lamb.

10. And he carried me away in the Spirit to a mountain great and high, and showed me the holy city Jerusalem,

U. coming down out of heaven from God, Having the glory of God: her light was like unto a stone most precious, as it were a jasper stone, clear as crystal 19. She had a wall great and high; she had twelve gates, and at the gates twelve angels; and names written thereon, which are the names of the twelve tribes of 13. the children of Israel. On the east were three gates; and on the north three gates; and on the south three 14. gates; and on the west three gates. And the wall of the city had twelve foundations, and on them the 16. twelve names of the twelve apostles of the Lamb.

And he that spake with me had for a measure a golden reed to measure the city, and the gates thereof, and the 16. wall thereof. And the city lieth foursquare, and the length thereof is as great also as the breadth; and he measured the city with the reed, twelve thousand furlongs: the length and the breadth and the height 17. thereof are equal. And he measured the wall thereof, a hundred and forty and four cubits, according to the measure of a man, that is, of an angel.

18. And the building of the wall thereof was jasper:

And the city was pure gold, like unto pure glass: Itsglorioui 19. And 1 the foundations of the wall of the city were cturc adorned with all manner of precious stones. appear

The first foundation was jasper; the second, sapphire; ance the third, chalcedony; 20. The fourth, emerald; the fifth, sardonyx; the sixth, sardius; The seventh, chrysolite; the eighth, beryl; the ninth, topaz; The tenth, chrysoprase; the eleventh, jacinth; the twelfth, amethyst 81. And the twelve gates were twelve pearls; Each one of the gates was of one pearl, And the street of the city was pure gold, transparent as glass. 2 22. And I saw no temple therein: No tc J"P lc For the Lord God Almighty is the temple thereof, JJJ And the Lamb is the ark of the covenant thereof 8. nor sun 23. And the city hath no need of the sun, nor yet of the r g n moon, to shine upon it: Ji ht, but

For the glory of the Lord doth lighten 4 it, God

And the lamp thereof is the Lamb.

84. And the nations shall walk by the light thereof: Umb

And the kings of the earth do bring their glory into it. Its g tes 26. And the gates thereof shall not be shut day or night. 6 " 0 1 Though A 025. 046 omit, it seems best, with Pr (gig) arm s 1- bo eth nations to read the copula. Ol ll? c 8 Or, " as it were transparent glass." eartn 1 A probable restoration; the original is lost. The English versions conceal this loss by transposing the words "And the Lamb" into the preceding sentence. Cf. xi. 19, where the temple and the ark of the covenant are spoken of as the headcentres of the manifestations of God. In the Heavenly Jerusalem God takes the place of the first, and the Lamb that of the second; see vol. ii. I7osq.

4 tt rruw is either the Greek timeless aorist, Moulton, Gr. 135 sq.; Robertson, Gr. 836 sq., or it is in our author's mind a rendering of the timeless Hebrew perfect a very common usage.

1 The text reads: " for there shall be no night there " a corruption due in part to xxii. 5. As in Isa. Ix II, the text clearly ran as I have emended: "Thy gates. shall not be shut day or night." The alternations of day and night still prevail on the earth. It is otherwise in xxii. J, where the New Jerusalem has come down from God to the new and glorified earth. Besides, the parallelism is against it; see vol. ii. 173.

THE REVELATION OF ST. JOHN XXII. 1-17.

86. And they shall bring the glory and the honour of the nations into it: 97. And there shall not enter into it t anything unclean or one t l that maketh an abomination or a lie: But only they that are written in the Lamb's book of life.

The river and tree of life

Fifth Beatitude for those who cleanse themselves and so have access to the tree of life in the City Invitation of the Spirit and the Bride

CHAPTER XXII. 1-2, 14-15, 17.

1. And he showed me a river of water of life, bright as crystal, 8. Proceeding out of the throne of God and of the Lamb, In the midst of the street thereof: And on this side of the river and on that was the tree 2 of life,

Bearing twelve (manner of) fruits, Yielding its fruit every month: And the leaves of the tree were for the healing of the nations.

14. Blessed are they that wash their robes,

That they may have the right to the tree of life, And may enter in by the gates into the city.

15. Without are the dogs, and the sorcerers,

And the fornicators, and the murderers, and the idolaters, And every one that loveth and maketh a lie.

17. And the Spirit and the bride 8 say, Come. And let him that heareth say, Come. And let him that is athirst come: Whosoever willeth let him take the water of life freely.

1 Primitive corruption for "any that is unclean or," cf, xrii. 15. Only persons are contemplated as the next line shows.

8 The term is u ed genetically. The text implies that there are two rows of trees, one on either side of the river; see vol. ii 176.

Since the term "bride" designates the Heavenly Jerusalem in our author (cf. xxi. 2, 9), it has no doubt the same meaning here, but the idea of the Christian community rather than of the city is here brought forward; see vol ii. 179.

CHAPTER XX. 4-15.

XX. 4-6. (Vision of the glorified martyrs who reign with Christ for a thousand years.) 4 c- And I saw the souls of them that had been Ki beheaded for the witness of Christ, of

And for the word of God, on earth, 4-6

And l had not worshipped the beast, Nor yet his image,

And had not received the mark upon their forehead And upon their hand; 4- b. And I saw thrones, and they seated themselves thereon, And judgment was given unto them. 1

And they lived and reigned with Christ a thousand years. 8 6 b. This is the first resurrection.

6. Blessed and holy is he that hath part in the first sixth resurrection: Beatitude

Over these the second death hath no power: the blessed-

But they shall be priests of God and of Christ, ness

And shall reign with him a thousand years. tha hlve part in

XX. 7-10. (Close of the Millennial Kingdom and of its the first evangelizing activities. Thereupon follows the loosing of Satan, esurrcc-the march of Gog and Magog against the beloved city, their llon destruction by supernatural means, and the casting of Satan into the lake of fire. The Seer does not say what became of the Heavenly Jerusalem, but its withdrawal from the earth before Ihe final judgment is presupposed. Since "the beloved city" in xx. 9 is the Heavenly Jerusalem, the saints referred to in the same verse must include the risen martyrs.) 7. And when the thousand years are fulfilled, Satan a Satan shall be loosed out of his prison, And shall loosed: his final 1 Text reads: "and that"; but see vol. ii. 183. efforts and 1

This couplet occurs immediately at the beginning of ver. 4, where alike overthrow, the context and the grammar are against them. 7-10 1 Here follows an interpolation, as Mr. Marsh has suggested: 5. "The rest of the dead lived not till the thousand years were fulfilled. See Greek text in he. By its removal the symmetry of the text is restored seven successive couplets.

come forth to deceive the nations which are in the four corners of the earth, Gog and Magog, to gather them together to the war: the number of whom is as 9. the sand of the sea. And they went 1 up over the breadth of the earth, and compassed the camp of the saints about, and the beloved city: and fire came down 10. out of heaven, and devoured them. And the devil that deceived them was cast into the lake of fire and brimstone, where are also the beast and the false prophet; and they shall be tormented day and night for ever and ever.

, 11-15. (Vision of the great throne and of Him that sat thereon, before whose presence the former heaven and the former earth forthwith vanish. Judgment of the dead. Death and hell cast into the lake of fire.)

Resurrec- H And I saw a great white throne, and him that sat tionofthe thereon; dead and And f rom his face the earth and the heaven fled away, judgment, And no P 1 06 was found for them

"-13 18. And I saw the dead, the great and the small, 8 standing before the throne, And books were opened: and another book was opened, which is (the book) of life:

And the dead were judged out of the things written in the books. 8 18. And the treasuries 4 gave up the dead which were in them; 4 1 The past verbs in 20 lte are to be explained from our author's use of Hebrew idiom, according to which Hebrew perfects (or imperfects with vav conversive) represent vividly the future events as things already accomplished.

8 Our author elsewhere writes: "the small and the great"; see vol. li. 194.

1 Tautological interpolation added here: " according to their works. 1 4 The text here reads " sea," but the context requires a reference to the abode of righteous souls, since Hades is the abode in our author only of wicked souls, and as such is cast into the lake of fire, xx. 14. The change of " treasuries " the normal word in Judaism (50-100 A. D.) for the abode of righteous souls, or of "mansions 1 (John xiv. 2), or "Paradise" (?) into " sea " was made in the interests of a bodily resurrection. But the sea has already vanished with the first heaven and earth (ver. n, xxi. i). According to the transmitted text only wicked souls have part in the General Resurrection and Final Judgment In 4 Ezra vii. the text dealing with the General Resurrection and Final Judgment has also been tampered with, with a view to enforcing belief in a physical resurrection The result of the tampering with the two texts is interesting: while m the Apocalypse only the wicked rise and are judged, in 4 Ezra only the righteous rise and are judged! see vol. ii. 194-198.

And death and Hades gave up the dead which were in them: And they were judged every man according to their works.

14. And death and Hades were cast into the lake of fire. 1 End of And all that were not found written in the book of life Jeat h and Were cast into the lake of fire.

XXL5 ft,4 d,5 b; XXL 1-4-; XXII. 3-6. (Declaration by God that the former things have passed away and that He creates all things new. Forthwith the Seer sees the new heaven and the new earth and the New 2 Jerusalem coming down, adorned as a bride for her husband. God tabernacles with men. No more grief or pain or tears or death. All the faithful are to reign with Christ for ever and ever (xxii. 5), whereas in the Millennial Kingdom only the risen martyrs were to reign for a thousand years.) 5. And he that sat upon the throne said, God 4 d. The former things have passed away; J? kes dl 5 b. Behold, I make all things new. 8 g new

XXI. 1. And I saw a new heaven and a new earth; New

For the first heaven and the first earth had passed heaven away; and new

Nor is there any more sea.

1 Text adds here a marginal gloss: " this is the second death, the lake of fire 1 drawn from xxi. 8f., where the clause is full of meaning; but it is wholly out of place here with regard to death and Hades.

8 Even the Heavenly City of xxi. 10, which had been withdrawn from the earth before the Judgment with Christ and the saints, is renewed or displaced by one of a higher nature.

Text contains the following intrusion: 5. " And he saith, Write: for these things are faithful and true. 6. And he said unto me, They have become." xxi. S doublet of xxii. 6 is in this edition restored after xxii 5 and immediately before xxi. 6 b. See next page. Hence correct note in vol. ii. 203 ad fin. 6 is an interpolation. The Seer does not require such an assurance in confirmation of God's own words. Nothing can intervene between the declaration of God, "Behold I make all things new," and the Seer's immediate recognition of their fulfilment: " And I saw a new heaven," cf. Gen. i. 3, "And God said, Let there be light: and there was light." This interpolation, xxi. 6, "And he said unto me, They have become," is an extremely idle one even with the traditional order of the text; for the Seer needs no such assurance, since tx kypotkesi he has in vision already seen the new heaven and the new earth and the New Jerusalem descending on the new Earth, xxi. 1-3. Further in xxi. b the words tta wd TOW rdrra do not refer to an accomplished fact, which the traditional order presupposes. If the Seer had so intended he would have said Mob? mrobpra vdrra (cf. iii. 8, tfod ftwa). These words refer to the present creative act. Hence the new creation, xxi. 1-3, follows after xxi. 5 b, and the Seer in the vision sees God's words at once translated into fact Cf. i Enoch xiv. 22 rfif Xdyos afroo tpyor.

444 REVELATION OF ST. JOHN XXI. 3-4; XXII. 3-5.

The New 9. And the holy city, New Jerusalem, I saw,

Jerusalem Coming down out of heaven from God,

Made ready as a bride adorned for her husband.

3. And I heard a great voice from the throne saying,

Behold, the tabernacle 1 of God is with men,

God And he shall dwell with them, dwells And they shall be his people, 8

Wlth racn And he shall be their God. 8 4. And God shall wipe away every tear from their cy t

Blessed- b. And death shall be no more: ness of, Neither shall there be mourning, nor crying, nor

G(X pain any more,

JEJJJJh, o. XXTT. 3. Neither shall there be any more curse.

"k 3-5 And the throne of God and of the Lamb shall be in it: And his servants shall serve him, 4. And they shall see his face,

And his name shall be on their foreheads.

5. And there shall be no more night,

And they have no need of light of lamp or light of sun, For the Lord God shall cause (his face) to shine upon them: 4 And they shall reign for ever and ever.

EPILOGUE AT THE GLOBE OF JOHNS VISION.

God's XXI 6 C, 6 b-8. (God's testimony to John's book: His testimony message to all men.) bokd XXI- 5- An H C saith, Write; for these words are faithful His and true.

6 b. I am the Alpha and the Omega, divine The beginning and the end: sonship I will give to him that thirsteth of the fountain of the

UUd. water oflife freely.

for the l t OK is probably "the Shekinah." There is no real English unfaithful equivalent. Perhaps we might render: " the Presence of God is with men "; the second or " the dwelling of God." In no case has "tabernacle " its ecclesiastical death, xxi. meaning or its traditional associations; see vol. it 205 sq. 5 6 b-8 See vol. ii. 207: crit. note on this line.

See vol. ii. 207 sq.: crit. note.

4 See vol. ii. 210 sq. tjharlfcif can, of course, be used intransitively, but John uses it only actively elsewhere: zviii. I, zxi. 23. Otherwise render: " shall shine upon them But in this sense we find urifetr with the dat 7. He that overcometh shall inherit these things, And I will be his God,

And he shall be my son.

8. But for the cravenhearted and unbelieving, And abominable and murderers,

And fornicators and sorcerers,

And idolaters and all liars

Their part shall be in the lake that burneth with fire and brimstone: Which is the second death.

CHAPTER XXII.

XXTT. 6-7, IB 16,13,12,10. (Here more than anywhere else in chaps, xx.-xxii. we have the disjecta membra of the Poet-Seer. I have restored the order of this section tentatively as above, xxii. u, i8 b-i9 are relegated to the footnotes as interpolations. See vol. ii. 211-213, 217.) (Christ's testimony to John's book: His speedy coming.) 6. And he said unto me, These words are faithful and Christ true: and the Lord, the God of the spirits of prophets, sent his angel to show unto his servants the 7. things which must shortly come to pass. And behold, 6-7,18 I come quickly. Blessed is he that keepeth the words seventh of the prophecy of this book. 1 Beatitude 18 l. To every one that heareth I testify the words of the prophecy of this book. 2 1 This sentence forms the seventh beatitude. There is a certain fitness in the order of the seven. The first (i. 3) declares the blessedness of those who read and keep the prophecy: the second (iii. 3, i. e., xvi. 15) of him who watcheth and keepeth his garments: the third (xiv. 12-13) f th se w. no die in the Lord: the fourth (xix. 9) of those who having so died are invited to the marriage supper of the Lamb: the fifth (xxii. 14) of those who had washed their garments that they might have access to the tree of life in the heavenly city: the sixth (xx. 6) of those who have actually part in the first resurrection: the seventh (xxii. 7) of those who keep the words of this Book.

s The following interpolation is inserted here: i8 b. If any man shall add unto them, God shall add unto him the plagues which are written in this book. 19. And if any man shall take away from the words of the book of this prophecy, God shall take away his part from the tree of life, and out of the holy city, which are written in this book "; see vol. ii. 222-224.

THE REVELATION OF ST. JOHN XXII 16-21.

His speedy

Advent

John's testimony: angel worship forbidden, xxii,8-9

Christ's final words and John's prayer and benediction, 20-21 16. I Jesus have sent mine angel to testify these things unto you in l the Churches: I am the root and the offspring of David, The bright and the morning star.

18. I am the Alpha and the Omega, The first and the last, The beginning and the end.

18. Behold, I come quickly; And my reward is with me, To render to each man according as his work is.

10. And he saith unto me, Seal not up the words of the prophecy of this book; for the time is at hand. l

XXTT. 8-9,80-81. (John's testimony: the closing words.) 8. And I John am he that heard and saw these things. And when I heard and saw, I fell down to worship before the feet of the angel which showed me these things. 9. And he saith unto me, See thou do it not: I am a fellow-servant with thee and with thy brethren the prophets, and with them which keep the words of this book: worship God.

80. He which testifieth these things saith, Yea: I come quickly.

Amen: come, Lord Jesus.

81. The grace of the Lord Jesus be with all the saints.

Amen. 8 l if. So A, etc. Other authorities hi =' concerning. M l Here the text adds: II. He that is unrighteous, let him do unrighteousness still: And he that is filthy, let him be made filthy still: And he that is righteous, let him do righteousness still: And he that is holy, let him be made holy still.

This verse refers to the Seer's contemporaries, and declares that the time for repentance is past. But, since xxi. 6-8 refer also to his contemporaries, there is still hope for them, if they repent; see vol. u. 221 sq.

l The text of this verse is very uncertain. I have followed AN in reading " the Lord Jesus." The fuller tide, "Lord Jesus Christ," has the support of 046 and most cursives, while the form " our Lord Jesus Christ" has the support of some cursives and nearly all the versions. Again, the Apocalypse cannot have ended with the words "with all" (A vg). Such a grace would be wholly it variance with the thought of the Seer. Only the saints or those seeking to be saints can receive such grace. Hence the reading of A vg is simply defective, and the choice must he between the reading of N (gig) "with the saints" and that of 046 sw- arm- bo "with all the saints." This last is most in keeping with our author's views: cf. viii. 3.

APPENDIX.

FOUR PAPYRUS AND VELLUM FRAGMENTS OF THE APOCALYPSE.
FRAGMENT I. (=
P. Oxy. viii. 1079.
(Late 3rd or 4th Cent Verso of a papyrus roll with Exodus on recto (ed. Hunt, 1911).)

TCUS cv TT; Ao ia x a p fywv KCU

Vf OTTO 0 (I)v K(U 0 Tjv fcCU 0 Cp Oic vos cat cwro T OV cirra irvcvia TOIV (?) crfwjTriov TOV dpovov av 5, TJov icat atTo IT; Xp o taprvs o irt crros o TrpaitOTOKos TCDV veicpo)

KOLL o ap aiv Td)v 3a(ri wv TTS

TO ayairwvti ipis icai Xvo-avri 17 ula? CK TDV axaprccuy IJAUV cv 6. r a atfuitt avrov KOI ctrottjo-cv j8a cr ta tav icpcts TOV 1 dvu) 2 xat avtoju avrw TO icpatOS KOI i; i 7. etc Tolu? ato)va aitnv tsov T J.

cp cjrai jucra TOI Kai o f Tai aurov iras i ai o ittics avrov c c 1 Correction in first hand.

1 Result of correction in first hand. Sic.
THE REVELATION OF ST. JOHN
FRAGMENT II. (= P).
P. Oxy. viii. 1080. (4th Cent Plate i. Leaf from vellum Codex iii. 19. w rj fs l ow KOI fitra 20. vorjvov ov ecmica CTTI TIK Ovpav KOI f 8 etcrcaewo uuu irpo? avrov cat Set imyoxu icr avrov ai av 21. TO? fter eiov o vewccov owco avrw ica curat ier eiov e v 019 icayw cat (Kaqi a 1 jura r o v

TTpf iov ev TI) tfpovai 22. avrov o e wv ovs aicov rar (o ri TO xpa Acy i (ed. Hunt, 1911).) ravra tsov KOI isov 0v pa avccoyicn; ev j ra ovpavoi KOI 1 " my i; rpwn;: cos eraairiyyos Aaj ier ctov Aeycav avafia (iov cai 8et u rot a Set ye eo r a i i cra ravra 2. jcjai 2 evtf TCD irw f vos CCCCTO ejv TO) owa icai tin TO V Opovov KO.

3. OrjfjLfvov Kat o KO eiri TOV pov ov 8 iicpova) c a 0an i A
OV cat 1 Correction by second hand.
cat 1 Second hand.
First hand wrote 8 The two missing lines are added by Ovpav wcuyfuviiw (?).
first hand at bottom of column, beginning Written by second hand.
noowa KT. This line is added by second hand
Added by second hand. (sic) between the lines.
FRAGMENT III. (= F 8).
P. Oxy. x. 1230. (Early 4th Cent. (ed. Grenfell and Hunt, 1914).)
Recto. T. 5.
avrjov c a i axi) v KOI ev ACO-O) TWV i wjs ca ayicvoi c wv Ktp ara
T TO irra TOV tfv airco raa i Aj cv neat ctai cv CK TT; S Sfef ia?
or c caa j3cv 1 A slip of the scribe for arerra.
Verso.
LTOv Srjvapiov KOLL
KOLL ro cxcov KCU TO 7. ore iv a v Tt v f Ko vra tfxdVTjv rov 8.
FRAGMENT IV. (= F). P. Oxy. vi. 848.
(5th Cent. Plate i. Fragment of papyrus Codex (ed. Grenfell and Hunt, 1908).)

Recto. Verso.

xvi. 17. rov vao v arro rov xvi. 19. Xrj cfjlvrj p-0ri ciw Opovov Xeyoiwra TTIOV TOW ffv Sou 18. yeyokev icai ry vat aim; TO Trony

VOVTO aotpatrat ptoi rov oivov icai avat cat yspo rov OVJJLOV TTJS

T U- K OI cr cto-xo9 y c ojpv 1?? avrfojv icu

NOTES ON THE ABOVE FRAGMENTS F 1.

i. 4-7. This fragment agrees word for word with A where it exists. It is true that it differs in the reading supplied by Professor Hunt in i. 4: i. e. Irwv a cifcujirtov. There is not room apparently for TWV roij v o irtqv as in A. The fragment agrees throughout with C save that with A 025 it omits TCDV cucnxov in i. 6, and perhaps rightly. It agrees generally with M save in two passages where K in i. 6 reads r. oicoi. roi aiwiav and in L 7 otwrat. It disagrees with 025 five times (i 4 a COTIP, i 5 ayatno-avtt, Aovcravri, airo (for eic), 1 Jatriaei? cat icpet) and with 046 four times (i 4 avo eov o WK, i 5 Aovo-atrt, atro, i 6

Thus this fragment, so far as it exists, attests the text of A(C) as already existing in its present form at the close of the 3rd cent, or early in the 4th. The transposition ro KHMTOS u rj So a in i. 6 is peculiar to this fragment. VOL. ii. 29 iii. ig-iv. 2. First of all A and F 2 (as well F 8 second hand in F 2) stand apart A has two peculiar readings in 4 1 waftrjoi and oast. Next A KU before curcacwroLiai in 3 20. Finally, F 1 " reads i wov in 3 19, avcwyxewy in 4, and KOL cv0ci? in 4 all against A. Thus F 2 multiplies by 75 per cent, the differences between A and F 2 (if we leave avafirjoi and xra out of consideration). F 8 reads i? Acvc in 3 as A.

K. F 8 is more closely related to K than to any other uncial. Thus K reads c u before c re cvrofuw in 3 and adds isov after icai 2 in 4 1. It reads A. COOW in 3 19 with F 2. The KOI (a Hebraism) in 3 20 is most probably original, but the other two are wrong.

025. This uncial KCU before curca. evo-0uuu against F J and reads ifxaxrov 3 19 and KCU evflews with F 2.

046. This uncial reads Xeve 3 and KOLI ctcrca. in 3 with F 2 both right, avcwyfjlcvtj in 4 1 with F 2, and does not insert ai before evflews in 4 2 as F 2 does.

From the above it follows that F 2 and F 2 " agree much more closely with K than with any other uncial, but have affinities with 025 and 026. 046 attests a better text here than ti or 025.

v. 5-8, vi. 5-8. F 3 agrees in 5 5 with A 025 in reading avoi cu, where 046 reads o avoiywv; in 5 with K 025. 046 in reading cv iccra, where A reads CAJICO-Q) and always elsewhere with C; in 5 with AN 046 in reading cxw, where 025 reads cxov (a correction), and 6 7 with AK in reading v v which C 025. 046 omit. Thus F 8 agrees so far as it goes with AK.

xvi. 17-18, 19. This fragment agrees word for word with A. Since 025 is defective here, we have only to consider the relation of F 4 to M and 046. While F 4 supports A in the right reading in l6 18 oonrpainu KGU ovu cat fyovrcu, K reads fipovrau. K. avrp. K. UK. K. jffpwroi, K ftp. K. currp. ic. u)v, and 046 aor9. ic. wv.

F 4 agrees with AM in i6 17 against 046, which adds rov ovpavov after yoov, and with A 046 in reading euro TOV Opovov against rov 0tov of M. Again, in x6 19 F 4 agrees with A 046 in reading Sowot against rov Soweu of K ro vonjpiov and rov otvov against M, which omits the article in both cases, and opyis avrov against K, which omits the avrov. Thus 046 is right five times with A against K.

This fragment is interesting. Like F 1, F 4 agrees word for word with A. But whereas F 1 gives considerable support to K, F 4 is with one exception against it. Next, whereas F 8 gives equal support to A and K, F 8 supports K more often than any other uncial.

The above fragments prove, so far as they go, the absolute pre-eminence of A. They furnish evidence for the early uncial character of certain deviations of 025 and for the antiquity of one or more false readings of 046. Next as regards, we see that, whereas it has considerable support from F 1 and the full support of F 8, it is far inferior to 046 in F F 4. Unfortunately 025 is defective for F 4. From this comparison 025 emerges with a bad record. Hence, if on the exiguous evidence of these fragments we arranged the uncials in the order of merit, we should have A, C, 046. 025. All the evidence given in the Introduction, which in the main is limited to the fragments of fl and the corresponding sections in the other Versions and MSS, uphold the following order: A, C, 025,, 046. An exhaustive examination of the MSS and Versions might place M before 025, but could not affect the primacy of A.

ADDITIONAL NOTE ON i3 llb.

THE text of this line in vol. ii. 317 should be restored as follows: AX V Kipara Svo OAOML rp apviy. The translation accordingly in vol. ii. 420 should be: " And he had two horns like the lamb." The term " lamb " is here a symbol for the Messiah as elsewhere in our author, and earlier in Judaism, as we shall see presently. There would be no sense in saying " he had two horns like a lamb"; for some lambs have horns and some have not. The whole point of i3 nb consists in this, that the second Beast or Antichrist is portrayed as a Satanic counterpart of Christ, just as in 13 s the first Beast or Antichrist is also represented as a Satanic counterpart of Christ; for he is described as icrjayp. cinr)v ck 0 varov. But (as I have shown in vol. i. 340-44) chapter 13 is derived from Jewish sources, and I3 11 18 cannot be understood apart from Jewish apocalyptic. Now, whereas in our author the Lamb is described as having "seven horns," 2 i. e. as a being of transcendent power, a Christian development of a Jewish conception, in this Jewish source the Messiah is symbolized by " a lamb with two horns, 1 which was definitely a Jewish conception. The explanation of this latter phrase is to be found in i Enoch and the Test. XII Patriarchs. In i Enoch 90 the Maccabean leaders are described as " horned lambs " as distinct from the rest of the religious Jews who are described as "lambs." In the pages referred to in the note 1 below, I have already shown how certain religious and military leaders of Israel were so symbolized in i Enoch 85-90. In the Test. Joseph i9 8 Jonathan the Maccabee, who is obviously regarded by the writer of that work as the Messiah, is symbolized by the term dtvo?. That for the corrupt " word M in i Enoch 9o 88 we must read " lamb," where the Messiah is referred to, I have shown in my second edition of that book. But I heiewith abandon Goldschmidt's emendation of the text which takes nte to be a corruption of T D, and which I then accepted, and also the hypothesis that 83-90 was originally written in Hebrew. I now regard 83-90 as derived from an Aramaic original, 5 and explain the meaningless term "word"in go as a rendering of IDX which was a corruption of "1BK = "lamb." There the Messiah is symbolized as a lamb of which it is said that it became great and horned: that is, it had two horns, since this is the natural number.

1 Hence raw in the source should have been read by the translator as nf p, not as n? f 1 See vol. i. p. cziii sq.

1 In my second edition, p. lxix, I left the question of the original language of 83-90 open, though inclining to the view that it was Hebrew. But like 6-36 and Daniel originally it was most probably written first in Aramaic. Later in the and cent B. C. such books were written in Hebrew.

ADDITIONAL NOTE ON THE LATIN VERSIONS 453

ADDITIONAL NOTE ON THE LATIN VERSIONS.

FRAGMENTS OF A LATIN VERSION OF THE APOCALYPSE PRESERVED IN THE SPECULUM (DESIGNATED M) AND FOUND IN ITS ENTIRETY IN THE CODEX GlgAS.

THESE fragments were first published by Mai in his Spiciugium Romanum 1843, x- 7 2 74 an(are reprinted here according to Weihrich's edition (Liber de divinis serif turts sive speculum Vienna, 1887). They do not represent any particular manuscript, but consist of a collection of proof passages from the O. or N. T. It is assigned to the vi-vii century. That m represents the same version as gig, a few examples will make clear.

From this comparison of versions, it will be seen that gig m represent one translation from the Greek and Cyp (i. e. Cyprian) Pr another. Occasionally I will append the readings of Tyc and vg. Unhappily fl is defective in the passages where m is preserved.

2 s8 qui scrutor (scruto m: scrutans Tyc vg) renes et corda, gig m Tyc vg: scrutator renis et cordis, Cyp Pr.

3 16 Neque calidus. aut calidus gig m vg: neque fervens . aut fervens Pr Tyc(?).

3 17 miserabilis et mendicus et nudus et caecus gig m: miser et pauper et caecus et nudus Cyp Tyc vg (Pr).

3 18 vestimenta. induaris gig m: vestiaris veste (Pr) confusio nuditatis gig m Tyc vg: foeditas nuditatis Cyp Pr. I4 10 in igne gig m: igne Cyp Pr Tyc vg. i8 4 et (Tyc) ne (ut non gig) conmunicetis peccatis ejus, et de (Tyc) plagis ejus (+ ut m) ne accipiatis (laeda-mini Tyc) gig m Tyc ne particeps sis delictorum ejus et ne perstringaris plagis ejus Cyp Pr.

i8 6 calicem quem (calice quo m Tyc) miscuit. miscite illi (ei m) duplum gig m Tyc: in quo poculo miscuit duplum remixtum est ei Cyp Pr Arm 2.

From the above, out of many like instances, it may be concluded that Cyp Pr and gig m are two independent translations of one and the same MS or possibly of two Greek MSS, which were generally in the closest agreement The example under 18 exhibits a divergence, which may represent a divergence in the Greek MSS. There are a few divergences between gig and m, which may be due to the influence of some other Latin version. Thus we have ditatus in 3 17 in gig Cyp and locupletatus in m (and Tyc vg). Here Pr is defective.

We might provisionally represent the relations of the Latin versions as follows:

Greek MS or MSS

Speculum (vi-vii cent).

a 1 Et angelo Ephesi ecclesiae scribe.

9 s8 Et sclent omnes ecclesiae quia ego sum qui scruto renes et corda.

3 14 Et angelo Laodiciae ecclesiae scribe: haec dicit ille amen, testis fidelis et verax, principium creaturae Dei. 16 Novi opera tua, quia neque frigidus neque calidus es. Utinam frigidus esses aut calidus! lfl Sed quoniam tepidus, evomam te ex ore meo. 17 Quia dicis: dives sum, et locupletatus sum, et nihil opus est mihi; et nescis quia tu es miser et miserabilis et mendicus et nudus et caecus. 18 Suadeo tibi a me emere aurum igne pro-batum, ut dives sis et locupleteris; et vestimenta mea alba, ut induaris, ut non appareat confusio nuditatis tuae. Et collurio inungue oculos tuos, ut videas. 19 Ego quoscumque amo, arguo et castigo. Aemulare igitur et age paenitentiam. Ecce sto ad januam et pulso. Si quis audierit vocem meam, et aperuent januam, introibo ad ilium, et caenabo cum illo et ille mecum. 91 Qui vincit, dabo illi sedere mecum in sede mea, quomodo et ego vici, et sedeo cum patre meo in sede ipsius.

14 Cecidit, cecidit Babylon magna. De vino fornicationis ejus biberunt omnes gentes. Si quis adorat bestiam et imaginem ejus, et accipit character in fronte sua aut in manu sua dextra, 10 et hie bibet de indignatione Dei, quae mixta est mera in calice irae ejus, et cruciabitur in igne et sulfore in conspectu angelorum et agnl 11 Et fumus et cruciatus eorum in saecula saeculorum ascendit Et non habent requiem die ac nocte qui adorant bestiam et imaginem ejus, et qui accepit character nominis illius, 18 Et audivi vocem de caelo dicentem mihi: scribe, beati mortui qui in Domino

ADDITIONAL NOTE ON THE LATIN VERSIONS 455 moriuntur amodo. Etiam didt spiritus, ut requiescant a laboribus suis: opera enim eorum sequuntur eos.

i7 M Aquae quas vidisti ubi meretrix sedet, populi et turbae et gentes et linguae sunt 18 Et audivi aliara vocem de caelo dicentem: exite de ea populus meus, et ne conmunicetis peccatis ejus, et de plagis ejus ut ne 1 accipiatis. 5 Quia adpropinqua-verunt peccata ejus usque ad caelum, et memoratus est Deus iniquitates ejus. Reddite ei sicut et ipsa reddidit, et duplicate duplicia secundum opera ejus. In calice quo miscuit vobis, miscite ei duplum. T Et quantum magnificavit se, et luxoriata est, tantum date ei tor mentum et luctum. Quia in corde suo dicit, sedeo regina, et luctum meum non videbo. 8 Propterea una hora veniet plaga ejus, mors et farais et luctus, et igne cremabitur. Quoniam fortis est dominus Deus qui judicat earn.

2o u Et vidi mortuos pusillos et magnos stantes in conspectu sedis. Et libri aperti sunt, et alius liber apertus est qui est vitae. Et judicati sunt mortui secundum ea quae scripta sunt in libris, et secundum opera sua. 18 Et dedit mare mortuos qui fuerunt in ipso, et mors et infernus dederunt mortuos qui fuerunt in ipsis. Et judicati sunt singuli secundum facta sua.

21 8 Dubiis autem et infidelibus et abominandis et homicidis et adulteris et maleficis et idolis servientibus et menda-cibus, pars illorum in stagno ignis ardentis et sulfore, quod est mors secunda.

22 16 Foras canes, et malifici, et adulteri, et idolis servientes.

18 Tester ego omni audienti verba prophetiae libri hujus. Si quis adjecerit supra haec, imponet Deus super eum plagas quae scriptae sunt in hoc libro.

19 Et si quis abstulerit verba prophetiae libri hujus, auferet Deus partem ejus de ligno vitae et de civitate sancta.

1 Ut ne (=fra jij). So Weihrich emends et- in Codex Sangaueiuu, MVLConu

THE REVELATION OF ST. JOHN

ADDITIONAL NOTE ON THE MILLENNIAL KINGDOM.

THE peculiar form that the Millennial Kingdom assumes in the Apocalypse is due to the results which, according to the Seer, would arise out of the conflicting claims of the Empire and the Christian Faith.

The main question at issue between them, a question which included all minor issues within it, originated in the demand that all loyal citizens of the Roman Empire should offer Divine worship to the Emperor. This claim to Divine honours was adopted by Rome with the object of unifying and consolidating all the diverse elements of the Roman Empire into a single whole. As Rome had already united all the civilized regions of the world in one universal commonwealth, so now it aimed at strengthening this bond of common citizenship by the still stronger tie of a common and universal religion, the one essential element of which was the worship of the Roman Emperor. Such a worship, of course, no Christian could render. Hence a collision of these two forces became inevitable, and in due course Rome proposed to itself definitely the task of exterminating Christianity on the ground that it was a Society guilty of high treason to the State. This came about first under Domitian. Thus there arose a conflict of two loyalties, loyalty to God and Christ on the one hand and loyalty to Caesar on the other, and our author was the first to set forth in all its seriousness the transcendent issues at stake, and to teach his brethren that to yield in any degree to such demands of the State was to be guilty of apostasy to God and the Christ who had redeemed them.

Under the conflict of his day the prophet clearly discerned the eternal issues at stake, and in this conflict he taught that no faithful follower of Christ would escape: in other words, he foretold a universal martyrdom. Herein our author may have found a fulfilment of the mysterious saying of our Lord: " When the Son of Man cometh, shall He find faith on the earth?"

This forecast of our author, however, was no more realized than numbers of the detailed prophecies of the O. T. But, though this element in his prophecy failed to be fulfilled, the larger spiritual truth embodied in his prophecy that the Kingdom of this world should become the Kingdom of the Lord and of His Christ is true for all time and all like crises in human affairs. While the human element falls away the divine remains.

But the Seer could not stop short with forecasting a universal martyrdom. For this forecast of a universal martyrdom naturally led to a recasting of the traditional expectation of

ADDITIONAL NOTE ON THE MILLENNIAL KINGDOM 457 the Millennial Kingdom. If the world was to be evangelized afresh, this evangelization could not be effected save through supernatural intervention, seeing that all the faithful were to be martyred before the advent of the Kingdom. Hence our Seer expected Christ to return on His Second Advent with all the blessed martyrs to destroy the enemies of the Kingdom (17 19 11 0) and to found the Millennial Kingdom in the Jerusalem that should come down from heaven, and so to evangelize the world afresh (2i-32 "16- 20).

But since John's expectation of a universal martyrdom in the immediate future was not realized, his expectation that the earth would be evangelized by Christ and the blessed martyrs from heaven, cannot be regarded as an essential element of the teaching of the N. T., seeing that the former expectation which gave it birth never itself came into being. The need for this supernatural method of Christianizing the world has not arisen. There has been no universal martyrdom of the Church. Hence since the faithful survive, Christ has committed into their hands the complete evangelization of the world.

But while the peculiar form of this expectation must be relegated to the region of unfulfilled prophecy, the truth at the base of this expectation is not thereby affected. And this truth is that ultimately the righteous shall inherit the earth. The entire Apocalypse is indeed in one respect an expansion of the two opening beatitudes of the Sermon on the Mount: 1 the first of these is, "Blessed are the poor in spirit: for theirs is the Kingdom of heaven " (Matt 5 s). The essential element of this beatitude is conveyed in many of the Seer's words, but especially in iii. 20. Behold I stand at the door and knock: If any man hear my voice and open the door, I will come in to him, and will sup with him, And he with me."

As for the second beatitude "Blessed are the meek: for they shall inherit the earth" (Matt. 5) the assurance of the truth of this beatitude shows itself in every song of the Apocalypse, whether sung by angels or saints, and this assurance gathers strength as the divine drama moves swiftly onwards, till at last in the closing millennium of the world's history the Kingdom of this world has become the Kingdom of the Lord and of His Christ.

The optimism of the man who believes in God and lives unto Him cannot be other than indomitable and unexpugnable.

1 The so-called second beatitude, "Blessed are they that mourn: for they shall be comforted," is an intrusion in Matthew's text V. should follow immediately on v. 1.

I. INDEX OF GREEK WORDS,

GIVING REFERENCES TO GREEK TEXT (VOL. n. PP. 236-385 TO INTRO-DUCTION (VOL. i. PP. XXI-CLXXXVII), TO COMMENTARY (VOL. I. PP. 1-373 AND VOL. II. PP. 1-226), AND TO ENGLISH

TRANSLATION (VOL. n. PP. 386-446), AND APPENDICES (PP. 447-457).

Order of verses in Greek Text according to which references are given in Index: l-3 f i6 M 3 7 7. fi. t gi. s s. s. is 7-iij p-i this

O. U.18

See restored Text, tol. U. 4 M, n. i.

s'. uisv , 9 U; L 245, 246., 9–" n IT 239-242. dlyaxXidw, I9 7; Ixxxvi; ii. 126., i f I2 11 20; xxix. 2-; xxix.

. S. 11 gs. 4. 9. U Fgs. M. ISj Ml. IL 14. If Io l. i. 7. S. 0. 10 i j W 2 7. S i6 i6-l 7 22-; i. 34, 2511.,,,,; li. 222.

yun, 3 7 4 8 55 6 lf 8 1 4 n 18 13 " 14" 17 i8- " i6 I9 8 2i 10 20- 21 22 22"; I 85, 145; ii.

wtf, 3 U 5 13 14 147; ii. 7, 8. ex 6t, 1 9 6" I2 M I9 10 22; L 21, 302, 326-328.;, i 6 20- "; i. 3, 169, 170; ii. 195-199. irfa, 2" 6 8 7 f f 9 C i. 3. 59, 191: fa-is 1.

Afywrrof, n a. oljtia, i s 6 10- M 7" 14 i6 4 I7 I8 a . I 23-. aww, la; 11. 124.

o4 w, 10 i8 n; L 262.

; Ixxu.

afeir, 2O 10 22"; 19"; I l6 u 17 is 1. 14".

I4 U M 370.

jll. IS Ql. S. S.0.7 IQ4. S ZI IS Z2 1S ijt I i6 I8-"18 I9 1 16 7 22 lte- a; xzxi; uses of, cxl; ii. 41.

I4 1f; budii; it 16, 17.

I. INDEX OF GREEK WORDS IQ 11 ai fc 22; xxxi, Ixxxviii, ex; i. 85,86. dxXd, f 9 io 7- 17" 2O 8; xxx, cxxxiv, i. 38. AXXijxowd, ig-; li. 119.

axxw, 2 6 7 1 8 io l I2 13" I4 8- 14 " 14 IS 1 I7 10 is4; clviii; i. 43, 238; ii. 12, 21, 22, 23. 20 1; 11. 141.

AX a, i 8 2i w 22 11; i. 20. dtaprfa, i 4. i5V5a-I2 U 20 8.

F, i8 u; ii. 104. s, I4 a; ii. 10. r, 2 M 14; cxxxiv; ii. 10. drd, prep., 4 7 17; adverb, 21 n; cxxviu; ii. 170.

da3curu, 4! 7 8 9 1 1 1 178 jgl 2Q; U. 189, 190.

d? rytirjkntw, I s; i. 7, 8. drdrawrtj, 4 14". drairafctf, 6 11 14"; i. 177.

wtj, 20 5-; ii. 184-185.

xurof, i 4 7 8" 9 7. 10. 16. 18. T j U j jlfc 18,51.8.9.18.11 51.1.1.

I9 11 20"; cxix, cxxvi; i. 136, 137.

tarrfiras, 2 1; i. 62.

dir prt, M; cxxxv.

xxix.

14; ii- 2, 5-7. 422 if. tuu, 9 11 10 ii" I2 17 l6 18" 2i 1; ii. 201. drqx0a, cxviii; i. 293. drurrot, 2i 8; ii. 216. drd, uses of, cxxvui, cxxix; i. 3, 222., 254, 301; ii. 25, 42. dr5 (36 times), I- W- 3! 6" 0. ft I3 M4, 3 8 14 i l4 tj, 4 4.

14 iffl IT. ii,78, gnuii I9 2Z M. IB (qumter) 2Q ll 2J 1 drd Tpwibrov, I2 U; i. 302, 330. 18 22 s- ls; Ixxvii.

i4(bh) , I 1; i. 4, 5. 7 1y; i. 212.

Hebraic use of Infinitive, i. 355-357. See also roo. u, 18 f AroxXtfwr, 9"; lii, Ivii; i. 246, 247. droorr XXw, I 1 f 22 8; i. 6-7, 142; ii.

219.

, 2 s 18 s0 2i 14., 17 2I W. 6 14; i. 181.

"Ap, i6 18; ii. 50. See Mayc04r., i8 l.

dpkOS, 13.

dpxa, o 9. M I3 8 n I4 1 " 4 14 I4 10 IS 1 I7 14 I9 7 1 2i 9-"— 22i- xx cxiii; i. 135, 140, 141, 152, 153, dprdfw, I2 8; i. 321. dpnp, I2 8-; cxlii; i. 303, 320. dpri, I2 10 14"; cxxxv; i. 301. dpxeuos, I2 9 20 2.

Xk 3 M 21 22 U; Ixxxv, cxi; i.

. 220.

Aora, I 4; i. 9. dtrrifrp, i 18- 2 1

Urrpomj, 4 8 u i6; Hi, clix; i. Il6.

rfa as emphatic pronoun, 3 14 19" 2i 7, ct. 2i 8; xxx, cxxii; other uses of, cxxii.

, ato-fl, cxxi, clvii; ii.

90, 98 (cf. rov, ii. 108), 207, 208. tpto, 22" y cxviii; i. 70. a, 2 4 80 ii., cxviii; i. 289.

I2 U I 4 i8 8; xxxi, cxxix, cxxxv; i. 38, 74, 302; ii. 4, 141. dxpt (ind.), 17"

I. INDEX OF GREEK WORDS 14" i6 u if Ixxxi, Ixxxvi; ii. 14.

Baxdr, 2".

8dxX, 2 w 14– 4 4 6" 8 8 S 7 8 I3 4.8. io. i8. i0. it r I4 M, 4 w I8 (war.) i8 19" 20-
". 3dtT, I 9; ii. 133. pdpat, 2; i. 74.

301, 317; ii. J. Poff(unori k 9 tf 14" is 7 10 16; i.

222; ii. 1 8. fcwrixefa, I 8 9 5 10 II 18 I2 10 i6 10 17"

1717. w. i xv ji XXX i xx xiv, clxvii; i. 16, 148, 326. 3urixefc, i 8 6 9 U lo 11 15
i6 18 i6 14 j 7 I.10.1S.14. H jgl.9, 9 16.18.19 2I a4.

i. 181,269; ii. 6a 71, 72, 75. jsartxetfw, 5 10 1 1 18-" I9 8 2O 4 " to 22; i. 294,
295. Scurlxurou, I8 7. Paffrdfa, 2 I7 7; xxxii. 3drpa X of f id"; ii. 4 7-rx I7 4 5 2I 17.
2 1 8; ii. 216.

Pifl apl5ior, 10 B 10; i. 260. fliHUw, i" 51-. ". a. 6 14 I0 8 Ixz, Ixxviii n.; i. 136.
8Xof, 3 20"; Ixxviii n. i. 84.

JXCKT W, I 3 l6–

P artijtjda t 2 IS 1- 10 17.

jsXArw, i u I6 18 (M 3) 3 c- 9" ii f 17 is 8 18 22 8; i. 24, 288. potjbto, I2 fc.
pbrpvt, I4 18.

3 Xw, u f; Ixxxvi; i. 285.

Pporrj, 4 8 6 1 8 lo 8- 11 I9 6; dix. S wof, i8- I9 8-"; i. 187; ii 89, 91, 115 "7 (neut.
17" 2I 1; xxx, cxxxv.

ii. 57, 61, 64. 428.

I,8. 7 3 10,8 8. 10. 18 6 4.8 6 8 6 18.1S. II 7!. 2. 8g5. ft 8 rj 9.4 IO S.6. f.8 1I 4.
W I2 4. 9. 12. 13.16 j L 8. 11. U. 18. 14 p 8. 18 1. 8. B. 2I 84 2Q8.9. 11, 7 8 1-8 8
7-8-" 11 18-18-u 12-M " 16- 4.10.17.18 ri6 i 18 fei 8! 22 8 L 22, 110, III.

rw, 2 28-M 3 9; ii. 393 n. r, 10-10.

io ii I3 7 I 4 itf I 7;1. i 47- 76xoj, i8 u u; ii. 101. 7Mi w, I 8- " u 2 1- 8- 1S- " 18 5
1 10 I3 8 14" I4 1 I7 fc8 I I9 W 2I 27 20 la- M 2i 6: 22 18-ypnyoptu, 3 s i6 15 (see f)
3; i. 79.

, i6 M (see 3 8) 3 17 17"., 3". 9 s I2 127.

7 1 20 8; Ixx.

f 9 i6 u 18; i. 254; ii.

47, 4, 95-ddicpvov, 7" 2i te. Aovcw, 3 7 5 6 22 16.

et, i 1 4 1 lo 11 II 8 I7 10 20 8 22 f; L 6. 8clkwvfjui i 1 4 1 I7 1 21 10 22 1; xxxii;
i. 2, 109.

dix; 2 W 12 1 i. 224., 347. 8i KCLTO, II 18 21.

, 6"; ex; i. 175. I7 1 21 9. Jeore, 19". ire)f, 2 11 4 7 6 s O 3- 4 II 14 led (ace.), i 4
13" if (Gen.), I. INDEX OF GREEK WORDS , a ll(W.). ll cliz; i. 224.; ii. 156.

riurfllTA. 91.

It4t, uses of; oodx; L 329; il 173. rouro, i. 302; ii. QI.

ii ai ftuurorfe, a u.

t, 1 1 1 1 2. 2I n; ii. 170.

ii. 395- ao 2i; cxl, odviii; i. 54, 87:= "to requite," 2; box, cxlviii; " to make," 3 f;
L 88; "to gran upon," 8 1; i. 230; "to commission," II s; i. 280; "to place," "put 3 8;
i.87, 36a;"togive up," 11. 198, 199. tttuu t various uses of, i. 278, 280.

128.

19" 22". 15 1 19"; czr; il 36, 91, 98,99- 7" 22" 2i; nzii.

ii. 172.

7" ii" i 4 15; mil; mi, bud, Ixxii i. 6, 206. 296: ii. 124, 125.

, 12 T. i. 11. istn c 4. 11 j i opii, i w fj 4"

15" 17 i8 I9 1; i. 149, 301, 3 0; . 9i 96. 9 11 22411.

topedr, 22" 2I; EDO.

rfdy, uses of; aanriv, CXZZT, dr. d with indie., 2 M 1 Mr (subj.), 2 3 fatal v (subj.
), 1 1 1. 9ffoi 4dv (subj.), I3 1. See teas. Jawrfc, 2- 3 6" 10 8 1 lo't u t 16" 2I M.
ii; 1.245.

(var.) 4 I6 1 i7 w I8- V 2I M. si 22 i JOB. mj. J.

Wrot, 2, uses of; xxxiv, cxxxv; L 284. cl W 4ij, 2 M; i. 65. c ftj t 2 17 9 i 17 14
19" 4 et rit, 11 1 i i y I3-w (") i

Subj. ii 8.

Indie., 11 8-i ewo, 17. ewor, i-11. IT. M- 4! el.

I2 is,31. s. u I4 i. a. 14 if ie- B nil. 17. IS 2O 21 20 20 2I 1- s; i. 106, 148,
161. ettwxtf vrof, 2 14- n; Ixxxiv; i. 63. tttwxoxdrwjj, 22 U 21. Wwxw, 9; i. 254,
255-etkocrt, 4 tfii ig.

used as aorist; bonr, czzvl; i.

39. 136. M3, 44, 3. 293. itprjica, used as aonst, czxvi; i. 212; ii. 120.

fjHiy. i 4; lniv; L9. eit, uses of; cuuz: ii. 24, 43. eb (78 times), i x-) 2- " 4 V. io. u
6. W 7 ii 8 f glS.7Klf IO-!!.!. If 12.

glS.7Klf IO- IS. 14 (bh) j a 251. S. S.

aoi. 19 (bte). 14.! 22 I eft, 224., 238.

I. INDEX OF GREEK WORDS , cxlviii; i. 154, 161, 247- =indef. article, cxxii;
i. 237, 247. eirfatymu, 3" II 11 15 2 1 7 22". fflya?, cxv ill. fe (135 times), I 2H. i.
io. u.

r 2 2sy s. t. it. it. it. it f 5 (bu. 7. t 6lb ft 4 6 1 14 Z t (ten. 7 (tar). t (tar), t (tar), t.
IS. 14. 17 g4. ft rglo gll gl. S (bb). I. If. 17. 18 (bu). JO. A (quater) IQ!. 4. It ji. 7.
ft, 1L IS I2 1S.! 13! 9. 11. I4 lt (bb). S. S. 10, 4 1S. 17 I4 B. St! (ten f. 7. (Mi) IO T.
10. Il (ter. IS (tor). U(bfc)! l. S. t(bb). S. ll! gl(bb). fbb). 4 (tar). Is. Iff. IQ S. U.
SI (bb) dr., partitive use; czz, cxxiz; i. 161, 288; li. 97; other uses of; cxxix, cxxx; U.
28, 33, 42, 95. "2. stbfe; ii. 57.

a ref, 2 tt S 8 6 11 2l" 22 J 2O 11 22 lf.?coror, 7 14 2I 17. d Xw, n.

6r 6w, 6 1 10; Ixxvui; i. 175; ii. 119.

2 M 2i; 1.330. 2; ii. 176. II U; czxii. I 7; Izviii; i. 1 8.

. 1. 1. ii. u. ss 22 it (17"; cxv.

u, i 4 9 17 u U B I6 14 22 1; ii. 48 timn, 6 11 ICQ.

; zxzvi, cxzi. 4ttopff, 18"- " 18 18"

19 22; ana.

(157 times), i-4,1.1 r,. it,.).

IS. ft. It (bb) 2 1 (tar). 7. t. IS. IS. M. If. SS. S4. S7, L 4 (bb). S. f. IS. 14. tt (bb)
4 l. S (bb) fit A S. t (bb). t. It (Us) gl. t 68 (tern-S. 14. li gl. IS Fg7. t gt. It– 9 17. b
(Wf) 9 1S 9 jo. 6 Iqulter,.

r. s. t. 10, ji. i. ii. is. it (bb). u. i 2 1. t. t. I. T. i. 10, 11,,.! ibto). IS I4 is. s. B. t
(bbi. 1.10 (Mi), u r I4 ii. in 5 (1W). I I 6.8 I7 S.4 1 I gt.7. t(bli.

ir (bu. Mb. S3 sw. ss. su. su. ss M IQ!. S. 11.14.16 (bb). 17 (Msi. SO(bb). SI 2,
lt. 7 22 S jo. 8. IS. IS (Ms). II 22 t 2, t 22 22 W 22 18 22 1.

A, uses of, cxxx, cxzxi; i. 135, 139, 147, 214, 221, 22211., 260, 272, 290, 314, 336, 359J ii-, 22, 90, 446. fraroi, 2I.

21. 15 19"., 2i u; ii. 164., 9 1.

, 22; ii. 176., 12" I 4; i. 369. is l 2" 3 " 7 i U.18 gs.4 8 S 9 is U 4. it I2 4. I3 is. is. u I4 s. 10 IS 4, 6 it I9 so xzx, cxxxi.

I?" W I4 L- c. r, 3 7" 2 i4; i. 217, 218.

tpxoptu, 3"6 4 0 I4 18 17 I4 18 1 2 s 6 9t. it. it If t I2 i 11 I4 18 16 17"- u 18 , 5 1 (twr.), II 14; cxxxi, cxxxv.

w, 6 20; cxxxi. (gen. 55 times), i 2 3 1 4" L X 7. ft. is (bb) 510. u ffibb). S. lit.

it gl U. 17t i 0 t (bts. 5 (bh). t (bb) t. t. 10 ibb) I2 1 j 3 ll,,8. 14 (bb). It I4 l. t. t, 4.16. ir, 6 lt I 7 l

M (dat. 13 times), 4 5" 7" 9" io (var) M (acc.73 times), i 7- 2 17- f- 4 S.4(ba) rl 5S.4f (D t.?). l. ttlt yl it. 11. 17 gt (te) rgio. lot 9 7. if (bb) I0 l ri ll (bb). 16 (bu) I2. It jjl T. It i 4 l. t (bb). f. 14 (bu) r X4 M, s f j S. S. f. It. IS. 14. 17. SI 2 8. ft. t iglfi. V. It jgll. IS I9 M I? 2I 20? 22. M (bb).

M, uses of, Ivii, xd, cxxiz, cxxxi-cxxxiii; i. 112, 113. rvt gen., i. 112, 113, 136, 191, 204, 206, 215, 223, 256, 262, 300, 301, 334. 335; " 2, 3, 12, I. INDEX OF GREEK WORDS

Witkdat.,. 113, 269; ii. 116,202. FKM OCT., i. 18, 112, 113, 136, 154, 191, 203, 215, 226, 252, 262, 301, 303, 334J 3, 15, i6, 22, 34. 43, 44, 51. 56, 57, 105, 116, 132, 137, 163,181-183, 190, 210, 211, 223. With gen. after coftprfec, li, liv., Ivii.

With ease varying with case of r, cxxxii; i. 112, 113. xaroucto.

, 21".

Irurhrrw, II 11. i 19 I7 M 17" 21; ci, cliv. clix; i. 8, 9, 25, 224, 272, 319; ii. 38, 39, 69. 2 i8 17; ii. 106. 2 IHOT, i".

tfxOfuu, I 4- i 8 2 s- M i6 M (M 3 s) 3 io. 11 4 s 5 7 1. 1. 1. 7. 17. u. M gs 9 n 2217. 7. 1J. K). cj 52; ii. 395 if. 6 Ipxlateiw. i. 10, ftrxoror, i 17 2 s- M I5 1 21 22 U; L 31.

r 0ns 4 s 5 l; i. 125, 137.

In, 3" 6 11 7 M 7 y f I2 l8"- 20 2I 1 4 22 22 11; CTXXT.

See ofcrc.

frot, ffvvccff, 4

JO 7 I4; cxl; L 266., 14?; il 12.

16. 18 2 I. 4. 7. IP. 1L U, 14. li. 17. It.-1. a 7. 8. 11. li. 17. VT.8 npq. 14. 17 r 9 1 j I0 i,, I2 i. 1. 1. it. 17 7.8. 18.1. j

Xw= finite verb; i. 124. wi, 6 U; czxzv. Icuj-dre, 6 10; i. 175.

vxcfr, 7 8.

i w 2 3 1 4- w 7 s 10 s I3 14 2o 4 20; i. 204, 205; U. 181, 183., 3 "; L 96.

, 6 1; i. 166.

4.7. y.8 7 11 14 IS 7 I9 4; Ixr.

toj, i 6 11 7- 8 1 9 I0 1 I2 1 2 10- 4 8 6" 7" " 9- " I4 if!6" i8 8 2i 20 10; i. 154, 183,237.

154, I2 14.

, 8 1; i. 224. r, A, i 4 i 8 48 n 17 i6W; ex, cxii, clii; i. 10, 295.

6, 8 i7. u. a 20 8 20 18 2I 1; Iv, dv; i. 117; ii. 194-196.

IS 1 IS 1 i6-'- "."-IB i6 j51l. SI,7!. S. S. IS jgl. S. It. 16. IS. IS. SI gl. S. S. IT. IS 2O 1 21 1 i " 20 11.1S 2I S. clviii; ii. 42,,94.

; i. 181, 182.

lo 4- f, 265, flckW,.

Aaf, 6- "; L 162.

ii 0 i7; L334 79 joi.

i" 2 4 J 5 cxlviii; i. 118, 119, 136, 140, 217; ii. 176.

pcffovpdvrum, 8" 14 19". turd (ace.), i 4 i w 71- 15 is 1 I9 1 20.

(gen.), I 7 11 a"-" 3 4. (bbmi 6 8 IO S,,7, 2 7.9. n,,4.7 I7 1. 1.11. 14 ebb) f gs. t 2I fcli 20 f 2I 8 b 21 22 1 n.

uerd, uses of; Ixxx, cxxxiii, cxxxiv; i. 18, 286, 301, 305, 370; ii. 406 n.

i. 39, 71, 254, 255. 1 21 1 lf 17; i.

276.

roro, 7 1 9 4 13 141- 22.

), with imperative, 2 U. with subj, 7 1 10 4 n 1 22 M. alone i9 10 22. 7j, uses of; cxxxvl 274- yvvfu, 8 T IS; L 233. icptt, 3 6" n" 13" 19 20"- M i- 43. 297, etc.

, 16"; ii. 52., 2 I7 li 18.

ii" 22"; Ixxvii, Ixxix; L 373-

Airxof, 7; i. 124. powucfc, i8 Mt; clii; ii. 109, IHX at, io; i. 261., 18 sl., 1 8"; Ixxv.

wmpior, i io 7 I7- f; had; I. 34, 264-266; ii. 65. i, 15.

retyot, a"; i. 73- I2 11 13 15 I7 14 2i 7; xxxii, cxlix; i. 45, 53, 54, 353-rucdw to, ii. 33. Ntjtoxatnp, 2 "; cxxi; L 52, rdrof, 2 1 11.

roof, 13" 17; i- 364- i8 2i 22 17 21"; ii. 179.

4 7 li C 8 " I2l 4 U 21" 20" 22; civ; L 236, 237, etc.

, 14" 16"; ii. 22.

6, 4, rrf, connecting noun with following phrase, i. 136, etc.

Moot, 17" 21 10.

; i. 334.!7 i8- I 3"i2 i6 14; j.

ii. 14, 15-ozbf, 16".

clviii; i.

6; i. 181. io 9; i. 262. iw-H 2" 4 t. 9 f- 1S 1, 3 1. II I4 14!! 2I U. II baudi, buudii, clii; i. 3, 27, 36, 37, 113; u. 106, 156.

UAr d Hirow, i. 3, 27; ii. 3, 19, 20.

J 244- I. INDEX OF GREEK WORDS yal I T 14" i6 7 22 M; i. 19, 20. wl6f 3 it 7 u Il i. t. it l4 i6. it l., i6L 1T 21"; i. 91, 215, 276, 277; ii- 37-ratfnji, is 17.

Hfro o 11-". reowfaf, I 7 io 1 u" 291.,7.

6tofos, 2" 8 1.

6toxoyw, 3; Ixxxr.

6Voua, 2 s- " 1T 3 1- 4- u 6

Qlljjlt, 18 I3 1. 6. 8. 17 i 4 l. U i 16 17 lo"l I0" " 2I v " 22 4; i. 81, 92, 291, 347, 34, 3545 n. 132, 133.

d 0s, i" 2" 14" i4 l7 1 14" IQ" i" 4 5 1; cxxxvi; L 137. x"(war.) 12" 13 +; cxxxvi, cl, cii; i. 305, 337, 351; ii-419 row, 2" II I2 f I4 4 I7 J 20 f; cxxxvi, clvi; i. 301, 304, 309, 310, 330; ii. io, 68. otr6pa, is 14; ii. 108. tpaait, , 6-" ii" 14" 16" 19"; i.

182, 183, 296; ii. 52. rw n"i2 17; i. 296.; ii. 107, 108.

i6 M I7 f 21"; tpvcor, 18 Ixxxiii.

fa j l (bu. 1.11. U iter). 90 38. 4. 8.11 4 l cb, 4 5 j6 58,18 7 X 9 (Us) IQ 4.6. 6.8 7 2 8-W iji. U. 14 (btt) I4. 8 I7 8 (Us). 11. U. 16. ft. 18 X g6 jg!9 iq 191 IO 2O 21 1 17 2O 11 2I 8 22. 6V 4x 00.

fadictf dk, II; cxxxvi; i. 272. flc-iot, I5 4 16; ex; ii. 29, 123. rof, i 2" 3" 13" i8 7-7 21". rrtj, i 7- " 2 9 4 II" 12" I7-" 19"

20 4; Ii, cxxii; L 73, 243, 287; 11. 119, 152, 183. 5rar, Fut. indie., 4.

Aor. indie., 8 1.

Aor. subj., 9 u 7 ia 4 17" ao 7.

Pres. subj., io 7 18. 5rox, uses of; cxxxvi, cxxxvii; i.

104, 127,223 dre, uses of; cxxxvil g Tt 2 t. 4.6.14. tt 3! (bb). 4. 8. 10. U. 4l6. 17 (t, 4 11,4.6 6 17 7 17 gll IQ 6 f, t. S0.17 I2 10.1t(te).18 I3 4– 1. tfc. II. 18. 18. to. I I9 i. 7 22 8 j!

uses of; cxxxvii.

o0=where, 17", cxxxvii.

06, uses of; cxxxvii.

o0 nfr, 2 11 3j" fc w 9 1 ij 4 I8 7 11 i8 14 fet, 8" 9" ii 4 12"

crxxvii, clviii.; L 238, 247, 302; ii. 90, 101.

om. om. ouw, 5; w. ottrf, oa o0W, uses of; i. 40, 21, rfddt, 2" 3- " 5. 7 14 15 iff"

otoc. r, ii. 91, 153. Mn, 10 l8 u iff; xxx, cxxxvii. ocr, i" 2 8 18 3; xxxi, cxxxvii; 3. 33. etc.

l; cxxxviii.

S t. It 511. 14 gl git

O 1 I0 4 8 11 8-1-! I 8 1 I2 1- 8 4. T. t. It. It j 3. It I4 I4 t. T I 4 1T iel jei 16 1- fl igl. 4. t. tt I9 i. 11.14 2f 2iw20 8- 2ii-; xci; i. 108, 303. W, 314, 3J3; 3J4, 329.

lxxxiv; L38. 0re, uses of; cxxxviii; i. 40.

otfre. otfre, 3" "5(tur.). oflre. o0re y 9-4 7i. fcm. M. I2 it r I4 4j, 4 4" it. tt,,4. t. it I2 i; it. it. 14, 8 i. t.

clviii.

2" 3 1-!! I6 it, gti. exor), 3"; L 95, 96. I-M 2" 3" 4 4 5 7 l I9 11 2I 4-. 114.

wcucuw, 3 W; Ixix; i. 99, loo., 716 9; i. 216, 243.

rtun-okpdrwp, i 4 n" 15 I6 14 l6 T, 9 t. it 2I. lvi Ixx CXj cxlvii clxii; i. 3, 20, 104, 127, 295, 387., 398.

, uses of; cxxxiv. Tapdjeiroj, 2 T; i. 55; ii. 157-161.

17; ii. 429. f 20. 14; ii. 8, 9, la af, i 2 W 4" 5- 6 14- 1 7 1 1 "" 7 4-t. u. it. it3trgno4 II t I2 t I3 T. t. it. it tb. tt. t4 j 9. IT. It. U 2I lt. IT 22 li 2I t. 4. 22 t 21 t aaito. n. j. 335f 33 g. ii. 155.

irardrrw, n 9 lo; Ixxviii, lzxiz L 285.

II 1 14" io f; L 270. i 2" 3- 141.

retr; cxix. recrdw, 7 lf; xxxti. Tetpdfw, 2- 3 ia; i. 58. Te V a ri6t, 3 10; i. 90. 20. 219.

, 18"-"-". (i8 f- 8f 21; ii. 99, 100, 431 n., 9- 1 i; 10; i. 224 n. u 2".

reif (ace.), - 18 4 7 f- " IO 1 II I2 I9 s. it. cxli; i. 82.

, 2 1 16 1 (see f) 3 9 2I M. 8 1 I2 14 14 lo 1; i. 302.

217; , 19; xxxii; ii. 139. Lrw, 8 11 io f- 1B; i. 235. rfrw, 141 i8 (var) 16. wlirru, i" 2 s 4 10 5- " 6 1- 1 7" 8 1 o 1 u" i 14 i6 I7 lf 18" io 1910 22 t. i. l8o 23 g t 239. H.

403. rfcrrw, 2 11 lt 13 I4 lf; xxix, cxv; 61, 335, 369. TUTT, i 2 l- M 3 14 I7 14 I9 11 2I 1 22 8; xxix, cxv; ii. 216 n. irxardw, 2 M 12 13"

rxorefa, ii 8 2 1 11 22. TXdrot, 2I 1C 20; Ixxix; ii. 190. rxto, l8 17.

rxirrt, o 11 " 1 1 I3 1 14 I5 llf I5 I6 t. n l8 4. t 21. 22 it.

f 2 W; cxxxviii. 3" 6"; i. 8a toj, 2 8 3" 6 13"

17-"

L INDEX OF GREEK WORDS; Ixix; i.

vxoorof, 5 11 i8; L 149. w, 7 1 22"; L 18 188, 214.

, I i" 2 7- " 3-4 4 i J 5 " u I3 M M" 16" I 14 17 I 1 19" 2i li 22 7-; Ixxxviii, cix, cxiv; i. 11-13, 53 I1O IU ii. 179, 218. irwuAancu)?, II. wife, 7 1- xxxii.; i. 336, 352, 353; ii. 14, 174, 178-wotfjutlvw, 2 17 7 17 12 19"; xxxi, Ixxv, Ixxviii, Ixxxviii, cxlvii; i. 75, 76, 2 1 6, 217; ii. 116. rocos, 3. roxet w, 2 1 12 7 13 I7 14 I9 11; i. 65; ii. 115. w6 pos, 9 7- u 7 I2 7-" I3 7 I6 14!

! 18 jglb, 16. It. II. 11 2 1 10. 14. II. Ii. W. l. 11. t. 22142 2,1 22"; U. I57-I6I.

, i 2" 5- " 7 8 8? io l 171 191. t. fo, 16.

i, I6 10 U 2i ff; ii. 41. roprefa, 2 U 9 U 14 17"- 17 18 I9 1; i. 255; ii. 61, 62, 65.

worfvpovs, 17 1 8"; zxxii; ii. 64, 91, 94., m.

f, 8 10 9" ii i6 4- 22 1-. tfywa, I2 11; i. 302, 330, 331. e, 6 1Q.

roriipior, I 4 w 16 17 i8; buuii, Ixxiv; ii. 16.

14 18" (wr.); ii. 96, 430.

row, iit. i 2"3 f I6 1 1 ii" I2 1 13"

I9 10 22; hcxi, cxlvii; i. 29, 256, 259, 260. rpwjstfrepof, 4- 5- 5" 5" 7"- II 16 14 19; i. 128-133. vp68aro, 18. xp6f (acc.), I 17 3 1C I2 8 u I3.

(Dat.), I.

rp6f, uses of; cxxxiv. wpwrevxt, S 8 1 8-. rparw w, 3 4" 5" 7" 4. t. ii. i1 t. u 4 154 l6 i 194! 19 20 22 s-; zxxii, cxli, clvi; i. 211, 212, 335; ii. 3, 128, 129, 139, 213. with dat. = " worship." with acc. = " do homage to." pwror, 4 7 6 7 U 9 T IO ll lf 12" 20" 22; xci, czzviii; i. 302, 305, 330.

22 18; L 272.

xo 11 II s, i. 269.

, 2" 22 1; Ixxxviii; i. 77. I 17 2 4- 4- 7 8 7 91 13" 20 i 2i i22"; i. 31; ii. 201. xpwr6rokOT, I 6; Ixxviii, Ixxxiv, cxlvii; i o Mi 38611. Trrfpvf, 4 9 12" TTWML,!!; i. 272, 286. 2 9.

17 i3 lf; 56,97., 2I- "- " 22"; ii. 162. p, i" 2" 3" 4 8 8 7- o 17- " 10 ii 13" 14" I4 1 IS 1 16 I7 1 i8 8 I? n. ft 20- 1- " 20 14 20 li 2I; cliv.

irup6w, I" 3"; i. 29, 98. rvpp6 t 6 12; i. 162., 18- li.

pd3dos, 2 s7 II 1 12 19". fr, 19" (wr.)., is 11; ii. 104. 5 22 I- 171.

22 11; ii., 22 11; ii.

222. 222.

II 1; i. 232. is 11.

2I 1B; il 169.

I. INDEX OF GREEK WORDS , 4 21; i. 114. v t 21; ii. 169. I7 9 19"-; ii. 74.

; ii. 104. I 1; xxxii; i. 6.

i. 300, 314. ty t 8 1; i.

223.

18".

2 1T 9 12 19. t, i8 19; ii. 91, 103, 115. o-trof, 6 18". 141.

r, 2 14. r evof, 2 17 l8 19. rap, 13 15 2I; cli; i. 353; ii 37, 38 205-207, 444 n. 0 i? rfo, 7 15 12" 13 2I; xndi; i. 215, 302, 329 J. 406 n.

ffkOTlfa 8.

ffkorfa, 9 1 I6 19.

, 4; i. 114, 115.

; 1.287,288.

, 5" 7" 13" 17; uiz; i. 149, 364.

, 6".?, I4 M 2l lf; ii. 25, 163.

oravpfa, II s. 14"

14"; Ixxxiv; i. 58, 59, 131, 163, 164; ii. 20., 15. 12; ii. 417.

, 6" 7–" 22; i. 1 irraxi), 213.

ffttfm, I" 2 3" 9"- " I0-12"- " I3- 84-188, 1910 22., 18; Izxzvi., i 9; L 21.

; L 77; il 393, 12.

0tf, 5- M 6- I3- i8; xxxii; i. 141, 143. 147. I??. 349; ii- "3–0Mpa, i6; zzzi; u. 53.-w-y w, 7. io 20 1 22 10; Ixxi, Irxn, Ixzxv.; i. 194-198. ftwyfr, 5- 61- " 7 8 9; ban.; i. 197, 198. 18"; il 104, 105., 7" 12" I9 1; bud; i 2II f 30, 326.

, 3"; i. 96, 97. raxayrtcubf, 16; il 53. ov, ao 3; u. 195-198., i 1 22.

, 2111. 14. ii. i7. ii. it., 2 M I2 4.

I0 7 1 1 7 I5M 15 17" 20 20 1- 20 7; i. 285.

, 2M 21 22 1; il 22O. T (Traxljcorra, 7 II 1 13 I4 1 1 21". rteffapet, 4- " 5- " 6 1- 7 l- 4. 11 51. ii! I4 i., 5 7 I9 4 2I it 20; L 11511., 22411.

16" (s 3) 3". " i2 I4 U 22 T 9; xzzii, baadvw., Ixxxviii; rlfuot t 17 18"- "21"-. Tifu6njt t is 19; clii; ii. 106, 107. ret, auril 5lm c(.

, T, 2-"– 9- 5 6"

I 3 4 Ibb), 5 4 I7 7, 18.

rordfcor 21". rof, 2 6" ia 9- 9 16" i8 ii. 105, 106. Tixroorot, l8 7 19. roo, and Inf. (Hebrew idiom); cxzvii, cxlvi, clviii n. t clxii; L 304, 305, 321-322. r c, 6 9 8 8" 9 19 1 1 9- i6 9 i6 9 I. INDEX OF GREEK WORDS 107 II 1 11 3 12 14 16 21"; L rp. ryd-,14"-"., 3 1T- f, 9"; i. 253. 21; ii. 170. MXtrot, 4 15. fexot, 21"-; cxlii. 0 w, i" 7" 8"-" n 12" 16 16 16" 17 17" 19 22."

fcrfc, II. utfe, I" 2"-" f I2 14 21"-; Ixviii, Ixzxiii; L 27; ii. 19, 20.

0UMOf.

rd-xw, I0 8 13" 14 16 I7 8 U; H.

42911.

6r6, uses of; cxxxiv; i. 171. 6 6"

1- w 6 f I2 l; czxziv. i 2-i." 3" 13" 14"; xxix, Ix if.; i. 21, 40, 49, 368.

21".

i" 8 11 i8 2I., 3" 15. a PM a la, 9" 18; i. 255. 4aiMur6f, 22" 21.

, 9 12 16 20".

2i; ii. 39. txa ex0a, I 11 3 T.

ta, 3" 22"; xxxii; L 99., I" 2" 19".

I"2 10 n" I4 T 15 19; U. I3. "i8 10. v 7; xxxii; L 21 1. 21. 1.255.

i 5- 7. n 13 i 4 i; i. 147.

14"; il 23.

U. u. ii 3 M 4 i. f 5. u. 11 51.1 f. it yi. it gi. ii Qt. u I0. t. i IZ U. U. It I2 l., 4 li.
I. I4 1IJ, 4 18 igl. If. IS f gl. 4. M. Me jol. 1. 17 2i; cxlii, cxlviii, cliii.

2I U; il 161-162. i8i 21" 22; Ixxvi, Uxvii,, cxlviii; ii. 210, 211, 444.

, 21"; ii. 169. Xaxfrox j8aiof, i" 2 11; i. 29., 18".

MM." I4." i6 19 20; i. 362.

X iptf, I 4 22 11; Ixxxiv, Ixxxvi; i. 9. 8 9" io. " 13"
clix.

f, 6" 19"; i. 182. Iljf, , 6 g 9; L 163., 168, 169.

, 6; i. 166.

, 8 9. 18". 3" 21" 22.

96; ii. 2IO.

i- 1 1" 12" 20-; Ixxii; i. 6, 294.

2 6" io 20"; i. 263., 3" 17 (var.) 18" 21". Xpvr i9ot, 21; ii. 169. ot, 2i w; ii. 170.
17 (w.) 18"., I 11- J- 2 I 4 5 8 9"

344; ii. 47.

; u.64.

16" 19 20; i. 342-14 2I 17 22".

12" x6 18". " 20.

22"; i. 20. ctte, 4 II" 13"-" 14" 17; cxxxviii; L 364.

12".

ex, cxii, clh; i. 10, 295., 31.10 911, 4 7 gu. if.; i. 81; ii. 71.

, jlo. 14 (b 14. 15 bis. 16. 17 (bis) Z Cbb. ML 14 n" I6 8; Ixxviii, I7 n 4 1. 7 r
gl 0. 11. II fljB. 10. 11 9. 3 98 9 7 (bk. 8 (bis). (Usi. IT I0 1 (Us). T. i. 10 I2 15 j
l (bb). B. 11 i 4 l(ter). S, Io wj, uses of; xxxi w., xxxiv, cxxxviii; i. 24, 30, 35. 36.
220., 244, 348, 349; ii. 19, 20, 32, 107, 155. without article; ii. 20, 32.

farep, 10; cxxxviii; i. 261.

II. HEBRAISMS. 1 drd wpoffirov, I2 14 =JBD, "because of"; p. cxlviii. jsdxXw.
elt K lw, 2 a ="tocast on a bed of suffering "; p. cxlvi. Dative rots ft fcixocs, 2i 8,
a Hebrew idiom; p. cxlviii. i56 u= nj, "to requite," 2 s8 (.= drojis at); p. cxlviii.
Sts6v(u= TU, "to set," 3 8 (=n at); p. cxlviii. rats Tpcxreuxatf, 8 1, "to offer upon the
prayers "; p. cxlviii. xdpayfmM(= 7jjv n)if 9, "to. set a mark upon"; vol. i. 362. =
iu, "to give up," 2O 18 (= Tapa-
Sisbai); vol. ii. 198 ad fin. Muuw r6 alfm,. fr, 6 10 io; vol.

i. 175. ptrt. tfffv, S 6 =P 31 P

"between. and "; p. cxlviii. M i =Sy, " because of"; p. cxlviii. Finite verb (atret)
instead of participle, I M; p. cxlvii. Futures to be rendered as presents or pasts, 4 8 " 10
I3 8; p. cxlviii sq.; vol. ii. 399.,420. fobwof (=w), "pestilence," 2 18 6 18. Infinitive
in principal or dependent clause=finite verb, I3 l; p. cxlvi. Infinitive preceded by rov,
12 7 =finite verb; cxlvi; vol. i. 321, 322. Infinitive resolved in succeeding clause into
finite verb, 13"; p. cxlvi. Kal in circumstantial clause = " seeing that," I2 U 18 19";
p. cxlviii.

in pieces"); p. cxlvii. 7wr0Yojrof, I 8; vol. i. p. 14. vibv dptrer, I2 8; p. cxlviii. ftrcrye Ad)3e, IO 8; p. cxlviii.

1 For the following transliterations of Hebrew words, see the Greek Index: Ajl xal introducing apodosis and therefore not to be translated, f io 7 14"; p. cxlviii. X yowof ws far) (for 0w), 6 1; p. cxlviii.

fda Ar, 6 1 =" first of"; p. cxlviii. Nominative standing in apposition to an oblique case, i 8 2 18 3" 8 9 o) 4 14" 20 9; p. cxhx sq. Nominativus pendens, 2 s8 f n 6; p. cxlix.

6vofm=6f6fmLTa 9 I7 8; p. cxlviii. 6 Ka6T? ifjl vot. abry 6 Qdvarot, 6 s; vol. i. 169 n.

6 0cfa 6 TravtOKpdrup; p. cxlvii. Participle resolved in succeeding clause into finite verb, i"

pp. cxliv-cxlvi.

Passages needing to be retranslated into Hebrew in order to discover the corruption or inadequate translation, I3 8 11 is 8 8 17 I8 8- 2 " 22; vol i. 337, 351, 358 sq., ii. 37 sq., 65, 100, 106, 109 sq., 210 sq., 431 it., 433. 452.

Pleonastic pronouns added in oblique cases after relatives, 3 8 7 iaf- M 138. "20 8; p cjj wtocs, io 1 (i. e. o ta=OTKii); p. cxlvii.

2 W I2 8 19" (= " to break IV. INDEX TO COMMENTARY III. PASSAGES IN OUR AUTHOR BASED ON THE O. T., THE PSEUDEPIGRAPHA AND THE N. T.

See vol. i. pp. Ixv-boocvl IV. INDEX TO COMMENTARY, VOLS I. AND II.

References to Introduction (Roman numerals) are given first, then references to the Commentary proper.

Abaddon, king of demonic locusts, i.

245-246.

Abbreviations, explained, czc-cxci; in Greek Text, ii. 233-235. Abyss, originally (i)=ocean that enfolded the earth, but is now restrained beneath earth, i. 240.

then (2)=abode of God's enemy, (3)=a great chasm, i. 240. In Enoch abysses are places of punishment.

I preliminary, for fallen angels; 2. final, for fallen angels and demons; 3. final, for Satan, angels, demons and wicked men, i. 241. In J ss preliminary place of punishment of fallen angels, demons, Beast and False Prophet, and prison for 1000 years of Satan, ii. 239-242. See Gehenna, Lake of Fire,

Punishment, Sheol. Accuser of the brethren, i. 327. See

Satan.

Additions. See Apocalypse. Advent, Second, description of, i.

17-19. expected imminently, i. 1,43, ii.

2l8, 221, 226.

suddenness of, i. 80, 81. Allegories, cviii. See Apocalypse, author's method. Almighty, cxlvii, i. 20, ii. 398. See

God, Titles of.

Alogi, rejected Apocalypse.

76-87- variously conceived (a) as individual, God-opposing, ii. 77; =Antiochus Epiphanes in Daniel, ii. 77.

= Pompey in Psalms of Solomon, ii. 78.

=? Caligula, ii. 78.

( ) collectively, as (i.) secular power Seleucid Syria, ii. 78; Rome, ii. 79; Rome under Nero redivivus, ii.

(ii.) religious power false teachers in Church (Johan-nine Epistles), ii. 79; or heathen priesthood of Emperor-worship = the Beast the False Prophet, ii. 80.

fused with Beliar myth as (i) a God-opposing man, armed with Satanic powers, restrained by Roman imperial power, ii. 80, 81, 82.

(2) a heathen priestly corporation, ii. 82.

(3) a purely Satanic power, ii.

fused with Neronic myth as (i) incarnation of Beliar as Antichrist in Nero still conceived as living, ii. 84.

(2) in form of dead Nero, in Ascension of Isaiah, ii. 84, 85.

(3) in Nero redivivus, in Sibylline Oracles, and Rev. xiii., xvii, ii. 85-87.

e. g. beast that died but was restored to life, ii. 54, 60, 68, and eighth horn which was yet one of the Seven (=Demonic Nero), i. 349, 350, ii. 70-71.

IV. INDEX TO COMMENTARY

Antichrist, B. Various conceptions of, in Apocalypse

Jewish view surviving (in nal sources of ii r w not John the Seer, i. 270-273), of Antichrist in Jerusalem (here only)=beast ascending from abyss (n 7), xxv, i. 257, 258, 269, 270, 285, 206 (in present context idea apparently is of demonic Nero Antichrist, i. 285, 286, ii. 83).

Twofold manifestation of Roman Antichrist, the two Beasts of chap xiii., one from sea=imperial power, I3 1, i. 332,333, 340-352.

one from land=Asiatic priesthood of imperial cult, 13", i. 357-361 (in original source =a Jewish Antichrist, i. 342, 343. See Beasts). Two conceptions of Roman Antichrist in chap, zvii., p. xxv, ii. 58-61, cf. L 339, ii. 77-79- (I)=Roman Empire, 17 etc.

(2)=Nero redivivus, to return from abyss, I7 8-" etc.

C. Conceptions variously referred by interpreters to Caligula, 1.338, 339, 349-35.2, 3 8 n.

Domitian, L 367, ii. 70-71 (but this impossible as he was not dead, or regarded as pre-existent or as slain, or one of seven, or about to ascend from abyss, or to lead Parthian hosts or muster nations against the Word of God, ii. 70, 70-

Nero redtvivusi i. 286, 333, 334, 339. 340, 35o f 359, 360, ii. 46, 54, 5, 81-87, 98, 107, 108.

Roman Empire, i. 339, 342, 345, ii. 58-72 (seven 1 (heads " are seven emperors, 69).

Titus, i. 367, ii. 69.

D. Characteristic acts of = blas- phemous claims, irresistible conquest and perse-cution of saints, i. 352,353-354-counterpart, Satanic, of Christ, i. 349, 358.

Antichrist, kingdom of = Third Woe, i. 264.

manifestation of, i. 20611., 243, 263-266, 292, 333.

Apocalypse, doctrines of works, cxv j relation of, to " White Garments," cxv, cxvi. See Garments, Works, of Resurrection, First and Second, cxvi. See Resurrection. of Millennium, cxvi. See Millennium, of Judgment, cxvi, cxvii. See Judgment

Editor of, 1-lv, a better Greek scholar, a Jew of Asia Minor, knew no Hebrew, 1, li; makes stupid interpolations, insists on celibacy, Hi; exalts angel above Son of Man, liii, lvi; empties Millennial Reign of significance, liv; removes "chambers" of souls, interpolates anathema, lv. Fulfilment, imminent, expected, i.

6, 8, ii. 218.

Grammar of, xxi, cxvii-clix. Table of contents of, cxvii. Parts of Speech, case, number, gender, cxvii-cxlii. Hebraic style of, cxlii, cxliii. Hebraisms in, cxliv-clii, clxil Unique expressions and Solecisms, clii-clvi. Order and combination of words, clvi-clix.

Interpolations i Dislocations, Lacunae and Dittographs, lyi-lxi. See also 1-lv. Peculiar constructions in, civ. Materials used in, (i) sources used in Greek, Hebrew, and some uncertain which, lxii-lxv.

(2) Old Testament Books quoted, lxv-lxxxii; on whole, translated directly from Hebrew, but some influenced by Septuagint and another Greek Version, lxvi-lxviii; Passages based directly on Hebrew, lxviii-lxxvii; based on Hebrew, but influenced by LXX, lxxviii-lxxix; based on Hebrew, but influenced by other versions, lxxx, lxxxi; reminiscent of O. T. passages, lxxxi, lxxxii.

(3) Pseudepigrapha, lxv, lxxxii, lxxxiii.

IV. INDEX TO COMMENTARY

Apocalypse, materials used in (4) New Testament Books, esp. Matt Luke, i Then. I and 2 Cor. Colos. Eph. Little Apocalypse (but not Mark, lxvi n lxv, lxvi,

Plan of, xxiii-xxviii; a Letter, xxiv; Prologue and Epilogue, organic parts of, xxiv; Sevenfold division of, xxiv, xxv; additions to, proleptic, xxv, i. 209, 269, ii. I (three 7 10-11 14).

Publication of, immediate, enjoined, unlike Jewish Apocalypses, ii. 221.

Relation of, a. to Fourth Gospel, xxix, xxxiv.

I. from different author difference in grammar, in diction, in words or forms of words, in meanings of same word or phrase, xxix-xxxii; in use of quotations, xxxvi. a. authors related to one another, by literary connection and theological affinities, xxxii-xxxiv. See Fourth Gospel. Ju to Johannine epistles xxxiv-xxxvii, xxxviii, xlii; from different author, no solecisms in latter, xxxiv; also different in constructions, xxxiv, xxxv. See John the Elder.

Skort Account of, xxv-xxviii.

Symbolism in, cvi-cvii.

Text of, (i) Interpolations in, lvi- lviii.

Dislocations of, lviii-lx. Lacunae in, lx, lxi. Dittographs in, lxi (2) original authorities, (i) uncials and some chief cursives, clx-clxxxiii; relative values of, clxxi-clxxvi; superiority of A, clx-clxvi.

(2) Versions short accounts of, clxxviii-clxxx; relative values of, clxvi-clxxi.

(3) Origen's scholia, clxxvi, (4) Papyrus fragments, ii. 447- 451-

Genealogical table of, authorities of, clxxxi.

Apocalypse, to be read in Church

Services, i. 7, ii. 226. Apocalypse, meanings a revealing of something hidden, i. 5. word not used as title of work before

John's Apocalypse, i. 4. Apocalypse of Jesus Christ=that given by Jesus Christ, i. 6. Apocalypse of John, given by God to

Christ, i. i, 5. sent by Christ through the angel to John, i. i, 5.

witnessed to by John, i. I, 5, 6. Apocalypse, the Little, i. 159; possibly known to John the

Seer, Ixvi. Apocalypses, why pseudonymous, xxxviii; early Christian ones not so, xxxix. Apocalyptic symbols e. g. lamps= stars, i. 123; star=angel, i. 239-

Apollyon, i. 246, 247. Apostle, title of, not claimed by John the Seer, xliii. Apostles, self-styled, not Judaizers, nor St. Paul or his followers, but Nicolaitans, i. 50. Archangels, relation of, to Seven

Spirits (of I 4), i. 11-13. to astral deities in Zend or

Babylonian religions, i. II, 12. the Seven, = Angels of the

Presence, i. 225. Ark, the heavenly, manifestation of, ushers in last Woe, i.

in Holy Jerusalem: the Lamb to be ark, ii. 171 (restoration).

Armageddon. See Har-Magedon.

Ascension, in cloud, of Two Witnesses, paralleled by that of Moses in Ascension of Moses, i. 291.

Asceticism. See Celibacy.

Asia, varying extension of term, i. 9.

Atonement, by martyrs' death, i. 173. See Redemption.

Authorship. See Apocalypse, Johannine Writings.

Authority over nations (s their destruction), i. 75-77-

Babylon, a symbol for Rome in 1st cent. A. p., ii. 14.

prophetic description of, reproduced for Rome, ii. 62, 63, 72.

IV. INDEX TO COMMENTARY

Babylonian origins of Dragon Myth, i. 311. See Dragon, Origins.

Balaamites, a variety of Gnostics, tempted to idolatry and licentiousness (as Balaam in Hebrew tradition), i. 63. contrary to commands of Apostolic Council at Jerusalem, i. 53; also known as Nicolaitans, i. 52, 64.

Baptism, the seal of, i. 197.

Baruch, II, Book of, nearly contemporary with Apocalypse, i. 5.

Beast, ascending from abyss (n 7)= originally Jewish Antichrist, appearing in Jerusalem; = in present context, Nero redi-vtvus, or demonic Antichrist, i. 285, 286.

Beast (in chap, xvii.), in present context = Nero redivivus, originally two descriptions in (i) Beast=Roman Empire, in (2) living Nero returning from East, ii. 55-61.

Beast, heads of = Roman emperors, why Seven, i. 346, 347. horns of =? same (diadems on horns), i. 346. In Daniel horns= king or dynasty.

Beasts, the Two (in chap, xiii.) derived from two Hebrew sources, L 332, 333, 338.

1. First Beast, from sea, denved from Dragon idea (see Dragon), and description based on Fourth Beast of Daniel, = Roman Empire (this interpretation as old as 1st

IV. INDEX TO COMMENTARY

Jesus Christ, i 22 31, ii. 446. King of kings and Lord of lords, I9 ir, ii. 75. Lamb, 5 8- 12-13 6 1- w 7 9-10-14"

2 9. 14788. as. 87 22 1 22 8, CXiii cxiv, i. 140, 141, ii. 452. Lion that is of tribe of Judah, 5 8, i. 140.

Lord Jesus, 22 90- n. Lord, their, II 8. Lord, the, 14". Lord of lords and King of kings, 17", ii. 75. Loveth us and loosed us from our sins, i 8, i. 15, 16. Man child, who shall break all the nations with a rod of iron, I2 8, i 320. Morning Star, 22", ii. 219. Root of David, 5, i. 140. Root and offspring of David, 22 16, ii. 219. Ruler of the kings of the earth, i 8, i. 14. Searcheth the reins and hearts,

He that, 2, i. 72, 73-Son of God, 2 18, i. 68 Son of Man, One like unto a, I 18 I4 14. i. 27, 35. 36, ii. 19, 20. True, 3 7, i. 85, 86. Walketh, He that, in the midst of the seven golden candlesticks, 2 1, i. 49.

Witness, Faithful, I 1, i. 13, 14. Witness, Faithful and True, 3",

Word of God, lo", ii. 134. Worship of, i. 17, 152. See Dox- ologies. See also Lamb,

VOL. II. 31

Messiah, Son of Man. Word of God.

Christian character, (i) a personal acquisition of the faithful, capable of being soiled or cleansed; (2) a gift of God. source of spiritual body, be stowed when character made perfect by martyrdom or at end of world, i. 97, 98, 184-188, 373, ii. 128.

Churches. See Angels of the Churches, Seven Churches.

City, the Beloved,., the Holy

City, ii. 190.

Great, = Rome, i6 w 17" i8 10 lf etc., ii. 52:= Jerusalem, II 8, i. 287. Holy, use of term by Seer, i. 279, 11. 157.

of God, or of gods, origin of conception, ii. 158, 159. See Jerusalem, Millennial.

Cloud. See Ascension.

Colossians, St. Paul's Epistle to, connected with Epistle to Lao-dicea, i. 94.

Commandments, Ten, order of, L 255-Commerce, Rome's, vastness and details of, ii. 101-105. Community, Jewish and Christian, represented by woman, i.

Copula, omission of, i. 43. Cosmic Woes, i. 154, 160, 218. Comological myth transformed into eschatological doctrine, i.

3i8, 358. Creation, due to divine will, i. 134;

Father author of, Christ principle of, ex, cxii;

New see Heaven and

Earth. Crown, reward of victory, i. 58; of righteous, i. 129; related to nimbus of heavenly beings, i. 58, 59- See ii. 20. Crown of life, i. e., belonging to the eternal life, i. 59. Cross, Sign of. See Sealing. Cryptogram, i. 364-368. Cup of wrath, ii. 14, 99. See Wine.

Wrath of God. Curse, = " accursed thing " in 22 s, ii.

IV. INDEX TO COMMENTARY

Dan, omission of, from list of Twelve Tribes, variously explained; idolatry of Dan, i. 208; Satan its prince, i. 193.; Antichrist to arise from it, i. 208, 209.

Date of work, xci-xcvii. See Apocalypse, Date of.

Day, great, of wrath or battle, i. 183, ii. 48, 49-Ixrd's. See Lord's Day.

Dead, Sovereign of=Jesus Christ, i. i, 14. See Firstborn.

Death, Christ's, i. 31. See Blood,

Redemption. Keys of. See Keys. Second, not = Lake of Fire, but the lot of those cast therein, ii. 199, 200; a Rabbinic expression, i. 59 to be annihilated at last, ii. 208. = pestilence in 6 s, etc., i. 170, ii. 402.

Demonic assault on Israel, to be repelled by Michael, i. 198 trials. See Sealing.

Demons, nature and origin of, not to be punished till final judgment, 11. 48.

Descent of Christ. See Hades.

Destroy the Earth, those who=Rome, or Beast, False Prophet and Satan, i. 296, 297, ii. 119.

Devil, identified with Satan, i. 325. See Satan.

Diadems, assigned to Christ, in 19"; to Dragon, in 12", i. 319, 347, ii. 132; to First Beast, in I3 1 only, i. 347.

Dionysius of Alexandria, xl, xli; his criticism of the Apocalypse, ci.

Disembodied souls, both non-martyred righteous and wicked have, i. 98.

at Resurrection non- martyred righteous receive spmtual bodies; but wicked do not, but are cast into Lake of Fire, i. 98, ii. 195-198.

Dislocations in Text, ii. 92, 93, 144-154. See Apocalypse, Text of.

Doctrine. See Apocalypse.

Dogs, use of term in Judaism, impure or heathen, ii. 178.

Domitian, xci-xcvii. See Antichrist,

Apocalypse, Date of. Door, w heaven, i. 107. See

Heaven.

of heart, Christ's knocking at, i. 100. open, = opportunity for missionary effort, not Christ Himself, nor right to enter into Messianic glory, i. 87. Doxology, indirect, ii. 122. Doxologies, to Christ, i. 15-17; as the Lamb, i. 144, 145, 149-151, etc.

by Cherubim Trisagion, i. 127. by Elders referring to creation, L 133. 134-ubim by Cherubim and Elders, i. 144, various attributes ascribed in, i. 149.

Dragon, identified with Serpent that tempted Eve, i. 325, ii. 141; with Devil and with Satan, 325- not destroyed by Christ in chap. xix., i. 309, ii. 140, 141.

Seven-headed, conception derived from Babylonian mythology, i. 317; vanous traditions, respecting, i. 317, 318; relation of, to primeval ocean chaos-monster, i. 318, 33i 358.

Seven heads, i. 31811., red, 318, 31911., ten horns (Daniel), 319.

persecutes woman, i. 331. Dragon and Woman with Child, = chap, xii., Semitic original of, i. 303-305.

meaning of, in present context woman = first Jewish and then Jewish-Christian com- mumt), i. 299, 30011.

rest of seed of woman=Gentile

Christians, i. 299, 332. non-Jewish and non Christian features, i. 300, 308. due to a second source beside the Jewish one, i. 307, 308. as I2 1 6 18 17 ultimately of heathen origin, i. 307, 309. Dragon speaking, impossible idea, cli, i. 358, 359.

Dragon myth, possible origins of, Babylonian, Zend, Greek, Egyptian, i.

IV. INDEX TO COMMENTARY

Eagle, the two wings of the, a lost tradition, L 330. Earth, those who dwell on, meanings of phrase, good and bad, 11.

12, 13.; literally used of inhabitants of Palestine, i.

289, 290. Earthquake Woe of Sixth Seal, i.

I79-I83- in Jerusalem, i. 291. in Rome, ii. 52.

Eating, supernatural gifts imparted by, i. 268.

Ecstatic condition, described twice over in 4 1J, i. 106-111. See Spirit.

Egyptian origin suggested for Dragon myth, i. 313.

Elder, use of title, xhi, xliii n.

Elders, Twenty-four, i. 115; subordinate to Cherubim, i. 116, 127; prostrate themselves at crises, i. 127; sit on thrones, crowned, act as angelic interpreters, present prayers of faithful, address and encourage Seer, praise God, i. 128, 129. one intervenes to explain a vision to Seer, Ixxxviin., i. 139. explanations of (i) glorified men, representatives of community, i. 129; but as they are enthroned prior to Judgment, they are not men but angels. Moreover, they act as Angeh interprets and offer men's prayers, i. 130.

(2) a college of angels, earlier were angehc assessors of God, originally 24 Babylonian star gods, i. 130, 131- (3) angelic representatives or heavenly counterparts of 24 priestly orders, and so offered sacrifice. This suits idea of heavenly temple and altar, L 132.

(4) but in present context are angelic representatives of whole body of faithful (c guardian angels), all of whom are priests and kings, i. 129, 133-Emerald = rock-crystal?, L 114,

Endurance, sustained characteristic of saints, i. 49, 50,89,368, 370.

Ephesus, government of, i. 47; a road terminus, i. 47; neo-corate of, i. 48; chief centre of Christianity in East, i. 48.

Epilogue of Book, declarations bv God, Jesus, and John, h.

211, 212.

Eternal, for ever and ever =1000 years, ii. 120. Evangelization of world by glorified martyrs during Millennial

Kingdom, liv, ii. 148, 172; origin of belief, ii. 149, 457. Exclusion from city of craven-hearted, faithless, impure, murderers, sorcerers, idolaters, liars, ii.

146, 173, 174, 177, 178, 215-217. Eye salve, symbol of new spiritual vision, i. 98, 99. Eyes, symbolize omniscience of Lamb, 1. 141. See Cherubim. Ezra, Fourth Book of, xxxiii and passim.

Faith, in Apoc. = faithfulness, fidelity, as well as belief, cxvi, i. 6l. Faithful. See Christ. False Prophet. See Beast, Second. False Teachers. Set Apostles. Famine, woe of Third Seal, i. 166- 168. Fear God's name, those who, = not proselytes, but Jewish or

Gentile Christians, i. 296, 297. Cf. ii. 125. Fear of God, essential part of Gospel, ii. 13. Fine linen, = spiritual bodies, the result of righteous acts, ii.

435. See Garments, Linen. First-born=sovereign (of the dead), L 14, ii. 386. " First-fruits," more properly rendered

"sacrifice, ii. 5-7,6 n. " Foot "SB leg, i. 259, 260. Fornication=unfaithfulness to Christ, and concessions to pflg" customs of trade-guildst i.

=immorality, i. 71. Fourth Gospel, by same author as I.

IV. INDEX TO COMMENTARY

Fourth Gospel and Epistles both free from solecisms, zxziv. common constructions, xxxiv, xxxv. common words and phrases, xxxv, xxxvi.

parallel expressions, xxxvi. absence of quotations, xxxvi. idiomatic Greek, xxxvi. Fragments, Papyrus and Vellum, ii.

447-451. Frogs, Zend belief in evil power of,

Future tense used of past or continuous action, frequentative, cxxiii, cxxiv, ii. 399 n.

Garment of Son of Man, i. 27,

Garments, whites spiritual bodies bestowed by God on faithful in resurrection life, cxv, cxvi, i. 81-83, 98, 184-188, 210-214.

not = righteousness (works) of saints, cxv, L 371-373, ii. 127-128.

Gehenna, not referred to, in Apocalypse, i. 240. but = Lake of Fire, ii. 139, 140. meaning of term, i. 24011. See

Punishment, Places of. Gematria, i. 364-368. Gnostic teaching at Thyatira, "the deep things of Satan," libertinism and emphasis on knowledge of intellectual mysteries, i. 73, 74. God, creative activity of, i. 263. description of, i. 113. doctrine of. See Apocalypse,

Doctrines.

face of, to be seen by His servants in Eternal Kingdom, ii 209, 210.

God, Titles of, Alpha and Omega, i 8 21, i. 2, 20, ii. 215. Created heaven. earth. sea. He who, xo, i. 263.

Father, i f 14, i. 17. God Almighty, 16" I9, cxlvii, i. 20, ii. 49, 398 n. God of heaven, n u 16", i. 292, ii. 46. Holy, 6 l id 5, i. 175, ii. 123 (different words).

God, of the nations, 15, ii.

Liveth for ever and ever, God who, is 7, ii. 39. He that, 4 9-lv io 6, i. 128.

Living God, 7, i. 204, 205.

Lord, IS 4.

Lord God, the, 22", ii. 211.

Lord God Almighty, i 8 4 ii 17 15 io 7 19 s 2i M, i. 20, 103, 104, 127, 295, ii. 36, 126, 170, 387., 398 n., cf. cxlvii.

Lord, the God of the Spirits of the prophets, 22 8, ii. 218.

Lord of the earth, 11 4, i. 284.

Master, 6 10, L 175.

my God, 3".

ourgod, 5 10 7 our Lord and God, 4", i.

133- our Lord, n 15, i. 294. sitteth on the throne, He that, 4. 10 5! 7 18 516 ylo. 10 jg4 21.

True, 6 10, i. 175.

which is and which was, 11 17 i6 B, i. 295, " 123-which is, and which i was, and which is to come, I 4 4 8, i. 2, io, 20, 103, 104, 127; not used of Christ, cxii; unin-flected, clii, i. io; Jewish and heathen parallels to this title, L io.

Gog and Magog, origin of names of, ii. 188, 189; duplicate attack on Jerusalem by, after Messianic Kingdom, ii. 188, 189 (close parallel to, in 4 Ezra, ii. 190, 191); comprehend all faithless on earth, ii. 189; destroyed by fire from heaven, ii. 191.

Gold tried in the fire, a gift acquired from Christ of a new heart or spirit, i. 97, 98.

Grace, form of, i. 9, ii. 226; "grace and peace," i. 9.

Grace and Works, i. 213, 214. See Garments, Works.

Grammar. See Apocalypse, Grammar of.

Greek origin of Dragon myth. St Dragon Myth, Origins.

Guilds. See Trade Guilds.

IV. INDEX TO COMMENTARY

Hades, as intermediate abode of unrighteous (or indifferent) souls only, ami., i. 32, 33, 15, 169, 170, ii. 140, 195, 196, 197, 199.

does not include Paradise, i. 32 (souls of righteous in "Treasuries").

Descent of Christ into, i. 32, 33.

inhabitants join in praise to Lamb, L 150.

intrusion in 6 s, i. 169, 170.

=Sheol, L 32. See Sheol. Harlot, the Great, Judgment of, ii. 54 sqq.

seated on Beast. See Antichrist.

to be destroyed by Beast and Ten Kings, ii. 55, 73, 74.

Rome, 11. 62, 75 (seated on waters owing to survival of Babylon description, ii. 62, 6 3 72); her name, ii. 65.

drunk with blood of martyrs, i. e. Neronic persecutions, ii. 65, 66.

HIT- Magedon, interpretation of phrase uncertain, "mountains of Megiddo," city of Megiddo, 8 "his fruitful mountain," " the desirable city" (= Jerusalem); but possibly due to some lost myth, ii. 50, 51. Scene of great world-battle, ii. 50.

Heads of Beast. See Beast. Heart, seat of thoughts, i 73. See

Heathen, evangelization of. See

Evangelization

Heathen myth, i. 143. See Origins. Heathen nations, two universal insurrections of, (l)at instigation of demons, Beast and False Prophet, before Messianic Kingdom, destroyed by Messiah, and Beast and False Prophet cast into Lake of Fire and lungs and armies slain, ii. 46, 47, 131. 35. 136, 139, 140.

(2) final, at instigation of Satan, after Messianic Kingdom, destroyed by fire from heaven, and Satan cast into Lake of Fire, ii. 46,47,13. 188-191.

Heathen, to be ruled (or destroyed) with rod of iron by Messiah and saints, i. 74-77. 320 Heaven, a single, in Apocalypse, L 108, but see i. 304, 329. creatures in, meaning of, i. 150. door into, by which Seer enters, i.

107. evil in, Satan still in, as in Job, etc., Eph. etc., L 324. war in, i. 321, 324. See Altar, Vision. Heaven and earth, present, to vanish, ii. 193.

new to come, conception of, in Judaism, ii. 203; Vision of, ii. 204.

Heavenly armies, composed of angels and glorified martyrs, who descend with Christ, ii.

35 136-r, Ark, J

See Altar, Ark, Jerusalem, Temple,

Throne. Horns, symbolize power, of Lamb, i. 141. See Beast. Horses, the Four, colours of, and their significance, i. 161, 162 n. White = war: by others variously interpreted of triumphant war, Parthian Empire,

Vologases, Rome, Messiah,

Gospel, i. 163-164. Red = international strife, i. 165, 1 66. Black = Famine, lack of bread, but not of oil or wine, i. 166-168. Pale = Pestilence, i. 168-171.

Idolaters, exclusion of, ii. 217. Idols, food sacrificed to, problem of, i. 63, 69, 70. Immorality, connection of, with demon-worship and idolatry, i. 255. Incense, added to prayers, to make them acceptable, i. 230, 231. symbolizes prayers of saints, L 145. See Censer.

Infinitive =? finite verb, cxzvii. Inspiration, imparted by eating, L 268, by visions, etc. S

Apocalypse, authors method,

Psychic experiences. Intercession of angels, i. 145, 230. Interpolations. See Apocalypse.

IV. INDEX TO COMMENTARY Interpretation, Methods of, dzzziii-clzzzvii

Contemporary-Historical, clzxziii.

Eschatological, clxzziv.

Chiliaslic, clxxziv.

Philological (earlier and later forms), clxxxiv clzzzvii.

Literary- Critical (Redactional, Sources, Fragmentary Hypotheses), clxxxv.

Traditional-Historical, clxxxvi.

Religious-Historical, clxzzvi.

Philosophical, clxzzvi.

Psychological, clzzzvii.

Recapitulatory, xziii. Itacisms, in Greek text, ii. 235.

Jasper, i. 114.

Jerusalem, the literal, called spiritually Sodom and Gomorrah, referred to in 11 7, Izii, zc, i. 279, 287, 288.

Jerusalem, Two descriptions of one Millennial (temporary), zc, i. 54, 55. ii- IS, 53- one eternal, in new heaven and new earth, when death abolished, ii. 153, 157, 158. Millennial (" Holy Jerusalem "), to descend in Millennium, ii. 145-150; before Final Judgment, at which it disappears, to be replaced by or transformed into New Jerusalem, ii. 158, 205; contains no Temple or Ark, replaced by God and the Lamb as centre of wornip, ii. 170, 171.

its foundations, gates, light, stones, ii. 161-170.

contains river of water of life and tree of life, ii. 174-177.

evil excluded from, ii. 177, 178.

relation of, to heathen idea of City of God or gods, ii. 158, are the true, i. 57, 159, 168. to Ezekie kiel's new city, ii. 159.

to conception of Paradise, ii 160, 161.

to conception of New Jeru- alem, ii. I6i.

Eternal (New Jerusalem), New, as opposed to Millennial, ii. 157-158; many features of, in traditional tezt properly refer to Millennial, ii. 144-148.

esus, use of personal name, czi. r, a title of honour in Apocalypse, ews, Christians oppose Christianity, i. 56-58., repentance or conversion to Christianity of, expected, i. 88, 291, 292.

Jewish Christian Apocalypse in gospels, influences conception of Second Coming in i 7, i. 19. See Apocalypse, Little.

Jewish and Christian Churches combined in description of Holy Jerusalem, ii. 163.

Jezebel, a name applied to a false teacher at Thyatira, a prophetess, who countenanced immorality as well as attendance at heathen guild feasts, i. 70, 71.

Johannine Epistles. See Fourth Gospel, John the Elder.

Johannine writings, authorship of, linguistic evidence, zziz-zxxvii; other evidence, xxxviii-1.

John, Gospel of. See Fourth Gospel.

John the Apostle, tradition of his residence at Ephesus not earlier than 180 A. D., zlv; martyred before 70 A. D., zlvi-1. See Apocalypse, author of.

John the Elder (Presbyter), author of, 2. 3 John and also I John and Fourth Gospel, zzxvui, xlii, zliii. wrongly stated to be author of Apocalypse in tradition and to-day, zli, xlii.

John the Seer, a prophet, zzziz, zliii; call of as, i. 2; a Jewish Christian, probably a native of Galilee, zzi, xliv; probably settled at Ephesus, zxi; a " brother " of the churches of Asia, zzziz, zliii, zliv; had authority over churches of Province of Asia, xxii; his style unique, strange Greek grammar, zzi, zliv, czvii-cliz; fiuniliar with Hebrew O. T., Septuagint, and a Theodotionic type of Ver- IV. INDEX TO COMMENTARY sion, xxi, etc.; his use of Jewish and Christian sources, xxii; hisdeathabout95 A. D., ii, 147-152; his work revised by unintelligent disciple, who interpolates some 22 verses and causes disarrangement of text, xxii, xxiii, 1 Iv, etc.

John the Seer, author of Apocalypse, xxi, xxxix; distinct from author of Gospel and Epistles. See Apocalypse, author of.

Jubilees, Book of, xxxiii.

J udgment, Christ's Second Coming to.

L 17-19.

His present judgment, ii. 393 n. of living on earth committed to Christ from Seven Seals to destruction of Gog and Magog, cxvi, ii. 192. final, by the Father alone, cxii; of all risen from the dead (martyrs exempt, also those who eat of Tree of Life during Millennium), cxvi, cxvii, ii. 192-194. See Abyss, Hades.

Judgments, First, Second, and Third series of, xxvi-xxviii. preceded by proclamations or anthems of praise, L 293; ct i.

222.

Key of David, Messianic significance of, authority to admit to or exclude from New Jerusalem, i. 86.

Keys of death and Hades, meaning of power to raise from dead, to free from Hades, i- 3, 33-Kingdom, and kingship of all the faithful, i. 16, 17. Millennial passes over into Eternal, no clear distinction, i. 294, 295.

Kings (kingdom) and priests, i. 16. Kings from the East. See Parthian Kings. Kings of the earth, ii 138, 140.

Lacunae. See Apocalypse, Text Lake of fire. See Punishment.

IV. INDEX TO COMMENTARY

L 199, 201, 205, 200. originally=entire body of blessed in heaven after Final Judgment, i. 201, 202. in present context=martyrs of last tribulation serving God in heaven before Millennial Kingdom, i. 201, 202.

Music, ii. 109, no. See Singer.

Mystery=" name to be interpreted symbolically,"ii. 65. =secret meaning, L 34. of God=whole purpose of God in history; otherwise interpreted of casting down of Satan or birth of Messiah; but cf. related uses of phrase =God's secret purpose of inclusion of Gentiles, or again the hidden working of evil, i. 26;, 266, 266. Mythology colouring eschatology, i. 253, 300, 311-3 4, 358, etc. See Origins.

Nakedness, of soul, = loss of spiritual body, i. 97, 98, 188. See

Garments. Name, inscribing of, on pillar of temple, on forehead of victor, i. 91, 92. significance of, = personality, ii.

391 hidden, magic powers of, ii. 132, 133. Messiah, new, = not new character, i. 6711., but (secret) name of God or

Christ, i. 67. Names of blasphemy, = divine titles of Emperors, e. g. Augustus, i-347, 348. Nature, praise of, conceived as offered by Elders, not Cherubim, i.

126, 127. Nero the only satisfactory solution of number 666 or 616, L 367.

redivivus, xcv-xcvii. See Antichrist, Apocalypse, Date of. Neronic myth stages of its development, ii. 80 sqq.

New, special significance of the word, i.9. 1.46, ii. 204. New Creation, IL 200, 201, 203, 204.

See Creation.

Heaven and Earth, ii. 203, 204. Jerusalem. See Jerusalem. New Testament, brv, Ixvi, Ixxxiii- Ixxxvi. See Apocalypse,

Materials used in. Nicolaitans, not followers of Nicolaus of Antioch, but Balaamites (2-), i. S 2, S3.,

Balaamites. Night, and darkness, to be abolished, ii. 210.

Nimbus, i. 115. See Crown. Number, idea of fixed, of martyrs, to be completed, i. 177-179. of name of Beast, i. 334, 364- 368. values of names, or isopsephinns, .36511., 366.

IV. INDEX TO COMMENTARY

Numerals, prepositive and postpositive use of, clix, i. 224 n.

Oath, method of swearing, i. 262, 263; by God of Creation, L 263. Old Testament, use of, Ixv-bnoril

Set Apocalypse, Materials used in. Olive Trees, Two (of Zechariah) identified with the Two

Candlesticks and Two Wit- nesses, i. 282, 283. Ophannim. See Cherubim. Order of Words, clvi-clix. See

Apocalypse, Grammar ol Origen's so-called text, clxxvi-

Origins and Parallels suggested, Babylonian, i. II, 12, 30, 32, 115, 118, 122, 123, 130, 163., 164, 198., 283., 308, 311, 3i3 3IS-3I9, 358, 365 11.63, 75. 1 59, 205. Egyptian, i. 91, 144, 198 if., 3 3, 316., 318., 325, ii. 75, 167, 205, 221 n.

Greek, i. 10, 115, 19811., 23911., 254, 308, 3", 324. 325," 220.

Persian, Zend, Mandaean, etc., L 10, ii, 30, 33, 83, 156-159., 184, 247, 250., 28211., 307, 308, 3", 319, 324, 37, ii- 47, 53, 75, 39. 142. Various, i. 123, 181., 244, 245, 28911., ii. 9, 51, 133, 138, 158, 159, 167, 1 68. See also clxxzvi.

Orphic Lpgion. See Beginning. Overcoming, special meaning of, L 45,53,54- 5 Victor." used of martyrs (only?), L 54.

Palm branches, symbol of victory, i.

211. Papias-traditions, xl-xliii, zlvl Set

Apocalypse, author of. Papyrus fragments. See Fragments. Paradise, not included in Hades, i.

32. equivalent to Heavenly Jerusalem, i. 55. See Jerusalem. not identified with third heaven, i.

or with abode of blessed departed, i-55-

Paradise, various views earthly and heavenly, 160.

abode of righteous after this life, or reserved till after Judgment, ii. 160-161. Parthian Empire, victory of, over

Rome. See Vologases. Parthian kings, in readiness to invade, at Euphrates, i 250. instruments of God's wrath against Rome, ii. 87. to join Nero redtvrvus in attack on Rome, ii. 46, 47, 55, 71-74-to be destroyed by Messiah, i.

133, 135- destruction of, omitted, ii. 114, 116, 117, 131, 43611.

Past tense, = prophetic future, ii. 414.

Patmos, John in, xzziz, i. 21, 22.

"People" and "peoples," ii. 207, 377

Perfect tense hi Greek, how to be rendered, cxrv-cxxvi, ii. 41411.

Pergamum, first centre of Caesar Worship (throne of Satan), i. 60, 61. description of, i. 60, 61.

Persecution, limited degree of, in

Seven Churches, i. 44, 4410.

world-wide, only once referred to in letters to Seven Churches, i. 44, 89. See Martyrdom.

economic, i. 334, 363, cf. ii. 86, 87.

Pestilence, woe of Fourth Seal, i 169-171.

Philadelphia, description of, i. 84, 85. Jewish opposition at, i. 88.

Pillar. See Temple of God.

Plagues. See Bowls.

Praise, in heaven, i. 125-128. See

Dozologies.

anthems of, at crises in coming of Kingdom,!. 293, 294-

Prayers, of souls under altar, for vengeance, become an instrument of divine wrath, i. 174-176, 178, ii. 4031.

Prayers of Saints, presented by angelic mediators not Elders (? by archangels as in Judaism), L 145, 146, 226; symbolized by incense, i. 145, and censed, i. 230.

IV. INDEX TO COMMENTARY

Predestination, of Lamb's sacrifice, i.

of saints in Book of Life, but not necessarily implied by that Book, onr, 1.354, 355.

Present tense future, u. 41411.

imperfect, ii. 4171. Priesthood, of til the faithful, i. 16, and kingship of martyrs, ii. 186. Priesthood, imperial=Second Beast.

See Beasts, work miracles, i. 359; making images speak, 361.

insist on worship of First Beast (Emperor) on penalty of death, i. 360, 361. Cf. zcv.

Proleptic passages, xxv, i. 203, 209, 256, 269-270, ii. i. Prologue. See Apocalypse, Plan of. Prophecy, a limited gift, i. 17. Prophets, Christian, ii. 112, 113;= God's servants, i. 6, 266 Set Seer.

spirits of, ii. 218. See Spirits. Pseudepigrapha, Izv, Ixxxii-lxxxiii. See Apocalypse, Materials used in.

Pseudonymous apocalypses, not so Apocalypse of John, xxxviii. Psychic experiences, i. Dreams-varying value set on, civ, cv.

ii. Visions, in sleep, in trance, with spiritual or bodily translation, waking visions, cv, 106, 107, 110, in, ii. 63; conventional use of " I saw," ox. value of, in Ethnic religions and in that of Israel, cv, cvi. literal descriptions of, hardly possible, hence use of symbolism, cvi, cvii. Cf. "Like."

Psychology, Jewish, L 73, ii. 73. Punishment, agents of angels of punishment, i. 250, 251 n. See Angels.

nature of, by fire and brimstone, in view of angels (parallels, Jewish and Christian), unceasing, ii. 17, 18. places of, preliminary, ii. 141, 142; and final, Lake of Fire, L 230, 240, ii. 139,200. Abyss, i. 239-242. See Abyss.

Punishment, places of, Gehenna, i. 240, 240. (replaced in Apocalypse by Lake of ire, 242).

Sheol, i. 24011., ii. 197. Lake of Fire. See above. (various, in i Enoch, i. 241). Purchase. Set Redemption.

Quotations, abundant in Apocalypse, rare in Fourth Gospel, xxxvi.

Reader, office of, in public worship,

Reaping symbol of Judgment in interpolation, U. 19, 24. See Vintaging. Reason, part played by, in Apoca- lyptic, cvii, cviii.

Recapitulation. See Interpretation. Redemption, by blood of Christ (as price), cxiv, L 16. idea of purchase, i. 16, 147, ii. 7, a loosing from sin, i. 15. a withdrawal from earth, ii. 7, 8. a washing, i. 213, 214. with view to kingdom and priest hood, i. 1 6, 148. Reign of Antichrist, 3 years, i. 279, 280, 289 n.

Reign of saints, not limited to Millennial Kingdom, i. 102. See Kingdom. Reinterpretation of older prophecy, L 273-Remnant, not referred to in I2 17, L

Repentance, of Jews expected, i. 88, 291, 292.

two witnesses to preach, i. 282. Repentance still possible, ii. 212, 215. time for, passed, and finality attained at End, ii. 212, 221, 222.

Reproof and chastisement, the outcome of love, i. 99, lop.

Resurrection, in literal not spiritual sense, ii. 184, 185. First, of martyrs only, as a reward for martyrdom, and to re-evangelize world during Millennium, cxvi, ii. 184, 185, 456, 457-

Second, for righteous (not martyred) and wicked, of righteous souls from "treasuries" or IV. INDEX TO COMMENTARY

spiritual apostasy, but against demonic trials, lxxxv., i. 89,90,195,196, 205, 206, 206 n.

outward manifestation of char acter, i. 206, 20611.

IV. INDEX TO COMMENTARY

Sealing, interpreted of Baptism, and of Sign of Cross, i. 197, 198. meaning of practice in ethnic religions, i. 198 1. Seals, the Seven, significance of, i. 137-the First Six, preliminary signs of

End, i. 153-183 relation of, to Messianic woes in Gospels, i. 157-161; but unlike those in Gospels, do not usher in End, 154. 1st four=social cataclysms, war, international strife, famine and pestilence; 5th, persecution; 6th, cosmic cataclysms, i. 158.

varying interpretations of Contemporary-Historical, etc., i. 155-160.

Seer. See John, Psychic Experiences.

Semitic original of chap, xh., i. 303- 305; chap, xiii., i. 334-338; chap, xvii., ii. 61-62; chap.

xvih., ii. 91.

Seraphim, i. 125, 126. See Cherubim.

Serpent. See Dragon. Servants of God=martyrs, ii. 124, 125.

=prophets, i. 6, 266. Service, spiritual, but not priestly, of martyrs, i. 214, 215. Seven, a sacred number to John, lxxxix it., i. 8, 9, 25. Seven Candlesticks=Seven Churches, 35, 37. See Candlestick.

Churches, reason for choice of particular churches unknown, L 8; probably because on great circular road, and so convenient postal centres, i. 24, 25.

identified with Seven Candlesticks, i. 35, 37. typical in circumstances of

Church as whole, i. 37. Letters to, written earlier than main part of work, i. 37; as survival expected to Second Advent and no reference (except 3 10) to world-wide persecution, i. 43, 44. Heads. See Heads. Horns. See Horns.

Seven Lamps of Fires Seven spirit!, i. 117. related originally to seven planets, i. 117.

Letters, originally addressed to Seven Churches of Asia under Vespasian, lxxxix; in final form of work addressed to all churches of Christendom, lxxxix M., xc. Plagues. See Bowls. Seals. See Seals. Spirits, represented by Seven Lamps, L 117; and Seven Eyes, i. 141-142. interpolated in i 4, i. 9. wrongly interpreted of Holy Spirit's sevenfold energies, =Seven Archangels, i. 11-13, or seven angelic beings possibly related to angels of Seven Churches, i. 12, 13. Stars, relation of, to Seven Spirits, to angels or heavenly ideals of Seven Churches, i. 2, 12, 5. See Stars, impel blasts, upon martyrs, i. 215, ii. 406. a periphrasis for Divine name, face, glory, hard to render in English, ii. 205-207, 444 n. Sheol, nature of, i. 32., 240., ii. 195 197 See Hades, Punishment. Shipmaster, ii. 105. Sign=a heavenly marvel, i. 314. =a miracle wrought by Antichrist, i. 314.

of cross, i. 197. of Son of Man, relation of, to seal, lxxi.

Silence, in heaven for prayers of saints to be heard, I 218, 223, 224. Sin, loosing from, i. 15, 16. See

Redemption. Singer, meaning of term, ii. 109,

Slave trade, ii. 104, 105. Smyrna, description of, Christians' poverty there, and Jews' bitter hostility, i. 56, 57. Solecisms. See Apocalypse, Grammar oi.

13, 3 34, 35-Trumpets. See Trumj Shekinah, to abide upoi IV. INDEX TO COMMENTARY

Son of Man, apparently equal or infenor to angel in interpolation, I4 18 17, hii, Ivi.

combines attributes of Ancient of Day and of Son of Man (Dan 7) and of nameless angel (Dan 10), i. 2, 28, 29.

"one Itke to a son of man," a Messianic designation of one not human but superhuman, i. 27, ii. 19.

judgment by, proleptically described in Vintaging of Earth, ii. 423, 42411.

judgment by, on heathen nations, ii. ifr-26.

title, origin of, in Daniel, i Enoch, the Gospels t 4 Ezra, ii. 19, 20.

titles of, i. 2, 31, etc. See Christ vision of, i. 2, 27-31.

See Messiah. Song, New, i. 146. Song of Lamb, ii. 34-36. See Moses,

Sorcery, a charge against Rome, ii.

112.

Souls, of wicked, disembodied, ii. 193,194. See Disembodied,

"treasuries" or chambers of (for righteous). See

Treasuries, finder altar, of martyrs, because already sacrificed thereon, i.

172, 173, 229, 230. a heavenly sacrifice, with atoning power, i. 173, 174, 173-Sources, Ixii-lxv. See Apocalypse,

Materials used in. Speculum=M, reprinted from Mai, contains same text as gig., ii. 452-455-

Spirit, use of word in Apocalypse. =life, ii. 179. Cf. i. 290. =personalized beings, men, angels, demons, ii. 179. Spirit of Christ, virtually

Christ, ii. 179; cf. L 53. giver of prophecy, i. 53. Holy, not represented by the Seven

Sprits of i 4, i. n. of prophecy,? marginal gloss, meaning uncertain, ii. 130, 131. to fall into or find oneself in=to fall into trance, i. 21.

Spirits, of the prophets, meaning of phrase uncertain, hardlya various angels sent to instruct them, rather = prophets' own spirits, ii. 218. three unclean, muster nations against Christ, ii. 427. Spiritual body given to martyrs at death, i. 176, 184-188,9 white robes of glory, i.

185. St. Paul's teaching as to, i. 185, 1 86. in a sense present possession of faithful, liable to defilement, capable of being cleansed, i.

187, 188.

Star; symbolizes angel, i. 13, 239. Star that fell from heaven and em- bittered waters, i. 235, 236. that fell from heaven and received key of abyss, i. 238, 239. Star-deities, relation of, to Arch- angels, i. ii, 12, 13. to Twenty-four Elders, i. 130, 131. See Morning Star. Stars, =heavenly ideals, i. 2, 34, 35; relation of, to angels, L 12, 13-Stars drawn to earth by Dragon =

Satan's angels, L 319, 320. State, conflicting claims of Chris- tianity and of, xcv, ciii, i. 44. "Stone," in i A corrupt for "Linen,"

ii- 3, 39-Stone, White, I. signifying acquittal.

2. admitting to free entertain- ment, 3. precious stones that fell with

scenery of, rainbow, etc., i. 114, ii; lightnings and thunders, hi, 116, 117; Seven Lamps of fire, 117; Twenty-four Elders, 115,116; Four Cherubim, i. 118,119 (in Daniel etc., also fiery streams under, i. 120). voice from, not of God, but of Elder or Cherub, ii. 124.

Thunder and lightning, clix, i. 116.

Thunders, Seven, revelation of, to be sealed and not written, L 261, 262.

Thyatira, a city notable for trade and craft guilds, i. 68. compromise with heathenism at, i. 69, 70, 72.

Time no longer, = delay no longer (io 7), i. 263, 264 n.

Time, times and half a time, origin of phrase, i. 330.

Titles of Christ, connection of, with messages to individual churches, i. 25-27, not always clear, i 45, 46, 48.

IV. INDEX TO COMMENTARY

Trade-guilds, importance of, at Thyatira, i. 68-70; their common meals and the problem of food sacrificed to idols, i. 69, 70, 72.

Traditional material, cviii. Su Origins.

Trance. Stt Spirit.

Translation of Spirit, and of body, i. no, in. See Heaven, Psychic Experiences, Vision.

Treasuries" in 20" deliberately altered to "sea,"ii. 194-199; souls of righteous guarded and resting in, Iv, cxvi, ii. 196, 197-

Tree of Life, symbol of immortality, i. 54, 55. in Paradise, i. e. in Holy Jerusalem, personal victory over evil alone entitles to, i. 54; not so with Water of Life, which is free, i. 55. See Water of Life.

in Millennial Kingdom, ii. 146.

description of, in 22 based on

Ezekiel, ii. 176, 177. Tribes, Twelve, order of, in list, i. 193,194,206-209. Dan. Tribulation, necessarily preceding Millennial Kingdom, i. 21, 90.

to affect only faithless and heathen, i. 90.

the Great, of martyrs, chiefly manifested in Satanic activity on earth, only secondarily in social and cosmic evils, i. 213.

See Ten Days. Trinity, doctrine of, not asserted by, i 4 5, i. 11-13.

Trisagion, derived from Isaiah, i. 127. True, not=genuine, but "true to one's word," i. 85, 86. Trumpet blasts, heptadic structure secondary, not original, i. 218, 219; first four colourless, with weak repetitions modelled on first four Bowls, 220; different from last three in diction and style, 22O, 221.

first four (interpolated)–) earth scorched, 4 sea turned to blood, J fresh waters embittered. J luminaries obscured, L 233-237.

Trumpet blasts, three last (=Three Demonic Woes), (i) locusts, i. 242-247; (2) horsemen and steeds, kill i men, i. 247-254 (origin of this idea, i. 53, 254); (3) casting down of Satan to earth and setting up of Antichrist's kingdom thereon, i. 292.

Unbelieving=faithless, ii. 216. Uncial texts. See Apocalypse, Text of.

Vengeance, prayer for, L 175, 176.

Versions. See Apocalypse, 7fe of.

Vespasian. See Apocalypse, Date of.

Victor, reward of, ii. 215. See "Overcoming."

Vintaging of earth (Judgment), assigned by Interpolator to nameless angel, but originally belonged to Son of Man, lii, liu, ii. 18, 19, 23, 423, 424 (same judgment assigned to Christ by John in i9-, Ivi, ii. 136, 137). to take place outside Jerusalem, not Rome, ii. 25.

Vision, new, formula of= " after this I saw and behold," ciz, i. 106. on earth, chaps. 1-3, 10, u 1 11 12, 13-14" 17-18 Iputoend.

in heaven, chaps. 4-8,11 15 " 18 14".

1M 15, 16, I9 1 10, i. 109. Visions. See Psychic Experiences. Vologases, Parthian Victory of, over

Romans in 62 A. D., i. 155, 163-

War, woe of First Seal, i. 163, 164.

See Seals.

in heaven. See Heaven. Watchfulness, duty of, enjoined on

Sardis, i. 79, 80, Si. Water of Life, a free gift, i. 55. =divine graces of forgiveness, truth and light, i. 55. reward of martyrs, i. 216, 217.

See Manna, River.

White, significance of colour, L 67, 165, 210, ii. 192, 193. See Horse, Garments, Stone, head and hair of Son of Man, 1.28.

IV. INDEX TO COMMENTARY

Wicked, final punishment of, in Lake of Fire, czvi. See Punishment.

Winds, destructive, plague of, 191., 192, 193 n. angels of, hold them in check, L 192., 204.

Wine, symbol of intoxicating and corrupting power of Rome, ii. 14.

"unmixed," symbol of concentrated or sheer judgments of God, ii. 16, 17, 136, 137 (possibly render "fermenting").

and oil, no shortage of, i. 167, 168; law against damaging vines and olive trees, ii. 402 n.

Witnesses, Two, abruptly introduced in ii 8, i. 258.

Moses and Elijah, not Enoch and Elijah, appear in Jerusalem as preachers of repentance, i. 280-282. Zoroastrian parallel not analogous, 282 ft.

identified with Two Olive Trees, etc, of Zechariah, 4 ", L 282-284.

Woes, Messianic. Sec Seals.

Woman with child=originally Jewish Community, which was to bring forth Messiah, while Dragon=Antichrist, i. 310 fleeing to wilderness, referred originally to Christians or Jews escaping from Jerusalem before 70 A. D., in present context to Christian exodus therefrom, while " rest of seed " refers not to Jews who stayed in Jerusalem, but Gentile Christians throughout Empire, i. 332.

Woman, Scarlet. See Harlot.

Word of God. See Messiah.

Word of Gods Apocalypse, i. i, 6, 7; xcpreaching of Gospel by John, i. 21, 22. x= martyrs' testimony to Jesus, i. 329.

Words, order of, clvi-clix, etc.

Works, doctrine of necessary, imply freewill, = moral character as manifested: symbolized by fine linen in an interpolation, cxv, ii. 127-128. following martyred saints, Zoroastrian parallel ideas and Jewish parallels, L 371; but in Apoc. the works are not separate, reserved in heaven, but accompany person, therefore = manifestation of inner life and character, i.

., 370-373. judgment by, u. 221. World, created because of God's will, i. 134.

World-Redeemer tradition, international at early date,.313. World-wide Evangelization, ii. 148, 149, 154, 155-Worship, two senses in which word used, cxli, i. 211, 212. Wrath, of God i. 296, ii. 14, 16, 24, rt 3i, 39. 52,96, 137-of Lamb, i. 182, 183.

Zeal, importance of, in Christian character, i. 100. Zealot 9 prophecy of inviolability of

Temple due to a, i. 278. Zend origin of Dragon-myth, i. 307, 308, 311, 312. See Origins. Zion, Mount, association of, with security and deliverance, ii.

4-Messiah to appear on-also a

Jewish expectation, ii. 5. Zodiac, signs of, i. 315, 316; connection of, with Cherubim, L 122, 123. See Stones.

TOL. n. Jt

The International Critical Commentary

ARRANGEMENT OF VOLUMES AND AUTHORS THE OLD TESTAMENT

GCNE3IS. The Rev. JOHN SKINNER, D. D., Principal and Professor of Old Testament Language and Literature, College of Presbyterian Church of England, Cambridge, England. Now Ready.

EXODUS. The Rev. A. R. S. KENNEDY, D. D., Professor of Hebrew, University of Edinburgh.

LEVITICUS. J. F. STENNING, M. A., Fellow of Waciham College, Oxford.

NUMBERS. The Rev. G. BUCHANAN GRAY, D. D., Professor of Hebrew, Mansfield College, Oxford. (Now Ready.

DEUTERONOMY. The Rev. S. R. DRIVER, D. D., D. Litt., sometime Regius Professor of Hebrew, Oxford. Now Ready.

JOSHUA. The Rev. GEORGE ADAM SMITH, D. D., LL. D., Principal of the University of Aberdeen.

JUDGES. The Rev. GEORGE F. MOORE, D D., LL. D., Professor of Theology, Harvard University, Cambridge, Mass. Now Ready.

SAMUEL. The Rev. H. P. SMITH, D. D., Librarian, Union Theological Seminary, New York. Now Ready.

KINGS. Author to be announced.

CHRONICLES. The Rev. EDWARD L. CURTIS, D. D., Professor of Hebrew, Yale University, New Haven, Conn. Now Ready.

EZRA AND N EH EM I AH. The Rev. L. W. BATTEN, Ph. D., D. D., Professor of Old Testament Literature, General Theological Seminary, New York City. Now Ready.

PSALMS. The Rev. CHAS. A. BRIGGS, D. D., D. Litt., sometime Graduate Professor of Theological Encyclopedia and Symbolics, Union Theological Seminary, New York. 2 vols. Now Ready.

PROVERBS. The Rev. C. H. TOY, D. D., LL. D., Professor of Hebrew, Harvard University, Cambridge, Mass. Now Ready.

JOS. The Rev. S. R. DRIVER, D. D., D. Litt., sometime Regius Professor of Hebrew, Oxford.

THE INTERNATIONAL CRITICAL COMMENTARY ISAIAH. Chaps. I-XXVII. The Rev. G. BUCHANAN GRAY, D. D., Professor of Hebrew, Mansfield College, Oxford. Now Ready.

ISAIAH. Chaps. XXVIII-XXXIX. The Rev. G. BUCHANAN GRAY, D. D. Chaps. LX-LXVI. The Rev. A. S, PEAKE, M. A., D. D., Dean of the Theological Faculty of the Victoria University and Professor of Biblical Exegesis in the University of Manchester, England.

JEREMIAH. The Rev. A. F. KIRKPATRICK, D. D., Dean of Ely, sometime Regius Professor of Hebrew, Cambridge, England.

EZEKIEL. The Rev. G. A. COOKE, M. A., Oriel Professor of the Interpretation of Holy Scripture, University of Oxford, and the Rev. CHARLES F. BURNBY, D. Litt., Fellow and Lecturer in Hebrew, St. John's College, Oxford.

DANIEL. The Rev. JOHN P. PETERS, Ph. D., D. D., sometime Professor of Hebrew, P. E. Divinity School, Philadelphia, now Rector of St. Michael's Church, New York Cky.

AMOS AND H08EA. W. R. HARPER, Ph. D., LL. D., sometime President of the University of Chicago, Illinois. Now Ready.

MIC AH, ZEPHANIAH, NAHUM, HABAKKUK, OBADIAH AND JOEL. Prof. JOHN M. P. SMITH, University of Chicago; W. HAYES WARD, D. D., LL. D., Editor of The Independent, New York; Prof. JULIUS A. BEWER, Union Theological Seminary, New York. Now Ready.

HAGQAI, ZECHARIAH, MALACHI AND JONAH. Prof. H. G. MITCHELL, D. D.; Prof. JOHN M. P. SMITH, Ph. D., and Prof. J. A. BEWER, Ph. D.
Now Ready.

ESTHER. The Rev. L. B. PATON, Ph. D., Professor of Hebrew, Hartford Theological Seminary. Now Ready.

ECCLE8IA8TE3. Prof. GEORGE A. BARTON, Ph. D., Professor of Biblical Literature, Bryn Mawr College, Pa. Now Ready.

RUTH, 80NQ OF 8ONQ8 AND LAMENTATIONS. Rev. CHARLES A. BRIGGS, D. D., D. Litt., sometime Graduate Professor of Theological Encyclopaedia and Symbolics, Union Theological Seminary, New York.

THE NEW TESTAMENT 8T. MATTHEW. The Rev. WUXOUGHBY C. ALLEN, M. A., Fellow and Lecturer hi Theology and Hebrew, Exeter College, Oxford. Now Ready.

ST. MARK. Rev. E. P. GOULD. D. D., sometime Professor of New Testament Literature, P. E. Divinity School, Philadelphia. Now Ready.

ST. LUKE. The Rev. ALFRED PLUIQCBR, D. D., late Master of University College, Durham. Now Ready.

THE INTERNATIONAL CRITICAL COMMENTARY

ST. JOHN. The Right Rev. JOHN HENRY BERNARD, D. D., Bishop of Ossory, Ireland.

HARMONY OF THE GOSPELS. The Rev. WIlLXAM SANDAY, D. D., LL. D., Lady Margaret Professor of Divinity, Oxford, and the Rev. WIL-LOUGHBY C. ALLEN, M. A., Fellow and Lecturer in Divinity and Hebrew, Exeter College, Oxford.

ACTS. The Rev. C. H. TURNER, D. D., Fellow of Magdalen College, Oxford, and the Rev. H. N. BATE, M. A., Examining Chaplain to the Bishop of London.

ROMANS. The Rev. WILLIAM SANDAY, D. D., LL. D., Lady Margaret Professor of Divinity and Canon of Christ Church, Oxford, and the Rev. A. C. HEADLAM, M. A., D. D., Principal of King's College, London. Now Ready.

I. CORINTHIANS. The Right Rev. ARCH ROBERTSON, D. D., LL. D., Lord Bishop of Exeter, and Rev. ALFRED PLUMMER, D. D., late Master of University College, Durham. Now Ready.

II. CORINTHIANS. The Rev. ALFRED PLUMMER, M. A., D. D., late Master of University College, Durham. Now Ready.

GALATIANS. The Rev. ERNEST D. BURTON, D. D., Professor of New Testament Literature, University of Chicago. In Press.

EPHESIANS AND COLOSSIANS. The Rev. T. K. ABBOTT, B. D. V D. Litt., sometime Professor of Biblical Greek, Trinity College, Dublin, now Librarian of the same. Now Ready.

PHILIPPIANS AND PHILEMON. The Rev. MARVIN R. VINCENT, D. D., Professor of Biblical Literature, Union Theological Seminary, New York City. Now Ready.

THESSALONIANS. The Rev. JAMES E. FR4ME, M. A, Professor of Libliral Theology, Union Theological Seminary, New Yoik City.

THE PASTORAL EPISTLES. The Rev. WALTER LOCK, D D., Warden of Keble College and Professor of Exegesis, Oxford.

HEBREWS. The Rev. JAMES MOFFATT, D. D., Minister United Free Church, Broughty Ferry, Scotland.

ST. JAMES. The Rev. JAMES H. ROPES, D. D., Bussey Professor of New Testament Criticism in Harvard University. Now Ready.

PETER AND JUDE. The Rev. CHARLES BIGG, D. D., sometime Regius Professor of Ecclesiastical History and Canon of Christ Church, Oxford. Now Ready.

THE JOHANNINE EPISTLES. The Rev. E. A. BROOKE, B. D., Fellow and Divinity Lecturer in King's College, Cambridge. Now Ready.

REVELATION. The Rev. ROBERT H. CHARLES, M. A., D. D., sometime Professor of Biblical Greek in the University of Dublin, awfr. Now Ready.

The International
Theological Library
ARRANGEMENT OF VOLUMES AND AUTHORS

THCOLOQICAL ENCYCLOPAEDIA. By CHARLES A. BxigGS, D. D., DXitt., sometime Professor of Theological Encyclopedia and Symbolics, Union Theological Seminary, New York.

AN INTRODUCTION TO THE LITERATURE OP THE OLD TESTA-MENT. By S. R. DRIVER, D. D., DXitt., sometime Regius Professor of Hebrew and Canon of Christ Church, Oxford.

Revised and Enlarged Edition.

CANON AND TEXT OP THE OLD TESTAMENT. By the Rev. TOHN SKIN-NER, D. D., Principal and Professor of Old Testament Language and Literature, College of the Presbyterian Church of England, Cambridge, England, and the Rev. OWEN WHTTEHOUSE, B. A., Principal and Professor of Hebrew, Chestnut College, Cambridge, England.

OLD TESTAMENT HISTORY. By HENRY PRESERVED SMITH, D. D., Librarian, Union Theological Seminary, New York. Now Ready.

CONTEMPORARY HISTORY OF THE OLD TESTAMENT.

Author to be announced.

THEOLOGY OP THE OLD TESTAMENT. By A. B. DAVIDSON, D. D., LL. D., sometime Professor of Hebrew, New College, Edinburgh.

Now Ready.

AN INTRODUCTION TO THE LITERATURE OP THE NEW TESTAMENT. By Rev. JAKES MOCTATT, B. D., Minister United Free Church, Brpughty Ferry, Scotland. Now Ready.

CANON AND TEXT OP THE NEW TESTAMENT. By CASPAR Rlnt GRE-GORY, DJX, LL. D. sometime Professor of New Testament Exegesis in the University of Leipzig. Now Ready.

THE LIFE OP CHRIST, By WILLIAM SANDAY, D. D., LL. D., Lady Margaret Professor of Divinity and Canon of Christ Church, Oxford.

THE INTERNATIONAL THEOLOGICAL LIBRARY

A HISTORY OF CHRISTIANITY IN THE APOSTOLIC AGE. By

ARTHUR C. McgifFERT, D. D., President Union Theological Seminary, New York. Now Ready.

CONTEMPORARY HISTORY OF THE NEW TESTAMENT. By FRANK C. PORTER, D. D., Professor of Biblical Theology, Yale University, New Haven, Conn.

THEOLOGY OF THE NEW TESTAMENT. By GEORGE B. STEVENS, D. D., sometime Professor of Systematic Theology, Yale University, New Haven, Conn. Now Ready.

BIBLICAL ARCHAEOLOGY. By G. BUCHANAN GRAY, D. D., Professor of Hebrew, Mansfield College, Oxford.

THE ANCIENT CATHOLIC CHURCH. By ROBERT RAINEY, D. D., LL. D., sometime Principal of New College, Edinburgh. Now Ready.

THE LATIN CHURCH IN THE MIDDLE AGES. By ANDRE LAGARDE.

Now Ready.

THE GREEK AND EASTERN CHURCHES. By W. F. ADENEY, D. D., Principal of Independent College, Manchester. Now Ready.

THE REFORMATION IN GERMANY. By T. M. LlnDSAY, D. D., Principal of the United Free College, Glasgow. Now Ready.

THE REFORMATION IN LANDS BEYOND GERMANY. By T. M. LINDSAY, D. D. Now Ready.

THEOLOGICAL SYMBOLICS. By CHARLES A. BRIC. GS, D. D., D. Lilt., sometime Professor of Theological Encyclopaedia and Symbolics, Union Theological Seminary, New York. Now Ready.

HISTORY OF CHRISTIAN DOCTRINE. By G. P. FlsHFR, D. I)., LL. D., sometime Professor of Ecclesiastical History, Yale University, New Haven, Conn. Revised and Enlarged Edition.

CHRISTIAN INSTITUTIONS. By A. V. G. ALLEN, D. D., sometime Professor of Ecclesiastical History, Protestant Episcopal Divinity School, Cambridge, Mass. Now Ready.

PHILOSOPHY OF RELIGION. By GEORGE GALLOWAY, D. D., Minister of United Free Church, Castle Douglas, Scotland. Now Ready.

HISTORY OF RELIGIONS. I. China, Japan, Egypt, Babylonia, Assyria, India, Persia, Greece, Rome. By GEORGE F. MOORE, D. D., LL. D., Professor in Harvard University. Now Ready.

HISTORY OF RELIGIONS. II. Judaism, Christianity, Mohammedanism. By GEORGE F. MOORE, D. D., LL. D., Professor in Harvard University.

Now Ready.

APOLOGETICS. By A, B. BRUCE, D. D., sometime Professor of New Testa-ment Exegesis, Free Church College, Glasgow. Revised and Enlarged Edition.

THE INTERNATIONAL THEOLOGICAL LIBRARY

THI CHRISTIAN DOCTRINE OF GOD. BywmiaMN. ClaKD, DJ). 1 sometime Professor of Systematic Theology, Hamilton Theological Seminary. Nmmy.

THE DOCTRINE OF MAN. By WniiaH P. PATERSON, D. D, Professor of Divinity, University ot Edinburgh.

THE DOCTRINE OF THE PERSON OF JESUS CHRIST, By H. R. MACKINTOSH, Ph. D., D. D., Professor of Theology, New I

THE CHRISTIAN DOCTRINE OF SALVATIOk. By GEORGE B. STEVENS, D. D., sometime Professor of Systematic Theology, Yale University.

Nm Ready.

THE DOCTRINE OF THE CHRISTIAN LIFE. By WILLIAM ADAMS BIOWN, D. D., Professor of Systematic Theology, Union Theological Seminary, New York.

CHRISTIAN ETHICS. By NEWMAN SMYTH, D. D, Pastor of Congregational Church, New Haven. Revised and Enlaryd Mm.

THE CHRISTIAN PASTOR AND THE WORKING CHURCH. By WASHING-TON GLADDEN, D D., sometime Pastor of Congregational Church, Columbus, Ohio. Now Ready.

THE CHRISTIAN PREACHER. By A. GARVE, D. D, Principal of New College, London, England.

HISTORY OF CHRISTIAN MISSIONS. By CHARLES HENRY ROBINSON, D. D., Hon. Canon of Ripon Cathedral and Editorial Secretary of the Society for the Propagation of the Gospel in Foreign Parts.

Him Ready.

CPSIA information can be obtained at www.ICGtesting.com
Printed in the USA
LVOW07s1821290814

401515LV00002B/392/P